The Theory and Practice of
investment
management

THE FRANK J. FABOZZI SERIES

The Theory and Practice of

investment

management

FRANK J. FABOZZI

HARRY M. MARKOWITZ

EDITORS

John Wiley & Sons, Inc.

contents

Frank J. Fabozzi is editor of the *Journal of Portfolio Management* and an adjunct professor of finance at Yale University's School of Management. He is a Chartered Financial Analyst and a Certified Public Accountant. Dr. Fabozzi is on the board of directors of the Guardian Life family of funds and the BlackRock complex of funds. He earned a doctorate in economics from the City University of New York in 1972 and in 1994 received an honorary doctorate of Humane Letters from Nova Southeastern University. Dr. Fabozzi is a Fellow of the International Center for Finance at Yale University. He is an Advisory Analyst for Global Asset Management (GAM) with responsibilities as Consulting Director for portfolio construction, risk control, and evaluation.

Harry M. Markowitz has applied computer and mathematical techniques to various practical decision making areas. In finance, in an article in 1952 and a book in 1959 he presented what is now referred to as MPT, "modern portfolio theory." This has become a standard topic in college courses and texts on investments, and is widely used by institutional investors for tactical asset allocation, risk control, and attribution analysis. In other areas, Dr. Markowitz developed "sparse matrix" techniques for solving very large mathematical optimization problems. These techniques are now standard in production software for optimization programs. He also designed and supervised the development of the SIMSCRIPT programming language. SIMSCRIPT has been widely used for programming computer simulations of systems like factories, transportation systems, and communication networks.

In 1989, Dr. Markowitz received The John von Neumann Award from the Operations Research Society of America for his work in portfolio theory, sparse matrix techniques, and SIMSCRIPT. In 1990, he shared the Nobel Prize in Economics for his work on portfolio theory.

contributing authors

James A. Abate	Global Asset Management (U.S.A.)
Mark J. P. Anson	CalPERS
Robert D. Arnott	First Quadrant LP
Bruce M.Collins	QuantCast LLC
Lev Dynkin	Lehman Brothers
Frank J. Fabozzi	Yale University
Bruce Feibel	Eagle Investment Systems
Gary L. Gastineau	ETF Advisors, LLC
James L. Grant	JLG Research/Baruch College (CUNY)
Francis Gupta	Credit Suisse Asset Management
Susan Hudson-Wilson	Property & Portfolio Research, LLC
Jay Hyman	Lehman Brothers
Robert R. Johnson	Association for Investment Management and Research
Frank J. Jones	The Guardian Life Insurance Company of America
Vadim Konstantinovsky	Lehman Brothers
Steven V. Mann	University of South Carolina
Harry M. Markowitz	Consultant
Pamela P. Peterson	Florida State University
Raman Vardharaj	The Guardian Life Insurance Company of America

Then and Now in Investing, and Why Now Is So Much Better

Peter L. Bernstein

As I read this book for the first time, I was constantly reminded of the contrast between the investment world of today and what professional investing was like at the beginning of my career fifty years ago. The revolution in investing over the past half century has been far more remarkable than most people with a shorter memory bank can realize.

While sophisticated investors back then understood a few of the basic ideas and principles that drive today's investment practices, their methods were crude, undisciplined, purely intuitive, and wildly inaccurate in terms of achieving what they hoped to accomplish. Entire areas and techniques of investment management had yet to be discovered, many destined to appear only twenty or thirty years later. The momentous Nobel-prize-winning theoretical innovations that did develop during the 1950s—Markowitz's principles of portfolio selection, Modigliani-Miller's contribution to corporate finance and the uses of arbitrage, and Tobin's insights into the risk/reward tradeoff—trickled at a snail's pace even into the academic world and were unknown to nearly all practitioners until many years later.

We did understand the importance of diversification, in both individual positions and in asset allocation. The diversification we provided, however, was determined by seat-of-the-pants deliberations, with no systematic evaluation beyond hunch. Although risk was an ever-present consideration, in our shop at least, the idea of attaching a number to investment risk was inconceivable. Performance measurement was a simple comparison to the Dow Jones Industrials. Institutional and tax-free investors were few and far between. Many of the individual clients who comprised our constituency kept their securities in safe deposit boxes instead of with brokers (risky) or custodian banks (costly), which was a major obstacle to making changes in portfolios, especially with bearer bonds.

We bought and sold stocks on the basis of their being "cheap" or "expensive," but we worked without any explicit methodology for quantifying what those words meant. The notion of growth as an investment consideration simply did not exist in the early 1950s, when stocks still yielded more than bonds. Although I attracted some attention with an article on the subject in the *Harvard Business Review* in 1956, growth as a central element of equity investing did not gain any traction until well into the 1960s.

We expected bond yields to rise and fall with business activity and stocks to do the opposite, which meant any suggestion of the two asset classes moving in tandem was unthinkable. Credit risk and interest rate risk were the only kinds of fixed-income risk we thought about; inflation played no part in decisions concerning asset allocation, market timing, or managing the bond portions of our portfolios. Everybody knew long bonds were riskier than short-term obligations, but precisely how much riskier and the structure of risk and return in the bond market were never part of our deliberations. The uses of the complex and fascinating mathematics of fixed-income securities were still largely undeveloped.

In any case, the fixed-income universe available to us consisted only of Treasuries, corporates, and municipals; many of the corporates traded on the Big Board instead of in the dealer markets that are so familiar today. But that did not matter much, because we acquired most of our clients' bonds on a buy-and-hold basis, as was the custom with all fixed-income securities purchased by sober investors like insurance companies, college endowments, trustees for widows and orphans, and the small number of fee-only investment counsel firms like ours.

With the invention of the money market fund still some twenty years in the future, and Treasuries difficult to trade in small or odd amounts, cash management consisted of advising clients to deposit or withdraw money from savings accounts. Once in the savings account, the money became "their" money rather than "our" money. And that meant we had to call even clients with discretionary accounts and engage in a debate whenever we wanted to make a purchase without an offsetting sale.

The volume of information of interest to investors was infinitesimal from today's vantage point. At ten minutes past every hour, a friendly broker would call on the phone to give us the latest hourly price of the Dow Jones Industrials and a rundown on the stocks we followed most closely. That was all we knew during the day about what was happening in the market. The Standard & Poor's averages were published only monthly, because calculating values for market-weighted indexes took too long for the result to be timely; searching the ticker tape for the thirty Dow stocks, jotting down their prices, adding them up, and then dividing by the divisor was a dreary task, but it could be accomplished in just a few minutes.

Research consisted primarily of the Value Line, which was way ahead of its time in working off a disciplined valuation procedure (although the saying went that if the stock's price did not move toward the Line after a while, the Line would manage to move toward the price). Wall Street research was spotty and superficial. As we and other leading investment advisors insisted that our clients choose their own brokers in order to avoid any odor of conflicts of interest, soft dollar research in such a world was nonexistent.

I need not elaborate on the difference the computer has made in preparing timely and elaborate client valuations, in organizing data for research purposes, and in speedy communication. But that was only the beginning: The computer has been the messenger of the investment revolution. If the world's stock of office equipment still consisted only of the slide-rules and hand-turned or electric (not electronic) desk-top calculators we used in the 1950s, the theories comprising the subject matter of this book, and that support today's investment practices, would never have moved beyond their pages in scholarly journals into the real world of investing.

■   ■   ■

To give you a flavor of the profound nature of the changes that have occurred, I suggest you peek ahead to a few chapters in this book. For example, skim through Chapter 3 on applying Markowitz's mean-variance analysis, Chapter 4 on asset pricing models, Chapter 22 on fixed-income portfolio strategies, and Chapter 31 on active asset allocation. Even a superficial view will reveal the radical difference between the way we managed portfolios in the 1950s and common practice today.

Markowitz won the Nobel prize for his emphasis on two ancient homilies—nothing ventured, nothing gained, but do not put all your eggs into one basket. Markowitz's memorable achievement was to transform these two basic investment guidelines into a rigorous analytical procedure for composing investment portfolios. His primary innovation, in fact, was to distinguish between risk in a portfolio setting and the risk an investor faces in selecting individual security positions.

Markowitz uses his quantitative definition of risk to provide a means of calculating—in hard numbers—the price of risk, or the amount of additional risk an investor must face in order to increase the portfolio's expected return by a given amount. Investors can now employ diversification (distributing the eggs in many baskets) to minimize the amount of "venture," or risk, relative to a given amount of expected "gain," or return. Or, with the same process, the investor can choose to maximize the gain to be expected from a given amount of venture. Markowitz characterizes such portfolios as "efficient," because they optimize the combination of input (risk) per unit of output (return). This pioneering analysis was only a starting point, but it is still the inspiration for an extensive set of novel approaches for arriving at the most critical decisions in the portfolio-building process.

Despite his contribution to the measurement and understanding of investment risk, Markowitz skipped over a full-dress definition of the other side of the equation—expected return. In Chapter 4 on asset pricing models, Fabozzi details striking advances in both defining and quantifying expected return. Nevertheless, the methodology in Chapter 4 is still a variation on Markowitz's theme, for risk continues to play a central role in the prices investors set on individual assets as they go about building their portfolios.

This approach is a quantum leap from the way I used to guess whether a security was "cheap" or "expensive." We limited ourselves to trying to figure out what P/E or dividend yield was appropriate for each stock we considered, a judgment that ignored the correlations between that security and all the other securities in the portfolio or between that security and the market as a whole. But Markowitz made it clear that the selection of issues for a portfolio is not the same thing as valuing individual securities. Those choices must be set in terms of the interaction between each individual security and the rest of the portfolio; later variations by William Sharpe and others, also described in Chapter 4, emphasized the importance of the interaction between individual securities and the market as a whole. Consequently, the models in Chapter 4 have an entirely different goal from the traditional valuation parameters covered in Chapters 9 through 11.

This entire structure of portfolio formation is by no means limited to selecting stocks: It is equally important in the management of fixed-income portfolios. Here, as you will see in Chapter 22, the many aspects of fixed-income strategies are even further removed from traditional investment practices than the modern approach to equity selections. The proliferation of new forms of fixed-income instruments has joined with the conversion of buy-and-hold into a broad set of active bond management strategies, creating a world of fixed-income investing unrecognizable to a Rip Van Winkle who went to sleep in the early 1950s and awoke in the early 2000s. Indeed, today's debt instruments are explicitly designed for agile and dynamic trading; the sanctified practice of holding bonds to maturity that I once knew would be dangerously inappropriate in today's world. As Fabozzi makes clear in this chapter, fixed-income instruments may still be less risky than equities, but they nevertheless offer an immense and widening span of risk and return tradeoffs. The result is a significant increase in total portfolio expected returns relative to the risks incurred. Here, too, portfolio efficiency can be enhanced.

Arnott's analysis of active asset allocation in Chapter 31 is also a long way from the intuitive approaches I was taught. We made changes in asset allocation based roughly on our forecast of the evolving business cycle, and that was the end of it. Arnott, on the other hand, begins by distinguishing between two types of allocation decisions: those designed for long-run considerations, which relate to an investor's risk aversion and the return required to achieve appointed goals over the long run, versus shorter-term allocation decisions designed to take advantage of continuing shifts in the valuation of one major asset class such as stocks, relative to another major asset class, such as bonds. Here, too, variety is the spice of life, for Arnott supplies the reader with an enticing assortment of solutions to these problems. Furthermore, most of these systems replace conventional asset return forecasts with the many devices of risk/return analysis displayed in the earlier chapters.

■   ■   ■

Despite my enthusiasm for the whole long story within the covers of this book, I warn the reader against expecting magic potions showering instant riches on anyone who masters these lessons. The future faced by investors is just as unpredictable as it ever was. Do not believe any boasts to the contrary. Risk is an inescapable companion in the investment process.

But that is just the point. By making risk an integral part of the decision-making process, and by incorporating the rigor and discipline of quantification, modern theories and applications clarify as never before the multifarious paths linking the risk of loss to opportunities for gain. One of the most exciting features to me is how a few dominant principles can spawn an apparently unlimited supply of variations on the basic themes, opening investment possibilities we never dreamed of fifty years ago. While this book does a great job of describing the cat, it also provides a broad menu of effective methods to skin the cat.

The transformation in investing over the past fifty years is comparable to stepping from Charles Lindbergh's Spirit of St. Louis into a modern commercial aircraft. Lindbergh's flight from New York to Paris made him a hero before the whole world. A flight from New York to Paris now takes place without notice every hour of the day and into the night. But it is not only distance and time that modern technology has conquered. A glance into the cockpit of a contemporary aircraft reveals a fantastic array of controls and instruments whose entire purpose is to prevent the kinds of crashes that were as routine in Lindbergh's day as they are headline news in our own time—and to do so without any loss of speed. The secret of success is in control of an airliner at altitudes and velocity Lindbergh never dreamed of.

The metaphor is apt. As this book makes abundantly clear, the striking difference between today's investment world and the world to which I was introduced is in control over the consequences of decision-making, under conditions of uncertainty, without any loss of opportunity. Indeed, the opportunity set has been greatly expanded. We will never know enough of what lies ahead to make greater wealth a certainty, but we can learn how to increase the odds and—equally important, I assure you—we can avoid losing our shirts because of foolish decisions.

The ideas in this book comprise a rich treasure. How I wish I had had it in my hands when I first entered the challenging world of investing back in 1951!

Foundations of
Investment Management

Investment Management

Frank J. Fabozzi, Ph.D., CFA
Adjunct Professor of Finance
School of Management
Yale University

Harry M. Markowitz, Ph.D.
Consultant

The purpose of this book is to describe the activities associated with *investment management*. Investment management—also referred to as *portfolio management* and *money management*—requires an understanding of:

1. how investment objectives are determined
2. the investment products to which an investor can allocate funds
3. the way investment products are valued so that an investor can assess whether or not a particular investment is fairly priced
4. the investment strategies that can be employed by an investor to realize a specified investment objective
5. the best way to construct a portfolio, given an investment strategy
6. the techniques for evaluating the performance of an investor

In this book, the contributors will explain each of these activities. In this introductory chapter, we set forth in general terms the *investment management process*. This process involves the following five steps:

Step 1: Setting investment objectives
Step 2: Establishing an investment policy

Step 3: Selecting an investment strategy
Step 4: Selecting the specific assets
Step 5: Measuring and evaluating investment performance

STEP 1: SETTING INVESTMENT OBJECTIVES

The first step in the investment management process, setting investment objectives, begins with a thorough analysis of the investment objectives of the entity whose funds are being managed. These entities can be classified as *individual investors* and *institutional investors*. Within each of these broad classifications is a wide range of investment objectives.

The objectives of an individual investor may be to accumulate funds to purchase a home or other major acquisition, to have sufficient funds to be able to retire at a specified age, or to accumulate funds to pay for college tuition for children. An individual investor may engage the services of a financial advisor/consultant in establishing investment objectives.

Institutional investors include

- pension funds
- depository institutions (commercial banks, savings and loan associations, and credit unions)
- insurance companies (life companies, property and casualty companies, and health companies)
- regulated investment companies (mutual funds)
- endowments and foundations
- treasury department of corporations, municipal governments, and government agencies

In general we can classify institutional investors into two broad categories—those that must meet contractually specified liabilities and those that do not. We can classify those in the first category as institutions with "liability-driven objectives" and those in the second category as "non-liability driven objectives." Some institutions have a wide range of investment products that they offer investors, some of which are liability driven and others that are non-liability driven. Once the investment objective is understand, it will then be possible to (1) establish a "benchmark" or "bogey" by which to evaluate the performance of the investment manager and (2) evaluate alternative investment strategies to assess the potential for realizing the specified investment objective.

A *liability* is a cash outlay that must be made at a specific time to satisfy the contractual terms of an issued obligation. An institutional investor is concerned with both the *amount* and *timing* of liabilities, because its assets must produce the cash flow to meet any payments it has promised to make in a timely way.

STEP 2: ESTABLISHING AN INVESTMENT POLICY

The second step in the investment management process is establishing policy guidelines to satisfy the investment objectives. Setting policy begins with the asset allocation decision. That is, a decision must be made as to how the funds to be invested should be distributed among the major classes of assets.

Asset Classes

Throughout this book we refer to certain categories of investment products as an "asset class." From the perspective of a U.S. investor, the convention is to refer the following as *traditional asset classes*:

    U.S. common stocks
    Non-U.S. (or foreign) common stocks
    U.S. bonds
    Non-U.S. (or foreign) bonds
    Cash equivalents
    Real estate

Cash equivalents are defined as short-term debt obligations that have little price volatility and are covered in Chapter 16.

Common stock and bonds are further divided into asset classes. For U.S. common stocks (also referred to as U.S. equities), the following are classified as asset classes:

    Large capitalization stocks
    Mid capitalization stocks
    Small capitalization stocks
    Growth stocks
    Value stocks

By "capitalization," it is meant the market capitalization of the company's common stock. This is equal to the total market value of all of the common stock outstanding for that company. For example, suppose that a company has 100 million shares of common stock outstanding and each share has a market value of $10. Then the capitalization of this company is $1 billion (100 million shares times $10 per share). The market capitalization of a company is commonly referred to as the "market cap" or simply "cap."

While the market cap of a company is easy to determine given the market price per share and the number of shares outstanding, how does one define "value" and "growth" stocks? We'll see how that is done in Chapter 8.

For U.S. bonds, also referred to as fixed-income securities, the following are classified as asset classes:

U.S. government bonds
Investment-grade corporate bonds
High-yield corporate bonds
U.S. municipal bonds (i.e., state and local bonds)
Mortgage-backed securities
Asset-backed securities

All of these securities are described in Chapters 16 and 17, where what is meant by "investment grade" and "high yield" are also explained. Sometimes, the first three bond asset classes listed above are further divided into "long term" and "short term."

For non-U.S. stocks and bonds, the following are classified as asset classes:

Developed market foreign stocks   Developed market foreign bonds
Emerging market foreign stocks   Emerging market foreign bonds

In addition to the traditional asset classes, there are asset classes commonly referred to as *alternative investments*. Two of the more popular ones are hedge funds and private equity. Hedge funds are covered in Chapter 29 and private equity is the subject of Chapter 30.

How does one define an asset class? One investment manager, Mark Kritzman, describes how this is done as follows:

> ...some investments take on the status of an asset class simply because the managers of these assets promote them as an asset class. They believe that investors will be more inclined to allocate funds to their products if they are viewed as an asset class rather than merely as an investment strategy.[1]

He then goes on to propose criteria for determining asset class status. We won't review the criteria he proposed here. They involve concepts

---

[1] Mark Kritzman, "Toward Defining an Asset Class," *The Journal of Alternative Investments* (Summer 1999), p. 79.

that are explained in later chapters. After these concepts are explained it will become clear how asset class status is determined. However, it should not come as any surprise that the criteria proposed by Kritzman involve the risk, return, and the correlation of the return of a potential asset class with that of other asset classes.

Along with the designation of an investment as an asset class comes a barometer to be able to quantify performance—the risk, return, and the correlation of the return of the asset class with that of another asset class. The barometer is called a "benchmark index," "market index," or simply "index." For example, listed below are the most popular indexes used to represent the various asset classes that fall into the equity area:

U.S. Equity	Wilshire 5000, Frank Russell 3000
U.S. Large Cap Equity	Standard & Poor's (S&P) 500
U.S. Large Cap Value	Frank Russell 1000 Value, S&P/Barra 500 Value
U.S. Large Cap Growth	Frank Russell 1000 Growth, S&P/Barra 500 Growth
U.S. Mid Cap Equity	Frank Russell Mid Cap
U.S. Small Cap Equity	Frank Russell 2000
U.S. Small Cap Value	Frank Russell 2000 Value
U.S. Small Cap Growth	Frank Russell 2000 Growth
International Equity	Morgan Stanley Capital International (MSCI) EAFE Salomon Smith Barney International, MSCI All Country World (ACWI) ex U.S.
Emerging Markets	MSCI Emerging Markets

For the U.S. fixed income (bond) asset class, the two commonly used indexes are the Lehman Brothers Aggregate Bond Index and the Salomon Brothers Broad Index.

As other asset classes are described in later chapters, the index used as a proxy for that asset class will be discussed.

If an investor wants exposure to a particular asset class, an investor must be able to buy a sufficient number of the individual assets comprising the asset class. Equivalently, the investor has to buy a sufficient number of individual assets comprising the index representing that asset class. This means that if an investor wants exposure to the U.S. large cap equity market and the S&P 500 is the index (consisting of 500 companies) representing that asset class, then the investor can't simply buy the shares of a handful of companies and hope to acquire the desired exposure to the large cap equity market. For institutional investors, acquiring a sufficient number of individual assets comprising an asset class is often not a serious problem and we will see how this can be done in later chapters. However, for individual investors, obtaining exposure to an asset class by buying individual assets is not simple. How can individual investors accomplish this?

Fortunately, there is an investment vehicle that can be used to obtain exposure to asset classes in a cost effective manner. The vehicle is a regulated investment company, more popularly referred to as a mutual fund. This investment vehicle is the subject of Chapter 26. For now, what is important to understand is that there are mutual funds that invest primarily in specific asset classes. Such mutual funds offer an investor the opportunity to gain exposure to an asset class without the investor having expertise in the management of the individual assets in that asset class and by investing a sum of money that in the absence of a mutual fund would not allow the investor to acquire a sufficient number of individual assets to obtain the desired exposure.

Constraints

There are some institutional investors that make the asset allocation decision based purely on their understanding of the risk-return characteristics of the various asset classes and expected returns. The asset allocation will take into consideration any investment constraints or restrictions. Asset allocation models are commercially available for assisting those individuals responsible for making this decision. Chapter 31 describes one such model.

In the development of an investment policy, the following factors must be considered:

- client constraints
- regulatory constraints
- tax and accounting issues

Client-Imposed Constraints

Examples of client-imposed constraints would be restrictions that specify the types of securities in which a manager may invest and concentration limits on how much or little may be invested in a particular asset class or in a particular issuer. Where the objective is to meet the performance of a particular market or customized benchmark, there may be a restriction as to the degree to which the manager may deviate from some key characteristics of the benchmark.

For example, in later chapters of this book the concepts of the beta of a common stock portfolio and the duration of a bond portfolio will be discussed. These risk measures provide an estimate of the exposure of a portfolio to changes in key factors that affect the portfolio's value—the market overall in the case of a portfolio's beta and the general level of interest rates in the case of a portfolio's duration. Typically, a client will not set a specific value for the level of risk exposure. Instead, the client restriction may be in the form of a maximum on the level of the risk exposure or a permissible range for the risk measure relative to the benchmark. For example, a client may restrict the portfolio's duration to be +0.5 or −0.5 of the client-specified benchmark. Thus, if the duration of the client-imposed benchmark is 4, the manager has the discretion of constructing a portfolio with a duration between 3.5 and 4.5.

Regulatory Constraints

There are many types of regulatory constraints. These involve constraints on the asset classes that are permissible and concentration limits on investments. Moreover, in making the asset allocation decision, consideration must be given to any risk-based capital requirements. For depository institutions and insurance companies, the amount of statutory capital required is related to the quality of the assets in which the institution has invested. There are two types of risk-based capital requirements: credit risk-based capital requirements and interest rate-risk based capital requirement. The former relates statutory capital requirements to the credit-risk associated with the assets in the portfolio. The greater the credit risk, the greater the statutory capital required. Interest rate-risk based capital requirements relate the statutory capital to how sensitive the asset or portfolio is to changes in interest rates. The greater the sensitivity, the higher the statutory capital required.

Tax and Accounting Issues

Tax considerations are important for several reasons. First, certain institutional investors such as pension funds, endowments, and foundations are exempt from federal income taxation. Consequently, the assets in which they invest will not be those that are tax-advantaged investments. Second, there are tax factors that must be incorporated into the investment policy. For example, while a pension fund might be tax-exempt, there may be certain assets or the use of some investment vehicles in which it invests whose earnings may be taxed.

Generally accepted accounting principles (GAAP) and regulatory accounting principles (RAP) are important considerations in developing investment policies. An excellent example is a defined benefit plan for a corporation. GAAP specifies that a corporate pension fund's surplus is equal to the difference between the market value of the assets and the present value of the liabilities. If the surplus is negative, the corporate sponsor must record the negative balance as a liability on its balance sheet. Consequently, in establishing its investment policies, recognition must be given to the volatility of the market value of the fund's portfolio relative to the volatility of the present value of the liabilities. Consider this. In 1994 the return on the S&P 500 and the Lehman Brothers Aggregate Bond Index was 1.29% and −2.92%, respectively. Interest rates rose in 1994. In 1995, the return on the S&P 500 was 37.52% and 18.47% on the Lehman Brothers Aggregate as a result of a decline in interest rates.[2] Most pension plans allocate the bulk of their funds to common stocks and bonds. Which was the best year for pension funds? It would seem that 1995 was the best year. Yet, The Pension Benefit Guaranty Corporation stated that underfunding by pension funds increased in 1995 but decreased in 1994. The reason is that the decline in interest rates increased the present value of liabilities in 1995 and decreased liabilities in 1994 due to a rise in interest rates. Thus, it is not just the performance of the assets that affects the performance of a pension fund but the relative performance of assets versus liabilities.

STEP 3: SELECTING A PORTFOLIO STRATEGY

Selecting a portfolio strategy that is consistent with the investment objectives and investment policy guidelines of the client or institution is the third step in the investment management process. Portfolio strategies can be classified as either active or passive.

An *active portfolio strategy* uses available information and forecasting techniques to seek a better performance than a portfolio that is simply diversified broadly. Essential to all active strategies are expectations about the factors that have been found to influence the performance of an asset class. For example, with active common stock strategies this may include forecasts of future earnings, dividends, or price-earnings ratios. With bond portfolios that are actively managed, expectations may involve forecasts of future interest rates and sector spreads. Active portfolio strategies involving foreign securities may require forecasts of local interest rates and exchange rates.

A *passive portfolio strategy* involves minimal expectational input, and instead relies on diversification to match the performance of some market index. In effect, a passive strategy assumes that the marketplace will reflect all available information in the price paid for securities. Between these extremes of active and passive strategies, several strategies have sprung up that have elements of both. For example, the core of a portfolio may be passively managed with the balance actively managed.

---

[2] The relationship between changes in interest rates and bond prices will be explained in Chapter 21.

In the bond area, several strategies classified as *structured portfolio strategies* have been commonly used. A structured portfolio strategy is one in which a portfolio is designed to achieve the performance of some predetermined liabilities that must be paid out. These strategies are frequently used when trying to match the funds received from an investment portfolio to the future liabilities that must be paid.

Given the choice among active and passive management, which should be selected? The answer depends on (1) the client's or money manager's view of how "price-efficient" the market is, (2) the client's risk tolerance, and (3) the nature of the client's liabilities. By marketplace price efficiency we mean how difficult it would be to earn a greater return than passive management after adjusting for the risk associated with a strategy and the transaction costs associated with implementing that strategy.

STEP 4: SELECTING THE SPECIFIC ASSETS

Once a portfolio strategy is selected, the next step is to select the specific assets to be included in the portfolio. It is in this phase of the investment management process that the investor attempts to construct an *efficient portfolio*. An efficient portfolio is one that provides the greatest expected return for a given level of risk, or equivalently, the lowest risk for a given expected return.

Inputs Required

To construct an efficient portfolio, the investor must be able to quantify risk and provide the necessary inputs. As will be explained in the next chapter, there are three key inputs that are needed: future expected return (or simply expected return), variance of asset returns, and correlation (or covariance) of asset returns. All of the investment tools described in the chapters that follow in this book are intended to provide the investor with information with which to estimate these three inputs.

There are a wide range of approaches to obtain the expected return of assets. Investors can employ various analytical tools that will be discussed throughout this book to derive the future expected return of an asset. For example, we will see in Chapter 4 that there are various asset pricing models that provide expected return estimates based on factors that historically have been found to systematically affect the return on all assets. Investors can use historical average returns as their estimate of future expected returns. Investors can modify historical average returns with their judgment of the future to obtain a future expected return. Another approach is for investors to simply to use their intuition without any formal analysis to come up with the future expected return.

In the next chapter, the reason why the variance of asset returns should be used as a measure of an asset's risk will be explained. This input can be obtained for each asset by calculating the historical variance of asset returns. There are sophisticated time series statistical techniques that can be used to improve the estimated variance of asset returns but they are not covered in this book. Some investors calculate the historical variance of asset returns and adjust them based on their intuition.

The covariance (or correlation) of returns is a measure of how the return of two assets vary together. Typically, investors use historical covariances of asset returns as an estimate of future covariances. But why is a covariance of asset returns needed? As well be explained in the next chapter, the covariance is important because the variance of a portfolio's return depends on it and the key to diversification is the covariance of asset returns.

Approaches to Portfolio Construction

Constructing an efficient portfolio based on the expected return for a portfolio (which depends on the expected return of all the asset returns in the portfolio) and the variance of the portfolio's return (which depends on the variance of the return of all of the assets in the portfolio and the covariance of returns between all pairs of assets in the portfolio) is referred to as "mean-variance" portfolio management. The term "mean" is use because the expected return is equivalent to the "mean" or "average value" of returns. This approach also allows for the inclusion of constraints such as lower and upper bounds on particular assets or assets in particular industries or sectors. The end result of the analysis is a set of efficient portfolios—alternative portfolios from which the investor can select that offer the maximum expected portfolio return for a given level of portfolio risk.

There are variations on this approach to portfolio construction. Mean-variance analysis can be employed by estimating risk factors that historically have explained the variance of asset returns. The basic principle is that the value of an asset is driven by a number of systematic factors (or, equivalently, risk exposures) plus a component unique to a particular company or industry. A set of efficient portfolios can be identified based on the risk factors and the sensitivity of assets to these risk factors. This approach is referred to the "multi-factor risk approach" to portfolio construction and is explained in Chapter 13 for common stock portfolio management and Chapter 24 for fixed-income portfolio management.

With either the full mean-variance approach or the multi-factor risk approach there are two variations. First, the analysis can be performed by investors using individual assets (or securities) or the analysis can be performed on asset classes. This will be illustrated for the full mean-variance approach in the next chapter.

The second variation is one in which the input used to measure risk is the tracking error of a portfolio relative to a benchmark index, rather than the variance of the portfolio return. By a benchmark index it is meant the benchmark that the investor's performance is compared against. As explained in Chapter 7, tracking error is the variance of the difference in the return on the portfolio and the return on the benchmark index. When this "tracking error multi-factor risk approach" to portfolio construction is applied to individual assets, the investor can identify the set of efficient portfolios in terms of a portfolio that matches the risk profile of the benchmark index for each level of tracking error. Selecting assets that intentionally cause the portfolio's risk profile to differ from that of the benchmark index is the way a manager actively manages a portfolio. In contrast, indexing means matching the risk profile. "Enhanced" indexing basically means that the assets selected for the portfolio do not cause the risk profile of the portfolio constructed to depart materially from the risk profile of the benchmark. This tracking error multi-factor risk approach to common stock and fixed-income portfolio construction will be explained and illustrated in Chapters 13 and 24, respectively.

At the other extreme of the full mean-variance approach to portfolio management is the assembling of a portfolio in which investors ignore all of the inputs—expected returns, variance of asset returns, and covariance of asset returns—and use their intuition to construct a portfolio. We refer to this approach as the "seat-of-the-pants approach" to portfolio construction. In a rising stock market, for example, this approach is too often confused with investment skill. It is not an approach we recommend.

STEP 5: MEASURING AND EVALUATING PERFORMANCE

The measurement and evaluation of investment performance is the last step in the investment management process. Actually, it is misleading to say that it is the last step since the investment management process is an ongoing process. This step involves measuring the performance of the portfolio and then evaluating that performance relative to some benchmark.

Although a portfolio manager may have performed better than a benchmark, this does not necessarily mean that the portfolio manager satisfied the client's investment objective. For example, suppose that a financial institution established as its investment objective the maximization of portfolio return and allocated 75% of its funds to common stock and the balance to bonds. Suppose further that the manager responsible for the common stock portfolio realized a 1-year return that was 150 basis points greater than the benchmark.[3] Assuming that the risk of the portfolio was similar to that of the benchmark, it would appear that the manager outperformed the benchmark. However, suppose that in spite of this performance, the financial institution cannot meet its liabilities. Then the failure was in establishing the investment objectives and setting policy, not the failure of the manager.

SUMMARY

The overview of the investment management process described in this chapter should help in understanding the activities that the portfolio manager faces and the need for the analytical tools that are described in the chapters that follow in this book.

---

[3] A basis point is equal to 0.0001 or 0.01%. This means that 1% is equal to 100 basis points.

CHAPTER 2

Portfolio Selection

Frank J. Fabozzi, Ph.D., CFA
Adjunct Professor of Finance
School of Management
Yale University

Harry M. Markowitz, Ph.D.
Consultant

Francis Gupta, Ph.D.
Vice President
Credit Suisse Asset Management

This chapter is an introduction to the theory of portfolio selection, which together with asset pricing theory, discussed in Chapter 4, provides the foundation and the building blocks for the management of portfolios. The goal of portfolio selection is the construction of portfolios that maximize expected returns consistent with individually acceptable levels of risk. Using both historical data and investor expectations of future returns, portfolio selection uses modeling techniques to quantify "expected portfolio returns" and "acceptable levels of portfolio risk," and provides methods to select an optimal portfolio.

The theory of portfolio selection presented in this chapter, popularly referred to as *mean-variance portfolio analysis* or simply *mean variance analysis*, is a normative theory. A normative theory is one that describes a standard or norm of behavior that investors should pursue in constructing a portfolio, in contrast to a theory that is actually followed. In the next chapter we illustrate how mean-variance analysis is applied in practice.

15

Asset pricing theory goes on to formalize the relationship that should exist between asset returns and risk if investors behave in a hypothesized manner. In contrast to a normative theory, asset pricing theory is a positive theory—a theory that hypothesizes how investors behave rather than how investors should behave. Based on that hypothesized behavior of investors, a model that provides the expected return (a key input into constructing portfolios based on mean-variance analysis) is derived and is called an *asset pricing model*.

Together, portfolio selection theory and asset pricing theory provide a framework to specify and measure investment risk and to develop relationships between expected asset return and risk (and hence between risk and required return on an investment). However, it is critically important to understand that portfolio selection theory is a theory that is independent of any theories about asset pricing. The validity of portfolio selection theory does not rest on the validity of asset pricing theory.

It would not be an overstatement to say that modern portfolio theory has revolutionized the world of investment management. Allowing managers to quantify the investment risk and expected return of a portfolio has provided the scientific and objective complement to the subjective art of investment management. More importantly, whereas at one time the focus of portfolio management used to be the risk of individual assets, the theory of portfolio selection has shifted the focus to the risk of the entire portfolio. This theory shows that it is possible to combine risky assets and produce a portfolio whose expected return reflects its components, but with considerably lower risk. In other words, it is possible to construct a portfolio whose risk is smaller than the sum of all its individual parts!

Though practitioners realized that the risks of individual assets were related, prior to modern portfolio theory they were unable to formalize how combining them into a portfolio impacted the risk at the entire portfolio level, or how the addition of a new asset would change the return/risk characteristics of the portfolio. This is because practitioners were unable to quantify the returns and risks of their investments. Furthermore, in the context of the entire portfolio, they were also unable to formalize the interaction of the returns and risks across asset classes and individual assets. The failure to quantify these important measures and formalize these important relationships made the goal of constructing an optimal portfolio highly subjective and provided no insight into the return investors could expect and the risk they were undertaking. The other drawback before the advent of the theory of portfolio selection and asset pricing theory was that there was no measurement tool available to investors for judging the performance of their investment managers.

SOME BASIC CONCEPTS

Portfolio theory draws on concepts from two fields: financial economic theory and probability and statistical theory. This section presents the concepts from financial economic theory used in portfolio theory. While many of the concepts presented here have a more technical or rigorous definition, the purpose is to keep the explanations simple and intuitive so the reader can appreciate the importance and contribution of these concepts to the development of modern portfolio theory.

Utility Function and Indifference Curves

In life there are many situations where entities (i.e., individuals and firms) face two or more choices. The economic "theory of choice" uses the concept of a utility function to describe the way entities make decisions when faced with a set of choices. A *utility function* assigns a (numeric) value to all possible choices faced by the entity. The higher the value of a particular choice, the greater the utility derived from that choice. The choice that is selected is the one that results in the maximum utility given a set of constraints faced by the entity.[1]

In portfolio theory too, entities are faced with a set of choices. Different portfolios have different levels of expected return and risk. Also, the higher the level of expected return, the larger the risk. Entities are faced with the decision of choosing a portfolio from the set of all possible risk/return combinations, where when they like return, they dislike risk. Therefore, entities obtain different levels of utility from different risk/return combinations. The utility obtained from any possible risk/return combination is expressed by the utility function. Put simply, the utility function expresses the preferences of entities over perceived risk and expected return combinations.

A utility function can be expressed in graphical form by a set of indifference curves. Exhibit 2.1 shows indifference curves labeled u_1, u_2, and u_3. By convention, the horizontal axis measures risk and the vertical axis measures expected return. Each curve represents a set of portfolios with different combinations of risk and return. All the points on a given indifference curve indicate combinations of risk and expected return that will give the same level of utility to a given investor. For example, on utility curve u_1, there are two points u and u', with u hav-

---

[1] The origins of utility theory date back to the 18th century. But it was not until 1944 that utility theory was formalized in a set of necessary and sufficient axioms by von Neumann and Morgenstern and applied to decision-making under risk and uncertainty. See J. von Neumann and Oskar Morgenstern, *Theory of Games and Economic Behavior* (Princeton, NJ: Princeton University Press, 1944).

ing a higher expected return than u', but also having a higher risk. Because the two points lie on the same indifference curve, the investor has an equal preference for (or is indifferent to) the two points, or, for that matter, any point on the curve. The (positive) slope of an indifference curve reflects the fact that, to obtain the same level of utility, the investor requires a higher expected return in order to accept higher risk.

For the three indifference curves shown in Exhibit 2.1, the utility the investor receives is greater the further the indifference curve is from the horizontal axis, because that curve represents a higher level of return at every level of risk. Thus, for the three indifference curves shown in the exhibit, u_3 has the highest utility and u_1 the lowest.

The Set of Efficient Portfolios and the Optimal Portfolio

Portfolios that provide the largest possible expected return for given levels of risk are called *efficient portfolios*. To construct an efficient portfolio, it is necessary to make some assumption about how investors behave when making investment decisions. One reasonable assumption is that investors are *risk averse*. A risk-averse investor is an investor who, when faced with choosing between two investments with the same expected return but two different risks, prefers the one with the lower risk.

EXHIBIT 2.1   Indifference Curves

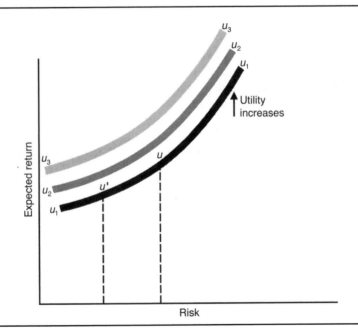

In selecting portfolios, an investor seeks to maximize the expected portfolio return given his tolerance for risk.[2] Given a choice from the set of efficient portfolios, an *optimal portfolio* is the one that is most preferred by the investor.

Risky Assets versus Risk-Free Assets

A risky asset is one for which the return that will be realized in the future is uncertain. For example, an investor who purchases the stock of Pfizer Corporation today with the intention of holding it for some finite time does not know what return will be realized at the end of the holding period. The return will depend on the price of Pfizer's stock at the time of sale and on the dividends that the company pays during the holding period. Thus, Pfizer stock, and indeed the stock of all companies, is a risky asset.

Securities issued by the U.S. government are also risky. For example, an investor who purchases a U.S. government bond that matures in 30 years does not know the return that will be realized if this bond is held for only one year. This is because changes in interest rates in that year will affect the price of the bond one year from now and that will impact the return on the bond over that year.

There are assets, however, for which the return that will be realized in the future is known with certainty today. Such assets are referred to as *risk-free* or *riskless assets*. The risk-free asset is commonly defined as a short-term obligation of the U.S. government. For example, if an investor buys a U.S. government security that matures in one year and plans to hold that security for one year, then there is no uncertainty about the return that will be realized. The investor knows that in one year, the maturity date of the security, the government will pay a specific amount to retire the debt. Notice how this situation differs for the U.S. government security that matures in 30 years. While the 1-year and the 30-year securities are obligations of the U.S. government, the former matures in one year so that there is no uncertainty about the return that will be realized. In contrast, while the investor knows what the government will pay at the end of 30 years for the 30-year bond, he does not know what the price of the bond will be one year from now.

MEASURING A PORTFOLIO'S EXPECTED RETURN

We are now ready to define the actual and expected return of a risky asset and a portfolio of risky assets.

---

[2] Alternatively stated, an investor seeks to minimize the risk that he is exposed to given some target expected return.

Measuring Single-Period Portfolio Return

The actual return on a portfolio of assets over some specific time period is straightforward to calculate using the following:

$$R_p = w_1 R_1 + w_2 R_2 + \ldots + w_G R_G \tag{1}$$

where,

R_p = rate of return on the portfolio over the period

R_g = rate of return on asset g over the period

w_g = weight of asset g in the portfolio (i.e., market value of asset g as a proportion of the market value of the total portfolio) at the beginning of the period

G = number of assets in the portfolio

In shorthand notation, equation (1) can be expressed as follows:

$$R_p = \sum_{g=1}^{G} w_g R_g \tag{2}$$

Equation (2) states that the return on a portfolio (R_p) of G assets is equal to the sum over all individual assets' weights in the portfolio times their respective return. The portfolio return R_p is sometimes called the *holding period return* or the *ex post return*.

For example, consider the following portfolio consisting of three assets:

Asset	Market value at the beginning of holding period	Rate of return over holding period
1	$6 million	12%
2	8 million	10%
3	11 million	5%

The portfolio's total market value at the beginning of the holding period is $25 million. Therefore,

w_1 = $6 million/$25 million = 0.24, or 24%   and $R_1 = 12\%$

w_2 = $8 million/$25 million = 0.32, or 32%   and $R_2 = 10\%$

w_3 = $11 million/$25 million = 0.44, or 44%   and $R_3 = 5\%$

Notice that the sum of the weights is equal to 1. Substituting into equation (1), we get the holding period portfolio return,[3]

$$R_p = 0.24(12\%) + 0.32(10\%) + 0.44(5\%) = 8.28\%$$

The Expected Return of a Portfolio of Risky Assets

Equation (1) shows how to calculate the actual return of a portfolio over some specific time period. In portfolio management, the investor also wants to know the expected (or anticipated) return from a portfolio of risky assets. The expected portfolio return is the weighted average of the expected return of each asset in the portfolio. The weight assigned to the expected return of each asset is the percentage of the market value of the asset to the total market value of the portfolio. That is,

$$E(R_p) = w_1 E(R_1) + w_2 E(R_2) + \ldots + w_G E(R_G) \qquad (3)$$

The $E(\ )$ signifies expectations, and $E(R_p)$ is sometimes called the *ex ante* return, or the expected portfolio return over some specific time period.

The expected return, $E(R_i)$, on a risky asset i is calculated as follows. First, a probability distribution for the possible rates of return that can be realized must be specified. A probability distribution is a function that assigns a probability of occurrence to all possible outcomes for a random variable. Given the probability distribution, the expected value of a random variable is simply the weighted average of the possible outcomes, where the weight is the probability associated with the possible outcome.

In our case, the random variable is the uncertain return of asset i. Having specified a probability distribution for the possible rates of return, the expected value of the rate of return for asset i is the weighted average of the possible outcomes. Finally, rather than use the term "expected value of the return of an asset," we simply use the term "expected return." Mathematically, the expected return of asset i is expressed as:

$$E(R_i) = p_1 R_1 + p_2 R_2 + \ldots + p_N R_N \qquad (4)$$

where,

R_n = the nth possible rate of return for asset i
p_n = the probability of attaining the rate of return n for asset i
N = the number of possible outcomes for the rate of return

---

[3] Note that since the holding period portfolio return is 8.28%, the growth in the portfolio's value over the holding period is given by ($25 million) $\times$ 0.0828 = $2.07 million.

EXHIBIT 2.2 Probability Distribution for the Rate of Return for Stock XYZ

n	Rate of Return	Probability of Occurrence
1	12%	0.18
2	10	0.24
3	8	0.29
4	4	0.16
5	−4	0.13
Total		1.00

How do we specify the probability distribution of returns for an asset? We shall see later on in this chapter that in most cases the probability distribution of returns is based on historical returns. Probabilities assigned to different return outcomes that are based on the past performance of an uncertain investment act as a good estimate of the probability distribution. However, for purpose of illustration, assume that an investor is considering an investment, stock XYZ, which has a probability distribution for the rate of return for some time period as given in Exhibit 2.2. The stock has five possible rates of return and the probability distribution specifies the likelihood of occurrence (in a probabilistic sense) of each of the possible outcomes.

Substituting into equation (4) we get

$$E(R_{XYZ}) = 0.18(12\%) + 0.24(10\%) + 0.29(8\%) + 0.16(4\%) + 0.13(-4\%)$$
$$= 7\%$$

Thus, 7% is the expected return or mean of the probability distribution for the rate of return on stock XYZ.

MEASURING PORTFOLIO RISK

The dictionary defines risk as "hazard, peril, exposure to loss or injury." With respect to investments, investors have used a variety of definitions to describe risk. Harry Markowitz quantified the concept of risk using the well-known statistical measures of variances and covariances.[4] He defined the risk of a portfolio as the sum of the variances of the investments and covariances among the investments. The notion of introducing the covariances among returns of the investments in the portfolio to measure the risk of a portfolio forever changed how the investment community thought about the concept of risk.

[4] See Harry Markowitz, "Portfolio Selection," *Journal of Finance* (March 1952), pp. 77–91 and *Portfolio Selection*, Cowles Foundation Monograph 16 (New York: John Wiley, 1959).

Variance and Standard Deviation as a Measure of Risk

The variance of a random variable is a measure of the dispersion or variability of the possible outcomes around the expected value (mean). In the case of an asset's return, the variance is a measure of the dispersion of the possible rate of return outcomes around the expected return.

The equation for the variance of the expected return for asset i, denoted $var(R_i)$, is

$$var(R_i) = p_1[r_1 - E(R_i)]^2 + p_2[r_2 - E(R_i)]^2 + \ldots + p_N[r_N - E(R_i)]^2$$

or,

$$var(R_i) = \sum_{i=1}^{N} p_n[r_n - E(R_i)]^2 \tag{5}$$

Using the probability distribution of the return for stock XYZ, we can illustrate the calculation of the variance:

$$var(R_{XYZ}) = 0.18(12\% - 7\%)^2 + 0.24(10\% - 7\%)^2 + 0.29(8\% - 7\%)^2$$
$$+ 0.16(4\% - 7\%)^2 + 0.13(-4\% - 7\%)^2 = 24.1\%$$

The variance associated with a distribution of returns measures the tightness with which the distribution is clustered around the mean or expected return. Markowitz argued that this tightness or variance is equivalent to the uncertainty or riskiness of the investment. If an asset is riskless, it has an expected return dispersion of zero. In other words, the return (which is also the expected return in this case) is certain, or guaranteed.

Standard Deviation

Since the variance is squared units, it is common to see the variance converted to the standard deviation by taking the positive square root of the variance:

$$SD(R_i) = \sqrt{var(R_i)}$$

For stock XYZ, then, the standard deviation is

$$SD(R_{XYZ}) = \sqrt{24.1\%} = 4.9\%$$

The variance and standard deviation are conceptually equivalent; that is, the larger the variance or standard deviation, the greater the investment risk.

There are two criticisms of the use of the variance as a measure of risk. The first criticism is that since the variance measures the dispersion of an asset's return around its expected return, it treats both the returns above and below the expected return identically. Investors, however, do not view return outcomes above the expected return in the same way as they view returns below the expected return. Whereas returns above the expected return are considered favorable, outcomes below the expected return are disliked. Because of this, some researchers have argued that measures of risk should not consider the possible return outcomes above the expected return.

Markowitz recognized this limitation and, in fact, suggested a measure of downside risk—the risk of realizing an outcome below the expected return—called the *semi-variance*. The semi-variance is similar to the variance except that in the calculation no consideration is given to returns above the expected return. However, because of the computational problems with using the semi-variance and the limited resources available to him at the time, he used the variance in developing portfolio theory.

Today, practitioners use various measures of downside risk.[5] However, regardless of the measure used, the basic principles of portfolio theory developed by Markowitz and set forth in this chapter are still applicable. That is, the choice of the measure of risk may affect the calculation but doesn't invalidate the theory.

The second criticism is that the variance is only one measure of how the returns vary around the expected return. When a probability distribution is not symmetrical around its expected return, then a statistical measure of the skewness of a distribution should be used in addition to the variance. Markowitz did not consider any such measure in developing portfolio theory. The use of only the variance can be justified based on empirical evidence that suggests that the historical distribution of the returns on stocks is approximately symmetrical.[6]

---

[5] See Vijay S. Bawa and E. B. Lindenberg, "Mean-Lower Partial Moments and Asset Prices," *Journal of Financial Economics* (June 1977), pp. 189–200; Peter C. Fishburn, "Mean-Risk Analysis with Risk Associated with Below-Target Variance," *American Economic Review* (March 1977), pp. 230–245; R. S. Clarkson, "The Measurement of Investment Risk," paper presented to the Faculty of Actuaries (British) on February 20, 1989; and Frank A. Sortino and Robert Van Der Meer, "Downside Risk," *Journal of Portfolio Management* (Summer 1991), pp. 27–31.

[6] See Chapters 1 and 2 in Eugene Fama, *Foundations of Finance* (New York: Basic Books, 1976).

Because expected return and variance are the only two parameters that investors are assumed to consider in making investment decisions, the Markowitz formulation of portfolio theory is often referred to as a "two-parameter model." It is also referred to as "mean-variance analysis." The relative ease of implementation is one of the major reasons why Markowitz's formulation of portfolio theory is so appealing and has become so popular. Not only is it intuitive, but it requires significantly less intellectual prowess and computing power to obtain the means and the variance-covariance matrix of a distribution of a series of returns than to estimate the entire joint distribution of those returns.

Measuring the Portfolio Risk of a Two-Asset Portfolio

Equation (5) gives the variance for an individual asset's return. The variance of a portfolio consisting of two assets is a little more difficult to calculate. It depends not only on the variance of the two assets, but also upon how closely the returns of one asset track those of the other asset. The formula is:

$$\text{var}(R_p) = w_i^2 \ \text{var}(R_i) + w_j^2 \ \text{var}(R_j) + 2w_i w_j \ \text{cov}(R_i, R_j) \tag{6}$$

where

$$\text{cov}(R_i, R_j) = \text{covariance between the return for assets } i \text{ and } j$$

In words, equation (6) states that the variance of the portfolio return is the sum of the squared weighted variances of the two assets plus two times the weighted covariance between the two assets. We will see that this equation can be generalized to the case where there are more than two assets in the portfolio.

Covariance

The covariance has a precise mathematical translation. Its practical meaning is the degree to which the returns on two assets co-vary or change together. The covariance is not expressed in a particular unit, such as dollars or percent. A positive covariance means the returns on two assets tend to move or change in the same direction, while a negative covariance means the returns tend to move in opposite directions. The covariance between any two assets i and j is computed using the following formula:

$$\text{cov}(R_i, R_j) = p_1[r_{i1} - E(R_i)] \ [r_{j1} - E(R_j)] + p_2[r_{i2} - E(R_i)] \ [r_{j2} - E(R_j)]$$
$$+ \ldots + p_N[r_{iN} - E(R_i)] \ [r_{jN} - E(R_j)] \tag{7}$$

where,

r_{in} = the nth possible rate of return for asset i
r_{jn} = the nth possible rate of return for asset j
p_n = the probability of attaining the rate of return n for assets i and j
N = the number of possible outcomes for the rate of return

To illustrate the calculation of the covariance between two assets, we use the two stocks in Exhibit 2.3. The first is stock XYZ from Exhibit 2.2 that we used earlier to illustrate the calculation of the expected return and the standard deviation. The other hypothetical stock is stock ABC whose data are shown in Exhibit 2.3. Substituting the data for the two stocks from Exhibit 2.3 in equation (7), the covariance between stocks XYZ and ABC is calculated as follows:

$$\text{cov}(R_{XYZ}, R_{ABC}) = 0.18(12\% - 7\%)\,(21\% - 10\%)$$
$$+ 0.24(10\% - 7\%)\,(14\% - 10\%) + 0.29(8\% - 7\%)\,(9\% - 10\%)$$
$$+ 0.16(4\% - 7\%)\,(4\% - 10\%) + 0.13(-4\% - 7\%)\,(-3\% - 10\%) = 34$$

Relationship between Covariance and Correlation

The correlation is analogous to the covariance between the expected returns for two assets. Specifically, the correlation between the returns for assets i and j is defined as the covariance of the two assets divided by the product of their standard deviations:

$$\text{cor}(R_i, R_j) = \text{cov}(R_i, R_j)/[\text{SD}(R_i)\,\text{SD}(R_j)] \tag{8}$$

EXHIBIT 2.3   Probability Distribution for the Rate of Return for Asset XYZ and Asset ABC

n	Rate of Return for Asset XYZ	Rate of Return for Asset ABC	Probability of Occurrence
1	12%	21%	0.18
2	10	14	0.24
3	8	9	0.29
4	4	4	0.16
5	−4	−3	0.13
Total			1.00
Expected return	7.0%	10.0%	
Variance	24.1%	53.6%	
Standard deviation	4.9%	7.3%	

The correlation and the covariance are conceptually equivalent terms. Dividing the covariance between the returns of two assets by the product of their standard deviations results in the correlation between the returns of the two assets. Because the correlation is a standardized number (i.e., it has been corrected for differences in the standard deviation of the returns), the correlation is comparable across different assets. The correlation between the returns for stock XYZ and stock ABC is

$$cor(R_{XYZ}, R_{ABC}) = 34/(4.9 \times 7.3) = 0.94$$

The correlation coefficient can have values ranging from +1.0, denoting perfect co-movement in the same direction, to –1.0, denoting perfect co-movement in the opposite direction. Also note that because the standard deviations are always positive, the correlation can only be negative if the covariance is a negative number. A correlation of zero implies that the returns are uncorrelated.

Measuring the Risk of a Portfolio Comprised of More than Two Assets

So far we have defined the risk of a portfolio consisting of two assets. The extension to three assets—i, j, and k—is as follows:

$$var(R_p) = w_i^2 \ var(R_i) + w_j^2 \ var(R_j) + w_k^2 \ var(R_k) + 2w_i w_j \ cov(R_i, R_j)$$
$$+ \ 2w_i w_k \ cov(R_i, R_k) + 2w_j w_k \ cov(R_j, R_k) \qquad (9)$$

In words, equation (9) states that the variance of the portfolio return is the sum of the squared weighted variances of the individual assets plus two times the sum of the weighted pair-wise covariances of the assets. In general, for a portfolio with G assets, the portfolio variance is given by,

$$var(R_p) = \sum_{g=1}^{G} w_g^2 var(R_g) + \sum_{g=1}^{G} \sum_{\substack{h=1 \\ \text{and } h \neq g}}^{G} w_g w_h cov(R_g, R_h) \qquad (10)$$

PORTFOLIO DIVERSIFICATION

Often, one hears investors talking about diversifying their portfolio. By this an investor means constructing a portfolio in such a way as to reduce portfolio risk without sacrificing return. This is certainly a goal that investors should seek. However, the question is how to do this in practice.

Some investors would say that including assets across all asset classes could diversify a portfolio. For example, a investor might argue that a portfolio should be diversified by investing in stocks, bonds, and real estate. While that might be reasonable, two questions must be addressed in order to construct a diversified portfolio. First, how much should be invested in each asset class? Should 40% of the portfolio be in stocks, 50% in bonds, and 10% in real estate, or is some other allocation more appropriate? Second, given the allocation, which specific stocks, bonds, and real estate should the investor select?

Some investors who focus only on one asset class such as common stock argue that such portfolios should also be diversified. By this they mean that an investor should not place all funds in the stock of one corporation, but rather should include stocks of many corporations. Here, too, several questions must be answered in order to construct a diversified portfolio. First, which corporations should be represented in the portfolio? Second, how much of the portfolio should be allocated to the stocks of each corporation?

Prior to the development of portfolio theory, while investors often talked about diversification in these general terms, they did not possess the analytical tools by which to answer the questions posed above. For example, in 1945, D.H. Leavens wrote:[7]

> An examination of some fifty books and articles on investment that have appeared during the last quarter of a century shows that most of them refer to the desirability of diversification. The majority, however, discuss it in general terms and do not clearly indicate why it is desirable.

Leavens illustrated the benefits of diversification on the assumption that risks are independent. However, in the last paragraph of his article, he cautioned:

> The assumption, mentioned earlier, that each security is acted upon by independent causes, is important, although it cannot always be fully met in practice. Diversification among companies in one industry cannot protect against unfavorable factors that may affect the whole industry; additional diversification among industries is needed for that purpose. Nor can diversification among industries

---

[7] D. H. Leavens, "Diversification of Investments," *Trusts and Estates* (May 1945), pp. 469–473.

protect against cyclical factors that may depress all industries at the same time.

A major contribution of the theory of portfolio selection is that using the concepts discussed above, a quantitative measure of the diversification of a portfolio is possible, and it is this measure that can be used to achieve the maximum diversification benefits.

The Markowitz diversification strategy is primarily concerned with the degree of covariance between asset returns in a portfolio. Indeed a key contribution of Markowitz diversification is the formulation of an asset's risk in terms of a portfolio of assets, rather than in isolation. Markowitz diversification seeks to combine assets in a portfolio with returns that are less than perfectly positively correlated, in an effort to lower portfolio risk (variance) without sacrificing return. It is the concern for maintaining return while lowering risk through an analysis of the covariance between asset returns, that separates Markowitz diversification from a naive approach to diversification and makes it more effective.

Markowitz diversification and the importance of asset correlations can be illustrated with a simple two-asset portfolio example. To do this, we will first show the general relationship between the risk of a two-asset portfolio and the correlation of returns of the component assets. Then we will look at the effects on portfolio risk of combining assets with different correlations.

Portfolio Risk and Correlation

In our two-asset portfolio, assume that asset C and asset D are available with expected returns and standard deviations as shown:

Asset	E(R)	SD(R)
Asset C	12%	30%
Asset D	18%	40%

If an equal 50% weighting is assigned to both stocks C and D, the expected portfolio return can be calculated as shown:

$$E(R_p) = 0.50(12\%) + 0.50(18\%) = 15\%$$

The variance of the return on the two-stock portfolio from equation (6) is:

$$var(R_p) = w_C^2 \ var(R_C) + w_D^2 w_D 2 \ var(R_D) + 2w_C w_D \ cov(R_C, R_D)$$
$$= (0.5)^2(30\%)^2 + (0.5)^2(40\%)^2 + 2(0.5)(0.5)cov(R_C, R_D)$$

From equation (8),

$$\text{cor}(R_C, R_D) = \text{cov}(R_C, R_D)/[\text{SD}(R_C)\ \text{SD}(R_D)]$$

so

$$\text{cov}(R_C, R_D) = \text{SD}(R_C)\ \text{SD}(R_D)\ \text{cor}(R_C, R_D)$$

Since $\text{SD}(R_C) = 30\%$ and $\text{SD}(R_D) = 40\%$, then

$$\text{cov}(R_C, R_D) = (30\%)(40\%)\ \text{cor}(R_C, R_D)$$

Substituting into the expression for $\text{var}(R_p)$, we get

$$\text{var}(R_p) = (0.5)^2(30\%)^2 + (0.5)^2(40\%)^2 \\ + 2(0.5)(0.5)(30\%)(40\%)\ \text{cor}(R_C, R_D)$$

Taking the square root of the variance gives

$$\text{SD}(R_p)$$

$$= \sqrt{(0.5)^2(30\%)^2 + (0.5)^2(40\%)^2 + 2(0.5)(0.5)(30\%)(40\%)\text{cor}(R_C, R_D)}$$

$$= \sqrt{625 + (600)\text{cor}(R_C, R_D)} \qquad\qquad (11)$$

The Effect of the Correlation of Asset Returns on Portfolio Risk

How would the risk change for our two-asset portfolio with different correlations between the returns of the component stocks? Let's consider the following three cases for $\text{cor}(R_C, R_D)$: +1.0, 0, and −1.0. Substituting into equation (11) for these three cases of $\text{cor}(R_C, R_D)$, we get

$\text{cor}(R_C, R_D)$	$E(R_p)$	$\text{SD}(R_p)$
+1.0	15%	35%
0.0	15	25
−1.0	15	5

As the correlation between the expected returns on stocks C and D decreases from +1.0 to 0.0 to −1.0, the standard deviation of the expected portfolio return also decreases from 35% to 5%. However, the expected portfolio return remains 15% for each case.

This example clearly illustrates the effect of Markowitz diversification. The principle of Markowitz diversification states that as the correlation (covariance) between the returns for assets that are combined in a portfolio decreases, so does the variance (hence the standard deviation) of the return for the portfolio. This is due to the degree of correlation between the expected asset returns.

The good news is that investors can maintain expected portfolio return and lower portfolio risk by combining assets with lower (and preferably negative) correlations. However, the bad news is that very few assets have small to negative correlations with other assets! The problem, then, becomes one of searching among large numbers of assets in an effort to discover the portfolio with the minimum risk at a given level of expected return or, equivalently, the highest expected return at a given level of risk.

The stage is now set for a discussion of efficient portfolios and their construction.

CHOOSING A PORTFOLIO OF RISKY ASSETS

Diversification in the manner suggested by Professor Markowitz leads to the construction of portfolios that have the highest expected return at a given level of risk. Such portfolios are called *efficient portfolios*. In order to construct efficient portfolios, the theory makes some basic assumptions about asset selection behavior by the entities. The assumptions are as follows:

Assumption 1: The only two parameters that affect an investor's decision are the expected return and the variance. (That is, investors make decisions using the two-parameter model formulated by Markowitz.)

Assumption 2: Investors are risk averse. (That is, when faced with two investments with the same expected return but two different risks, investors will prefer the one with the lower risk.)

Assumption 3: All investors seek to achieve the highest expected return at a given level of risk.

Assumption 4: All investors have the same expectations regarding expected return, variance, and covariances for all risky assets. (This is referred to as the *homogeneous expectations assumption*.)

Assumption 5: All investors have a common one-period investment horizon.

Constructing Efficient Portfolios

The technique of constructing efficient portfolios from large groups of stocks requires a massive number of calculations. In a portfolio of G securities, there are $(G^2 - G)/2$ unique covariances to calculate. Hence, for a portfolio of just 50 securities, there are 1,224 covariances that must be calculated. For 100 securities, there are 4,950. Furthermore, in order to solve for the portfolio that minimizes risk for each level of return, a mathematical technique called *quadratic programming* must be used. A discussion of this technique is beyond the scope of this chapter. However, it is possible to illustrate the general idea of the construction of efficient portfolios by referring again to the simple two-asset portfolio consisting of assets C and D.

Recall that for two assets, C and D, $E(R_C) = 12\%$, $SD(R_C) = 30\%$, $E(R_D) = 18\%$, and $SD(R_D) = 40\%$. We now further assume that $cor(R_C, R_D) = -0.5$. Exhibit 2.4 presents the expected portfolio return and standard deviation for five different portfolios made up of varying proportions of C and D.[8]

Feasible and Efficient Portfolios

A *feasible portfolio* is any portfolio that an investor can construct given the assets available. The five portfolios presented in Exhibit 2.4 are all feasible portfolios. The collection of all feasible portfolios is called the *feasible set of portfolios*. With only two assets, the feasible set of portfolios is graphed as a curve that represents those combinations of risk and expected return that are attainable by constructing portfolios from all possible combinations of the two assets.

EXHIBIT 2.4   Portfolio Expected Returns and Standard Deviations for Five Mixes of Assets C and D

Asset C: $E(R_C) = 12\%$, $SD(R_C) = 30\%$
Asset D: $E(R_D) = 18\%$, and $SD(R_D) = 40\%$
Correlation between Asset C and D = $cor(R_C, R_D) = -0.5$

Portfolio	Proportion of Asset C	Proportion of Asset D	$E(R_p)$	$SD(R_p)$
1	100%	0%	12.0%	30.0%
2	75	25	13.5%	19.5%
3	50	50	15.0%	18.0%
4	25	75	16.5%	27.0%
5	0	100	18.0%	40.0%

---

[8] These calculations are simple enough to verify using a calculator.

EXHIBIT 2.5   Feasible and Efficient Portfolios for Assets C and D

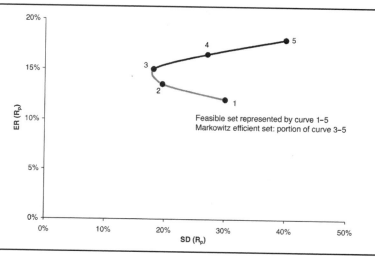

Feasible set represented by curve 1–5
Markowitz efficient set: portion of curve 3–5

Exhibit 2.5 presents the feasible set of portfolios for all combinations of assets C and D. As mentioned earlier, the portfolio mixes listed in Exhibit 2.4 belong to this set and are shown by the points 1 through 5, respectively. Starting from 1 and proceeding to 5, asset C goes from 100% to 0%, while asset D goes from 0% to 100%—therefore all possible combinations of C and D lie between portfolios 1 and 5, or on the curve labeled 1–5. In the case of two assets, any risk/return combination not lying on this curve is not attainable, since there is no mix of assets C and D that will result in that risk/return combination. Consequently, the curve 1–5 can also be thought of as the feasible set.

In contrast to a feasible portfolio, an *efficient portfolio* is one that gives the highest expected return of all feasible portfolios with the same risk. An efficient portfolio is also said to be a *mean-variance efficient portfolio*. Thus, for each level of risk there is an efficient portfolio. The collection of all efficient portfolios is called the *efficient set*.

The efficient set for the feasible set presented in Exhibit 2.5 is differentiated by the bold curve section 3–5. Efficient portfolios are the combinations of assets C and D that result in the risk/return combinations on the bold section of the curve. These portfolios offer the highest expected return at a given level of risk. Notice that two of our five portfolio mixes—portfolio 1 with $E(R_p) = 12\%$ and $SD(R_p) = 20\%$ and portfolio 2 with $E(R_p) = 13.5\%$ and $SD(R_p) = 19.5\%$—are not included in the efficient set. This is because there is at least one portfolio in the efficient set (for example, portfolio 3) that has a higher expected return and lower risk than both of them. We can also see that portfolio 4 has a higher expected return and lower risk than portfolio 1. In fact, the whole curve section 1–3 is not efficient. For any given risk/return combination on this curve section, there is a combination (on the curve section 3–5) that has the same risk and a higher return, or the same return and a lower risk, or both. In other words, for any portfolio that results in the return/risk combination on the curve section 1–3 (excluding portfolio 3), there exists a portfolio that dominates it by having the same return and lower risk, or the same risk and a higher return, or a lower risk and a higher return. For example, portfolio 4 dominates portfolio 1, and portfolio 3 dominates both portfolios 1 and 2.

Exhibit 2.6 shows the feasible and efficient sets when there are more than two assets. In this case, the feasible set is not a line, but an area. This is because, unlike the two-asset case, it is possible to create asset portfolios that result in risk/return combinations that not only result in combinations that lie on the curve I–II–III, but all combinations that lie in the shaded area. However, the efficient set is given by the curve II–III. It is easily seen that all the portfolios on the efficient set dominate the portfolios in the shaded area.

The efficient set of portfolios is sometimes called the *efficient frontier*, because graphically all the efficient portfolios lie on the boundary of the set of feasible portfolios that have the maximum return for a given level of risk. Any risk/return combination above the efficient frontier cannot be achieved, while risk/return combinations of the portfolios that make up the efficient frontier dominate those that lie below the efficient frontier.

EXHIBIT 2.6   Feasible and Efficient Portfolios with More Than Two Assets*

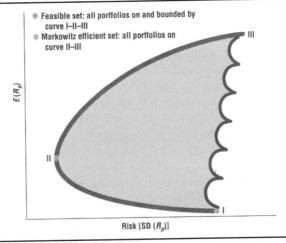

* The picture is for illustrative purposes only. The actual shape of the feasible region depends on the returns and risks of the assets chosen and the correlation among them.

EXHIBIT 2.7   Selection of the Optimal Portfolio

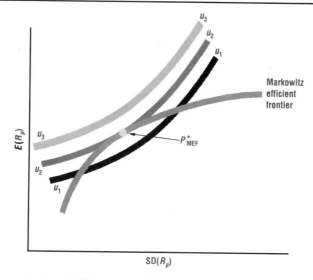

$u_1, u_2, u_3 = $ indifference curves with $u_1 < u_2 < u_3$

$P^*_{MEF} = $ optimal portfolio on Markowitz efficient frontier

Choosing the Optimal Portfolio in the Efficient Set

Now that we have constructed the efficient set of portfolios, the next step is to determine the optimal portfolio.

Since all portfolios on the efficient frontier provide the greatest possible return at their level of risk, an investor or entity will want to hold one of the portfolios on the efficient frontier. Notice that the portfolios on the efficient frontier represent trade-offs in terms of risk and return. Moving from left to right on the efficient frontier, the risk increases, but so does the expected return. The question is which one of those portfolios should an investor hold? The best portfolio to hold of all those on the efficient frontier is the *optimal portfolio*.

Intuitively, the optimal portfolio should depend on the investor's preference over different risk/return trade-offs. As explained earlier, this preference can be expressed in terms of a utility function.

In Exhibit 2.7, three indifference curves representing a utility function and the efficient frontier are drawn on the same diagram. An indifference curve indicates the combinations of risk and expected return that give the same level of utility. Moreover, the farther the indifference curve from the horizontal axis, the higher the utility.

EXHIBIT 2.8   Selection of Optimal Portfolio with Different Indifference Curves
(Utility Function)

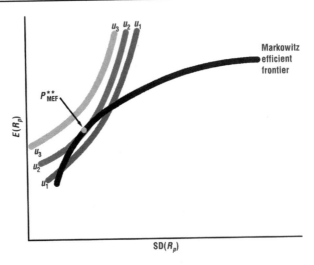

u_1, u_2, u_3 = indifference curves with $u_1 < u_2 < u_3$
P^{**}_{MEF} = optimal portfolio on Markowitz efficient frontier

From Exhibit 2.7, it is possible to determine the optimal portfolio
for the investor with the indifference curves shown. Remember that the
investor wants to get to the highest indifference curve achievable given
the efficient frontier. Given that requirement, the optimal portfolio is
represented by the point where an indifference curve is tangent to the
efficient frontier. In Exhibit 2.7, that is the portfolio P^*_{MEF}. For example, suppose that P^*_{MEF} corresponds to portfolio 4 in Exhibit 2.5. We
know from Exhibit 2.4 that this portfolio is made up of 25% of asset C
and 75% of asset D, with an $E(R_p) = 16.5\%$ and $SD(R_p) = 27.0\%$.
    Consequently, for the investor's preferences over risk and return as
determined by the shape of the indifference curves represented in
Exhibit 2.7, and expectations for asset C and D inputs (returns and variance-covariance) represented in Exhibit 2.4, portfolio 4 is the optimal
portfolio because it maximizes the investor's utility. If this investor had
a different preference for expected risk and return, there would have
been a different optimal portfolio. For example, Exhibit 2.8 shows the
same efficient frontier but three other indifference curves. In this case,
the optimal portfolio is P^{**}_{MEF}, which has a lower expected return and
risk than P^*_{MEF} in Exhibit 2.7. Similarly, if the investor had a different
set of input expectations, the optimal portfolio would be different.

At this point in our discussion, a natural question is how to estimate an investor's utility function so that the indifference curves can be determined. Unfortunately, there is little guidance about how to construct one. In general, economists have not been successful in measuring utility functions.

The inability to measure utility functions does not mean that the theory is flawed. What it does mean is that once an investor constructs the efficient frontier, the investor will subjectively determine which efficient portfolio is appropriate given his or her tolerance to risk.

INDEX MODEL'S APPROXIMATIONS TO THE COVARIANCE STRUCTURE

The inputs to mean-variance analysis include expected returns, variance of returns, and either covariance or correlation of returns between each pair of securities. For example, an analysis that allows 200 securities as possible candidates for portfolio selection requires 200 expected returns, 200 variances of return, and 19,900 correlations or covariances. An investment team tracking 200 securities may reasonably be expected to summarize their analyses in terms of 200 means and variances, but it is clearly unreasonable for them to produce 19,900 carefully considered correlations or covariances.

It was clear to Markowitz that some kind of model of covariance structure was needed for the practical application of normative analysis to large portfolios. He did little more than point out the problem and suggest some possible models of covariance for research.

One model Markowitz proposed to explain the correlation structure among security returns assumed that the return on the ith security depends on an "underlying factor, the general prosperity of the market as expressed by some index." Mathematically, the relationship is expressed as follows:[9]

$$r_i = \alpha_i + \beta_i F + u_i \qquad (12)$$

where

r_i = the return on security i
F = value of some index[10]
u_i = error term

---

[9] See pages 96–101 and in particular footnote 1 on page 100 of Markowitz, *Portfolio Selection*.

[10] Markowitz used the notation I in proposing the model given by equation (12).

The expected value of u_i is zero and u_i is uncorrelated with F and every other u_j.

The parameters α_i and β_i are parameters to be estimated. When measured using regression analysis, β_i is the ratio of the covariance of asset i's return and F to the variance of F.

Markowitz further suggested that the relationship need not be linear and that there could be several underlying factors.

Single Index Market Model

In 1963, William Sharpe tested equation (12) as an explanation of how security returns tend to go up and down together with general market index, F.[11] For the index in the market model he used a market index for F. Specifically, Sharpe estimated using regression analysis the following model:

$$r_{it} = \alpha_i + \beta_i\, r_{mt} + u_{it} \qquad (13)$$

where

r_{it} = return on asset i over the period t

r_{mt} = return on the market index over the period t

α_i = a term that represents the nonmarket component of the return on asset i

β_i = the ratio of the covariance of the return of asset i and the return of the market index to the variance of the return of the market index

u_{it} = a zero mean random error term

The model given by equation (13) is called the *single index market model* or simply the *market model*. It is important to note that when Markowitz discussed the possibility of using equation (12) to estimate the covariance structure, the index he suggested was not required to be a market index.

Regression analysis is used to calculate the values for β_i and α_i. Suppose that the S&P 500 is used to represent the market index. Exhibit 2.9 shows 60 monthly returns for five companies and for the S&P 500 for the period January 1996 to December 2000. We will not demonstrate how to calculate β_i and α_i here because this can be easily done using the built-in feature available on most electronic spreadsheets. At the bottom of the exhibit the output of the regression analysis is reported for each company. There are statistical tests that are used to determine if the esti-

---

[11] William F. Sharpe, "A Simplified Model for Portfolio Analysis," *Management Science* (January 1963), pp. 277–293.

mated values for beta and alpha are statistically significant. These tests are based on the Student-t test reported in the exhibit. A discussion of these tests is beyond the scope of this chapter. The beta for all five companies is statistically different from zero, which means that there is a relationship between the return on the stock of each company and the return on the S&P 500. The coefficient of determination, denoted by R-squared, indicates the strength of the relationship. Specifically, it measures the percentage of the variation in the return on the stock explained by the return on the S&P 500.

EXHIBIT 2.9   Return Data and Historical Betas for Five Stocks

	Month	S&P500	General Electric	McGraw Hill	IBM	General Motors	Xerox
1	31-Jan-96	0.03262	0.06597	0.02152	0.18741	−0.00473	−0.09763
2	29-Feb-96	0.00693	−0.01629	−0.01084	0.13249	−0.01853	0.06063
3	29-Mar-96	0.00792	0.03755	−0.00715	−0.09276	0.03902	−0.03647
4	30-Apr-96	0.01343	−0.00803	0.01729	−0.03146	0.01878	0.16733
5	31-May-96	0.02285	0.07120	0.06980	−0.00603	0.02350	0.07423
6	28-Jun-96	0.00226	0.04834	−0.02400	−0.07260	−0.04989	0.02539
7	31-Jul-96	−0.04575	−0.04657	−0.14754	0.08586	−0.06921	−0.05841
8	30-Aug-96	0.01881	0.01064	0.05974	0.06721	0.02615	0.08933
9	30-Sep-96	0.05417	0.10027	0.03963	0.08852	−0.03275	−0.01749
10	31-Oct-96	0.02613	0.06319	0.09971	0.03614	0.11719	−0.13520
11	29-Nov-96	0.07338	0.07494	−0.02229	0.23818	0.08205	0.05660
12	31-Dec-96	−0.02151	−0.04428	0.01374	−0.04941	−0.03254	0.07990
13	31-Jan-97	0.06132	0.04678	0.07859	0.03548	0.05830	0.11401
14	28-Feb-97	0.00593	−0.00604	0.04995	−0.08143	−0.01059	0.06610
15	31-Mar-97	−0.04261	−0.03018	−0.01446	−0.04522	−0.04320	−0.08488
16	30-Apr-97	0.05841	0.11839	−0.00489	0.16940	0.04515	0.08132
17	30-May-97	0.05858	0.08784	0.08324	0.08037	0.00000	0.10163
18	30-Jun-97	0.04345	0.07660	0.07420	0.04335	−0.02832	0.16893
19	31-Jul-97	0.07812	0.08285	0.15303	0.17175	0.10987	0.04279
20	29-Aug-97	−0.05745	−0.10784	−0.09054	−0.03948	0.02222	−0.08207
21	30-Sep-97	0.05315	0.09207	0.10398	0.04562	0.06673	0.11930
22	31-Oct-97	−0.03448	−0.05051	−0.03416	−0.07075	−0.04108	−0.05791
23	28-Nov-97	0.04459	0.14313	0.05235	0.11371	−0.04284	−0.02049
24	31-Dec-97	0.01573	−0.00271	0.08128	−0.04452	0.05804	−0.04496
25	30-Jan-98	0.01015	0.05622	−0.05659	−0.05615	−0.04630	0.08799
26	27-Feb-98	0.07045	0.00323	0.08885	0.05962	0.19849	0.10575
27	31-Mar-98	0.04995	0.11238	0.00579	−0.00539	−0.01723	0.20166
28	30-Apr-98	0.00908	−0.01160	0.01808	0.11552	−0.00554	0.06635
29	29-May-98	−0.01883	−0.02128	0.01472	0.01592	0.07421	−0.09361
30	30-Jun-98	0.03944	0.08996	0.04237	−0.02287	−0.07043	−0.00865
31	31-Jul-98	−0.01162	−0.01252	0.00537	0.15406	0.08232	0.03875
32	31-Aug-98	−0.14580	−0.10552	−0.06459	−0.14834	−0.18928	−0.16815

EXHIBIT 2.9 (Continued)

	Month	S&P500	General Electric	McGraw Hill	IBM	General Motors	Xerox
33	30-Sep-98	0.06240	−0.00172	0.03934	0.14095	−0.05591	−0.03078
34	30-Oct-98	0.08029	0.09976	0.13486	0.15564	0.15148	0.15118
35	30-Nov-98	0.05913	0.03286	−0.00053	0.11343	0.11375	0.10186
36	31-Dec-98	0.05638	0.13250	0.13827	0.11658	0.02415	0.10102
37	29-Jan-99	0.04101	0.02819	0.06135	−0.00610	0.25415	0.05085
38	26-Feb-99	−0.03228	−0.04350	0.01612	−0.07247	−0.07451	−0.10988
39	31-Mar-99	0.03879	0.10629	−0.00400	0.04418	0.05435	−0.05187
40	30-Apr-99	0.03794	−0.04746	0.01376	0.18018	0.02371	0.12710
41	28-May-99	−0.02497	−0.03499	−0.05719	0.11020	−0.08379	−0.04362
42	30-Jun-99	0.05444	0.11125	0.03976	0.11422	−0.04348	0.05473
43	30-Jul-99	−0.03205	−0.03230	−0.05678	−0.02756	−0.07386	−0.17249
44	31-Aug-99	−0.00625	0.03039	0.02020	−0.00800	0.09202	−0.01918
45	30-Sep-99	−0.02855	0.05876	−0.06409	−0.02860	−0.05000	−0.12099
46	29-Oct-99	0.06254	0.14286	0.23256	−0.18802	0.11917	−0.32340
47	30-Nov-99	0.01906	−0.03967	−0.04566	0.05020	0.02928	−0.03524
48	31-Dec-99	0.05784	0.19239	0.08710	0.04669	0.00955	−0.16393
49	31-Jan-00	−0.05090	−0.13651	−0.09026	0.04056	0.10834	−0.07989
50	29-Feb-00	−0.02011	−0.00935	−0.08834	−0.08356	−0.04965	0.04192
51	31-Mar-00	0.09672	0.17873	−0.10565	0.14842	0.08874	0.20460
52	28-Apr-00	−0.03080	0.01044	0.15385	−0.05508	0.13057	0.01923
53	31-May-00	−0.02192	0.00517	−0.01576	−0.03583	−0.24032	0.03113
54	30-Jun-00	0.02393	0.00593	0.04982	0.02037	−0.17788	−0.23502
55	31-Jul-00	−0.01634	−0.02690	0.10069	0.02624	−0.01938	−0.28313
56	31-Aug-00	0.06070	0.14095	0.04601	0.17514	0.27662	0.09328
57	29-Sep-00	−0.05348	−0.01471	0.02624	−0.14773	−0.09957	−0.06226
58	31-Oct-00	−0.00495	−0.04984	0.00983	−0.12444	−0.04423	−0.43983
59	30-Nov-00	−0.08007	−0.09578	−0.16869	−0.04944	−0.19517	−0.17185
60	29-Dec-00	0.00405	−0.02956	0.10353	−0.09091	0.02904	−0.33333
	Beta		1.24	0.86	1.22	1.11	1.27
	t-value		9.70	4.77	5.39	4.71	3.70
	Alpha		0.0100	0.0093	0.0105	−0.0051	−0.0319
	t-value		1.62	1.07	0.97	−0.45	−1.94
	R-squared		0.62	0.28	0.33	0.28	0.19

While we explained how to estimate the beta for an asset, the beta for a portfolio can also be determined. For a portfolio of assets, the beta (β_p) is simply a weighted average of the computed betas for the individual assets (α_i) in the portfolio, where the weight is the percentage of the market value of the individual asset relative to the total market value of the portfolio. That is,

$$\beta_p = \sum_{i=1}^{G} w_i \beta_i$$

where G is the number of assets.

So, for example, the beta for a portfolio comprised of the following:

Company	Weight
General Electric	20%
McGraw Hill	25%
IBM	15%
General Motors	10%
Xerox	30%

would have the following beta:

portfolio beta
= 20%(1.24) + 25%(0.86) + 15%(1.22) + 10%(1.11) + 30%(1.27) = 1.14

Notice that in equation (13) the parameter to be estimated is β, beta. In Chapter 4, we will see another parameter that is an input for an asset pricing model identified as "beta." As will be explained in that chapter, they are not the same constructs. The importance of differentiating these two "beta" measures will be explained in that chapter.

Multi-Index Market Models

Sharpe concluded that equation (12) was as complex a covariance as seemed to be needed. This conclusion was supported by research of Kalman Cohen and Gerald Pogue.[12] Benjamin King found strong evidence for industry factors in addition to the marketwide factor.[13] Barr Rosenberg found other sources of risk beyond a marketwide factor and industry factor.[14] We will discuss other factor models that can be used to construct an optimal portfolio in Chapter 13.

---

[12] Kalman J. Cohen and Gerald A. Pogue, "An Empirical Evaluation of Alternative Portfolio Selection Models," *Journal of Business* (April 1967).

[13] Benjamin F. King, "Market and Industry Factors in Stock Price Behavior," *Journal of Business*, Supplement (January 1966).

[14] Barr Rosenberg, "Extra-Market Components of Covariance in Security Returns," *Journal of Financial and Quantitative Analysis* (March 1974).

In Chapter 1 the range of approaches to portfolio construction was described. One approach to full mean-variance analysis is the use of these multi-index or factor models to obtain the covariance structure.

SUMMARY

In this chapter we have introduced portfolio theory. Developed by Harry Markowitz, this theory explains how investors should construct efficient portfolios and select the best or optimal portfolio from among all efficient portfolios. The theory differs from previous approaches to portfolio selection in that he demonstrated how the key parameters should be measured. These parameters include the risk and the expected return for an individual asset and a portfolio of assets. Moreover, the concept of diversifying a portfolio, the goal of which is to reduce a portfolio's risk without sacrificing expected return, can be cast in terms of these key parameters plus the covariance or correlation between assets. All these parameters are estimated from historical data and other sources of information and draw from concepts in probability and statistical theory.

A portfolio's expected return is simply a weighted average of the expected return of each asset in the portfolio. The weight assigned to each asset is the market value of the asset in the portfolio relative to the total market value of the portfolio. The variance or the standard deviation of an asset's returns measures its risk. Unlike the portfolio's expected return, a portfolio's risk is not a simple weighting of the standard deviation of the individual assets in the portfolio. Rather, the covariance or correlation between the assets that comprise the portfolio affects the portfolio risk. The lower the correlation, the smaller the risk of the portfolio.

Markowitz has set forth the theory for the construction of an efficient portfolio, which has come to be called a efficient portfolio—a portfolio that has the highest expected return of all feasible portfolios with the same level of risk. The collection of all efficient portfolios is called the efficient set of portfolios or the efficient frontier.

The optimal portfolio is the one that maximizes an investor's preferences with respect to return and risk. An investor's preference is described by a utility function, which can be represented graphically by a set of indifference curves. The utility function shows how much an investor is willing to trade off between expected return and risk. The optimal portfolio is the one where an indifference curve is tangent to the efficient frontier.

CHAPTER 3

Applying Mean-Variance Analysis

Frank J. Fabozzi, Ph.D., CFA
Adjunct Professor of Finance
School of Management
Yale University

Francis Gupta, Ph.D.
Vice President
Credit Suisse Asset Management

Harry M. Markowitz, Ph.D.
Consultant

In the previous chapter, we explained mean-variance analysis. In this chapter, we move from theory to practice by illustrating how mean-variance analysis is applied. We begin with the problem of using historical data to estimate the inputs required by the model. The application we employ is to asset allocation among asset classes. (In Chapters 13 and 24 we will see how multi-factor risk models are used to select individual securities.) We then demonstrate how to implement the optimal portfolio.

USING HISTORICAL DATA TO ESTIMATE INPUTS

As noted earlier, the inputs required for portfolio theory are generally estimated from historical observations on the rate of returns.[1] (Because

---

[1] There have been other methods proposed for estimating expected returns which are described in the next chapter.

spreadsheets have a built-in feature for calculating the historical mean rate of return, the variance of an asset, and the historical covariance for the rate of return between two assets, and the formulas are available in elementary statistics textbooks, we do not present the formulas here.) Given the calculated variance and covariances, the historical correlation can be calculated using equation (8). The assumption is that the values obtained from historical observations are reasonable estimates for the expected returns, standard deviations, and correlations in the future. Or, in some case, the time period chosen to obtain the estimates may indeed be the best representation of the beliefs of the future performance of the asset classes.

Historical returns are calculated from either monthly data or weekly data. Regardless of the time interval used to calculate a historical return, the following formula is used:

$$\text{Historical return} = \frac{\text{adjusted ending-period price} - \text{adjusted beginning-period price}}{\text{beginning-period price}}$$

where "adjusted prices" are those that correct for cash dividends and stock splits.

For example, let's look at how to calculate the historical return for the Ford Motor Company for the month of January 1996. The required information is given below:

adjusted beginning-period price (beginning of 1/96) = $15.79
adjusted ending-period price (end of 1/96)   = $16.13

Historical return for the Ford Motor Company for January 1996
$$= \frac{\$16.13 - \$15.79}{\$16.13} = 2.15\%$$

Exhibit 3.1 presents data on 60 monthly returns for two actual stocks, the Ford Motor Company and the Coca-Cola Company, for the time period January 1996 to December 2000. Exhibit 3.1 shows the mean, standard deviation, correlation, and covariance for these two stocks. As can be seen, there is a positive correlation, but not a perfect one, between the return on the stock of Ford and Coca-Cola.

Some Thoughts on Inputs Based on Historical Performance

Exhibit 3.2 used five years of monthly returns to compute the historical returns, risks, and correlations for two stocks—Ford and Coca-Cola. Similarly, Exhibit 3.3 uses monthly returns over different and varying time periods to present the annualized historical returns for four market indexes. Market indexes are used to broadly represent the performance of a market portfolio that is made up of a set of predefined securities. The Lehman Brothers Aggregate Bond Index represents the U.S. government and corporate bond market and will be discussed in Chapter 22. The S&P 500 index is made up of 500 stocks and is supposed to closely mimic the performance of large U.S. firms. As explained in Chapter 6, the Morgan Stanley Capital International (MSCI) EAFE index represents the performance of the equity markets in Europe and Japan, while the EM Free index captures the performance of equity markets of the emerging economies.

EXHIBIT 3.1 Historical Monthly Returns for Ford and Coca-Cola: Five Years Ending December 2000

	1996	1997	1998	1999	2000
FORD					
January	2.15	−0.40	5.01	4.67	−6.68
February	5.95	2.33	10.90	−3.45	−16.35
March	9.95	−4.56	14.61	−4.44	10.36
April	4.42	10.72	−29.31	12.80	19.18
May	1.73	7.95	13.25	−10.66	−11.29
June	−11.32	1.32	13.74	−1.18	−11.44
July	0.00	7.56	−3.41	−14.09	8.29
August	3.50	5.23	−21.71	7.50	−9.22
September	−6.71	4.93	5.33	−3.61	5.45
October	0.00	−3.20	15.40	9.20	3.65
November	4.80	−1.59	1.52	−7.96	−12.90
December	−1.51	12.97	6.61	5.57	3.00
COCA-COLA					
January	1.51	9.97	−2.90	−2.52	−1.40
February	7.12	5.40	5.99	−2.19	−15.34
March	2.81	−8.39	13.06	−3.68	−3.11
April	−1.53	14.12	−2.01	10.91	0.65
May	12.90	7.67	3.30	0.63	12.98
June	6.80	−0.53	9.28	−9.27	7.96
July	−4.33	1.66	−5.84	−2.32	6.72
August	6.66	−17.09	−19.10	−1.24	−14.14
September	2.00	6.71	−11.31	−19.09	5.06
October	−0.74	−7.18	17.25	22.26	9.51
November	1.48	10.62	3.92	14.38	4.03
December	2.94	6.69	−4.37	−13.46	−2.70

Source: Yahoo

EXHIBIT 3.2   Monthly Mean, Variance, Standard Deviation, Correlation, and Covariance for Ford and Coca-Cola: Five Years Ending December 2000

Parameter	Ford	Coca-Cola
Mean	1.08%	1.32%
Variance	91.04%	81.02%
Standard Deviation	9.54%	9.00%
Correlation Between Ford and Coca-Cola	0.35	
Covariance Between Ford and Coca-Cola	29.85	

EXHIBIT 3.3   Annualized Returns Using Historical Performance Depend on the Time Period

Period	Lehman Aggregate	S&P 500	MSCI EAFE	MSCI EM Free
Five-Year				
1991–1995	9.2%	15.9%	10.5%	16.3%
1996–2000	6.3	18.3	8.2	0.1
Ten-Year				
1991–2000	7.7	17.1	9.3	8.2

One drawback of using the historical performance to obtain estimates is clearly evident from this exhibit. Based on historical performance, a portfolio manager looking for estimates of the expected returns for these four asset classes to use as inputs for obtaining the set of efficient portfolios at the end of 1995 would have used the estimates from the five-year period, 1991–1995. Then according to the portfolio manager's expectations, over the next five years, only the U.S. equity market (as represented by the S&P 500) outperformed (i.e., had the highest return), while U.S. bonds, Europe and Japan, and emerging markets all underperformed. In particular, the performance of emerging markets was dramatically different from its expected performance (actual performance of 0.1% versus an expected performance of 16.3%). This finding is disturbing, because if portfolio managers cannot have faith in the inputs that are used to solve for the efficient portfolios, then it is not possible for them to have much faith in the outputs (i.e., the make-up and expected performance of the efficient and optimal portfolios).

EXHIBIT 3.4   Annualized Standard Deviations Using Historical Performance Depend on the Time Period

Period	Lehman Aggregate	S&P 500	MSCI EAFE	MSCI EM Free
Five-Year				
1991–1995	4.0%	10.1%	15.5%	18.0%
1996–2000	4.8	17.7	15.6	26.6
Ten-Year				
1991–2000	3.7	13.4	15.0	22.3

Portfolio managers who were performing the exercise at the beginning of 2001 faced a similar dilemma. Should they use the historical returns for the 1996–2000 period? That would generally imply that the optimal allocation has a large holding of U.S. equity (since that was the asset class that performed well), and an underweighting to U.S. bonds and emerging markets equity. But then what if the actual performance over the next five years is more like the 1991–1995 period?[2] In that case, the optimal portfolio is not going to perform as well as a portfolio that had a good exposure to bonds and emerging markets equity. (Note that emerging markets equity outperformed U.S. equity under that scenario.) Or, should portfolio managers use the estimates computed by using 10 years of monthly performance?

The truth is that, in fact, there is no right answer. This is because we are dealing with the world of uncertainty. This is also true for the cases of obtaining estimates for the variances and correlations. Exhibit 3.4 presents the standard deviations for the same indexes over the same time periods. Though the risk estimates for the Lehman Aggregate and EAFE indexes are quite stable, the estimates for the S&P 500 and EM Free are significantly different over different time periods. However, the volatility of the indexes does shed some light into the problem of estimating expected returns as presented in Exhibit 3.3. MSCI EM Free, the index with the largest volatility, also has the largest difference in the estimate of the expected return. Intuitively, this makes sense—the greater the volatility of an asset, the harder, or longer the data required to predict its future performance.

Exhibit 3.5 shows the five-year rolling correlation between the S&P 500 and MSCI EAFE. In January 1996, the correlation between the returns of the S&P 500 and EAFE was about 0.45 over the past five

---

[2] Similarly, there are other methods for estimating the variances and covariances. See Chapters 13 and 24 on multi-factor risk models. See also Louis K.C. Chan, Jason Karceski, and Josef Lakonishok, "On Portfolio Optimization: Forecasting Covariances and Choosing the Risk Model," Review of *Financial Studies* (1999).

years (1991–1995). Consequently, a portfolio manager would have expected the correlation over the next five years to be around that estimate. However, for the five-year period ending December 2000, the correlation between the assets slowly increased to 0.73. Historically, this was an all-time high. In January 2001, should the portfolio manager assume a correlation 0.45 or 0.73 between the S&P 500 and EAFE over the next five years? Or does 0.59, the correlation over the entire 10-year period (1991–2000) sound more reasonable?

Again, the truth is that there is no right answer. In reality, as mentioned earlier, if portfolio managers believe that the inputs based on the historical performance of an asset class is not a good reflection of the future expected performance of that asset class, they may objectively or subjectively alter the inputs. Different portfolio managers may have different beliefs, in which case the alterations will be different.[3] The important thing here is that all alterations have theoretical justifications, which in turn ultimately leads to an optimal portfolio that closely aligns to the future expectations of the portfolio manager.

EXHIBIT 3.5   Correlation Between Returns of the S&P 500 and MSCI EAFE Indexes

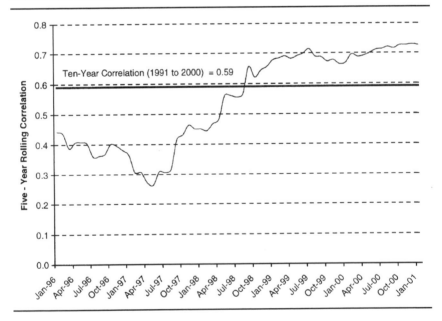

___

[3] It is quite common that the optimal strategic bond/equity mix within a portfolio differs significantly across portfolio managers.

EXHIBIT 3.6   Histories Vary for the Commonly Used Indexes for Asset Classes

Index	Asset Class	Inception Date
U.S. 30-Day Treasury Bill	U.S. Cash	1/26
Lehman Brothers Aggregate Bond	U.S. Bonds	1/76
S&P 500	U.S. Large Cap Equity	1/26
Russell 2000	U.S. Small Cap Equity	1/79
MSCI EAFE	Europe/Japan Equity	1/70
MSCI EM Free	Emerging Markets Equity	1/88

There are some purely objective arguments as to why we can place more faith in the estimates obtained from historical data for some assets than others. Exhibit 3.6 presents the commonly used indexes for some asset classes and their respective inception dates. Since there are varying lengths of histories available for different assets (for instance, U.S. and European markets not only have longer histories, but their data are also more accurate), inputs of some assets can generally be estimated more precisely than the estimates of others.[4]

When solving for the efficient portfolios, the differences in precision of the estimates should be explicitly incorporated into the analysis. But modern portfolio theory assumes that all estimates are as precise or imprecise, and therefore, treats all assets equally. Some practitioners of mean-variance optimization incorporate their beliefs on the precision of the estimates by imposing constraints on the maximum exposure of some asset classes in a portfolio.[5] The asset classes on which these constraints are imposed are generally those whose expected performances are either harder to estimate, or those whose performances are estimated less precisely. A different approach taken by other practitioners is to increase the volatility of the asset classes so as to reflect their uncertainty in the expected return estimates of those asset classes. The end result is the same: the higher volatility makes those asset classes less attractive in a mean-variance framework and therefore those asset classes receive smaller allocations in optimal portfolios.

The extent to which we can use personal judgment to subjectively alter estimates obtained from historical data depends on our under-

---

[4] Statistically, the precision of an estimate is inversely proportional to the amount of information that is used to estimate it. That is, the more the data used to obtain an estimate, the greater the precision of the estimate.

[5] For a further discussion of the benefits and costs of constraining the allocation to an asset class, see Francis Gupta and David Eichorn, "Mean-Variance Optimization for Practitioners of Asset Allocation," Chapter 4 in Frank J. Fabozzi (ed.), *Handbook of Portfolio Management* (New Hope, PA: Frank J. Fabozzi Associates, 1998).

standing of what factors influence the returns on assets, and what is their impact. The political environment within and across countries, monetary and fiscal policies, consumer confidence, and the business cycles of sectors and regions are some of the key factors that can assist in forming future expectations of the performance of asset classes.

To summarize, it would be fair to say that using historical returns to estimate parameters that can be used as inputs to obtain the set of efficient portfolios depends on whether the underlying economies giving rise to the observed outcomes of returns are strong and stable. Strength and stability of economies comes from political stability and consistency in economic policies. It is only after an economy has a lengthy and proven record of a healthy and consistent performance under varying (political and economic) forces that impact free markets that historical performance of its markets can be seen as a fair indicator of their future performance.

APPLICATION OF PORTFOLIO THEORY TO ASSET ALLOCATION

Now that we are familiar with the theoretical concepts and various building blocks of modern portfolio theory, we will use an example to illustrate how portfolio managers use this theory to build optimal portfolios for their clients. In this example we will construct an efficient frontier made up of U.S. bonds and U.S. and international equity, and shed some light into the selection of an optimal portfolio.

Asset Classes and Inputs

By now we know that the first decision to be made is the assets we would like to include in the portfolio and their corresponding returns, risks (standard deviations), and correlations to be used as inputs in the mean-variance optimization. For our purposes, we are going to build a portfolio made up of four asset classes—three domestic and one international. As discussed earlier, these asset classes have associated indexes and those indexes can be used when implementing the optimal portfolio. Exhibit 3.7 presents the forward-looking assumptions for the four asset classes.

These inputs are an example of estimates that are *not* totally based on historical performance of these asset classes.[6] The risk and correlation figures are mainly historical.

---

[6] The expected return estimates are created using a risk premium approach (i.e., obtaining the historical risk premiums over the risk-free rate of return of bonds, large cap, mid cap, small cap, and international equity) and then subjectively altered to include the asset manager's expectations regarding the future long-run (5 to 10 years) performance of these asset classes.

EXHIBIT 3.7 Forward Looking Inputs (Expected Returns, Standard Deviations, and Correlations)

E(R)	SD(R)	Asset Classes	Asset	Correlations			
				1	2	3	4
6.4%	4.7%	U.S. Bonds	1	1.00			
10.8	14.9	U.S. Large Cap Equity	2	0.32	1.00		
11.9	19.6	U.S. Small Cap Equity	3	0.06	0.76	1.00	
11.5	17.2	EAFE International Equity	4	0.17	0.44	0.38	1.00

EXHIBIT 3.8 The Efficient Frontier Using Only U.S. Bonds and U.S. Large Cap Equity from Exhibit 3.7

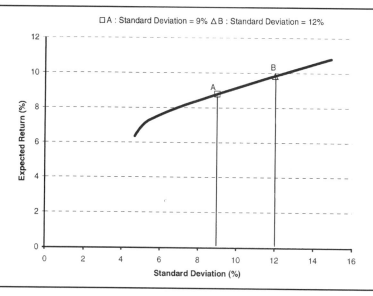

The Efficient Frontier

The next step is to use a software package to perform the optimization that results in the efficient frontier. For purposes of exposition, Exhibit 3.8 first presents the efficient frontier using only two of the four asset classes from Exhibit 3.7—U.S. bonds and large cap equity. (This efficient frontier is very similar to the efficient frontier presented in Exhibit 2.5 which was made up of assets C and D.) Starting with only two asset classes will enable us to understand how the addition of more asset classes may be desirable to the building of an optimal portfolio. Because it is efficient, the corresponding portfolio on the efficient frontier for any given level of risk will result in the highest possible expected return. We show two such portfolios: A and B corresponding to standard deviations of 9% and 12%, respectively. Portfolio B has the higher risk, but it also has the higher expected return.

In addition to the trade-off between return and risk among the efficient portfolios, the other factor that determines an entity's optimal portfolio is the entity's risk aversion, or appetite for risk. Therefore, depending on the entity's risk aversion, any one of the portfolios on the efficient frontier could be a candidate optimal portfolio. However, for purposes of exposition, we will concentrate on portfolios A and B.

Exhibit 3.9 presents the compositions of portfolios A and B, and some important characteristics that may assist us in understanding how risk averse individuals choose an optimal portfolio from the set of efficient portfolios.

As one would expect, the more conservative portfolio (A), allocates more to the more conservative asset class. Portfolio A allocated a little more than 45% of the portfolio to fixed income, while portfolio B only allocates 22% to that asset class. This results in a significantly higher standard deviation for portfolio B (12% versus 9%). In exchange for the 3% (or 300 basis points) of higher risk, portfolio B results in 104 basis points of higher expected return (9.83% versus 8.79%). This is the risk/ return trade-off that we discussed earlier. The question that a risk averse individual faces when choosing an optimal portfolio is this: Does the increase in the expected return compensate me for the increased risk that I will be bearing? If it does, then the individual will choose portfolio B.

EXHIBIT 3.9   Growth of $100 Illustrates the Risk/Return Trade-Off of Portfolios A and B

Characteristic	Portfolio A	Portfolio B
U.S. Fixed Income	45.8%	22.0%
U.S. Large Cap Equity	54.2	78.0
Expected Return	8.79%	9.83%
Standard Deviation (Risk)	9.00%	12.00%
Return Per Unit of Risk	98 Basis points (bps)	82 Basis points (bps)

Growth of $100	1 Year	5 Years	10 Years	1 Year	5 Years	10 Years
95th Percentile (Upside)	$124	$203	$345	$131	$232	$424
Average (Expected)	109	152	232	110	160	255
5th Percentile (Downside)	95	111	146	91	104	137

Though we know that the standard deviation is a measure of risk, in reality it is a difficult concept to comprehend. We can get around this by expressing risk in terms of the distribution of wealth over time. The higher the risk, the wider the spread of the distribution. A wider spread implies a greater upside and a greater downside. The key to translating risk into something more comprehensible is to quantify the upside and downside.[7]

Exhibit 3.9 also presents the 95th percentile, expected, and 5th percentiles for every $100 invested in portfolios A and B over 1, 5, and 10 years, respectively. Over a one-year period, there is a 1 in 20 chance that the $100 invested in portfolio A will grow to $124, but there is also a 1 in 20 chance that the portfolio will lose $5 (i.e., it will it shrink to $95). In comparison, for portfolio B there is a 1 in 20 chance that $100 will grow to $131 (the upside is $6 more than if invested in portfolio A). But there is also a 1 in 20 chance that the portfolio will shrink to $91 (the downside is $4 more than if invested in portfolio A). If the investment horizon is one year, is this investor willing to accept a 1 in 20 chance of losing $9 instead of $4 for a 1 in 20 chance of gaining $31 instead of $24?[8] The answer depends on the investor's risk aversion.

As the investment horizon becomes longer, the chances that a portfolio will lose its principal keep declining. Over 10 years, there is a 1 in 20 chance that portfolio A will grow to $345, but there is also a 1 in 20 chance that the portfolio will only grow to $146 (the chances that the portfolio results in a balance less than $100 are much smaller). In comparison, over 10 years, there is a 1 in 20 chance that portfolio B will grow to $424 (the upside is $79 more than if invested in portfolio A)! And even though there is a 1 in 20 chance that the portfolio will only grow to $137—that is only $7 less than if invested in portfolio A! Also portfolio B's average (expected) balance over 10 years is $23 more than portfolio A's ($255 versus $232). Somehow, compounding makes the more risky portfolio seems more attractive over the longer run. In other words, a portfolio that may not be acceptable to the investor over a short run may be acceptable over a longer investment horizon. *In summary, it is sufficient to say that the optimal portfolio depends not only on risk aversion, but also on the investment horizon.*

---

[7] Though easier to understand, the computation of the wealth distribution over multiple periods entails simulations, and is also best left to an off-the-shelf software package.

[8] It may be useful to mention here that more recently researchers in behavioral finance have found some evidence to suggest that investors view the upside and downside differently. In particular, they equate each downside dollar to more than one upside dollar.

EXHIBIT 3.10   Expanding the Efficient Frontier Using All Asset Classes from Exhibit 3.7

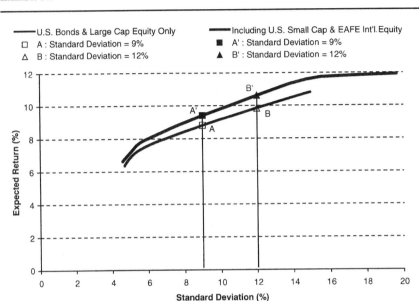

Expanding the Efficient Frontier

Exhibit 3.10 compares the efficient frontier using two asset classes, namely, U.S. bonds and large cap equity with one obtained from using all four asset classes from Exhibit 3.7 in the optimization. The inclusion of U.S. small cap and EAFE international equity into the mix makes the opportunity set bigger (i.e., the frontier covers a larger risk/return spectrum). It also moves the efficient frontier outwards (i.e., the frontier results in a larger expected return at any given level of risk, or conversely, results in a lower risk for any given level of expected return). The frontier also highlights portfolios A′ and B′—the portfolios with the same standard deviation as portfolios A and B, respectively.

Exhibit 3.11 shows the composition of the underlying portfolios that make up the frontier. Interestingly, U.S. small cap and EAFE international equity—the more aggressive asset classes—are included in all the portfolios. Even the least risky portfolio has a small allocation to these two asset classes. On the other hand, U.S. large cap equity—an asset class that is thought of as the backbone of a domestic portfolio—gets excluded from the more aggressive portfolios.

EXHIBIT 3.11   Composition of the Efficient Frontier

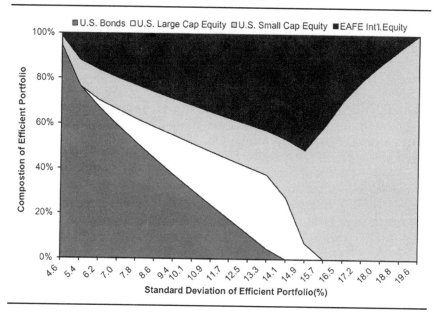

EXHIBIT 3.12   Composition of Equally Risky Efficient Portfolios in the Expanded Frontier

Asset Class	Standard Deviation = 9.0%		Standard Deviation = 12.0%	
	A	A′	B	B′
U.S. Fixed Income	34.3%	40.4%	22.0%	15.1%
U.S. Large Cap Equity	18.7	15.8	78.0	27.8
U.S. Small Cap Equity	—	16.1	—	18.6
EAFE International Equity	—	27.7	—	38.5
Expected Return	8.79%	9.39%	9.83%	10.61%
Standard Deviation (Risk)	9.00%	9.00%	12.00%	12.00%
Return Per Unit of Risk	98 bps	104 bps	82 bps	88 bps

Exhibit 3.12 compares the composition and expected performance of portfolios A and B to A′ and B′, respectively. Both the new portfolios, A′ and B′, find U.S. small cap and EAFE international equity very attractive and replace a significant proportion of U.S. large cap equity with those asset classes. In B′, the more aggressive mix, the allocation to U.S. bonds also declines (15.1% versus 22%).

Inclusion of U.S. small cap and EAFE international equity results in sizable increases in the expected return and return per unit of risk. In particular, the conservative portfolio A′, has an expected return of 9.39% (60 basis points over portfolio A) and the aggressive portfolio B′ has an expected return of 10.61% (78 basis points over portfolio B). Note also the increases in the returns per unit of risk.

It is conceivable that the huge allocations to U.S. small cap and EAFE international equity in A′ and B′ may be uncomfortable for some investors. U.S. small cap equity is the most risky asset class and EAFE international equity is the second most aggressive asset class. The conservative portfolio allocates more than 40% of the portfolio to these two assets, while the aggressive allocates more than 50%. As explained in the section when we discussed inputs based on historical returns, these two would also be the asset classes whose expected returns, because of the large volatilities, would be harder to estimate. Consequently, investors may not want to allocate more than a certain amount of their portfolios to these two asset classes.

On a separate note, investors in the United States may also want to limit their exposure to EAFE international equity because of psychological reasons. Familiarity to domestic asset classes leads them to believe that those asset classes are "less" risky.[9] Exhibit 3.13 presents the composition of the efficient frontier when the maximum allocation to EAFE is constrained at 10% of the portfolio, implying a 90% allocation to domestic asset classes. As a result of this constraint, all the portfolios now receive an allocation of U.S. large cap equity.

Exhibit 3.14 compares the composition A′ and B′ to A″ and B″ the respective equally risky portfolios that lie on the constrained efficient frontier. In the conservative portfolio A″, the combined allocation to U.S. small cap and EAFE international equity has declined to 30% (from 43.8%) and in B″ it has fallen to 34.8% (from 57.1%). Also, now the bond allocation increases for both of the portfolios.

The decline in the expected return can be used to quantify the cost of this constraint. The conservative portfolio's expected return fell from 9.39% to 9.20%—a decline of 19 basis points—a cost that may be well worth it for an investor whose optimal appetite for risk is 9%. The more aggressive portfolio pays more for the constraint (10.61% − 10.26% = 35 basis points).

---

[9] Similarly, investors in Europe may believe that EAFE equity is "less" risky than U.S. equity and may want to limit their exposure to U.S. asset classes. This is often referred to as the "domestic asset class bias."

EXHIBIT 3.13   Composition of the Constrained Efficient Frontier
Maximum Allocation to EAFE International Equity = 10%

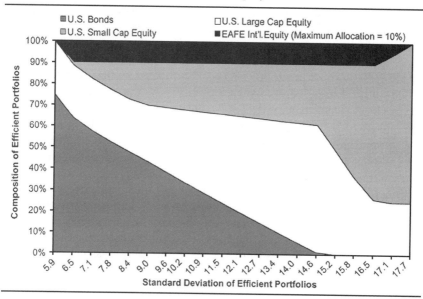

EXHIBIT 3.14   The Benefits and Costs of Constraining an Efficient Frontier

Asset Class	Unconstrained		Maximum Allocation to EAFE International Equity = 10.0%	
	A′	B′	A″	B″
U.S. Fixed Income	40.4%	15.1%	43.1%	20.1%
U.S. Large Cap Equity	15.8	27.8	26.9	45.1
U.S. Small Cap Equity	16.1	18.6	20.0	24.8
EAFE International Equity	27.7	38.5	10.0	10.0
Expected Return	9.39%	10.61%	9.20%	10.26%
Standard Deviation	9.00%	12.00%	9.00%	12.00%
Cost of Constraint	—	—	19 bps	35 bps

IMPLEMENTATING THE OPTIMAL PORTFOLIO

Now that we understand the process of obtaining the optimal portfolio, the next step in portfolio management deals with implementing the optimal portfolio. The optimal portfolio that we derived was made up of asset classes, but asset classes by themselves cannot be invested in. To implement the optimal portfolio, the investor has to purchase either market indexes (that the asset classes represent), or mutual funds (that are supposed to represent those asset classes), or if an investor is more sophisticated, she can buy individual securities that broadly represent the asset classes that comprise the optimal portfolio. In this section we will limit ourselves to implementing the optimal portfolio using market indexes and/or mutual funds.

Passive Implementation of the Optimal Portfolio

For purposes of exposition, let's assume that B″ (from Exhibit 3.14) is the optimal portfolio. As stated earlier, one easy way to implement this portfolio is to buy the index funds that represent the respective asset classes that make up the optimal portfolio. This is equivalent to purchasing the index. Since none of these index funds are actively managed (i.e., they perfectly track the index), gaining exposure to the asset classes using index funds is referred to as *passive* implementation of the optimal portfolio. Exhibit 3.15 shows the indexes used to gain exposure to the various asset classes in the optimal portfolio, passively.

Since there are many indexes for each asset class, it is important to note that the choice of the index used to gain exposure to an asset class is a matter of personal taste. Each index has its pros and cons as to how well it replicates the asset class it is supposed to represent.

Another aspect of portfolio implementation has to do with rebalancing the portfolio back to its strategic weights (i.e., the weights in the optimal portfolio). Due to the differences in returns of the various holdings over time, weights of the various asset classes within the portfolio may start to differ markedly from those in the optimal portfolio. This not only changes the risk profile of the portfolio,[10] but at any given time the "current" portfolio may not even be efficient. To rebalance, the asset classes that are overweight are sold and the asset classes that are underweight are bought. Thus, rebalancing generally incurs trading costs.

EXHIBIT 3.15 Passive Implementation of the Optimal Portfolio B″ from Exhibit 3.14

Asset Class	Index	Allocation to B″
U.S. Fixed Income	Lehman Aggregate	20.1%
U.S. Large Cap Equity	S&P 500	45.1%
U.S. Small Cap Equity	FR 2000	24.8%
EAFE International Equity	MSCI EAFE	10.0%

---

[10] Remember, the optimal portfolio was dependent on the investor's appetite for risk. A portfolio with different weights from the optimal may have a risk that is very different from what the investor is willing to tolerate.

EXHIBIT 3.16   Growth of $100 Differs by the Frequency of Rebalancing

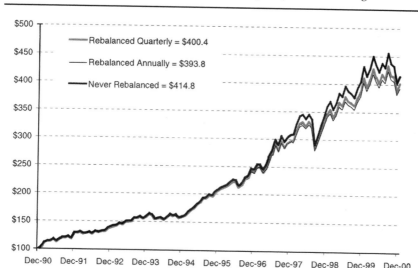

Frequency of Rebalancing	Annual Return	Annual Standard Deviation
Quarterly	14.88%	10.56%
Annually	14.69	10.75
Never	15.29	11.54

Note: Uses monthly returns for the indexes.

Exhibit 3.16 shows the growth of a $100 investment in the optimal portfolio B″ for three different rebalancing frequencies over the 10-year period, 1991–2000.[11] Notice, that no clear relationship exists between the frequency of rebalancing and the performance of a portfolio. In our example the quarterly rebalanced portfolio outperforms the one that is rebalanced annually, implying that the higher the frequency of rebalancing, the better the return. But then the portfolio that is never rebalanced over the 10 years results in the biggest ending balance. Also notice that

---

[11] This means that in the beginning of 1991, $100 was allocated among the indexes shown in Exhibit 3.15. As already discussed, these indexes represent the asset classes that make up the optimal portfolio. The allocation to each index is meant to reflect the weight of its respective asset class in the optimal portfolio. Therefore, of the $100 invested in the portfolio, $20.1 was invested in the Lehman Brothers Aggregate Bond Index, $45.1 was invested in the S&P 500 stock index, $24.8 in the Frank Russell 2000, and $10 in the MSCI EAFE index.

the quarterly rebalanced portfolio has the least risk as measured by the standard deviation, whereas the portfolio that is never rebalanced is the most risky, indicating some relationship between the frequency of rebalancing and the volatility. For our purposes, it would not be an understatement to say that all individuals who are serious about practicing portfolio management should understand that the issue of rebalancing is an important component of portfolio implementation and is worth giving some serious thought.[12]

Implementation Using Active Strategies

Gaining exposure to the optimal portfolio using passive strategies is relatively easy. Investors first decide which indexes best represent the asset classes that comprise the optimal portfolio and allocate their total portfolio among the indexes so as to replicate the asset class weights. Then all they need to worry about is rebalancing. In terms of performance they know what to expect. Since their entire portfolio is invested in indexes, the return on the portfolio is a weighted average of the return on the indexes, where the weights are the relative dollar amounts invested in the respective indexes. But some investors may believe that their portfolios can outperform the broad market. Therefore, they may implement their optimal portfolios by picking individual securities that they feel will outperform the market.[13] Or, they may invest in strategies that actively focus on picking a group of stocks with the hope that the manager of the strategy (i.e., the portfolio manager) will be able to generate some excess return over and above the market. These strategies are marketed to investors as *active mutual funds*. Exhibit 3.17 presents the performance of all mutual funds within the Lipper Universe for the asset classes that make up our optimal portfolio B″.

Within the domestic fixed income asset class, only 16.1% of all funds with a track record of one year or more beat the Lehman Aggregate in 2001. Over the long-run, the statistic improves: 28.5% of all domestic fixed income funds with a track record of 10 years or more beat the Lehman Aggregate over a 10-year period ending 2001. For domestic large cap equity, 31.7% of the funds with a track record of 10 years or more beat the S&P 500 over a 10-year period ending 2001. Those numbers jump to 82.6% and 86.1% for domestic small cap funds and international equity funds, respectively.

---

[12] Instead of using a time frequency for rebalancing, some investors use rules based on asset class weights. For example, a simple rule would be one which rebalances the portfolio whenever any asset classes' weight differs by more than 10% from its optimal weight.

[13] As mentioned, we will not consider this case.

EXHIBIT 3.17 Mutual Fund Return Performance: Lipper Universe

	U.S. Fixed Income	U.S Large Cap Equity	U.S. Small Cap Equity	International Equity
1-Year				
Total # of Funds	3,504	1,894	943	1,240
% Outperformed Benchmark	16.1%	36.7%	56.2%	54.4%
3-Years				
Total # of Funds	2,957	1,265	675	894
% Outperformed Benchmark	16.1%	60.6%	82.7%	82.3%
5-Years				
Total # of Funds	2,232	792	395	547
% Outperformed Benchmark	16.2%	42.2%	76.2%	68.7%
10-Years				
Total # of Funds	800	243	92	108
% Outperformed Benchmark	28.5%	31.7%	82.6%	86.1%
Return Evaluated Against (Index)	Lehman Aggregate	S&P 500	FR 2000	MSCI EAFE

Note: Uses gross returns as of year-end 2001. U.S. Fixed Income funds include all domestic fixed income funds except for short duration funds. International Equity funds include all international equity funds except for emerging markets funds.

61

EXHIBIT 3.18   U.S. Large Cap Equity Funds: 5-Year Performance
(Performance Benchmark = S&P 500)

Number of Funds with ...	Greater Risk than S&P 500	Lower Risk than S&P 500	Totals
Greater Return than S&P 500	237	97	334 (42.2%)
Lower Return than S&P 500	277	181	458 (57.8%)
Totals	514 (64.9%)	278 (35.1%)	792 (100.0%)

Note: Uses gross returns as of year-end 2001. Lipper Universe.

At first the picture looks very optimistic. It seems that investors have a pretty good chance to outperform a portfolio solely invested in indexes by picking actively managed funds. But this conclusion is not that obvious: whereas passive implementation of a portfolio is a relatively easy and straightforward task, implementing an optimal portfolio using active strategies can be quite complicated. There are three major concerns that have to be kept in mind while implementing a portfolio using active strategies.

First is the issue of fees. Active funds require more skill to manage than passive/index funds, therefore typically their fees are much higher than those of index funds. Sometimes, this higher fee may quickly erode away the excess return that the strategy is adding. Therefore, it is important to remember when selecting an actively managed mutual fund that the investor only receives net of fees returns.

Second is the issue of selecting an outperforming mutual fund. Though it seems that in every asset class there are a significant number of funds that outperform the indexes, in reality picking a "winner" is relatively hard. Also, it is harder to pick a winner within some asset classes (such as such as domestic large cap equity) than other asset classes (international equity). This is because the funds in those asset classes have weaker consistency in performance and therefore it makes it harder to use past results as an indicator of future performance.

Third, and this is even more important than the two mentioned above: Sometimes active strategies are significantly more risky than the asset classes they represent. Exhibit 3.18 shows a performance breakdown of the 792 domestic large cap equity mutual funds with a track record of 5 years or more (from Exhibit 3.17). Of the 334 funds that resulted in a 5-year annual return greater than the S&P 500, 237 took on greater risk. Overall, about two-thirds of the funds (64.9%) were more risky than the S&P 500. In addition, even for the funds that added excess returns, the average excess return was much smaller than the average increase in the volatility.

The reason that active strategies add more risk is simple: In a quest to beat the index many funds are very concentrated and hold many fewer securities than those included in the index.[14] Sometimes they may just focus on a particular sector (such as sector funds). Some funds also hold securities that are not part of the index. For instance a U.S. large cap equity fund may hold small cap securities. Because mutual funds may be gaining exposure to securities outside their asset class, using active strategies to implement an optimal portfolio may pose a challenge to investors. Furthermore, the holdings of a fund are not easily accessible,[15] thus making it very hard for investors to correct for the "asset class" biases within a fund.

This problem was first formalized by William Sharpe.[16] He proposed a very elegant solution that did not require fund holdings but used the readily available fund returns to understand its style. In other words, if a domestic fixed income fund was holding some domestic large cap equity then its returns would not only look "similar" to the Lehman Aggregate Bond Index, but they would also look "similar" to the S&P 500 index. The "similarity" was measured in terms of correlations.[17] In fact, the more large cap equity it held, the more its return would look like the S&P 500 (i.e., the greater would be its correlation with the S&P 500). Conversely, the returns of a domestic fixed income fund that was true to its style (e.g., a Lehman Aggregate index fund) would track the index perfectly—with a correlation of one.

Exhibit 3.19 shows the style of Fidelity's Magellan fund, an actively managed fund and the Vanguard S&P 500 index fund, a passive fund. These are two of the largest domestic large cap equity mutual funds in the world.

Fidelity Magellan's style has varied with time. As of March 2002, 10% of the variation in the fund's return can be explained by the variation in the returns of the Frank Russell 2000 (FR 2000) index.[18] Consequently, if this fund is used to gain exposure to domestic large cap in the

---

[14] Of course, the concentrations are in securities that the fund manager feels are going to outperform the index.

[15] Giving away the holdings and the weights would be equivalent to giving away the active strategy.

[16] See, William F. Sharpe, "Asset Allocation: Management Style and Performance Measurement." *Journal of Portfolio Management* (Winter 1992).

[17] A multiple regression is used to explain the variability in the fund's returns using the variability of the indexes' returns.

[18] This does not necessarily mean that the fund was holing U.S. small cap equity. That determination only can be made by looking into the holdings of the fund. What it does mean is that the fund does own securities whose returns are correlated to that of the FR 2000 index.

optimal portfolio, by default the portfolio will gain exposure to the FR 2000 index. These are the nuances that have to be kept in mind when investors use active strategies to implement their optimal portfolio.

Coming back to our optimal portfolio: If we had decided to use Fidelity Magellan in our optimal portfolio and had to allocate $100 to the portfolio, a $50 investment in the Fidelity Magellan fund would result in a $45 exposure to the S&P 500 (90% of $50) and a $5 exposure to the FR 2000 (10% of $50) index. Since this would already give us the approximate optimal exposure to U.S. large cap equity (45.1%) with a 5% exposure to U.S. small cap equity, we would only need to invest $19.8 more in the FR 2000 index to obtain the optimal allocation of 24.8% to U.S. small cap equities.

EXHIBIT 3.19   Styles of an Active and Passive Fund Differ Dramatically

Fidelity Magellan Fund

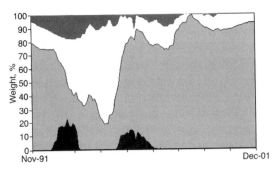

Vanguard 500 Index Fund

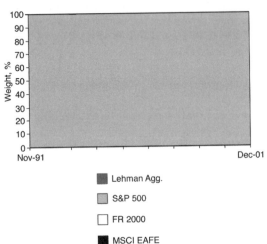

CHAPTER 4

Asset Pricing Models

Frank J. Fabozzi, Ph.D.,CFA
Adjunct Professor of Finance
School of Management
Yale University

In Chapter 2, a normative theory of portfolio selection, mean-variance analysis, was explained. As emphasized in that chapter and its application in Chapters 2 and 3, a key input into a portfolio construction model is the expected return for each security. In this chapter we will explain hypotheses about a security's expected return based on asset pricing models.

CHARACTERISTICS OF AN ASSET PRICING MODEL

In well-functioning capital markets, an investor should be rewarded for accepting the various risks associated with investing in an asset. Throughout this book we be discussing these risks and how, if possible, to quantify them. Risks are also referred to as "risk factors" or "factors."

We can express an asset pricing model in general terms as follows:

$$E(R_i) = f(F_1, F_2, F_3, \ldots, F_N) \tag{1}$$

where

$$
\begin{aligned}
E(R_i) &= \text{expected return for asset } i \\
F_k &= \text{risk factor } k \\
N &= \text{number of risk factors}
\end{aligned}
$$

Equation (1) says that the expected return is a function of N risk factors. The trick is to figure out what the risk factors are and to specify the precise relationship between expected return and the risk factors.

We can fine-tune the asset pricing model given by equation (1) by thinking about the minimum expected return we would want from investing in an asset. As explained in Chapter 16, there are securities issued by the U.S. Department of the Treasury that offer a known return if held over some period of time. The expected return offered on such securities is called the *risk-free return* or the *risk-free rate*. By investing in an asset other than such securities, investors will demand a premium over the risk-free rate. That is, the expected return that an investor will demand is

$$E(R_i) = R_f + \text{risk premium}$$

where R_f is the risk-free rate.

The "risk premium" or additional return expected over the risk-free rate depends on the risk factors associated with investing in the asset. Thus, we can rewrite the general form of the asset pricing model given by equation (1) as follows:

$$E(R_i) = R_f + f(F_1, F_2, F_3, \ldots, F_N) \qquad (2)$$

Risk factors can be divided into two general categories. The first category is risk factors that cannot be diversified away via Markowitz diversification, discussed in Chapter 2. That is, no matter what the investor does, the investor cannot eliminate these risk factors. These risk factors are referred to as *systematic risk factors* or *nondiversifiable risk factors*. The second category is risk factors that can be eliminated via diversification. These risk factors are unique to the asset and are referred to as *unsystematic risk factors* or *diversifiable risk factors*.

CAPITAL ASSET PRICING MODEL

The first asset pricing model derived from economic theory was developed by William Sharpe and is called the *capital asset pricing model* (CAPM).[1] The CAPM has only one systematic risk factor—the risk of

---

[1] William F. Sharpe, "Capital Asset Prices," *Journal of Finance* (September 1964), pp. 425–442. Others who reached a similar conclusion regarding the pricing of risk assets include: John Lintner, "The Valuation of Risk Assets and the Selection of Risky Investments in Stock Portfolio and Capital Budgets," *Review of Economics and Statistics* (February 1965), pp. 13–37; Jack L. Treynor, "Toward a Theory of Market Value of Risky Assets," unpublished paper, Arthur D. Little, Cambridge, MA, 1961; and, Jan Mossin, "Equilibrium in a Capital Asset Market," *Econometrica* (October 1966), pp. 768–783.

the overall movement of the market. This risk factor is referred to as "market risk." So, in the CAPM, the terms "market risk" and "systematic risk" are used interchangeably. By "market risk" it is meant the risk associated with holding a portfolio consisting of all assets, called the "market portfolio." As will be explained later, in the market portfolio an asset is held in proportion to its market value. So, for example, if the total market value of all assets is $X and the market value of asset j is $Y, then asset j will comprise $Y/$X of the market portfolio.

The CAPM is given by the following formula:

$$E(R_i) = R_f + \beta_i[E(R_M) - R_f] \qquad (3)$$

where

$E(R_M)$ = expected return on a "market portfolio"
β_i = measure of systematic risk of asset i relative to the "market portfolio"

We will derive the CAPM later. For now, let's look at what this asset pricing model says.

The expected return for an asset i according to the CAPM is equal to the risk-free rate plus a risk premium. The risk premium is

$$\text{risk premium in the CAPM} = \beta_i[E(R_M) - R_f]$$

First look at *beta* (β_i) in the risk premium component of the CAPM. Beta is a measure of the sensitivity of the return of asset i to the return of the market portfolio. A beta of 1 means that the asset or a portfolio has the same quantity of risk as the market portfolio. A beta greater than 1 means that the asset or portfolio has more market risk than the market portfolio and a beta less than 1 means that the asset or portfolio has less market risk than the market portfolio. Later in this chapter we will see how beta is estimated.[2]

The second component of the risk premium in the CAPM is the difference between the expected return on the market portfolio, $E(R_M)$, and the risk-free rate. It measures the potential reward for taking on the risk of the market above what can earned by investing in an asset that offers a risk-free rate.

Taken together, the risk premium is a product of the quantity of market risk (as measured by beta) and the potential compensation of taking on market risk (as measured by $[E(R_M) - R_f]$).

---

[2] While the term "beta" is a measure referred to in Chapter 2 when describing the market model, we will see later in this chapter that the beta in the CAPM is not the same.

Let's use some values for beta to see if all of this makes sense. Suppose that a portfolio has a beta of zero. That is, the return for this portfolio has no market risk. Substituting zero for β in the CAPM given by equation (3), we would find that the expected return is just the risk-free rate. This makes sense since a portfolio that has no market risk should have an expected return equal to the risk-free rate.

Consider a portfolio that has a beta of 1. This portfolio has the same market risk as the market portfolio. Substituting 1 for β in the CAPM given by equation (3) results in an expected return equal to that of the market portfolio. Again, this is what one should expect for the return of this portfolio since it has the same market risk exposure as the market portfolio.

If a portfolio has greater market risk than the market portfolio, beta will be greater than 1 and the expected return will be greater than that of the market portfolio. If a portfolio has less market risk than the market portfolio, beta will be less than 1 and the expected return will be less than that of the market portfolio.

Derivation of the CAPM

The CAPM is an equilibrium asset pricing model derived from a set of assumptions. Here we demonstrate how the CAPM is derived.

Assumptions

The CAPM is an abstraction of the real world capital markets and, as such, is based upon some assumptions. These assumptions simplify matters a great deal, and some of them may even seem unrealistic. However, these assumptions make the CAPM more tractable from a mathematical standpoint. The CAPM assumptions are as follows:

Assumption 1: Investors make investment decisions based on the expected return and variance of returns.

Assumption 2: Investors are rational and risk averse.

Assumption 3: Investors subscribe to the Markowitz method of portfolio diversification.

Assumption 4: Investors all invest for the same period of time.

Assumption 5: Investors have the same expectations about the expected return and variance of all assets.

Assumption 6: There is a risk-free asset and investors can borrow and lend any amount at the risk-free rate.

Assumption 7: Capital markets are completely competitive and frictionless.

The first five assumptions deal with the way investors make decisions. The last two assumptions relate to characteristics of the capital market.

Some of these assumptions require further explanation. In Markowitz portfolio theory, presented in Chapter 2, it is assumed that investors make investment decisions based on two parameters, the expected return and the variance of returns. Assumption 1 indicates that in the CAPM the same two parameters are used by investors. Assumption 2 indicates that in order to accept greater risk, investors must be compensated by the opportunity of realizing a higher return. We refer to such investors as *risk averse*. This is an oversimplified definition. Actually, a more rigorous definition of risk aversion is described by a mathematical specification of an investor's utility function. However, this complexity need not be of concern here. What is important is that if an investor faces a choice between two portfolios with the same expected return, the investor will select the portfolio with the lower risk. Certainly, this is a reasonable assumption.

The CAPM assumes (Assumption 3) that the risk-averse investor will ascribe to Markowitz's methodology of reducing portfolio risk by combining assets with counterbalancing covariances or correlations. By Assumption 4, all investors are assumed to make investment decisions over some single-period investment horizon. How long that period is (i.e., six months, one year, two years, etc.) is not specified. In reality, the investment decision process is more complex than that, with many investors having more than one investment horizon. Nonetheless, the assumption of a one-period investment horizon is necessary to simplify the mathematics of the theory. To obtain the Markowitz efficient frontier which we will be used in developing the CAPM, it will be assumed that investors have the same expectations with respect to the inputs that are used to derive the efficient portfolios: asset returns, variances, and covariances. This is Assumption 5 and is referred to as the "homogeneous expectations assumption."

As we will see, the existence of a risk-free asset and unlimited borrowing and lending at the risk-free rate (Assumption 6) is important in deriving the CAPM. This is because efficient portfolios are created for portfolios consisting of risky assets. No consideration is given as to how to create efficient portfolios when a risk-free asset is available. In the CAPM, it is assumed not only that there is a risk-free asset but that an investor can borrow funds at the interest paid on a risk-free rate.

Finally, it is assumed that the capital market is perfectly competitive (Assumption 7). In general, this means the number of buyers and sellers is sufficiently large, and all investors are small enough relative to the market so that no individual investor can influence an asset's price. Consequently, all investors are price takers, and the market price is determined where there is equality of supply and demand. In addition, according to Assumption 7, there are no transaction costs or impediments that interfere with the supply of and demand for an asset. Economists refer to these various costs and impediments as "frictions." The costs associated with frictions generally result in buyers paying more than in the absence of frictions and/or sellers receiving less.

Capital Market Line

To derive the CAPM, we begin with the efficient frontier. In creating this efficient frontier, there was no consideration of a risk-free asset. In the absence of a risk-free rate, efficient portfolios can be constructed based on expected return and variance, with the optimal portfolio being the one portfolio that is tangent to the investor's indifference curve. The efficient frontier changes, however, once a risk-free asset is introduced and assuming that investors can borrow and lend at the risk-free rate (Assumption 6). This is illustrated in Exhibit 4.1.

EXHIBIT 4.1   The Capital Market Line

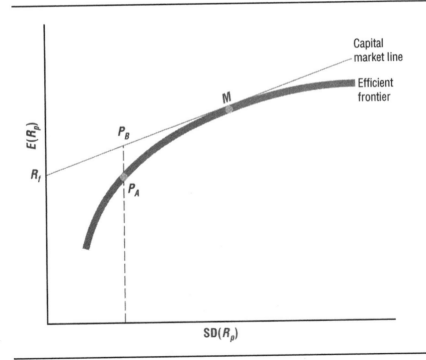

Every combination of the risk-free asset and the efficient portfolio denoted by point M is shown on the line drawn from the vertical axis at the risk-free rate tangent to the efficient frontier. The point of tangency is denoted by M which represents portfolio M. All the portfolios on the line are feasible for the investor to construct. Portfolios to the left of portfolio M represent combinations of risky assets and the risk-free asset. Portfolios to the right of M include purchases of risky assets made with funds borrowed at the risk-free rate. Such a portfolio is called a *leveraged portfolio* since it involves the use of borrowed funds. The line from the risk-free rate that is tangent to portfolio M is called the *capital market line* (CML).

Let's compare a portfolio on the CML to a portfolio on the efficient frontier with the same risk. For example, compare portfolio P_A, which is on the efficient frontier, with portfolio P_B, which is on the CML and therefore is comprised of some combination of the risk-free asset and the efficient portfolio M. Notice that for the same risk the expected return is greater for P_B than for P_A. By Assumption 2, a risk-averse investor will prefer P_B to P_A. That is, P_B will dominate P_A. In fact, this is true for all but one portfolio on the CML: portfolio M which is on the efficient frontier.

With the introduction of the risk-free asset, we can now say that an investor will select a portfolio on the CML which represents a combination of borrowing or lending at the risk-free rate and the efficient portfolio M. The particular efficient portfolio on the CML that the investor will select will depend on the investor's risk preference. This can be seen in Exhibit 4.2 which is the same as Exhibit 4.1 but has the investor's indifference curves included. The investor will select the portfolio on the CML that is tangent to the highest indifference curve, u_3 in the exhibit. Notice that without the risk-free asset, an investor could only get to u_2, which is the indifference curve that is tangent to the efficient frontier. Thus, the opportunity to borrow or lend at the risk-free rate results in a capital market where risk-averse investors will prefer to hold portfolios consisting of combinations of the risk-free asset and some portfolio M on the efficient frontier.

We can derive a formula for the CML algebraically. Based on the assumption of homogeneous expectations (Assumption 5), all investors can create an efficient portfolio consisting of w_f placed in the risk-free asset and w_M in the market portfolio, where w represents the corresponding percentage (weight) of the portfolio allocated to each asset. Thus,

$$w_f + w_M = 1 \quad \text{or} \quad w_f = 1 - w_M$$

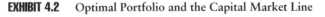

EXHIBIT 4.2   Optimal Portfolio and the Capital Market Line

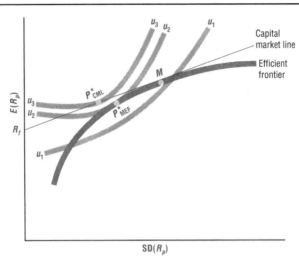

u_1, u_2, u_3 = indifference curves with $u_1 < u_2 < u_3$

M = Market portfolio

R_f = risk-free rate

P^*_{CML} = optimal portfolio on capital market line

P^*_{MEF} = optimal portfolio on efficient frontier

As we explained in Chapter 2, the expected return is equal to the weighted average of the expected return of the two assets. Therefore, the expected portfolio return, $E(R_p)$, is equal to

$$E(R_p) = w_f R_f + w_M E(R_M)$$

Since we know that $w_f = 1 - w_M$, we can rewrite $E(R_p)$ as follows:

$$E(R_p) = (1 - w_M) R_f + w_M E(R_M)$$

This can be simplified as follows:

$$E(R_p) = R_f + w_M [E(R_M) - R_f] \tag{4}$$

The variance of the portfolio consisting of the risk-free asset and portfolio M can be found using the formula for the variance of a two-asset portfolio given in Chapter 2. It is

$$\mathrm{var}(R_p) = w_f^2\ \mathrm{var}(R_f) + w_M^2\ \mathrm{var}(R_M) + 2w_f\,w_M\ \mathrm{cov}(R_f, R_M)$$

We know that the variance of the risk-free asset, $\mathrm{var}(R_f)$, is equal to zero. This is because there is no possible variation in the return since the future return is known. The covariance between the risk-free asset and portfolio M, $\mathrm{cov}(R_f, R_M)$, is zero. This is because the risk-free asset has no variability and therefore does not move at all with the return on portfolio M which is a risky portfolio. Substituting these two values into the formula for the portfolio's variance, we get

$$\mathrm{var}(R_p) = w_M^2\ \mathrm{var}(R_M)$$

In other words, the variance of the portfolio is represented by the weighted variance of portfolio M.

We can solve for the weight of portfolio M by substituting standard deviations for variances. Since the standard deviation is the square root of the variance, we can write

$$\mathrm{SD}(R_p) = w_M\ \mathrm{SD}(R_M)$$

and therefore

$$w_m = \frac{\mathrm{SD}(R_p)}{\mathrm{SD}(R_M)}$$

If we substitute the above result for w_M in equation (4) and rearrange terms we get the CML:

$$E(R_p) = R_f + \left[\frac{E(R_M) - R_f}{\mathrm{SD}(R_M)}\right]\mathrm{SD}(R_p) \qquad (5)$$

What is Portfolio M?   Now that we know that portfolio M is pivotal to the CML, we need to know what portfolio M is. That is, how does an investor construct portfolio M? Eugene Fama demonstrated that portfolio M must consist of all assets available to investors, and each asset must be held in proportion to its market value relative to the total market value of all assets.[3] That is, portfolio M is the "market portfolio" described

---

[3] Eugene F. Fama, "Efficient Capital Markets: A Review of Theory and Empirical Work," *Journal of Finance* (May 1970), pp. 383–417.

earlier. So, rather than referring to the market portfolio, we can simply refer to the "market."

Risk Premium in the CML   With homogeneous expectations, $SD(R_M)$ and $SD(R_p)$ are the market's consensus for the expected return distributions for portfolio M and portfolio p. The risk premium for the CML is

$$\left[\frac{E(R_M) - R_f}{SD(R_M)}\right]SD(R_p)$$

Let's examine the economic meaning of the risk premium.

The numerator of the first term is the expected return from investing in the market beyond the risk-free return. It is a measure of the reward for holding the risky market portfolio rather than the risk-free asset. The denominator is the market risk of the market portfolio. Thus, the first term measures the *reward per unit of market risk*. Since the CML represents the return offered to compensate for a perceived level of risk, each point on the CML is a balanced market condition, or equilibrium. The slope of the CML (i.e., the first term) determines the additional return needed to compensate for a unit change in risk. That is why the slope of the CML is also referred to as the *equilibrium market price of risk*.

The CML says that the expected return on a portfolio is equal to the risk-free rate plus a risk premium equal to the market price of risk (as measured by the reward per unit of market risk) times the quantity of risk for the portfolio (as measured by the standard deviation of the portfolio). That is,

$$ER_p = R_f + \text{market price of risk} \times \text{quantity of risk}$$

Systematic and Unsystematic Risk

Now we know that a risk-averse investor who makes decisions based on expected return and variance should construct an efficient portfolio using a combination of the market portfolio and the risk-free rate. The combinations are identified by the CML. Based on this result, Sharpe derived an asset pricing model that shows how a risky asset should be priced. In the process of doing so, we can fine-tune our thinking about the risk associated with an asset. Specifically, we can show that the appropriate risk that investors should be compensated for accepting is not the variance of an asset's return but some other quantity. In order to do this, let's take a closer look at risk.

We can do this by looking at the variance of the portfolio. It can be demonstrated that the variance of the market portfolio containing N assets can be shown to be equal to:[4]

$$\text{var}(R_M)$$
$$= w_{1M} \, \text{cov}(R_1, R_M) + w_{2M} \, \text{cov}(R_2, R_M) + \ldots + w_{NM} \, \text{cov}(R_N, R_M) \quad (6)$$

where w_{iM} is equal to the proportion invested in asset i in the market portfolio.

Notice that the portfolio variance does not depend on the variance of the assets comprising the market portfolio but their covariance with the market portfolio. Sharpe defines the degree to which an asset covaries with the market portfolio as the asset's *systematic risk*. More specifically, he defined systematic risk as the portion of an asset's variability

---

[4] The proof is as follows. The variance of a portfolio consisting of N assets is equal to:

$$\text{var}(R_p) = \sum_{i=1}^{N} \sum_{j=1}^{N} w_i w_j \text{cov}(R_i, R_j)$$

If we substitute M (market portfolio) for p and denote by w_{iM} and w_{jM} the proportion invested in asset i and j in the market portfolio, then the above equation can be rewritten as:

$$\text{var}(R_M) = \sum_{i=1}^{N} \sum_{j=1}^{N} w_{iM} w_{jM} \text{cov}(R_i, R_j)$$

It can be demonstrated that the above equation can be expressed as follows:

$$\text{var}(R_M)$$
$$= w_{1M} \sum_{j=1}^{N} w_{jM} \text{cov}(R_1, R_j) + w_{2M} \sum_{j=1}^{N} w_{jM} \text{cov}(R_2, R_j)$$
$$+ \ldots + w_{NM} \sum_{j=1}^{N} w_{NM} \text{cov}(R_N, R_j)$$

The covariance of asset i with the market portfolio, $\text{cov}(R_i, R_M)$, is expressed as follows:

$$\text{cov}(R_i, R_M) = \sum_{j=1}^{N} w_{jM} \text{cov}(R_j, R_j)$$

Substituting the right-hand side of the left-hand side of the equation into the prior equation, gives equation (6)

that can be attributed to a common factor. Systematic risk is the minimum level of risk that can be obtained for a portfolio by means of diversification across a large number of randomly chosen assets. As such, systematic risk is that which results from general market and economic conditions that cannot be diversified away.

Sharpe defined the portion of an asset's variability that can be diversified away as *nonsystematic risk*. It is also sometimes called *unsystematic risk, diversifiable risk, unique risk, residual risk*, and *company-specific risk*. This is the risk that is unique to an asset.

Consequently, total risk (as measured by the variance) can be partitioned into systematic risk as measured by the covariance of asset i's return with the market portfolio's return and nonsystematic risk. The relevant risk is the systematic risk. We will see how to measure the systematic risk later.

How diversification reduces nonsystematic risk for portfolios is illustrated in Exhibit 4.3. The vertical axis shows the variance of the portfolio return. The variance of the portfolio return represents the *total risk* for the portfolio (systematic plus nonsystematic). The horizontal axis shows the number of holdings of different assets (e.g., the number of common stock held of different issuers). As can be seen, as the number of asset holdings increases, the level of nonsystematic risk is almost completely eliminated (i.e., diversified away). Studies of different asset classes support this. For example, for common stock, several studies suggest that a portfolio size of about 20 randomly selected companies will completely eliminate nonsystematic risk leaving only systematic risk.[5] In the case of corporate bonds, generally less than 40 corporate issues are needed to eliminate nonsystematic risk.[6]

Security Market Line

The CML represents an equilibrium condition in which the expected return on a portfolio of assets is a linear function of the expected return on the market portfolio. Individual assets do not fall on the CML. Instead, it can be demonstrated that the following relationship holds for individual assets:[7]

---

[5] The first empirical study of this type was by Wayne H. Wagner and Sheila Lau, "The Effect of Diversification on Risks," *Financial Analysts Journal* (November–December 1971), p. 50.

[6] See Richard W. McEnally and Calvin M. Boardman, "Aspects of Corporate Bond Portfolio Diversification," *Journal of Financial Research* (Spring 1979), pp. 27–36.

[7] For the proof, see William F. Sharpe, *Portfolio Theory and Capital Markets* (New York, NY: McGraw Hill, 1970), pp. 86–91.

EXHIBIT 4.3   Systematic and Unsystematic Portfolio Risk

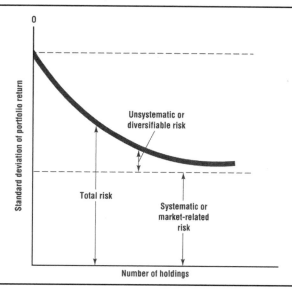

$$E(R_i) = R_f + \left[\frac{E(R_i) - R_f}{\text{var}(R_M)}\right]\text{cov}(R_i, R_M) \tag{7}$$

Equation (7) is called the *security market line* (SML).

In equilibrium, the expected return of individual securities will lie on the SML and *not* on the CML. This is true because of the high degree of nonsystematic risk that remains in individual assets that can be diversified out of portfolios. In equilibrium, only efficient portfolios will lie on both the CML and the SML.

The SML also can be expressed as

$$E(R_i) = R_f + [E(R_i) - R_f]\frac{\text{cov}(R_i, R_M)}{\text{var}(R_M)} \tag{8}$$

How can the ratio in equation (8) be estimated for each asset? It can be estimated empirically using return data for the market portfolio and the return on the asset. The empirical analogue for equation (8) is:

$$r_{it} - r_{ft} = \alpha_i + \beta_i [r_{Mt} - r_{ft}] + e_{it} \tag{9}$$

where e_{it} is the error term. Equation (9) is called the *characteristic line*.

β_i, beta, in equation (9) is the estimate of the ratio in equation (8); that is,

$$\beta_i = \frac{\text{cov}(R_i, R_M)}{\text{var}(R_M)} \tag{10}$$

Substituting β_i into the SML given by equation (8) gives the beta-version of the SML:

$$E(R_i) = R_f + \beta_i \, [E(R_M) - R_f] \tag{11}$$

This is the CAPM form given by equation (3). This equation states that, given the assumptions of the CAPM, the expected return on an individual asset is a positive linear function of its index of systematic risk as measured by beta. The higher the beta, the higher the expected return.

In Chapter 1, we discussed how an investor pursuing an active strategy will search for underpriced securities to purchase or retain and overpriced securities to sell or avoid (if held in the current portfolio, or sold short if permitted). If an investor believes that the CAPM is the correct asset pricing model, then the SML can be used to identify mispriced securities. A security is perceived to be underpriced (i.e., undervalued) if the "expected" return projected by the investor is greater than the "required" return stipulated by the SML. A security is perceived to be overpriced (i.e., overvalued), if the "expected" return projected by the investor is less than the "required" return stipulated by the SML. Said another way, if the expected return plots above (over) the SML, the security is "underpriced;" if it plots below the SML, it is "overpriced."

Two Betas, Two Theories

We have seen the term beta used in two ways in our development of portfolio theory. In Chapter 2, we used the market model to estimate beta. Beta was used in that instance as a proxy measure of the covariance with an index so that the full mean-variance analysis need not be performed. The approach was mentioned by Markowitz,[8] but investigated by Sharpe.[9] The market model is repeated below:

$$r_{it} = \alpha_i + \beta_i \, r_{mt} + u_{it} \tag{12}$$

---

[8] Harry M. Markowitz, *Portfolio Selection: Second Edition* (Cambridge, MA: Basil Blackwell Ltd., 1991), p. 100.
[9] William F. Sharpe, "A Simplified Model for Portfolio Analysis," *Management Science* (January 1963), pp. 277–293.

Note that the index need not be a market portfolio [hence the use of m rather than M) in equation (12)]. When Sharpe estimated the market model, he used a stock market index.

Now we see the term beta used again in the CAPM. The beta is estimated from the characteristic line given by equation (9). The market model and the characteristic line look almost identical. The difference is simply that the characteristic line measures the return relative to the risk-free rate in each period. In the case of the characteristic line, a proxy for the market portfolio is used. This is in contrast to the market model where the index need not be the market portfolio.

This distinction between the beta in the market model and the beta in the characteristic line is important. Critics of portfolio selection and the CAPM have incorrectly made statements about the drawbacks of these theories because they fail to understand the distinction between these two betas. Adding to the confusion was that Sharpe introduced both of these beta concepts around the same time (1963 and 1964).

Estimating the Characteristic Line

As with the market model, the characteristic line is estimated using regression analysis. In fact, all the data required are the same except for the risk-free rate each period. Many practitioners typically ignore the risk-free rate and effectively use the market model to estimate beta—further leading to confusion about the beta in the market model and the characteristic line.

In Chapter 2, the market model is applied to five companies. The results of the beta estimates and one other important statistic are given below:

	General Electric	McGraw Hill	IBM	General Motors	Xerox
Beta	1.24	0.86	1.22	1.11	1.27
R-squared	0.62	0.28	0.33	0.28	0.19

The coefficient of determination, denoted by R-squared, indicates the strength of the relationship. Specifically, it measures the percentage of the variation in the return on a stock explained by the return by the market portfolio (proxied by the S&P 500 in our illustration). The value ranges from 0 to 1. The higher the R-squared, the greater the proportion of systematic risk relative to total risk. For individual stocks, the R-squared is typically in the 0.3 area. That is, for individual stocks systematic risk is small relative to nonsystematic risk. For well-diversified portfolios, the R-squared is typically greater than 0.9.

Performance Measures

In the Markowitz framework adopted by the CAPM, investors make investment decisions based on expected return and the standard deviation. The standard deviation is a measure of risk. Portfolio managers and their clients have used several measures to evaluate the performance of managers assuming that there is a linear relationship between a portfolio's return and the return on some broad-based market index. The three most common measures are the Treynor measure,[10] the Sharpe measure,[11] and the Jensen measure.[12]

Treynor Measure

The *Treynor measure* is a measure of the excess return per unit of risk. The excess return is defined as the difference between the portfolio's return and the risk-free rate of return over the some evaluation period. The risk measure used is the relative systematic risk as measured by the portfolio's beta. Treynor argues that this is the appropriate risk measure since in a well-diversified portfolio, the unsystematic risk is close to zero.

In equation form, the Treynor measure is:

$$\frac{\text{Portfolio return} - \text{Risk-free rate}}{\text{Portfolio's beta}}$$

Sharpe Measure

As with the Treynor measure, the *Sharpe measure* is a gauge of the reward/risk ratio. The numerator is the same as in the Treynor measure. The risk of the portfolio is measured by the standard deviation of the portfolio's return. The Sharpe measure is thus:

$$\frac{\text{Portfolio return} - \text{Risk-free rate}}{\text{Standard deviation of portfolio's return}}$$

Consequently, the Sharpe index is a measure of the excess return relative to the total variability of the portfolio. The Sharpe and Treynor measures will give identical performance rankings if the portfolios evaluated

---

[10] Jack Treynor, "How to Rate Management of Investment Funds," *Harvard Business Review* (January–February 1965), pp. 63–75.
[11] William F. Sharpe, "Mutual Fund Performance," *Journal of Business* (January 1966), pp. 119–138.
[12] Michael C. Jensen, "The Performance of Mutual Funds in the Period 1945–1964," *Journal of Finance* (May 1968), pp. 389–416.

are well diversified. If they are poorly diversified, the rankings could be quite different.

Jensen Measure

The *Jensen measure* uses the CAPM to empirically determine whether the portfolio manager outperformed a market index. Using time-series data for the return on the portfolio and the market, this is done by estimating the following relationship using regression analysis:

$$r_{pt} - r_{ft} = \alpha_p + \beta_p \left[r_{Mt} - r_{ft} \right] + e_{pt}$$

where r_{pt}, r_{ft}, and r_{Mt} are the observed returns for the portfolio, the risk-free rate, and the return on the market; e_{pt} is the error term; and α_p and β_p are the parameters to be estimated using regression analysis.

The intercept term alpha, α_p, is the unique return realized by the manager. The Jensen measure is the alpha or unique risk that is estimated from the above regression. If the alpha is not statistically different from zero, there is no unique return. A statistically significant alpha that is positive means that the manager outperformed the market; a negative value means that the manager underperformed the market.

As with the Treynor measure, the Jensen measure assumes that the portfolio is fully diversified so that the only risk remaining in the portfolio is systematic risk.

Tests of the CAPM

Now that's the theory. The question is whether or not the theory is supported by empirical evidence. There has been probably more than 1,000 academic papers written on the subject. (Almost all studies use common stock to test the theory.) These papers cover not only the empirical evidence but the difficulties of testing the theory.

Let's start with the empirical evidence. There are two important results of the empirical tests of the CAPM that question its validity. First, it has been found that stocks with low betas have exhibited higher returns than the CAPM predicts and stocks with high betas have been found to have lower returns than the CAPM predicts. Second, market risk is not the only risk factor priced by the market. Several studies have discovered other factors that explain stock returns.[13] We will discuss these risk factors in later chapters.

---

[13] See, for example, Eugene Fama and Kenneth French, "The Cross-Section of Expected Returns," *Journal of Finance* (June 1992), pp. 427– 465.

While on the empirical level there are serious questions raised about the CAPM, there is an important paper challenging the validity of these empirical studies. The paper, authored by Richard Roll and titled "A Critique of the Asset Pricing Theory's Tests,"[14] demonstrates that the CAPM is not testable until the exact composition of the "true" market portfolio is known, and the only valid test of the CAPM is to observe whether the *ex ante* true market portfolio is mean-variance efficient. As a result of his findings, Roll states that he does not believe there ever will be an unambiguous test of the CAPM. He does not say that the CAPM is invalid. Rather, Roll says that there is likely to be no unambiguous way to test the CAPM and its implications due to the non-observability of the true market portfolio and its characteristics.

Modifications of the CAPM

Several researchers have modified the CAPM. Here we will briefly describe two modifications.

Suppose that there is no risk-free rate and that investors cannot borrow and lend at the risk-free rate (Assumption 6). How does that affect the CAPM? Fischer Black examined how the original CAPM would change if there is no risk-free asset in which the investor can borrow and lend.[15] He demonstrated that neither the existence of a risk-free asset nor the requirement that investors can borrow and lend at the risk-free rate is necessary for the theory to hold. Black's argument was as follows. The beta of a risk-free asset is zero. Suppose that a portfolio can be created such that it is uncorrelated with the market. That portfolio would then have a beta of zero, and Black labeled that portfolio a "zero-beta portfolio." He set forth the conditions for constructing a zero-beta portfolio and then showed how the CAPM can be modified accordingly. Specifically, in equation (3), the return on the zero-beta portfolio is substituted for the risk-free rate.

Now let's look at the assumption that the only relevant risk is the variance of asset returns (Assumption 1). That is, it is assumed that the only risk factor that an investor is concerned with is the uncertainty about the future price of a security. Investors, however, usually are concerned with other risks that will affect their ability to consume goods and services in the future. Three examples would be the risks associated with future labor income, the future relative prices of consumer goods, and future investment opportunities. Consequently, using the variance of expected returns as the sole measure of risk would be inappropriate

---

[14] Richard Roll, "A Critique of the Asset Pricing Theory's Tests," *Journal of Financial Economics* (March 1977), pp. 129–176.
[15] Fischer Black, "Capital Market Equilibrium with Restricted Borrowing," *Journal of Business* (July 1972), pp. 444–455.

in the presence of these other risk factors. Recognizing these other risks that investors face, Robert Merton modified the CAPM based on consumers deriving their optimal lifetime consumption when they face such non-market risk factors.[16]

The Role of the CAPM in Investment Management Applications

In 1980, a highly regarded magazine published an article with the title "Is Beta Dead?"[17] In response to this article, in its Winter 1981 issue *The Journal of Portfolio Management* published a series of articles. The article by Barr Rosenberg in particular provides an excellent discussion of the CAPM and its role.[18]

The key to the CAPM's contribution to investment management theory is clearly stated by Rosenberg:

> The CAPM is theory, but, paradoxically, the role of the CAPM as "theory" leading to application has been less important than its role in mobilizing attention and defining constructs. We should keep in mind that the CAPM is not "true," since many of its assumptions are not exactly satisfied in the real world. Indeed, the CAPM rules out active management and investment research, and thus abolishes most applications at the stroke of a pen, by virtue of the unrealistic assumptions that it makes. [p. 5]

That is, even though the CAPM is not true it does not mean that the constructs introduced by the theory are not important. Constructs introduced in the development of the theory include the notion of a market portfolio, systematic risk, diversifiable risk, and beta. As Rosenberg notes: "These ideas play an important role in the methods of 'modern portfolio theory'."

In the next section we will discuss another asset pricing model that introduces risk factors other than market risk. In Chapter 13, we will discuss other models that consider non-market risk factors. However, these do not invalidate the important constructs developed by the CAPM. Rosenberg concludes his article with the following statement:

> The question of rewards for factors other than equity market risk has been the subject of active study and controversy for a decade—

---

[16] Robert C. Merton, "An Intertemporal Capital Asset Pricing Model," *Econometrica* (September 1973), pp. 867–888.

[17] Anise Wallace, "Is Beta Dead?" *Institutional Investor* (July 1980), pp. 23–30.

[18] Barr Rosenberg, "The Capital Asset Pricing Model and the Market Model," *The Journal of Portfolio Management* (Winter 1981), pp. 5–16.

and no doubt will continue to be so in the decades to come. Nevertheless, no one has refuted the existence of equilibrium reward for equity market risk; indeed, it has rarely been questioned, although the magnitude has been in doubt. The concept of reward to equity market risk (or beta) is a theoretical insight, that, in my view, is likely to endure. (p. 16).

Fast forward a little more than two decades since the publication of the Rosenberg article and his conclusions still hold.[19]

Moreover, Markowitz has explained that the major reason for the debate is the confusion between the beta that is associated with the market model (estimated to avoid having to compute all covariances for assets in a portfolio) and the beta in the CAPM.[20] We have emphasized the difference between these two betas.

ARBITRAGE PRICING THEORY MODEL

An alternative to the equilibrium asset pricing model just discussed, an asset pricing model based purely on arbitrage arguments was derived by Stephen Ross.[21] The model, called the *Arbitrage Pricing Theory* (APT) *Model*, postulates that an asset's expected return is influenced by a variety of risk factors, as opposed to just market risk as suggested by the CAPM. The APT model states that the return on a security is linearly related to H risk factors. However, the APT model does *not* specify what these risk factors are, but it is assumed that the relationship between asset returns and the risk factors is linear. Moreover, unsystematic risk can be eliminated so that an investor is only compensated for accepting the systematic risk factors.

Arbitrage Principle

Since the model relies on arbitrage arguments, we will digress at this point to define what is meant by arbitrage. In its simple form, arbitrage

---

[19] These sentiments were echoed in a presentation by Peter Bernstein in a keynote address on the occasion of the fifth anniversary of the establishment of the International Center for Financial Management & Engineering (FAME) in Geneva on February 7, 2002. (See: "How Modern is Modern Portfolio Theory?" *Economics and Portfolio Strategy*, Peter L. Bernstein, Inc., March 15, 2002.)

[20] Harry M. Markowitz, "The 'Two Beta' Trap," *The Journal of Portfolio Management* (Fall 1984), pp. 12–20.

[21] Stephen A. Ross, "The Arbitrage Theory of Capital Asset Pricing," *Journal of Economic Theory* (December 1976), pp. 343–362.

is the simultaneous buying and selling of an asset at two different prices in two different markets. The arbitrageur profits without risk by buying cheap in one market and simultaneously selling at the higher price in the other market. Investors don't hold their breath waiting for such situations to occur, because they are rare. In fact, a single arbitrageur with unlimited ability to sell short could correct a mispricing condition by financing purchases in the underpriced market with proceeds of short sales in the overpriced market. (Short-selling means selling an asset that is not owned in anticipation of a price decline. The mechanism for doing this is described in Chapter 6.) This means that riskless arbitrage opportunities are short-lived.

Less obvious arbitrage opportunities exist in situations where a *package of assets* can produce a payoff (expected return) identical to an asset that is priced differently. This arbitrage relies on a fundamental principle of finance called the *law of one price* which states that a given asset must have the same price regardless of the means by which one goes about creating that asset. The law of one price implies that if the payoff of an asset can be synthetically created by a package of assets, the price of the package and the price of the asset whose payoff it replicates must be equal.

When a situation is discovered whereby the price of the package of assets differs from that of an asset with the same payoff, rational investors will trade these assets in such a way so as to restore price equilibrium. This market mechanism is assumed by the APT model, and is founded on the fact that an arbitrage transaction does not expose the investor to any adverse movement in the market price of the assets in the transaction.

For example, let us consider how we can produce an arbitrage opportunity involving the three assets A, B, and C. These assets can be purchased today at the prices shown below, and can each produce only one of two payoffs (referred to as State 1 and State 2) a year from now:

Asset	Price	Payoff in State 1	Payoff in State 2
A	$70	$50	$100
B	60	30	120
C	80	38	112

While it is not obvious from the data presented above, an investor can construct a portfolio of assets A and B that will have the identical return as asset C in both State 1 or State 2. Let w_A and w_B be the proportion of assets A and B, respectively, in the portfolio. Then the payoff (i.e., the terminal value of the portfolio) under the two states can be expressed mathematically as follows:

if State 1 occurs: $\$50\ w_A + \$30\ w_B$
if State 2 occurs: $\$100\ w_A + \$120\ w_B$

We create a portfolio consisting of A and B that will reproduce the payoff of C regardless of the state that occurs one year from now. Here is how: For either condition (State 1 and State 2) we set the expected payoff of the portfolio equal to the expected payoff for C as follows:

State 1: $\$50\ w_A + \$30\ w_B\quad = \$\ 38$
State 2: $\$100\ w_A + \$120\ w_B = \$112$

we also know that $w_A + w_B = 1$.

If we solved for the weights for w_A and w_B that would simultaneously satisfy the above equations, we would find that the portfolio should have 40% in asset A (i.e., $w_A = 0.4$) and 60% in asset B (i.e., $w_B = 0.6$). The cost of that portfolio will be equal to

$$(0.4)(\$70) + (0.6)(\$60) = \$64$$

Our portfolio (i.e., package of assets) comprised of assets A and B has the same payoff in State 1 and State 2 as the payoff of asset C. The cost of asset C is $80 while the cost of the portfolio is only $64. This is an arbitrage opportunity that can be exploited by buying assets A and B in the proportions given above and shorting (selling) asset C.

For example, suppose that $1 million is invested to create the portfolio with assets A and B. The $1 million is obtained by selling short asset C. The proceeds from the short sale of asset C provide the funds to purchase assets A and B. Thus, there would be no cash outlay by the investor. The payoffs for States 1 and 2 are shown below:

Asset	Investment	Payoff in State 1	Payoff in State 2
A	$400,000	$285,715	$571,429
B	600,000	300,000	1,200,000
C	−1,000,000	−475,000	−1,400,000
Total	0	110,715	371,429

In either State 1 or 2, the investor profits without risk. The APT model assumes that such an opportunity would be quickly eliminated by the marketplace.

APT Model Formulation

The APT model postulates that an asset's expected return is influenced by a variety of risk factors, as opposed to just market risk of the CAPM. That is, the APT model asserts that the return on an asset is linearly related to H "factors." The APT does not specify what these factors are, but it is assumed that the relationship between asset returns and the factors is linear. Specifically, the APT model asserts that the rate of return on asset i is given by the following relationship:

$$R_i = E(R_i) + \beta_{i,1}F_1 + \beta_{i,2}F_2 + \dots + \beta_{i,H}F_H + e_i$$

where

R_i = the rate of return on asset i

$E(R_i)$ = the expected return on asset i

F_h = the h-th factor that is common to the returns of all assets ($h = 1, \dots, H$)

$\beta_{i,h}$ = the sensitivity of the i-th asset to the h-th factor

e_i = the unsystematic return for asset i

For equilibrium to exist, the following conditions must be satisfied: Using no additional funds (wealth) and without increasing risk, it should not be possible, on average, to create a portfolio to increase return. In essence, this condition states that there is no "money machine" available in the market.

Ross derived the following relationship which is what is referred to as the APT model:

$$E(R_i) = R_f + \beta_{i,F1}[E(R_{F1}) - R_F] + \beta_{i,F2}[E(R_{F2}) - R_F]$$
$$+ \dots + \beta_{i,FH}[E(R_{FH}) - R_F] \tag{13}$$

where $[E(R_{Fj}) - R_f]$ is the excess return of the jth systematic risk factor over the risk-free rate, and can be thought of as the price (or risk premium) for the jth systematic risk factor.

The APT model as given by equation (13) asserts that investors want to be compensated for all the risk factors that *systematically* affect the return of a security. The compensation is the sum of the products of each risk factor's systematic risk ($\beta_{i,Fh}$), and the risk premium assigned to it by the financial market $[E(R_{Fh}) - R_f]$. As in the case of the CAPM, an investor is not compensated for accepting unsystematic risk.

It turns out that the CAPM is actually a special case of the APT model. If the only risk factor in the APT model as given by equation (13) is market risk, the APT model reduces to the CAPM. Now contrast the APT model given by equation (3). They look similar. Both say that investors are compensated for accepting all systematic risk and no non-systematic risk. The CAPM states that systematic risk is market risk, while the APT model does not specify the systematic risk.

Supporters of the APT model argue that it has several major advantages over the CAPM or multi-factor CAPM. First, it makes less restrictive assumptions about investor preferences toward risk and return. As explained earlier, the CAPM theory assumes investors trade off between risk and return solely on the basis of the expected returns and standard deviations of prospective investments. The APT model, in contrast, simply requires some rather unobtrusive bounds be placed on potential investor utility functions. Second, no assumptions are made about the distribution of asset returns. Finally, since the APT model does not rely on the identification of the true market portfolio, the theory is potentially testable.

MULTI-FACTOR RISK MODELS IN PRACTICE

The APT model provides theoretical support for an asset pricing model where there is more than one risk factor. Consequently, models of this type are referred to as *multi-factor risk models*. As we will see in later chapters where these models are applied to equity portfolio management (in Chapter 13) and bond portfolio management (in Chapter 24), they provide the tools for quantifying the risk profile of a portfolio relative to a benchmark, for constructing a portfolio relative to a benchmark, and controlling risk. For now, we provide a brief review of the multifactor risk models used in equity portfolio management. The three types are statistical factor models, macroeconomic factor models, and fundamental factor models.[22]

Statistical Factor Models

In a *statistical factor model,* historical and cross-sectional data on stock returns are tossed into a statistical model. The goal of the statistical model is to best explain the observed stock returns with "factors" that are linear return combinations and uncorrelated with each other.

For example, suppose that monthly returns for 5,000 companies for ten years are computed. The goal of the statistical analysis is to produce "factors" that best explain the variance of the observed stock returns. For example, suppose that there are six "factors" that do this. These "factors" are statistical artifacts. The objective in a statistical factor

---

[22] Gregory Connor, "The Three Types of Factor Models: A Comparison of Their Explanatory Power," *Financial Analysts Journal* (May–June 1995), pp. 42–57.

model then becomes to determine the economic meaning of each of these statistically derived factors.

Because of the problem of interpretation, it is difficult to use the factors from a statistical factor model for valuation, portfolio construction, and risk control. Instead, practitioners prefer the two other models described next, which allow them to prespecify meaningful factors, and thus produce a more intuitive model.

Macroeconomic Factor Models

In a *macroeconomic factor model*, the inputs to the model are historical stock returns and observable macroeconomic variables. These variables are called *raw descriptors*. The goal is to determine which macroeconomic variables are pervasive in explaining historical stock returns. Those variables that are pervasive in explaining the returns then become the factors and are included in the model. The responsiveness of a stock to these factors is estimated using historical time series data.

An example of a proprietary macroeconomic factor model is the Burmeister, Ibbotson, Roll, and Ross (BIRR) model.[23] In this model, there are five macroeconomic factors that reflect unanticipated changes in the following macroeconomic variables: investor confidence (confidence risk); interest rates (time horizon risk); inflation (inflation risk); real business activity (business cycle risk); and a market index (market timing risk). For each stock, the sensitivity of the stock to a factor risk is statistically estimated. In addition, for each factor risk a market price for that risk is statistically estimated. Given these two estimates, the expected return can be projected.

Fundamental Factor Models

Fundamental factor models use company and industry attributes and market data as raw descriptors. Examples are price/earnings ratios, book/price ratios, estimated economic growth, and trading activity. The inputs into a fundamental factor model are stock returns and the raw descriptors about a company. Those fundamental variables about a company that are pervasive in explaining stock returns are then the raw descriptors retained in the model. Using cross-sectional analysis, the sensitivity of a stock's return to a raw descriptor is estimated.

There are several fundamental factor models available from vendors. Fundamental factor models are the subject of Chapter 13. Consequently, a discussion of this type of mutifactor risk model will be postponed until then.

---

[23] Edwin Burmeister, Roger Ibbotson, Richard Roll, and Stephen A. Ross, "Using Macroeconomic Factors to Control Portfolio Risk," unpublished paper.

CHAPTER 5

Calculating Investment Returns

Bruce Feibel
Director, Performance Measurement Technology
Eagle Investment Systems

After investment objectives have been set, strategy determined, assets allocated, and trades are made, the next task is to value the portfolio and begin the process of performance measurement. Whether an investor makes his own investing decisions or delegates this duty to advisors, all parties are interested in calculating and weighing the results. The first stage in the performance measurement process is to compute a *return*, which is the income and profit earned on the capital that the investor places at risk in the investment.

Suppose $100 is invested in a fund and the fund subsequently increases in value such that the investor receives $130 back. What was the return on this investment? The investor gained $30. Taking this *dollar return* and dividing it by the $100 invested, and multiplying the decimal result 0.3 by 100 gives us the return expressed as a percentage; that is, 30%.

A *rate of return* is the gain received from an investment over a period of time expressed as a percentage. Returns are a ratio relating how much was gained given how much was risked. We interpret a 30% return as a gain over the period equal to almost ⅓ of the original $100 invested.

Although it appears that no special knowledge of investments is required to calculate and interpret rates of return, several complications make the subject worthy of further investigation:

- Selection of the proper inputs to the return calculation
- Treatment of additional client contributions and withdrawals to and from the investment account

91

■ Adjusting the return to reflect the timing of these contributions and withdrawals
■ Differentiating between the return produced by the investment manager and the return experienced by the investor
■ Computing returns spanning multiple valuation periods
■ Averaging periodic rates of return

These are the issues that we will address in this chapter. In it, we summarize what has evolved to be the investment industry standard approach to calculating and reporting portfolio rates of return. Individual and institutional investors, investing via separate and commingled accounts, using a myriad of strategies and asset classes, use the methodology presented in this chapter to calculate the returns earned by their investment portfolios. The tools covered here are relevant whether you are an individual monitoring the performance of your own personal brokerage account, a financial planner providing advice to many individuals, the manager of a mutual fund, or a plan sponsor overseeing dozens of specialist investment managers. In the illustrations that are used to explain the various concepts presented in the chapter, a spreadsheet format is used so that it is easier for the reader to replicate the calculations.

SINGLE PERIOD RATE OF RETURN

Why do we compute rates of return to describe the performance of an investment when we could simply judge our performance by the absolute dollars gained over time? After all, there is no better judge than money in the bank! There are several reasons that returns have emerged as the preferred statistic for summarizing investment performance:

■ The rate of return concentrates a lot of information into a single statistic. Individual data points about the beginning and ending market values, income earned, cash contributions and withdrawals, and trades for all of the holdings in the portfolio are compressed into a single number.
■ This single number, the return, is a ratio. It is faster for an investor to analyze proportions than absolute numbers. For example, if an investor is told she earned an 8% rate of return, she can instantly begin to judge whether she is happy with this result, compared to the need to pore over valuation and transaction statements first.
■ Returns are comparable even if the underlying figures are not. An investor can compare returns even when the portfolios have different

base currencies or have different sizes. For example, if an investor puts $100 to work and gains $10, she has earned the same return as an investor who put $1 million to work and ended up with $1.1 million.

■ Returns calculated for different periods are comparable; that is, an investor can compare this year's return to last year's.

■ The interpretation of the rate of return is intuitive. Return is the value reconciling the beginning investment value to the ending value over the time period we are measuring. An investor can take a reported return and use it to determine the amount of money he would have at the end of the period given the amount invested:

$$MVE = MVB \times (1 + \text{Decimal return})$$

where

MVE = market value at the end of the period
MVB = market value at the start of the period

For example, if we were to invest $100 at a return of 40%, we would have $140 at the end of the period: $100 × (1.40) = $140. Adding one to the decimal return before multiplying gives a result equal to the beginning value plus the gain/loss over the period. Multiplying by the return of 0.4 gives the gain/loss over the period ($40).

Let's look closer at the calculation of return. In our introductory example we earned a $30 gain on an investment of $100. By dividing the gain by the amount invested we derive the 30% return using:

$$\text{Return in percent} = \left(\frac{\text{Gain or Loss}}{\text{Investment made}} \right) \times 100$$

Suppose that instead of investing and then getting our money back within a single period, we held an investment worth $100 at the beginning of the period and continued to hold it at the end of the period when it was valued at $130. Multiplying the first ratio by 100 transforms the decimal fraction into a percentage gain; 30% in our example (0.3 × 100 = 30%).

The same return can be calculated whether an investor buys and then liquidates an investment within a period or carries it over from a prior period and holds on to it. When we measure the return on an investment that we buy and hold across periods, we treat the beginning market value as if it were a new investment made during the period, and the ending market value as if it were the proceeds from the sale of the investment at the end of the period.

We have used two forms of the return calculation so far. It does not matter which one we use. The two methods are equivalent.

$$\left(\frac{\text{Gain or Loss}}{\text{Investment made}}\right) \times 100 = \left[\left(\frac{\text{Current value}}{\text{Investment made}}\right) - 1\right] \times 100$$

We can demonstrate that the two forms are same by deriving the second form of the calculation from the first.

$$\left(\frac{\text{MVE} - \text{MVB}}{\text{MVB}}\right) \times 100 \rightarrow \left(\frac{\text{MVE}}{\text{MVB}} - \frac{\text{MVB}}{\text{MVB}}\right) \times 100 \rightarrow \left(\frac{\text{MVE}}{\text{MVB}} - 1\right) \times 100$$

Using the first form, the numerator of the rate of return calculation is the *unrealized gain or loss:* the difference between the starting and ending market value. If there were income earned during the period, we also add it into the numerator, making the numerator more properly the market value plus accrued income. In either form of the calculation the denominator is the *investment made.* The number we select for the denominator represents the *money at risk* during the period. For the first measurement period, the investment made is equal to the amount originally invested in the portfolio. In subsequent periods, it is equal to the ending market value of the previous period. The calculation of a return where we invested $100 at the end of December and it rises to $110 in January and then $120 in February is provided in the following spreadsheet.

	A	B	C	D
1	Month End	Market Value	Dollar Return	Percent Return
2	31-Dec-2000	100		
3	31-Jan-2000	110	10	10.00
4	28-Feb-2000	120	10	9.09
5				↑
6			=B4-B3	=((C4/B3)*100)

Notice that even though we earned the same $10 dollar return in January and February, the percent return is higher in January (10/100 = 10.00%) than it was in February (10/110 = 9.09%). The reason for the lower February return is that the money at risk in the fund for February equals not only the original investment of $100 but also the $10 gained in January. With more money put at risk, the same dollar gain results in a lower return to the investment.

By using the *market value* of the investment to calculate returns, we recognize a gain on the investment even though it is not actually *realized* by selling it at the end of the period. To calculate returns that include unrealized gains, we value the portfolio at the end of each measurement period. These dates are the periodic *valuation dates*. A return calculated between two valuation dates is called a *single period, holding period,* or *periodic* return. The periodicity of single period returns is related to the frequency of portfolio valuation. For example, single period returns can be calculated on a daily basis for mutual funds which are valued at the close of the market each night, but may be calculated only monthly for institutional separate accounts, or quarterly for a share in a real estate partnership, as these types of holdings are not valued as frequently. Valuations are performed at least as often as participants are allowed to move money into or out of a commingled fund.

Components of Single Period Returns

When there are no transactions into or out of an investment account and no income earned, to calculate a single period return, we simply divide the ending market value by the beginning market value. Total portfolio market values are derived by summing up the values of the underlying investments within the fund. If we are calculating the return earned on our share of a commingled portfolio, such as a mutual fund, the market value equals the sum of the shares we own multiplied by the unit value of each share on the valuation date. Unit values are calculated by dividing the sum of the individual security market values that comprise the fund by the number of shares outstanding. Portfolio holdings are determined on a trade date basis. With *trade date accounting* we include securities in the portfolio valuation on the day the manager agrees to buy or sell the securities, as opposed to waiting for the day the trades are settled with the broker.

The *market value* of each security is the amount we would expect to receive if the investment were sold on the valuation date. It is calculated using observed market prices and exchange rates wherever possible. Determining market value is easy for instruments like exchange-traded equities, but we need to estimate the current value of other investment types. For example, bonds that do not trade often are marked to market by reference to the price of similar bonds that did trade that day. Although it is possible, say for liquidity reasons, that we could not actually realize the observed market closing price used in the valuation if we were to actually sell the investment, this method avoids introducing subjective estimates of trading impact into return calculations. If the fund holds cash, it too is included the valuation of the fund.

The individual security market values include a measure of income earned or *accrued income* on the investment. Accrued income is income earned but not yet received. For example, if an investor sells a bond between coupon dates, the investor sells the interest accrued from the last payment date to the buyer of the bond. Because the interest sold would be part of the proceeds if the security were sold on the valuation date, we also include it in the calculation of market value. Returns that reflect both the change in market value and the income earned during the period are called *total returns*. In a similar manner, the total portfolio market value is adjusted for accrued receivables and payables to and from the fund. For example, the accrued management fee payable to the investment manager is subtracted from the total market value.

While it is outside the scope of this chapter to itemize the finer points of valuing every type of security the fund could invest in, the principles of market quote driven, trade date, accrual based valuation are used to judge the worth of each security in the portfolio, which are then summed to the portfolio level and result in the single period return calculation formula:

Percent Rate of Return

$$= \left[\left(\frac{\text{Ending Market Value} + \text{Ending Accrued Income}}{\text{Beginning Market Value} + \text{Beginning Accrued Income}} \right) - 1 \right] \times 100$$

It is worthwhile to note what factors we do not explicitly include in the return calculation. The *cost of investments* is *not* considered in performance measurement after the first period's return calculation (except for securities that are valued at their amortized cost). For each subsequent period, the ending market value for the previous period is used as the beginning market value for the next period. The justification for this practice is that we assume that the investment cycle begins afresh with each valuation period, and it is the current market value, and not the original cost, that is invested, or put at risk again, in the next period.

The return calculation makes no reference to gains *realized* in the course of security sales during the period. In fact the portfolio beginning and ending market values include both *unrealized* and *realized capital appreciation* generated by trading within the portfolio during the period. Consider a portfolio with this sequence of activity:

December 31, 2000
▪ Holds 100 shares Stock A priced at $1 per share = $100 MVB

January 31, 2001
▪ Stock A valued at $110 for a (10/100 = 10%) return in January

February 28, 2001
▪ Stock A valued at $115 for a (5/110 = 4.55%) return in February

March 1, 2001
- 50 shares of Stock A are sold for $1.15 per share, netting $57.50
- The realized gain on the sale is $7.50 ($57.50 − $50 = $7.50)
- 10 Shares of Stock B at $5.75 a share are purchased with the proceeds

March 31, 2001
- Stock A valued at (50 shares × $1 = $50)
- Stock B valued at (10 shares × $5 = $50)
- The total portfolio is worth $100, for a (−15/115 = −13.04%) loss in March

The spreadsheet below shows that we do not explicitly use the realized gain of $7.50 in the return calculation for March.

	A	B	C	D	E	F
1	Date	MV Stock A	MV Stock B	Total MV	Gain/Loss	% Return
2	31-Dec-2000	100.00	0.00	100.00		
3	31-Jan-2001	110.00	0.00	110.00	10.00	10.00
4	28-Feb-2001	115.00	0.00	115.00	5.00	4.55
5	01-Mar-2001	57.50	57.50	115.00		
6	31-Mar-2001	50.00	50.00	100.00	-15.00	-13.04
7					↑	↑
8					=D6-D5	=((E6/D5)*100)

The realized gain on the sale of Stock A was committed to the purchase of Stock B, which was then marked to market at the end of the March. We explicitly calculate the unrealized market value change during the period (−15.00), and this market value change implicitly includes any realized gains/losses on securities sold during the period.

It is possible that the manager might not reinvest the sale proceeds via the purchase of another security. In this case, we still do not explicitly include the realized gain in the calculation of return. Instead, we include the cash received on the sale in the total fund market value. The following spreadsheet illustrates the fact that we do not need to know about the transactions *within* the portfolio during the valuation period in order to calculate portfolio level performance.

	A	B	C	D	E	F
1	Date	MV Stock A	Cash	Total MV	Gain/Loss	% Return
2	31-Dec-2000	100.00	0.00	100.00		
3	31-Jan-2001	110.00	0.00	110.00	10.00	10.00
4	28-Feb-2001	115.00	0.00	115.00	5.00	4.55
5	01-Mar-2001	57.50	57.50	115.00		
6	31-Mar-2001	50.00	57.90	107.90	-7.10	-6.17
7					↑	↑
8					=D6-D5	=((E6/D5)*100)

Transactions within the portfolio during the period do not affect the total fund level return calculation because they have an equal and opposite impact on performance—a purchase of one security is a sale of another (cash). This is also true of income received during the period. Income received on a security is an outflow from that security but an inflow of cash. To calculate portfolio level performance when there are no additional contributions and withdrawals, we only need to calculate the market value of all of the securities in the fund and cash balances at the beginning and end of the holding period.

Return on Investment (ROI)

So far we have looked at the calculation of a single period return for situations where the market value of our holdings is made available for investment at the start of the next period. Individual and institutional investors also make periodic additional investments, or *contributions* to, and *withdrawals* from investment accounts. These net contributions to the fund are *not* included as a component of investment return; they represent an increase of capital at risk but not a capital gain on our investment. For this reason, when a fund receives new money, it is not possible to measure performance by simply observing the change in market value.

These asset transfers into and out of the fund are sometimes called *cash flows*. Cash flow is a generic term for different transaction types. For a defined benefit pension plan, the cash flows include periodic corporate contributions to fund the plan and withdrawals to service retirees. For a mutual fund, cash flows include purchases or liquidations of fund shares and exchanges of shares between funds.

The value of the cash flow is the amount of money deposited or withdrawn. A positive cash flow is a flow into the fund. A negative cash flow is a flow out of the fund. Sometimes contributions are made in securities and not cash; this occurs, for example, when a portfolio is transitioned to a new investment manager. The monetary value of these "in-kind" contributions is measured by the current value of the assets transferred at the time of the contribution. In these situations it is important to use the current market value rather than the original cost. If the original cost were used, the return calculation for the first period after the contribution would credit the entire return to date as earned in the first period after the transfer.

When there are cash flows, we need to adjust the calculation of gain/loss in the numerator of the return calculation to account for the fact that the increase in market value was not entirely due to investment earnings. For example, suppose we have a portfolio with an MVB of 100 and a MVE of 130. What is the gain if we invested an additional $10 during the period? We started off with $100 and ended up with $130. We subtract out the additional investment before calculating the gain.

$$\text{Gain/Loss} = (\text{Current Value} - \text{Original Investment} \\ - \text{Net Cash Inflows} + \text{Net Cash Outflows})$$

The gain in this case is $20 (130 − 100 − 10 + 0). The $20 gain/loss during the period combines two amounts—the gain on the original $100 and the gain on the additional $10 invested. If instead of a net inflow, we had a net outflow because we took money out of the portfolio during the period, the second component would be the gain earned up until the money was withdrawn.

When there are cash flows, in addition to modifying the numerator, we need to modify the denominator of the return calculation to account for additional capital invested or withdrawn during the measurement period. We can modify the rate of return calculation to account for additional investment or withdrawals. The result is the *return on investment* (ROI) formula. ROI is the gain or loss generated by an investment expressed as a percentage of the amount invested, adjusted for contributions and withdrawals.

$$\text{ROI in percent} = \left(\frac{(\text{EMV} + \text{NOF}) - (\text{BMV} + \text{NIF})}{\text{BMV} + \text{NIF}} \right) \times 100$$

where NIF are the net inflows and NOF are the net outflows. The following spreadsheet shows the calculation of the ROI.

	A	B	C	D	E
1	MVB	In Flows	Out Flows	MVE	Return on Investment %
2	100.00	10.00	0.00	130.00	18.18
3					
4		=(((D2+C2)-(A2+B2))/(A2+B2))*100			

The first expression in the numerator (EMV + NOF) replaces the EMV used in the ROR calculation. We adjust the ending market value for any withdrawals from the portfolio. Notice that this increases the numerator and the resulting return. Withdrawals are treated as a *benefit* to performance. In the second expression, we are subtracting the amount invested in order to calculate the gain. The inflows are treated as an investment, which reduces the gain. Contributions are treated as a *cost* to performance. The total amount invested (BMV + NIF) is the ROI denominator. By adding the contributions to the BMV we reduce the return, because we are dividing the same gain by a larger number.

Is 18.18% a fair return to account for the case where BMV = 100, EMV = 130, and there was a NIF = 10? The answer is: It depends. Note that there is an implicit assumption that the NIF was available for investing, or at risk, for the complete period. If the additional inflow was put into the fund at the beginning of the period, the investor did not have use of the money for the entire period. The investor would expect a higher fund return to compensate for this as compared to his keeping the money and investing in the fund only at the end of the period. So, returns should take into account the timing of the additional cash flows. If the investment were made sometime during the period, the investor did have use of the capital for some part of the period. For example, if the measurement period was a month and the $10 contribution came midway through the month, the fund had $100 of invested capital for the first half of the month and $110 for the second half. The gain of $20 was made on a smaller invested balance; therefore the return credited to the account should be *higher* than 18.18%.

While ROI adjusts for portfolio contributions and withdrawals, it does not adjust for the *timing* of these cash flows. Because of the assumption that contributions were available for the whole period, ROI will give the same return no matter when in the period the flows occur. Another drawback of the ROI as a measure of investment performance is that it does not adjust for the *length* of the holding period. The ROI calculation gives the same result whether the gain was earned over a day, a year, or 10 years. For these reasons, we need a measure of return that reflects both the timing of cash flows and the length of the period for which the assets were at risk. Both adjustments are derived from concepts related to the time value of money, which we review next.

Time Value of Money

Returns can be equated to the interest rates used in the calculation of the future value of a fixed income investment. However, unlike returns, interest rates are known ahead of time, so we can project the future value at the beginning of the period. The future value of an investment equals the present value plus the interest and other gains earned over the period.

$$FV = PV \times (1 + R)^N$$

where

$$
\begin{aligned}
FV &= \text{value at end of period} \\
PV &= \text{current value of the investment} \\
R &= \text{rate of income earned per period} \\
N &= \text{number of valuation periods}
\end{aligned}
$$

In return calculations, it is the R that is unknown. We calculate this rate R using observations of the beginning and ending market values. To derive the equivalent of the future value, which is the MVE of an investment during a single period, we multiply the MVB by 1 plus the interest rate.

Ending Market Value = Beginning Market Value × (1 + Interest Rate)

The difference between the ending and beginning market values is the income earned. *Compounding* is the reinvestment of income to earn more income in subsequent periods. In a *simple interest* scenario, the income earned is not reinvested in order for it to compound in the following periods. For example, if an MVB = 1,000 is put to work for a period of 4 months at an interest rate = 5% per month, we calculate an ending value of 1,200.

Ending market value = Beginning market value
$$\times [1 + (\text{Rate in percent} / 100) \times \text{No. of time periods invested}]$$
$$= 1,000 \times [1 + (5\% / 100) \times 4] = 1,200$$

We use the simple interest calculation if the investor withdraws the income earned at the end of each period. In this example, the total gain over the four months is 200. Dividing by the $1,000 invested gives a 20% return for the four-month period. This equals the monthly periodic dollar return multiplied by four.

If the income and gains are retained within the investment vehicle or *reinvested*, they will accumulate and increase the starting balance for each subsequent period's income calculation. For example, $100 invested at 7% for 10 years, assuming yearly compounding, produces an ending value of $196.72.

Unfortunately, the reinvestment assumption is not realistic for all investors. For example, any taxable investor investing outside a vehicle shielded from taxes, such as a qualified retirement account, will have to pay taxes on income earned. The taxes reduce the income available for reinvestment in the next period. Given this fact, one of the trends in performance measurement is the incorporation of taxes into the return calculation.

The reinvestment assumption is important because the power of investing lies in the *compound interest*, the interest on the interest earned in prior periods. Given the 10-year investment earning a 7% yearly return, the interest on interest component comprises 14% of the terminal value. With a 30-year investment at 7%, the interest on interest will approach 60% of the ending value.

When interest earnings are withdrawn after each period, the simple interest calculation is a better measure of the situation. If income is left to earn more income, then compound interest is the better measure. Compound interest is assumed in almost all investment applications. With interest rates, we usually assume that interest is reinvested at the same interest rate for subsequent periods. The difference between working with returns instead of interest rates is that in return calculations, while we also assume that the income is reinvested, we recognize that the periodic returns fluctuate over time.

Returns that Take Time Into Account

Given the fact that money has a time value, let's return to a question that we considered earlier: What is the proper holding period return to attribute to a fund where the MVB equals $100, we invest an additional $10 during the period, and the MVE = $130?

No matter when in the period the investment was made, the dollar gain is $20 ($130 − $100 − $10) for the period. The return over the period depends on the timing of the additional investment. The return could be as low as 18.18% or as high as 20%. If the $10 were invested at the *beginning of the period*, capital employed equals the original investment of $100 plus the additional investment of $10.

$$\left(\frac{130 - 100 - 10}{100 + 10}\right) \times 100 \rightarrow \left(\frac{130 - 110}{110}\right) \times 100 \rightarrow \left(\frac{20}{110}\right) \times 100 = 18.18\%$$

If instead the additional investment were made precisely at the *end of the period*, the capital employed during the period is just $100, so the return is 20%.

$$\left(\frac{130 - 100 - 10}{100}\right) \times 100 \rightarrow \left(\frac{130 - 110}{100}\right) \times 100 \rightarrow \left(\frac{20}{100}\right) \times 100 = 20\%$$

Given the same dollar gain, we should credit the overall investment with a higher return as the contribution is made closer to the end of the period. If the investment is made at the end of the period, the additional contribution is not included in the denominator. The same numerator divided by a smaller denominator leads to the higher return. The higher return is justified when the contribution is made at the end of the period because the capital at risk during the period was lower, yet we earned the same dollar gain.

This example shows that it is important to track the time when contributions or withdrawals are made into an investment account in order to accurately determine returns. We always adjust the numerator for the additional contributions or withdrawals during the period. We either include the full amount of the contribution in the denominator, none of it, or a partial amount, depending on the timing of the cash flow. When the denominator of a return calculation is adjusted for contributions or withdrawals we refer to the denominator as the *average capital employed* or the *average invested balance.*

PERFORMANCE OF AN INVESTMENT: MONEY WEIGHTED RETURNS

In this section we establish the need to recognize the effects of both investor and manager decisions when calculating the return earned by the investor, but isolating the effects of investor decisions when calculating the return to be attributed to the manager. The dollar, or money weighted return (MWR) is the performance of the investment portfolio and incorporates the effects of both decisions.

Timing of Investor Decisions

In addition to the time value of money, the *market timing* of the investor contributions and withdrawals will affect realized returns. The capital markets provide us with positive long-term returns but volatile periodic returns. Market timing is a term that relates the time an investor makes his investment to the market cycle—that is, is the investor buying low and selling high.

For example, suppose we are investing via a mutual fund—an investment vehicle described in Chapter 26—and during the month the fund's net asset value per share (NAV) varied between 10.00 and 12.00 and there were no distributions.

Date	NAV per share
5/31	10.00
6/10	12.00
6/20	10.00
6/30	11.00

The monthly return that will be published for this fund is (11/10 = 10%). The following spreadsheet shows the calculation of various holding period returns for the month.

	A	B	C	D	E	F
1	Period	Return From	Calculated As	Return	% Return	
2	1	5/31 – 6/10	((12 / 10) – 1) x 100	0.20	20.00	
3	2	5/31 – 6/20	((10 / 10) –1) x 100	0.00	0.00	Published Return
4	3	5/31 – 6/30	((11 / 10) – 1) x 100	0.10	10.00	
5	4	6/10 – 6/20	((10 / 12) –1) x 100	-0.17	-16.67	
6	5	6/10 – 6/30	((11 / 12) – 1) x100	0.09	9.09	
7	6	6/20 – 6/30	((11 / 10) – 1 x 100	0.10	10.00	

The investor with perfect foresight, or luck, invested on 5/31 and withdrew on 6/10 to earn a 20% return. The investor with poor timing, who bought at the high on 6/10 and sold at the bottom on 6/20, had a −16.67% return. This spread of 36.67% represents the return differential due to the timing of the cash flows. The important point for investment performance measurement is that these cash flows were at the *discretion of the investor*, not the manager. Actions of the investment manager would have had no impact on this differential return; the manager would have put the money to work according to his mandate.

In the example above, the advertised return for the period would be the 10% return, which was measured from the start of the monthly period to the end. Even though different investors experienced different returns, the investment manager for the mutual fund had no control over these timing decisions; therefore 10% is an accurate representation of his performance. It is the appropriate return to use when comparing the performance to a peer group average or to a benchmark.

Timing of Investment Manager Decisions

When we calculate returns, we can also consider the timing of decisions that are the responsibility of the manager. Consider two managers starting with the same $100 portfolio at the beginning of the month. Both receive $10 client contributions. Their strategies differ only in that Manager 1 attempts to time the market as shown in this example. Assume that the market moves down 10% during the month. Manager 1 leaves the contribution in cash. The following spreadsheet shows that Manager 1's return is −9.05%.

	A	B	C	D
1	Segment	MVB	Percent Return	MVE
2	Cash	10	0.01	10.05
3	Equity	100	-0.10	90.00
4	Total	110	-9.05	100.05
5				
6			=((D4/B4)-1)*100	

The following spreadsheet shows that Manager 2 invests the contribution in equities at the beginning of the month and realizes a −10.00% return.

	A	B	C	D
1	Segment	MVB	Percent Return	MVE
2	Cash	0.00	0.01	0.00
3	Equity	110.00	-0.10	99.00
4	Total	110.00	-10.00	99
5			↑	
6			=((D4/B4)-1)*100	

Despite the negative returns, Manager 1 earned 95 basis points [–9.05% – (–10%)] in *value added* over Manager 2 due to the beneficial decision to leave the contribution in the relatively higher yielding cash segment during the month.

Segregating Investor and Manager Timing Decisions

It is often the case that the manager and the investor are two different people. The preceding sections illustrate a performance measurement problem: Decisions made by the investor and the investment manager must be segregated in order to properly calculate returns that reflect their respective responsibilities.

The ideal performance statistic for measuring the return experienced by the investor would include effects of both:

- The timing of investor decisions to make an investment into the portfolio
- The decisions made by the manager to allocate assets and select securities within the portfolio

The *money weighted return* (MWR) is used when we need to measure the performance as experienced by the investor. MWR is a performance statistic reflecting how much money was earned during the measurement period. This amount is influenced by the timing of decisions to contribute or withdraw money from a portfolio, as well as the decisions made by the manager of the portfolio. The MWR is contrasted with the performance statistic used to measure manager performance, the *time weighted return* (TWR), which is discussed later. As we will see, the MWR is important even if we are interested only in evaluating manager performance, because they are sometimes used in the estimation of the TWR.

MWR is the return an investor actually experiences after making an investment. It reconciles the beginning market value and additional cash flows into the portfolio to the ending market value. To accurately reflect these transactions, the MWR takes into account not only the amount of the cash flows but also the timing of the cash flows. Different investors into a portfolio will invest different amounts and make their investment on different dates. Because of the differences in cash flow timing and magnitude, it is not appropriate to compare the MWR calculated for two different investors.

When there are no cash flows, the return is calculated as the ending market value over the beginning market value. If there were a cash flow, we need to take into account the amount and the timing of the flow. To account for the timing of the flow, we calculate a weighting adjustment, which will be used to adjust the cash flow for the portion of the period that the cash flow was invested. The spreadsheet below shows that if we are calculating a MWR for a 1-year period and there are two cash flows, the first at the end of January and the second at the end of February, the flows will be weighted by 0.92 for the January month end flow (the flow will be available to be invested for 92% of the year) and 0.83 for the February month end flow (the flow will be available to be invested for 83% of the year).

	A	B	C	D
1	Date	Time into Total Period	Months Invested	Period Weight
2	31-Dec-2000	0	12	1.00
3	31-Jan-2001	1	11	0.92
4	28-Feb-2001	2	10	0.83
5			↑	
6			=12-B4	=C4/12

Internal Rate of Return (IRR)

Suppose we invest $100 at the beginning of the year and end up with $140 at the end of the year. We made cash flows of $10 each at the end of January and February. What is the MWR return for this situation? The MWR we are looking for will be the value that solves this equation:

$$100 \times (1 + MWR) + 10 \times (1 + MWR)^{0.92} + 10 \times (1 + MVR)^{0.83} = 140$$

The return that reconciles the beginning value and intermediate cash flows to the ending value is the *internal rate of return* or *IRR*. The return is the value that solves for IRR in this equation:

$$MVE = MVB \times (1 + IRR) + CF_1 \times (1 + IRR)^1 \ldots CF_N \times (1 + IRR)^N$$

where

CF = amount of the cash flow in or out of the portfolio
N = percentage of the period that the CF was available for investment

The IRR is the rate implied by the observed market values and cash flows. For all but the simplest case, we cannot solve for the IRR directly. Unfortunately, we cannot use algebra to rearrange the terms of the equation to derive the solution. The IRR is calculated using a trial and error process where we make an initial guess and then iteratively try successive values informed by how close we were to the solution in the last try, until we solve the problem.

Techniques have been developed to perform the iteration efficiently and converge on a solution quickly. The following spreadsheet shows the calculation of the IRR using the Excel solver utility.

	A	B	C	D	E	F
1	Date	Months Invested	Period Weight	Value	Future Value of Flow	
2	Dec-31-2000	12	1.00	100	117.05	=D2*((1+E8)^C2)
3	Jan-31-2001	11	0.92	10	11.55	=D3*((1+E8)^C3)
4	Feb-28-2001	10	0.83	10	11.40	=D4*((1+E8)^C4)
5	Dec-31-2001			140	140.00	=SUM(E2:E4)
6						
7		IRR calculated using solver		Difference:	0.00	=D5-E5
8				IRR:	0.1705	
9				Percent Return:	17.05	=E8*100

Here, we set the difference between the ending market value in cell D5 equal to the sum of the future values in cell E5. We then solved for the IRR in cell E8. The IRR is 17.05% because, as demonstrated below, it is the interest rate that resolves the flows to the ending market value.

$$100 \times (1 + 0.1705) + 10 \times (1 + 0.1705)^{0.92} + 10 \times (1 + 0.1705)^{0.83} = 140$$

Notice that there is an assumption embedded in the IRR formula: The rate of return is assumed to be constant within the period. In this example, each cash flow is compounded at 17.05% for the complete portion of the year invested.

Problems with the IRR

We classify the IRR as an MWR because it takes into account both the timing and size of cash flows into the portfolio. It is an appropriate measure of the performance of the investment as experienced by the investor. The fact that the IRR needs to be calculated via iteration used to make the IRR an expensive calculation, because of the computer time used by the iteration algorithm. This is not a problem today. But, the historical problem led to the development of various creative methods to cheaply estimate the IRR. One of these methods, the Modified Dietz method, is still the most common method used by analysts to compute MWRs and, as we will see, estimate returns between valuation dates when we are calculating a TWR.

Modified Dietz Return

The *Modified Dietz return* is a simple interest estimate of the MWR. The Modified Dietz calculation is the same as the ROI calculation, except the cash flows added to the beginning market value are adjusted according to the time they were invested in the portfolio.

$$\text{Modified Dietz Return} = \frac{\text{MVE} - \text{MVB} - \text{CF}}{\text{MVB} + \{[(\text{CD} - C_i)/\text{CD}] \times \text{CF}_i\}} \times 100$$

where

  CF = net amount of the cash flows for the period
  CD = total days in the period
  C_i = the day of the cash flow
  CF_i = the amount of the net cash flow on C_i

The calculation is named for the developer, Peter Dietz, who was associated with the Frank Russell pension consulting company. The original Dietz method, not currently used, makes the assumption that cash flows occurred midway through the period.

To illustrate the calculation of a Modified Dietz return, consider the following situation

  Begin Market Value + Accrued Income   MVB 100
  End Market Value + Accrued Income   MVE 120
  Sum (Client Contribution/Withdrawal) CF   10 on the 20th of a
                                              30-day month

To calculate the Modified Dietz return as shown, first we calculate the *adjustment factor*, which is 0.33, assuming that the flow occurs at the end of the day on the 20th.

$$\frac{30 - 20}{30} = 0.33$$

Then we adjust the cash flow by multiplying the amount by the adjustment factor: $0.33 \times \$10 = \$3.33$. We then add the modified flow to the beginning market value in the denominator, and calculate the Modified Dietz return, 9.68%.

$$9.68\% = \frac{120 - 100 - 10}{100 + 3.33} \times 100$$

Both the IRR and Modified Dietz formulas are money weighted returns. MWR results *are* affected by the timing and magnitude of the cash flows during the period. The return statistics that completely eliminate the impact of investor cash flows are time weighted returns.

PERFORMANCE OF THE INVESTMENT MANAGER: TIME WEIGHTED RETURNS

A rate of return is the percentage change in the value of an asset over some period of time. Total returns are calculated by dividing the capital gain/loss and income earned by the value of the investment at the beginning of the period. As we saw earlier in this chapter, investors experience different returns investing in the same fund depending on the timing and magnitude of their cash flows into and out of the portfolio. Returns are used in evaluating the performance of an investment manager, but he (usually) has no control over the timing and amount of investor flows, so we need a performance measure that negates the effect of these cash flows. The desired return would judge the manager by the return on money invested over the whole period and eliminate the effect of client cash flows.

Time Weighted Return

The *time weighted return* (TWR) is a form of total return that measures the performance of a dollar invested in the fund over the complete measurement period. The TWR eliminates the timing effect that external portfolio cash flows have on performance, leaving only the effects of the market and manager decisions.

To calculate a time weighted return, we break the period of interest into subperiods, calculate the returns earned during the subperiods, and then compound these subperiod returns to derive the TWR for the whole period. The subperiod boundaries are the dates of each cash flow. Specifically, the steps to calculate a TWR are as follows.

1. Begin with the market value at the beginning of the period.
2. Move forward through time toward the end of the period.
3. Note the value of the portfolio immediately before a cash flow into or out of the portfolio.
4. Calculate a *subperiod return* for the period between the valuation dates.
5. Repeat 3 and 4 for each cash flow encountered.
6. When there are no more cash flows, calculate a subperiod return for the last period using the end of period market value.
7. Compound the subperiod returns by taking the product of (1 + the subperiod returns).

The last step is called *geometric linking*, or *chain linking*, of the returns. Chain linking has the same function as compounding in the future value calculation. We employ chain linking instead of the future value formula when the periodic returns change from subperiod to subperiod.

$$\text{Time Weighted Return} = [(1 + R_1) \times (1 + R_2) \times \ldots (1 + R_N) - 1] \times 100$$

where R_N are the subperiod returns.

The TWR assumes compounding and reinvestment of the gains earned in the previous subperiods. The expression (1 + the subperiod return) is called a *wealth relative* or *growth rate*, which represents the increase in capital over the subperiod. For example, if a portfolio is worth $100 at the beginning of the subperiod, and $105 at the end of the subperiod before the next cash flow, the subperiod return is 5% and the growth rate for the subperiod equals 1.05.

Below we will illustrate the steps to calculate a TWR. We calculate the TWR for a month where fund market values were:

Date	End of Day Valuation
5/31	1000
6/9	1100
6/19	1200
6/30	1200

And there were two cash flows during the month:

Date	Cash Flow
6/10	200
6/20	-100

Divide the Period into Subperiods

The first step in the TWR calculation is to divide the period we are interested in into subperiods, where the subperiods are segregated by the cash flow dates. The next step is to note the value of the portfolio before each cash flow. If we are working with a beginning of day cash flow assumption, we use the valuation performed on the night prior to the cash flow.

Date	Beginning of Day Valuation	Cash Flow	End of Day Valuation
5/31			1000
6/9			1100
6/10	1100	200	
6/19			1200
6/20	1200	−100	
6/30	1200		1200

We have two cash flows and three subperiods.

1. 5/31 to the end of day 6/9
2. 6/10 to the end of day 6/19
3. 6/20 to the end of day 6/30

Note that there are (1 + the number of cash flow dates) subperiods.

Calculate Subperiod Returns

Next we calculate a single period return for each subperiod. The time of day assumption governs the treatment of the cash flows in the subperiod return formula. Here we assume that cash flows occur at the beginning of the day. With a beginning of day assumption, we add the cash flow to the beginning day market value to form the denominator of the return. Cash flows into the portfolio are added to the denominator, cash flows out of the portfolio are subtracted. If there is more than one cash flow during the day we net the flows together.

$$\text{Sub Period Return (start of day flow assumption)} = \frac{\text{MVE}}{\text{MVB} + \text{Net Cash Inflows}}$$

The effect of the cash flow adjustment is to negate the effect of the contributions/withdrawals from the return calculation. The calculation of the three subperiod returns, 10.00%, −7.69%, and 9.09%, is shown in the following spreadsheet.

	A	B	C	D	E	F	G
1	Sub Period	Return From	BMV	CF	EMV	Percent Return	Growth Rate
2	1	5/31 – 6/10	1000	0	1100	10.00	1.10
3	2	6/10 – 6/20	1100	200	1200	-7.69	0.92
4	3	6/20 – 6/30	1200	-100	1200	9.09	1.09
5				=((E4/(C4 + D4))-1)*100		=1+(F4/100)	
6							

EXHIBIT 5.1 Time Weighted Return

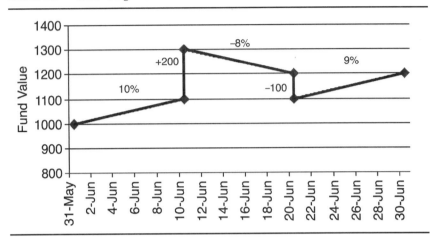

Calculate Multiple Period Returns

The percentage return for the month is calculated by chain linking the subperiod returns.

$$[(1.1000) \times (0.9231) \times (1.0909) - 1] \times 100 = 10.77\%$$

By calculating the return in this way, we have completely eliminated from the return the impact of the cash flows into and out of the portfolio. Exhibit 5.1 provides a way to visualize how the TWR eliminates cash flow effects from the return calculation.

Estimating the Time Weighted Return

There is a potential hurdle to implementing this methodology. TWR requires a valuation of the portfolio before each cash flow. Unfortunately, these periodic valuations are not always available. For example, many institutional separate accounts are valued on a monthly frequency, but the client may deposit or withdraw from the account at any time during the month. While industry trends lean in the direction of daily valuations, until these are available for all investment vehicles, we need a way of estimating the true TWR when contributions and withdrawals are made in between valuation dates.

We can approximate a TWR by calculating a MWR for each subperiod between valuation dates and compounding them over longer periods using the chain linking method used to link subperiod returns into a TWR. This linked MWR estimate of TWR provides a reliable approximation of the TWR in situations where the cash flows are small relative to the portfolio size and there is low return volatility within the subperiod. If the cash flows are large and the market is volatile during the period, the MWR estimate of TWR will be inaccurate. So it is important to note that the linked MWR is an *estimate* of the TWR over the longer period. While the cash flows are weighted within the subperiod, the cash flows are still influencing the returns. The linking process does not remove the effect of the cash flows from the cumulative return calculation. A compromise solution to calculating a TWR is to perform a special valuation whenever there are large cash flows and then link the subperiod MWR.

MULTIPLE PERIOD RETURN CALCULATION

We can compute rates of return over multiple periods by compounding the single period returns. We are often interested in an average of the periodic returns that reflects the compounding function. The average returns are often restated to an annual average basis. These topics are covered in this section.

Cumulative Returns

We saw the compounding process at work when we employed subperiod returns in the chain linking process to create a multiperiod TWR. In this same way, we can derive cumulative returns for any period of interest, such as month-to-date, year-to-date, first quarter of the year, 1-year, 3-year, and since-account-inception. To compound the returns, we multiply (1 + decimal return) for each period.

$$\text{Cumulative Return} = [(\text{Growth Rate}_1) \times (\text{Growth Rate}_2) \ldots - 1] \times 100$$

The following spreadsheet shows the calculation of a cumulative 5-year return given the series of yearly returns 9%, 6%, –2%, 8%, and – 4%.

	A	B	C	D	E
1				Growth Rates	
2	Year	Return	Single Period	Compounded	Cumulative %
3	1	0.09	1.09	1.09	
4	2	0.06	1.06	1.16	
5	3	-0.02	0.98	1.13	=PRODUCT(C3:C7)
6	4	0.08	1.08	1.22	
7	5	-0.04	0.96	1.17	17.40
8				=(D7-1)*100	
9					

By compounding the returns we find that the cumulative 5-year return is 17.40%.

Since we often are interested in the performance of an investment over time, we can maintain *cumulative growth rates*. Cumulative growth rates are useful for quickly calculating the cumulative return over multiple periods because we do not need to reference the intermediate returns or growth rates. Cumulative growth rates are calculated by taking the previous period ending cumulative growth rate and multiplying by (1 + current period return). We can use cumulative growth rates to calculate the expected value of an investment by multiplying it by the cumulative growth factor. For example, $100 invested into a fund with a compound 5-year growth rate of 1.2568 will result in an ending value of $125.68.

$$100 \times (1.2568) = 125.68$$

Growth rates also can also be used to derive the return between any two dates.

$$\text{Return} = \left[\left(\frac{\text{End Period Growth Rate}}{\text{Begin Period Growth Rate}} \right) - 1 \right] \times 100$$

We calculate cumulative returns when we are interested in the performance of investments over long-term time periods. Note that cumulative returns incorporate the assumption that investment gains are reinvested into the fund and compounded over time. The appreciation at the end of each period, as measured by the return, is treated as if it is income that is reinvested into the portfolio in the next period.

Arithmetic Mean Return

Often, we are interested in calculating average, or mean, investment returns. Average returns can be used to compare the performance of investment managers or funds over time. There are two methods for calculating the average of a series of returns: the arithmetic and geometric methods. As a measure of the average return, a mean return can be calculated by adding the periodic returns together and dividing by the number of returns.

$$\text{Arithmetic Mean Return} = \frac{\text{Sum (Periodic Returns)}}{\text{Count of Returns}}$$

The periodicity of the returns must be the same for each of the returns (i.e., all of the returns must be daily, monthly, or yearly returns). The arithmetic mean return cannot be used in all applications. For example, we may want to use an average yearly return to project the future value of an investment. One problem with using arithmetic mean returns is that they do not take into account the compounding of returns over time. For example, if we have two yearly returns:

Year	Return
1	10%
2	20%

The arithmetic mean return is 15% [(20 + 10)/2]. The compound 2-year return is 32%.

$$[(1.10) \times (1.20) - 1] \times 100 = 32.00\%$$

If we take the arithmetic mean return and plug it into the compounding formula we will get a higher result than we did using the actual periodic returns.

$$[(1.15) \times (1.15) - 1] \times 100 = 32.25\%$$

Use of the arithmetic mean return to reconcile the beginning to ending investment value overstates the ending value. The average return we use in this application should be lower than the arithmetic mean return in order to account for the compounding process.

Geometric Mean Return

When we multiply the average yearly return by the total number of years, it does not equal the compounded return because it does not take into account the income earned by reinvesting the prior period income. In the previous example, the 20% return in Year 2 was earned by reinvesting the 10% Year 1 return, but that is not accounted for in the arithmetic average. To fix this, instead of taking the arithmetic mean return we calculate the geometric mean return. The *geometric mean return* is the nth root of the compound return, where n is the number of periods used to calculate the compound cumulative return. That is:

$$\text{Geometric Mean Return} = [\sqrt[N]{(1 + \text{Cumulative Return})} - 1] \times 100$$

(Note that finding the root is the inverse of multiplying the growth rates.)

The following spreadsheet shows that the geometric average yearly return derived from a two-year compound return of 32% equals 14.89%.

	A	B	C	D	E
1				**Growth Rates**	
2	Year	Return	Single Period	Compounded	Cumulative %
3	1	0.10	1.10	1.10	
4	2	0.20	1.20	1.32	32.00
5		=PRODUCT(C3:C4)			
6				Arithmetic yearly average:	15.00
7				Geometric yearly average:	14.89
8			=((D4^(1/2))-1)*100		
9					

In Excel, to take the nth root, we raise the compound growth rate to the (1/N) power.

$$(\sqrt[2]{1.32} - 1) \times 100 \rightarrow (1.1489 - 1) \times 100 = 14.89\%$$

Plugging the geometric mean return into the compound growth formula yields the compound return for the period.

$$\text{Compound Return} = \{[1 + (\text{Geometric Mean Return}/100)]^N - 1\} \times 100$$

We can back into the 32% compound return for two months using the geometric average return of 14.89%.

$$\{[1 + (14.89/100)]^2 - 1\} \times 100 \rightarrow [(1.1489)^2 - 1] \times 100$$
$$\rightarrow (1.32 - 1) \times 100 \rightarrow 32\%$$

Or:

$$\{[(1.1489) \times (1.1489)] - 1\} \times 100 = 32\%$$

Column C in the spreadsheet that follows shows that one advantage of using average returns is that we do not need to know the actual periodic returns in order to calculate a future value:

	A	B	C	D	E
1	Year	Actual Return	Geometric Average Return		
2	1	0.15	0.0534	=((1+(B6/100))^(1/3))-1	
3	2	0.07	0.0534	=C2	
4	3	-0.05	0.0534	=C2	
5					
6	Year 1-3 in %	16.90	16.90	=((1+C2)*(1+C3)*(1+C4)-1)*100	
7		=((1+B2)*(1+B3)*(1+B4)-1)*100			
8					

Annualizing Returns Greater than a Year

If the multiperiod compound return that we are annualizing was calculated for a period greater than a year, the rate is restated to an annual basis using the inverse of the compounding formula. The inverse of taking a number and raising it to a power n is to take the nth root of the number.

$$\{[^{\#\text{ of years}}\sqrt{(1 + \text{Period rate})}] - 1\} \times 100$$

For example, if an investment earned 19.1% over a 3-year period, the return can be quoted as an annual average return of 6% by finding the third root of the cumulative growth rate.

$$\{[\sqrt[3]{(1.19102)}] - 1\} \times 100 = 6.00$$

Notice that we calculate the annualized return by first taking the root of the cumulative growth rate as opposed to taking the nth root of the cumulative return. The nth root of the growth rate is the geometric average growth rate. To transform the average growth rate into a geometric average return we subtract 1 and multiply by 100.

We usually need to calculate an annualized return for cumulative periods that are not exact multiples of a year. To calculate annualized returns for such odd periods, we can calculate the actual number of calendar days in the cumulative period and divide by 365.25 to calculate an annualized equivalent.

$$\text{Annualized Return} = \left[\left(^{\frac{\text{Number of Days}}{365.25}}\sqrt{\text{Linked Growth Rates}}\right) - 1\right] \times 100$$

For example, the annualized equivalent of a 14% return earned over 16 months is equal to 10.37%.

SUMMARY

In this chapter we outlined the procedures for calculating and interpreting the meaning of investment returns. Periodic portfolio valuation and cash flow figures are transformed into single period returns. Time weighted returns measure the results attributable to the investment manager. Dollar weighted returns reflect both the performance of the manager and the timing of investor transactions.

Rates of return are a description of one facet of investment performance. Performance measurement is also concerned with measuring the risks taken to earn these returns, and the attribution of returns to market activity and active management. As the investment cycle turns, the return, risk, and attribution statistics we calculate in performance measurement are the inputs to the next round of asset allocation and security selection decisions.

Investing in Common Stock

Common Stock Markets, Trading Arrangements, and Trading Costs

Frank J. Fabozzi, Ph.D., CFA
Adjunct Professor of Finance
School of Management
Yale University

Frank J. Jones, Ph.D.
Chief Investment Officer
The Guardian Life Insurance Company of America

Robert R. Johnson, Ph.D., CFA
Senior Vice President
Association for Investment Management and Research

Bruce M.Collins, Ph.D.
CEO
QuantCast LLC

In this chapter we discuss the investment characteristics of common stock, explain the markets where common stock is traded, the costs associated with trading common stock, and the arrangements made for the trading of common stock by retail (i.e., individual) and institutional investors.

COMMON STOCK VERSUS PREFERRED STOCK

Common stocks are also called *equity securities*. Equity securities represent an ownership interest in a corporation. Holders of equity securities are entitled to the earnings of the corporation when those earnings are distributed in the form of *dividends*; they are also entitled to a pro rata share of the remaining equity in case of liquidation.

Common stock is only one type of equity security. Another type is preferred stock. The key distinction between the two forms of equity securities is the degree to which their holders may participate in any distribution of earnings and capital and the priority given to each class in the distribution of earnings. Typically, preferred stockholders are entitled to a fixed dividend, which they receive before common stockholders may receive any dividends. Therefore, we refer to preferred stock as a senior corporate security, in the sense that preferred stock interests are senior to the interests of common stockholders.

WHERE STOCK TRADING OCCURS

Investors express their opinions about the economic prospects of a company through the trades they make in the market for common stock. The aggregate of these trades provides the market consensus opinion of the price of the stock.

In the United States, secondary market trading in common stocks occurs in two different ways. The first is on organized exchanges, which are specific geographical locations called trading floors, where representatives of buyers and sellers physically meet. The trading mechanism on exchanges is the auction system, characterized by the presence of many competing buyers and sellers assembled in one place.

The second type is via over-the-counter (OTC) trading, which results from geographically dispersed traders or market-makers linked to one another via telecommunication systems. That is, there is no trading floor. This trading mechanism is a negotiated system whereby individual buyers negotiate with individual sellers.

Exchange markets are called central auction specialist systems and OTC markets are called multiple market maker systems. In recent years a new method of trading common stocks via independently owned and operated electronic communications networks (ECNs) has developed and is growing quickly.

In the United States there are two national stock exchanges: (1) the New York Stock Exchange (NYSE), commonly called the "Big Board," and (2) the American Stock Exchange (AMEX or ASE), called the "Curb." National stock exchanges trade stocks of both U.S. and non-U.S. corporations. In addition to the national exchanges, there are regional stock exchanges in Boston, Chicago (called the Midwest Exchange), Cincinnati, San Francisco (called the Pacific Coast Exchange) and Philadelphia. Regional exchanges primarily trade stocks from corporations based within their geographic region.

The major OTC market in the U.S. is Nasdaq (the National Association of Securities Dealers Automated Quotation System), which is owned and operated by the NASD (the National Association of Securities Dealers), although it is in the process of becoming independent. The NASD is a securities industry self-regulatory organization (SRO) that operates subject to the oversight of the Securities and Exchange Commission (SEC). Nasdaq is a national market. During 1998, Nasdaq and AMEX merged to form the Nasdaq-AMEX Market Group, Inc.

The NYSE is the largest exchange in the world with the shares of approximately 3,000 companies listed. The AMEX is the second largest national stock exchange in the U.S., with over 750 issues listed for trading. Nasdaq has a greater number of listed stocks but with much lower market capitalization than the NYSE.

According to the Securities Act of 1934, there are two categories of traded stocks. The first is exchange traded stocks (also called "listed" stocks). The second is OTC stocks which are non-exchange traded stocks and are, thus, by inference, "non-listed." However, as we describe later in this chapter, Nasdaq stocks have listing requirements (the Nasdaq National Market and the Nasdaq Small Capitalization Market). Thus, a more useful and practical categorization of these categories is as follows:

1. Exchange listed stocks (national and regional exchanges)
2. Nasdaq listed OTC stocks
3. Non-Nasdaq OTC stocks

We focus on each of these markets later in this section.

The four major types of markets on which stocks are traded are referred to as follows:

■ First Market—trading on exchanges of stocks listed on an exchange
■ Second Market—trading in the OTC market of stocks not listed on an exchange
■ Third Market—trading in the OTC market of stocks listed on an exchange

■ Fourth Market—private transactions between institutional investors who deal directly with each other without utilizing the services of a broker-dealer intermediary

These types of markets are discussed below.

Exchanges

Stock exchanges are formal organizations, approved and regulated by the SEC. They are comprised of "members" that use the exchange facilities and systems to exchange or trade "listed" stocks. These exchanges are physical locations where members assemble to trade. Stocks that are traded on an exchange are said to be *listed stocks*, which means they are individually approved by the exchange for trading on the exchange. To be listed, a company must apply for and satisfy requirements established by the exchange for minimum capitalization, shareholder equity, average closing share price, and other criteria. Even after being listed, exchanges may delist a stock if it no longer meets the exchange requirements. To have the right to trade securities or make markets on an exchange floor, firms or individuals must become a *member* of the exchange, which is accomplished by buying a *seat* on the exchange.

The NYSE

The NYSE is organized as a centralized continuous auction market at a designated location on the trading floor, called a "post," with brokers representing the buy and sell orders of their customers. A single *specialist* is the market maker for each stock. A member firm may be designated as a specialist for the common stock of more than one company. While several stocks can trade at the same post, only one specialist is designated for the common stock of each listed company.

A specialist for each stock stands at a trading position around one of the 17 NYSE "posts." Each post is essentially an auction site where orders (bids and offers) arrive. Most orders arrive from floor brokers and over an electronic delivery system called the SuperDot (Super Designated Order Turnaround). SuperDot is an electronic order routing and reporting system linking member firms electronically worldwide directly to the specialist's post on the trading floor of the NYSE. The majority of NYSE orders are processed electronically through SuperDot.

In addition to the single specialist market-maker on an exchange, other firms that are members of an exchange can trade for themselves or on behalf of their customers. NYSE member firms, which are broker-dealer organizations that serve the investing public, are represented on the trading floor by brokers who serve as fiduciaries in the execution of customer orders.

Specialists are dealers or market makers assigned by the NYSE to conduct the auction process and maintain an orderly market in one or more designated stocks. Specialists may act as both a broker (agent) and a dealer (principal). In their role as a broker or agent, specialists represent customer orders in their assigned stocks, which arrive at their post electronically or are entrusted to them by a floor broker to be executed if and when a stock reaches a price specified by a customer (limit or stop order). As a dealer or principal, specialists buy and sell shares in their assigned stocks for their own account as necessary to maintain an orderly market. Specialists must always give preference to public orders over trading for their own account.

In general, public orders for stocks traded on the NYSE, if they are not sent to the specialist's post via SuperDot, are sent from the office of the member firm to its representative on the exchange floor, who attempts to execute the order in the trading crowd. Later in this chapter we discuss the various types of orders that an investor can ask a broker to execute. There are certain types of orders where the order will not be executed immediately on the trading floors. These are limit orders and stop orders. If the order is a limit order or a stop order and the member firm's floor broker cannot transact the order immediately, they can wait in the trading crowd or give the order to the specialist in the stock, who will enter the order in that specialist's *limit order book* (or simply, *book*) for later execution based on the relationship between the market price and the price specified in the limit or stop order. The book is the list arranged by size from near the current market price to further away from it, which specialists keep the limit and stop orders given to them. While the book was formerly an actual physical paper book, it is now maintained electronically. Only the specialist can view the orders in the book for their stock. This exclusivity with respect to the limit order book is an obvious advantage to the specialist, which to some degree offsets their obligation to make fair and orderly markets. However, at the time of this writing, the NYSE was planning to make specialists' books available to investors electronically.

NYSE-assigned specialists have four major roles:

1. As dealers, they trade for their own accounts when there is a temporary absence of public buyers or sellers, and only after the public orders in their possession have been satisfied at a specified price.
2. As agents, they execute market orders entrusted to them by brokers, as well as orders awaiting a specific market price.
3. As catalysts, they help to bring buyers and sellers together.

4. As auctioneers, they quote current bid/asked prices that reflect total supply and demand for each of the stocks assigned to them.

In carrying out their duties, specialists may act as either an agent or a principal. When acting as an *agent*, the specialist simply fills customer market orders, limit or stop orders (either new orders or orders from their book) by opposite orders (buy or sell). When acting as a *principal*, the specialist is charged with the responsibility of maintaining a *fair and orderly market*. Specialists are prohibited from engaging in transactions in securities in which they are registered unless such transactions are necessary to maintain a fair and orderly market. Specialists profit only from those trades in which they are involved; that is, they realize no revenue for trades in which they are an agent.

The term "fair and orderly market" means a market in which there is price continuity and reasonable depth. Thus, specialists are required to maintain a reasonable spread between bids and offers and small changes in price between transactions. Specialists are expected to bid and offer for their own account if necessary to promote such a fair and orderly market. They cannot put their own interests ahead of public orders and are obliged to trade for their own accounts against the market trend to help maintain liquidity and continuity as the price of a stock fluctuates. They may purchase or sell stock for their investment account only if such purchases or sales are necessary to ensure a fair and orderly market.

Specialists are responsible for balancing buy and sell orders at the opening of the trading day in order to arrange an equitable opening price for the stock. Specialists are only expected to participate in the opening of the market to the extent necessary to balance supply and demand for the security to effect a reasonable opening price. While trading throughout the day is via a continuous auction-based system, the opening is conducted via a single-price call auction system. Specialists conduct the call and determine the single price.

If there is an *imbalance* between buy and sell orders either at the opening or during the trading day and the specialist cannot maintain a fair and orderly market, then under restricted conditions, they may close the market in that stock (that is, discontinue trading) until they are able to determine a price at which there is a balance of buy and sell orders. Such closes of trading can occur either during the trading day or more commonly at the opening, and can last for minutes or days. Closings of a day or more may occur when, for example, there is an acquisition of one firm by another or when there is an extreme announcement by the corporation (for this reason, many firms choose to make announcements after the close of trading).

The Over-the-Counter Market

The OTC market is called the market for "unlisted stocks." As explained earlier, while there are listing requirements for exchanges, there are also "listing requirements" for the Nasdaq National and Small Capitalization OTC markets, discussed below. Nevertheless, exchange traded stocks are called "listed," and stocks traded on the OTC markets are referred to as "unlisted."

There are three parts of the OTC market—two under the aegis of NASD (the Nasdaq markets) and a third market for truly unlisted stocks, the non-Nasdaq OTC markets.

Nasdaq Stock Market

Nasdaq is essentially a telecommunication network linking thousands of geographically-dispersed market making participants. Nasdaq is an electronic quotation system providing price quotations to market participants on Nasdaq listed stocks. While there is no central trading floor, Nasdaq has become an electronic "virtual trading floor." There are more than 4,700 common stocks with a total market value of over $3.5 trillion included in the Nasdaq system. Some 535 dealers, known as market makers, representing some of the world's largest securities firms, provide competing bids to buy and offers to sell Nasdaq stocks to investors.

The Nasdaq stock market has two broad tiers of securities: (1) the Nasdaq National Market (NNM) and the Small Capitalization Market. Newspapers have separate sections for these two tiers of stocks (sections labeled the "Nasdaq National Market" and the "Nasdaq Small Capitalization Market"). The Nasdaq NMS is the dominant OTC market in the U.S.

Other OTC Markets

While the Nasdaq stock markets are the major parts of the U.S. OTC markets, the vast number of OTC issues (about 8,000) do not trade on either of the two Nasdaq systems. There are two types of markets for these stocks. The securities traded on these markets have no listing requirements. Thus, these two OTC markets are not "issuer services." Rather, they are "subscriber services"—that is subscribers can make bids and offers for any stock not listed on exchanges or Nasdaq.

The first of these two non-Nasdaq OTC markets is the OTC Bulletin Board (OTCBB), sometimes called simply the "Bulletin Board." OTCBB is owned and operated by Nasdaq and regulated by NASD. The OTCBB displays real-time quotes, last-sale prices and volume information for approximately 5,500 securities. It includes stocks not traded on NYSE, AMEX, or Nasdaq.

The second non-Nasdaq OTC market is the "Pink Sheets," a market owned and operated by the National Quotation Bureau. Prior to the creation of Nasdaq in 1971, dealer quotations were disseminated by paper copy only. These copies were printed on pink paper for which reason these OTC securities were called "pink sheet stocks." The Pink Sheets are still published weekly. In addition, an electronic version of the Pink Sheets is updated daily and disseminated over market data vendor terminals. In order to provide greater visibility to these issues, many of which are low priced and thinly traded, transactions in Pink Sheet issues are subject to price and volume reporting under NASD Schedule D. These Pink Sheet securities are often pejoratively called "penny stocks."

These two markets are subscriber markets only—that is, any subscriber can enter quotes for securities on the systems. However, the trades on these markets are executed not on these systems but via the telephone. If the trades are conducted by NASD members, which is typically the case, they are reported to NASD and disseminated by ACT (the Nasdaq trade reporting system).

The OTCBB, however, tends to trade more active stocks than the Pink Sheets. OTCBB trades approximately the most active 4,000 stocks.

The Third Market

A stock may be both listed on an exchange and also traded in the OTC market, called the *third market*. Like Nasdaq, the third market is a network of broker-dealers that aggregates quotation information and provides inter-participant order routing tools, but leaves order execution to market participants. Dealers that make markets in the third market operate under the regulatory jurisdiction of the NASD. While the third market is not owned by the NASD, market makers in the third market use some of the facilities provided by Nasdaq. When the NASD created Nasdaq in 1971, it included substantially similar functionality for third market listed trading.

Alternative Trading Systems—The Fourth Market

It is not necessary for the two parties to a transaction to use an intermediary. That is, the services of a broker or a dealer are not required to execute a trade. The direct trading of stocks between two customers without the use of a broker is called the *fourth market*. This market grew for the same reasons as the third market—excessively high minimum commissions established by exchanges.

A number of proprietary alternative trading systems (ATSs), which comprise the fourth market, are operated by the NASD members or member affiliates. These fourth market ATSs are for-profit "broker's brokers" that match investor orders and report trading activity to the marketplace via Nasdaq or the third market. In a sense, ATSs are similar to exchanges because they are designed to allow two participants to meet directly on the system and are maintained by a third party who also serves a limited regulatory function by imposing requirements on subscribers.

Broadly, there are two types of ATSs: electronic communications networks and crossing networks.

Electronic Communications Networks

Electronic communications networks (ECNs) are privately owned broker–dealers that operate as market participants within the Nasdaq system. They display quotes that reflect actual orders and provide institutions and Nasdaq market makers with an anonymous way to enter orders. Essentially, an ECN is a limit order book open for continuous trading that is widely disseminated to subscribers who may enter and access orders displayed on the ECN. ECNs offer transparency, anonymity, automated service, and reduced prices, and are therefore effective means for handling small orders. ECNs are used to disseminate firm commitments to trade (firm bids or offers) to participants, or subscribers, who have typically either purchased or leased hardware for the operation of the ECN or have built a custom connection to the ECN. ECNs may also be linked into the Nasdaq marketplace via a quotation representing the ECN's best buy and sell quote. In general, ECNs use the internet to link buyers and sellers, bypassing brokers and trading floors.

Since ECNs are part of the Nasdaq execution, their volume is counted as part of the Nasdaq volume. ECNs account for over 30% of Nasdaq trading in exchange trading.

Instinet (Institutional Networks Corporation), the first ECN, began operating in 1969, and continues to be a very large ECN in terms of activity. Instinet was acquired by Reuters Holdings in 1987. Instinet is an NASD member broker-dealer and trades both Nasdaq and exchange-listed stocks. Instinet was originally intended as a system through which institutional investors could cross trades (that is, a crossing network). However, market makers are now significant participants in Instinet. Instinet usage for Nasdaq securities (that is, usage as an ECN), began to grow in the mid-1980s when market makers were allowed to subscribe.

Since 1969, nine additional ECNs have been created: Island, Archipelago, REDI Book, Bloomberg Tradebook, BRASS Utility, Strike, Attain, NexTrade, and Market XT. Two of the ECNs, Archipelago and Island, have applied to the SEC to become exchanges.

Crossing Networks

Systems have been developed that allow institutional investors to "cross" trades—that is, match buyers and sellers directly—typically via computers. Crossing networks are batch processes that aggregate orders for execution at prespecified times. They provide anonymity and reduced cost, and are specifically designed to minimize a trading cost (market impact cost) that we will describe later. Crossing networks vary considerably in their approach to market structure, including the type of order information that can be entered by the subscriber and the amount of pre-trade transparency available to participants.

At present, there are three major crossing networks: ITG Posit, the Arizona Stock Exchange (AZX), and Optimark. Instinet, the original crossing network, operates a fourth crossing network in addition to its current ECN offering.

Instinet is an interactive *hit-and-take* system, which means that participants search for buyers or sellers electronically, and negotiate and execute trades. It is a computerized execution service registered with the SEC. The service permits subscribers to search for the opposite side of a trade without the cost of brokerage during Instinet's evening crossing network. Many mutual funds and other institutional investors use Instinet.

ITG Posit is more than a simple order-matching system. It matches the purchase and sale of portfolios in a manner that optimizes system liquidity. ITG's hourly POSIT operates only during the trading day.

The Phoenix-based AZX, which commenced trading in March 1992, has been an after-hours electronic marketplace where anonymous participants trade stocks via personal computers. This exchange provides a call auction market which accumulates bids and offers for a security and, at designated times, derives a single price that maximizes the number of shares to be traded. It conducts call auctions at 9:30 a.m., 10:30 a.m., 12:30 p.m., 2:30 p.m., and 4:30 p.m. EST.[1]

TRADING MECHANICS

Next we describe the key features involved in trading stocks. Later in the chapter, we discuss trading arrangements (block trades and program trades) that developed specifically for coping with the needs of institutional investors.

Types of Orders and Trading Priority Rules

When an investor wants to buy or sell a share of common stock, the price and conditions under which the order is to be executed must be commu-

---

[1] For a discussion of the concepts underlying the Arizona Stock Exchange, see the AZX website www.azx.com.

nicated to a broker. The simplest type of order is the market order, an order to be executed at the best price available in the market. If the stock is listed and traded on an organized exchange, the best price is assured by the exchange rule that when more than one order on the same side of the buy/sell transaction reaches the market at the same time, the order with the best price is given priority. Thus, buyers offering a higher price are given priority over those offering a lower price; sellers asking a lower price are given priority over those asking a higher price.

Another priority rule of exchange trading is needed to handle receipt of more than one order at the same price. Most often, the priority in executing such orders is based on the time of arrival of the order—first orders in are the first orders executed—although there may be a rule that gives higher priority to certain types of market participants over other types of market participants seeking to transact at the same price. For example, on exchanges, orders can be classified as either *public orders* or orders of those member firms dealing for their own account (both nonspecialists and specialists). Exchange rules require that public orders be given priority over orders of member firms dealing for their own account.

The danger of a market order is that an adverse move may take place between the time the investor places the order and the time the order is executed. To avoid this danger, the investor can place a *limit order* that designates a price threshold for the execution of the trade. A *buy limit order* indicates that the stock may be purchased only at the designated price or lower. A *sell limit order* indicates that the stock may be sold only at the designated price or higher. The key disadvantage of a limit order is that there is no guarantee that it will be executed at all; the designated price may simply not be obtainable. A limit order that is not executable at the time it reaches the market is recorded in the limit order book described earlier in this chapter.

The limit order is a *conditional order*: It is executed only if the limit price or a better price can be obtained. Another type of conditional order is the *stop order*, which specifies that the order is not to be executed until the market moves to a designated price, at which time it becomes a market order. A *buy stop order* specifies that the order is not to be executed until the market rises to a designated price, that is, until it trades at or above, or is bid at or above, the designated price. A *sell stop order* specifies that the order is not to be executed until the market price falls below a designated price—that is, until it trades at or below, or is offered at or below, the designated price. A stop order is useful when an investor cannot constantly monitor the market. Profits can be preserved or losses minimized on a stock position by allowing market movements to trigger a trade. In a sell (buy) stop order, the designated price is lower (higher) than the current market price of the stock. In a sell (buy) limit order, the designated price is higher (lower) than the current market price of the stock. The relationships between the two types of conditional orders, and the market movements which trigger them, appear in Exhibit 6.1.

There are two dangers associated with stop orders. Stock prices sometimes exhibit abrupt price changes, so the direction of a change in a stock price may be quite temporary, resulting in the premature trading of a stock. Also, once the designated price is reached, the stop order becomes a market order and is subject to the uncertainty of the execution price noted earlier for market orders.

A *stop-limit order*, a hybrid of a stop order and a limit order, is a stop order that designates a price limit. In contrast to the stop order, which becomes a market order if the stop is reached, the stop-limit order becomes a limit order if the stop is reached. The stop-limit order can be used to cushion the market impact of a stop order. The investor may limit the possible execution price after the activation of the stop. As with a limit order, the limit price may never be reached after the order is activated, which therefore defeats one purpose of the stop order—to protect a profit or limit a loss.

EXHIBIT 6.1 Conditional Orders and the Direction of Triggering Security Price Movements

Price of Security	Limit Order	Market if Touched Order	Stop Limit Order	Stop Order
Higher price	Price specified for a *sell limit order*.	Price specified for a *sell market if touched order*.	Price specified for a limit *buy stop order*.	Price specified for a *buy stop order*.
Current Price	—	—	—	—
Lower Price	Price specified for a *buy limit order*.	Price specified for a *buy market if touched order*.	Price specified for a *sell stop limit order*.	Price specified for a *sell stop order*.
Comment	Can be filled only at price or better (that is, does not become a market order when price is reached).	Becomes market order when price is reached.	Does not become a market order when price is reached; can be executed only at price or better.	Becomes market order when price is reached.

An investor may also enter a *market if touched order*. This order becomes a market order if a designated price is reached. A market if touched order to buy becomes a market order if the market falls to a given price, while a stop order to buy becomes a market order if the market rises to a given price. Similarly, a market if touched order to sell becomes a market order if the market rises to a specified price, while the stop order to sell becomes a market order if the market falls to a given price. We can think of the stop order as an order designed to get out of an existing position at an acceptable price (without specifying the exact price), and the market if touched order as an order designed to get into a position at an acceptable price (also without specifying the exact price).

Orders may be placed to buy or sell at the open or the close of trading for the day. An opening order indicates a trade to be executed only in the opening range for the day, and a closing order indicates a trade is to be executed only within the closing range for the day.

An investor may enter orders that contain order cancellation provisions. A *fill or kill order* must be executed as soon as it reaches the trading floor or it is immediately canceled. Orders may designate the time period for which the order is effective—a day, week, month, or perhaps by a given time within the day. An open order, or good till canceled order, is good until the investor specifically terminates the order.

Orders are also classified by their size. One round lot is typically 100 shares of a stock. An *odd lot* is defined as less than a round lot. A *block trade* is defined on the NYSE as an order of 10,000 shares of a given stock or a total market value of $200,000 or more.

Both the major national stock exchanges and the regional stock exchanges have systems for routing orders of a specified size (that are submitted by brokers) through a computer directly to the specialists' posts where the orders can be executed. On the NYSE, this system is the SuperDot system. The AMEX's Post Execution Reporting system allows orders of up to 2,000 shares to be routed directly to specialists. The regional stock exchanges have computerized systems for routing small orders to specialists. The Small Order Execution system of the Nasdaq routes and executes orders of up to 1,000 shares of a given stock.

Short Selling

Short selling involves the sale of a security not owned by the investor at the time of sale. The investor can arrange to have her broker borrow the stock from someone else, and the borrowed stock is delivered to implement the sale. To cover her short position, the investor must eventually purchase the stock and return it to the party that lent the stock.

Let us look at an example of how a short sale is done. Suppose Ms. Stokes believes that Wilson Steel common stock is overpriced at $20 per share and wants to be in a position to benefit if her assessment is correct. Ms. Stokes calls her broker, Mr. Yats, indicating that she wants to sell 100 shares of Wilson Steel. Mr. Yats will do two things: (1) sell 100 shares of Wilson Steel on behalf of Ms. Stokes, and (2) arrange to borrow 100 shares of that stock to deliver to the buyer. Suppose that Mr. Yats is able to sell the stock for $20 per share and borrows the stock from Mr. Jordan. The shares borrowed from Mr. Jordan will be delivered to the buyer of the 100 shares. The proceeds from the sale (ignoring commissions) will be $2,000. However, the proceeds do not go to Ms. Stokes because she has not given her broker the 100 shares. Thus, Ms. Stokes is said to be "short 100 shares."

Now, let's suppose one week later the price of Wilson Steel stock declines to $15 per share. Ms. Stokes may instruct her broker to buy 100 shares of Wilson Steel. The cost of buying the shares (once again ignoring commissions) is $1,500. The shares purchased are then delivered to Mr. Jordan, who lent 100 shares to Ms. Stokes. At this point, Ms. Stokes has sold 100 shares and bought 100 shares. So, she no longer has any obligation to her broker or to Mr. Jordan—she has covered her short position. She is entitled to the funds in her account that were generated by the selling and buying activity. She sold the stock for $2,000 and bought it for $1,500. Thus, she realizes a profit before commissions of $500. Commissions are subtracted from this amount.

Two more costs will reduce the profit further. First, a fee will be charged by the lender of the stock. Second, if there are any dividends paid by Wilson Steel while the stock is borrowed, Ms. Stokes must compensate Mr. Jordan for the dividends he is entitled to.

If the price of Wilson Steel stock rises instead of falling, Ms. Stokes will realize a loss if she is forced to cover her short position. For example, if the price rises to $27, Ms. Stokes will lose $700, to which must be added commissions, the cost of borrowing the stock, and possibly dividends.

Exchanges impose restrictions as to when a short sale may be executed; these so-called *tick-test rules* are intended to prevent investors from destabilizing the price of a stock when the market price is falling. A short sale can be made only when either (1) the sale price of the particular stock is higher than the last trade price (referred to as an *uptick trade*), or (2) if there is no change in the last trade price of the particular stock (referred to as a *zero uptick*), the previous trade price must be higher than the trade price that preceded it. For example, if Ms. Stokes wanted to short Wilson Steel at a price of $20, and the two previous trade prices were $20⅛, and then $20, she could not do so at this time because of the uptick trade rule. If the previous trade prices were $19⅞, $19⅞, and then

$20, she could short the stock at $20 because of the uptick trade rule. Suppose that the sequence of the last three trades is: $19⅞, $20, and $20. Ms. Stokes could short the stock at $20 because of the zero uptick rule.

Margin Transactions

Investors can borrow cash to buy securities and use the securities themselves as collateral. For example, suppose Mr. Boxer has $10,000 to invest and is considering buying Wilson Steel, which is currently selling for $20 per share. With his $10,000, Mr. Boxer can buy 500 shares. Suppose his broker can arrange for him to borrow an additional $10,000 so that Mr. Boxer can buy an additional 500 shares. Thus, with a $20,000 investment, he can purchase a total of 1,000 shares. The 1,000 shares will be used as collateral for the $10,000 borrowed, and Mr. Boxer will have to pay interest on the amount borrowed.

A transaction in which an investor borrows to buy shares using the shares themselves as collateral is called buying on margin. By borrowing funds, an investor creates financial leverage. Note that Mr. Boxer, for a $10,000 investment, realizes the consequences associated with a price change of 1,000 shares rather than 500 shares. Compared to borrowing no funds, he will benefit if the price rises but be worse off if the price falls.

To illustrate, we examine what happens if the price subsequently changes. If the price of Wilson Steel rises to $29 per share, ignoring commissions and the cost of borrowing, Mr. Boxer will realize a profit of $9 per share on 1,000 shares, or $9,000. Had Mr. Boxer not borrowed $10,000 to buy the additional 500 shares, his profit would be only $4,500. Suppose, instead, the price of Wilson Steel stock decreases to $13 per share. In this case, by borrowing to buy 500 additional shares, he lost $7 per share on 1,000 shares instead of $7 per share on just 500 shares.

The funds borrowed to buy the additional stock will be provided by the broker, who gets the money from a bank. The interest rate that banks charge brokers for these funds is the *call money rate* (also referred to as the *broker loan rate*). The broker charges the borrower the call money rate plus a service charge.

Margin Requirements

The brokerage firm is not allowed to lend as much as it wishes to investors to buy securities. The Securities Exchange Act of 1934 prohibits brokers from lending more than a specified percentage of the market value of the securities. The *initial margin requirement* is the proportion of the total market value of the securities that the investor must pay as an equity share, and the remainder is borrowed from the broker. The 1934 act gives the Board of Governors of the Federal Reserve (the Fed) the responsibility to set initial margin requirements. The initial margin requirement is 50% as of this writing, but has been below 40%.

The Fed also establishes a maintenance margin requirement. This is the minimum proportion of (1) the equity in the investor's margin account to (2) the total market value. If the investor's margin account falls below the minimum maintenance margin (which may happen if the share price fell substantially), the investor is required to put up additional cash. The investor receives a margin call from the broker specifying the additional cash to be put into the investor's margin account. If the investor fails to put up the additional cash, the broker has the authority to sell the securities in the investor's account.

The following example illustrates maintenance margin. Assume an investor buys 100 shares of stock at $60 per share for $6,000 on 50% margin and the maintenance margin is 25%. By purchasing $6,000 of stock on 50% margin, the investor must put up $3,000 of cash (or other equity) and, thus, borrows $3,000 (referred to as the debit balance). The investor, however, must maintain 25% of margin. To what level must the stock price decline to hit the maintenance margin level? The price is $40. At this price, the stock position has a value of $4,000 ($40 × 100 shares). With a loan of $3,000, the equity in the account is $1,000 ($4,000 − $3,000), or 25% of the account value ($1,000/$4,000 = 25%). If the price of the stock decreases below $40, the investor must deposit more equity to bring the equity level up to 25%. In general, if the maintenance margin is 25%, the account level has to decrease to 4/3 times the amount borrowed (the debit balance) to reach the minimum maintenance margin level.

There are also margin requirements for short selling. Consider a similar margin example for a short position. An investor shorts (borrows and sells)100 shares of stock at $60 for total stock value of $6,000. With an initial margin of 50%, the investor must deposit $3,000 (in addition to leaving the $6,000 from the sale in the account). This leaves the investor with a *credit balance* of $9,000 (which does not change with the stock price since it is in cash). However, the investor owes 100 shares of the stock at the current market price. To what level must the stock price increase to hit the maintenance margin level, assumed to be 30% (which is the equity in the account as a percentage of the market value of the stock)? The answer is $69.23, for a total stock value of $6,923. If the stock is worth $6,923, there is $2,077 of equity in the account ($9,000 − $6,923), which represents 30% of the market value of the stock ($2,077/$6,923 = 30%). If the maintenance margin is 30%, the value of the stock which triggers the maintenance level is calculated by multiplying the credit balance by 10/13 (10/13 × $9,000 = $6,923).

A summary of the long and short margin requirements is provided in the following table:

Margin	Long	Short
Initial	50%	50%
Maintenance	25%	30%
Multiple of Debit (Long) or credit (Short) Balance to require maintenance	4/3	10/13

Price Limits and Collars

Trading or price limits specify a minimum price below which the market index level may not decline due to an institutionally mandated termination of trading, at least at prices below the specified price (the price limit) for a specified period of time. For example, if the DJIA was trading at 11,000 and its price limit was 500 points below that, then no trades could occur below 10,500. This pause in trading is intended to "give the market a breather" to at least calm emotions. Trading limits had previously been used in the futures markets but not in the stock market. These price limits have been modified several times since their implementation soon after the stock market crash of 1987.

TRADING COSTS

A critical element in investment management is controlling the trading costs necessary to implement a strategy. While important, the measurement of trading costs is very difficult.

We begin by defining trading costs. Trading costs can be decomposed into two major components: *explicit costs* and *implicit costs*. Explicit costs are the direct costs of trading, such as broker commissions, fees, and taxes. Implicit costs represent such indirect costs as the price impact of the trade and the opportunity costs of failing to execute in a timely manner or at all. Whereas explicit costs are associated with identifiable charges, no such reporting of implicit costs occurs.

Explicit Costs

The main explicit cost is the commission paid to the broker for execution. Commission costs are fully negotiable and vary systematically by broker type and market mechanism. The commission may depend on both the price per share and the number of shares in the transaction. In addition to commissions, there may be other explicit costs. These explicit costs include custodial fees (the fees charged by an institution holding securities in safekeeping for an investor) and transfer fees (the fees associated with transferring an asset from one owner to another).

With the introduction of negotiated commissions in May 1975, the opportunity arose for the development of discount brokers. These brokers charge commissions at rates substantially less than those charged by full service brokers, while offering little or no advice or any other service apart from execution of the transaction.

In general, commissions began a downward trend in 1975 which continued through 1996, when they reached 4.5¢ per share. Based on a study by the Plexus Group, after increasing during 1997, commissions reached 4.5¢ per share again in the first quarter of 1999. Only small, easily traded orders have become cheaper, not the larger and more difficult trades. Commissions for larger trades (over 10,000 shares) have been relatively stable at about 4.8¢ per share. Commissions for trades under 10,000 shares on the other hand, have declined to 2.8¢ per share.[2]

The Plexus Group study also found that the commissions on capital committing trades—trades which require a commitment of the dealer's own capital to accomplish the trade rather than simply executing the trade by matching two customer orders on an agency basis—are higher and have not declined. Investors should expect to pay for the use of the dealer's capital and the associated risk. Similarly, soft dollar trades, discussed below, have high and stable commissions. Consequently, investors may be penalized for not being able to "shop around" for lower commissions. Overall, it is the commissions on agency trades (trades on which the dealer need not commit capital) and non-soft dollar trades (for which the customer can shop around) that are the lowest and have declined the most.

There are also two other issues that relate to transactions costs—"soft dollars" and "payment for order flow." These issues are discussed below.

Soft Dollars

Investors often choose their broker–dealer based on who will give them the best execution at the lowest transaction cost on a specific transaction, and also based on who will provide complementary services (such as research) over a period of time. Order flow can also be "purchased" by a broker-dealer from an investor with "soft dollars." In this case, the broker–dealer provides the investor, without explicit charge, services such as research or electronic services, typically from a third party for which the investor would otherwise have had to pay "hard dollars" to the third party. Of course, the investor pays the broker–dealer for the execution service.

---

[2] Plexus Group, "Withering Commissions, Winning Brokers: Who Will Survive?"

According to such a relationship, the investor preferentially routes their order to the broker–dealer specified in the soft dollar relationship and does not have to pay "hard dollars," or real money, for the research or other services. This practice is called paying "soft dollars" (i.e., directing their order flow) for the ancillary research. For example, client A preferentially directs his order flow to broker–dealer B (often a specified amount of order flow over a specified period, such as a month or year) and pays the broker–dealer for these execution services. In turn, broker/dealer B pays for some research services provided to client A. Very often the research provider is a separate firm, say, firm C. Thus, soft dollars refer to money paid by an investor to a broker–dealer or a third party through commission revenue rather than by direct payments.

The disadvantage to the broker–dealer is that they have to pay hard dollars (to the research provider) for the client's order flow. The disadvantage to the client is that they are not free to "shop around" for the best bid or best offer, net of commissions, for all their transactions, but have to do an agreed amount of transaction volume with the specific broker–dealer. In addition, the research provider may give a preferential price to the broker–dealer. Thus, each of these participants in the soft dollar relationship experiences some advantage, but also an offsetting disadvantage.

The SEC has imposed formal and informal limitations on the type and amount of soft dollar business institutional investors can conduct. For example, while an institutional investor can accept research in a soft dollar relationship, they cannot accept furniture or vacations. SEC disclosure rules, passed in 1995, require investment advisors to disclose, among other things, the details on any product or services received through soft dollars.

Payment for Order Flow

In payment for order flow arrangements, an OTC market maker may offer a cash payment to other brokerage firms which have customer order flow in exchange for the right to execute the broker's order flow, thus providing a reason for the broker preferencing trades to certain market makers for each stock. Such payment for order flow has occurred mainly on Nasdaq on which there are several market makers for each stock. Rebates are typically on a per-share basis and have historically been about 2¢ a share.

The reasons for payment for order flow remain controversial. One possible reason is that it is a device for price discrimination based on the information content of the order. Specifically, market makers may pay for orders that are placed by "uninformed traders," and hence are more profitable to execute; but may not pay for orders placed by "informed traders," which are less profitable. In general, retail order flow is considered to be uninformed, and institutional and professional order flow to be informed. In fact, most payment for order flow arrangements are with retail brokerage houses and the average size of purchased orders is significantly below the overall average trade size. Obviously small retail trades are preferred by the market makers who pay for order flow and are considered uninformed order flow. The data appear to be consistent with the uniformed/informed trader hypothesis.

Inter-market market-maker competition and inter-exchange competition via payment for order flow remains controversial.[3] The relevant policy question is whether retail broker–dealers are diverted from sending their retail orders to the best markets, thereby disadvantaging their customers, or whether a portion of the payment accrues to the customer, thereby benefiting the customer. The advent of decimalization during 2000, discussed below, has permitted smaller bid–offer spreads and reduced the degree of payment for order flow. Overall, both soft dollars and payment for order flow remain controversial.

Implicit Costs

Implicit trading costs include impact costs, timing costs, and opportunity costs.

Impact Costs

The impact cost of a transaction is the change in market price due to supply/demand imbalances as a result of the trade. Bid-ask spread estimates, although informative, fail to capture the fact that large trades—those that exceed the number of shares the market maker is willing to trade at the quoted bid and ask prices—may move prices in the direction of the trade. That is, large trades may increase the price for buy orders and decrease the price for sell orders. The resulting market impact or price impact of the transaction can be thought of as the deviation of the transaction price from the "unperturbed price" that would have prevailed had the trade not occurred. As discussed above, crossing networks are designed to minimize impact costs.

Timing Cost

The *timing cost* is measured as the price change between the time the parties to the implementation process assume responsibility for the trade and the time they complete the responsibility. Timing costs occur when orders are on the trading desk of a buy side firm (e.g., an invest-

---

[3] Floyd Norris, "Wall St. Said to Gain Most in Policy Shift," *New York Times* (Dec. 20, 2000), pp. C1, C6.

ment management firm), but have not been released to the broker because the trader fears that the trade may swamp the market.

Opportunity Costs [4]

The opportunity cost is the "cost" of securities not traded. This cost results from missed or only partially completed trades. These costs are the natural consequence of the release delays. For example, if the price moves too much before the trade can be completed, the manager will not make the trade. In practice, this cost is measured on shares not traded based on the difference between the market price at the time of decision and the closing price 30 days later.

While commissions and impact costs are actual and visible out-of-pocket costs, opportunity costs and timing costs are the costs of foregone opportunities and are invisible. Opportunity costs can arise for two reasons. First, some orders are executed with a delay, during which the price may move against the investor. Second, some orders incur an opportunity cost because they are only partially filled or are not executed at all.

Classification of Trading Costs

Thus far we have classified four main trading costs—commissions, impact costs, timing costs, and opportunity costs—as explicit or implicit trading costs. This categorization is based on whether or not the costs are identifiable accounting costs. Another categorization of these costs is execution costs versus opportunity costs. This categorization is based on whether or not the trades are completed. A schematic diagram of trading costs using this categorization is shown in Exhibit 6.2.

The categorization of the four costs according to the two criteria is as follows.

Explicit vs. Implicit	Execution vs. Opportunity
Explicit	*Execution*
Commission	Commission
	Impact
Implicit	*Opportunity*
Impact	Timing
Timing	Opportunity
Opportunity	

---

[4] The other side of opportunity costs is referred to as *adverse selection* and is often ignored in the measurement process. Adverse selection is a result of trading too soon when a better execution price could have been obtained by waiting. The decision to trade is a balance between fear of trading too soon (adverse selection) and the fear of trading too late (opportunity costs).

EXHIBIT 6.2   Diagram of Types of Trading Costs

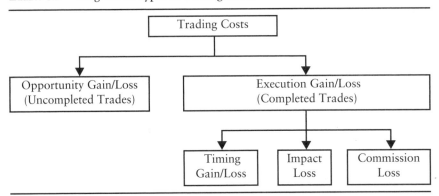

Source: "Alpha Capture," *Plexus Group*, Second Quarter, 1999.

Measuring Transaction Costs[5]

The measurement of transaction costs is critical for portfolio managers in formulating investment strategies and for clients in assessing the performance of managers. There are three dimensions to measuring trading costs: commissions for a particular stock or trading style, determination of a benchmark for execution costs and opportunity costs, and separation of the influence of the trade from other factors.

Commission rates, taxes, and fees are readily observable and fixed for a transaction. This component of costs is negotiated on a pre-trade basis and is known and measurable.

The measurement of other components of transaction costs, particularly the impact component, has no unique solution. Impact cost arises when a trade induces a temporary price movement. This is the result of either immediate liquidity demands or the actions of a market maker who perceives that an investor's trade contains useful information. There are alternative approaches to measuring execution costs that capture useful information about the transaction process. In general, the cost of transacting is the difference between the execution price (i.e., the actual price at which the trade was executed) and a fair market benchmark. That is,

$$\text{Costs} = \text{execution price} - \text{fair price}$$

The fair price of a security is the price that would have prevailed had an investor's trade not taken place. However, since that price is not observable,

---

[5] For a further discussion, see Bruce M. Collins and Frank J. Fabozzi, "A Methodology for Measuring Transactions Costs," *Financial Analysts Journal* (March–April 1991), pp. 27–36.

the fair price must be estimated or inferred. There are several working definitions of a fair price benchmark among practitioners. The choice of a benchmark may involve choosing either a price that represents the fair value of a stock in the absence of the investor from the market or a price that represents the consequence of the investor's presence in the market. We present three different approaches to measuring impact cost, which are referred to as pre-trade benchmarks, post-trade benchmarks, and average benchmarks.

Pre-trade benchmarks are prices occurring before or at the decision to trade, while *post-trade benchmarks* are prices occurring after the decision to trade. *Average benchmarks*, also referred to as *across-day benchmarks*, use the average or representative price of a large number of trades. Essentially, all three benchmarks are attempts to measure the fair value of a stock at a point in time. Transaction costs emerge when the execution price deviates from the fair price. To the extent that any price represents an unbiased estimate of a fair price, the concept is valid. It does, however, assume that markets are price efficient, a concept discussed in the next chapter.

Pre-Trade Benchmarks

Pre-trade benchmarks utilize a price that existed prior to the trade as a benchmark.[6] This price may be the previous night's close or the price at which the stock last traded. The premise behind pre-trade benchmarks is that the only way of knowing the impact of an investor's trade on the price of the stock is by comparing it with conditions prior to his or her arrival in the marketplace. One way to accomplish this is by comparing the execution price with the price at which the stock last traded. Alternatively, when a time lag to last sale exists, the midpoint of the bid-ask can be used. In either case, the argument follows that market conditions before the time of execution represent the reference point for evaluating any price movement induced by an investor's entrance into the marketplace. A positive difference between the execution price and the benchmark is regarded as a cost.

Critics of pre-trade benchmarks argue that prior prices are not good measures of cost because the benchmark might not be independent of the trading decision, which is a fundamental requirement for a good measure of execution costs. In other words, the investor should not be able to game the trade. Gaming in this context refers to structuring a trade in such a way that it satisfies or accommodates a particular cost measure. That is, gaming is rigging the apparent costs by the person accountable

---

[6] See André F. Perold, "The Implementation Shortfall: Paper versus Reality," *Journal of Portfolio Management* (April 1988), pp. 4–9 and Gary Beebower, "Evaluating Transaction Costs," Chapter 11 in Wayne H. Wagner (ed.), *The Complete Guide to Securities Transactions* (New York: John Wiley & Sons, 1989), for a discussion of pre-trade measures.

for these costs so that the manager can show low costs by rigging the measurement criteria—and the client is none the wiser. A simple example of gaming is to execute easy trades and not difficult trades.

Post-Trade Benchmarks

A second approach to measuring impact costs is using post-trade benchmarks.[7] The premise underlying the use of a post-trade benchmark is that it avoids the problem of gaming because it is independent of the trading decision. One requirement, however, is a benchmark that lies outside the influence of the trade. Thus, the measurement interval is another parameter to consider. As is the case with pre-trade benchmarks, there are several choices for post-trade benchmarks. These include the next trade immediately after a trade, the closing price on the trade date, or any price subsequent to the time of execution.

Average Measures

A final approach to establishing a fair price benchmark is to establish a representative price for the trade date. Two such measures are the average of the high and low and the trade-weighted average price.[8] The weakness of both measures as benchmarks for measuring execution costs is that they are subject to gaming.[9] These averages are better indicators of the market timing portion of costs rather than execution costs. However, proponents argue that average cost benchmarks are better measures than market impact benchmarks because the former are more representative of an equilibrium price.[10]

---

[7] For a discussion of post-trade benchmark measure of impact cost, see Beebower "Evaluating Transaction Costs" and G. Beebower and W. Priest, "The Tricks of the Trade," *Journal of Portfolio Management* (Winter 1980), pp. 36–42.

[8] See S. Berkowitz and D. E. Logue, "Study of the Investment Performance of ERISA Plans," U.S. Dept. of Labor, July 1986, and S. Berkowitz, D. E. Logue, and E. A. Noser, "The Total Cost of Transactions on the N.Y.S.E.," *Journal of Finance* (March 1988), pp. 97–112, for a discussion of these measures.

[9] For example, the trade-weighted average price is gamed by spreading a trade out across the trading day—periodically transacting. A major proportion of the desired trade might be transacted around the opening, closing, and large-block trades. The trader participates but does not originate a trade. The trading style is reactive and not proactive. Thus, the use of this benchmark is essentially a promise by the trader to be mediocre and may not produce the best results.

[10] Peter Bernstein, consulting editor of the *Journal of Portfolio Management*, argues that the only reliable benchmarks are "representative price" benchmarks, which are essentially some form of average price, because they are more likely to represent an equilibrium price. Alternative benchmarks might incorporate market impact from competitive trades other than the one being evaluated.

EXHIBIT 6.3 Cost Measurement Techniques

Method	Benchmarks	Advantages	Disadvantages
Pretrade	Last sale Previous close	Captures current market: ½ bid-ask spread	May affect trading decision
Posttrade	Next sale Trade date close N-day close	Avoids gaming	Neglects pretrade information that is based on market effects
Intraday	Avg. high/low Weighted average	Measures daily market timing	Subject to gaming
Factor-adjusted	Market Industry	Captures residual effects	Difficult to measure

Other Factors

Other factors have been used to adjust costs. The movement of prices can be induced by general market movements.[11] For example, suppose several portfolio managers would like to increase their exposure to the stock market. Suppose further that they all enter orders to buy certain stocks at the same time. As a result of these orders, the price may move between the time the order is entered and the time it is executed. Consequently, the cost of execution should be adjusted for changes in the market or other factors assumed to affect prices. The premise underlying this approach is to specify an unbiased estimate of a fair price in the manager's absence from the market. The measure captures the residual effects of a manager's trade on the movement in price by adjusting the benchmark. A positive residual is indicative of a cost. The expression below is an example of a cost estimator using this approach.

Cost = execution price − benchmark − market factor adjustment

Exhibit 6.3 summarizes the different approaches to measuring execution costs along with advantages and disadvantages.

Research on Transaction Costs

Overall, while the trading commission is the most obvious, measurable and discussed trading cost, it is only one of the four types of trading costs and, as discussed below, may in fact be the smallest. The implicit trading costs are much more difficult to measure.

---

[11] See Kathleen A. Condon, "Measuring Equity Transactions Costs," *Financial Analyst Journal* (September 1981), pp. 57–60, for a specification of this type of adjustment. See Stephen Bodurtha and T. Quinn, "Does Patient Trading Really Pay?" *Financial Analyst Journal* (April–May 1990), pp. 35–42, for an example of how to implement an adjustment for market changes.

Recent studies in transactions costs allow several conclusions. They are:

1. Although considerable debate still surrounds how to measure trading costs, the consensus is that implicit trading costs are economically significant relative to explicit costs (and also relative to realized portfolio returns).
2. Equity trading costs vary systematically with trade difficulty and order-placement strategy.
3. Differences in market design, investment style, trading ability and reputation are important determinants of trading costs.
4. Even after researchers control for trade complexity and trade venue, trading costs are found to vary considerably among managers.
5. Accurate prediction of trading costs requires more detailed data on the entire order-submission process than is generally available, especially information on pre-trade decision variables.

These findings suggest that the concept of "best execution" for institutional traders is difficult to measure and hence to enforce.[12]

TRADING ARRANGEMENTS FOR RETAIL AND INSTITUTIONAL INVESTORS

Trades are executed by both individuals, called retail investors, and institutions. There are several differences in the way each group trades. The first is size: Institutions typically transact much larger orders than individuals. The second is commissions: Consistent with their larger size, institutions typically pay lower commissions than individuals. While institutional commissions have declined since 1975, some retail commissions have also declined significantly recently as a result of the advent of discount brokers.

The third difference is the method of order execution. While both an individual and an institution may trade through a broker–dealer, the manner in which their orders are entered and executed may be considerably different, even if the trades are through the same broker–dealer. An individual trading through a broker–dealer typically goes through a stockbroker (financial consultant). These orders go to a retail exchange execution desk and from there to the NYSE (usually through SuperDot) or to the OTC execution desk where they will be transacted with another market maker on Nasdaq.

---

[12] Donald B. Keim and Ananth Madhavan, "The Cost of Institutional Equity Trades," *Financial Analysts Journal* (July/August 1998), pp.50–59.

Retail investors receive a "confirm" (confirmation) of the trade, typically in the mail. Institutional investors generally give their order directly to the institutional broker–dealer execution desk for both exchange and OTC orders. Exchange orders may be sent to the broker–dealer's floor broker, and OTC orders may be transacted with another broker–dealer or internalized at a competitive bid–offer. Competing bids or offers are typically obtained in all cases.

Retail Stock Trading

Historically, there has been a decline in the direct household ownership of common stock. This decline does not necessarily lead to the conclusion that households have decreased their common stock holdings. Rather, it means that households are holding more common stock through intermediaries such as mutual funds rather than directly. While households hold more total common stock than before, they hold less common stock directly, and, thus, increasingly the stock executions are done by institutions, such as mutual funds, rather than by individuals.

One of the reasons for individuals owning stock through mutual funds rather than directly involves transaction costs; that is, institutions can transact stocks more cheaply than individuals. While this advantage for institutions remains, transaction costs for individuals have declined significantly during the last decade.

Since May Day 1975, stock trading commissions have declined both for institutions and individuals. However, prior to 1990, individuals traded stocks mainly through so-called "full service brokers," where commissions reflected not only the stock trade execution, but also the counsel of a stockbroker and perhaps research. The largest full service broker–dealers are also known as "wirehouses." These firms typically do institutional trading and investment banking as well as retail business. The commissions for these full service brokers have declined since 1975.

In addition, a "discount broker" industry developed in which the stockbroker provided no advice and no research. Individuals entered their orders via a telephone. More recently, individuals could enter their orders via their personal computer—these are called "online" or "Web based" brokerage firms. Consistent with the lower provision of service by discount brokers and online brokers, stock trading commissions decreased significantly. Thus, individuals could trade and own stocks more efficiently.

To remain competitive to a wide range of clients in this environment, the traditional full service brokerage firms responded by offering customers alternative means of transacting common stock. For example, many full service brokerage firms offer the traditional services of a stockbroker and research at a high commission, and, in addition, offer direct order entry only at a lower commission. Conversely, some discount brokers have begun to offer more service at a higher commission.

Thus, there continue to be ebbs and flows in the balance between more service and low commissions in the retail trading of common stock. Both online brokers, who offer no service and low commissions, and managers of segregated accounts, who offer enhanced services for a large fee, are growing along with full service stock brokerages and mutual funds.

Despite paying higher commissions than institutions, individual investors may have some advantages over institutions. Because individuals usually transact smaller orders, they will incur smaller impact costs. In addition, if individual investors transact online, they may have shorter time lags. It is for these and other reasons that "packaged products" of individual stocks such as "folios" and exchange-traded funds are becoming more attractive.

Institutional Trading

With the increase in trading by institutional investors, trading arrangements more suitable for these investors were developed. Institutional needs include trading in large size and trading groups of stocks, both at a low commission and with low market impact. This has resulted in the evolution of special arrangements for the execution of certain types of orders commonly sought by institutional investors: (1) orders requiring the execution of a trade of a large number of shares of a given stock and (2) orders requiring the execution of trades in a large number of different stocks at as near the same time as possible. The former types of trades are called *block trades*; the latter are called *program trades*. An example of a block trade would be a mutual fund seeking to buy 15,000 shares of IBM stock. An example of a program trade would be a pension fund wanting to buy shares of 200 names (companies) at the end of a trading day ("at the close").

The institutional arrangement that has evolved to accommodate these two types of institutional trades is the development of a network of trading desks of the major securities firms and other institutional investors that communicate with each other by means of electronic display systems and telephones. This network is referred to as the upstairs market. Participants in the upstairs market play a key role by (1) providing liquidity to the market so that such institutional trades can be executed, and (2) by arbitrage activities that help to integrate the fragmented stock market.

Block Trades

On the NYSE, block trades are defined as either trades of at least 10,000 shares of a given stock, or trades of shares with a market value of at least $200,000, whichever is less. Since the execution of large numbers of block orders places strains on the specialist system in the NYSE, special procedures have been developed to handle them. Typically, an institutional customer contacts its salesperson at a brokerage firm, indicating that it wishes to place a block order. The salesperson then gives the order to the block execution department of the brokerage firm. Note that the salesperson does not submit the order to be executed to the exchange where the stock might be traded or, in the case of an unlisted stock, try to execute the order on the Nasdaq system. The sales traders in the block execution department contact other institutions to attempt to find one or more institutions that would be willing to take the other side of the order. That is, they use the upstairs market in their search to fill the block trade order. If this can be accomplished, the execution of the order is completed.

If the sales traders cannot find enough institutions to take the entire block (for example, if the block trade order is for 40,000 shares of IBM, but only 25,000 can be "crossed" with other institutions), then the balance of the block trade order is given to the firm's market maker. The market maker must then make a decision as to how to handle the balance of the block trade order. There are two choices. First, the brokerage firm may take a position in the stock and buy the shares for its own account. Second, the unfilled order may be executed by using the services of competing market makers. In the former case, the brokerage firm is committing its own capital.

NYSE Rule 127 states that if a member firm receives an order for a large block of stock that might not be readily absorbed by the market, the member firm should nevertheless explore the market on the floor, including, where appropriate, consulting with the specialist as to his interest in the security. If a member firm intends to cross a large block of stock for a public account at a price that is outside of the current quote, it should inform the specialist of its intention.

Program Trades

Program trades involve the buying and/or selling of a large number of names simultaneously. Such trades are also called basket trades because effectively a "basket" of stocks is being traded. The NYSE defines a program trade as any trade involving the purchase or sale of a basket of at least 15 stocks with a total value of $1 million or more. The rationale for treating a portfolio or basket of stocks as a single asset is that it diversifies the risk of trading and thus reduces costs. Brokers can offer a much lower commission rate if the portfolio is submitted as a single asset rather than submitting each individual name. In addition, the trades are typically motivated by an investor's desire for broad market exposure and are therefore "informationless," which should not result in large price concessions.

The two major applications of program trades are asset allocation and index arbitrage. With respect to asset allocation trades, some examples of why an institutional investor may want to use a program trade are deployment of new cash into the stock market; implementation of a decision to move funds invested in the bond market to the stock market (or vice versa); and rebalancing the composition of a stock portfolio due to a change in investment strategy. For example, a mutual fund money manager can move funds quickly into or out of the stock market for an entire portfolio of stocks through a single program trade. All these strategies are related to asset allocation.

The growth of mutual fund sales and massive equity investments by pension funds and insurance companies during the 1990s have all given an impetus to such methods to trade baskets or bundles of stocks efficiently. Other reasons for which an institutional investor may have a need to execute a program trade should be apparent when an investment strategy called indexing is discussed in the next chapter.

There are several commission arrangements available to an institution for a program trade, and each arrangement has numerous variants. Considerations in selecting one (in addition to commission costs) are the risk of failing to realize the best execution price, and the risk that the brokerage firms to be solicited about executing the program trade will use their knowledge of the program trade to benefit from the anticipated price movement that might result—in other words, that they will frontrun the transaction (for example, buying a stock for their own account before filling the customer buy order).

From a dealer's perspective, program trades can be conducted in two basic ways, namely on an agency basis or on a principal basis. An intermediate type of program trade, the agency incentive arrangement, is a third alternative. A program trade executed on an agency basis involves the selection by the investor of a brokerage firm solely on the basis of commission bids (cents per share) submitted by various brokerage firms. The brokerage firm selected uses its best efforts as an agent of the institution to obtain the best price. Such trades have low explicit commissions. To the investor, the disadvantage of the agency program trade is that, while commissions may be the lowest, the execution price may not be the best due to impact costs and the potential frontrunning by the brokerage firms solicited to submit a commission bid. The investor knows in advance the commission paid, but does not know the price at which the trades will be executed. Another disadvantage is that there is increased risk of adverse selection of the counter-party in the execution process.

Related to the agency basis is an *agency incentive arrangement*, in which a benchmark portfolio value is established for the group of stocks in the program trade. The price for each "name" (i.e., specific stock) in the program trade is determined as either the price at the end of the previous day or the average price of the previous day. If the brokerage firm can execute the trade on the next trading day such that a better-than-benchmark portfolio value results—a higher value in the case of a program trade involving selling, or a lower value in the case of a program trade involving buying—then the brokerage firm receives the specified commission plus some predetermined additional compensation. In this case the investor does not know in advance the commission or the execution price precisely, but has a reasonable expectation that the price will be better than a threshold level.

What if the brokerage firm does not achieve the benchmark portfolio value? It is in such a case that the variants come into play. One arrangement may call for the brokerage firm to receive only the previously agreed-upon commission. Other arrangements may involve sharing the risk of not realizing the benchmark portfolio value with the brokerage firm. That is, if the brokerage firm falls short of the benchmark portfolio value, it must absorb a portion of the shortfall. In these risk-sharing arrangements, the brokerage firm is risking its own capital. The greater the risk sharing the brokerage firm must accept, the higher the commission it will charge.

The brokerage firm can also choose to execute the trade on a principal basis. In this case, the dealer would commit its own capital to buy or sell the portfolio and complete the investor's transaction immediately. Since the dealer incurs market risk, it would also charge higher commissions. The key factors in pricing principal trades are: liquidity characteristics, absolute dollar value, nature of trade, customer profile, and market volatility. In this case, the investor knows the trade execution price in advance, but pays a higher commission.

To minimize frontrunning, institutions often use other types of program trade arrangements. They call for brokerage firms to receive, not specific names and quantities of stocks, but only aggregate statistical information about key portfolio parameters. Several brokerage firms then bid on a cents per share basis on the entire portfolio (also called "blind baskets"), guaranteeing execution at either closing price (termed "market-at-close") or a particular intra-day price to the customer. Note that this is a principal trade. Since mutual fund net asset values are calculated using closing prices, a mutual fund that follows an indexing strategy (i.e., an index fund), for instance, would want guaranteed market-at-close execution to minimize the risk of not performing as well as the stock index. When the winning bidder has been selected, it receives the details of the portfolio. While the commission in this type of transaction is higher, this procedure increases the risk to the brokerage firm of successfully executing the program trade. However, the brokerage firm can use stock index futures to protect itself from market-wide movements if the characteristics of the portfolio in the program trade are similar to the index underlying the stock index futures contract.

STOCK MARKET INDICATORS

Stock market indicators have come to perform a variety of functions, from serving as benchmarks for evaluating the performance of professional money managers to answering the question "How did the market do today?" Thus, stock market indicators (indexes or averages) have become a part of everyday life. Even though many of the stock market indicators are used interchangeably, it is important to realize that each indicator applies to, and measures, a different facet of the stock market.

The most commonly quoted stock market indicator is the Dow Jones Industrial Average (DJIA). Other popular stock market indicators cited in the financial press are the Standard & Poor's 500 Composite (S&P 500), the New York Stock Exchange Composite Index (NYSE Composite), the Nasdaq Composite Index, and the Value Line Composite Average (VLCA). There are a myriad of other stock market indicators such as the Wilshire stock indexes and the Russell stock indexes, which are followed primarily by institutional money managers.

In general, market indexes rise and fall in fairly similar patterns. Although the correlations among indexes are high, the indexes do not move in tandem at all times. The differences in movement reflect the different manner in which the indexes are constructed. Three factors enter into that construction: the universe of stocks represented by the sample underlying the index, the relative weights assigned to the stocks included in the index, and the method of averaging across all the stocks.

Some indexes represent only stocks listed on an exchange. Examples are the DJIA and the NYSE Composite, which represent only stocks listed on the NYSE or Big Board. By contrast, the Nasdaq includes only stocks traded over the counter. A favorite of professionals is the S&P 500 because it is a broader index containing both NYSE-listed and OTC-traded shares. Each index relies on a sample of stocks from its universe, and that sample may be small or quite large. The DJIA uses only 30 of the NYSE-traded shares, while the NYSE Composite includes every one of the listed shares. The Nasdaq also includes all shares in its universe, while the S&P 500 has a sample that contains only 500 of the more than 8,000 shares in the universe it represents.

The stocks included in a stock market index must be combined in certain proportions (i.e., each stock must be given a weight). The three main approaches to weighting are: (1) weighting by the market capitalization, which is the number of shares times price per share; (2) weighting by the price of the stock; and (3) equal weighting for each stock, regardless of its price or its firm's market value. With the exception of the Dow Jones averages (such as the DJIA) and the VLCA, nearly all of the most widely used indexes are market-value weighted. The DJIA is a price-weighted average, and the VLCA is an equally weighted index.

Stock market indicators can be classified into three groups: (1) those produced by stock exchanges based on all stocks traded on the exchanges; (2) those produced by organizations that subjectively select the stocks to be included in indexes; and (3) those where stock selection is based on an objective measure, such as the market capitalization of the company. The first group includes the New York Stock Exchange Composite Index, which reflects the market value of all stocks traded on the NYSE. While it is not an exchange, the Nasdaq Composite Index falls into this category because the index represents all stocks traded on the Nasdaq system.

The three most popular stock market indicators in the second group are the Dow Jones Industrial Average, the Standard & Poor's 500, and the Value Line Composite Average. The DJIA is constructed from 30 of the largest blue-chip industrial companies traded on the NYSE. The companies included in the average are those selected by Dow Jones & Company, publisher of The Wall Street Journal. The S&P 500 represents stocks chosen from the two major national stock exchanges and the OTC market. The stocks in the index at any given time are determined by a committee of Standard & Poor's Corporation, which may occasionally add or delete individual stocks or the stocks of entire industry groups. The VLCA, produced by Value Line Inc., covers a broad range of widely held and actively traded NYSE, AMEX, and OTC issues selected by Value Line.

In the third group we have the Wilshire indexes produced by Wilshire Associates (Santa Monica, California) and Russell indexes produced by the Frank Russell Company (Tacoma, Washington), a consultant to pension funds and other institutional investors. The criterion for inclusion in each of these indexes is solely a firm's market capitalization. The most comprehensive index is the Wilshire 5000, which actually includes more than 6,700 stocks now, up from 5,000 at its inception. The Wilshire 4500 includes all stocks in the Wilshire 5000 except for those in the S&P 500. Thus, the shares in the Wilshire 4500 have smaller capitalization than those in the Wilshire 5000. The Russell 3000 encompasses the 3,000 largest companies in terms of their market capitalization. The Russell 1000 is limited to the largest 1,000 of those, and the Russell 2000 has the remaining smaller firms.

In the next chapter, investment "styles" are discussed. The specialized common stock market indexes that represent styles are discussed in the next chapter.

INTERNATIONAL EQUITY INVESTING

The purpose of investing in stocks of companies outside an investor's home country is to enhance returns and to reduce risk through diversification. Chapter 2 illustrated how these objectives may be achieved. In fact, some of the international stock market indexes discussed in this section were used in the application of mean-variance analysis illustrated in the Chapter 2 discussion.

Exhibits 6.4 and 6.5 provide the countries included in each index and the size, in U.S. dollars, of two major world stock indexes. Both indexes are products of Morgan Stanley Capital International (MSCI) and are the most widely used indexes of their type. Exhibit 6.4 provides the Europe, Australasia, and the Far East Index (EAFE Index). As the name indicates, EAFE includes the world's developed countries (with the exception of the United States and Canada). Japan has the largest market capitalization with the United Kingdom second. At the bottom of Exhibit 6.4 is the MSCI World Index, which includes EAFE as well as the United States and Canada. The United States comprises more than half of the MSCI World Index. Exhibit 6.5 provides the composition of the MSCI Emerging Market Index (EM), which covers developing countries in Asia, Latin America, Europe, and the Middle East. Note that Taiwan, Brazil, and Mexico have the highest market capitalization in the EM Index.

Multiple Listings on National Markets

Stocks of corporations can be listed for trading on exchanges in other countries as well as multiple exchanges in their home country. Stocks of some very large corporations are listed on exchanges in several countries. As an example, the number of stocks of firms from other countries that were listed on the German national exchange (Deutsche Bourse) is more than 7,500 (compared to only about 1,000 German domestic companies).

An important question is whether or not a share traded in different markets has different prices in those markets. The answer is "no" because investors can buy or sell the shares in any of the markets, and will arbitrage any meaningful differences in prices. To "arbitrage" is to exploit the presence of different prices for the same item in different markets. That is, if the price of a stock were significantly lower in country X than in country Y, investors would buy as many shares as they could in country X and sell shares in country Y. Investors would do this until the pressure they were putting on prices in both markets would drive the prices together. A decreasing gap in prices means that the arbitrage profits decline. Investors stop arbitraging when profits due to the price differences approximately equaled the costs of the transactions. Therefore, when the various transactions costs, including commissions, taxes, and costs of exchanging currencies, are fully considered, the price of any share tends to be the same across the different markets in which it is traded. In fact, the law of one price demands that securities of similar risk be priced identically to avoid arbitrage.

EXHIBIT 6.4   Capitalization of Stock Markets Included in the Morgan Stanley Capital International Indexes
(Data as of 12/31/01; Figures in $ Billions)

Europe and Far East (EAFE) Index

Market	Estimated Market Cap of the Country (in Billions)	Market Cap Included in the EAFE Index (in Billions)	% of Total EAFE Index
Europe			
United Kingdom	2,214.6	1,678.3	25.3%
France	1,167.6	699.2	10.5%
Germany	1,089.6	523.2	7.9%
Switzerland	620.2	493.1	7.4%
Netherlands	561.0	382.3	5.8%
Italy	528.4	272.5	4.1%
Spain	364.2	216.5	3.3%
Sweden	235.3	158.8	2.4%
Finland	193.9	153.8	2.3%
Belgium	152.8	73.9	1.1%
Denmark	85.3	57.5	0.9%
Ireland	70.7	54.0	0.8%
Norway	69.6	33.4	0.5%
Portugal	49.4	30.4	0.5%
Greece	83.2	23.8	0.4%
Austria	20.9	9.0	0.1%
Asia and Far East			
Japan	2,490.1	1,334.0	20.1%
Australia	372.3	244.7	3.7%
Hong Kong	275.0	129.4	2.0%
Singapore	116.7	58.2	0.9%
New Zealand	17.8	8.4	0.1%
Total	10,778.6	6,634.4	100.0%

World Index

Market	Estimated Market Cap	Market Cap Included in the World Index	% of Total World Index
U.S.	13,886.5	8,934.1	56.1%
EAFE	10,778.6	6,634.4	41.7%
Canada	611.1	346.8	2.2%
Total	25,276.2	15,915.3	100.0%

Notes:
1. Actual total market cap of a country is larger than what is included in the index.
2. MSCI indexes are now based on free float.
Source: Morgan Stanley Capital International, Blue Book, December 2001.

EXHIBIT 6.5   Capitalization of Stock Markets Included in the Morgan Stanley Capital International Index (Data as of 12/31/01; Figures in $ Billions)

Emerging Markets (EM) Index

Market	Estimated Market Cap of the Country	Market Cap Included in the EM Index	% of Total EM Index
Asia			
Korea	200.7	122.7	16.9%
Taiwan	286.4	108.5	15.0%
Malaysia	120.2	46.6	6.4%
China	141.8	44.6	6.2%
India	111.9	41.9	5.8%
Thailand	31.3	11.2	1.5%
Indonesia	29.9	5.3	0.7%
Philippines	44.6	5.0	0.7%
Pakistan	4.6	1.2	0.2%
Sri Lanka	1.4	0.3	0.0%
Latin America			
Mexico	136.7	73.0	10.1%
Brazil	188.4	66.6	9.2%
Chile	56.2	18.9	2.6%
Argentina	23.0	7.9	1.1%
Peru	10.8	2.8	0.4%
Venezuela	6.4	2.0	0.3%
Colombia	7.8	1.0	0.1%
Europe & Middle East			
South Africa	149.1	71.9	9.9%
Israel	58.6	31.2	4.3%
Russia	52.2	24.1	3.3%
Turkey	46.5	13.5	1.9%
Poland	24.9	8.1	1.1%
Hungary	10.4	6.7	0.9%
Czech Republic	9.8	4.4	0.6%
Morocco	9.0	1.9	0.3%
Egypt	22.3	1.4	0.2%
Jordan	6.2	1.3	0.2%
Total	1,791.1	724.0	100.0%

Notes:
1. Actual total market cap of a country is larger than what is included in the index.
2. MSCI indexes are now based on free float.
Source: Morgan Stanley Capital International, Red Book, December 2001.

Global Diversification: Correlation of World Equity Markets

The theoretical reason for the potential benefit of global diversification is provided in Chapter 2. Specifically, the inclusion of securities from other countries may increase a portfolio's expected return without increasing portfolio risk or variability in returns. The basis of the benefits from diversification is that international capital markets are less than perfectly positively correlated; that is, their returns do not increase and decrease in unison.

This dissimilarity in changes in market returns is not surprising. Different countries tend to have different experiences in such important areas as taxation, monetary management, banking policies, political goals and stability, population growth, and so on. And, because the primary factors influencing local stock prices are domestic or local events and policies, the prices of groups of stocks from different geographic regions tend to move up or down at somewhat different times and to somewhat different degrees. This pattern of dissimilar security price changes allows investors to diversify away a certain amount of individual country risk and creates the benefits of international or global investing.

Studies of correlations between countries reveal some interesting points. First, as just noted, international stock markets behave quite differently from one another; that is the correlation between their returns tends to be substantially less than unity. While the highest historical correlation has been between the United States and Canada (around 0.70), many correlation coefficients between countries have been less than 0.50. Thus, investors can diversify their holdings by spreading their portfolio across various global markets.

The second notable point is that geography and political alliances do influence correlations between markets. On average, stock prices in Germany and Japan move less similarly (historically the correlation has been a little more than 0.30) than do the stock prices between Germany and France (historically the correlation has been in the 0.60–0.70 range). Consequently, investors seeking diversification must choose carefully from among the various markets.

Finally, it is interesting that all the correlations are typically positive and well above zero. This implies the absence of complete dissimilarity in the movement of stock prices. The positive values mean that the world's stock prices are, like their economies, somewhat integrated. Thus, the benefit of international diversification has limits. In other words, the markets of the world are members of a somewhat loosely connected system of economies, and allocating funds among the various economies provides some, but not complete, reduction of variability in returns on securities. Furthermore, the benefits of diversification are diminished by global exogenous events such as the September 11, 2002 attack on the World

Trade Center in New York City. Under theses circumstances, global market influences dominate country-specific events.

There are two factors, however, that have tended to increase the correlation among the various countries' stock markets over time; that is, these factors have tended to reduce the advantages of diversification among the world's equity markets. One of these factors is behavioral and the other is due to the structure of the economies and their stock markets. The first relates to the behavior of investors during times of financial crisis, the times when investors would find diversification potentially the most beneficial. During such times, the reasoning goes, investors become very risk averse and flee to safety and liquidity. If a crisis starts in one country for a legitimate fundamental reason, investors will sell stocks in not just that country or region alone, but in many or all other countries as well. This "flight to quality" will result in unusually high temporary demand for low risk, high liquidity assets, and a simultaneous decrease in the demand for and price of all risky assets. Such a crisis mentality increases the correlation among all or most risky assets and does so at a time when diversification is needed most. This phenomenon is called "contagion."

The second factor that may increase international market correlations relates to the structure of national economies and their stock markets. A country's economy can be postulated to be composed of two sectors, a *global sector* and a *country sector*. The global sector provides goods and services to the global economy through international trade. Thus, the companies in a country's global sector respond more to global forces than to national or local forces. Microchip manufacturing, automobile manufacturing, and telecommunications are examples of global sectors. Economic forces affect microchip manufacturers across countries much more than they affect nonglobal companies in the same country. In contrast, the country sector produces goods and services mainly for local consumption. Companies in this sector are affected by economic forces more like the other local economy companies in the same country than like the global companies in that country. Railroads, retailing, and construction are examples of country sectors.

The conclusion is that companies in global sectors tend to follow the global market for their goods and services rather than their local economy and consequently do not contribute to global diversification. For example, the stocks of telecommunications companies all over the world declined significantly during 2000. Companies in the country sector, in contrast, follow the indigenous economy more closely. These stocks, therefore, would be more effective diversifying elements of a global portfolio. An application of this concept is that a U.S. stock investor should not buy the Finland stock index to pursue international stock diversification since Nokia, which manufactures telecommunications equipment, represents approximately 67% of the Finland stock index.

The evidence indicates that the share of global sectors has been increasing relative to country sectors in most developed countries during the last several years. As a result, globally diversified portfolios currently provide less market diversification than they did previously.[13] Overall, however, global diversification continues to provide a benefit to an investment portfolio, although the global diversification process may need to be performed more carefully by considering both the country and sector effects.

Stock Market Indexes

There are many stock indexes that chart and measure the performance of foreign stock markets. In every country where stock trading takes place, there is at least one index that measures general share price movements. If a country has more than one stock exchange, each exchange usually has its own index. Also, news organizations and financial advisory services create indexes.

In Japan, there are two major indexes, the Tokyo Stock Price Index (TOPIX), which is produced by the Tokyo Stock Exchange, and the Nikkei 225, which is calculated and published by the financial information firm Nihon Keizai Shimbun, Inc. The TOPIX is a composite index that is based on all the shares in the Tokyo market's First Section, a designation reserved for the established and large companies whose shares are the most actively traded and widely held. (The TOPIX is computed based on the included firms' market value, not just their prices.) The Nikkei 225 Stock Average (computed as a price weighted index in the same way as the Dow Jones 30) is based on 225 of the largest companies in the First Section.

The United Kingdom's London Stock Exchange is covered by several widely followed indexes. The Financial Times Industrial Ordinary Index is based on the prices of shares of 30 leading companies and is known as the FT 30. A broader index is the Financial Times–Stock Exchange 100, which is a market-value index and is commonly referred to as the FTSE 100 (and pronounced "Footsie 100"). This index is based on the shares of the largest 100 U.K. firms, whose market value makes up a majority of the market value of all U.K. equities. The Financial Times and the Institute for Actuaries produce indexes for different

---

[13] See Stefano Cavaglia, Christopher Brightman, and Michael Akid, "The Increasing Importance of Industry Factors," *Financial Analysts Journal* (September/October, 2000), pp. 41–54, and Sean P. Baca, Brian L. Garbe, and Richard Weiss, "The Rise of Sector Effects in Major Equity Markets," *Financial Analysts Journal*, (September/October 2000), pp. 34–40.

sectors and a composite index across sectors. These FT-A indexes are very broadly based, with the composite including more than 700 shares.

The primary German stock index is the DAX, which stands for the Deutscher Aktienindex, produced by the Frankfurt Stock Exchange. (The German name for this exchange is the Frankfurter Wertpapier börse. Some financial services regularly refer to the exchange by its initials, FWB.) The DAX is based on the 30 most actively traded shares listed on the Frankfurt exchange. The FAZ Index is another popular German index. Compiled by the daily newspaper the Frankfurter Allgemeine Zeitung, the FAZ Index is computed from the share prices of the 100 largest companies listed on the Frankfurt exchange.

In France, a national association of stockbrokers and the Paris Bourse produce an index based on the shares of 40 large and prominent firms traded on the exchange. The index is known as the CAC 40 Index, after the name of the Bourse's electronic trading system.

Other widely followed national stock indexes include the Hang Seng Index produced by the Stock Exchange of Hong Kong, the TSE 300 Composite of the Toronto Stock Exchange, and the Swiss Performance Index (SPI), which includes almost 400 firms and is published by the stock exchanges in that country.

To meet the increased interest in global equity investing, financial institutions have crafted several respected international equity indexes. The international equity index followed most by U.S. pension funds is the Morgan Stanley Capital International Europe, Australasia, and the Far East Index (EAFE Index). This index, started by Capital International in 1968 and acquired by Morgan Stanley in 1986, covers more than 2,000 companies in 21 countries. Relatively new international equity indexes include the Financial Times World Index (a joint product of the Institute of Actuaries in the United Kingdom, Goldman Sachs & Co., and Wood MacKenzie & Co.), the Salomon Smith Barney–Russell Global Equity Index (a joint product of Salomon Smith Barney and Frank Russell, Inc.), and the Global Index (a joint product of First Boston Corporation and London-based *Euromoney* magazine).

Global Depositary Receipts

When a corporation's equities are traded in a foreign market, whether they were issued in the foreign market or not, they are typically in the form of a *Global Depositary Receipt* (GDR). Banks issue GDRs as evidence of ownership of the underlying stock of a foreign corporation that the bank holds in trust. Each GDR may represent ownership of one or more shares of common stock of a corporation. The advantage of the GDR structure to the corporation is that the corporation does not have to comply with all of the regulatory issuing requirements of the foreign country where the stock is to be traded. GDRs are typically, but as discussed below not always, sponsored by the issuing corporation. That is, the issuing corporation will work with a bank to offer its common stock in a foreign country via the sale of GDRs.

As an example, consider the U.S. version of the GDR, the American Depositary Receipt (ADR). The combination of GDRs and ADRs for a given company is called simply a DR (Depository Receipt). ADRs are denominated in U.S. dollars and pay dividends in U.S. dollars. Although ADRs are priced in U.S. dollars and their dividends are paid in U.S. dollars, the basis for these payments is the local currency of the underlying stock. Thus, a change in the exchange rate between the local currency of the underlying corporation and the U.S. dollar will affect the U.S. dollar price and dividend of the ADR.

ADRs can be created in one of two ways. First, one or more banks or brokerage firms can assemble a large block of the shares of a foreign corporation and issue ADRs without the participation of the foreign corporation. These are nonsponsored ADRs. More typically, however, the foreign corporation that seeks to have its stock traded in the United States sponsors the ADR. In these instances, there is only one depositary bank that issues the ADR. Periodic financial reports (in English) are provided by the issuing corporation to the holders of the ADR. The Bank of New York is the leading U.S. depository bank for ADRs.

ADRs can either be traded on one of the two major organized stock exchanges (the New York Stock Exchange and the American Stock Exchange) or traded on the over-the-counter market. The nonsponsored ADR is typically traded on the over-the-counter market. Since ADRs can be continuously created to meet investor demand, they provide the same trading liquidity as the home market securities they represent.

There are several advantages to a U.S. investor of the purchase an ADR of an international company rather than holding the international stock directly. First, the investor can trade the stock on a U.S. market (exchange or OTC) during U.S. hours and according to U.S. trading practices. Second, the investor makes and receives payments in U.S. dollars rather than foreign currency, although as indicated above, the investor is subject to foreign exchange risk. Finally, the U.S. investor can use a U.S., rather than a global, custodian, which can be easier and save costs and, in some cases, avoid country-specific taxes.

As U.S. investors, both institutional and individual, have become more open to international investing, the popularity of U.S. ADRs has increased significantly. There are such a large number of ADRs listed in the United States that Merrill Lynch has constructed ADR indexes for various regions, countries, and sectors. In addition, the Bank of New

York has created a group of ADR indexes, a Composite Index, three regional subindexes (Europe, Asia, and Latin America), three market subindexes (Developed, Emerging, and Euroland), and 20 country indexes. These indexes are capitalization weighted and are calculated continuously throughout the trading day.

CHAPTER 7

Tracking Error and Common Stock Portfolio Management

Raman Vardharaj
Senior Quantitative Analyst
The Guardian Life Insurance Company of America

Frank J. Jones, Ph.D.
Chief Investment Officer
The Guardian Life Insurance Company of America

Frank J. Fabozzi, Ph.D., CFA
Adjunct Professor of Finance
School of Management
Yale University

Tracking error is a key concept in understanding the potential performance of a common stock portfolio relative to a benchmark index and the actual performance of a common stock portfolio relative to a benchmark index. Tracking error can be used to measure the degree of active management by a portfolio manager. In this chapter, we will describe this measure, explain how tracking error is computed, and identify some of the factors that affect tracking error. We will see how tracking error is applied in common portfolio management—both common stock and fixed income portfolio management—in later chapters.

163

DEFINITION OF TRACKING ERROR

As explained in Chapter 2, the risk of a portfolio can be measured by the standard deviation of portfolio returns. This statistical measure provides a range around the average return of a portfolio within which the actual return over a period is likely to fall with some specific probability. The mean return and standard deviation (or volatility) of a portfolio can be calculated over a period of time. For example, the standard deviation of some common stock market indexes during the 10-year period ending November 2001 based on monthly index returns are shown below:

Index	Annual Standard Deviation
S&P 500	14.4%
S&P MidCap 400	16.6%
Russell 2000	18.2%
Wilshire 5000	14.7%

The standard deviation or volatility of a portfolio or a market index is an absolute number. A portfolio manager or client can also ask what the variation of the return of a portfolio is relative to a specified benchmark. Such variation is called the portfolio's *tracking error.*

Specifically, tracking error measures the dispersion of a portfolio's returns relative to the returns of its benchmark. That is, tracking error is the standard deviation of the portfolio's *active return* where active return is defined as:

active return = portfolio's actual return − benchmark's actual return

A portfolio created to match the benchmark index (i.e., an index fund) that regularly has zero active returns (that is, always matches its benchmark's actual return) would have a tracking error of zero. But a portfolio that is actively managed that takes positions substantially different from the benchmark would likely have large active returns, both positive and negative, and thus would have an annual tracking error of, say, 5% to 10%.

To find the tracking error of a portfolio, it is first necessary to specify the benchmark. The tracking error of a portfolio, as indicated, is its standard deviation relative to the benchmark, *not* its total standard deviation. For example, an index fund that exactly matches the S&P 500 would have a tracking error of 0% but an overall standard deviation of 14.4% (as noted above), which is the standard deviation of its benchmark. Exhibit 7.1 presents the information used to calculate the tracking error for a hypothetical portfolio and benchmark using 30 weekly observations. The fourth column in the exhibit shows the active return for the week. It is from the data in this column that the tracking error is computed. As reported in the exhibit, the standard deviation of the weekly active returns is 0.54%. This value is then annualized by multiplying by the square root of 52—52 representing the number of weeks in a year.[1] This gives a value of 3.89%.

Given the tracking error, a range for the possible portfolio active return and corresponding range for the portfolio can be estimated assuming that the active returns are normally distributed. For example, assume the following:

> benchmark = S&P 500
> expected return on S&P 500 = 20%
> tracking error relative to S&P 500 = 2%

then[2]

Number of Standard Deviations	Range for Portfolio Active Return	Corresponding Range for Portfolio Return	Probability
1	±2%	18%–22%	67%
2	±4%	16%–24%	95%
3	±6%	14%–26%	99%

Tracking Error for an Active/Passive Portfolio

As explained in the previous chapter, a manager can pursue a blend of an active and passive (i.e., indexing) strategy. That is, a manager can construct a portfolio such that a certain percentage of the portfolio is indexed to some benchmark index and the balance actively managed. Assume that the passively managed portion (i.e., the indexed portion) has a zero tracking error relative to the index. For such a strategy, we can show (after some algebraic manipulation) that the tracking error for the overall portfolio would be as follows:

> portfolio tracking error relative to index
> = (percent of portfolio actively managed)
> × (tracking error of the actively managed portion relative to index)

---

[1] If the observations were monthly rather than weekly, the monthly tracking error would be annualized by multiplying by the square root of 12.
[2] The probabilities are based on a normal probability distribution.

EXHIBIT 7.1   Data and Calculation for Active Return, Alpha, and
Information Ratio

Week	Weekly Returns (%)		
	Portfolio	Benchmark	Active
1	3.69%	3.72%	−0.02%
2	−0.56	−1.09	0.53
3	−1.41	−1.35	−0.06
4	0.96	0.34	0.62
5	−4.07	−4.00	−0.07
6	1.27	0.91	0.37
7	−0.39	−0.08	−0.31
8	−3.31	−2.76	−0.55
9	2.19	2.11	0.09
10	−0.02	−0.40	0.37
11	−0.46	−0.42	−0.05
12	0.09	0.71	−0.62
13	−1.93	−1.99	0.06
14	−1.91	−2.37	0.46
15	1.89	1.98	−0.09
16	−3.75	−4.33	0.58
17	−3.38	−4.22	0.84
18	0.60	0.62	−0.02
19	−10.81	−11.60	0.79
20	6.63	7.78	−1.15
21	3.52	2.92	0.59
22	1.24	1.89	−0.66
23	−0.63	−1.66	1.03
24	3.04	2.90	0.14
25	−1.73	−1.58	−0.15
26	2.81	3.05	−0.23
27	0.40	1.64	−1.23
28	1.03	1.03	0.01
29	−0.94	−0.95	0.00
30	1.45	1.66	−0.21

Average of active returns = 0.04%
Standard deviation of active returns = 0.54%

Annualizing
Annual average = Weekly average × 52
Annual variance = Weekly variance × 52
Annual std dev = Weekly std dev × ($52^{0.5}$)

Hence, on an annual basis,
alpha   = 1.83% (= 0.04% × 52 = annualized average of weekly active returns)
tracking error = 3.89% (= 0.54% × [$52^{0.5}$] = annualized std dev of weekly active returns)
information ratio = alpha/tracking error = 1.83%/3.89% = 0.47

An enhanced index fund differs from an index fund in that it deviates from the index holdings in small amounts and hopes to slightly outperform the index through those small deviations. In terms of an active/passive strategy, the manager allocates a small percentage of the portfolio to be actively managed. The reason is that in case the bets prove detrimental, then the underperformance would be small. Thus, realized returns would always deviate from index returns only by small amounts. There are many enhancing strategies. Suppose that a manager whose benchmark is the S&P 500 pursues an enhanced indexing strategy allocating only 5% of the portfolio to be actively managed and 95% indexed. Assume further that the tracking error of the actively managed portion is 15% with respect to the S&P 500. The portfolio would then have a tracking error calculated as follows:

> percent of portfolio actively managed relative to S&P 500 = 5%
> tracking error relative to S&P 500 = 15%
> portfolio's tracking error relative to S&P 500 = 5% × 15% = 0.75%

COMPONENTS OF TRACKING ERROR

As explained in the previous chapter, there are two distinct approaches to portfolio selection. The first is a top-down approach. Here the manager tries to pick broad economic themes such as sectors, style, size, etc., which are likely to outperform in the coming periods and holds stocks that are consistent with the chosen theme. The second is a bottom-up approach, where the manager picks each individual stock in the portfolio on its own merit.

Insofar as the themes or stocks emphasized in the portfolio differ from those in the benchmark (through overweights and underweights), there will be a tracking error. We can then view the tracking error as arising partly from the theme-picking and partly from the stock-picking.

Since top-down managers believe they can add value mainly through discerning trends in returns associated with broad themes, they would want to reduce the portion of their portfolio's tracking error that arises from stock-specific reasons.

Bottom-up managers believe it is difficult, if not impossible, to forecast trends in themes. Returns associated with such broad themes tend to be volatile and this can amplify mistakes. Such managers believe it is more prudent to place a lot of small bets via stock selection than to place a few large bets via theme selection. Bottom-up managers would, therefore, seek to reduce the portion of the tracking error of their portfolios that comes from theme-specific reasons.

To answer the needs of these two types of managers, it would be useful to decompose a portfolio's tracking error along these lines. Fortunately, this can be done. BARRA's portfolio risk analysis software, for example, permits such a decomposition.

FORWARD LOOKING VERSUS BACK LOOKING TRACKING ERROR

In Exhibit 7.1 the tracking error of the hypothetical portfolio is shown based on the active returns reported. However, the performance shown is the result of the portfolio manager's decisions during those 30 weeks with respect to portfolio positioning issues such as beta, sector allocations, style tilt (i.e., value versus growth), stock selections, etc. Hence, we can call the tracking error calculated from these trailing active returns a *backward looking tracking error*. It is also called the *ex-post tracking error*.

One problem with a backward looking tracking error is that it does not reflect the effect of current decisions by the portfolio manager on the future active returns and hence the future tracking error that may be realized. If, for example, the manager significantly changes the portfolio beta or sector allocations today, then the backward looking tracking error that is calculated using data from prior periods would not accurately reflect the current portfolio risks going forward. That is, the backward looking tracking error will have little predictive value and can be misleading regarding portfolio risks going forward.

The portfolio manager needs a forward looking estimate of tracking error to accurately reflect the portfolio risk going forward. The way this is done in practice is by using the services of a commercial vendor that has a model, called a multi-factor risk model, that has defined the risks associated with a benchmark index. Such a model is described in Chapter 13. Statistical analysis of the historical return data of the stocks in the benchmark index are used to obtain the factors and quantify their risks. (This involves the use of variances and correlations.) Using the manager's current portfolio holdings, the portfolio's current exposure to the various factors can be calculated and compared to the benchmark's exposures to the factors. Using the differential factor exposures and the risks of the factors, a *forward looking tracking error* for the portfolio can be computed. This tracking error is also referred to as the *predicted tracking error* or *ex ante tracking error*.

There is no guarantee that the forward looking tracking error at the start of, say, a year would exactly match the backward looking tracking error calculated at the end of the year. There are two reasons for this.

The first is that as the year progresses and changes are made to the portfolio, the forward looking tracking error estimate would change to reflect the new exposures. The second is that the accuracy of the forward looking tracking error depends on the extent of the stability in the variances and correlations that were used in the analysis. These problems notwithstanding, the average of forward looking tracking error estimates obtained at different times during the year will be reasonably close to the backward looking tracking error estimate obtained at the end of the year.

Each of these estimates has its use. The forward looking tracking error is useful in risk control and portfolio construction. The manager can immediately see the likely effect on tracking error of any intended change in the portfolio. Thus, she can do a what-if analysis of various portfolio strategies and eliminate those that would result in tracking errors beyond her tolerance for risk. The backward looking tracking error can be useful for assessing actual performance analysis, such as the information ratio discussed next.

INFORMATION RATIO

Alpha is the average active return over a time period. Since backward looking tracking error measures the standard deviation of a portfolio's active return, it is different from alpha. A portfolio does not have backward looking tracking error simply because of outperformance or underperformance. For instance, consider a portfolio that outperforms (or underperforms) its benchmark by exactly 10 basis points every month. This portfolio would have a backward looking tracking error of zero and a positive (negative) alpha of 10 basis points. In contrast, consider a portfolio that outperforms its benchmark by 10 basis points during half the months and underperforms by 10 bp during the other months. This portfolio would have a backward looking tracking error that is positive but an alpha equal to zero. (Note that in some texts, alpha and tracking error are calculated respectively as the average and the standard deviation of the beta-adjusted active return, instead of the total active return.)

The *information ratio* combines alpha and tracking error as follows:

$$\text{Information ratio} = \frac{\text{alpha}}{\text{Backward looking tracking error}}$$

The information ratio is essentially a reward-to-risk ratio. The reward is the *average* of the active return, that is, alpha. The risk is the standard deviation of the active return, the tracking error, and, more specifically, backward looking tracking error. The higher the information ratio, the better the manager performed relative to the risk assumed.

To illustrate the calculation of the information ratio, consider the active returns for the hypothetical portfolio shown in Exhibit 7.1. The weekly average active return is 0.04%. Annualizing the weekly average active return by multiplying by 52 gives an alpha of 1.83%. Since the backward tracking error is 3.89%, the information ratio is 0.47 (1.83%/ 3.89%)

DETERMINANTS OF TRACKING ERROR

There are several factors that affect the level of tracking error. In the following sections we discuss the major factors: number of stocks in the portfolio, portfolio market capitalization and style difference relative to the benchmark, sector deviation from the benchmark, market volatility, and portfolio beta.

Number of Stocks in the Portfolio

Tracking error decreases as the portfolio progressively includes more of the stocks that are in the benchmark index. This effect is illustrated in Exhibit 7.2 which shows the effect of portfolio size for a large cap portfolio benchmarked to the S&P 500, a mid cap portfolio benchmarked to the S&P 400, and a small cap portfolio benchmarked to the S&P 600.[3] Notice that an optimally chosen portfolio of just 50 stocks can track the S&P 500 within 2.3%. For mid cap and small cap stocks, the corresponding tracking errors are 3.5% and 4.3%.

In contrast, tracking error increases as the portfolio progressively includes more stocks that are not in the benchmark. This effect is illustrated in Exhibit 7.3. In this case, the benchmark index is the S&P 100 and the portfolio progressively includes more and more stocks from the S&P 500 that are not in the S&P 100. The result is that the tracking error with respect to the S&P 100 rises.

---

[3] The tracking errors for the various portfolios were obtained from BARRA Aegis software. These are forward-looking tracking errors rather than backward-looking tracking errors. Also, the portfolios were optimally constructed to minimize tracking error.

EXHIBIT 7.2   Tracking Error versus the Number of Benchmark Stocks in the Portfolio

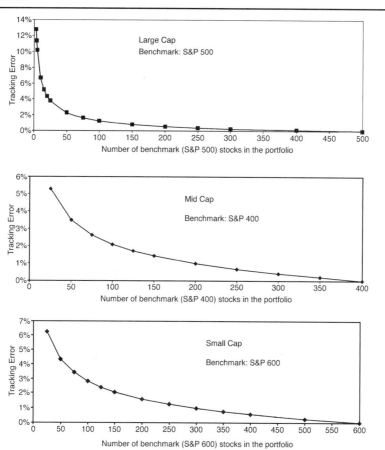

EXHIBIT 7.3   Tracking Error versus the Number of Non-Benchmark Stocks in the Portfolio

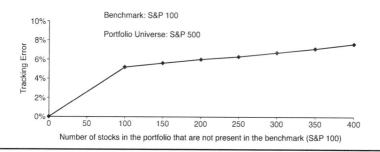

EXHIBIT 7.4   The Effects of Market Cap and Style on Tracking Error

Portfolios used for comparison with S&P 500[a]
Investment Valuation

Value	Blend	Growth	Size (Cap)
S&P 500 Value	S&P 500	S&P 500 Growth	Large
S&P 400 Value	S&P 400	S&P 400 Growth	Medium
S&P 600 Value	S&P 600	S&P 600 Growth	Small

Tracking Error with respect to S&P 500
Investment Valuation

Value	Blend	Growth	Size (Cap)
3.34%	0.36%[b]	2.83%	Large
7.56%	7.07%	7.97%	Medium
9.03%	8.55%	9.59%	Small

[a] Portfolio is restricted to 250 stocks, chosen to minimize tracking error.
[b] This number would be 0% if the portfolio is not restricted to 250 names and is allowed to hold all 500 names.

Portfolio Market Cap and Style Difference Relative to the Benchmark

In Chapter 8 the concept of equity styles and Morningstar's equity style classification system for mutual funds based on market capitalization ("cap") of large, medium, and small and style of value, blend, and growth was explained. We will use the Morningstar classification system here to see how tracking error is related to market capitalization and overall style (growth versus value). The benchmark index used is the S&P 500. Portfolios with a maximum of 250 stocks are chosen from universes of various cap sizes and styles and compared with the S&P 500.

The results are shown in Exhibit 7.4. It can be seen that tracking error increases as the average market cap of the portfolio deviates from that of the benchmark index. Tracking error also increases as the overall style (growth/value) of the portfolio deviates from that of the benchmark index.

First, holding style constant, tracking error rises when the cap size difference increases. For example, a mid cap blend portfolio has a tracking error of 7.07% while a small cap blend portfolio has a tracking error of 8.55% with respect to the S&P 500, which is a large cap blend portfolio. Second, for a given cap size, tracking error is greater when the style is either growth or value than when it is the blend.

The top half Exhibit 7.5 shows portfolios that deviate from the S&P 500 either in cap size or in style and have the same tracking error. As can be seen, the farther a portfolio is from the center of the Morningstar equity fund box for large cap blend stocks (proxied by S&P 500), the greater is its tracking error. The bottom half of Exhibit 7.5 illustrates the same phenomenon for small cap stocks.

EXHIBIT 7.5 Size and Style versus Tracking Error

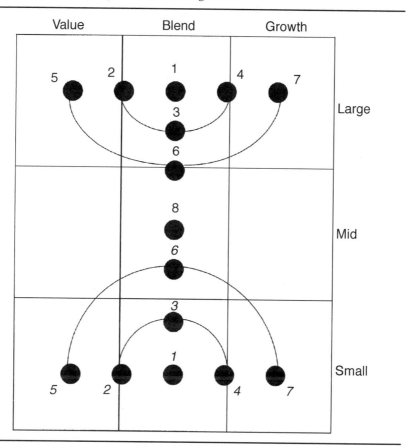

Investment valuation is along the horizontal axis and market cap (size) is along the vertical axis.

Large Cap

Portfolio 1 has a tracking error of 0%. Portfolios 2, 3, 4 have nearly similar tracking errors of around 2.1%. Portfolios 5, 6, 7 have nearly similar tracking errors of around 4.2%. Portfolio 8 has a tracking error of 8.5%.

Small Cap

Portfolio 1 has a tracking error of 0%. Portfolios 2, 3, 4 have nearly similar tracking errors of around 1.7%. Portfolios 5, 6, 7 have nearly similar tracking errors of around 3.4%. Portfolio 8 has a tracking error of 4.9%.

EXHIBIT 7.6   Tracking Error Increases as Sector Bets Increase

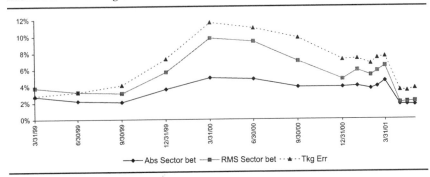

Sector deviation is defined as the fund portfolio weight in a sector in excess of the benchmark weight in that sector. By definition, the sum of all sector deviations as well as their average would be zero. We define the "Abs Sector Bet" as the average of the absolute values of the sector deviations. The "RMS Sector Bet" is the root mean square sector deviation. That is, the sector deviations are squared and then averaged. Then, the square root of this average is computed. This is the RMS sector bet. The Abs Sector Bet and the RMS sector bet are two indicators of the overall level of sector bets in the portfolio.

Sector Deviation from the Benchmark

When a portfolio's allocations to various economic sectors differ from those of its benchmark, it results in tracking error. In general, when the differences in sector allocation increase, the tracking error increases.

To present a real world example of the effect of sector bets on tracking error, we analyzed an actual mutual fund portfolio's sector bets (i.e., differences between the portfolio and the benchmark in the percentages allocated to various sectors) and tracking error over a 2-year period covering March 31, 1999 to March 31, 2001. The results are shown in Exhibit 7.6. We define sector deviation as the portfolio's weight in a sector in excess of the benchmark weight in that sector. By definition, the sum of all sector deviations as well as their average would both be zeros, so a measure must be devised to avoid this. There are two measures shown in the exhibit that overcome this problem and the measures are explained in the note to the exhibit. As can be seen from Exhibit 7.6, in general, the tracking error increased as the level of sector bets increased.

Market Volatility

Managed portfolios generally hold only a fraction of the assets in their benchmark. Given this, a highly volatile benchmark index (as measured in terms of standard deviation) would be harder to track closely than a generally less volatile benchmark index.

EXHIBIT 7.7   Tracking Error and Dramatic Shortfall

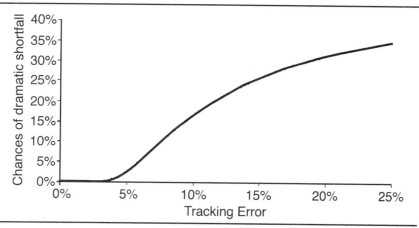

This can be seen by using the market model. Tracking error based on the SMM is:

$$\text{Tracking error} = [(\beta - 1)^2 \, \text{Var}(R_m)^2 + \text{Var}(e)]^{\frac{1}{2}}$$

As can be seen from the above equation, tracking error increases with market volatility, $\text{Var}(R_m)^2$. Substituting a market index for the market in the equation above demonstrates that tracking error increases with the volatility of the index.

As market volatility rises, the portfolio tracking error increases. This correspondingly increases the probability of "dramatic underperformance," by which we mean an underperformance of 10% or more. This can be seen in Exhibit 7.7. On the horizontal axis of the exhibit is the tracking error and on the vertical axis is the probability of a shortfall of 10% or more from the benchmark index.[4]

As the tracking error rises, the probability of dramatic outperformance increases just as much as the probability of dramatic underperformance. But, the portfolio management consequences of these two types of extreme relative performances are not symmetric—dramatic underperformance can cause a manager to be terminated. Another implication is that since an increase in market volatility increases tracking error and thereby the chances of dramatic underperformance, there is an increased need for managers to monitor the portfolio tracking error more frequently and closely during periods of high market volatility.

---

[4] In this calculation, we assumed normal distribution of active returns and an alpha of -0.26%, which is the average alpha for domestic stock mutual funds.

EXHIBIT 7.8   Tracking Error and Beta

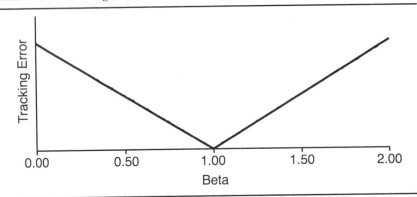

Portfolio Beta

The beta for the market portfolio is 1 and beta for the risk-free portfolio (cash) is zero. Suppose an investor holds a combination of cash and the market portfolio. Then, the portfolio beta falls below 1. The managed portfolio is less sensitive to systematic risk than the market, and is therefore less risky than the market. Conversely, when the investor holds a leveraged market portfolio, by borrowing at the risk-free rate and investing in the market portfolio, the beta is above 1, and the portfolio is more risky than the market.

To quantify the relationship between portfolio beta and tracking error, look again at the formula for the tracking error from the SMM given above. As can been, the portfolio tracking error with respect to the market portfolio, increases both when the beta falls below 1 and when the beta rises above 1. So, as the portfolio increases the proportion of cash held, even though its absolute risk falls, its tracking error risk rises. As shown in Exhibit 7.8, tracking error rises linearly as the beta deviates from 1.

In the above example, we make the simplistic assumption that the manager only chooses between holding the market portfolio and cash when making changes to its beta. In the more general case where the fund can hold any number of stocks in any proportion, its beta can differ from 1 due to other reasons. But, even in this general case, the tracking error increases when the portfolio beta deviates from the market beta.

MARGINAL CONTRIBUTION TO TRACKING ERROR

Since tracking error arises from various bets (some intentional and some unintentional) placed by the manager through overweights and underweights relative to the benchmark index, it would be useful to understand how sensitive the tracking error is to small changes in each of these bets.

Suppose, for example, a portfolio initially has an overweight of 3% in the semiconductor industry relative to its benchmark index, and that the tracking error is 6%. Suppose that the tracking error subsequently increases to 6.1% due to the semiconductor industry weight in the portfolio increasing by 1% (and hence the overweight goes to 4%). Then, it can be said that this industry adds 0.1% to tracking error for every 1% increase in its weight. That is, its *marginal contribution to tracking error* is 0.1%. This would hold only at the margin, i.e., for a small change, and not for large changes.

Marginal contributions can be also calculated for individual stocks. If the risk analysis employs a multi-factor risk model, then similar marginal contribution estimates can be obtained for the risk factors also.

Generally, marginal contributions would be positive for overweighted industries (or stocks) and negative for underweighted ones. The reason is as follows. If a portfolio already holds an excess weight in an industry, then increasing this weight would cause the portfolio to diverge further from the benchmark index. This increased divergence adds to tracking error, leading to a positive marginal contribution for this industry. Suppose, however, the portfolio has an underweight in an industry. Then, increasing the portfolio weight in this industry would make the portfolio converge towards the benchmark, thus reducing tracking error. This leads to a negative marginal contribution for this industry.

An analysis of the marginal contributions can be useful for a manager who seeks to alter the portfolio tracking error. Suppose a manager wishes to reduce the tracking error, then she should reduce portfolio overweights in industries (or stocks) with the highest positive marginal contributions. Alternatively, she can reduce the underweights (i.e., increase the overall weights) in industries (or stocks) with the most negative marginal contributions. Such changes would be most effective in reducing the tracking error while minimizing the necessary turnover and the associated expenses.

RISK BUDGETS

Thus far our focus has been on tracking error for common stock portfolios. Applications involving tracking error for fixed income portfolio management are provided in Section Three of this book. We conclude this chapter by explaining how an institutional investor such as a pension fund or an insurance company that invests in several asset classes can use tracking error.

Managers of portfolios that include investments in multiple asset classes often employ separate specialist managers for each asset class whose performances are judged relative to the appropriate benchmarks (e.g., S&P 500 for the stock portfolio manager, Lehman Aggregate bond index for the bond portfolio manager, etc.) The overall portfolio may have a custom benchmark that is a weighted combination of these individual benchmarks (for e.g., 30% of the S&P 500 plus 40% of the Lehman Aggregate etc.). Typically, in the management of such portfolios, the chief investments officer (CIO) is responsible for the asset allocation decision—that is, the decision as to the percentage of the portfolio that should be invested in each asset class. The individual asset class managers (the specialists) are responsible for the security selection decisions within their asset classes. Both these decisions have an effect on the tracking error of the overall portfolio.

An interesting question in such a context is: Given a *target* tracking error for the overall portfolio, what are the implied targets for the individual asset class portfolios? Such targets are also referred to as "budgets." How should the tracking error budgets be chosen for each of the specialist managers? A simple solution would be to enforce a common tracking error target for each portfolio. But, that ignores various issues such as correlations, asset class weights, alphas, and information ratios.

A second solution would be to maximize the overall portfolio information ratio. As mentioned earlier, this is the ratio of the portfolio alpha to its tracking error. A third solution would be to maximize the overall portfolio utility, which is the excess of the portfolio expected return over its risk (scaled by risk tolerance). The solutions to these maximization problems can then be used to calculate the optimal tracking error for each manager. In these approaches, the allowable tracking error for a manager would increase with the manager's expected information ratio and expected alpha. The problem with these approaches, however, is that implementation requires robust and predictive estimates for alphas and information ratios. In reality, these estimates are hard to obtain.

Tracking errors for the overall portfolio and the asset class portfolios need to be periodically monitored to check if they are in line with the budgets. If, for example, the stock portfolio tracking error rises beyond its budget, what should the CIO do? This would depend on whether the stock portfolio manager's perceived ability (i.e., expected alpha) has risen in line with the rise in tracking error. If not, something needs to be done, though it is not clear what. One of the following could be done: (1) the CIO could ask the stock portfolio manager to reduce tracking error; (2) the CIO could reduce the allocation to that asset class; or (3) the CIO could seek to alter the correlation of the stock portfolio with the other asset class portfolios.

An interesting finding from such analyses is that, under reasonable assumptions, most of the tracking error risk of the overall portfolio comes from the asset allocation decision, and only a small proportion comes from the security selection decisions of the individual portfolio managers.[5]

SUMMARY

Tracking error measures the variation of a portfolio's return relative to its benchmark index. As the portfolio differs from its benchmark index in terms of the number of stocks held, their average market caps, sector allocations, and beta, its tracking error rises. Tracking error also rises in volatile markets. For a portfolio manager, the risk of heavily underperforming the benchmark rises as the tracking error increases. Thus tracking error is an important indicator of portfolio performance and should be monitored frequently.

---

[5] See David C. Blitz and Jouke Hottinga, "Tracking Error Allocation," *Journal of Portfolio Management* (Summer 2001) and William F. Sharpe, "Budgeting and Monitoring the Risk of Defined Benefit Funds," September 2001, on website www.stanford.edu/~wfsharpe.

CHAPTER 8

Common Stock Portfolio Management Strategies

Frank J. Fabozzi, Ph.D., CFA
Adjunct Professor of Finance
School of Management
Yale University

James L. Grant, Ph.D.
JLG Research/Adjunct Professor of Finance
Baruch College (CUNY)

In this chapter we review strategies for equity portfolios, taking a close look at active and passive management, the decision as to whether or not to pursue an active or passive management, style investing, and the different types of active strategies that can be employed. We begin the chapter with a discussion of the equity portfolio management process.

INTEGRATING THE EQUITY PORTFOLIO MANAGEMENT PROCESS

In Chapter 1, the investment management process was described as a series of five distinct steps. In practice, portfolio management requires an integrated approach. There must be recognition that superior investment performance results when valuable ideas are implemented in a cost-efficient manner. The process of investing—as opposed to the process of investment—includes innovative stock selection and portfolio strategies as well as efficient cost structures for the implementation of any portfolio strategy.[1] Exhibit 8.1 highlights the importance of an integrated approach to managing equity portfolios. It recognizes that the value added by the manager is the result of information value less the implementation cost of trading. This difference in value is referred to as "captured value," a term coined by Wayne Wagner and Mark Edwards.[2]

This view that an investing process requires an integrated approach to portfolio management is reinforced by BARRA, a vendor of analytical systems used by portfolio managers. BARRA emphasizes that superior investment performance is the product of careful attention paid by equity managers to the following four elements:

- Forming reasonable return expectations
- Controlling portfolio risk to demonstrate investment prudence
- Controlling trading costs
- Monitoring total investment performance

Accordingly, the investing process that includes these four elements are all equally important in realizing superior investment performance. In Chapter 4, several quantitative models for general expected returns were described. As for the second element, we will discuss the process of controlling risk in this chapter and in more detail in Chapter 13. Trading costs were explained in Chapter 6 and in Chapter 13, monitoring the total investment performance of an equity portfolio is explained.

EXHIBIT 8.1   The Investing Process

Source: See Wayne H. Wagner and Mark Edwards, "Implementing Investment Strategies: The Art and Science of Investing," Chapter 11 in Frank J. Fabozzi (ed.), *Active Equity Portfolio Management* (New Hope, PA: Frank J. Fabozzi Associates, 1998).

---

[1] Wayne H. Wagner and Mark Edwards, "Implementing Investment Strategies: The Art and Science of Investing," Chapter 11 in Frank J. Fabozzi (ed.), *Active Equity Portfolio Management* (New Hope, PA: Frank J. Fabozzi Associates, 1998).
[2] Wagner and Edwards, "Implementing Investment Strategies: The Art and Science of Investing."

CAPITAL MARKET PRICE EFFICIENCY

Later in this chapter we will explain the two major types of portfolio strategies: active versus passive. The decision as to which of the two approaches to pursue depends on the price efficiency of the market. A price efficient market is one in which security prices at all times fully reflect all available information that is relevant to their valuation. When a market is price efficient, investment strategies pursued to outperform a broad-based stock market index will not consistently produce superior returns after adjusting for risk and transaction costs.

Numerous studies have examined the pricing efficiency of the stock market. While it is not our intent in this chapter to provide a comprehensive review of these studies, we can summarize the basic findings and implications for common stock portfolio management strategies.

Forms of Efficiency

There are three different forms of pricing efficiency: (1) weak form, (2) semi-strong form, and (3) strong form. The distinctions among these forms rests in the relevant information that is believed to be taken into consideration in the price of the security at all times. Weak-form efficiency means that the price of the security reflects the past price and trading history of the security. Semi-strong–form efficiency means that the price of the security fully reflects all public information (which, of course, includes but is not limited to, historical price and trading patterns). Strong-form efficiency exists in a market where the price of a security reflects all information, whether it is publicly available or known only to insiders such as the firm's managers or directors.

The preponderance of empirical evidence supports the claim that the U.S. common stock market is efficient in the weak form. The evidence emerges from numerous sophisticated tests that explore whether or not historical price movements can be used to project future prices in such a way as to produce returns above what one would expect from market movements and the risk class of the security. Such returns are known as *positive abnormal returns*. The implications are that investors who follow a strategy of selecting common stocks solely on the basis of price patterns or trading volume—such investors are referred to as *technical analysts* or *chartists*—should not expect to do better than the market. In fact, they may fare worse because of higher transactions costs associated with frequent buying and selling of stocks.

Evidence on price efficiency in the semi-strong form is mixed. Some studies support the proposition of efficiency when they suggest that investors who select stocks on the basis of fundamental security analysis—which consists of analyzing financial statements, the quality of management, and the economic environment of a company—will not outperform the market. This result is certainly reasonable. There are so many analysts using the same approach, with the same publicly available data, that the price of the stock remains in line with all the relevant factors that determine value. On the other hand, a sizable number of studies have produced evidence indicating that there have been instances and patterns of pricing inefficiency in the stock market over long periods of time. Economists and financial analysts often label these examples of inefficient pricing as "anomalies" in the market, that is, phenomena that cannot be easily explained by accepted theory.

Empirical tests of strong form pricing efficiency fall into two groups: (1) studies of the performance of professional money managers, and (2) studies of the activities of insiders (individuals who are either company directors, major officers, or major stockholders). Studying the performance of professional money managers to test the strong form of pricing efficiency has been based on the belief that professional managers have access to better information than the general public. Whether or not this is true is moot because the empirical evidence suggests professional managers have been unable to outperform the market consistently. In contrast, evidence based on the activities of insiders has generally revealed that this group often achieves higher risk-adjusted returns than the stock market. Of course, insiders could not consistently earn those high abnormal returns if the stock prices fully reflected all relevant information about the values of the firms. Thus, the empirical evidence on insiders argues against the notion that the market is efficient in the strong-form sense.

Implications for Investing in Common Stock

Common stock investment strategies can be classified into two broad categories: active strategies and passive strategies. Active strategies are those that attempt to outperform the market by one or more of the following: (1) timing market transactions, such as in the case of technical analysis, (2) identifying undervalued or overvalued stocks using fundamental security analysis, or (3) selecting stocks according to one of the market anomalies. Obviously, the decision to pursue an active strategy must be based on the belief that there is some type of gain from such costly efforts, but gains are possible only if pricing inefficiencies exist. The particular strategy chosen depends on why the investor believes this is the case.

Investors who believe that the market prices stocks efficiently should accept the implication that attempts to outperform the market cannot be systematically successful, except by luck. This implication does not mean that investors should shun the stock market, but rather that they should pursue a passive strategy, one that does not attempt to outperform the market. Is there an optimal investment strategy for someone who holds this belief in the pricing efficiency of the stock market? Indeed there is. The theoretical basis rests on modern portfolio theory and capital market theory. According to modern portfolio theory, the market portfolio offers the highest level of return per unit of risk in a market that is price efficient. A portfolio of financial assets with characteristics similar to those of a portfolio consisting of the entire market—the market portfolio—will capture the pricing efficiency of the market.

But how can such a passive strategy be implemented? More specifically, what is meant by a market portfolio, and how should that portfolio be constructed? In theory, the market portfolio consists of all financial assets, not just common stock. The reason is that investors compare all investment opportunities, not just stock, when committing their capital. Thus, our principles of investing must be based on capital market theory, not just stock market theory. When the theory is applied to the stock market, the market portfolio has been interpreted as consisting of a large universe of common stocks. But how much of each common stock should be purchased when constructing the market portfolio? Theory states that the chosen portfolio should be an appropriate fraction of the market portfolio; hence, the weighting of each stock in the market portfolio should be based on its relative market capitalization. Thus, if the aggregate market capitalization of all stocks included in the market portfolio is T and the market capitalization (i.e., number of shares times the share price) of one of these stocks is A, then the fraction of this stock that should be held in the market portfolio is A/T.

The passive strategy that we have just described is called *indexing*. As pension fund sponsors in the 1990s increasingly came to believe that managers were unable to outperform the stock market, the amount of funds managed using an indexing strategy has grown substantially.

ACTIVE VERSUS PASSIVE PORTFOLIO MANAGEMENT

While we just distinguished between the extremes of equity portfolio management—passive versus active—in practice there are investors who pursue different degrees of active management and different degrees of passive management. It would be helpful to have some way of quantifying the degree of active or passive management. Fortunately, there is a way to do that.

EXHIBIT 8.2   Measures of Management Categories

	Indexing	Active Management	Enhanced Indexing
Expected Alpha	0%	2.0% or higher	0.5% to 2.0%
Tracking Error	0% to 0.2%	4% or higher	0.5% to 2.0%

Source: Exhibit 2 in John S. Loftus, "Enhanced Equity Indexing," Chapter 4 in Frank J. Fabozzi (ed.), *Perspectives on Equity Indexing* (New Hope, PA: Frank J. Fabozzi Associates, 2000), p. 84.

John Loftus of Pacific Investment Management Company (PIMCO) has suggested that one way of classifying the various types of equity strategies is in terms of two measures—alpha and tracking error.[3] These measures begin with the calculation of the *active return* for a period. The active return is the difference between the actual portfolio return for a given period (say, a month) and the benchmark index return for the same period.[4] *Alpha* is defined as the average active return over some time period. So, if there are 12 monthly active returns observed, then the average of the 12 monthly active returns is the alpha. *Tracking error* is the standard deviation of the active return. The previous chapter is devoted entirely to the subject of tracking error and is important in common stock portfolio management. As explained in that chapter, tracking error occurs because the risk profile of a portfolio differs from that of the risk profile of the benchmark index.

Based on these measures, Loftus proposes the classification scheme shown in Exhibit 8.2. While there may be disagreements as to the values proposed by Loftus, the exhibit does provide some guidance. In an indexing strategy, the portfolio manager seeks to construct a portfolio that matches the risk profile of the benchmark index, the expected alpha is zero and, except for transaction costs and other technical issues discussed later when we cover the topic of indexing, the tracking error should be, in theory, zero. Due to these other issues, tracking error will be a small positive value. At the other extreme, a manager who pursues an active strategy by constructing a portfolio that significantly differs from the risk profile of the benchmark portfolio has an expected alpha of more than 2% and a large tracking error—a tracking error of 4% or higher.

Using tracking error as our guide and the fact that a manager can construct a portfolio whose risk profile can differ to any degree from the

---

[3] John S. Loftus, "Enhanced Equity Indexing," Chapter 4 in Frank J. Fabozzi (ed.), *Perspectives on Equity Indexing* (New Hope, PA: Frank J. Fabozzi Associates, 2000).

[4] The decomposition of return into an active return and a risk-free return is explained in Chapter 13.

risk profile of the benchmark index, we have a conceptual framework for understanding common stock portfolio management strategies. For example, there are managers that will construct a portfolio with a risk profile close to that of the benchmark index but intentionally not identical to it. Such a strategy is called *enhanced indexing*. This strategy will result in the construction of a portfolio that has greater tracking error relative to an indexing strategy. In the classification scheme proposed by Loftus, for an enhanced indexer the expected alpha does not exceed 2% and the tracking error is 0.5% to 2%.

EQUITY STYLE MANAGEMENT

Before we discuss the various types of active and passive strategies, let's discuss an important topic regarding what has come to be known as *equity investment styles*. Several academic studies found that there were categories of stocks that had similar characteristics and performance patterns. Moreover, the returns of these stock categories performed differently than other categories of stocks. That is, the returns of stocks within a category were highly correlated and the returns between categories of stocks were relatively uncorrelated. As a result of these studies, practitioners began to view these categories of stocks with similar performance as a "style" of investing. Using size as a basis for categorizing style, some managers became "large cap" investors while others "small cap" investors. ("Cap" means market capitalization.) Moreover, there was a commonly held belief that a manager could shift "styles" to enhance performance return.

Today, the notion of an equity investment style is widely accepted in the investment community. Next we look at the popular equity style types and the difficulties of classifying stocks according to style.

Types of Equity Styles

Stocks can be classified by style in many ways. The most common is in terms of one or more measures of "growth" and "value." Within a growth and value style there is often a sub-style based on some measure of size. The motivation for the value/growth style categories can be explained in terms of the most common measure for classifying stocks as growth or value—the price-to-book value per share (P/B) ratio.[5] Earnings growth will increase the book value per share. Assuming no

---

[5] Support for the use of this measure is provided in Eugene F. Fama and Kenneth R. French, "Common Risk Factors on Stocks and Bonds," *Journal of Financial Economics* (February 1993), pp. 3–56.

change in the P/B ratio, a stock's price will increase if earnings grow—as higher book value times a constant P/B ratio leads to higher stock price. A manager who is growth oriented is concerned with earnings growth and seeks those stocks from a universe of stocks that have higher relative earnings growth. The growth manager's risks are that growth in earnings will not materialize and/or that the P/B ratio will decline.

For a value manager, concern is with the price component rather than with the future earnings growth. Stocks would be classified as value stocks within a universe of stocks if they are viewed as cheap in terms of their P/B ratio. By cheap it is meant that the P/B ratio is low relative to the universe of stocks. The expectation of the manager who follows a value style is that the P/B ratio will return to some normal level and thus even with book value per share constant, the price will rise. The risk is that the P/B ratio will not increase.

Within the value and growth categories there are sub-styles. In the value category, there are three sub-styles: low price-to-earnings (P/E) ratio, contrarian, and yield.[6] The *low-P/E manager* concentrates on companies trading at low prices relative to their P/E ratio.[7] (The P/E ratio can be defined as the current P/E, a normalized P/E, or a discounted future earnings.) The *contrarian manager* looks at the book value of a company and focuses on those companies that are selling at low valuation relative to book value. The companies that fall into this category are typically depressed cyclical stocks or companies that have little or no current earnings or dividend yields. The expectation is that the stock is on a cyclical rebound or that the company's earnings will turn around. Both these occurrences are expected to lead to substantial price appreciation. The most conservative value managers are those that look at companies with above average dividend yields that are expected to be capable of increasing, or at least maintaining, those yields. This style is followed by a manager who is referred to as a *yield manager*.

Growth managers seek companies with above average growth prospects. In the growth manager style category, there tends to be two major sub-styles.[8] The first is a growth manager who focuses on high-quality companies with consistent growth. A manager who follows this sub-style

---

[6] Jon A. Christopherson and C. Nola Williams, "Equity Style: What It Is and Why It Matters," Chapter 1 in T. Daniel Coggin, Frank J. Fabozzi, and Robert D. Arnott (eds.), *The Handbook of Equity Style Management: Second Edition* (New Hope, PA: Frank J. Fabozzi Associates, 1997).

[7] For a discussion of an approach based on low price-earnings, see Gary G. Schlarbaum, "Value-Based Equity Strategies," Chapter 7 in *The Handbook of Equity Style Management*.

[8] Christopherson and Williams, "Equity Style: What It Is and Why It Matters."

is referred to as a *consistent growth manager.* The second growth sub-style is followed by an *earnings momentum growth manager.* In contrast to a consistent growth manager, an earnings momentum growth manager prefers companies with more volatile, above-average growth. Such a manager seeks to buy companies in expectation of an acceleration of earnings.

There are some managers who follow both a growth and value investing style but have a bias (or tilt) in favor of one of the styles. The bias is not sufficiently identifiable to categorize the manager as either a growth or value manager. Most managers who fall into this hybrid style are described as *growth at a price managers* or *growth at a reasonable price managers.* These managers look for companies that are forecasted to have above-average growth potential selling at a reasonable value.

Style Indexes

In Chapter 6, the various types of stock market indexes are discussed. With the notion of style investing came stock market indexes that could be used to represent different styles. There are three major services that provide popular style indexes based on capitalization. Standard & Poor's together with BARRA publishes cap-based growth and value indexes based on three S&P indexes: the S&P 500 Index (also called the S&P Composite Index), the Mid Cap 400 Index, and the Small Cap 600 indexes. Based on its Russell 1000, Russell 3000, and Russell Top 200, Frank Russell publishes three large cap style indexes. It also produces a mid-cap index and a small cap based on both the Russell 2000 and Russell 2500 indexes. A large, mid, and small cap set of indexes is also produced by Wilshire Associates.

Style Classification Systems

Now that we have a general idea of the two main style categories, growth and value, and the further refinement by size, let's see how a portfolio manager goes about classifying stocks that fall into the categories. We call the methodology for classifying stocks into style categories as a *style classification system.* Vendors of style indices have provided direction for developing a style classification system. However, managers will develop their own system.

Developing such a system is not a simple task. To see why, let's take a simple style classification system where we just categorize stocks into value and growth using one measure, the price-to-book value ratio. The lower the P/B ratio the more the stock looks like a value stock. The style classification system would then be as follows:

Step 1: Select a universe of stocks.

Step 2: Calculate the total market capitalization of all the stocks in the universe.

Step 3: Calculate the P/B ratio for each stock in the universe.

Step 4: Sort the stocks from the lowest P/B ratio to the highest P/B ratio.

Step 5: Calculate the accumulated market capitalization starting from the lowest P/B ratio stock to the highest P/B ratio stock.

Step 6: Select the lowest P/B stocks up to the point where one-half the total market capitalization computed in Step 2 is found.

Step 7: Classify the stocks found in Step 6 as value stocks.

Step 8: Classify the remaining stocks from the universe as growth stocks.

While this style classification system is simple, it has both theoretical and practical problems. First, from a theoretical point of view, in terms of the P/B ratio there is very little distinguishing the last stock on the list that is classified as value and the first stock on the list classified as growth. From a practical point of view, the transaction costs are higher for implementing a style using this classification system. The reason is that the classification is at a given point in time based on the prevailing P/B ratio and market capitalizations. At a future date, P/B ratios and market capitalizations will change, resulting in a different classification of some of the stocks. This is often the case for those stocks on the border between value and growth that could jump over to the other category. This is sometimes called "style jitter." As a result, the manager will have to rebalance the portfolio to sell off stocks that are not within the style classification sought.

There are two refinements that have been made to style classification systems in an attempt to overcome these two problems. First, more than one categorization variable has been used in a style classification system. Categorization variables that have been used based on historical and/or expectational data include dividend/price ratio (i.e., dividend yield), cash flow/price ratio (i.e., cash flow yield), return on equity, and earnings variability, and earnings growth. As an example of this refinement, consider the style classification system developed by one firm, Frank Russell, for the Frank Russell style indices. The universe of stocks included (either 1,000 for the Russell 1000 index or 2,000 for the Russell 2000 index) were classified as part of their value index or growth index using two categorization variables. The two variables are the B/P ratio and a long-term growth forecast of earnings.[9]

The second refinement has been to develop better procedures for making the cut between growth and value. This involves not classifying every stock into one category or the other. Instead, stocks may be classified into three groups: "pure value," "pure growth," and "middle-of-the-road" stocks. The three groups would be such that they each had one third of the total market capitalization. The two extreme groups, pure value and pure growth, are not likely to face any significant style jitter. The middle-of-the road stocks are assigned a probability of being value or growth.

Thus far our focus has been on style classification in terms of value and growth. As we noted earlier, sub-style classifications are possible in terms of size. Within a value and growth classification, there can be a model determining large value and small value stocks, and large growth and small growth stocks. The variable most used for classification of size is a company's market capitalization. To determine large and small, the total market capitalization of all the stocks in the universe considered is first calculated. The cutoff between large and small is the stock that will give an equal market capitalization. Even here though, one might worry about "size jitter."

Range of Equity Style Opportunities

There are different styles used by managers of mutual funds, an investment vehicle that will be explained in Chapter 26. There are organizations that classify managers based on several broad style classifications. One of these organizations is Morningstar which classifies equity mutual funds on the basis of size—in terms of market capitalization of the stocks held—and style—value versus growth. Based on size and style, Morningstar classifies mutual funds according to the following 3 × 3 (or nine-box) matrix range of equity styles:

	Value	Blend	Growth
Large Cap	Lge V	Lge B	Lge G
Mid Cap	Mid V	Mid B	Mid G
Small Cap	Sm V	Sm B	Sm G

Morningstar believes that combining these two variables offers investors a broad view of a mutual fund's holdings and risk. The style classi-

---

[9] "Russell Equity Indices: Index Construction and Methodology," Frank Russell Company, July 8, 1994 and September 6, 1995.

fication system, referred to as the Morningstar equity style box, is based on a mutual fund's most recent holdings.[10]

In the case of U.S. domestic stocks, size is a measure of the average market cap of a mutual fund's holdings as it compares to the average market cap of stocks in the Morningstar equity database of the 5,000 largest domestic stocks. On this basis, Morningstar places the mutual fund into large cap, mid cap, or small cap groups. Style of each stock is a score based on a composite of its P/E ratio and P/B ratio. An average of such scores is computed for each of the size categories. The average style score of a mutual fund's holdings is then compared to the average for its size category. Mutual funds whose average style scores are well above the average are categorized as "growth," and those with score that are well below the average are categorized as "value." This classification system is supported by the observation that growth stocks (i.e., stocks with higher than average earnings growth rates) have high P/E and P/B ratios, while value stocks have low P/E and P/B ratios.

In terms of equity style definitions, conventional wisdom holds that large cap stocks have an average market capitalization of more than $5 billion.[11] Mid cap stocks often range from $1 to $5 billion on the size scale, while small caps have an equity capitalization of less than $1 billion.

The following 5×3 matrix expands the range of opportunities for style-based equity investors:

	Value	Blend	Growth
Maxi Cap	*Max V*	*Max B*	*Max G*
Large Cap	Lge V	Lge B	Lge G
Mid Cap	Mid V	Mid B	Mid G
Small Cap	Sm V	Sm B	Sm G
Micro Cap	*Mic V*	*Mic B*	*Mic G*

In this context, *maxi*-capitalization value- and growth-stock opportunities have been added to the style matrix to recognize that another equity size classification is needed—namely "giant cap" stocks—as many U.S.

---

[10] However, because of the difficulty of classifying a manager into any one of the generic investment styles, William Sharpe has suggested that a benchmark can be constructed using multiple regression analysis from various specialized market indexes. In this enhanced style approach, a benchmark can be statistically created that adjusts for a manager's index-like tendencies. Such a benchmark is called a Sharpe benchmark. For a complete explanation, see William F. Sharpe, "Determining a Fund's Effective Asset Mix," *Investment Management Review* (September/October 1988), pp. 16–29.

[11] These are broad equity capitalization ranges used by Morningstar.

large capitalization firms such as Cisco Systems, Coca-Cola, General Electric, and Microsoft have market values well in excess of $100 billion. For examples, in early December 2001, the equity cap for Coca-Cola, General Electric, and Microsoft were about $115 billion, $370 billion, and $365 billion, respectively. These figures are dramatically higher than the traditional $5 billion starting point for large cap stocks. Moreover, in terms of the possible creation of additional style passive (or active) opportunities, it is noteworthy that at the lowest end of the equity size spectrum, *micro-cap* stocks have an equity cap of about $250 million, or less.

PASSIVE STRATEGIES

There are two types of passive strategies: a buy-and-hold strategy and an indexing strategy. In a *buy-and-hold strategy*, a portfolio of stocks based on some criterion is purchased and held to the end of some investment horizon. There is no active buying and selling of stocks once the portfolio is created. While referred to as a passive strategy, there are elements of active management. Specifically, the investor who pursues this strategy must determine which stock issues to buy.

An indexing strategy is the more commonly followed passive strategy. With this strategy, the manager does not attempt to identify undervalued or overvalued stock issues based on fundamental security analysis. Nor does the manager attempt to forecast general movements in the stock market and then structure the portfolio so as to take advantage of those movements. Instead, an indexing strategy involves designing a portfolio to track the total return performance of a benchmark index. Next we explain how that is done.

Constructing an Indexed Portfolio

In constructing a portfolio to replicate the performance of the benchmark index, sometimes referred to as the *indexed portfolio* or the *tracking portfolio*, there are several approaches that can be used. One approach is to purchase all stock issues included in the benchmark index in proportion to their weightings. A second approach, referred to as the *capitalization approach*, is one in which the manager purchases a number of the largest capitalized names in the benchmark index and equally distributes the residual stock weighting across the other issues in the benchmark index. For example, if the top 150 highest-capitalization stock issues are selected for the replicating portfolio and these issues account for 70% of the total capitalization of the benchmark index, the remaining 30% is evenly proportioned among the other stock issues.

Another approach is to construct an indexed portfolio with fewer stock issues than the benchmark index. Two methods used to implement this approach are the cellular (or stratified sampling) method and the multi-factor risk model method.

In the *cellular method*, the manager begins by defining risk factors by which the stocks that make up a benchmark index can be categorized. A typical risk factor is the industry in which a company operates. Other factors might include risk characteristics such as beta or capitalization. The use of two characteristics would add a second dimension to the stratification. In the case of the industry categorization, each company in the benchmark index is assigned to an industry. This means that the companies in the benchmark have been stratified by industry. The objective of this method is then to reduce residual risk by diversifying across all industries in the same proportion as the benchmark index. Stock issues within each cell or stratum, or in this case industry, can then be selected randomly or by some other criterion such as capitalization ranking.

The second method is using a multi-factor risk model to construct a portfolio that matches the risk profile of the benchmark index. By doing so, a predicted tracking error close to zero can be obtained. In the case of smaller portfolios, this approach is ideal since the manager can assess the tradeoff of including more stock issues versus the higher transaction costs for constructing the indexed portfolio. This can be measured in terms of the effect on predicted tracking error.

ACTIVE INVESTING

In contrast with passive investing, active investing makes sense when a moderate to low degree of capital market efficiency is present in the financial markets (or areas thereof). This happens when the active investor has (1) better information than most other investors (namely, the "consensus" investors), and/or (2) the investor has a more productive way of looking at a given information set to generate active rewards.

In general, active strategies can be classified as either a top-down approach or a bottom-up approach. We discuss each approach below.

Top-down Approaches to Active Investing

Before delving into the "top-down" approach to investing, it should be noted that those who actually use portfolio analysis to select portfolios do so in one of two major ways:

1. Top-down approach
2. All-at-once approach

In the top-down approach, a "top-down" portfolio analysis is performed at the asset class level. Then, the asset class allocation is implemented either passively or actively. If implemented actively, this can be done quantitatively or informally. If done quantitatively, then the asset class index becomes the benchmark for the manager with this mandate. In this approach to portfolio analysis, expected returns for asset classes can be based on macroeconomic models or considerations. This was demonstrated in Chapter 3 using mean-variance analysis. In the "all-at-once" approach to portfolio analysis, means, variances, and covariances are supplied at the individual stock level and an efficient frontier is computed at the security level rather than at the asset class level.

With this background, we can now distinguish between two types of top-down active investing—namely, (1) top-down active that involves the utilization and forecasts of key variables that impact the macroeconomic outlook (such as consumer confidence, commodity prices, interest rates, inflation, and economic productivity), and (2) top-down active investing by equity management styles such as value or growth. We'll look at the macroeconomic outlook approach to top-down active investing with recognition that active investing (or tilting) by equity styles such as value or growth is to some degree a byproduct of the former approach to top-down active investing.

Macroeconomic Approach to Top-Down Investing

With the macroeconomic variables approach to top-down active investing, an equity manager[12] begins by assessing the macroeconomic environment and forecasting its near-term outlook. Based on this assessment and forecast, an equity manager decides on how much of the portfolio's funds to allocate among the different sectors of the equity market and how much to cash equivalents (i.e., short-term money market instruments).

Given the amount of the portfolio's funds to be allocated to the equity market, the manager must then decide how much to allocate among the sectors and industries of the equity market. The sectors of the equity market can be classified as follows: basic materials, communications, consumer staples, financials, technology, utilities, capital goods, consumer cyclical, energy, health care, and transportation.[13] Industry classifications give a finer breakdown and include, for example, alumi-

---

[12] In the discussion that follows, we take an institutional perspective where the active portion of the client's portfolio (pension fund, endowment, etc.) is managed by a professional money manager.

[13] These are the categories used by Standard & Poor's Corporation. There is another sector labeled "miscellaneous" that includes stocks that do not fall into any of the other sectors.

num, paper, international oil, beverages, electric utilities, telephone and telegraph, and so forth.

In making the active asset allocation decision, a manager who follows a macroeconomic approach to top-down investing often relies on an analysis of the equity market to identify those sectors and industries that will benefit the most on a relative basis from the anticipated economic forecast. Once the amount to be allocated to each sector and industry is made, the manager then looks for the individual stocks to include in the portfolio. The top-down approach looks at changes in several macroeconomic factors to assess the expected active return on securities and portfolios. As noted before, prominent economic variables include changes in commodity prices, interest rates, inflation, and economic productivity.

Additionally, the macroeconomic outlook approach to top-down investing can be both quantitative and qualitative in nature. From the former perspective, equity managers employ factor models in their top-down attempt at generating abnormal returns (that is, positive alpha). Three of the more sophisticated and proprietary *macro*-factor models are the Burmeister, Ibbotson, Roll and Ross (BIRR) model, the Salomon Brothers RAM (Risk Attribute Model) model, and the Northfield Macroeconomic Risk Model. Although these macro-factor models differ in terms of their input and output, they effectively capture the risk of a portfolio by estimating the sensitivity of its return to a statistically determined set of macroeconomic risk measures.

The power of top-down factor models is that given the macroeconomic risk measures and factor sensitivities, a portfolio's risk exposure profile can be quantified and controlled. In this way, it is possible to see why a portfolio is likely to generate abnormally high or low returns in the marketplace. However, one of the practical limitations of these quantitatively based approaches to equity management is that there can be considerable disagreement about the "just right" number of macro-risk pricing factors.

Style Active Approach to Top-Down Investing

Tilting or rotating by equity style—such as value or growth—is another form of top-down active investing. In this context, the enhanced equity style matrix presented earlier in this chapter has several active management implications. For example, if abnormal return opportunities exist in the giant cap or maxi-cap universe—due perhaps to leftover corporate restructurings and or acquisitions—then investors could tilt their portfolios in the relevant "giant cap" value or growth direction. Also, if untapped opportunities exist way down in "micro-cap land," then active equity allocations can be tilted toward micro-cap stocks having a value or growth orientation.

From a style-active perspective, it is interesting to note that several studies document the risk-adjusted return superiority of a value style of investing over a growth style. While the empirical evidence seems compelling regarding the performance superiority of a value style of investing, the findings are problematic in several respects. First, the empirical findings contradict the long-established view in finance that investors should be compensated for bearing market or systematic risk. Second, according to one study,[14] there is ample reason to believe that equity styles per se—such as value, growth, and small cap—reflect both macroeconomic and monetary influences. Third, the findings on value versus growth investing imply that active value managers may be penalized over active growth managers for their low-risk investment successes because their equity style benchmarks—due to unexplained empirical regularities—have comparatively *high*-expected returns.[15]

Bottom-Up Approaches to Active Investing

The "bottom-up" approach to active investing makes sense when numerous pricing inefficiencies exist in the capital markets (or components thereof). An investor who follows a bottom-up approach to investing focuses either on (1) technical aspects of the market or (2) the economic and financial analysis of individual companies, giving relatively less weight to the significance of economic and market cycles.

The investor who pursues a bottom-up strategy based on certain technical aspects of the market is said to be basing stock selection on technical analysis. The primary research tool used for investing based on economic and financial analysis of companies is called *security analysis*. We will describe security analysis next and technical analysis later.

---

[14] See, Gerald R. Jensen, Robert R. Johnson, and Jeffrey M. Mercer, "The Inconsistency of Small-Firm and Value Stock Premiums, *Journal of Portfolio Management* (Winter, 1998).

[15] One study supports the empirical view that it may be easier for growth managers to outperform their equity-style benchmarks, while value managers have an added measure of return responsibility. See T. Daniel Coggin and Charles Trzcinka, "Analyzing the Performance of Equity Managers: A Note on Value versus Growth," in *The Handbook of Equity Style Management*, pp. 167–170. Coggin, Fabozzi, and Rahman find that institutional equity managers not only outperformed the stock market in general, but that their active performance measures (alpha) for benchmarked-growth portfolios were higher than the corresponding security-selection measures for value-focused managers. See, T. Daniel Coggin, Frank J. Fabozzi, and Shafiqur Rahman, "The Investment Performance of U.S. Equity Pension Fund Managers: An Empirical Investigation," *Journal of Finance* (July 1993) pp. 1039–1055.

The following three types of security analysis can now be distinguished in practice:

- Traditional fundamental analysis
- Quantitative fundamental analysis
- Value-based metric analysis

Each type of security analysis is briefly described below. They are covered in more detail in later chapters.

Traditional Fundamental Analysis

Traditional fundamental analysis often begins with the financial statements of a company in order to investigate its revenue, earnings, and cash flow prospects, as well as its overall corporate debt burden. Growth in revenue, earnings, and cash flow on the income statement side (current and pro-forma) and the relative magnitude of corporate leverage (namely, debt-to-capital ratio among others) from current and anticipated balance sheets are frequently used by fundamental equity analysts in forming an opinion of the investment merits of a particular company's stock.

In this type of security analysis, the investor also looks at the firm's product lines, the economic outlook for the products (including existing and potential competitors), and the industries in which the company operates. Based on the growth prospects of earnings, the fundamental analyst attempts to determine the fair market value (or the "intrinsic value") of the stock, using, for example, a price-to-earnings or price-to-book value multiplier. The estimated "fair value" of the firm is then compared to the actual market price to see if the stock is correctly priced in the capital market. "Cheap stocks," or potential buy opportunities, have a current market price below the estimated intrinsic value, while "expensive" or overvalued stocks have a market price that exceeds the calculated present worth of the stock. Benjamin Graham and David Dodd developed the classical approach to equity securities analysis.[16] Notable investors who have successfully employed the traditional approach to equity security analysis include Warren Buffet of Berkshire Hathaway, Inc. and Peter Lynch of Fidelity Management & Research Co.

Traditional fundamental analysis is covered in Chapters 9, 10, and 11.

Quantitative Fundamental Analysis

Quantitative fundamental analysis seeks to assess the value of securities using a statistical model derived from historical information about secu-

---

[16] See, Benjamin Graham and David Dodd, *Security Analysis* (New York: McGraw-Hill Book Co., Inc.: 1934 original edition).

rity returns. The most commonly used model is the *fundamental multifactor risk model* or simply fundamental factor model. The most widely used fundamental factor model is the BARRA model which is described in Chapter 13. Without getting into the statistical details here, this model is both jointly quantitative and fundamental in nature because it has several systematic *non*-market or "common factors" measures that are used in traditional fundamental analysis such as equity size, book-to-price, dividend yield, earnings growth rate, among others, as well as many industry classifications that can be used to identify active rewards on individual securities and portfolios.

To see the potential benefit of a fundamental factor model, consider the following factor model:

$$ER = \alpha + \beta_M(\text{Market return}) + \beta_1(\text{Equity capitalization})$$
$$+ \beta_2(\text{Book-to-price ratio}) + \beta_3(\text{Dividend yield})$$
$$+ \beta_4(\text{Industrial}) + \beta_5(\text{Non-industrial})$$

where ER is the expected return. In this factor model the β_1, β_2, and β_3 represent the stock or portfolio return sensitivities to the set of fundamental factors (the common factors)—equity capitalization (a measure of size), book-to-price ratio, and dividend yield factors—shown in the model. In addition, the industry effect is provided by β_4 and β_5.[17]

According to BARRA, common factors such as equity capitalization (size), book yield, and dividend yield (among other common factors) are systematic *non*-market factors that may be used by active investors to generate active returns.

In addition to identifying the expected return for a security, a fundamental factor model can be used to construct a portfolio or rebalance a portfolio. This is demonstrated in Chapter 13.

Bruce Jacobs and Kenneth Levy refer to strategies that employ quantitative methods to select stocks and to construct portfolios that have the same risk profile as a benchmark index but provide the opportunity to enhance returns relative to that benchmark index at appropriate incremental level as an "engineered approach" to portfolio management.[18]

Value-Based Metrics Analysis

A rapidly emerging form of security analysis is based on an "economic profit" measure called EVA (for Economic Value Added). Stern Stewart

---

[17] For those familiar with regression analysis, the industrial variables are included as what are called dummy variables; that is, they have a value of either one or zero.

[18] Bruce I. Jacobs and Kenneth N. Levy, "Investment Management: An Architecture for the Equity Market," Chapter 1 in *Active Equity Portfolio Management*.

& Company developed EVA commercially during the early 1980s as a modern financial tool for measuring corporate success.[19] EVA (and its close associate, CFROI, for Cash Flow Return on Investment[20]) falls into the realm of security analysis because this profit measure is directly related to the firm's underlying net present value (NPV).[21] In this context, EVA is a new approach to looking at the firm's real profitability, as corporate earnings are calculated net of the overall dollar-cost of debt *and* equity capital. Companies having discounted positive EVA—or equivalently, positive NPV—are viewed as "wealth creators," while firms with discounted negative economic value added are viewed as wealth wasters due to their negative NPV outcomes. In terms of stock selection, companies with positive EVA momentum are considered buy opportunities, while the stocks of negative-average EVA companies are possible sell or short-sell candidates.

Brokerage firms such as C.S. First Boston and Goldman Sachs U.S. Research are using EVA measurement tools to evaluate the performance of companies, industries, and even market economies. Investment management companies are beginning to see the benefits of an economic profit or value-based approach to security analysis and common stock portfolio management. For example, Global Asset Management and Oppenheimer Capital have successfully integrated economic profit measurement in their security selection and portfolio construction processes. To date, corporate players like Alcan, Coca-Cola, Diageo, Guidant, and Nestle have embraced economic profit measurement as an innovative tool for measuring corporate financial success.

Security analysis based on value-based metrics is explained in Chapter 12.[22]

---

[19] Economic value added (EVA®) is a registered trademark of Stern Stewart & Co. See G. Bennett Stewart III, *The Quest for Value* (New York: Harper Collins, 1991).

[20] For an explanation of CFROI®, see Bartley J. Madden, *CFROI Valuation: A Total Systems Approach to Valuing the Firm* (Woburn, MA: Butterworth-Heinemann, 1999).

[21] Indeed, the NPV of any company is equal to the present value of its expected EVA. This implies that wealth creators have positive average EVA while wealth destroyers have negative average EVA. Given market inefficiencies, active investors could reap abnormal profits by buying the stocks of companies having positive economic profit momentum and selling or shorting the stocks of companies with discounted negative economic profit happenings.

[22] A foundation on the emerging value-based (or economic profit) approach to common stock portfolio management is also provided in James L. Grant, "Foundations of EVA for Investment Managers," *Journal of Portfolio Management* (Fall 1996), pp. 41–48, and James L. Grant, *Foundations of Economic Value Added* (New Hope, PA: Frank J. Fabozzi Associates, 1997).

Fundamental Law of Active Management

The information ratio is the ratio of alpha to the tracking error. It is a reward (as measured by alpha) to risk (as measured by tracking error) ratio. The higher the information ratio, the better the performance of the manager. Two portfolio managers, Richard Grinold and Ronald Kahn, have developed a framework—which they refer to as the "fundamental law of active management"—for explaining how the information ratio changes as a function of:[23]

1. The *depth* of an active manager's skill
2. The *breadth* or number of independent insights or investment opportunities.

In formal terms, the information ratio can be expressed as:

$$IR = IC \times BR^{0.5}$$

IR = the information ratio
IC = the information coefficient
BR = the number of independent insights or opportunities available to the active manager

In the above expression, the information ratio (IR) is the reward-to-risk ratio for an active portfolio manager. (This measure is explained in Chapter 7.) In turn, the information coefficient (IC) is a measure of the depth of an active manager's skill. On a more formal basis, IC measures the "correlation" between actual returns and those predicted by the portfolio manager. According to the fundamental law of active management, the information ratio also depends on breadth (BR), which reflects the number of creative insights or active investment opportunities available to the investment manager.

There are several interesting implications of the fundamental law of active management. First, we see that the information ratio goes up when manager skill level rises for a given number of independent insights or active opportunities. This fact should be obvious, as a more skillful manager should produce higher risk-adjusted returns, compared with a less skilled manager whose performance is evaluated over the *same* set of investment opportunities (possibly securities). Second, a prolific manager with a large number of independent insights for a given skill level can, in principle, produce a higher information ratio than a manager with the same skill but a limited number of investment opportunities.

---

[23] For a practical discussion of this active management "law," see Ronald N. Kahn, "The Fundamental Law of Active Management," *BARRA Newsletter* (Winter 1997).

Equally important, the fundamental law of active management suggests that a manager with a high skill level but a limited set of opportunities may end up producing the *same* information ratio as a manager having a relatively lower level of skill but more active opportunities. According to Ronald Kahn,[24] a market timer with an uncanny ability to predict the market may end up earning the same information ratio on the average as a somewhat less skillful stock picker. This might happen because the stock picker has numerous potentially mispriced securities to evaluate, while the otherwise successful market timer may be constrained by the number of realistic market forecasts per year (due, perhaps, to quarterly forecasting or macroeconomic data limitations). Thus, the ability to profitably evaluate an investment opportunity (skill) and the number of independent insights (breadth) is key to successful active management.

With an understanding of the fundamental law of active management, we can now look at the risk of failing to produce a given level of active portfolio return. In this context, Bruce Jacobs and Kenneth Levy suggest that even traditional equity managers face a portfolio management dilemma involving a trade-off between the depth, or "goodness," of their equity management insights and the breadth or scope of their equity management ideas.[25] According to Jacobs and Levy, the breadth of active research conducted by equity managers is constrained in practical terms by the number of investment ideas (or securities) that can be implemented (researched) in a timely and cost efficient manner. This trade-off is shown in Exhibit 8.3.

The exhibit displays the relationship between the depth of equity manager insights (vertical axis) and the breadth of those insights (horizontal axis). The depth of equity manager insights is measured in formal terms by the information coefficient (IC, on the vertical axis), while the breadth (BR) of manager insights can be measured by the potential number of investment ideas or the number of securities in the manager's acceptable universe. When the breadth of equity manager insights is low—as in the case of traditional equity management, according to Jacobs and Levy—then the depth, or "goodness" of each insight needs to be high in order to produce a constant level of active reward-to-active risk (information ratio, IR). Exhibit 8.3 shows that this low breadth/high depth combination produces the same level of active reward that would be associated with a pair-wise high number of investable ideas (or securities) and a relatively low level of equity manager "goodness" or depth per insight.

---

[24] See Kahn, "The Fundamental Law of Active Management."
[25] Jacobs and Levy, "Investment Management: An Architecture for the Equity Market."

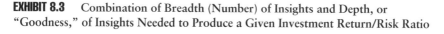

EXHIBIT 8.3 Combination of Breadth (Number) of Insights and Depth, or "Goodness," of Insights Needed to Produce a Given Investment Return/Risk Ratio

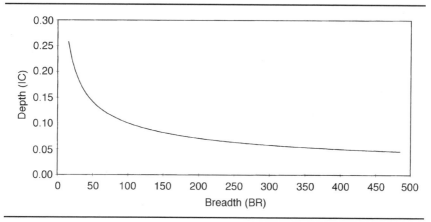

Source: See Bruce I. Jacobs and Kenneth N. Levy, "Investment Management: An Architecture for the Equity Market," Chapter 1 in Frank J. Fabozzi (ed.), *Active Equity Portfolio Management* (New Hope, PA: Frank J. Fabozzi Associates, 1998).

In a risk management context, one can say that the probability of failure to achieve a given level of active reward is quite high when the breadth of investment ideas or securities to be analyzed is very low. If the market is price efficient, that scenario is likely in the traditional fundamental analysis approach to active equity management discussed earlier. On the other hand, the risk of not achieving a given level of active reward is low when the breadth of implementable manager ideas is high. This can happen in a world where active managers employ an engineered approach to active portfolio management. However, if the capital market is largely price efficient, then the probability of failing to produce any level of active reward is high (near one). With market efficiency, investable ideas are transparent, and their active implications are already fully impounded in security prices.

It is interesting to note that over the 10-year period 1987 to 1996 one mutual fund (the Vanguard Index 500) that follows an indexing strategy (i.e., a passive strategy) outperformed about 80% of actively managed portfolios. If equity managers have good stock selection skills, then why are they losing to more passive oriented strategies? According to Wagner and Edwards, the cost of implementing valuable investment ideas has been both misunderstood and underestimated—such that equity managers have incurred sub-par performance despite the presence of better than average investment ideas. Hence, this is the reason that a good deal of discussion in Chapter 6 was devoted to the topic of trading costs. This is why at the outset of this chapter it was stated that all elements in an integrated common stock portfolio management process—controlling costs being one of them—are equally important in producing superior returns.

Strategies Based on Technical Analysis

Given the preceding developments, we would be remiss for not shedding some insight on active strategies based on technical analysis. In this context, various common stock strategies that involve only historical price movement, trading volume, and other technical indicators have been suggested since the beginning of stock trading. Many of these strategies involve investigating patterns based on historical trading data (past price data and trading volume) to forecast the future movement of individual stocks or the market as a whole. Based on observed patterns, mechanical trading rules indicating when a stock should be bought, sold, or sold short are developed. Thus, no consideration is given to any factor other than the specified technical indicators. This approach to active management is called *technical analysis*. Because some of these strategies involve the analysis of charts that plot price and/or volume movements, investors who follow a technical analysis approach are sometimes called *chartists*. The overlying principle of these strategies is to detect changes in the supply of and demand for a stock and capitalize on the expected changes.

Dow Theory

The grandfather of the technical analysis school is Charles Dow. During his tenure as editor of the *Wall Street Journal*, his editorials theorized about the future direction of the stock market. This body of writing is now referred to as the "Dow Theory." This theory rests on two basic assumptions. First, according to Charles Dow, "The averages in their day-to-day fluctuations discount everything known, everything foreseeable, and every condition which can affect the supply of or the demand for corporate securities." This assumption sounds very much like the efficient market theory. But there's more. The second basic assumption is that the stock market moves in trends—up and down—over periods of time. According to Charles Dow, it is possible to identify these stock price trends and predict their future movement.

According to the Dow Theory, there are three types of trends or market cycles. The "primary trend" is the long-term movement in the market. Primary trends are basically four-year trends in the market. From the primary trend a trend line showing where the market is heading can be derived. The secondary trend represents short-run departures of stock prices from the trend line. The third trend is day-to-day fluctuations in stock prices. Charles Dow believed that upward movements in the stock market were tempered by fallbacks that lost a portion of the previous gain. A market turn occurred when the upward movement was not greater than the last gain. In assessing whether or not a gain did in fact occur, he suggested examining the comovements in different stock market indexes such as the Dow Jones Industrial Average and the Dow Jones Transportation Average. One of the averages is selected as the primary index and the other as the "confirming index." If the primary index reaches a high above its previous high, the increase is expected to continue if it is confirmed by the other index also reaching a high above its previous high.

Simple Filter Rules

The simplest type of technical strategy is to buy and sell on the basis of a predetermined movement in the price of a stock; the rule is basically if the stock increases by a certain percentage, the stock is purchased and held until the price declines by a certain percentage, at which time the stock is sold. The percentage by which the price must change is called the "filter." Each investor pursuing this technical strategy decides his or her own filter.

Moving Averages

Some technical analysts make decisions to buy or sell a stock based on the movement of a stock over an extended period of time (for example, 200 days). An average of the price over the time period is computed, and a rule is specified that if the price is greater than some percentage of the average, the stock should be purchased; if the price is less than some percentage of the average, the stock should be sold. The simplest way to calculate the average is to calculate a simple moving average. Assuming that the time period selected by the technical analyst is 200 days, then the average price over the 200 days is determined. A more complex moving average can be calculated by giving greater weight to more recent prices.

Advance/Decline Line

On each trading day, some stocks will increase in price or "advance" from the closing price on the previous trading day, while other stocks will decrease in price or decline from the closing price on the previous trading day. It has been suggested by some market observers that the cumulative number of advances over a certain number of days minus the cumulative number of declines over the same number of days can be used as an indicator of short-term movements in the stock market.

Relative Strength

The *relative strength* of a stock is measured by the ratio of the stock price to some price index. The ratio indicates the relative movement of the stock to the index. The price index can be the index of the price of stocks in a given industry or a broad-based index of all stocks. If the ratio rises, it is presumed that the stock is in an uptrend relative to the index; if the ratio falls, it is presumed that the stock is in a downtrend relative to the index. Similarly, a relative strength measure can be calculated for an industry group relative to a broad-based index. Relative strength is also referred to as *price momentum* or *price persistence*.

Short Interest Ratio

Some technical analysts believe that the ratio of the number of shares sold short relative to the average daily trading volume is a technical signal that is valuable in forecasting the market. This ratio is called the *short interest ratio*. However, the economic link between this ratio and stock price movements can be interpreted in two ways. On one hand, some market observers believe that if this ratio is high, this is a signal that the market will advance. The argument is that short sellers will have to eventually cover their short position by buying the stocks they have shorted and, as a result, market prices will increase. On the other hand, there are some market observers who believe this a bearish signal being sent by market participants who have shorted stocks in anticipation of a declining market.

Market Overreaction

To benefit from favorable news or to reduce the adverse effect of unfavorable news, investors must react quickly to new information.[26] According to cognitive psychologists, people tend to overreact to extreme events. People tend to react more strongly to recent information and they tend to heavily discount older information.

The question is, do investors follow the same pattern? That is, do investors overreact to extreme events? The *overreaction hypothesis* suggests that when investors react to unanticipated news that will benefit a company's stock, the price rise will be greater than it should be given that information, resulting in a subsequent decline in the price of the stock. In contrast, the overreaction to unanticipated news that is expected to adversely affect the economic well-being of a company will force the price down too much, followed by a subsequent correction that will increase the price.

---

[26] Werner DeBondt and Richard Thaler, "Does the Market Overreact?" *Journal of Finance* (July 1985), pp. 793–805.

If, in fact, the market does overreact, investors may be able to exploit this to realize positive abnormal returns if they can (1) identify an extreme event, and (2) determine when the effect of the overreaction has been impounded in the market price and is ready to reverse. Investors who are capable of doing this will pursue the following strategies. When positive news is identified, investors will buy the stock and sell it before the correction to the overreaction. In the case of negative news, investors will short the stock and then buy it back to cover the short position before the correction to the overreaction.

Nonlinear Dynamic Models: Chaos Theory

Some market observers—like Edgar Peters of PanAgora Asset Management[27]—believe that the pattern of stock price behavior is *so* complex that *linear* (simple, or otherwise) mathematical models are insufficient for detecting historical price patterns and developing models for forecasting future return volatility. While stock prices may appear to change randomly, there could be an undiscovered *nonlinear* pattern that is missed when using simple mathematical tools. Scientists have developed complex mathematical models for detecting patterns from observations of some phenomenon that appear to be random. Generically, these models are called *nonlinear dynamic models* because the mathematics used to detect any structure or pattern is based on a system of nonlinear equations.

Nonlinear dynamic models have been suggested for analyzing stock price patterns. In recent years, there have been several studies that suggest that stock prices exhibit the characteristics of a nonlinear dynamic model.[28] The particular form of nonlinear dynamic models that has been suggested is *chaos theory*. At this stage, the major insight provided by chaos theory is that stock price movements that appear to be random may in fact have a structure that can be used to generate abnormal returns. However, some market observers caution that the actual application of nonlinear return models falls short of the mark. Interviews with market players by Sergio Focardi and Caroline Jonas in 1996 found that "chaos theory is conceptually too complex to find much application in finance today."[29]

---

[27] See, Edgar E. Peters, *Chaos and Order in the Capital Markets: A New View of Cycles, Prices, and Market Volatility* (New York: John Wiley & Sons, 1991).

[28] See, José Scheinkman and Blake LeBaron, "Nonlinear Dynamics and Stock Returns," *Journal of Business* (1989), pp. 311–337, and Peters, *Chaos and Order in the Capital Markets*.

[29] See, Sergio Focardi and Caroline Jonas, *Modeling the Market: New Theories and Techniques* (New Hope, PA: Frank J. Fabozzi Associates, 1997), p. 14.

CHAPTER 9

Traditional Fundamental Analysis I: Sources of Information

Pamela P. Peterson, Ph.D., CFA
Professor of Finance
Florida State University

Frank J. Fabozzi, Ph.D., CFA
Adjunct Professor of Finance
School of Management
Yale University

As explained in Chapter 8, security analysis is used by an active manager pursuing a bottom-up approach. One form of security analysis is traditional fundamental analysis. The purpose of such analysis which involves the selection, evaluation, and interpretation of financial data and other pertinent information to assist in evaluating the operating performance and financial condition of a company or an industry. The operating performance of a company is a measure of how well a company has used its resources—its assets, both tangible and intangible—to produce a return on its investment. The financial condition of a company is a measure of its ability to satisfy its obligations, such as the payment of interest in a timely manner.

In this chapter and the two that follow we will discuss traditional fundamental analysis. In this chapter our focus is on the sources of information available. There is a wealth of financial information about companies available to analysts and investors. The popularity of the Internet as a means of delivery has made vast amounts of information available to everyone. Consider the amount of information available about Microsoft Corporation. Not only can investors find annual reports, quarterly reports, press releases, and links to the company's filings with regulators on Microsoft's web site, anyone can download data for analysis and listen-in on Microsoft's conversations with analysts. Although the availability and convenience afforded information gathering has eased one aspect of traditional fundamental analysis, what remains is the more challenging task of analyzing this information in a meaningful way in order to properly assess the value of a company. That task is described in the next two chapters.

The analysis of information requires the analyst to apply the tools of financial analysis. These tools include financial ratio analysis, the subject of Chapter 10, and the analysis of earnings, cash flow, and dividends, the subject of Chapter 11. We conclude Chapter 11 with a discussion of a dividend discount model for valuing a stock.

SOURCES OF FINANCIAL INFORMATION

There are many sources of information available to analysts. One source of information is the company itself, preparing documents for regulators and distribution to shareholders. Another source is information prepared by government agencies that compile and report information about industries and the economy. Still another source is information prepared by financial service firms that compile, analyze, and report financial and other information about the company, the industry, and the economy.

The basic information about a company can be gleaned from publication (both print and Internet), annual reports, and sources such as the federal government and commercial financial information providers. The basic information about a company consists of the following:

- Type of business (e.g., manufacturer, retailer, service, utility)
- Primary products
- Strategic objectives
- Financial condition and operating performance
- Major competitors (domestic and foreign)
- Competitiveness of the industry (domestic and foreign)
- Position of the company in the industry (e.g., market share)
- Industry trends (domestic and foreign)
- Regulatory issues (if applicable)
- Economic environment

A thorough financial analysis of a company requires examining events that help explain the firm's present condition and effect on its future prospects. For example, did the firm recently incur some extraordinary losses? Is the firm developing a new product, or acquiring another firm? Current events can provide useful information to the financial analyst. A good place to start is with the company itself and the disclosures that it makes—both financial and otherwise.

Most of the company-specific information can be picked up through company annual reports, press releases, and other information that the company provides to inform investors and customers about itself. Information about competitors and the markets for the company's products must be determined through familiarity with the products of the company and its competitors. Information about the economic environment can be found in many available sources. In the following sections, we will take a brief look at the different types of information.

INFORMATION PREPARED BY THE COMPANY

Documents prepared by a company can be divided into two groups:

1. Disclosures required by regulatory authorities, including documents that a corporation prepares and files with the Securities and Exchange Commission (SEC), and
2. Documents that a corporation prepares and distributes to shareholders.

Though both types of documents provide financial and related information about the company, the documents prepared for regulators differ from those prepared for shareholders in terms of the depth of information and form of presentation.

Disclosures Required by Regulatory Authorities

Companies whose stock is traded in public markets are subject to a number of securities laws that require specific disclosures. Publicly traded companies are required by securities laws to disclose information through filings with the SEC. The SEC, a federal agency that administers federal securities laws, established by the Securities and Exchange Act of 1934, carries out the following activities:

- Issues rules that clarify securities laws or trading procedure issues
- Requires disclosure of specific information
- Makes public statements on current issues
- Oversees self-regulation of the securities industry by the stock exchanges and professional groups such as the National Association of Securities Dealers

The publicly traded company must make a number of periodic and occasional filings with the SEC. In addition, major shareholders and executives must make periodic and occasional filings. A number of these filings are described in the next sections.

10-K and 10-Q Filings

The 10-K filing contains the information provided in the annual report plus additional requirements, such as the management discussion and analysis (MDA), and must be filed within 90 days after close of a corporation's fiscal year.

The 10-K comprises five parts:

Part I Covers business, properties, legal proceedings, principal security holders, and security holdings of management

Part II Covers selected financial data, management's discussion and analysis of financial conditions and results of operations, financial statements, and supplementary data

Part III Covers directors and executive officers and remuneration of directors and officers

Part IV Provides complete, audited annual financial information

Part V Schedule of various items provided

The MDA is required by the SEC Regulation S-K, Item 303. This regulation requires information and discussion regarding:

Type of Information	Disclosures
Liquidity	• Trends and commitments, events and uncertainties that are likely to affect the company's liquid resources
Capital resources	• Commitments for capital expenditures • Trends in capital resources • Changes in debt, equity, and off-balance sheet financing
Results of operations	• Significant economic events, changes, or uncertainties that likely affect income from operations • Significant revenues or expenses • Detail increases in revenues regarding price and quantities of goods sold • Impact of inflation on revenues and income from continuing operations

In addition to the specific information, the MDA should include any other information that is necessary to understand a company's operating results, financial condition, and changes in financial condition.

The MDA provides a discussion of risks, trends, and uncertainties that pertain to the company and is a useful device for management to explain the financial results in terms of the company's strategies, recent actions (e.g., mergers), and the company's competitors.

Proxy Statements

In addition to the financial statement and management discussion information available in the periodic 10-Q and 10-K filings, useful non-financial information is available in proxy statements. The proxy statement notifies designated classes of shareholders of matters to be voted upon at a shareholders' meeting. The proxy statement provides an array of information on issues such as:

- the reappointment of the independent auditor,
- compensation (salary, bonus, and options) of the top five executives, and
- stock ownership of executives and directors.

Some of this information is innocuous (e.g., reappointment of the auditor), yet some raises a "red flag" suggesting a significant financial problem or situation. Red flags include:

- Compensation committee interlocks (i.e., member of management is a member of the board of director's compensation committee)
- Self-dealing (i.e., the company is doing business with other companies for which a member of the company's management has a financial interest)
- A change in auditors
- Transactions with related parties (e.g., look for family members who are managers of subsidiaries or divisions)
- Anti-takeover provisions (often referred to as "shareholders' rights plans")
- Management compensation that continues to increase even though the company's performance has declined
- Three or more different types of compensation plans for the same managers
- A board of directors that consists of a majority of inside and affiliated directors. Inside directors are current employees of the company. Affiliated directors are either former employees or are employees of firms that do business with the company (e.g., the company's banker)

And the information can sometimes reveal rather interesting (and perhaps unusual) information about the company's management and their decisions. Consider a few examples from proxy statements:

- The $195,000 expenditure in 1990 by Occidental Petroleum to finance a book about Armand Hammer, its chairman at the time.
- In 1990, an Executive Vice-President of W. R. Grace and Chief Executive Officer of the subsidiary, National Medical Care, consented to the entry of a misdemeanor finding and to the payment of a fine for his importation of skins of endangered species in violation of federal law.
- The president and chief executive officer and a director of the Einstein Noah Bagel Corporation was also employed by Boston Chicken "to undertake various special projects for Boston Chicken." Following this arrangement, Mr. Goldston became Vice Chairman of the Board and a director of Boston Chicken. It is comforting that "Boston Chicken has agreed to structure Mr. Goldston's future projects so that his employment with Boston Chicken will not interfere with his duties" with Einstein Noah Bagel.

8-K Filing

The 8-K statement is an occasional filing that provides useful information about the company that is not generally found in the financial statements. The 8-K statement is filed by a company if there is a significant event. The specific events that require filing this statement are:

- A change in control of the company
- An acquisition or disposition of a significant amount of assets
- The bankruptcy or receivership of the company
- A change in the company's auditing firm
- A resignation of a member of the board of directors because of a disagreement with the company's operations, policies, or practices

For example, in Discovery Zone's June 3, 1996 8-K filing, they reported information regarding their auditors that provides a "red flag."

On June 3, 1996, Discovery Zone, Inc. (the "Registrant") was informed by its independent accountants, Price Waterhouse LLP ("PW"), that PW declined to stand for re-election as the Registrant's independent accountants for the year ending December 31, 1996. The Board of Directors of the Registrant did not recommend or approve the change in independent accountants.

In addition, any other event that the company deems important to shareholders may be reported using an 8-K filing. Because 8-K filings are triggered by major company events, it is useful for the analyst to keep abreast of any such filings for the companies that they follow.

Registration Statement and Prospectus

When a corporation offers a new security to the public, the SEC requires that the corporation prepare and file a registration statement. The registration statement presents financial statement data, along with detailed information about the new security. A condensed version of this statement, called a *prospectus*, is made available to potential investors.

Documents Distributed to Shareholders

The financial reports to shareholders are not simply a presentation of the basic financial statements—the balance sheet, the income statement, and the statement of cash flows—but also communicate additional non-financial information, such as information about the relevant risks and uncertainties of the company. To that end, accounting standards have broadened the extent and type of the information presented within the financial statements and in notes to the financial statements. For example, companies are now required to disclose risks and uncertainties related to their operations, how they use estimates in the preparation of financial statements, and the vulnerability of the company to geographic and customer concentrations.

The annual report is the principal document used by corporations to communicate with shareholders. It is not an official SEC filing; consequently, companies have significant discretion in deciding on what types of information are reported and the way it is presented. The annual report presents the financial statements (the income statement, the balance sheet, and the statement of cash flows), notes to these statements, a discussion of the company by management, the report of the independent accountants, and financial information on operating segments, product and services, geographical areas, and major customers. Along with this basic information, annual reports may present 5- or 10-year summaries of key financial data, quarterly data, and other descriptions of the business or its products.

Because of the wide latitude that companies have in presenting the information to shareholders, the reports range from the austere to the lavish. Quarterly reports to shareholders provide limited financial information on operations. These reports are simpler and more compact in presentation than their annual counterpart.

In addition to the annual and quarterly reports, companies provide information through press releases using commercial wire services such as PR Newswire (www.prnewswire.com), Business Wire (www.businesswire.com),

First Call (www.firstcall.com), or Dow Jones (bis.dowjones.com). The wire services then distribute this information to print and Internet mediums. The information provided in press releases include earnings, dividend, new product, and acquisition announcements.

Letter to Shareholders

The letter to shareholders included in the annual and quarterly reports are sometimes dismissed by analysts and investors as unimportant because the management discussion analysis in the 10-K and shareholder reports provide more detailed information. Moreover, management has less flexibility in preparing the MDA. If management is found to materially mislead investors in the MDA, SEC action can be taken. In contrast, no SEC action will be taken by the SEC if the chief executive officer's letter to shareholders—typically prepared by the firm's investor relations or public relations staff—is optimistic despite the financial difficulties currently facing the firm.

It is because of the flexibility that management has in preparing the letter to shareholders that there may be a material difference between the statements made in the MDA and the letter to shareholders. Thornton O'Glove, former publisher of the *Quality of Earnings Report*, refers to this as "differential disclosure." For example, consider the perspectives on operating profit used in PepsiCo. Inc's 1997 annual report and 10-K. Factually correct data can be presented in both the annual report and the 10-K, but interpreted with different emphasis. In PepsiCo Inc.'s annual report's Letter from the Chairman,

> "In snacks and beverages—called "continuing operations in the financial pages"—our operating profit grew 30% and earnings per share grew 62%. Operating profit margins improved by almost three percentage points."

A 30% increase in operating profits is quite impressive. In the MDA of the 10-K, a slightly different—and slightly less "rosy"—reading of the data is presented, with the 30% increase in reported profit and only a 13% increase in ongoing operations' profit:

	Operating Profit ($ in millions)			% Growth Rates	
	1997	1996	1995	1997	1996
Reported	$2,662	$2,040	$2,606	30	(22)
Ongoing[1]	$2,952	$2,616	$2,672	13	(2)

[1] Ongoing excludes the effect of the unusual items (see Note 2).

And although the operating profit margin improved from 10.0% to 12.7% (the "almost three percentage points"), using data that is presented in both the annual report and the 10-K the analyst can calculate that 1997's margin was lower than 1995's margin of 13.7%.

The point is that the analyst may find the letter to shareholders interesting. However, the MDA may identify where potential problems may exist, while the letter to shareholders may present a more rosy picture of the future prospects of the firm.

Issues in Using Financial Statement Data

There are a number of issues that should be considered in using the data in a company's financial statements and quarterly reports. Three important ones are: (1) restatement of prior years' data, (2) "off-balance sheet" activity, and (3) pro forma.

The Restatement of Prior Years' Data

When a company reports financial data for more than one year, which is often the case, previous years' financial data are restated to reflect any changes in accounting methods or acquisitions that have taken place since the previous data had been reported. Consider the case of Harnischfeger Industries, Inc. shown in Exhibit 9.1. The originally reported data for 1991 are shown alongside the restated 1991 data reported in the 1995 financial statements. So which data are correct? Both. The 1991 data has simply been restated in 1995 to reflect accounting changes and acquisitions since 1991 to make the data comparable to the current 1995 data. Therefore, the analyst must consider which data are most appropriate to use in the analysis. If, for example, the analyst is looking at Harnischfeger and its competitive position in 1991, the analyst would want to use the as-reported 1991 data. If, on the other hand, the analyst is looking at trends in some of the data in an effort to forecast future operating performance or financial condition, the restated 1991 data are more appropriate.

Of course, some restatements are not due to accounting changes, but may be due to corrections of prior years' statements. Consider the case of Enron Corporation, which made an accounting error and had failed to report the financial activities of unconsolidated entities. The restatements resulted in a reduction of shareholders' equity of almost $1.2 billion, as detailed in Exhibit 9.2.

"Off-Balance Sheet" Activity

There have always been some corporate investing or financing activities that simply do not show up in financial statements. Though there have been improvements in accounting standards that have moved much of this activity to the financial statements (e.g., leases, pension benefits, post-retirement benefits), opportunities remain to conduct business that is not represented adequately in the financial statements. An example is the case of joint ventures. As long as the investing corporation does not have a controlling interest in the joint venture, the assets and financing of the venture can remain off of the balance sheet. Limited information is provided in footnotes to the statements, but this information is insufficient to adjudge the performance and risks of the joint venture. The opportunity to keep some information from the financial statements places a greater burden on the analyst to dig deep into the company's notes to the financial statements, filings with the SEC, and the financial press.

EXHIBIT 9.1   Selected Financial Data for Harnischfeger Industries, Inc., 1991

Dollar Amounts in Thousands Except per Share Amounts	As Reported in 1991	As Restated for 1991 in 1995
Net sales	$1,584,114	$1,863,703
Operating income	$120,920	$194,682
Net income	$64,610	$79,966
Total assets	$1,506,882	$2,135,627
Earnings per share	$2.08	$1.90
Book value per share	$19.82	$11.98
Number of employees	11,600	17,100

Source: Harnischfeger Industries, Inc., 1991 Annual Report, pp. 34–35, and Harnischfeger Industries, Inc., 1995 Annual Report, pp. 46–47.

EXHIBIT 9.2   Selected Financial Data for Enron Corporation, 2000 in Millions Except for per Share Data

Item	As Reported for 2000	As Restated in November 2001 for 2000
Net income	$979	$847
Diluted earnings per share	$1.12	$0.97
Total assets	$65,503	$64,775
Debt	$10,229	$10,857
Equity	$11,470	$10,306

Source: Form 8-K filed with the Securities and Exchange Commission November 8, 2001.

Pro Forma Statements

In recent years, many companies have developed a practice of reporting pro forma financial information. Pro forma financial information is financial data that may be based on accounting methods other than generally accepted accounting principles (GAAP).[1] This information may be limited to earnings per share or span an entire financial statement. The difficulty that pro forma financial data presents is that there is no uniform method applied so that one company's pro forma earnings, for example, may be calculated quite differently than another company's pro forma earnings. The pro forma data may obscure the financial information that is determined using GAAP or it may simply focus on one element in the financial statements (e.g., earnings before interest, taxes, depreciation, and amortization) and ignore all others. Often the pro forma information is derived from statements created by applying GAAP, but the information is extracted through selective editing or restatement.

Interpreting pro forma financial information requires understanding the methods used to produce the information. Whereas pro forma financial information itself is not misleading, presenting pro forma information without an adequate description of how this information deviates from GAAP is potentially misleading.

Key to using any pro forma financial results is understanding the assumptions made, identifying what information is revealed and what information is not revealed, and determining how these results compare with GAAP results. The financial analyst must therefore look beyond the pro formas and examine the financial information prepared according to GAAP in order to have information that is comparable across companies and time.

INTERVIEWING COMPANY REPRESENTATIVES

Interviewing representatives of company may produce additional information and insight into the company's business. The starting place for the interview is the company's investors' relations (IR) office, which is generally well-prepared to address the analyst's questions.

The key is for the analyst to prepare before meeting with the IR officer so that the interview questions can be well focused. This preparation includes understanding the company's business, its products, the industry in which it operates, and its recent financial disclosures. The

---

[1] In the context of financial planning, pro forma statements are statements for future periods that are estimates of what may occur. This differs from the current practice of pro forma financial information.

analyst must understand the industry-specific terminology and any industry-specific accounting methods. In the telecommunications industry, for example, the analyst must understand measures such as gigahertz and minutes-in-use, and such terms as bandwidth, point-of-presence, and spectrum. As another example, an analyst for the oil and gas industry should understand that a degree day is a measure of temperature variation from a reference temperature.

The analyst must keep in mind that the IR officer has an obligation to treat all investors in a fair manner, which means that the IR officer cannot give a financial analyst material information that is not also available to others.[2] There is also information that the IR officer cannot give the analyst. For example, in a very competitive industry it may not be appropriate to give monthly sales figures for specific products. The analyst must understand the competitive nature of the industry and understand what information is typically not revealed in the industry.

Because the analyst comes armed with knowledge of the company's financial statements, the questions should focus on taking a closer look at the information provided by these disclosures:

- Extraordinary or unusual revenues and expenses
- Large differences between earnings from cash flows
- Changes in how data is reported
- Explanations for deviations from consensus earnings expectations
- How the company values itself versus the market's valuation
- Sales to major customers

An analyst that uses a statistical model to develop forecasts for the company or its industry may, of course, require very specific data that may not be readily available in the financial statements.

It is sometimes useful to determine what the company expects to earn in the future. Though companies may be reluctant to provide a specific earnings forecast, they will sometimes respond to a query regarding analysts' consensus earnings forecasts. In their response about analysts' forecasts, the company may reveal its own forecast. If a company provides a forecasts of its earnings, the analyst must consider the forecast in light of the company's previous forecasting; for example, some companies may consistently underestimate future earnings in order to avoid a negative earnings surprise. Further, the company's forecast or response to a consensus forecast may be accompanied by significant defensive disclosures that concern the risks that the company may not meet projected earnings.

---

[2] The Securities and Exchange Commission's Regulation FD, adopted on August 10, 2000 and effective on October 23, 2000, requires that any information that a company discloses be disclosed publicly, available to all investors at the same time.

INFORMATION PREPARED BY GOVERNMENT AGENCIES

Federal and state governmental agencies provide a wealth of information that may be useful in analyzing a company, its industry, or the economic environment.

Company-Specific Information

One of the most prominent innovations in the delivery of company information is the Securities and Exchange Commission's Electronic Data Gathering and Retrieval (EDGAR) system that is available on the Internet (www.sec.gov). The EDGAR system provides on-line access to most SEC filings for all public domestic companies from 1994 forward. The primary financial statement filings, such as the 10-K and 10-Q, are required EDGAR filings, though some filings (e.g., insider security ownership and 10-K filings of foreign corporations) are optional. The EDGAR system provides access within 24 hours of filing, providing up-to-date information that is accessible to everyone.

In addition to the EDGAR system at the SEC site, several financial service companies provide free or fee access to the information in the EDGAR system in different database forms that assist in searching or database creation tasks.

Industry Data

The analysis of a company requires that the analyst look at the other firms that operate in the same line of business. The purpose of examining these other companies is to get an idea of the market in which the company's products are sold: What is the degree of competition? What are the trends? What is the financial condition of the company's competitors?

Several government agencies provide information that is useful in an analysis of an industry. The primary governmental providers of industry data are the U.S. Bureau of the Census and the Bureau of Economic Analysis, an agency of the U.S. Department of Commerce. A recent innovation is the creation of Stat-USA, a fee-based collection of governmental data. Stat-USA is an electronic provider of industry and sector data that is produced by the U.S. Department of Commerce. The available data provided for different industries include gross domestic product, shipments of products, inventories, orders, and plant capacity utilization.

The government classification of businesses into industries is based on the North American Industry Classification System (NAICS). NAICS is a system of industry identification, replacing the Standard Industrial Classification (SIC). The NAICS is a 6-digit system that classifies businesses using 350 different classes and is now the basis for the classification of industry-specific data produced by governmental agencies.

Economic Data

Another source of information for financial analysis is economic data, such as the gross domestic product and consumer price index, which may be useful in assessing the recent performance or future prospects of a firm or industry. For example, suppose an analyst is evaluating a firm that owns a chain of retail outlets. What information will the analyst need to judge the firm's performance and financial condition? The analyst needs financial data, but they do not tell the whole story. The analyst also needs information on consumer spending, producer prices, and consumer prices. These economic data are readily available from government sources.

INFORMATION PREPARED BY FINANCIAL SERVICE COMPANIES

A whole industry exists to provide financial and related information about individual companies, industries, and the economy. The ease and low cost of providing such data on the Internet has fostered a proliferation of information providers. However, the prominent providers in today's Internet-based world are some of the same providers that were prominent in print medium.

Company-Specific Information

Information about an individual company is available from a vast number of sources, including the company itself through its own web pages. In addition to relaying the company's financial information that is presented by the company through its communication with shareholders and regulators, there are many financial service firms that compile the financial data and present analyses.

Several sources of data on individual companies are listed in Exhibit 9.3. This is by no means an exhaustive listing because of the large and growing number of information providers. The providers distinguish themselves in the market for information through the breadth of coverage (in terms of the number of companies in their database), the depth of coverage (in terms of the extensive nature of their data for individual companies), or their specialty (e.g., the collection of analyst recommendations and forecasts).

EXHIBIT 9.3 Sources of Individual Company Financial Data

Financial Reporting Service	Product	Brief Description
Disclosure www.disclosure.com	Global Access	Electronic database of companies' financial statements and financial analyst forecasts
Dun & Bradstreet www.dnb.com	Principal International Businesses	Electronic database of selected information on 50,000 companies in 140 countries
Fitch IBCA www.fitchibca.com	BankScope	Comprehensive database of financials on 10,000 international banks
	CreditDisk	International bank rating service on CD-ROM
	Fitch IBCA Research	In-depth research on U.S. corporations
	International Bank Rating Review	Ratings, key financial statistics, background, and one-page credit assessments of 650 banks around the world
Moody's Investor Services www.moodys.com	Company Data Direct	An online database of information on a companies' history, financial statements, and long-term debt
	Company Data with EDGAR	An electronic database consisting of company SEC filings
Standard and Poor's, McGraw-Hill, Inc. www.standardpoor.com	Compustat	Electronic database of annual and quarterly financial statement and market data coverage for over 18,000 North American and 11,000 global companies
	Market Insight	Web-based access to individual company financial statement data on the Standard & Poor's universe of companies
	EDGAR from Compustat	A searchable electronic database consisting of company 10-K and 10-Q filings
Value Line, Inc. www.valueline.com	DataFile	Electronic database with annual and quarterly financial statement and monthly market price data for over 5,000 securities on an "as reported" basis since 1955
	Estimates & Projections File	Electronic data with Value Line's proprietary estimates of earnings and dividends for the 1,700 companies
Zacks Investment Research www.zacks.com	Zacks Historical Data	Electronic database comprised of financial statement data, analyst forecasts, earnings surprise and stock recommendations
	Zacks Research System (ZRA)	An electronic database that includes financial statement, price, and earnings data for over 6,000 companies

Industry Data

The first step in analyzing the industry is to define the company's industry. The NAICS is a system of classification of companies, yet it does not classify companies—it simply sets up a coding system that once the company's productive activities are identified by the analyst, a company can then be classified into a specific, coded industry. Though it may seem a simple task, the fact that most companies operate in more than one line of business complicates the definition of the industry and the analysis process. Consider RJR Nabisco which operates in both the tobacco and the food industries, contributing 49% and 51% of net sales, respectively. Because it operates in two different industries, it is difficult to classify the RJR Nabisco into one or another NAICS code. As a result of its operating significantly in two industries, the financial analyst must analyze both of these industries.

The classification of companies into industries is based on judgment and different financial reporting services and different analysts may classify the same company into different industries. One provider may classify a company based on the line of business that generates the largest percentage of sales, whereas another provider may classify a company according to the largest percentage of assets in that industry. The analyst must be aware of how the reporting service classifies companies into industries when using industry data.

In addition to the classification problem, another problem arises in the calculation of industry statistics that may be used as inputs into the analysis. Consider an industry comprised of the following four companies:

Company	Return on assets
A	23%
B	20%
C	15%
D	10%

What is this industry's return on assets? Is it the arithmetic average of 17%? That's one way of looking at it. But what if the companies are quite different in terms of size? If company A has $10 million in assets and companies B, C, and D each have only $1 million, the simple average of 17% does not appear to adequately represent the industry's return. It seems reasonable that some type of weighting be applied to reflect the difference in size, though the choice of weights is left to the judgment of the analyst. If the analyst is using industry averages that are prepared by someone else, it is important for the analyst to understand how the average is derived.

Aside from the financial statement data, the analyst may need to collect additional information about a company and industry that is industry-specific. For example, in analyzing the airline industry, the load factor (the percentage of seats sold) is an indicator of activity that is related to an airline's performance.

A number of financial information providers offer industry-specific data and compile financial data by industry. Some services, such as Standard & Poor's Compustat and Value Line, provide industry data based on their large universe of stocks covered in their database of individual company financial data.

Economic Data

Much of the economic data that is used in financial analysis is taken from government sources, though some information is independently produced through surveys and research. There are many commercial services that collect and disseminate this and other information. These services include AP Business News (www.ap.org), Bridge (www.bridge.com), and Business Wire (www.businesswire.com). Financial publications, such as the *Wall Street Journal* (www.wsj.com), *Investors Business Daily* (www.investors.com), and the *Financial Times* (www.ft.com), provide economic data in both in print and electronic forms. In addition, databases, such as McGraw-Hill's DRI U.S. Central Data Base (USCEN), collect and market historical series of U.S. economic and financial data.

RELATIONSHIP TO FUNDAMENTAL MULTI-FACTOR RISK MODELS

As explained in Chapter 13, another tool for the bottom up active manager is using a fundamental multi-factor risk model. This approach makes the equity selection and portfolio construction decisions based on quantitative models without relying on analysts. The portfolio construction process is purely "by the numbers" produced by the model. However, the inputs are obtained from an analysis of financial statements.

For example, a fundamental factor model uses company and industry attributes and market data as raw descriptors to explain a company's historical stock returns. Those variables that are found to be pervasive in explaining stock returns are then the raw descriptors that become "factors" in the model. In the fundamental factor model of BARRA described in Chapter 13, the inputs obtained taken from a company's current and historical financial statements in constructing factors include price/earnings ratio, book/price ratio, variance in earnings, cash flow, debt-to-asset ratio. Yet, as we shall see, the quality of some of these numbers taken from financial statements may be questionable or the data may not be comparable over time for a given company or across companies. The portfolio manager must be aware of these input problems in model development and employment of the model's output in portfolio construction.

The concern with respect to relying solely on the output of fundamental factor models without an assessment by an analyst has led some portfolio managers to modify the results of their models. Specifically, in developing fundamental factor models, some portfolio managers include as an input their equity analysts' view on the company's future operating performance and financial condition. A good is example is the Goldman Sachs Asset Management Factor Model. This firm, a subsidiary of the investment banking firm Goldman Sachs, includes a factor that is based on an assessment by its equity analysts who have performed traditional equity analysis.

The equity portfolio manager must even understand the limitations of financial accounting data used today in classifying stocks. Specifically, today the notion of an "investment style" is well accepted in the industry. Companies are classified by capitalization (e.g., large cap, medium cap, small cap, and micro cap). Classification by size doesn't present a problem since it relies on market price and number of shares. However, when companies are classified in terms of what is popularly referred to as "growth" and "value," information from the financial statements is required to classify stocks and therefore subject to the problem of the quality of the financial data used.

The key point here is that an understanding of financial statements and their limitations are essential to even today's quantitative portfolio manager. The development of quantitative models doesn't mean that a portfolio manager can ignore the basic source of information. Unfortunately, too often quantitative portfolio managers are more concerned with whether their models satisfy some obscure statistical property rather than whether the inputs for some companies are truly representative of the measure of interest. Sometimes the reason for a significant error term in model projections lies with the inputs.

CHAPTER 10

Traditional Fundamental Analysis II: Financial Ratio Analysis

Pamela P. Peterson, Ph.D., CFA
Professor of Finance
Florida State University

Frank J. Fabozzi, Ph.D., CFA
Adjunct Professor of Finance
School of Management
Yale University

In this chapter, one of the tools of traditional fundamental analysis is explained—financial ratio analysis. This involves selecting the relevant information—primarily the financial statement data—and evaluating it. We show how to incorporate market data and economic data in the analysis and interpretation of financial ratios. Finally, we show you how to interpret financial ratio analysis, warning of the pitfalls that occur when it's not done properly.

Financial ratio analysis is one of the many tools useful in valuation based on traditional fundamental analysis because it helps the analyst gauge returns and risks. We begin the analysis with a fictitious firm as our example, allowing us to use simplified financial statements and allowing you to become more comfortable with the tools of financial analysis. After we cover the basics, we use these same tools with data from an actual firm in an integrative example.

RATIOS AND THEIR CLASSIFICATIONS

A *ratio* is a mathematical relation between two quantities. Suppose you have 200 apples and 100 oranges. The ratio of apples to oranges is 200/100, which we can conveniently express as 2:1 or 2. A financial ratio is a comparison between one bit of financial information and another. Consider the ratio of current assets to current liabilities, which we refer to as the current ratio. This ratio is a comparison between assets that can be readily turned into cash—current assets—and the obligations that are due in the near future—current liabilities. A current ratio of 2 or 2:1 means that we have twice as much in current assets as we need to satisfy obligations due in the near future.

Ratios can be classified according to the way they are constructed and the financial characteristic they are describing. For example, we will see that the current ratio is constructed as a coverage ratio (the ratio of current assets—available funds—to current liabilities—the obligation) that we use to describe a firm's liquidity (its ability to meet its immediate needs).

There are as many different financial ratios as there are possible combinations of items appearing on the income statement, balance sheet, and statement of cash flows. We can classify ratios according to how they are constructed or according to the financial characteristic that they capture.

Ratios can be constructed in the following four ways:

1. As a *coverage ratio*. A coverage ratio is a measure of a firm's ability to "cover," or meet, a particular financial obligation. The denominator may be any obligation, such as interest or rent, and the numerator is the amount of the funds available to satisfy that obligation.
2. As a *return ratio*. A return ratio indicates a net benefit received from a particular investment of resources. The net benefit is what is left over after expenses, such as operating earnings or net income, and the resources may be total assets, fixed assets, inventory, or any other investment.
3. As a *turnover ratio*. A turnover ratio is a measure of how much a firm gets out of its assets. This ratio compares the gross benefit from an activity or investment with the resources employed in it.
4. As a *component percentage*. A component percentage is the ratio of one amount in a financial statement, such as net profit, to the total of amounts in that financial statement, such as sales.

In addition, we can also express financial data in terms of time—say, how many days' worth of inventory we have on hand—or on a per share basis—say, how much a firm has earned for each share of common stock. Both are measures we can use to evaluate operating performance or financial condition.

When we assess a firm's operating performance, we want to know if it is applying its assets in an efficient and profitable manner. When we assess a firm's financial condition, we want to know if it is able to meet its financial obligations. We can use financial ratios to evaluate five aspects of operating performance and financial condition:

1. Return on investment
2. Liquidity
3. Profitability
4. Activity
5. Financial leverage

There are several ratios reflecting each of the five aspects of a firm's operating performance and financial condition. We apply these ratios to the Fictitious Corporation, whose balance sheets, income statements, and statement of cash flows are shown in Exhibits 10.1, 10.2, and 10.3, respectively. The ratios we introduce now are by no means the only ones that can be formed using financial data, though they are some of the more commonly used. After becoming comfortable with the tools of financial analysis, you will be able to create ratios that serve your particular evaluation objective.

RETURN-ON-INVESTMENT RATIOS

Return-on-investment ratios compare measures of benefits, such as earnings or net income, with measures of investment. For example, if you want to evaluate how well the firm uses its assets in its operations, you could calculate the *return on assets*—sometimes called the *basic earning power ratio*—as the ratio of earnings before interest and taxes (EBIT)—operating earnings—to total assets:

$$\text{Basic earning power} = \frac{\text{Earnings before interest and taxes}}{\text{Total assets}}$$

For Fictitious Corporation, for 1999:

$$\text{Basic earning power} = \frac{\$2,000,000}{\$11,000,000} = 0.1818 \text{ or } 18.18\%$$

For every dollar invested in assets, Fictitious earned about 18 cents in 1999. This measure deals with earnings from operations; it does not consider how these operations are financed.

Another return-on-assets ratio uses net income—operating earnings less interest and taxes—instead of earnings before interest and taxes:[1]

EXHIBIT 10.1 Fictitious Corporation Balance Sheets for Years Ending December 31, in Thousands

	1999	1998
ASSETS		
Cash	$400	$200
Marketable securities	200	0
Accounts receivable	600	800
Inventories	1,800	1,000
Total current assets	$3,000	$2,000
Gross plant and equipment	$11,000	$10,000
Accumulated depreciation	(4,000)	(3,000)
Net plant and equipment	7,000	7,000
Intangible assets	1,000	1,000
Total assets	$11,000	$10,000
LIABILITIES AND SHAREHOLDERS' EQUITY		
Accounts payable	$500	$400
Other current liabilities	500	200
Long-term debt	4,000	5,000
Total liabilities	$5,000	$5,600
Common stock, $1 par value;		
Authorized 2,000,000 shares		
Issued 1,500,000 and 1,200,000 shares	1,500	1,200
Additional paid-in capital	1,500	800
Retained earnings	3,000	2,400
Total shareholders' equity	6,000	4,400
Total liabilities and shareholders' equity	$11,000	$10,000

[1] In actual application the same term, return on assets, is often used to describe both ratios. It is only in the actual context or through an examination of the numbers themselves that we know which return ratio is presented. We use two different terms to describe these two return-on-asset ratios in this chapter simply to avoid any confusion.

EXHIBIT 10.2   Fictitious Corporation Income Statements for Years Ending December 31 (in Thousands)

	1999	1998
Sales	$10,000	$9,000
Cost of goods sold	(6,500)	(6,000)
Gross profit	$3,500	$3,000
Lease expense	(1,000)	(1,000)
Administrative expense	(500)	(500)
Earnings before interest and taxes (EBIT)	$2,000	$2,000
Interest	(400)	(500)
Earnings before taxes	$1,600	$1,500
Taxes	(400)	(500)
Net income	$1,200	$1,000
Preferred dividends	(100)	(100)
Earnings available to common shareholders	$1,100	$900
Common dividends	(500)	(400)
Retained earnings	$600	$500

$$\text{Return on assets } = \frac{\text{Net income}}{\text{Total assets}}$$

For Fictitious in 1999:

$$\text{Return on assets } = \frac{\$1,200,000}{\$11,000,000} = 0.1091 \text{ or } 10.91\%$$

Thus, without taking into consideration how assets are financed, the return on assets for Fictitious is 18%. Taking into consideration how assets are financed, the return on assets is 11%. The difference is due to Fictitious' financing part of its total assets with debt, incurring interest of $400,000 in 1999; hence, the return-on-assets ratio excludes 1999 taxes of $400,000 from earnings in the numerator.

If we look at Fictitious' liabilities and equities, we see that the assets are financed in part by liabilities ($1 million short term, $4 million long term) and in part by equity ($800,000 preferred stock, $5.2 million common stock). If we look at the information as investors, we may not be interested in the return the firm gets from its *total* investment (debt plus equity), but rather shareholders are interested in the return the firm can generate on their investment. The *return on equity* is the ratio of the net income shareholders receive to their equity in the stock:

EXHIBIT 10.3 Fictitious Company Statement of Cash Flows, Years Ended December 31, in Thousands

	1999	1998
Cash Flow From (Used For) Operating Activities		
Net income	$1,200	$1,000
Add or deduct adjustments to cash basis:		
Change in accounts receivables	$200	$(200)
Change in accounts payable	100	400
Change in marketable securities	(200)	200
Change in inventories	(800)	(600)
Change in other current liabilities	300	0
Depreciation	1,000	1,000
	600	800
Cash flow from operations	$1,800	$1,800
Cash Flow From (Used For) Investing Activities		
Purchase of plant and equipment	$(1,000)	$0
Cash flow from (used for) investing activities	$(1,000)	$0
Cash Flow From (Used For) Financing Activities		
Sale of common stock	$1,000	$0
Repayment of long-term debt	(1,000)	(1,500)
Payment of preferred dividends	(100)	(100)
Payment of common dividends	(500)	(400)
Cash flow from (used for) financing activities	(600)	(1,900)
Increase (decrease) in cash flow	$200	$(100)
Cash at the beginning of the year	200	300
Cash at the end of the year	$400	$200

$$\text{Return on equity} = \frac{\text{Net income}}{\text{Book value of shareholders' equity}}$$

For Fictitious Corporation, there is only one type of shareholder: common. For 1999:

$$\text{Return on equity} = \frac{\$1,200,000}{\$6,000,000} = 0.2000 \text{ or } 20.00\%$$

Recap: Return-on-Investment Ratios

The return-on-investment ratios for Fictitious Corporation for 1999 are:

Basic earning power = 18.18%
Return on assets   = 10.91%
Return on equity   = 20.00%

These return-on-investment ratios tell us:

- Fictitious earns over 18% from operations, or about 11% overall, from its assets.
- Shareholders earn 20% from their investment (measured in book value terms).

These ratios do not tell us:

- Whether this return is due to the profit margins (that is, due to costs and revenues) or to how effectively Fictitious uses its assets.
- The return shareholders earn on their actual investment in the firm, that is, what shareholders earn relative to their actual investment, not the book value of their investment. For example, you may invest $100 in the stock, but its value according to the balance sheet may be more or less than $100.

The Du Pont System

The returns on investment ratios give us a "bottom line" on the performance of a company, but don't tell us anything about the "why" behind this performance. For an understanding of the "why," the analyst must dig a bit deeper into the financial statements. A method that is useful in examining the source of performance is the Du Pont system. The *Du Pont system* is a method of breaking down return ratios into their components to determine which areas are responsible for a firm's performance. To see how it's used, let's take a closer look at the first definition of the return on assets:

$$\text{Basic earning power} = \frac{\text{Earnings before interest and taxes}}{\text{Total assets}}$$

Suppose the return on assets changes from 20% in one period to 10% the next period. We do not know whether this decreased return is due to a less efficient use of the firm's assets—that is, lower activity—or to less effective management of expenses (i.e., lower profit margins). A lower return on assets could be due to lower activity, lower margins, or both. Since we are interested in evaluating past operating performance to evaluate different aspects of the management of the firm and to predict future performance, knowing the source of these returns is valuable.

Let's take a closer look at the return on assets and break it down into its components: measures of activity and profit margin. We do this by relating both the numerator and the denominator to sales activity. Divide both the numerator and the denominator of the basic earning power by sales:

$$\text{Basic earning power} = \frac{\text{Earnings before interest and taxes}/\text{Sales}}{\text{Total assets}/\text{Sales}}$$

which is equivalent to:

$$\text{Basic earning power} = \left(\frac{\text{Earnings before interest and taxes}}{\text{Sales}}\right)\left(\frac{\text{Sales}}{\text{Total assets}}\right)$$

This says that the earning power of the company is related to profitability (in this case, operating profit) and a measure of activity (total asset turnover).

Basic earning power = (Operating profit margin) (Total asset turnover)

If we are analyzing a change in basic earning power, we therefore know that we could look at this breakdown to see the change in its components: operating profit margin and total asset turnover.

This method of analyzing return ratios in terms of profit margin and turnover ratios, referred to as the Du Pont System, is credited to the E.I. du Pont Corporation, whose management developed a system of breaking down return ratios into their components.[2]

Let's look at the return on assets of Fictitious for 1998 and 1999. Its returns on assets were 20% in 1998 and 18.18% in 1999. We can decompose the firm's returns on assets for the two years, 1998 and 1999, to obtain:

Year	Basic Earning Power	Operating Profit Margin	Total Asset Turnover
1998	20.00%	22.22%	0.9000 times
1999	18.18	20.00	0.9091 times

---

[2] American Management Association, *Executive Committee Control Charts*, AMA Management Bulletin No. 6, 1960, p. 22.

We see that operating profit margin declined from 1998 to 1999, yet asset turnover improved slightly, from 0.9000 to 0.9091. Therefore, the return-on-assets decline from 1998 to 1999 is attributable to lower profit margins.

The return on assets can be broken down into its components in a similar manner:

$$\text{Return on assets} = \left(\frac{\text{Net income}}{\text{Sales}}\right)\left(\frac{\text{Sales}}{\text{Total assets}}\right)$$

or

$$\text{Return on assets} = (\text{Net profit margin})\,(\text{Total asset turnover})$$

We can relate the basic earning power ratio to the return on assets, recognizing that:

$$\text{Net income} = \text{Earnings before tax}\,(1 - \text{Tax rate})$$

$$\text{Net income} = \text{Earnings before interest and taxes}$$
$$\times \left(\frac{\text{Earnings before taxes}}{\text{Earnings before interest and taxes}}\right)(1 - \text{Tax rate})$$

$$\uparrow \qquad\qquad\qquad\qquad\qquad \uparrow$$
$$\text{equity's share of earnings} \qquad \text{tax retention \%}$$

The ratio of earnings before taxes to earnings before interest and taxes reflects the interest burden of the company, where as the term $(1 - \text{tax rate})$ reflects the company's tax burden. Therefore,

$$\text{Return on assets} = \left(\frac{\text{Earnings before interest and taxes}}{\text{Sales}}\right)\left(\frac{\text{Sales}}{\text{Total assets}}\right)$$
$$\times \left(\frac{\text{Earnings before taxes}}{\text{Earnings before interest and taxes}}\right)(1 - \text{Tax rate})$$

or

$$\text{Return on assets} = (\text{Operating profit margin})(\text{Total asset turnover})$$
$$\times (\text{Equity's share of earnings})(\text{Tax retention \%})$$

   The breakdown of a return-on-equity ratio requires a bit more decomposition because instead of total assets as the denominator, we want to use shareholders' equity. Since activity ratios reflect use of all of the assets, not just the proportion financed by equity, we need to adjust the activity ratio by the proportion that assets are financed by equity (i.e., the ratio of the book value of shareholders' equity to total assets):

$$\text{Return on equity} = (\text{Return on assets})\left(\frac{\text{Total assets}}{\text{Shareholders' equity}}\right)$$

$$\text{Return on equity} = \left(\frac{\text{Net income}}{\text{Sales}}\right)\left(\frac{\text{Sales}}{\text{Total assets}}\right)\left(\frac{\text{Total assets}}{\text{Shareholders' equity}}\right)$$

$$\uparrow$$
$$\text{equity multiplier}$$

The ratio of total assets to shareholders' equity is referred to as the *equity multiplier*. The equity multiplier, therefore, captures the effects of how a company finances its assets, referred to as its financial leverage. Multiplying the total asset turnover ratio by the equity multiplier allows us to break down the return-on-equity ratios into three components: profit margin, asset turnover, and financial leverage. For example, the return on equity can be broken down into three parts:

   Return on equity
      = (Net profit margin)(Total asset turnover)(Equity multiplier)

Applying this breakdown to Fictitious for 1998 and 1999:

Year	Return on Equity	Net Profit Margin	Total Asset Turnover	Total Debt to Assets	Equity Multiplier
1998	22.73%	11.11%	0.9000 times	56.00%	2.2727
1999	20.00	12.00	0.9091	45.45%	1.8332

We see that the return on equity decreased from 1998 to 1999 because of a lower operating profit margin *and* less use of financial leverage.
   We can decompose the return on equity further by breaking out the equity's share of before-tax earnings (represented by the ratio of earnings before and after interest) and tax retention% (one minus the tax rate):

$$\text{Return on equity} = \left(\frac{\text{Earnings before interest and taxes}}{\text{Sales}}\right)\left(\frac{\text{Sales}}{\text{Total assets}}\right)$$
$$\times \left(\frac{\text{Earnings before taxes}}{\text{Earnings before interest and taxes}}\right)(1 - \text{Tax rate})$$
$$\times \frac{\text{Total assets}}{\text{Shareholders' equity}}$$

This decomposition allows the financial analyst to take a closer look at the factors that are controllable by a company's management (e.g., asset turnover) and those that are not controllable (e.g., tax retention). As you can see, the breakdowns lead the analyst to information on both the balance sheet and the income statement. And this is not the only breakdown of the return ratios—further decomposition is possible.

LIQUIDITY

Liquidity reflects the ability of a firm to meet its short-term obligations using those assets that are most readily converted into cash. Assets that may be converted into cash in a short period of time are referred to as *liquid assets*; they are listed in financial statements as current assets. Current assets are often referred to as *working capital*, since they represent the resources need for the day-to-day operations of the firm's long-term capital investments. Current assets are used to satisfy short-term obligations, or current liabilities. The amount by which current assets exceed current liabilities is referred to as the *net working capital*.

The Operating Cycle

How much liquidity a firm needs depends on its operating cycle. The *operating cycle* is the duration from the time cash is invested in goods and services to the time that investment produces cash. For example, a firm that produces and sells goods has an operating cycle comprising four phases:

1. Purchase raw material and produce goods, investing in inventory
2. Sell goods, generating sales, which may or may not be for cash
3. Extend credit, creating accounts receivable
4. Collect accounts receivable, generating cash

The four phases make up the cycle of cash use and generation. The operating cycle would be somewhat different for companies that produce services rather than goods, but the idea is the same—the operating cycle is the length of time it takes to *generate* cash through the *investment* of cash.

What does the operating cycle have to do with liquidity? The longer the operating cycle, the more current assets are needed (relative to current liabilities) since it takes longer to convert inventories and receivables into cash. In other words, the longer the operating cycle, the greater the amount of net working capital required.

To measure the length of an operating cycle we need to know:

1. The time it takes to convert the investment in inventory into sales (that is, cash → inventory → sales → accounts receivable)
2. The time it takes to collect sales on credit (that is, accounts receivable → cash)

We can estimate the operating cycle for Fictitious Corporation for 1999, using the balance sheet and income statement data. The number of days Fictitious ties up funds in inventory is determined by the total amount of money represented in inventory and the average day's cost of goods sold. The current investment in inventory—that is, the money "tied up" in inventory—is the ending balance of inventory on the balance sheet. The *average day's cost of goods sold* is the cost of goods sold on an average day in the year, which can be estimated by dividing the cost of goods sold (which is found on the income statement) by the number of days in the year. The average day's cost of goods sold for 1999 is:

$$\text{Average day's cost of good sold} = \frac{\text{Cost of goods sold}}{365 \text{ days}}$$

$$= \frac{\$6,500,000}{365 \text{ days}} = \$17,808 \text{ per day}$$

In other words, Fictitious incurs, on average, a cost of producing goods sold of $17,808 per day.

Fictitious has $1.8 million of inventory on hand at the end of the year. How many days' worth of goods sold is this? One way to look at this is to imagine that Fictitious stopped buying more raw materials and just finished producing whatever was on hand in inventory, using available raw materials and work in process. How long would it take Fictitious to run out of inventory?

We compute the *number of days of inventory* by calculating the ratio of the amount of inventory on hand (in dollars) to the average day's cost of goods sold (in dollars per day):

$$\text{Number of days of inventory} = \frac{\text{Amount of inventory on hand}}{\text{Average day's cost of goods sold}}$$

$$= \frac{\$1,800,000}{\$17,808 \text{ per day}} = 101 \text{ days}$$

In other words, Fictitious has approximately 101 days of goods on hand at the end of 1999. If sales continued at the same price, it would take Fictitious 101 days to run out of inventory.

If the ending inventory is representative of the inventory throughout the year, then it takes about 101 days to convert the investment in inventory into sold goods. Why worry about whether the year-end inventory is representative of inventory at any day throughout the year? Well, if inventory at the end of the fiscal year-end is lower than on any other day of the year, we have understated the number of days of inventory. Indeed, in practice most companies try to choose fiscal year-ends that coincide with the slow period of their business. That means the ending balance of inventory would be *lower* than the typical daily inventory of the year. To get a better picture of the firm, we could, for example, look at quarterly financial statements and take averages of quarterly inventory balances. However, here for simplicity we make a note of the problem of representatives and deal with it later in the discussion of financial ratios.[3]

We can extend the same logic for calculating the number of days between a sale—when an account receivable is created—to the time it is collected in cash. If we assume that Fictitious sells all goods on credit, we can first calculate the *average credit sales per day* and then figure out how many days' worth of credit sales are represented by the ending balance of receivables.

The average credit sales per day are:

$$\text{Credit sales per day} = \frac{\text{Credit sales}}{365 \text{ days}} = \frac{\$10,000,000}{365 \text{ days}} = \$27,397 \text{ per day}$$

---

[3] As an attempt to make the inventory figure more representative, some suggest taking the average of the beginning and ending inventory amounts. This does nothing to remedy the representativeness problem because the beginning inventory is simply the ending inventory from the previous year and, like the ending value from the current year, is measured at the low point of the operating cycle. A preferred method, if data are available, is to calculate the average inventory for the four quarters of the fiscal year.

Therefore, Fictitious generates $27,397 of credit sales per day. With an ending balance of accounts receivable of $600,000, the *number of days of credit* in this ending balance is calculated by taking the ratio of the balance in the accounts receivable account to the credit sales per day:

$$\text{Number of days of credit} = \frac{\text{Accounts receivable}}{\text{Credit sales per day}}$$

$$= \frac{\$600,000}{\$27,397 \text{ per day}} = 22 \text{ days}$$

If the ending balance of receivables at the end of the year is representative of the receivables on any day throughout the year, then it takes, on average, approximately 22 days to collect the accounts receivable. In other words, it takes 22 days for a sale to become cash.

Using what we have determined for the inventory cycle and cash cycle, we see that for Fictitious:

$$\text{Operating cycle} = \text{Number of days of inventory} + \text{Number of days of credit}$$
$$= 101 \text{ days} + 22 \text{ days} = 123 \text{ days}$$

We also need to look at the liabilities on the balance sheet to see how long it takes a firm to pay its short-term obligations. We can apply the same logic to accounts payable as we did to accounts receivable and inventories. How long does it take a firm, on average, to go from creating a payable (buying on credit) to paying for it in cash?

First, we need to determine the amount of an *average day's purchases* on credit. If we assume all the Fictitious purchases are made on credit, then the total purchases for the year would be the cost of goods sold less any amounts included in cost of goods sold that are not purchases. For example, depreciation is included in the cost of goods sold yet is not a purchase. Since we do not have a breakdown on the company's cost of goods sold showing how much was paid for in cash and how much was on credit, let's assume for simplicity that purchases are equal to cost of goods sold less depreciation. The average day's purchases then become:

$$\text{Average day's purchases} = \frac{\text{Cost of goods sold} - \text{Depreciation}}{365 \text{ days}}$$

$$= \frac{\$6,500,000 - \$1,000,000}{365 \text{ days}} = \$15,068 \text{ per day}$$

The number of days of purchases represented in the ending balance in accounts payable is calculated as the ratio of the balance in the accounts payable account to the average day's purchases:

$$\text{Number of days of payables} = \frac{\text{Accounts payable}}{\text{Average day's purchases}}$$

For Fictitious in 1999:

$$\text{Number of days of payables} = \frac{\$500,000}{\$15,068 \text{ per day}} = 33 \text{ days}$$

This means that on average Fictitious takes 33 days to pay out cash for a purchase.

The operating cycle tells us how long it takes to convert an investment in cash *back into* cash (by way of inventory and accounts receivable). The number of days of payables tells us how long it takes to pay on purchases made to create the inventory. If we put these two pieces of information together, we can see how long, on net, we tie up cash. The difference between the operating cycle and the number of days of purchases is the *net operating cycle*:

Net operating cycle = Operating cycle – Number of days of payables

Or, substituting for the operating cycle,

Net operating cycle = Number of days of inventory
+ Number of days of credit
– Number of payables

The net operating cycle for Fictitious in 1999 is:

Net operating cycle = 101 + 22 – 33 = 90 days

The net operating cycle is how long it takes for the firm to get cash back from its investments in inventory and accounts receivable, considering that purchases may be made on credit. By not paying for purchases immediately (that is, using trade credit), the firm reduces its liquidity needs. Therefore, the longer the net operating cycle, the greater the required liquidity.

Measures of Liquidity

We can describe a firm's ability to meet its current obligations in several ways. The *current ratio* indicates the firm's ability to meet or cover its current liabilities using its current assets:

$$\text{Current ratio } = \frac{\text{Current assets}}{\text{Current liabilities}}$$

For the Fictitious Corporation, the current ratio for 1999 is the ratio of current assets, $3 million, to current liabilities, the sum of accounts payable and other current liabilities, or $1 million.

$$\text{Current ratio } = \frac{\$3,000,000}{\$1,000,000} = 3.0 \text{ times}$$

The current ratio of 3.0 indicates that Fictitious has three times as much as it needs to cover its current obligations during the year. However, the current ratio groups all current asset accounts together, assuming they are all as easily converted to cash. Even though, by definition, current assets can be transformed into cash within a year, not all current assets can be transformed into cash in a short period of time.

An alternative to the current ratio is the *quick ratio*, also called the *acid-test ratio*, which uses a slightly different set of current accounts to cover the same current liabilities as in the current ratio. In the quick ratio, the least liquid of the current asset accounts, inventory, is excluded. Hence:

$$\text{Quick ratio } = \frac{\text{Current assets} - \text{Inventory}}{\text{Current liabilities}}$$

We typically leave out inventories in the quick ratio because inventories are generally perceived as the least liquid of the current assets. By leaving out the least liquid asset, the quick ratio provides a more conservative view of liquidity.

For Fictitious, in 1999:

$$\text{Quick ratio } = \frac{\$3,000,000 - 1,800,000}{\$1,000,000} = \frac{\$1,200,000}{\$1,000,000} = 1.2 \text{ times}$$

Still another way to measure the firm's ability to satisfy short-term obligations is the *net working capital-to-sales ratio*, which compares net working capital (current assets less current liabilities) with sales:

$$\text{Net working capital-to-sales ratio } = \frac{\text{Net working capital}}{\text{Sales}}$$

This ratio tells us the "cushion" available to meet short-term obligations relative to sales. Consider two firms with identical working capital of $100,000, but one has sales of $500,000 and the other sales of $1,000,000. If they have identical operating cycles, this means that the firm with the greater sales has more funds flowing in and out of its current asset investments (inventories and receivables). The firm with more funds flowing in and out needs a larger cushion to protect itself in case of a disruption in the cycle, such as a labor strike or unexpected delays in customer payments. The longer the operating cycle, the more of a cushion (net working capital) a firm needs for a given level of sales.

For Fictitious Corporation:

$$\text{Net working capital-to-sales ratio } = \frac{\$3,000,000 - 1,000,000}{\$10,000,000}$$
$$= 0.2000 \text{ or } 20\%$$

The ratio of 0.20 tells us that for every dollar of sales, Fictitious has 20 cents of net working capital to support it.

Recap: Liquidity Ratios

Operating cycle and liquidity ratio information for Fictitious, using data from 1999, in summary, is:

Number of days of inventory	=	101 days
Number of days of credit	=	22 days
Operating cycle	=	123 days
Number of days of payables	=	33 days
Net operating cycle	=	90 days
Current ratio	=	3.0
Quick ratio	=	1.2
Net working capital-to-sales ratio	=	20%

Given the measures of time related to the current accounts—the operating cycle and the net operating cycle—and the three measures of liquidity—current ratio, quick ratio, and net working capital-to-sales ratio—we know the following about Fictitious Corporation's ability to meet its short-term obligations:

■ Inventory is less liquid than accounts receivable (comparing days of inventory with days of credit).
■ Current assets are greater than needed to satisfy current liabilities in a year (from the current ratio).
■ The quick ratio tells us that Fictitious can meet its short-term obligations even without resorting to selling inventory.
■ The net working capital "cushion" is 20 cents for every dollar of sales (from the net working capital-to-sales ratio.)

What don't ratios tells us about liquidity? They don't provide us with answers to the following questions:

■ How liquid are the accounts receivable? How much of the accounts receivable will be collectible? Whereas we know it takes, on average, 22 days to collect, we do not know how much will never be collected.
■ What is the nature of the current liabilities? How much of current liabilities consists of items that recur (such as accounts payable and wages payable) each period and how much of occasional items (such as income taxes payable)?
■ Are there any unrecorded liabilities (such as operating leases) that are not included in current liabilities?

PROFITABILITY RATIOS

We have seen that liquidity ratios tells us about a firm's ability to meet its immediate obligations. Now we extend our analysis skills by adding profitability ratios, which helps us gauge how well a firm is managing its expenses. *Profit margin ratios* compare components of income with sales. They give us an idea of what factors make up a firm's income and are usually expressed as a portion of each dollar of sales. For example, the profit margin ratios we discuss here differ only in the numerator. It's in the numerator that we can evaluate performance for different aspects of the business.

For example, suppose the analyst wants to evaluate how well production facilities are managed. The analyst would focus on gross profit (sales less cost of goods sold), a measure of income that is the direct result of production management. Comparing gross profit with sales produces the *gross profit margin*:

$$\text{Gross profit margin} = \frac{\text{Sales} - \text{Cost of goods sold}}{\text{Sales}}$$

This ratio tells us the portion of each dollar of sales that remains after deducting production expenses. For Fictitious Corporation for 1999:

$$\text{Gross profit margin} = \frac{\$10,000,000 - \$6,500,000}{\$10,000,000} = \frac{\$3,500,000}{\$10,000,000}$$
$$= 0.3500 \text{ or } 35\%$$

For each dollar of sales, the firm's gross profit is 35 cents. Looking at sales and cost of goods sold, we can see that the gross profit margin is affected by:

■ Changes in sales volume, which affect cost of goods sold *and* sales
■ Changes in sales price, which affect sales
■ Changes in the cost of production, which affect cost of goods sold

Any change in gross profit margin from one period to the next is caused by one or more of those three factors. Similarly, differences in gross margin ratios among firms are the result of differences in those factors.

To evaluate operating performance, we need to consider operating expenses in addition to the cost of goods sold. To do this, we remove operating expenses (e.g., selling and general administrative expenses) from gross profit, leaving us with operating profit, also referred to as earnings before interest and taxes (EBIT). The *operating profit margin* is therefore:

$$\text{Operating profit margin} = \frac{\text{Sales} - \text{Cost of goods sold} - \text{Operating expenses}}{\text{Sales}}$$
$$= \frac{\text{Earnings before interest and taxes}}{\text{Sales}}$$

For Fictitious in 1999:

$$\text{Operating profit margin} = \frac{\$2,000,000}{\$10,000,000} = 0.20 \text{ or } 20\%$$

Therefore, for each dollar of sales, Fictitious has 20 cents of operating income. The operating profit margin is affected by the same factors as gross profit margin, plus operating expenses such as:

■ Office rent and lease expenses
■ Miscellaneous income (for example, income from investments)
■ Advertising expenditures
■ Bad debt expense

Most of these expenses are related in some way to sales, though they are not included directly in the cost of goods sold. Therefore, the difference between the gross profit margin and the operating profit margin is due to these indirect items that are included in computing the operating profit margin.

Both the gross profit margin and the operating profit margin reflect a company's operating performance. But they do not consider how these operations have been financed. To evaluate both operating *and* financing decisions, we need to compare net income (that is, earnings after deducting interest and taxes) with sales. Doing so, we obtain the *net profit margin*:

$$\text{Net profit margin} = \frac{\text{Net income}}{\text{Sales}}$$

The net profit margin tells us the net income generated from each dollar of sales; it considers financing costs that the operating profit margin doesn't consider. For Fictitious, for 1999:

$$\text{Net profit margin} = \frac{\$1,200,000}{\$10,000,000} = 0.12 \text{ or } 12\%$$

For every dollar of sales, Fictitious generates 12 cents in profits.

Recap: Profitability Ratios

The profitability ratios for Fictitious in 1999 are:

Gross profit margin   = 35%
Operating profit margin = 20%
Net profit margin   = 12%

They tell us the following about the operating performance of Fictitious:

- Each dollar of sales contributes 35 cents to gross profit and 20 cents to operating profit.
- Every dollar of sales contributes 12 cents to owners' earnings.
- By comparing the 20-cent operating profit margin with the 12-cent net profit margin, we see that Fictitious has 8 cents of financing costs for every dollar of sales.

What these ratios do not tell us about profitability is the sensitivity of gross, operating, and net profit margins to:

■ Changes in the sales price
■ Changes in the volume of sales

Looking at the profitability ratios for one firm for one period gives us very little information that can be used to make judgments regarding future profitability. Nor do these ratios give us any information about why current profitability is what it is. We need more information to make these kinds of judgments, particularly regarding the future profitability of the firm. For that, we turn to activity ratios, which are measures of how well assets are being used.

ACTIVITY RATIOS

Activity ratios—for the most part, turnover ratios—can be used to evaluate the benefits produced by specific assets, such as inventory or accounts receivable or to evaluate the benefits produced by the totality of the firm's assets.

Inventory Management

The *inventory turnover ratio* indicates how quickly a firm has used inventory to generate the goods and services that are sold. The inventory turnover is the ratio of the cost of goods sold to inventory:[4]

$$\text{Inventory turnover ratio} = \frac{\text{Cost of goods sold}}{\text{Inventory}}$$

For Fictitious, for 1999:

$$\text{Inventory turnover ratio} = \frac{\$6,500,000}{\$1,800,000} = 3.61 \text{ times}$$

This ratio tells us that Fictitious turns over its inventory 3.61 times per year. On average, cash is invested in inventory, goods and services are produced, and these goods and services are sold 3.6 times a year. Looking back to the number of days of inventory, we see that this turn-

---

[4] A common alternative to this is the ratio of sales to inventory. But there is a problem with this alternative: The numerator is in terms of sales (based on selling prices), whereas the denominator is in terms of costs. By including the sales price in the numerator, the result is not easily interpreted.

over measure is consistent with the results of that calculation: We have 101 calendar days of inventory on hand at the end of the year; dividing 365 days by 101 days, or 365/101 days, we find that inventory cycles through (from cash to sales) 3.61 times a year.

Accounts Receivable Management

In much the same way we evaluated inventory turnover, we can evaluate a firm's management of its accounts receivable and its credit policy. The *accounts receivable turnover ratio* is a measure of how effectively a firm is using credit extended to customers. The reason for extending credit is to increase sales. The downside to extending credit is the possibility of default—customers not paying when promised. The benefit obtained from extending credit is referred to as *net credit sales*—sales on credit less returns and refunds.

$$\text{Accounts receivable turnover} = \frac{\text{Net credit sales}}{\text{Accounts receivable}}$$

Looking at the Fictitious Corporation income statement, we see an entry for sales, but we do not know how much of the amount stated is on credit. This is often the case when we analyze companies from the outside looking in. Let's assume that the entire sales amount represents net credit sales. For Fictitious, for 1999:

$$\text{Accounts receivable turnover} = \frac{\$10,000,000}{\$600,000} = 16.67 \text{ times}$$

Therefore, almost 17 times in the year there is, on average, a cycle that begins with a sale on credit and finishes with the receipt of cash for that sale. In other words, there are 17 cycles of sales to credit to cash during the year.

The number of times accounts receivable cycle through the year is consistent with the number of days of credit (22) that we calculated earlier—accounts receivable turn over 17 times during the year, and the average number of days of sales in the accounts receivable balance is 365 days/16.67 times = 22 days.

Overall Asset Management

The inventory and accounts receivable turnover ratios reflect the benefits obtained from the use of specific assets (inventory and accounts receivable). For a more general picture of the productivity of the firm, we can compare the sales during a period with the total assets that generated these sales.

One way is with the *total asset turnover ratio* which tells us how many times during the year the value of a firm's total assets is generated in sales:

$$\text{Total assets turnover} = \frac{\text{Sales}}{\text{Total assets}}$$

For Fictitious Corporation in 1999:

$$\text{Total assets turnover} = \frac{\$10,000,000}{\$11,000,000} = 0.91 \text{ times}$$

The turnover ratio of 0.91 indicated that during 1999, every dollar invested in total assets generates 91 cents of sales. Or, stated differently, the total assets of Fictitious "turn over" almost once during the year. Since total assets include both tangible and intangible assets, this turnover tells us how efficiently all assets were used.

An alternative is to focus only on fixed assets, the long-term, tangible assets of the firm. The *fixed asset turnover* is the ratio of sales to fixed assets:

$$\text{Fixed asset turnover ratio} = \frac{\text{Sales}}{\text{Fixed assets}}$$

For Fictitious Corporation for 1999:

$$\text{Fixed asset turnover ratio} = \frac{\$10,000,000}{\$7,000,000} = 1.43 \text{ times}$$

Therefore, for every dollar of fixed assets, Fictitious is able to generate $1.43 of sales.

Recap: Activity Ratios

The activity ratios for Fictitious Corporation are:

Inventory turnover ratio	=	3.61 times
Accounts receivable turnover ratio	=	16.67 times
Total asset turnover ratio	=	0.91 times
Fixed asset turnover ratio	=	1.43 times

From these ratios we can determine that:

- Inventory flows in and out almost four times a year (from the inventory turnover ratio).
- Accounts receivable are collected in cash, on average, 22 days after a sale (from the number of days of credit). In other words, accounts receivable flow in and out almost 17 times during the year (from the accounts receivable turnover ratio).

What theses ratios do not tell us about the firm's use of its assets:

- The number of sales not made because credit policies are too stringent
- How much of credit sales is not collectible
- Which assets contribute most to the turnover

FINANCIAL LEVERAGE RATIOS

A firm can finance its assets with equity or with debt. Financing with debt legally obligates the firm to pay interest and to repay the principal as promised. Equity financing does not obligate the firm to pay anything because dividends are paid at the discretion of the board of directors. There is always some risk, which we refer to as business risk, inherent in any business enterprise. But how a firm chooses to finance its operations—the particular mix of debt and equity—may add financial risk on top of business risk. *Financial risk* is risk associated with a firm's ability to satisfy its debt obligations, and is often measured using the extent to which debt financing is used relative to equity.

Financial leverage ratios are used to assess how much financial risk the firm has taken on. There are two types of financial leverage ratios: component percentages and coverage ratios. Component percentages compare a firm's debt with either its total capital (debt plus equity) or its equity capital. Coverage ratios reflect a firm's ability to satisfy fixed financing obligations, such as interest, principal repayment, or lease payments.

Component Percentage Ratios

A ratio that indicates the proportion of assets financed with debt is the *debt-to-assets ratio*, which compares total liabilities (short-term + long-term debt) with total assets:

$$\text{Total debt-to-assets ratio} = \frac{\text{Debt}}{\text{Total assets}}$$

For Fictitious in 1999:

$$\text{Total debt-to-assets ratio} = \frac{\$5,000,000}{\$11,000,000} = 0.4546 \text{ or } 45.46\%$$

This ratio tells us that 45% of the firm's assets are financed with debt (both short-term and long-term).

We may also look at the financial risk in terms of the use of debt relative to the use of equity. The *debt-to-equity ratio* tells us how the firm finances its operations with debt relative to the book value of its shareholders' equity:

$$\text{Debt-to-equity ratio} = \frac{\text{Debt}}{\text{Book value of shareholders' equity}}$$

For Fictitious, for 1999, using the book-value definition:

$$\text{Debt-to-equity ratio} = \frac{\$5,000,000}{\$6,000,000} = 0.8333 \text{ or } 83.33\%$$

For every one dollar of book value of shareholders' equity, Fictitious uses 83 cents of debt.

Both of these ratios can be stated in terms of total debt, as above, or in terms of long-term debt. And it is not always clear which form—total or long term debt—the ratio is calculated. Additionally, it is often the case that the current portion of long-term debt is excluded in the calculation of the long-term versions of these debt ratios.

Book Value versus Market Value

One problem with using a financial ratio based on the book value of equity to analyze financial risk is that there is seldom a strong relationship between the book value and market value of a stock. We can see the distortion in values on the balance sheet by looking at the book value of equity and comparing it with the market value of equity. The book value of equity consists of:

1. The proceeds to the firm of all the stock issues since it was first incorporated, less any stock repurchased by the firm
2. The accumulative earnings of the firm, less any dividends, since it was first incorporated

Let's look at an example of the book value versus the market value of equity. IBM was incorporated in 1911. So the book value of its equity represents the sum of all its stock issued and all its earnings, less any dividends paid since 1911. As of the end of 2001, IBM's book value was $22 billion, yet its market value was over $200 billion.

Book value generally does not give a true picture of the investment of shareholders in the firm for the following reasons:

1. Earnings are recorded according to accounting principles, which may not reflect the true economics of transactions
2. Because of inflation, the earnings and proceeds from stock issued in the past do not reflect today's values

Market value, on the other hand, is the value of equity as perceived by investors. It is what investors are willing to pay. So why bother with book value? For two reasons: First, it is easier to obtain the book value than the market value of a firm's securities, and second, many financial services report ratios using book value rather than market value.

However, any of the ratios presented in this chapter that use the book value of equity can be restated using the market value of equity. For example, instead of using the book value of equity in the debt-to-equity ratio, you can use the market value of equity to measure the firm's financial leverage.

Coverage Ratios

The ratios that compare debt to equity or debt to assets tell us about the amount of financial leverage, which enables us to assess the financial condition of a firm. Another way of looking at the financial condition and the amount of financial leverage used by the firm is to see how well it can handle the financial burdens associated with its debt or other fixed commitments.

One measure of a firm's ability to handle financial burdens is the *interest coverage ratio*, also referred to as the *times interest-covered ratio*. This ratio tells us how well the firm can cover or meet the interest payments associated with debt. The ratio compares the funds available to pay interest (that is, earnings before interest and taxes) with the interest expense:

$$\text{Interest coverage ratio} = \frac{\text{EBIT}}{\text{Interest expense}}$$

The greater the interest coverage ratio, the better able the firm is to pay its interest expense. For Fictitious, for 1999:

$$\text{Interest coverage ratio} = \frac{\$2,000,000}{\$400,000} = 5 \text{ times}$$

An interest coverage ratio of 5 means that the firm's earnings before interest and taxes are five times greater than its interest payments.

The interest coverage ratio tells us about a firm's ability to cover the interest related to its debt financing. However, there are other costs that do not arise from debt but which nevertheless must be considered in the same way we consider the cost of debt in a firm's financial obligations. For example, lease payments are fixed costs incurred in financing operations. Like interest payments, they represent legal obligations.

What funds are available to pay debt and debt-like expenses? We can start with EBIT and *add back* expenses that were deducted to arrive at EBIT. The ability of a firm to satisfy its fixed financial costs—its fixed charges—is referred to as the *fixed charge coverage ratio*. One definition of the fixed charge coverage considers only the lease payments:

$$\text{Fixed charge coverage ratio} = \frac{\text{Earnings before interest and taxes} + \text{Lease expense}}{\text{Interest} + \text{Lease expense}}$$

For Fictitious Corporation, for 1999:

$$\text{Fixed charge coverage ratio} = \frac{\$2,000,000 + \$1,000,000}{\$400,000 + \$1,000,000} = 2.14 \text{ times}$$

This ratio tells us that Fictitious' earnings can cover its fixed charges (interest and lease payments) more than two times over.

What fixed charges to consider is not entirely clear-cut. For example, if the firm is required to set aside funds to eventually or periodically retire debt—referred to as *sinking funds*—is the amount set aside a fixed charge? As another example, since preferred dividends represent a fixed financing charge, should they be included as a fixed charge? From the perspective of the common shareholder, the preferred dividends must be covered to enable either the payment of common dividends or to retain earnings for future growth. Since debt principal repayment and preferred stock dividends are paid on an after-tax basis—paid out of dollars remaining after taxes are paid—we must translate this fixed charge into equivalent before-tax dollars. The fixed charge coverage ratio can be expanded to accommodate the sinking funds and preferred stock dividends as fixed charges.

Up to now we considered earnings before interest and taxes as funds available to meet fixed financial charges. The EBIT we have used thus far included noncash items such as depreciation and amortization. Since we are trying to compare funds available to meet obligations, a better measure of available funds is cash flow from operations, which we can find in the statement of cash flows. A ratio that considers cash flows from operations as funds available to cover interest payments is referred to as the *cash flow interest coverage ratio.*

$$\text{Cash flow interest coverage ratio} = \frac{\text{Cash flow from operations} + \text{Interest} + \text{Taxes}}{\text{Interest}}$$

The amount of cash flow from operations that is in the statement of cash flows is net of interest and taxes. So we have to add back interest and taxes to cash flow from operations to arrive at the cash flow amount *before* interest and taxes in order to determine the cash flow available to cover interest payments.

For Fictitious Corporation in 1999:

$$\text{Cash flow interest coverage ratio} = \frac{\$1,800,000 + \$400,000 + \$400,000}{\$400,000}$$

$$= \frac{\$2,600,000}{\$400,000} = 6.5 \text{ times}$$

This coverage ratio tells us that, in terms of cash flows, Fictitious has 6.5 times more cash than is needed to pay its interest. This is a better picture of interest coverage than the five times reflected by EBIT. Why the difference? Because cash flow considers not just the accounting income, but non-cash items as well. In the case of Fictitious, depreciation is a non-cash charge that reduced EBIT but not cash flow from operations—it is added back to net income to arrive at cash flow from operations.

Recap: Financial Leverage Ratios

Summarizing, the financial leverage ratios for Fictitious Corporation for 1999 are:

Debt-to-assets ratio	= 45.45%
Debt-to-equity ratio	= 83.33%
Interest coverage ratio	= 5.00 times
Fixed charge coverage ratio	= 2.14 times
Cash flow interest coverage ratio	= 6.50 times

These ratios tells us Fictitious uses its financial leverage as follows:

- Assets are 45% financed with debt, measured using book values.
- Long-term debt is approximately two-thirds of equity. When equity is measured in market value terms, long-term debt is approximately one-sixth of equity.

These ratios do not tell us:

- What other fixed, legal commitments the firm has that are not included on the balance sheet (for example, operating leases).
- What the intentions of management are regarding taking on more debt as the existing debt matures.

COMMON SIZE ANALYSIS

We have looked at a firm's operating performance and financial condition through ratios that relate various items of information contained in the financial statements. Another way to analyze a firm is to look at its financial data more comprehensively.

Common-size analysis is a method of analysis in which the components of a financial statement are compared with each other. The first step in common-size analysis is to break down a financial statement—either the balance sheet or the income statement—into its parts. The next step is to calculate the proportion that each item represents relative to some benchmark. In common-size analysis of the balance sheet, the benchmark is total assets. For the income statement, the benchmark is sales.

Let's see how it works by doing some common-size financial analysis for the Fictitious Corporation. The company's balance sheet is restated in Exhibit 10.4. This statement does not look precisely like the balance sheet we have seen before. Nevertheless, the data are the same but reorganized. Each item in the original balance sheet has been restated as a proportion of total assets for the purpose of common size analysis. Hence, we refer to this as the *common-size balance sheet*.

In this balance sheet, we see, for example, that in 1999 cash is 3.6% of total assets, or $400,000/$11,000,000 = 0.036$. We can also see that the largest investment is in plant and equipment, which comprises 63.6% of total assets. On the liabilities side, we can see that current liabilities are a small portion (9.1%) of liabilities and equity.

The common-size balance sheet tells us in very general terms how Fictitious has raised capital and where this capital has been invested. As with financial ratios, however, the picture is not complete until we look at trends and compare these proportions with those of other firms in the same industry.

In the income statement, as we did in the balance sheet, we can restate items as a proportion of sales; this statement is referred to as the *common-size income statement*. The common-size income statements for Fictitious for 1999 and 1998 are shown in Exhibit 10.5. For 1999, we see that the major costs are associated with goods sold (65%); lease expense, other expenses, interest, taxes, and dividends make up smaller portions of sales. Looking at gross profit, EBIT, and net income, we see that these proportions are the profit margins we calculated earlier. The common-size income statement provides information on the profitability of different aspects of the firm's business. Again, the picture is not complete until we look at trends over time and comparisons with other companies in the same industry.

EXHIBIT 10.4   Fictitious Corporation Common-Size Balance Sheets for Years Ending December 31

	1999		1998	
Asset Components				
Cash	3.6%		2.0%	
Marketable securities	1.8%		0.0%	
Accounts receivable	5.5%		8.0%	
Inventory	16.4%		10.0%	
Current assets		27.3%		20.0%
Net plant and equipment		63.5%		70.0%
Intangible assets		9.1%		10.0%
Total assets		100.0%		100.0%
Liability and shareholders' equity components				
Accounts payable	4.6%		4.0%	
Other current liabilities	4.6%		1.0%	
Long-term debt	36.4%		50.0%	
Total liabilities		45.4%		56.0%
Shareholders' equity		54.6%		44.0%
Total liabilities and shareholders' equity		100.0%		100.0%

EXHIBIT 10.5 Fictitious Corporation Common Size Income Statement for Years Ending December 31

	1999	1998
Sales	100.0%	100.0%
Cost of goods sold	65.0%	66.7%
Gross profit	35.0%	33.3%
Lease and administrative expenses	15.0%	16.7%
Earnings before interest and taxes	20.0%	16.7%
Interest expense	4.0%	5.6%
Earnings before taxes	16.0%	16.7%
Taxes	4.0%	5.7%
Net income	12.0%	11.1%
Common dividends	6.0%	5.6%
Retained earnings	6.0%	5.5%

USING FINANCIAL RATIO ANALYSIS

Financial analysis provides information concerning a firm's operating performance and financial condition. This information is useful to an analyst in evaluating a firm's operations and to an investor in evaluating the risk and potential returns to investing in a firm's securities.

But financial ratio analysis cannot tell the whole story and must be interpreted and used with care. When we discussed each ratio, we noted what we need to assume or what it might not tell us. For example, in calculating inventory turnover, we need to assume that the inventory shown on the balance sheet is representative of inventory throughout the year. Another example is in the calculation of accounts receivable turnover. We assumed that all sales were on credit. If we are on the outside looking in—that is, evaluating a firm based on its financial statements only—and therefore do not have data on credit sales, we have to start making assumptions, which may or may not be correct.

In addition, there are other areas of concern you should be aware of in using financial ratios:

- Limitations in the accounting data used to construct the ratios, as discussed in a previous chapter
- Selection of an appropriate benchmark firm or firms for comparison purposes
- Interpretation of the ratios

■ Pitfalls in forecasting future operating performance and financial condition based on past trends

Let's take a closer look at some of these concerns.

Example: Wal-Mart, 1996–1997

Applied to a fictitious company, the ratio calculations are rather straightforward: We form a ratio of two items derived from the balance sheet or the income statement. However, it is usually not as straightforward when applying these tools to an actual company. Let's look at the case of Wal-Mart and its ratios for a two-year period. Wal-Mart's balance sheets for the 1997 and 1996 fiscal years (years ending January 31, 1998 and 1997, respectively) are shown in Exhibit 10.6 and Wal-Mart's income statements for these same fiscal years are shown in Exhibit 10.7.

Selected financial ratios for Wal-Mart Stores for the two years are shown in Exhibit 10.8. As you can see by comparing the financial ratios and the financial statement data, not all figures are taken directly from these statements. For example, gross profit is not given, so the analyst must calculate that as the difference between total revenues and cost of sales. As another example, total debt is not given as a subtotal on the balance sheet, so the analyst must combine the different debt items to arrive at the total debt amount that is used in the financial leverage ratios.

Using a Benchmark

To interpret a firm's financial ratios we need to compare them with the ratios of other firms in the industry since these other firms are in a similar line of business and face some of the same market pressures—for example, competition in the input and output markets—as the firm we are evaluating.

But finding the appropriate comparable firms is difficult for many large firms that have operations spanning many different lines of business. For example, in 2000, the Walt Disney Company reported the following:[5]

(in millions)

Business Segment	Revenues	Operating Income	Assets
Media networks	$9,615	$2,298	$20,049
Studio entertainment	5,994	110	7,295
Parks and resorts	6,803	1,620	10,820
Consumer products	2,622	455	1,105
Internet group	368	−402	1,955

---

[5] *The Walt Disney Company Annual Report 2000*, pp. 49 and 73.

EXHIBIT 10.6   Wal-Mart Stores' Balance Sheets for 1997 and 1996 (in millions)

	1997	1996
Assets		
Current Assets		
Cash and cash equivalents	$1,447	$883
Receivables	976	845
Inventories	16,497	15,897
Prepaid expenses and other	432	368
Total current assets	$19,352	$17,993
Property Plant and Equipment		
Land	$4,691	$3,689
Building and improvements	14,646	12,724
Fixtures and equipment	7,636	6,390
Transportation equipment	403	379
Total	$27,376	$23,182
Accumulated depreciation	(5,907)	(4,849)
Net property, plant, and equipment	$21,469	$18,333
Property under capital lease	$3,040	$2,782
Accumulated amortization	(903)	(791)
Net property under capital lease	$2,137	$1,991
Other assets and deferred charges	2,426	1,287
Total assets	$45,384	$39,604
Liabilities and Shareholders' Equity		
Current Liabilities		
Accounts payable	$9,136	$7,628
Accrued liabilities	3,628	2,413
Accrued income taxes	565	298
Long-term debt due within one year	1,039	523
Obligations under capital leases due within one year	102	95
Total current liabilities	$14,460	$10,957
Non-current Liabilities		
Long-term Debt	$7,191	$7,709
Long-term Obligations under Capital Leases	2,483	2,307
Deferred Income Taxes and Other	809	463
Minority Interest	1,938	1,025
Shareholders' Equity		
Preferred stock	$0	$0
Common stock	224	228
Capital in excess of par value	585	547
Retained earnings	18,167	16,768
Foreign currency translation adjustment	(473)	(400)
Total shareholders' equity	$18,503	$17,143
Total Liabilities and Shareholders' Equity	$45,384	$39,604

EXHIBIT 10.7   Wal-Mart Stores' Income Statements for the 1997 and 1996 Fiscal Year (in millions)

	1997	1996
Revenues		
Net sales	$117,958	$104,859
Other income—net	1,341	1,319
Total revenues	$119,299	$106,178
Costs and expenses		
Cost of sales	93,438	83,510
Operating, selling, and general and administrative expenses	19,358	16,936
Interest costs		
Debt	555	629
Capital leases	229	216
Total expenses	$113,580	$101,301
Income before income taxes, minority interest, and equity in unconsolidated subsidiaries	$5,719	$4,877
Provision for income taxes		
Current	2,095	974
Deferred	20	(180)
	$2,115	$1,794
Income before minority interest and equity in unconsolidated subsidiaries	$3,604	$3,083
Minority interest and equity in unconsolidated subsidiaries	(78)	(27)
Net income	$3,526	$3,056

EXHIBIT 10.8   Selected Financial Ratios for Wal-Mart Stores for 1997 and 1996 Fiscal Years

Ratio	1997	1996
Return		
Basic earning power	$6,503/$45384 = 14.33%	$5,732/39,604 = 14.47%
Return on assets	$3,526/$45,384 = 7.77%	$3,056/$39604 = 7.72%
Return on equity	$3,526/$18,503 = 19.06%	$3,056/$17,143 = 17.83%
Liquidity		
Current ratio	$19,352/$14,460 = 1.34 times	$17,993/$10,957 = 1.64 times
Quick ratio	$3,526/$18,503 = 0.19 times	$2,096/$10,957 = 0.19 times
Profitability		
Gross profit margin	$25,861/$119,299 = 21.68%	$22,668/$106,178 = 21.35%
Operating profit margin	$6,503/$119,299 = 5.45%	$5,732/$106,178 = 5.40%
Net profit margin	$3,526/$119,299 = 2.96%	$3,056/$106,178 = 2.88%
Activity		
Inventory turnover	$93,438/$16,497 = 5.66 times	$83,510/$15,897 = 5.25 times
Total asset turnover	$119,299/$45,384 = 2.63 times	$106,178/$39,604 = 2.68 times
Financial leverage		
Total debt-to-assets ratio	$26,881/$45,384 = 59.23%	$22,461/$39,604 = 56.71%
Total debt-to-equity ratio	$26,881/$18,503 = 145.28	$22,461/$17,143 = 131.02%
Interest coverage ratio	$6,503/$784 = 8.29 times	$5,732/$845 = 6.78 times

In what industry do we classify the Walt Disney Company? Media networks, where it has invested almost 50% of its assets but derives only 38% of its revenues? Entertainment? Consumer products? What are the comparable companies? It is not always clear. In the case of Disney, there are no companies with the same *mix* of lines of business, so we end up comparing it with similar companies, such as Time Warner, that are in the same lines of business—amusements and film entertainment (i.e., creative contents)—but with different revenue, income, and asset mixes.

Suppose we find a comparable firm or set of firms. The average ratios of these comparable firms do not necessarily constitute a good benchmark. Finding that a firm is about average is not necessarily the same as saying that it is doing well. A better comparison may be with those firms that are in similar lines of business and are also the industry's leaders.

Selecting and Interpreting Ratios

It is difficult to say whether a comparison is good or bad. Suppose we find a firm that has a current ratio greater than the industry leaders. This could mean the firm is more liquid than the others and there is less risk that it cannot meet its near-term obligations. But it may also mean that the company is tying up its assets in low- or no-earning assets, which reduces its profitability.

Since ratios cannot be viewed in isolation, we need to look at several different characteristics of a firm *at the same time* in order to make judgments regarding its operating performance and financial condition. Statistical models have been developed that incorporate several aspects of a firm's operating performance and financial conditions at the same time in order to make assessments of a firm's creditworthiness. With the help of computers, these models enable us to translate financial ratios into meaningful measures.

Another issue of interpretation is the appropriateness of particular ratios to the firm. Consider an electric utility whose sole line of business is generating electricity. The only inventory that such a utility has on hand will be nuts, bolts, and a few spare parts—which do not amount to much. Calculating an inventory turnover doesn't make sense for this type of firm—and any attempts to do so will result in an absurd inventory turnover, perhaps over 2,000 times! The selection of ratios must make sense for the firm being analyzed.

Still another issue is trying to make sense out of ratios that are out of reasonable bounds. Suppose a firm that has a negative book value of equity—it can happen. If we calculate its total debt-to-assets ratio, we get a value greater than 1.0, meaning that more than 100% of the firm's assets are financed with debt. In this case, some other ratio—say, total debt-to-market-value of equity—should be used instead.

INTEGRATIVE EXAMPLE: FINANCIAL ANALYSIS OF WAL-MART STORES[6]

Now that you are familiar with the concepts behind the financial ratios, we will demonstrate how to look at ratios over time and across an industry, using data for an actual firm that has a past (and a future). Let's look at and analyze the financial ratios of Wal-Mart Stores as of 1997. But first, we'll take a brief look at the business of Wal-Mart, the industry, and the economy, which we must always do to properly analyze any financial ratio.

The Business

Sam Walton founded Wal-Mart Stores in 1945. Its main business is operating discount department stores (Wal-Mart stores and Wal-Mart Supercenters) and wholesale clubs (Sam's Clubs). By the end of 1997, Wal-Mart had 1,921 department stores, 441 supercenters, and 443 wholesale clubs and was the largest retailer in the United States in terms of dollar sales. It operates over 628 foreign stores, mostly in Canada and Latin America. Wal-Mart leases the vast majority of its stores from developers and local governments.

Most of Wal-Mart's new stores in the United States will be supercenters, which sell grocery products in addition to general consumer goods. The grocery line of business traditionally has smaller profit margins than the general consumer goods.

The Industry

Wal-Mart is a discount retailer. Other discount retailers include Kmart, Dayton Hudson (Target Stores), and Costco. Kmart was once the industry leader, but in years prior to 1997 it retrenched, closing stores and restructuring; in 1992, Kmart had over 4,000 stores, but in 1997 Kmart had less than 2,200. (And filed for bankruptcy in 2002.)

Traditionally, retailers such as Sears Roebuck and Company and J. C. Penney did not compete with the discount retailers, but in the years prior to 1997 they entered the fray, making for a very competitive retail industry. The leaders in the industry and the breakdown of the industry's sales for 1997 are shown in Exhibit 10.9. The minor players (classified in "Others" in Exhibit 10.9) included Dillard Department Stores, Family Dollar Stores, Inc., Dollar General Corporation, Fred Meyer, Inc., Kohl's Corporation, and Nordstrom, Inc.

---

[6] The sources of information used in this analysis were the annual reports for various years and various issues of *Value Line Investment Survey* published by Value Line Inc. *This integrative example was written prior to the filing of bankruptcy by Kmart in January 2002. This should be kept clearly in mind when reviewing this example.*

EXHIBIT 10.9   Retail Industry Sales, 1997

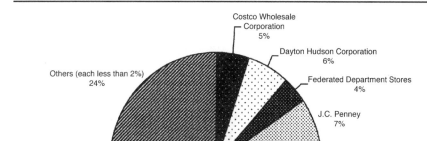

Source: Based on data obtained from *Value Line Investment Survey*

Much of Wal-Mart's growth in the 1970s and 1980s was at the expense of small, local retailers. In the 1990s, Wal-Mart's competition consisted of the other behemoth retail companies; growth could no longer come from mom-and-pop stores because many of these smaller stores had gone out of existence.

Because most of these retailers expanded as far as they could in the United States, future growth required expansion outside of the United States or expansion into different lines of business. Wal-Mart just prior to 1997 had opened stores in China and Germany, though the initial success was limited.

Several retailers were shifting more of their stocked goods to private-label brands, which could provide much lower, competitive prices. Further, several retailers were focusing on operating efficiencies in warehousing, distribution, and accounting, which might pay off in lowering operating costs.

A big uncertainty at the time of the analysis was whether Kmart would be able to turn around its situation through the then-current downsizing and restructuring. At the time, it was expected that it would be a number of years before analysts would know whether Kmart would regain its leadership position in the industry.

EXHIBIT 10.10   Annual Percentage Change in Sales and Net Income for Wal-Mart Stores, 1993–1997

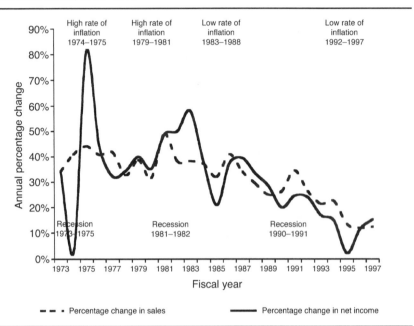

The Economy

To evaluate Wal-Mart's financial condition and operating performance with an eye on the future, we need to look at how it has done under different economic conditions: Has the firm fared well during recessions? Has it fared well during periods of high inflation? How has it done during periods of economic prosperity?

To gain a perspective on the firm's management under different economic conditions, we have to evaluate the financial ratios within the economic climate over which they are measured. To do this, we could look back at economic history, mapping out the indicators, such as gross domestic product (GDP), which is a measure of the goods and services produced in a nation, and the consumer price index (CPI), which measures the general level of prices, to get an idea of economic conditions and how Wal-Mart fared under different conditions.

The changes in annual sales and net income for Wal-Mart over the 25-year period 1973–1997 are shown in Exhibit 10.10, with economic climates indicated. We see that Wal-Mart did well in poor economic climates: The growth in sales and net income is strongest during recessionary and inflationary periods. This makes sense, because consumers are likely to seek out discounts when their personal financial condition worsens.

At the end of 1997 (the point of reference for this analysis), inflation was forecasted to remain low, yet the economy was showing signs of slowing in response to the economic problems in Asia. These conditions are favorable for Wal-Mart.

Financial Ratios of the Firm and the Industry

To analyze Wal-Mart Stores, we have graphed selected ratios for Wal-Mart over the 10-year period, 1988–1997, along with the corresponding average ratio for the industry. We have included four companies as defining the "industry" at that time by which we make comparisons with Wal-Mart: Sears, Roebuck and Company, J. C. Penney, Kmart, and Dayton Hudson.

Return

Exhibit 10.11 shows that Wal-Mart's return on equity was better than the industry's. We attribute a company's return on equity to: (1) its efficiency in using assets (turnover), (2) its ability to manage expenses (profit margin), (3) its use of financial leverage (debt ratios), (4) the tax burden, and (5) the interest burden.

EXHIBIT 10.11   Return on Equity for Wal-Mart Stores and the Industry, 1988–1997

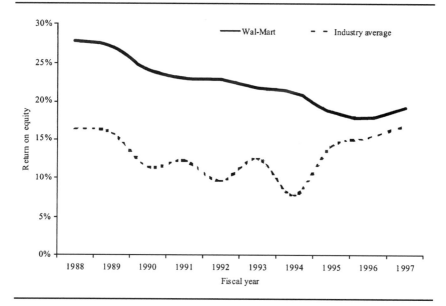

We can use the Du Pont system to analyze Wal-Mart's returns on equity. For example, we see that Wal-Mart's return on equity in 1988 differs from that for 1997 (27.83% versus 19.06%). Using the Du Pont breakdown of the return on equity,

$$\text{Return on equity} = \left(\frac{\text{Earnings before interest and taxes}}{\text{Sales}}\right)\left(\frac{\text{Sales}}{\text{Total assets}}\right)$$

$$\times \left(\frac{\text{Earnings before taxes}}{\text{Earnings before interest and taxes}}\right)(1 - \text{Tax rate})$$

$$\times \frac{\text{Total assets}}{\text{Shareholders' equity}}$$

we can breakdown Wal-Mart's 1997 return on equity into its components:

$$
\begin{aligned}
\text{Return on equity} = &\ (\text{Operating profit margin})(\text{Total asset turnover}) \\
&\ (\text{Equity share of before-tax earnings}) \\
&\ (\text{Tax retention})(\text{Equity multiplier})
\end{aligned}
$$

$$19.06\% = \left(\frac{\$6,503}{\$119,299}\right)\left(\frac{\$119,299}{\$45,384}\right)\left(\frac{\$5,719}{\$6,503}\right)\left(1 - \frac{\$2,193}{\$5,719}\right)\left(\frac{\$45,384}{\$18,503}\right)$$

Getting to the root of the difference using the Du Pont system results in the following:

Characteristic	1988	1997
Return on equity	27.83%	19.06%
Operating profit margin	6.41%	5.45%
Total asset turnover	3.59 times	2.63 times
Equity share of before-tax earnings	90.89%	87.94%
Tax retention	63.06%	61.65%
Equity multiplier	2.11 times	2.45 times

This information tells the analyst that the difference is attributed to many factors, including a lower profit margin and a lower asset utilization in 1997. But as you can see, the increased tax burden and the increased use of debt also contributed to the decline in the return on equity. However, the comparison of these two years does not give a complete picture of Wal-Mart and its return. A more thorough analysis would compare these components for Wal-Mart for each year and compare Wal-Mart's component ratios with those of the industry.

Understanding the industry's trends may also help explain the changes in performance and financial condition over time. The increased competitiveness in the industry is apparent in the declining return on equity for both Wal-Mart and its competitors. If the industry remains very competitive, we should expect to see further convergence in the return on equity for Wal-Mart and its competitors.

Liquidity

The current ratios for Wal-Mart and the retail store industry are graphed in Exhibit 10.12. We can easily see that Wal-Mart was less liquid than the other companies, as indicated by its lower current ratios. Both the industry and Wal-Mart experienced declining liquidity over time.

EXHIBIT 10.12   Current Ratio for Wal-Mart and the Industry, 1988–1997

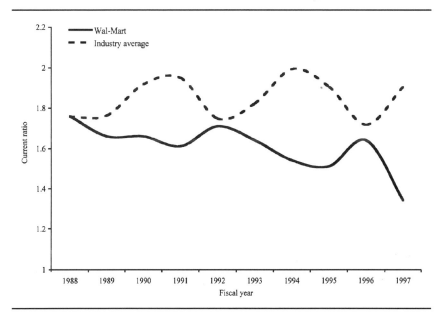

   We can't tell whether this is good or bad because we are looking at only one piece of the puzzle. On the one hand, relatively lower liquidity could mean that Wal-Mart was having difficulty meeting its short-term obligations, perhaps forcing it to seek additional short-term financing. On the other hand, relatively lower liquidity could mean that Wal-Mart was managing its current assets efficiently. Since current assets provide a low return—a firm earns less from its current assets than from its investment in plant and equipment—a smaller investment in current assets may mean that Wal-Mart was investing in non-current assets that provided a higher return. So let's withhold judgment on a declining current ratio until we examine Wal-Mart's profitability.

Profitability

The gross profit margins and operating profit margins for both Wal-Mart and the industry are graphed in Exhibit 10.13. We see that Wal-Mart had lower gross margins than the rest of the industry. This may be attributed to the inclusion in the industry average of traditionally non-discounters such as J. C. Penney, which typically had a gross margin around 33%. The lower gross profit margins combined with about the same operating profit margins as the industry tells us that Wal-Mart was better at managing its operating costs (e.g., the day-to-day operating costs of running its stores) than its competitors.

EXHIBIT 10.13   Gross Profit Margin and Operating Profit Margin for Wal-Mart Stores and the Industry, 1988–1997

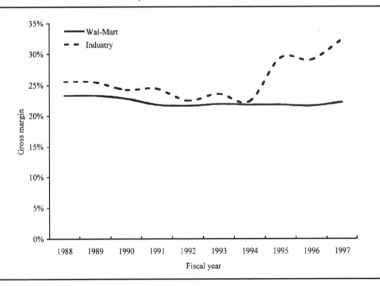

EXHIBIT 10.13   (Continued)

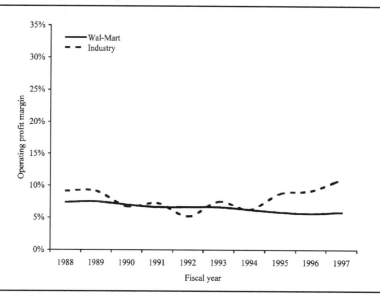

Wal-Mart's gross margins declined from around 25% to 22%. The declining gross margins for Wal-Mart and the rest of the industry from 1988–1994 may have been the result of the increased competition as traditional non-discounters (e.g., J. C. Penney) began to compete with the discount retailers. Further, Wal-Mart's entry into grocery items (through its supercenters) may have accounted for the slightly lower margins since grocery retailers typically have gross margins in the 21%–25% range. The increased gross and operating profit margins in the industry from 1995–1997 may reflect some retailers' shift to higher-margin goods.

Activity

The inventory turnover for Wal-Mart and the industry is shown in Exhibit 10.14. Inventory turnover was slower for Wal-Mart than the rest of the industry. This indicates that there may be a difference between either the type of inventory or the inventory management systems of Wal-Mart and its competitors.

One of the aspects that helped Wal-Mart grow and become profitable was its warehousing system. By using distribution warehousing and its own fleet of trucks, Wal-Mart was able to maintain a relatively low level of inventory. Wal-Mart's inventory turnover is, in fact, higher than most firms in the industry, but the inclusion of Sears in the industry average obscures the industry statistics. Before 1994, Sears had a cata-log system, which allowed it to keep less inventory on hand in its stores and in its warehouses, resulting in a high inventory turnover (around 13 times). The drop in the industry average turnover in 1995 illustrates the sensitivity of the industry average to Sear's dropping its catalog busi-ness.

Was the slower turnover bad? Not necessarily. A slower turnover may be good news (lower risk of stock-outs) or bad news (less efficient use of existing assets). Whether good news or bad news is determined by looking at the whole picture.

Financial Leverage

Exhibit 10.15 shows the long-term-debt-equity ratio for Wal-Mart and the industry. We see that for most of the time, Wal-Mart had a lower debt-equity ratio than the industry, but Wal-Mart's use of debt increased after 1991 only to decline once again after 1994. The industry debt-equity ratio increased after 1994 because of changes in two companies: Kmart restructuring at the time, which required it to take on additional debt and close many stores, and Sears discontinuing its catalog and sell-ing 80% of Allstate Insurance, reducing its assets but not its level of debt.

EXHIBIT 10.14   Inventory Turnover for Wal-Mart Stores and the Industry, 1988–1997

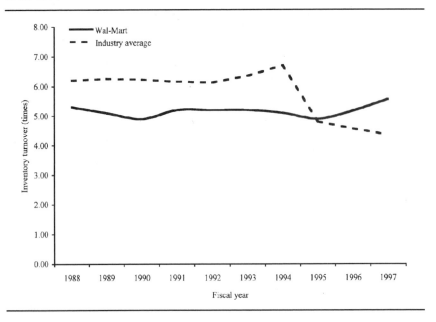

EXHIBIT 10.15   Long-Term Debt to Equity Ratios for Wal-Mart and the Industry, 1988–1997

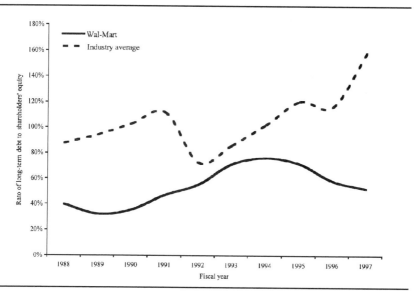

Common Size Analysis

A thorough common-size analysis requires looking at financial statement components over time. Exhibit 10.16 uses a bar graph to represent each of the three major components of Wal-Mart's assets as a proportion of total assets (panel A) and to represent the three major components of liabilities and equity as proportions of total liabilities and equity (panel B).

As we see in Exhibit 10.16, current assets (which consisted primarily of inventory) had diminished in importance over the years, especially after 1991, as Wal-Mart shifted more of its investment towards plant assets (buildings). As we also see in this exhibit, Wal-Mart had increased its reliance on long-term debt to finance its expansion, substituting longer-term sources (in particular, notes payable) for shorter-term sources (trade credit, as represented by accounts payable).

Other Factors

In addition to the financial statement data and economic forecasts, there are factors that should be considered by the financial analyst in addressing the performance and condition of the companies in this industry. Factors that should be included in the analysis of companies in the retail industry include the following:

EXHIBIT 10.16   Common Size Balance Sheets for Wal-Mart Stores, 1988–1997

Panel A

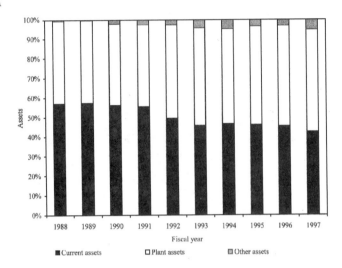

Panel B

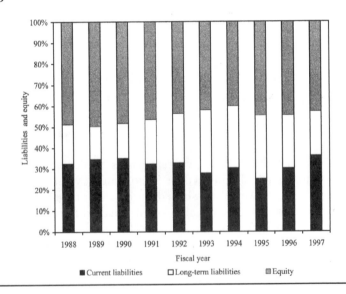

- Same store's sales, where upward movement in this indicator is perceived as favorable
- Changes in the number of stores, relative to competitors
- Progress or success in strategies to alter sales mix (e.g., Sear's "softer
  side" campaign)

- Market share nationally, internationally, and in specific geographic or demographic markets
- Mergers or acquisitions within the industry (e.g., Proffitt's acquisitions of Carson Pirie Scott and Saks Holdings) that may alter the market share of both minor and major firms in the industry
- Effects of "category killers," specialty stores that may take away sales in specific product lines (e.g., electronics)

Financial Analysis of Wal-Mart: Summary

Using the information about Wal-Mart and its competitors and looking at not only the ratios of the most recent fiscal years available at the time but a time-series of these financial ratios, an analyst could have drawn a number of conclusions regarding Wal-Mart and its operating performance and financial condition:

- Wal-Mart appeared to do best in periods of high inflation and recession.
- The industry was comprised of large national chains: Wal-Mart's major competitors at the time were Dayton Hudson, Kmart, J. C. Penney, and Sears Roebuck & Co. Both Kmart and Sears, troubled companies in 1993–1995, appeared to be recovering and it appeared were becoming stronger competitors for Wal-Mart.
- Wal-Mart provided superior return on equity (relative to its competitors), most likely because of its operating efficiency; compared to its competitors, Wal-Mart had lower gross margins yet similar operating profit margins.
- The industry had become more competitive in years leading up to the time of the analysis, which was reflected in lower operating margins, return on equity, and price-to-earnings.
- Wal-Mart had shifted its use of assets toward plant assets and away from current assets, which was reflective of its growth through opening more stores.
- Wal-Mart had shifted its mix of liabilities, using more long-term sources and less short-term funds.
- The analysis suggests that the prospects for Wal-Mart continued to be good, but the growth in sales and profits had slowed considerably. The increased degree of competitiveness was expected to affect all firms in the industry, resulting in lower profit margins and returns in the future.

CHAPTER 11

Traditional Fundamental Analysis III: Earnings Analysis, Cash Analysis, Dividends, and Dividend Discount Models

Pamela P. Peterson, Ph.D., CFA
Professor of Finance
Florida State University

Frank J. Fabozzi, Ph.D., CFA
Adjunct Professor of Finance
School of Management
Yale University

What determines the market price of a share of common stock? Like anything, price depends on what people are willing to pay. The price of a share of stock today depends on what investors believe is today's value of all the cash flows that will accrue in the entire future from that share of stock. In other words, no one is going to pay any more today for a share of stock than they think it is worth—based on what they get out of it in terms of future cash flows. What people are willing to pay for a share of stock today determines its market value.

The theory of stock prices makes sense. If we could accurately forecast a company's cash flows in the future, we could determine the value of the company's stock today and determine whether the stock is over-

or undervalued by the market. But forecasting future cash flows is difficult. As an alternative, what is typically done is to examine the historical and current relation between stock prices and some fundamental value, such as earnings or dividends, using this relation to estimate the value of a share of stock.

In this chapter we take a closer look at the fundamental factors of earnings, cash flows, and dividends and their relations with share price as expressed in such commonly-used ratios as the price-earnings ratio and the dividend yield. In the last section of this chapter, we describe the valuation of stock based on the present value of projected future dividends. This approach to the valuation of common stock is referred to the discounted cash flow approach and the models used are referred to as dividend discount models.

EARNINGS ANALYSIS

A commonly used measure of a company's performance over a period of time is its earnings, which is often stated in terms of a return—earnings scaled by the amount of the investment. But earnings can really mean many different things depending on the context. If an analyst is evaluating the performance of a company's operations, the focus is on the operating earnings of the company—its *earnings before interest and taxes*, EBIT. If the analyst is evaluating the performance of a company overall, the focus is upon net income, which is essentially EBIT less interest and taxes. If the analyst is evaluating the performance of the company from a common shareholder's perspective, the earnings are the earnings available to common shareholders—EBIT less interest, taxes, and preferred stock dividends. Muddying the financial waters further is the issue of nonrecurring earnings or losses. Should the analyst focus on earnings before nonrecurring items or after? Therefore, it is useful to be very specific in the meaning of "earnings."

Can Earnings Be Managed?

There is a possibility that reported financial information may be managed or manipulated by the judicious choice of accounting methods and timing. In particular, earnings can be manipulated using a number of devices, including the selection of inventory method (e.g., FIFO versus LIFO) and the selection of depreciation method and lives. The possibility of manipulation exists, so the burden is on the analyst to understand a company's financial reporting, accounting methods, and the likelihood of manipulation.

EXHIBIT 11.1   Volume and High-Low-Closing Stock Prices for Qualcomm for Trading Days Surrounding the July 22, 1998 Positive Earnings Surprise

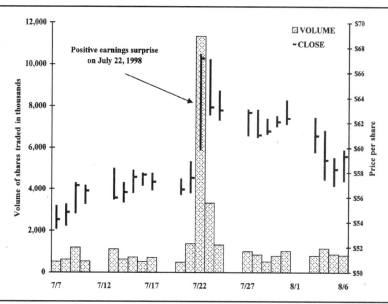

Source: Microsoft Investor, investor.msn.com

There are many pressures that a company may face that affect the likelihood of manipulation. These pressures include:

■ Reporting ever-increasing earnings, especially when the business is subject to variations in the business cycle
■ Meeting or beating analyst forecasts
■ Executive compensation based on earnings targets

It is informative to look at the second pressure listed above for managing earnings, meeting or beating analysts' forecasts. We know from the wealth of empirical evidence that stock prices react to *earnings surprises*, where surprises are defined as a difference between expected and actual earnings. In general, the price of a company's stock will jump upward at the announcement of better-than-expected earnings and the price of a company's stock will fall quickly at the announcement of worse-than-expected earnings.

The typical reaction to a positive earnings surprise is shown in Exhibit 11.1 for the case of Qualcomm, which reported third quarter 1998 earnings per share of $0.33, compared to the forecasted $0.26 per share. As you can see in this graph, both the volume of shares traded and the share prices jumped upward in response to the earnings surprise. Negative earnings surprises are similar in nature, with increased volume yet lower share prices associated with the earnings announcement. However, there is usually a lot else going on in the market, so earnings surprises may not always be accompanied by large price adjustments. For example, many 1998 quarterly earnings announcements were tempered with gloomy forecasts about the effects of the Asian crisis on future earnings, dampening any price reaction to a positive earnings surprise for many companies.

Because there is a market reaction to surprises—negative for earnings less than expected and positive for earnings better than expected—companies have an incentive to manage earnings to meet or exceed forecasted earnings. Frustrating the efforts to beat analysts forecasts is the tendency of analysts to be overly optimistic about earnings. In fact, the overestimation of earnings is more pronounced in cases in which companies report negative earnings.

Even with the potential for managed earnings, is there a relation between earnings and stock value? Consider General Electric's earnings and prices over the period 1987–1998, as illustrated in Exhibit 11.2. As can be seen, the market value of GE's common stock moves along in tandem with GE's net earnings, yet the relation between market value and earnings before discontinued items is not as strong.

EXHIBIT 11.2   General Electric's Earnings and Market Value of Equity, 1987–1997

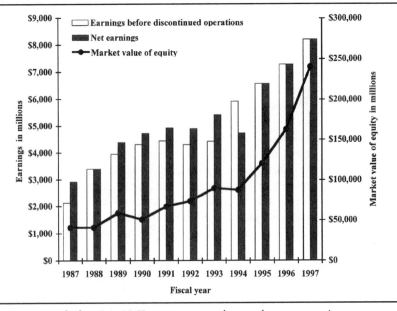

Source: General Electric's 10-K statements and annual reports, various years.

Though the example using General Electric illustrates the relation for one company over a specific range of years, the issue is whether earnings and market value are related for most companies. The research into the relation between earnings and value concludes the following:

- Stock prices change in response to an announcement of unexpected earnings, and
- Accounting earnings are correlated with stock returns, especially returns measured over a long horizon following the release of earnings.

The strong relation between earnings and stock prices may be due to reported earnings being strongly correlated with true earnings (that is, earnings in absence of management). Or the earnings-stock price relation may be due to stocks' valuation being dependent on *reported* earnings.

Earnings Per Share

We often refer to earnings in terms of the amount per share of stock, rather than as a total dollar amount generated in a period. Expressing a company's net income in terms of income per share allows us to compare it with the company's market price per share. *Earnings per share* (EPS) is earnings available for common shareholders, divided by the number of common shares outstanding:

$$\text{Earnings per share} = \frac{\text{Earnings available to common stockholders}}{\text{Number of common shares outstanding}}$$

This ratio indicates each share's portion of how much is earned by the firm in a given accounting period:

Suppose a company has $5 million of earnings and 4 million shares outstanding. Its earnings per share is:

$$\text{Earnings per share} = \frac{\$5,000,000}{4,000,000 \text{ shares}} = \$1.25 \text{ per share}$$

This company earned $1.25 for each common share outstanding.

The EPS doesn't tell us anything about the preferred shareholders. And that's acceptable because preferred shareholders, in most cases, receive a fixed dividend amount. Because the common shareholders are the residual owners of the firm—they are the last ones in line after creditors and preferred shareholders—we are interested in seeing just what is left over for them.

When we see an amount given for EPS, we have to be sure we know what it really means. But what is there to interpret? Net income available to common shares is pretty clear-cut (with some exceptions). What about the number of common shares outstanding? Can that change during the period of time under consideration? It can, affecting the calculated value of earnings per share. The number of common shares outstanding can change for two reasons:

1. *Timing:* Net income is earned over a specific period of time, yet the number of shares outstanding may change over this period.
2. *Dilutive securities:* The company may have securities outstanding that can be converted into common stock or employee stock options and warrants that may be exercisable (i.e., potentially dilutive securities), so the number of shares of common stock that potentially may share in this net income is greater than the number reported as outstanding.

The methodology for handling timing is straightforward—calculating the weighted average number of shares outstanding during the period. For a company having securities that are dilutive—meaning they could share in net income—there are two earnings per share amounts that are reported in financial statements: basic earnings per share and diluted earnings per share. Basic earnings per share are earnings (minus preferred dividends), divided by the average number of shares outstanding. Diluted earnings per share is earnings (minus preferred dividends), divided by the number of shares outstanding considering all dilutive securities (e.g., convertible debt, options).

Analysts' Forecasts

There are many financial services firms offering projections on different aspects of a firm's performance. The most common financial ratio forecast is future earnings per share of a firm, though projections of cash flows and stock prices are available. For most companies whose stock is publicly-traded, there are a number of analysts who analyze the stock and make forecasts regarding earnings in the future.

In addition to the forecasts made by individual analysts, several service providers collect and report statistics of analysts' forecasts. Several service providers are listed below:

Service provider	Address
First Call	www.firstcall.com
Institutional Brokers Estimate System (I/B/E/S)	www.ibes.com
Multex	www.multexnet.com
Zacks Investment Research[a]	www.zacks.com

[a] Zacks' analysts' forecast information is available through other sites, including Yahoo! Finance [biz.yahoo.com/zacks/]

One of the most common statistics is the *consensus earnings forecast*. The consensus earnings forecast is the average of the earnings per share forecasts for a given stock. Services that provide analyst forecast information also provide earnings surprise analysis—the difference between actual earnings per share and the forecasted earnings per share, where the consensus forecast is used as the forecasted earnings per share.

There are three issues related to using analysts forecasts in traditional fundamental analysis. First, different providers define actual and forecasted earnings differently. There are different earnings per share amounts historically (basic and diluted) and different analysts will forecast for different earnings per share. Second, analysts' forecasts are made at different points in time. Not all analysts sit down at the same time to make forecasts, so consensus forecasts are an average of forecasts made at different point in time. Since we know that analysts' forecasts are more accurate as the time approaches to release actual earnings, this means that a set of forecasts at a point in time is a collection of forecasts that have different degrees of accuracy. Finally, there are differing degrees of analyst following. There are some companies for which few analysts make forecasts, whereas other companies have many analysts following. An earnings surprise in a company for which there are few analysts following it may have a different stock market reaction as compared to a surprise of similar magnitude for a well-followed company. For example, there are 26 analysts reporting forecasts to Zacks Investment Research for the 1998 fiscal year for Walt Disney Company, compared to four analysts for OEA Inc.

Consensus earnings forecasts and the forecasts of individual analysts are used to compute several measures that researchers have found to be important factors in explaining stock returns. The first measure is *earnings momentum*. This is a measure of consensus earnings growth found by computing the growth in earnings based on actual earnings for the current period and the consensus earnings forecasts for the next period. Some analysts and services refer to this as *earnings torpedo*. A second measure is the number of analysts that have increased their estimate of earnings less the number that have decreased their estimate of earnings, divided by the total number of analysts who have provided estimates. A variant of this measure is the percentage of analysts who have revised upwards their earnings estimate for the next period.

Analyst Forecasting Ability

A study by Elton, Gruber, and Gultekin demonstrated the value of accurate forecasts.[1] They found that if an investor was armed with per-

---

[1] Edwin Elton, Martin Gruber, and M. Gultekin, "Expectations and Share Prices," *Management Science* (September 1981).

fect information about the growth of earnings that would occur, an investor could have generated significant abnormal positive returns. Given the value of good forecasts, let's look at how well analysts do in forecasting EPS.

There has been extensive research dating back to the late 1960s that have investigated how well analysts do in forecasting earnings. The general findings are that (1) the forecast errors are too large to make the forecasts useful in models that rely on earnings estimates and (2) the forecasts tend to have an optimistic bias.

Forecasts Based on Extrapolative Statistical Models

Our discussion focused only on analyst forecasts, not on how analysts develop their forecasts. Some analysts use the techniques of traditional fundamental analysis. Today, some analysts use statistical models to extrapolate future earnings. The models range from very simple regression models in which time is the explanatory variable and earnings per share is the dependent variable to much more sophisticated time series statistical models.

The question is how good are EPS forecasts based on extrapolative statistical models compared to analysts' forecasts based on traditional fundamental analysis. There is an extensive literature that supports the view that analyst forecasts do not outperform forecasts based on naive extrapolative statistical models. But there are some studies that do suggest superiority because of the advantages that analysts have in utilizing more current information.[2] The preponderance of the evidence, however, certainly supports what two researchers found back in 1972, "... mechanical techniques have been shown to do about as good a job of forecasting earnings as do security analysts."[3]

Why might extrapolative statistical models do better in forecasting earnings than fundamental analysis? Daniel Coggin suggests, based on studies in the area of clinical psychology, why forecasts from statistical models might be superior to that of trained experts.[4] Specifically, he cites studies that show that for classifying subjects, statistical models outperformed psychologists. The reason proferred is that statistical models are not biased by human judgment and other imperfections in processing information. Another reason is that researchers find that in forecasting

---

[2] For an overview of this literature, see T. Daniel Coggin, "The Analysts and the Investment Process: An Overview," in Frank J. Fabozzi (ed.), *Managing Institutional Assets* (New York, NY: Harper & Row, 1990).

[3] Edwin Elton and Martin Gruber, "Earnings Estimates and the Accuracy of Expectational Data," *Management Science* (April 1972), p. B-423.

[4] Coggin, "The Analysts and the Investment Process: An Overview."

earnings, analysts do not employ time series properties of earnings correctly.[5]

Most of the studies have used simple or naive extrapolative statistical models. Statisticians have developed more complex models for forecasting time series data. Do such complex models do a better job of forecasting earnings than simple or naive models? The evidence does not suggest that complex statistical models lead to significantly better forecasts.[6]

Price-Earnings Ratio

Many investors are interested in how the earnings are valued by the market. A measure of how these earnings are valued is the *price-earnings ratio* (P/E). This ratio compares the price per common share with earnings per common share:

$$\text{Price-earnings ratio} = \frac{\text{Market price per share}}{\text{Earnings per share}}$$

The result is a multiple—the value of a share of stock expressed as a multiple of earnings per share. The inverse of this measure is referred to as the *earnings yield*, or E/P:[7]

$$\text{Earnings yield} = \frac{\text{Earnings per share}}{\text{Market price per share}}$$

Because investors are forward-looking in their valuation, earnings per share in this ratio represents the *expected normal earnings per share* for the stock. If a company has a share price of $17 and earnings per share of 80 cents, the price-earnings ratio is:

$$\text{Price-earnings ratio} = \frac{\$17.00}{\$0.80} = 21.25 \text{ times}$$

---

[5] Jeffrey S. Abarbanell and Victor Bernard, "Tests of Analysts' Overreaction/Underreaction to Earnings Information as an Explanation for Anomalous Stock Price Behavior," *Journal of Finance* (July 1992), pp. 1181–1208.
[6] Robert Conroy and Robert Harris, "Consensus Forecasts of Corporate Earnings: Analysts Forecasts and Time Series Methods," *Management Science* (June 1987), pp. 724–738.
[7] Though the earnings yield provides the same information as the price-earnings ratio, it is often used to avoid the problem of dividing by zero in the cases in which earnings are zero.

and the earnings yield is:

$$\text{Earnings yield} = \frac{\$0.80}{\$17.00} = 4.71\%$$

If the market value of the stock represents today's forecast of future earnings to common shareholders and if current earnings are an indication of future earnings, this ratio tells us that each dollar of earnings represents $21.25 of value today.

An interesting issue arises in deciding the appropriate inputs to the P/E ratio. The numerator is rather straightforward: Use a recent market price per share. The denominator presents a number of issues. Aside from the issue of whether the denominator is the basic or diluted earnings per share, an important issue is over what period to measure earnings per share. At any point in time, the most recently ending annual period or quarter's earnings may not be available. Further muddying the waters is whether the P/E ratio should be measured over a historical period (backward-looking) or measured using forecasted earnings (forward-looking). So what is the analyst to do? There are several approaches that are used:

- The sum of the latest available four reported quarters
- Estimated earnings for the next fiscal year
- Earning per share averaged over several historical, annual periods

The last approach is suggested by Graham and Dodd and uses an EPS that is the average of EPS for "not less than five years, preferably seven or ten years."[8]

As pointed out by Eugene Fama and Kenneth French in their study of the relation between stock returns and fundamental factors, E/P (or its inverse P/E) includes the stock price in its construction and hence should be correlated with stock returns.[9] This has been supported in research that finds that E/P explains stock returns.[10] Additional evidence can be seen in Chapter 9 where we discuss fundamental factor models.

---

[8] Benjamin Graham and David L. Dodd. *Security Analysis*, first edition (New York: McGraw-Hill, 1934), p. 452.

[9] Eugene F. Fama and Kenneth R. French. "The Cross-Section of Expected Stock Returns," *Journal of Finance* (June 1992), pp. 427–465.

[10] See, as an example, the following study: Sanjoy Basu, "The Relationship Between Earnings Yield, Market Value, and Return for NYSE Common Stocks: Further Evidence," *Journal of Financial Economics* (1983), pp. 129–156.

CASH FLOW ANALYSIS

Some of the most important financial data are provided by the company in its annual and quarterly financial statements. However, the choices available in the accrual accounting system make it difficult to compare companies' performance. These choices also provide the opportunity for the management of financial numbers through judicious choice of accounting methods. For example, $1 of net income for one company may not be equivalent to $1 of net income of another company. Cash flows provide the analyst with a way of transforming net income based on an accrual system to a more comparable medium. Additionally, cash flows are essential ingredients in valuation: The value of a company today is the present value of its expected future cash flows. Therefore, understanding past and current cash flows may help the analyst in forecasting future cash flows and hence, determine the value of the company. Moreover, understanding cash flow allows an analyst to assess the ability of a firm to maintain current dividends and its current capital expenditure policy without relying on external financing.

Difficulties with Measuring Cash Flow

The primary difficulty with measuring cash flow is that it is a flow: Cash flows into the company (cash inflows) and cash flows out of the company (cash outflows). At any point in time there is a stock of cash on hand, but the stock of cash on hand varies among companies because of the size of the company, the cash demands of the business, and a company's management of working capital. So what is cash flow? Is it the total amount of cash flowing into the company during a period? Is it the total amount of cash flowing out of the company during a period? Is it the net of the cash inflows and outflows for a period? Well, there is no specific definition of cash flow—and that's probably why there is so much confusion regarding the measurement of cash flow. Ideally, the analyst needs a measure of the company's operating performance that is comparable among companies—something other than net income (e.g., net cash flow).

A simple, yet crude method of calculating cash flow requires simply adding non-cash expenses (e.g., depreciation and amortization) to the reported net income amount to arrive at cash flow. This amount is not really a cash flow, but simply earnings before depreciation and amortization. Is this a cash flow that analysts should use in valuing a company? Though not a cash flow, this estimated cash flow does allow a quick comparison of income across firms that may use different depreciation methods and depreciable lives.

The problem with this measure is that it ignores the many other sources and uses of cash during the period. Consider the sale of goods for credit. This transaction generates sales for the period. Sales and the accompanying cost of goods sold are reflected in the period's net income and the estimated cash flow amount. However, until the account receivable is collected, there is no cash from this transaction. If collection does not occur until the next period, there is a misalignment of the income and cash flow arising from this transaction. Therefore, the simple estimated cash flow ignores some cash flows that, for many companies, are significant.

Another estimate of cash flow that is simple to calculate is EBITDA—earnings before interest, taxes, depreciation, and amortization. However, this measure suffers from the same accrual-accounting bias as the previous measure, which may result in the omission of significant cash flows. Additionally, EBITDA does not consider interest and taxes, which may also be substantial cash outflows for some companies.

These two rough estimates of cash flows are used in practice not only for their simplicity, but because they experienced widespread use prior to the disclosure of more detailed information in the statement of cash flows. Currently, the measures of cash flow are wide-ranging, including the simplistic cash flows measures, measures developed from the statement of cash flows, and measures that seek to capture the theoretical concept of "free cash flow."

Cash Flows and the Statement of Cash Flows

Companies are required to prepare and report a statement of cash flows that is consistent with the actual cash flows (inflows and outflows). This statement requires the company to classify cash flows into three categories, based on the activity: operating, investing, and financing. Cash flows are summarized by activity and within activity by type (e.g., asset dispositions are reported separately from asset acquisitions). The classification of cash flows into the three types of activities provides useful information that can be used by the analyst to see, for example, whether the company is generating sufficient cash flows from operations to sustain its current rate of growth.

Looking at the relation among the three cash flows in the statement gives the analyst a sense of the activities of the company. A young, fast growing company may have negative cash flows from operations, yet positive cash flows from financing activities (i.e., operations may be financed to a large part with external financing). As a company grows, it may rely to a lesser extent on external financing. The typical, mature company generates cash from operations and reinvests part or all of it back into the company. Therefore, cash flow related to operations is positive (i.e., a source of cash) and cash flow related to investing activities is negative (i.e., a use of cash). As a company matures, it may seek less financing externally and may even use cash to reduce its reliance on external financing (e.g., repay debts). We can classify companies on the basis of the pattern of their sources of cash flows, as shown below:

	Financing Growth Externally and Internally	Financing Growth Internally	Mature	Temporary Financial Downturn	Financial Distress	Downsizing
Cash flow: operations	+	+	+	−	−	+
Cash flow: investing activities	−	−	−	+	−	+
Cash flow: financing activities	+	−	+ or −	+	−	−

Though we can classify a company based on the sources and uses of cash flows, more data are needed to put this information in perspective. What is the trend in the sources and uses of cash flows? What market, industry, or company-specific events affect the company's cash flows? How does the company being analyzed compare with other companies in the same industry in terms of the sources and uses of funds?

Lets take a closer look at the incremental information provided by cash flows. Consider Wal-Mart Stores, Inc., which had growing sales and net income from 1988 to 1997, as summarized in Exhibit 11.3. We see that net income grew each year, with the exception of 1995, and that sales grew each year. We get additional information by looking at the cash flow and their sources, as graphed in Exhibit 11.4. We see that the growth in Wal-Mart was supported by both internally generated funds and, to a lesser extent, through external financing. Wal-Mart's pattern of cash flows suggests that Wal-Mart is a mature company that has become less reliant on external financing in recent years, funding most of its recent growth with internally generated funds.

Free Cash Flow

Cash flows without any adjustment may be misleading because they do not reflect the cash outflows that are necessary for the future existence of a firm. An alternative measure is *free cash flow*.[11] In theory, free cash flow is the cash flow left over after the company funds all positive net

---

[11] Michael Jensen, "Agency Costs of Free Cash Flow, Corporate Finance, and Takeovers," *American Economic Review* (May 1986), pp. 323–329.

present value projects. Positive net present value projects are those projects (i.e., capital investments) for which the present value of expected future cash flows exceeds the present value of project outlays, all discounted at the cost of capital. In other words, free cash flow is the cash flow of the firm, less capital expenditures necessary to stay in business (i.e., replacing facilities as necessary) and grow at the expected rate (which requires increases in working capital).

EXHIBIT 11.3   Wal-Mart Stores, Inc., Net Income and Sales for the Years 1988–1997

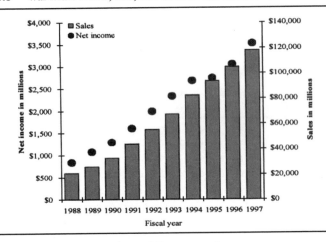

Source: Wal-Mart Stores, Inc., Annual Report, various years

EXHIBIT 11.4   Wal-Mart Stores, Inc., Sources of Cash Flow, 1988–1997

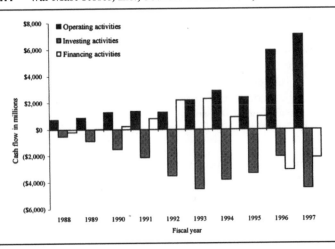

Source: Wal-Mart Stores, Inc., Annual Report, various years

By itself, the fact that a company generates free cash flow is neither good nor bad. What the company does with this free cash flow is what is important. And this is where it is important to measure the free cash flow as that cash flow in excess of profitable investment opportunities. Consider the simple numerical exercise with the Winner Company and the Loser Company:

	Winner Company	Loser Company
Cash flow before capital expenditures	$1,000	$1,000
Capital expenditures, positive net present value projects	(750)	(250)
Capital expenditures, negative net present value projects	0	(500)
Cash flow	$250	$250
Free cash flow	$250	$750

These two companies have identical cash flows and the same total capital expenditures. However, the Winner Company spends only on profitable projects (in terms of positive net present value projects), whereas the Loser Company spends on both profitable projects and wasteful projects. The Winner Company has a lower free cash flow than the Loser Company, indicating that they are using the generated cash flows in a more profitable manner. The lesson is that the existence of a high level of free cash flow is not necessarily good—it may simply suggest that the company is either a very good takeover target or the company has the potential for investing in unprofitable investments.

Positive free cash flow may be good or bad news; likewise, negative free cash flow may be good or bad news:

	Good News	Bad News
Positive free cash flow	The company is generating substantial operating cash flows, beyond those necessary for profitable projects.	The company is generating more cash flows than it needs for profitable projects and may waste these cash flows on unprofitable projects.
Negative free cash flow	The company has more profitable projects than it has operating cash flows and must rely on external financing to fund these projects.	The company is unable to generate sufficient operating cash flows to satisfy its investment needs for future growth.

Therefore, once the analyst calculates free cash flow, other information (e.g., trends in profitability) must be considered to evaluate the operating performance and financial condition of the firm.

There is some confusion when this theoretical concept is applied to actual companies. The primary difficulty is that the amount of capital expenditures necessary to maintain the business at its current rate of growth is generally not known; companies generally do not report this item and may not even be able to determine how much of a period's capital expenditures are attributed to maintenance and how much is attributed to expansion. Some analysts estimate free cash flow by assuming that all capital expenditures are necessary for the maintenance of the current growth of the company. Though there is little justification in using all expenditures, this is a practical solution to an impractical calculation. This assumption allows us to estimate free cash flows using published financial statements.

Another issue in the calculation is defining what is truly "free" cash flow. Generally we think of "free" cash flow as that being leftover after all necessary financing expenditures are paid; this means that free cash flow is after interest on debt is paid. Some calculate free cash flow before such financing expenditures, others calculate free cash flow after interest, and still others calculate free cash flow after both interest and dividends (assuming that dividends are a commitment, though not a legal commitment).

There is no one correct method of calculating free cash flow and different analysts may arrive at different estimates of free cash flow for a company. The problem is that it is impossible to measure free cash flow as dictated by the theory, so many methods have arisen to calculate this cash flow.

Net Free Cash Flow

There are many variations in the calculation of cash flows that are used in analyses of companies' financial condition and operating performance. As an example of these variations, consider the alternative to free cash flow developed by Fitch, a company that rates corporate debt instruments. This cash flow measure, referred to as *net free cash flow* (NFCF), is free cash flow less interest and other financing costs, and taxes. In this approach, free cash flow is defined as earnings before depreciation, interest, and taxes, less capital expenditures. Capital expenditures encompass all capital spending, whether for maintenance or expansion and no changes in working capital are considered.

The basic difference between NFCF and free cash flow is that the financing expenses—interest and, in some cases dividends—are deducted. If preferred dividends are perceived as non-discretionary—that is, investors come to expect the dividends—dividends may be included with the interest commitment to arrive at net free cash flow. Otherwise, dividends are deducted from net free cash flow to produce cash flow. Another difference is that NFCF does not consider changes in working capital in the analysis. Furthermore, cash taxes are deducted to arrive at net free cash flow. Cash taxes is the income tax expense restated to reflect the actual cash flow related to this obligation, rather than the accrued expense for the period. Cash taxes are the income tax expense (from the income statement) adjusted for the change in deferred income taxes (from the balance sheets).

Net free cash flow gives the analyst an idea of the unconstrained cash flow of the company. This cash flow measure may be useful from a creditor's perspective in terms of evaluating the company's ability to fund additional debt. From a shareholder's perspective, net cash flow (i.e., net free cash flow net of dividends) may be an appropriate measure because this represents the cash flow that is reinvested in the company.

The Usefulness of Cash Flows and in Financial Analysis

The usefulness of cash flows for financial analysis depends on whether cash flows provide unique information or provide information in a manner that is more accessible or convenient for the analyst. The cash flow information provided in the statement of cash flows, for example, is not necessarily unique because most, if not all, of the information is available through analysis of the balance sheet and income statement. What the statement does provide is a classification scheme that presents information in a manner that is easier to use and, perhaps, more illustrative of the company's financial position.

An analysis of cash flows and the sources of cash flows can reveal information to the analyst, including:

■ The sources of financing the company's capital spending. Does the company generate internally (i.e., from operations) a portion or all of the funds needed for its investment activities? If a company cannot generate cash flow from operations, this may indicate problems up ahead. Reliance on external financing (e.g., equity or debt issuance) may indicate a company's inability of to sustain itself over time.
■ The company's dependence on borrowing. Does the company rely heavily on borrowing that may result in difficulty in satisfying future debt service?
■ The quality of earnings. Large and growing differences between income and cash flows suggests a low quality of earnings.

Consider financial results of OEA, Inc., a manufacturer of propellants and pyrotechnic devices (such as those used in air bags), as presented in Exhibit 11.5. As we can see in this exhibit, both operating income and net income are growing over time, with a slight interruption of this growth in 1992. If an analyst looked at cash flows rather than income, a much different picture of the company would apper, as shown in Exhibit 11.6. As we can see in this exhibit, the growth in investment expenditures has continued over time, yet the company is less able to generate funds from operations; in fact, in 1997 OEA relied entirely on external financing. This difficulty is associated with the concerns at the time over air bags, the re-engineering of air bags, and OEA's heavy reliance on the airbags for its revenues (80%). OEA's financial challenges were not reflected in the income figures, but can be detected with an analysis of the sources of cash flows.

Ratio Analysis

One use of cash flow information is in ratio analysis, much like we did in the previous chapter primarily with the balance sheet and income statement information. In that chapter we used a cash flow-based ratio, the cash flow interest coverage ratio, as a measure of financial risk. There are a number of other cash flow-based ratios that the analyst may find useful in evaluating the operating performance and financial condition of a company.

A useful ratio to help further assess a company's cash flow is the cash flow to capital expenditures ratio, or *capital expenditures coverage ratio*:

$$\text{Cash flow-to-capital expenditures} = \frac{\text{Cash flow}}{\text{Capital expenditures}}$$

EXHIBIT 11.5   OEA Inc., Operating and Net Income 1988–1997

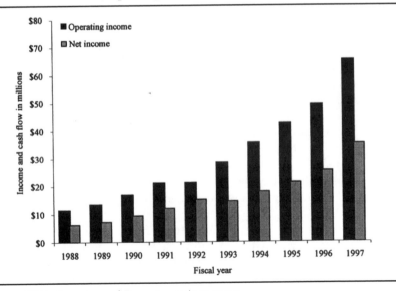

Source: OEA, Inc., Annual Reports, various years

EXHIBIT 11.6   OEA, Inc., Sources of Cash Flows, 1988–1997

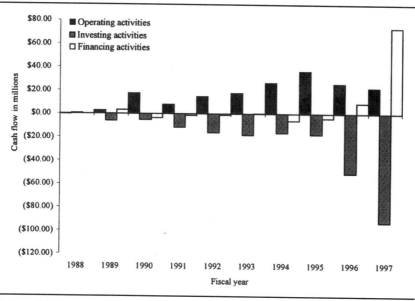

Source: OEA, Inc., Annual Reports, various years

This ratio gives the analyst information about the financial flexibility of the company and is particularly useful for capital-intensive firms and utilities. The larger the ratio, the greater the financial flexibility. The analyst, however, must carefully examine the reasons why this ratio may be changing over time and why it might be out of line with comparable firms in the industry. For example, a declining ratio can be interpreted in two ways. First, the firm may eventually have difficulty adding to capacity via capital expenditures without the need to borrow funds. The second interpretation is that the firm may have gone through a period of major capital expansion and therefore it will take time for revenues to be generated that will increase the cash flow from operations to bring the ratio to some normal long-run level.

Another useful cash flow ratio is the cash flow to debt ratio:

$$\text{Cash flow-to-debt} = \frac{\text{Cash flow}}{\text{Debt}}$$

where debt can be represented as total debt, long-term debt, or a debt measure that captures a specific range of maturity (e.g., debt maturing in 5 years). This ratio gives a measure of a company's ability to meet maturing debt obligations.

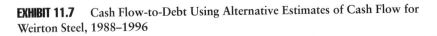

EXHIBIT 11.7 Cash Flow-to-Debt Using Alternative Estimates of Cash Flow for Weirton Steel, 1988–1996

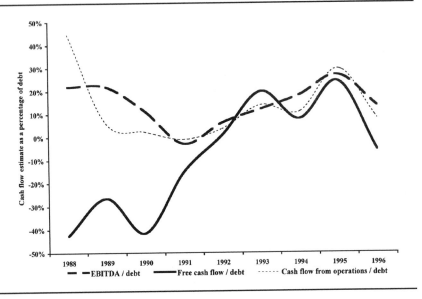

Source: Weirton Steel's 10-K reports, various years

Using Cash Flow Information

The analysis of cash flows provides information that can be used along with other financial data to help the analyst assess the financial condition of a company. Consider the cash flow-to-debt ratio calculated using three different measures of cash flow—EBITDA, free cash flow, and cash flow from operations (from the statement of cash flows)—each compared with long-term debt, as shown in Exhibit 11.7 for Weirton Steel. The effect of capital expenditures in the 1988–1991 period can be seen by the difference between the free cash flow measure and the other two measures of cash flow; both EBITDA and cash flow from operations ignore capital expenditures, which were substantial outflows for this company in the earlier period.

Cash flow information may help the analyst identify companies that may encounter financial difficulties. Consider the findings of a study that analyzed the financial statements of W.T. Grant during the 1966–1974 period preceding its bankruptcy in 1975 and ultimate liquidation.[12] They noted that financial indicators such as profitability ratios, turnover

---

[12] J.A. Largay III and C.P. Stickney, "Cash Flows, Ratio Analysis and the W.T. Grant Company Bankruptcy," *Financial Analysts Journal* (July/August 1980), pp. 51–54.

ratios, and liquidity ratios showed some down trends, but provided no definite clues to the company's impending bankruptcy. A study of cash flows from operations, however, revealed that company operations were causing an increasing drain on cash, rather than providing cash. This necessitated an increased use of external financing, the required interest payments on which exacerbated the cash flow drain. Cash flow analysis clearly was a valuable tool in this case since W.T. Grant had been running a negative cash flow from operations for years. Yet none of the traditional ratios discussed above take into account the cash flow from operations. Use of the cash flow-to-capital expenditures ratio and the cash flow-to-debt ratio would have highlighted the company's difficulties.

DIVIDENDS AND DIVIDEND DISCOUNT MODELS

Dividends are cash payments made by a corporation to its owners. Though cash dividends are paid to both preferred and common shareholders, most of the focus of the attention is on the dividends paid to the residual owners of the corporation, the common shareholders. Dividends paid to common and preferred shareholders are not legal obligations of a corporation and some corporations do not pay cash dividends. But for those companies that pay dividends, changes in dividends are noticed by investors—increases in dividends are viewed favorably and are associated with increases in the company's stock price, whereas decreases in dividends are viewed quite unfavorably and are associated with decreases in the company's stock price.

There is no requirement that companies pay cash dividends. We observe, however, that many companies do pay cash dividends and, once they pay dividends only reluctantly (in cases of financial distress) lower or eliminate cash dividends. It is often the case, however, that relatively young, fast-growing companies do not pay dividends; as the companies mature they begin to pay dividends. At the present time, Internet companies and companies in high-tech industries, such as Microsoft, pay little or no dividends.

Dividend Measures

Dividends are measured using three different measures: dividends per share, dividend yield, and dividend payout ratio.

Dividends Per Share

The value of a share of stock today is the investors' assessment of today's worth of future cash flows for each share. Because future cash flows to shareholders are dividends, we need a measure of dividends for each share of stock to estimate future cash flows per share. The *dividends per share* is the dollar amount of dividends paid out during the period per share of common stock:

$$\text{Dividends per share} = \frac{\text{Dividends}}{\text{Number of shares outstanding}}$$

Some companies appear to follow a policy of paying ever-increasing cash dividends. Other companies pay dividends per share that increase over time, but not at a constant rate. And still other companies pay dividends such that the dividends per share amount does not follow any particular pattern.

Dividend Yield

The *dividend yield*, also referred to the *dividend-price ratio*, is the the ratio of dividends to price:

$$\text{Dividend yield} = \frac{\text{Annual cash dividends per share}}{\text{Market price per share}}$$

In an exhaustive study of the relation between dividend yield and stock prices, John Campbell and Robert Shiller find that:[13]

- There is a weak relation between the dividend yield and subsequent 10-year dividend growth
- The dividend yield does not forecast future dividend growth
- The dividend yield predicts future price changes

The weak relation between the dividend yield and future dividends may be attributed to the effects of the business cycle on dividend growth. The tendency for the dividend yield to revert to its historical mean has been observed by researchers.[14]

Dividend Payout Ratio

Another way of describing dividends paid out during a period is to state the dividends as a portion of earnings for the period. This is referred to as the *dividend payout ratio*:

---

[13] See John Y. Campbell and Robert J. Shiller, "Valuation Ratios and the Long-Run Stock Market Outlook," *Journal of Portfolio Management* (Winter 1998), p. 11.
[14] Campbell and Shiller, "Valuation Ratios and the Long-Run Stock Market Outlook."

$$\text{Dividend payout ratio} = \frac{\text{Dividends}}{\text{Earnings available to common shareholders}}$$

For example, a dividend payout ratio 30%, means that the company paid out 30% of its earnings to shareholders.

The proportion of earnings paid out in dividends varies by company and industry. For example, the companies in the steel industry typically pay out 25% of their earnings in dividends, whereas the electric utility companies pay out approximately 75% of their earnings in dividends.

If companies focus on dividends per share in establishing their dividends (e.g., a constant dividends per share), the dividend payout will fluctuate along with earnings. We generally observe that companies set the dividend policy such that dividends per share grow at a relatively constant rate, resulting in dividend payouts that fluctuate.

Dividends and Stock Prices

If an investor buys a common stock, he or she has bought shares that represent an ownership interest in the corporation. Shares of common stock are a perpetual security—there is no maturity. The investor who owns shares of common stock has the right to receive a certain portion of any dividends—but dividends are not a sure thing. Whether or not a corporation will pay dividends is up to its board of directors—the representatives of the common shareholders. Typically we see some pattern in the dividends companies pay: Dividends are either constant or grow at a constant rate. But there is no guarantee that dividends will be paid in the future.

It is reasonable to figure that what an investor pays for a share of stock should reflect what he or she expects to receive from it—return on the investor's investment. What an investor receives are cash dividends in the future. How can we relate that return to what a share of common stock is worth? Well, the value of a share of stock should be equal to the present value of all the future cash flows an investor expects to receive from that share. To value stock, therefore, an investor must project future cash flows, which, in turn, means projecting future dividends. This approach to the valuation of common stock is referred to the discounted cash flow approach and the models used are referred to as dividend discount models.

Dividend discount models are not the only approach to valuing common stock. There are fundamental factor models that will be described in Chapter 13 and value-based approaches that we cover in Chapter 12.

Dividend Discount Models

As discussed above, the basis for the *dividend discount model* (DDM) is simply the application of present value analysis, which asserts that the fair price of an asset is the present value of the expected cash flows.[15] In the case of common stock, the cash flows are the expected dividend payouts. The basic DDM model can be expressed mathematically as:

$$P = \frac{D_1}{(1 + r_1)^1} + \frac{D_2}{(1 + r_2)^2} + \dots \tag{1}$$

where

P = the fair value or theoretical value of the common stock
D_t = the expected dividend for period t
r_t = the appropriate discount or capitalization rate for period t

The dividends are expected to be received forever.

Practitioners rarely use the dividend discount model given by equation (1). Instead, one of the DDMs discussed in the following sections is typically used.

The Finite Life General Dividend Discount Model

The DDM given by equation (1) can be modified by assuming a finite life for the expected cash flows. In this case, the expected cash flows are the expected dividend payouts and the expected sale price of the stock at some future date. The expected sale price is also called the *terminal price* and is intended to capture the future value of all subsequent dividend payouts. This model is called the *finite life general DDM* and is expressed mathematically as:

$$P = \frac{D_1}{(1 + r_1)^1} + \frac{D_2}{(1 + r_2)^2} + \dots + \frac{D_N}{(1 + r_N)^N} + \frac{P_N}{(1 + r_N)^N} \tag{2}$$

where

P_N = the expected sale price (or terminal price) at the horizon period N
N = the number of periods in the horizon

and P, D_t, and r_t are the same as defined above.

---

[15] John B. Williams, *The Theory of Investment Value* (Cambridge, MA: Harvard University Press, 1938).

Assuming a Constant Discount Rate A special case of the finite life general DDM that is more commonly used in practice is one in which it is assumed that the discount rate is constant. That is, it is assumed each r_t is the same for all t. Denoting this constant discount rate by r, equation (2) becomes:

$$P = \frac{D_1}{(1+r)^1} + \frac{D_2}{(1+r)^2} + \dots + \frac{D_N}{(1+r)^N} + \frac{P_N}{(1+r)^N} \qquad (3)$$

Equation (3) is called the *constant discount rate version* of the finite life general DDM. When practitioners use any of the DDM models presented in this chapter, typically the constant discount rate version form is used.

Let's illustrate the finite life general DDM assuming a constant discount rate assuming each period is a year. Suppose that the following data are determined for stock XYZ by a financial analyst:

$D_1 = \$2.00 \quad D_2 = \$2.20 \quad D_3 = \$2.30 \quad D_4 = \$2.55 \quad D_5 = \$2.65$
$P_5 = \$26 \quad N = 5 \quad r = 0.10$

Based on these data, the fair price of stock XYZ is

$$P = \frac{\$2.00}{(1.10)^1} + \frac{\$2.20}{(1.10)^2} + \frac{\$2.30}{(1.10)^3} + \frac{\$2.55}{(1.10)^4} + \frac{\$2.65}{(1.10)^5} + \frac{\$26.00}{(1.10)^5} = \$24.895$$

Required Inputs The finite life general DDM requires three forecasts as inputs to calculate the fair value of a stock:

1. the expected terminal price (P_N)
2. the dividends up to the assumed horizon $(D_1$ to $D_N)$
3. the discount rates $(r_1$ to $r_N)$ or r (in the case of the constant discount rate version)

Thus the relevant question is, How accurately can these inputs be forecasted?

The terminal price is the most difficult of the three forecasts. According to theory, P_N is the present value of all future dividends after N; that is, $D_{N+1}, D_{N+2}, \dots, D_{\text{infinity}}$. Also, the future discount rate (r_t) must be forecasted. In practice, forecasts are made of either dividends (D_N) or earnings (E_N) first, and then the price P_N is estimated by assigning an "appropriate" requirement for yield, price-earnings ratio, or capitalization rate. Note that the present value of the expected terminal price $P_N/(1 + r)^N$ becomes very small if N is very large.

The forecasting of dividends is "somewhat" easier. Usually, past history is available, management can be queried, and cash flows can be projected for a given scenario. The discount rate r is the required rate of return. Forecasting r is more complex than forecasting dividends, although not nearly as difficult as forecasting the terminal price (which requires a forecast of future discount rates as well). As noted above, in practice for a given company, r is assumed to be constant for all periods and typically generated from the capital asset pricing model (CAPM). The CAPM provides the expected return for a company based on its systematic risk (beta).

Assessing Relative Value Given the fair price derived from a dividend discount model, the assessment of the stock proceeds along the following lines. If the market price is below the fair price derived from the model, then the stock is *undervalued* or *cheap*. The opposite holds for a stock whose market price is greater than the model-derived price. In this case, the stock is said to be *overvalued* or *expensive*. A stock trading equal to or close to its fair price is said to be *fairly valued*.

There are three shortcomings with using the DDM for relative value analysis. First, the DDM does not tell an analyst when the price of the stock should be expected to move to its fair price. That is, the model says that based on the inputs generated by the analyst, the stock may be cheap, expensive, or fair relative to the model. However, it does not tell the analyst that if it is mispriced how long it will take before the market recognizes the mispricing and corrects it. As a result, an investor may hold on to a stock perceived to be cheap for an extended period of time and may underperform a benchmark during that period.

The second shortcoming is that while a stock may be mispriced, an investor must also consider how mispriced it is in order to take the appropriate action (buy a cheap stock and sell or sell short an expensive stock). This will depend on by how much the stock is trading from its fair value after considering transaction costs.

Finally, and this is a major shortcoming from a theoretical perspective, is that the DDM fails to look at the stock in the context of a portfolio. In Chapter 1, several approaches to portfolio construction are discussed. A naive approach is to evaluate a stock in isolation—that is, failing to take into account the covariance of the return of the stock being analyzed with the return of other stocks that are candidates for inclusion in a portfolio. In this sense, the DDM is a naive approach since it looks at stocks in isolation. This should be kept in mind in the discussion that follows when we refer to a stock as being overvalued, undervalued, or fairly priced.

Constant Growth Dividend Discount Model

If future dividends are assumed to grow at a constant rate (g) and a single discount rate (r) is used, then the finite life general DDM assuming a constant growth rate given by equation (3) becomes:

$$P = \frac{D_0(1+g)^1}{(1+r)^1} + \frac{D_0(1+g)^2}{(1+r)^2} + \frac{D_0(1+g)^3}{(1+r)^3} + \ldots + \frac{D_0(1+g)^N}{(1+r)^N} + \frac{P_N}{(1+r)^N}$$

and it can be shown that if N is assumed to approach infinity, equation (4) is equal to:

$$P = \frac{D_0(1+g)}{r-g} \qquad (4)$$

Equation (5) is called the *constant growth dividend discount model.*[16] An equivalent formulation for the constant growth DDM is:

$$P = \frac{D_1}{r-g} \qquad (5)$$

where D_1 is equal to $D_0(1+g)$.

Consider a company that currently pays dividends of $3.00 per share. If the dividend is expected to grow at a rate of 3% per year and the discount rate is 12%, what is the value of a share of stock of this company? Using equation (5),

$$P = \frac{\$3.00(1+0.03)}{0.12-0.03} = \frac{\$3.09}{0.09} = \$34.33$$

If the growth rate for this company's dividends is 5%, instead of 3%, the current value is $45.00:

---

[16] Myron Gordon and E. Shapiro, "Capital Equipment Analysis: The Required Rate of Profit," *Management Science* (October 1956), pp. 102–110. The model was first developed in Williams, *The Theory of Investment Value.*

$$P = \frac{\$3.00(1 + 0.05)}{0.12 - 0.05} = \frac{\$3.15}{0.07} = \$45.00$$

Therefore, the *greater* the expected growth rate of dividends, the *greater* the value of a share of stock.

In this last example, if the discount rate is 14% instead of 12% and the growth rate of dividends is 3%, the value of a share of stock is:

$$P = \frac{\$3.00(1 + 0.03)}{0.14 - 0.03} = \frac{\$3.09}{0.11} = \$28.09$$

Therefore, the *greater* the discount rate, the *lower* the current value of a share of stock.

Let's apply the model as given by equation (5) to estimate the price of three utilities, Bell Atlantic, BellSouth, and Cincinnati Bell, as of 1997. The discount rate for each telephone utility was estimated using the capital asset pricing model assuming (1) a market risk premium of 5% and (2) a risk-free rate of 6%.[17] The beta estimate for each telephone utility was obtained from the Value Line Investment Survey: 0.95 for Bell Atlantic, 0.95 for BellSouth, and 0.90 for Cincinnati Bell. The discount rate, r, for each telephone utility based on the CAPM was then:

Bell Atlantic $r = 0.06 + 0.95 (0.05) = 0.1075$ or 10.75%
BellSouth $r = 0.06 + 0.95 (0.05) = 0.1075$ or 10.75%
Cincinnati Bell $r = 0.06 + 0.90 (0.05) = 0.1050$ or 10.50%

The dividend growth rate can be estimated by using the compounded rate of growth of historical dividends. The dividend history for the three telephone utilities ending in 1997 is shown in Exhibit 11.8. The data needed for the calculations are summarized below, adjusted for stock splits and dividends:

---

[17] These are the same three utilities analyzed by William J. Hurley and Lewis D. Johnson in "A Realistic Dividend Valuation Model," *Financial Analysts Journal* (July-August 1994), pp. 50–54. The market risk premium is based on the historical spread between the return on the market (often proxied with the return on the S&P 500 Index) and the risk-free rate. Historically, this spread has been approximately 5%. The risk-free rate is often estimated by the yield on U.S. Treasury securities, most often using the rate on a 1-year Treasury bill or a Treasury bond with a 10-year maturity. At the end of 1997, the 1-year rate was 5.63% and 10-year Treasury securities were yielding approximately 6.35%. We use 6% as an estimate for the purposes of this illustration.

EXHIBIT 11.8   Annual Dividend and Dividend Changes for Bell Atlantic, BellSouth, and Cincinnati Bell

Year	Bell Atlantic Dividend	% change	BellSouth Dividend	% change	Cincinnati Bell Dividend	% change
1977					$0.11	22.73%
1978					$0.14	11.11%
1979					$0.15	6.67%
1980					$0.16	3.13%
1981					$0.17	3.03%
1982					$0.17	2.94%
1983					$0.18	5.71%
1984	$0.80		$0.86		$0.19	13.51%
1985	$0.85	6.25%	$0.94	9.30%	$0.21	4.76%
1986	$0.90	5.88%	$1.02	8.51%	$0.22	9.09%
1987	$0.96	6.67%	$1.10	7.84%	$0.24	16.67%
1988	$1.02	6.25%	$1.18	7.27%	$0.28	21.43%
1989	$1.10	7.84%	$1.26	6.78%	$0.34	11.76%
1990	$1.18	7.27%	$1.34	6.35%	$0.38	5.26%
1991	$1.26	6.78%	$1.38	2.99%	$0.40	0.00%
1992	$1.30	3.17%	$1.38	0.00%	$0.40	0.00%
1993	$1.34	3.08%	$1.38	0.00%	$0.40	0.00%
1994	$1.38	2.99%	$1.38	0.00%	$0.40	0.00%
1995	$1.40	1.45%	$1.41	2.17%	$0.40	0.00%
1996	$1.43	2.14%	$1.44	2.13%	$0.40	0.00%
1997	$1.49	4.20%	$1.44	0.00%	$0.40	0.00%

Note: Dividends have been adjusted for stock dividends and stock splits up through October 1998.
Source: Value Line Investment Survey, various issues

Company	Dividends Starting in:	Dividend	1997 Dividend	Number of Years
Bell Atlantic	1984	$0.80	$1.49	13
BellSouth	1984	$0.86	$1.44	13
Cincinnati Bell	1977	$0.11	$0.40	20

The compound growth rate, g, is found using the following formula:[18]

$$g = \left(\frac{1997 \text{ dividend}}{\text{Starting dividend}} \right)^{1/\text{no. of years}} - 1$$

Substituting the values for the starting and ending dividend amounts and the number of periods into the formula, we get:

$$g \text{ for Bell Atlantic} = \left(\frac{\$1.49}{\$0.80} \right)^{1/13} - 1 = 4.900\%$$

$$g \text{ for BellSouth} = \left(\frac{\$1.44}{\$0.86} \right)^{1/13} - 1 = 4.045\%$$

$$g \text{ for Cincinnati Bell} = \left(\frac{\$0.40}{\$0.11} \right)^{1/20} - 1 = 6.668\%$$

The value of D_0, the estimate for g, and the discount rate r for each utility are summarized below:

	D_0	g	r
Bell Atlantic	$1.49	4.900%	10.75%
BellSouth	$1.44	4.045%	10.75%
Cincinnati Bell	$0.40	6.668%	10.50%

Substituting these values into equation (5) we obtain:

$$\text{Bell Atlantic estimated price} = \frac{\$1.49(1.049)}{0.1075 - 0.049} = \frac{\$1.5630}{0.0585} = \$26.72$$

$$\text{BellSouth estimated price} = \frac{\$1.44(1.04045)}{0.1075 - 0.04045} = \frac{\$1.49832}{0.06705} = \$22.35$$

---

[18] This formula is equivalent to calculating the geometric mean of 1 plus the percentage change over the number of years. Using time value of money math, the 1997 dividend is the future value, the starting dividend is the present value, the number of years is the number of periods; solving for the interest rate produces the growth rate.

$$\text{Cincinnati Bell estimated price} = \frac{\$0.40(1.06668)}{0.1050 - 0.06668} = \frac{\$0.42667}{0.03832} = \$11.13$$

A comparison of the estimated price and the actual price is given below:[19]

	Estimated Price End of 1997	Actual Price End of 1997
Bell Atlantic	$26.72	$45½
BellSouth	$22.35	$56⁵⁄₁₆
Cincinnati Bell	$11.13	$31

Notice that the constant growth DDM is considerably off the mark for all three companies. The reasons can be seen in Exhibit 11.8: (1) the dividend growth pattern for none of the three utilities appears to suggest a constant growth rate, and (2) the growth rate of dividends in recent years has been much slower than earlier years (and, in fact, zero for Cincinnati Bell), causing growth rates estimated from the long time periods to overstate future growth. And this pattern is not unique to these utilities.

Another problem that arises in using the constant growth rate model is that the growth rate of dividends may exceed the discount rate, r. Consider the following three companies and their dividend growth over the 10-year period 1987–1997, with r estimated using a risk-free rate of 6% and a market risk premium of 5%:

	1987 Dividends	1997 Dividends	g	Beta	r
Coca-Cola	$0.14	$0.56	14.87%	1.10	11.5%
Texaco	$0.38	$1.75	16.50%	0.70	9.5%
Tootsie Roll	$0.04	$0.16	14.87%	0.60	9.0%

For these three companies, the growth rate of dividends over the prior 10 years is greater than the discount rate. If we substitute the D_0 (the 1997 dividends), the g, and the r into equation (5), the estimated price at the end of 1997 is negative, which doesn't make sense. Therefore, there are some cases in which it is inappropriate to use the constant rate DDM.

---

[19] Stated in number of shares as of October 1998, which reflects the June 1998 2-for-1 split for Bell Atlantic.

The potential for mis-valuation using the constant rate DDM is highlighted by Russell Fogler in his illustration using ABC prior to its being taken over by Capital Cities in 1985.[20] He estimated the value of ABC stock to be $53.88, which was less than its market price at the time (of $64) and less than the $121 paid per share by Capital Cities.

Multiphase Dividend Discount Models

The assumption of constant growth is unrealistic and can even be misleading. Instead, most practitioners modify the constant growth DDM by assuming that companies will go through different growth phases. Within a given phase, dividends are assumed to grow at a constant rate.

Two-Stage Growth Model   The simplest form of a multiphase DDM is the two-stage growth model. A simple extension of equation (4) uses two different values of g. Referring to the first growth rate as g_1 and the second growth rate as g_2 and assuming that the first growth rate pertains to the next four years and the second growth rate refers to all years following, equation (4) can be modified as:

$$P = \frac{D_0(1+g_1)^1}{(1+r)^1} + \frac{D_0(1+g_1)^2}{(1+r)^2} + \frac{D_0(1+g_1)^3}{(1+r)^3} + \frac{D_0(1+g_1)^4}{(1+r)^4}$$
$$+ \frac{D_0(1+g_1)^5}{(1+r)^5} + \frac{D_0(1+g_1)^6}{(1+r)^6} + \dots$$

which simplifies to:

$$P = \frac{D_0(1+g_1)^1}{(1+r)^1} + \frac{D_0(1+g_1)^2}{(1+r)^2} + \frac{D_0(1+g_1)^3}{(1+r)^3} + \frac{D_0(1+g_1)^4}{(1+r)^4} + P_4$$

Because dividends following the fourth year are presumed to grow at a constant rate g_2 forever, the value of a share at the end of the fourth year (that is, P_4) is determined by using equation (5), substituting $D_0(1+g_1)^4$ for D_0 (because period 4 is the base period for the value at end of the fourth year) and g_2 for the constant rate g:

---

[20] H. Russell Fogler, "Security Analysis, DDMs, and Probability," in *Equity Markets and Valuation Methods* (Charlottesville, VA: The Institute of Chartered Financial Analysts, 1988), pp. 51–52.

$$P = \frac{D_0(1 + g_1)^1}{(1 + r)^1} + \frac{D_0(1 + g_1)^2}{(1 + r)^2} + \frac{D_0(1 + g_1)^3}{(1 + r)^3} + \frac{D_0(1 + g_1)^4}{(1 + r)^4}$$

$$+ \left[\frac{1}{(1 + r)^4} \left(\frac{D_0(1 + g_1)^4(1 + g_2)}{r - g_2} \right) \right] \qquad (6)$$

Suppose a company's dividends are expected to grow at a 4% for the next four years and then 8% thereafter. If the current dividend is $2.00 and the discount rate is 12%,

$$P = \frac{\$2.08}{(1 + 0.12)^1} + \frac{\$2.16}{(1 + 0.12)^2} + \frac{\$2.25}{(1 + 0.12)^3} + \frac{\$2.34}{(1 + 0.12)^4}$$

$$+ \left[\frac{1}{(1 + 0.12)^4} \left(\frac{\$2.53}{0.12 - 0.08} \right) \right] = \$46.87 \qquad (7)$$

If this company's dividends are expected to grow at the rate of 4% forever, the value of a share is $26.00; if this company's dividends are expected to grow at the rate of 8% forever, the value of a share is $52.00. But because the growth rate of dividends is expected to increase from 4% to 8% in four years, the value of a share is between those two values, or $46.87.

As you can see from this example, the basic valuation model can be modified to accommodate different patterns of expected dividend growth.

Three-Stage Growth Model   The most popular multiphase model employed by practitioners appears to be the *three-stage DDM*.[21] This model assumes that all companies go through three phases, analogous to the concept of the product life cycle. In the *growth phase*, a company experiences rapid earnings growth as it produces new products and expands market share. In the *transition phase*, the company's earnings begin to mature and decelerate to the rate of growth of the economy as a whole. At this point, the company is in the *maturity phase*, in which earnings continue to grow at the rate of the general economy.

---

[21] The formula for this model is derived in Eric Sorensen and David Williamson, "Some Evidence on the Value of Dividend Discount Models," *Financial Analysts Journal* (November–December 1985), pp. 60–69.

Different companies are assumed to be at different phases in the three-phase model. An emerging growth company would have a longer growth phase than a more mature company. Some companies are considered to have higher initial growth rates and hence longer growth and transition phases. Other companies may be considered to have lower current growth rates and hence shorter growth and transition phases.

In the typical investment management organization, analysts supply the projected earnings, dividends, growth rates for earnings, and dividend and payout ratios using the fundamental security analysis described throughout this book. The growth rate at maturity for the entire economy is applied to all companies. As a generalization, approximately 25% of the expected return from a company (projected by the DDM) comes from the growth phase, 25% from the transition phase, and 50% from the maturity phase. However, a company with high growth and low dividend payouts shifts the relative contribution toward the maturity phase, while a company with low growth and a high payout shifts the relative contribution toward the growth and transition phases.

Stochastic Dividend Discount Models

As we noted in our discussion and illustration of the constant growth DDM, an erratic dividend pattern such as that of Cincinnati Bell can lead to quite a difference between the estimated price and the actual price. In the case of Cincinnati Bell, the estimated price of $11.13 was considerably less than the actual price of $31, suggesting that this telephone utility was trading significantly below its true value.

William Hurley and Lewis Johnson have suggested a new family of valuation model.[22] Their model allows for a more realistic pattern of dividend payments. The basic model generates dividend payments based on a model that assumes that either the firm will increase dividends for the period by a constant amount or keep dividends the same. The model is referred to as a *stochastic DDM* because the dividend can increase or be constant based on some estimated probability of each possibility occurring. The dividend stream used in the stochastic DDM is called the *stochastic dividend stream*.

There are two versions of the stochastic DDM. One assumes that dividends either increase or decrease at a constant growth rate. This version is referred to as a *binomial stochastic DDM* because there are two possibili-

---

[22] William Hurley and Lewis Johnson, "A Realistic Dividend Valuation Model;" "Generalized Markov Dividend Discount Models," *Journal of Portfolio Management* (Fall 1998), and "Confidence Intervals for Stochastic Dividend Discount Models," unpublished paper.

ties for dividends. The second version is called a *trinomial stochastic DDM* because it allows for an increase in dividends, no change in dividends, and a cut in dividends. We discuss each version in the sections that follow.

Binomial Stochastic Model For both the binomial and trinomial stochastic DDM, there are two versions of the model—the *additive growth model* and the *geometric growth model*. The former model assumes that dividend growth is additive rather than geometric. This means that dividends are assumed to grow by a constant dollar amount. So, for example, if dividends are $2.00 today and the additive growth rate is assumed to be $0.25 per year, then next year dividends will grow to $2.25, in two years dividends will grow to $2.50, and so on. The second model assumes a geometric rate of dividend growth. This is the same growth rate assumption used in the earlier DDMs presented in this chapter.

The binomial additive stochastic model is expressed as follows:

$$D_{t+1} = \begin{cases} D_t + C \text{ with probability } p \\ D_t \text{ with probability } 1-p \end{cases} \quad \text{for } t = 1, 2, \ldots$$

where

D_t = dividend in period t
D_{t+1} = dividend in period $t+1$
C = dollar amount of the dividend increase
p = probability that the dividend will increase

Hurley and Johnson have shown that the theoretical value of the stock based on the additive stochastic DDM assuming a constant discount rate is equal to:

$$P = \frac{D_0}{r} + \left[\frac{1}{r} + \frac{1}{r^2}\right]Cp \tag{8}$$

For example, consider once again Cincinnati Bell. In the illustration of the constant growth model, we used D_0 of $0.84 and g of 8.2%. Hurley and Johnson used as the probability of an increase in dividends the historical percentage of annual dividend increases. The estimate for C is obtained by calculating the dollar increase in dividends for each year that had a dividend increase and then taking the average dollar dividend increase.

For 14 of the 20 years, the dividend increased and the average dividend increase was $0.0207. Because dividends increased 17 of the 20 years, a value of 14/20 or 0.70% is used. Substituting these values into equation (8), we find the estimated price to be:

$$P = \frac{\$0.40}{0.105} + \left[\left(\frac{1}{0.105} + \frac{1}{0.105^2}\right)(\$0.0207)\left(\frac{14}{20}\right)\right]$$

$$= \frac{\$0.40}{0.105} + \$1.4523 = \$5.26$$

Now let's look at the binomial geometric stochastic model. Letting g be the growth rate of dividends, then the geometric dividend stream is:

$$D_{t+1} = \begin{cases} D_t(1+g) \text{ with probability } p \\ D_t \text{ with probability } 1-p \end{cases} \text{ for } t = 1, 2, \ldots$$

Hurley and Johnson show that the price of the stock in this case is:

$$P = \frac{D_0(1+pg)}{r-pg} \tag{9}$$

Equation (9) is the binomial stochastic DDM assuming a geometric growth rate and a constant discount rate.

Let's apply equation (9) to Cincinnati Bell. The growth rate used here is the geometric average of the percentage dividend increases for those years in which dividends increased.[23] Based on the figures reported in Exhibit 11.8, g is 1.69%. Using a growth rate of 1.69% and the previous values of D_0, r, and p, the estimated price using equation (9) is:

$$P = \frac{\$0.40[1 + (0.70)(0.0787)]}{0.105 - [(0.70)(0.0787)]} = \$8.46$$

Trinomial Stochastic Models   The trinomial stochastic DDM allows for dividend cuts. Within the Hurley-Johnson stochastic DDM framework, Yulin Yao derived this model that allows for a cut in dividends.[24] He

---

[23] Letting g_t be the percent change in dividend (in decimal form) and $N+$ the years of years of a dividend increase, then the geometric average is found as follows: $[g_1 \times g_2 \times g_3 \times \ldots \times g_{N+}]^{1/N+}$

[24] Yulin Yao, "A Trinomial Dividend Valuation Model," *Journal of Portfolio Management* (Summer 1997).

notes that it not uncommon for a firm to cut dividends temporarily. In fact, an examination of the dividend record of the electric utilities industry as published in *Value Line Industry Review* found that in the aggregate firms cut dividends three times over a 15-year period.

The trinomial additive stochastic model allows for dividend cuts as follows:

$$D_{t+1} = \begin{cases} D_t + C \text{ with probability } p_U \\ D_t - C \text{ with probability } p_D \\ D_t \text{ with probability } 1 - p_C = 1 - p_U - p_D \end{cases} \quad \text{for } t = 1, 2, \dots$$

where

p_U = probability that the dividend will increase
p_D = probability that the dividend will decrease
p_C = probability that the dividend will be unchanged

The theoretical value of the stock based on the trinomial additive stochastic DDM then becomes:

$$P = \frac{D_0}{r} + \left[\frac{1}{r} + \frac{1}{r^2} \right] C(p_U - p_D) \tag{10}$$

Notice that when p_D is zero (that is, there is no possibility for a cut in dividends), equation (10) reduces to equation (8).

For the trinomial geometric stochastic DDM allowing for a possibility of cuts, we have:

$$D_{t+1} = \begin{cases} D_t(1 + g) \text{ with probability } p_U \\ D_t(1 - g) \text{ with probability } p_D \\ D_t \text{ with probability } 1 - p_C = 1 - p_U - p_D \end{cases} \quad \text{for } t = 1, 2, \dots$$

and the theoretical price is:

$$P = \frac{D_0[1 + (p_U - p_D)]}{r - (p_U - p_D)g} \tag{11}$$

Once again, substituting zero for p_D, equation (11) reduces to equation (9)—the binomial geometric stochastic DDM.

EXHIBIT 11.9   Dividend History and Beta for Five Electric Utilities

Year	Rochester G&E	United Illum.	Ohio Edison	Montana Power	Sierra Pacific
1979	1.33	2.62	1.76	1.03	1.28
1980	1.40	2.68	1.76	1.06	1.43
1981	1.49	2.76	1.76	1.17	1.46
1982	1.75	2.92	1.76	1.27	1.46
1983	1.84	3.08	1.80	1.46	1.50
1984	2.04	2.30	1.84	1.30	1.57
1985	2.20	2.08	1.88	1.00	1.63
1986	2.20	2.32	1.92	1.26	1.69
1987	2.03	2.32	1.96	1.34	1.74
1988	1.50	2.32	1.96	1.35	1.77
1989	1.52	2.32	1.96	1.39	1.81
1990	1.58	2.32	1.73	1.44	1.84
1991	1.62	2.44	1.50	1.50	1.84
1992	1.68	2.56	1.50	1.55	1.48
1993	1.72	2.66	1.50	1.55	1.12
1994	1.76	2.76	1.50	1.59	1.12
Beta	0.60	0.60	0.75	0.75	0.60

Source: Exhibit 2 in Yulin Yao, "A Trinomial Dividend Valuation Model," *Journal of Portfolio Management* (Summer 1997), p. 102. This copyrighted material is reprinted with permission from Institutional Investor, Inc., *The Journal of Portfolio Management*, 488 Madison Avenue, New York, NY 10022.

Applications of the Stochastic DDM   Yao applied the stochastic DDMs to five electric utility stocks that had regular dividends from 1979 to 1994 and had a temporary reduction of dividends in some period: Rochester G&E, United Illum., Ohio Edison, Montana Power, and Sierra Pacific. The historical dividends and the beta for each electric utility are reported in Exhibit 11.9. The discount rate is determined from the capital asset pricing model assuming a market risk premium of 5%, a risk-free rate of 6%, and the beta for the electric utility shown in Exhibit 11.9. The value for the dollar amount of the dividend change and the growth rate are estimated from the past pattern of dividend changes. The probabilities are based on the number of years of dividend increases, decreases, and no changes.

EXHIBIT 11.10 Valuation and Actual Prices of Five Electric Utilities Using the Stochastic DDM and Ignoring the Probability of Bankruptcy

Company	Actual Price	Binomial Stochastic Model (Ignoring Dividend Cuts)		Trinomial Stochastic Model (Allowing for Dividend Cuts)	
		Additive Model	Geometric Model	Additive Model	Geometric Model
Rochester G&E	$23	$27.91	$40.50	$24.63[1]	$28.39
United Illum.	35	40.63	46.87	36.79[1]	39.09
Ohio Edison	19	19.74	19.82	18.73	18.74[a]
Montana Power	24	19.68	33.02	17.40	21.91[a]
Sierra Pacific	19	21.88	24.60	19.58[1]	20.27

[a] Indicates the best fit model.
Source: Adapted from Exhibit 3 in Yulin Yao, "A Trinomial Dividend Valuation Model," *Journal of Portfolio Management* (Summer 1997). This copyrighted material is reprinted with permission from Institutional Investor, Inc., *The Journal of Portfolio Management*, 488 Madison Avenue, New York, NY 10022.

The estimates for the four stochastic DDMs are reported in Exhibit 11.10. For all five electric utility stocks, a model allowing for a cut in dividends (i.e., the trinomial model) provided a better estimate of the price. Notice that there was no superiority of the geometric or additive model for dividends. In the case of the Montana Power, the pattern of dividends reported in Exhibit 11.9 is best described by a geometric model; the geometric DDM was the best fit. For Sierra Pacific, the pattern of dividends payments is best described by an additive DDM and the additive model in fact provided an estimate closer to the actual price.

The stochastic DDM developed by Hurley and Johnson is a powerful tool for the analyst because it allows the analyst to generate a probability distribution for a stock's value.

Hurley and Johnson show how the stochastic DDM can be used to overcome this limitation of traditional DDMs. An analyst can use the derived probability distribution from the stochastic DDM to assess the probability that the stock is undervalued (again subject to the limitation that the stock is being evaluated in isolation). For example, an analyst may find from a probability distribution that the probability that the stock is greater than $35 (the market price) is 90%.

To employ a stochastic DDM an analyst must be prepared to make subjective assumptions about the uncertain nature of future dividends.

The Monte Carlo simulation, available on a spreadsheet (@RISK in Excel, for example), can then be used to generate the probability distribution.[25]

Expected Returns and Dividend Discount Models

Thus far we have seen how to calculate the fair price of a stock given the estimates of dividends, discount rates, terminal prices, and growth rates. The model-derived price is then compared to the actual price and the appropriate action is taken.

The analysis can be recast in terms of expected return, an estimate that can be used as an input in mean-variance analysis. This is found by calculating the return that will make the present value of the expected cash flows equal to the actual price. Mathematically, this is expressed as follows:

$$P_A = \frac{D_1}{(1+ER)^1} + \frac{D_2}{(1+ER)^2} + \ldots + \frac{D_N}{(1+ER)^N} + \frac{P_N}{(1+ER)^N} \qquad (12)$$

where

P_A = actual price of the stock
ER = expected return

The expected return (ER) in equation (12) is found by trial-and-error. For example, consider the following inputs used at the outset of this chapter to illustrate the finite life general DDM as given by equation (3). For stock XYZ, the inputs assumed are:

$D_1 = \$2.00$ $D_2 = \$2.20$ $D_3 = \$2.30$ $D_4 = \$2.55$ $D_5 = \$2.65$
$P_5 = \$26$ $N = 5$

We calculated a fair price based on equation (3) to be $24.90. Suppose that the actual price is $25.89. Then the expected return is found by solving the following equation for ER:

$$\$25.89 = \frac{\$2.00}{(1+ER)} + \frac{\$2.20}{(1+ER)^2} + \frac{\$2.30}{(1+ER)^3} + \frac{\$2.55}{(1+ER)^4}$$
$$+ \frac{\$2.65}{(1+ER)^5} + \frac{\$26.00}{(1+ER)^5}$$

By trial and error, it can be determined that the expected return is 9%.

---

[25] Hurley and Johnson, "Confidence Intervals for Stochastic Dividend Discount Models" and William J. Hurley and Lewis D. Johnson, "Stochastic Two-Phase Dividend Discount Models," *Journal of Portfolio Management* (Summer 1997).

EXHIBIT 11.11   The Relation Between the Fair Value of a Stock and the Stock's Expected Return

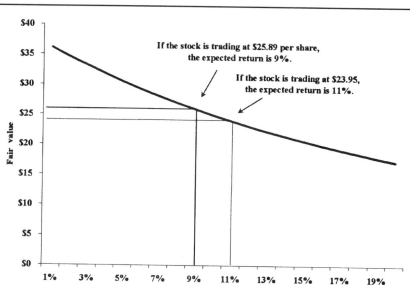

The expected return is the discount rate that equates the present value of the expected future cash flows with the present value of the stock. This rate is also referred to as the *internal rate of return*. The higher the expected return—for a given set of future cash flows—the lower the current value. The relation between the fair value of a stock and the expected return of a stock is shown in Exhibit 11.11.

Given the expected return and the required return (that is, the value for *r* from an asset pricing model), any mispricing can be identified. If the expected return exceeds the required return, then the stock is under-valued; if it is less than the required return then the stock is overvalued. A stock is fairly valued if the expected return is equal to the required return. In our illustration, the expected return (9%) is less than the required return (10%); therefore, stock XYZ is overvalued.

With the same set of inputs, the identification of a stock being mis-priced or fairly valued will be the same regardless of whether the fair value is determined and compared to the market price or the expected return is calculated and compared to the required return. In the case of XYZ stock, the fair value is $24.90. If the stock is trading at $25.89, it is overvalued. The expected return if the stock is trading at $25.89 is 9%, which is less than the required return of 10%. If, instead, the stock price is $24.90, it is fairly valued. The expected return can be shown to be 10%, which is the same as the required return. At a price of $23.95, it can be shown that the expected return is 11%. Since the required return is 10%, stock XYZ would be undervalued.

While the illustration above uses the basic DDM, the expected return can be computed for any of the models. In some cases, the calculation of the expected return is simple since a formula can be derived that specifies the expected return in terms of the other variables. For example for the constant growth DDM given by equation (5), the expected return (r) can be easily solved to give:

$$r = \frac{D_1}{P} + g$$

Rearranging the constant growth model to solve for the expected return, we see that the required rate of return can be specified as the sum of the dividend yield and the expected growth rate of dividends.

CHAPTER 12

Security Analysis Using Value-Based Metrics

James A. Abate, CPA, CFA
Investment Director
Global Asset Management (U.S.A.)

James L. Grant, Ph.D.
JLG Research/Adjunct Professor of Finance
Baruch College (CUNY)

The world of security analysis is undergoing a revolution of sorts with increased focus on "value-based" metrics that are designed to give shareholders their due. Chief among these measures of corporate financial success is a metric called *economic value added* (EVA[1]). EVA and related value-based measures such as *cash flow return on investment* (CFROI[2]) are now making significant inroads into the realm of security analysis and equity portfolio management. These metrics are also paving the way for a "modern" school of equity fundamental analysis that

---

[1] EVA® is a registered trademark of Stern Stewart & Co. For a discussion and application of their value-based (economic profit) measure in a corporate finance setting, see G. Bennett Stewart III, *The Quest for Value* (New York: Harper Collins, 1991), and Al Ehrbar, *EVA: The Real Key to Creating Wealth* (New York: John Wiley & Sons, 1998).

[2] CFROI® is a value-based metric of HOLT Value Associates, L.P. For a discussion of the CFROI approach to measuring economic profit, see Bartley J. Madden, *CFROI Valuation: A Total Systems Approach to Valuing the Firm* (Woburn, MA: Butterworth-Heinemann, 1999).

departs from the traditional method, with its prior focus on accounting measures such as earnings per share and return on equity.

Perhaps the best-known value-based metric among today's corporate and investment players is EVA. Introduced in 1982 by Joel Stern and G. Bennett Stewart, this economic profit measure gained early acceptance among the corporate financial community because of its innovative way of looking at profitability net of the dollar weighted cost of debt *and* equity capital. Indeed, many firms—including corporate giants like AT&T, Coca-Cola, Diageo, Guidant, and SPX—have used an EVA platform to design incentive pay schemes that lead managers to make wealth-enhancing investment decisions for the shareholders. EVA is also gaining popularity in the investment community. For example, Goldman Sachs U.S. Research, and C.S. First Boston use EVA to evaluate the performance potential of many sectors of the economy. Also, Global Asset Management and Oppenheimer Capital have successfully used economic profit principles to actively manage investment portfolios from a "bottom-up" fundamental perspective.

We'll begin the chapter with a look at how to estimate EVA in a basic setting. This will allow us to see the benefits of a value-based framework without getting tangled up in a plethora of value-based accounting adjustments. We'll then look at standard accounting adjustments that are necessary to estimate economic profit in practice. This entails a closer look at how to estimate a company's net operating profit after tax (NOPAT) as well as the dollar weighted average cost of capital, $WACC. Next, we'll examine the basic link between EVA and its close associate, CFROI. We'll then explain how a multi-factor EVA risk model can be used to obtain improved estimates of the required return on common stock (equivalently, the cost of equity capital). This risk measurement innovation is important in light of the empirical limitations of CAPM that were mentioned in Chapter 4. Finally, we'll see how value-based metrics such as EVA can be used to evaluate companies in a stock selection context.

A WORD ON LEVERED AND UNLEVERED FIRMS

Central to the basic economic profit calculation is the distinction between a *levered* firm and an *unlevered* firm. A levered firm, like most real-world companies, is one that is financed with both debt and equity sources of capital. In contrast, an equivalent business-risk unlevered firm is one that, in principle, is 100% equity financed. This firm-type classification is helpful to understanding the economic profit calculation because EVA is measured by subtracting a company's dollar cost of invested capital—a reflection of its weighted average cost of debt and equity capital—from its unlevered net operating profit after tax (noted as NOPAT, versus LNOPAT for levered net operating profit). With this distinction, the firm's EVA is generally defined as:

$$EVA = NOPAT - \$WACC$$

NOPAT is used in the EVA formulation for two reasons. First, an economic profit emphasis on this term serves as a modern-day reminder that a company largely receives profits from the desirability, or lack thereof, of its overall products and services. Along this line, the risk or uncertainty of NOPAT is a reflection of the firm's inherent business risk. Second, since most firms have some form of business debt outstanding, they receive a yearly interest tax subsidy—measured by the corporate tax rate *times* a company's interest expense—that is already reflected in the dollar cost of capital, $WACC.

As we'll see shortly, an incorrect focus by managers or investors on the levered firm's net operating profit after tax, LNOPAT, rather than its unlevered net operating profit, NOPAT, would lead to an *upward* bias in the company's reported economic profit. By recognizing the possible "double counting" of a firm's debt-interest tax subsidies (on both debt and debt equivalents such as operating leases), the manager or investor avoids imparting a *positive* bias in the firm's EVA, and, ultimately, its enterprise value and stock price.

THE BASIC EVA FORMULATION

Before getting immersed in a sea of value-based accounting adjustments, we'll look at the key features of economic profit measurement in a *basic* setting. In this context, we'll unfold EVA into its two basic ingredients—namely, NOPAT, which represents a company's unlevered net operating profit after tax, and $WACC, which represents a firm's dollar cost of invested capital. We'll first look at NOPAT.

In the absence of any EVA accounting adjustments, the firm's NOPAT can be expressed in terms of its tax-adjusted earnings before interest and taxes, EBIT, according to:[3]

$$NOPAT = EBIT \times (1 - t) = [S - COGS - SG\&A - D] \times (1 - t)$$

---

[3] We'll provide an overview of the conventional accounting adjustments to estimating EVA later. For an exhaustive discussion of EVA accounting adjustments, see Stewart, *The Quest for Value.*

In this expression, EBIT × (1 − t) is the unlevered firm's net operating profit after tax. This basic EVA term is a reflection of the firm's earnings before interest and taxes, EBIT, less *unlevered* business taxes—measured by EBIT less t times EBIT. Likewise, the terms, S, COGS, and SG&A in the NOPAT specification refer to the firm's sales, cost of goods sold, and selling, general and administrative expenses, respectively. In principle, the depreciation term, D, should be a charge that reflects the *economic* obsolescence of the firm's assets. In this context, using an estimate of economic depreciation rather than accounting depreciation when the NOPAT differences are meaningful.[4]

In turn, the firm's dollar cost of capital, $WACC, can be expressed as:

$$\$WACC = WACC \times C$$

In this expression, WACC is the weighted-average cost of debt *and* equity capital (expressed as a required rate in decimal form), and C is the firm's invested capital. In turn, the weighted average cost of capital, WACC, is given by:

$$WACC = \text{After-tax Debt Cost} \times \text{Debt Weight} + \text{Equity Cost} \times \text{Equity Weight}$$

Taken together, these financial developments show that the firm's EVA can be expressed in basic terms as:

$$\begin{aligned} EVA &= NOPAT - \$WACC \\ &= EBIT \times (1-t) - WACC \times C \\ &= (S - COGS - SG\&A - D) \times (1-t) - WACC \times C \end{aligned}$$

In the next section, we'll look at a simple income statement and balance sheet to show how to measure a firm's "EVA," absent value-based accounting adjustments that will be explained later.

"OK BEVERAGE COMPANY"

In an attempt to reinforce the concept of value-based measurement, we'll now apply the basic EVA formulation to a hypothetical firm called

---

[4] See, Stephen F. O'Byrne, "Does Value-Based Management Discourage Investment in Intangibles?" Chapter 5 in Frank J. Fabozzi and James L. Grant (eds.), *Value-Based Metrics: Foundations and Practice* (New Hope, PA: Frank J. Fabozzi Associates, 2000).

"OK Beverage Company." Exhibits 12.1 and 12.2 show the standard income statement and balance sheets for the beverage producer at an established point in time.

EXHIBIT 12.1 OK Beverage Company Income Statement

	Status Quo Position
Sales	$125,000
COGS	86,000
SG&A	22,000
Interest Expense	3,312
Pretax Profit	13,688
Taxes (at 40%)	5,475
Net Income	$8,213
Shares Outstanding	6,250
EPS	$1.31

EXHIBIT 12.2 OK Beverage Company Balance Sheet

Cash	750	Accounts Payable	10,000
U.S. Govt. Securities	1,250	Wages Payable	2,000
Accounts Receivable	17,000	Tax Accruals	2,000
Inventory	63,000	Current Liabilities	14,000
Current Assets	82,000	(*non*-interest bearing)	
Property (Land)	4,000	Long-Term Debt	41,400
Net Plant	15,000	(8% Coupon)	
Net Equipment	51,000		
Net Fixed Assets	70,000	Common Stock at Par	625
		Addit'l. Paid in Capital	14,375
		Retained Earnings	81,600
		Stockholders' Equity	96,600
		Liabilities and	
Total Assets	152,000	Stockholders' Equity	152,000

Looking at OK Beverage Company's financial statements from a traditional accounting perspective, it seems that the firm is a profitable beverage producer. Based on the income statement shown in Exhibit 12.1, the firm reports *positive* net income and earnings per share, at $8,213 and $1.31, respectively. In addition, with Stockholders' Equity at $96,600 the beverage producer's rate of return on equity (ROE) is positive, at 8.5% ($8,213/96,600 \times 100$). Moreover, this accounting ROE results from multiplying OK-B's positive return on assets (ROA), at 5.4%, by its equity-leverage multiplier (Assets/Equity) of 1.57.

OK-B's Economic Profit

To see if OK Beverage Company is truly a profitable company—that is, a wealth creator with (discounted) positive EVA—we'll first estimate the firm's *unlevered* net operating profit after tax, NOPAT. Upon substituting the beverage producer's sales; cost of goods sold; selling, general, and administrative expenses, and tax rate figures into the NOPAT formulation, we obtain:[5]

$$NOPAT = (S - COGS - SG\&A) \times (1 - t)$$
$$= (125,000 - 86,000 - 22,000) \times (1 - 0.4) = \$10,200$$

In order to calculate OK-B's projected *dollar* cost of capital, the manager or investor needs to know something about (1) the after-tax cost of debt, (2) the estimated cost of equity capital, and (3) the "target" debt weight, *if any*,[6] in the firm's capital structure, and (4) the amount of invested capital employed in the beverage business. With respect to the first requirement, OK-B's after-tax cost of debt can be estimated according to:

$$After\text{-}tax\ Debt\ Cost = Pre\text{-}tax\ Debt\ Cost \times (1 - t)$$
$$= 0.08 \times (1 - 0.4) = 0.048\ or\ 4.8\%$$

In this expression, the pre-tax debt cost, at 8%, is taken as the firm's average coupon rate on the balance sheet (for simplicity, we assume that the firm's bonds are trading at par value). In this context, OK-B's pre-tax

[5] For convenience, we assume that depreciation is included in selling, general, and administrative expense account of OK Beverage.
[6] The "optimal" mix (if any) of debt and equity capital on a firm's balance sheet is a controversial issue in the study of corporate finance. An economic profit interpretation of the Miller-Modigliani hypothesis on capital structure is explained in Frank J. Fabozzi and James L. Grant, "Value-Based Metrics in Financial Theory," Chapter 2 in *Value-Based Metrics: Foundations and Practice*.

borrowing cost of 8% can also be obtained by dividing the firm's interest expense, $3,312, by the face amount of its long term debt, at $41,400.

In turn, we'll use the Capital Asset Pricing Model (CAPM)[7] to estimate OK-B's cost of equity capital despite its limitations discussed in Chapter 4. With a risk-free interest rate of 6.5%, a market-driven equity risk premium of 6%, and a common stock beta of 1.0, the firm's CAPM-based cost of equity capital becomes:

$$\text{Expected return} = \text{Risk-free rate} + \text{Market risk premium} \times \text{Beta}$$
$$= 0.065 + 0.06 \times 1.0 = 0.125 \text{ or } 12.5\%$$

Moreover, if we assume that OK-B's "target" debt-to-capital ratio is, say, 30%, the firm's weighted average cost of capital can be measured according to:

$$\text{WACC} = \text{After-tax debt cost} \times \text{Debt weight} + \text{Equity cost} \times \text{Equity weight}$$
$$= 0.048 \times (0.3) + 0.125 \times (0.7) = 0.102 \text{ or } 10.2\%$$

Repackaging the Balance Sheet

With knowledge of OK-B's operating capital it is possible to calculate the dollar cost of invested capital, $WACC.[8] In this context, it is helpful to recognize that the firm's balance sheet can be "repackaged" in a way that shows the *equivalency* of the firm's operating and financial capital. Exhibit 12.3 illustrates this result.

Exhibit 12.3 shows that OK-B's operating *and* financing capital is $138,000. The operating capital (left hand side of balance sheet) is equal to net working capital plus net plant, property, and equipment. Likewise, in the absence of EVA accounting adjustments, the financing capital is just long-term debt plus stockholders' equity. Hence, the firm's overall dollar-cost of capital can be calculated by applying the weighted average cost of capital, at 10.2%, to either the firm's tangible operating capital or its equivalent financing source of invested capital. Whatever side of the EVA balance sheet is chosen, OK-B's *dollar* cost of capital is $14,076:

$$\$WACC = WACC \times C = 0.102 \times 138,000 = \$14,076$$

---

[7] William F. Sharpe, "Capital Asset Prices: A Theory of Market Equilibrium under Conditions of Risk," *Journal of Finance* (September 1964), pp. 425–442.

[8] In this basic EVA application, we use the terms operating capital and invested capital interchangeably. In practice, operating capital is generally viewed as invested capital *less* goodwill arising from premiums paid in acquisitions. For an insightful discussion of the difference between these capital measures, see Tom Copeland, Tim Koller, and Jack Murrin, *Valuation: Measuring and Managing the Value of Companies* (New York: John Wiley & Sons, 1996).

EXHIBIT 12.3   OK Beverage Company Operating and Financial Capital (Aggregate Results)

Operating Capital:		Financing Capital:	
Net Working Capital			
Current Assets	82,000		
Current Liabilities	(14,000)		
(*non*-interest bearing)			
	68,000	Long-Term Debt	41,400
Net Fixed Assets	70,000	Stockholders' Equity	96,600
Totals:	138,000		138,000

Most importantly, since OK-B's dollar cost of financing, $WACC, is higher than its unlevered net operating profit after tax, NOPAT, the firm has *negative* economic profit:

$$EVA = NOPAT - \$WACC = 10,200 - 14,076 = -\$3,876$$

While OK-B *looks* like a profitable beverage producer from a traditional accounting perspective, the EVA insight reveals that the firm is a (potential[9]) wealth destroyer. This happens because the firm's net operating profitability is not sufficient enough to cover the weighted average cost of debt *and* equity capital.

OK-B's Residual Return on Capital (RROC)

We can also show that OK-B has negative EVA because its underlying "residual (or surplus) return on capital," RROC, is negative. This wealth-wasting situation occurs when a firm's after-tax return on invested capital, ROC, falls short of the weighted average capital cost, WACC. To illustrate this, simply define RROC as the firm's EVA-to-Capital ratio. At −2.8%, one sees that OK-B's adverse *surplus* return on invested capital is caused by its negative economic profit:

$$RROC = EVA/Capital = -3,876/138,000 = -0.028 \text{ or } -2.8\%$$

Likewise, since EVA can be expressed as the firm's invested capital, C, times the residual return on capital, RROC, this same result is obtained by focusing on the *spread* (also referred to as the "EVA spread") between

---

[9] Wealth destruction occurs when persistently adverse EVA leads to negative net present value. This of course results in a decline in a company's enterprise value and its stock price.

the firm's after-tax return on invested capital, ROC, and its weighted average cost of debt and equity capital, WACC:

$$RROC = EVA/C = (ROC - WACC)$$
$$= (0.074 - 0.102) = -0.028 \text{ or } -2.8\%$$

In this expression, ROC, at 7.4%, results from dividing NOPAT, $10,200, by the firm's invested capital, $138,000. The WACC is the familiar cost of capital percentage of 10.2%.

OK-B's Interest Tax Subsidy

As we noted before, when looking at a firm's economic profit, it is important to use unlevered net operating profit after tax, NOPAT, in the first step of the EVA calculation. This is important because the dollar cost of invested capital (step two in the EVA calculation) already reflects the interest tax subsidy (if any) received on the firm's outstanding debt obligations. By double counting this debt-induced tax subsidy, the manager or investor would not only overestimate the firm's operating profit, but one would also impart a positive bias in the firm's enterprise value and its stock price.

To show leverage-induced bias, it is helpful to note that the levered firm's net operating profit after tax, LNOPAT, can be expressed in terms of the equivalent business-risk unlevered firm's net operating profit, NOPAT, *plus* a yearly interest tax subsidy. Looking at OK-B in this levered (with debt) and unlevered (without debt) fashion yields:

$$LNOPAT = NOPAT + t \times Interest$$
$$= \$10,200 + 0.4 \times \$3,312 = \$11,525$$

In this expression, $t \times$ Interest (at $1,325) is the yearly interest tax subsidy that OK-B receives as a levered firm, as opposed to a debt-free company. However, this *same* interest tax benefit is already reflected in the firm's dollar cost of capital through the reduced cost of corporate debt financing.

To show this, recall that OK-B's after tax cost of debt was previously expressed as:

$$After\text{-}tax \; debt \; cost = Pre\text{-}tax \; debt \; cost \times (1 - t)$$
$$= 0.08 \times (1 - 0.4) = 0.048 \text{ or } 4.8\%$$

In this formulation, the firm's pre-tax cost of debt, 8%, is reduced by 320 basis points due to the tax benefit that OK-B receives from deductibility of its debt interest expense. Expressing this leverage-induced reduction in the firm's dollar cost of capital yields the same yearly interest tax benefit that is already reflected in the beverage company's levered operating profit:

$$\text{\$WACC tax subsidy} = t \times (\text{Pre-tax debt cost}) \times \text{Debt}$$
$$= 0.4 \times (3,312/41,400) \times 41,400 = \$1,325$$

Thus, to avoid imparting leverage-induced bias, OK-B's economic profit must be calculated by *first* estimating what its net operating profit after tax, NOPAT, would be as an equivalent business-risk unlevered firm—namely, an "OK-B like" company with no business debt—and *then* subtracting the overall dollar cost of debt and equity capital from this unlevered net operating profit figure.

OK-B's EVA on a Pre-Tax Basis

If the manager or investor were inclined to calculate OK Beverage Company's EVA on a pretax basis, then the beverage producer's unlevered net operating profit before taxes, at $17,000, would be used in conjunction with the *pre*-tax dollar cost of capital. The only complication here is that the after-tax cost of equity capital needs to be "grossed up" by one *minus* the business tax rate to convert it to a pre-tax financing rate.[10] To see how this works, note that OK-B's weighted average cost of capital can be expressed on a before tax basis as:

Pre-tax WACC
= Debt Weight × Pre-tax Debt Cost + Equity Weight × Pre-tax Equity Cost
= $0.3 \times 0.08 + 0.7 \times 0.125/(1 - 0.4) = 0.17$ or 17%

In this formulation, the firm's *pre-tax* cost of equity capital is 20.8%, and its pre-tax cost of invested capital is 17%. With this development, OK-B's *pre-tax* EVA is:

$$\text{Pre-tax EVA} = \text{Pre-tax net operating profit} - \text{Pre-tax \$WACC}$$
$$= \text{EBIT} - \text{Pre-tax WACC} \times \text{C}$$
$$= \$17,000 - 0.17 \times \$138,000 = -\$6,460$$

---

[10] The pre-tax approach to estimating a firm's economic profit is helpful because the manager or investor focuses *directly* on the unlevered firm's cash operating profit without getting tangled up with tax issues arising from depreciation and other accounting complexities. However, tax considerations *do* arise when converting the after-tax cost of equity capital (CAPM or otherwise) to a pre-tax required rate of return.

Likewise, the firm's pre-tax EVA is equal to its after-tax EVA "grossed up" by one *minus* the business tax rate, t:

$$\text{Pre-tax EVA} = \text{After-tax EVA}/(1-t)$$
$$= (-\$3,876)/(1-0.4) = -\$6,460$$

OK-B's Growth Opportunities

Given that OK Beverage Company has negative economic profit, the firm has a clear incentive to find a *positive* growth opportunity. In this context, let's suppose that the firm's managers discover that they can invest \$20,000 in a new product distribution system that will increase yearly sales by \$40,000. In turn, suppose that OK-B's cost of goods sold and selling, general, and administrative expenses will rise by \$25,000 and \$5,000 per annum, respectively. With these assumptions, the firm's estimated annual NOPAT will go up by \$6,000:

$$\Delta\text{NOPAT} = \Delta(S - \text{COGS} - \text{SG\&A}) \times (1-t)$$
$$= (40,000 - 25,000 - 5,000) \times (1-0.4) = \$6,000$$

Since the beverage producer's operating capital rises by \$20,000 to support the higher sales forecast, OK-B's estimated (annual) capital costs rise by \$2,040:

$$\Delta\$\text{WACC} = \text{WACC} \times \Delta C = 0.102 \times 20,000 = \$2,040$$

If sustainable, the changes in NOPAT and \$WACC reveal that OK-B's growth opportunity is a desirable investment for its shareholders.[11] With these figures, OK-B's EVA rises by \$3,960:

$$\Delta\text{EVA} = \Delta\text{NOPAT} - \Delta\$\text{WACC} = \$6,000 - \$2,040 = \$3,960$$

As a result of OK Beverage Company's investment opportunity, it is interesting to see that the firm has moved from a wealth-destroyer to a wealth-neutral position. That is, at \$84 (−3,876 + \$3,960), *total* EVA now exceeds zero. Among other things, this implies that the firm's revised return on invested capital, 10.3% (16,200/158,000), is now close to the overall cost of capital, 10.2%. Likewise, in this wealth neutral situation, the firm's residual return on capital, RROC, is nearly zero. Of course, with further growth opportunities, OK-B has the *potential* to become a wealth creator with *discounted* positive economic profit. In the

---

[11] In other words, the investment opportunity has discounted positive EVA (equivalently, positive NPV).

next section, we'll look at the valuation consequences of OK-B's growth opportunity, including a basic estimate of the firm's enterprise value.

Valuation Considerations

Up to this point, we used the income and balance sheets for "OK Beverage Company" to calculate economic profit (EVA) in a basic setting. However, nothing was said about the market value of OK-B as an ongoing company. Without getting into detailed valuation considerations,[12] some simple pricing insights are obtained by assuming that investors pay an NPV (net present value) multiple of, say, *10-times* the estimated EVA[13] of "OK-B-like" companies. In the ensuing pricing application, we'll express the firm's enterprise value, V_F, as the sum of (1) the total operating capital employed in the business, C, *plus*, (2) the net present value (NPV=MVA[14]) derived from the firm's existing assets and future growth opportunity:

$$V_F = C + NPV$$

With an EVA multiplier of *10-times* OK-B's aggregate EVA of \$84 (recall, −3,876 + 3,960), the firm's market value added is \$840. Upon adding this NPV figure to its revised operating capital (with the \$20,000 growth opportunity), we obtain:

$$V_F = C + NPV = 158,000 + \$840 = \$158,840$$

Summarizing these basic valuation findings: With the positive EVA growth opportunity, OK-B has moved from a wealth-waster to a wealth-neutral position. The firm's zero-expected *total* EVA is generated by a return on invested capital, ROC, that now approximately equals the weighted average cost of capital—even though ROC is higher than the firm's pre- and post-tax cost of corporate debt financing. Because of OK-B's wealth-neutral position, the firm's enterprise value-to-capital (or, in more popular terms, the "price-book" ratio) is near unity. At this point, OK-B's profitability index ratio (ROC/WACC) is also close to one.

---

[12] For an explanation of the economic profit approach to enterprise and stock valuation, see James L. Grant and James A. Abate, *Focus on Value: A Corporate and Investor Guide to Wealth Creation* (New York: John Wiley & Sons, 2001).

[13] In practice, we would *first* need to make the necessary value-based accounting adjustments that we explain in an upcoming section before attempting to measure the firm's NPV, enterprise value, and of course its stock price.

From a valuation perspective, it is worth noting that multiplying a firm's EVA by a NPV multiple of "10" is tantamount to discounting its EVA perpetuity at a rate of 10%.

[14] MVA, for market value added, is the popular equivalent of NPV. These value-added terms are used interchangeably in the EVA literature.

Moreover, with further EVA growth opportunities, the firm has the potential to become a wealth creator and thus witness a noticeably sharp improvement in its enterprise value and stock price. Managers and investors should take note of such positive EVA growth opportunities!

WAYS TO INCREASE EVA

We see that basic EVA is helpful for managers and investors because it provides a transparent look at the key features of economic profit measurement. In this context, basic EVA reveals that a company is not economically profitable until it covers its usual operating expenses and all of its financial capital costs—namely, the dollar cost of debt *and* equity capital. In this fundamental sense, EVA is superior to traditional accounting profit measures such as net income, earnings per share and return on equity. Additionally, we can use basic EVA to gain some strategic insight on the steps that managers must take to permanently improve the economic profit outlook and, thereby, shareholder wealth. Active investors can also benefit by earning abnormal returns ("alpha") to the extent that a company's successful effort to improve the EVA outlook is not already impounded in stock price.[15]

There are several meaningful ways that a company can improve its economic profit outlook.[16] In this context, the basic EVA formulation suggests that wealth conscious managers should take steps to:

- Increase revenue
- Reduce operating expenses where prudent
- Use less capital to produce the same amount of goods and services
- Use more capital in the presence of *positive* growth opportunities
- Reduce WACC

Expanding a firm's market share is of course captured by rising sales levels in the basic EVA formula. All other things being the same (operating expenses and capital costs), higher revenue means higher margins and thus economic profit. It should also be no surprise that reducing a company's operating expenses via cost cutting and/or achieving tax efficiency enhances economic profit because the SG&A and tax accounts go

---

[15] We'll look at company (or stock) selection using value-based principles in a later section.

[16] The first four ways to improve economic profit are consistent with those emphasized in Shawn Tully, "The Real Key to Creating Wealth," *Fortune*, September 20, 1993.

down. However, when using cost cutting as a tool to improve the EVA outlook, managers (and investors) must be cautioned that too much cost cutting, "cuts" the fabric of a company's future economic profit—and in so doing, reduces the enterprise value of the firm and its stock price.

Also, if EVA is to be taken seriously as an improvement over traditional accounting profit measures, then it must do more than just show that increasing revenue and/or reducing operating expenses will improve the firm's enterprise value and its stock price. Fortunately, this is where economic profit and traditional accounting measures depart since EVA fully "accounts" for the dollar cost of capital in terms of both the amount of operating capital employed in a business and the opportunity cost of that invested capital.

EVA emphasizes the role of invested capital as shown in the basic EVA formulation. Clearly, anything that managers can do to (1) improve inventory and net PP&E (plant, property, and equipment) turnover ratios on the balance sheet, and (2) reduce business uncertainty (as reflected in a decline in NOPAT volatility) will have beneficial dollar cost of capital implications via the impact on C and WACC, respectively. Moreover, we used the basic EVA formula to show that investing more capital in *positive* economic profit growth opportunities is really what shareholder value creation is all about.

On balance, EVA links the income statement and balance sheets with a value-based focus on net operating profit (NOPAT, from adjusted income statement) and invested capital (C, from adjusted balance sheet). Unlike accounting profit, EVA measures the dollar cost of capital by multiplying the amount of invested capital by the *overall* cost of capital. Hence, EVA measures economic profit in the classical economists notion of "profit" because the business owners' normal return on invested capital is "fully reflected" in the profit calculation. Since accounting profit accounts only for the dollar cost of debt financings, via interest expense, it completely misses the dollar cost of equity capital. This cost of financing omission is particularly important for companies that typically finance their growth opportunities with mostly equity capital—such as firms in the technology and health care fields.

EVA MEASUREMENT CHALLENGES

The basic EVA formulation is helpful in showing how a *value-based* metric like EVA differs from a traditional accounting measure of profit such as net income. However, the basic EVA illustration belies the *complexity* of the economic profit calculation in practice. In this context, C.S. First Boston, Goldman Sachs U.S. Equity Research, and Stern Stewart & Co. point out that there are some 160 accounting adjustments that can be made to a firm's financial statements (income and balance sheets) to convert them to a *value-based* format emphasizing cash operating profit and asset replacement cost considerations.[17] Many of the potential accounting adjustments can have a material impact on a manager or investor's estimate of a company's after-tax return on capital through their *joint* impact on NOPAT and invested capital. Additionally, there are significant empirical anomalies and academic issues that embroil the weighted average cost of capital, WACC—primarily, the cost of equity, which we touch on later.

As mentioned before, the firm's after-tax return on capital is calculated by dividing its *unlevered* net operating profit after tax, NOPAT, by the amount of invested capital employed in the business. In practice, however, there are numerous accounting items that *jointly* impact the numerator and the denominator of the ROC ratio. These potential distortions arise from the accounting-versus-economic treatment of depreciation, intangibles (including research and development and goodwill arising from corporate acquisitions), deferred income taxes, inventory costing (LIFO versus FIFO), and other equity reserve adjustments. Such EVA measurement issues are important because they impact the analyst's estimate of cash operating profit in the numerator of the after-tax return on capital (e.g., profit impact of accounting depreciation *versus* economic obsolescence) and the invested capital estimate used in the denominator of the ROC ratio (e.g., impact of net fixed assets on the balance sheet *versus* economic replacement cost of assets).[18]

NOPAT ADJUSTMENTS

To help reduce the complexity of the EVA calculation, Bennett Stewart offers a practical guide to estimating a firm's net operating profit after tax (NOPAT) and its invested capital.[19] In this context, he shows equivalent "bottom-up and top-down" approaches to estimating a company's net operating profit after taxes along with equivalent "asset and financing" approaches to estimating invested capital. Exhibit 12.4 shows some of the key accounting

---

[17] For example, see Steven G. Einhorn, Gabrielle Napolitano, and Abby Joseph Cohen, "EVA: A Primer," *U.S. Research* (Goldman Sachs, September 10, 1997).

[18] However, managers and investors must be careful not to get overly caught up in value-based accounting adjustments and, in so doing, miss the "big picture" perspective of economic profit measurement and valuation.

[19] See Stewart, *The Quest for Value*. Also, for a recent application of EVA with accounting adjustments, see Pamela Peterson, "Value-Based Measures of Performance," Chapter 4 in *Value-Based Metrics: Foundations and Practice*.

adjustments in the equivalent NOPAT approaches recommended by Stewart, while Exhibit 12.5 shows the companion accounting adjustments that must be made when estimating a company's invested capital in practice.

EXHIBIT 12.4   Calculation of NOPAT from Financial Statement Data

---

A. Bottom-up approach

Begin:

   Operating profit after depreciation and amortization

Add:

   Implied interest expense on operating leases
   Increase in LIFO reserve
   Increase in capitalized research and development
   Increase in accumulated goodwill amortization
   Increase in cumulative write-offs of special items *

Equals:

   Adjusted operating profit before taxes

Subtract:

   Cash operating taxes

Equals:

   NOPAT

B. Top-down approach

Begin:

   Sales

Subtract:

   Cost of goods sold
   Selling, general, and administrative expenses
   Depreciation

Add:

   Implied interest expense on operating leases
   Increase in equity reserve accounts (see above listing)
   Other operating income

Equals:

   Adjusted operating profit before taxes

Subtract:

   Cash operating taxes

Equals:

   NOPAT

---

* To the extent that write-offs are included in operating results rather than an extraordinary or unusual item.

Note: Exhibit based on information in G. Bennett Stewart III, *The Quest for Value* (New York: Harper Collins, 1991).

EXHIBIT 12.5   Calculation of Capital Using Accounting Financial Statements

---

A. Asset approach

Begin:

    Net short term operating assets

Add:

    Net plant and equipment
    Other assets
    LIFO reserve
    Capitalized research and development
    Accumulated goodwill amortization
    Cumulative write-offs of special items
    Present value of operating leases

Equals:

    Capital

B. Sources of financing approach

Begin:

    Book value of common equity

Add equity equivalents:

    Preferred stock
    Minority interest
    Deferred income tax
    Equity reserve accounts (see above listing)

Add debt and debt equivalents:

    Interest-bearing short-term debt
    Long-term debt
    Present value of operating leases

Equals:

    Capital

Note: Exhibit based on information in G. Bennett Stewart III, *The Quest for Value* (New York: Harper Collins, 1991).

In the "bottom-up" approach to estimating NOPAT (Exhibit 12.4), the manager or investor begins with operating profit after depreciation and amortization. This is just the familiar earnings before interest and taxes (EBIT) figure on a company's income statement. To this amount, several value-based accounting adjustments are made to arrive at a closer approximation of the firm's pre-tax cash operating profit. For examples, the rise in the LIFO reserve account is added back to operating profit to adjust for the overstatement of cost of goods sold—due to an overstatement of product costing—in a period of rising prices, while the net increase in research and development expenditure is added back to operating profit to recognize that R&D investment generates a *future* stream of benefits.[20]

Likewise, the change in accumulated goodwill amortization is added back to pre-tax operating profit to reflect the fact that goodwill is a form of capital investment that needs to earn a cost of capital return just like expenditures on physical capital. In a value-based (economic profit) context, annual corporate restructuring write-offs (a "special item") get added back since they are viewed as a form of restructuring "investment." Also, the implied interest expense on operating leases is added back to pre-tax operating profit to recognize that leasing is a form of debt financing. In other words, the implied interest expense on operating leases should be reflected in the firm's cost of debt financing, rather than showing up in its *unlevered* net operating profit. However, in industries where operating leases are common and similar in financial magnitude, such as in certain segments of retail for example, the manager or investor should use judgment to decide whether the leasing adjustment will materially enhance the accuracy of the economic profit calculation for company comparisons.

From an EVA tax perspective, the rise in a company's deferred tax account (obtained from the balance sheet) should be subtracted from reported income taxes to adjust for the overstatement of actual cash taxes. Also, the tax subsidies received on debt financings (including debt equivalents such as operating leases) should be added back to reported income taxes to arrive at a more accurate representation of the cash taxes paid by an *unlevered* firm. As we explained before, tax subsidies received by a company from debt financings show up in the after-tax cost of debt and must therefore be excluded in the estimation of NOPAT. Upon making the "bottom-up" accounting adjustments, Exhibit 12.4 shows that the manager or investor arrives at a company's NOPAT by subtracting cash operating taxes from adjusted operating profit before taxes.

Exhibit 12.4 also shows the "top-down" approach to estimating NOPAT. In this approach, the manager or investor begins with sales or revenue. Usual income statement items such as cost of goods sold, selling, general and administrative expenses, and depreciation[21] are then subtracted from this figure. Next, the EVA items that we mentioned before—including the rise in "equity reserve" accounts (e.g. increase in LIFO reserve and accumulated goodwill amortization) as well as the

---

[20] In a value-based framework, R&D expenditures are generally capitalized and amortized over a useful time period such as five years—rather than expensed in the current year as if these expenditures have no future cash flow benefits.

[21] In principle, an estimate of economic depreciation should be used on EVA financial statements.

implied interest expense on operating leases—are added to the EVA income statement to obtain a more accurate measure of the firm's pre-tax cash operating profit. As with the bottom-up approach, cash operating taxes are then subtracted from adjusted operating profit before taxes to arrive at a company's net operating profit after tax (NOPAT).

Invested Capital

A look at Exhibit 12.5 reveals the companion EVA accounting adjustments that must be made to arrive at invested capital. Based on the "assets" approach, the manager or investor begins with net short-term operating capital. This reflects moneys tied up in current asset accounts like accounts receivables and inventories as well as a *normal* amount of cash needed for operations.[22] Current liability accounts such as accounts payable, accrued expenses, and taxes payable are netted from the short-term operating asset accounts. Notes payable are excluded from net short-term operating capital because they represent a source of debt financing. Also, their interest cost is reflected in the calculation of a company's dollar cost of capital.

Net plant, property, and equipment is then added to capital along with other assets and several equity-based reserve accounts. Some managers or investors may choose to adjust property, plant, and equipment to a *gross* basis by adding back accumulated depreciation in an effort to eliminate differing depreciation policies and to approximate replacement cost of assets. Obviously, the accumulated depreciation adjustment would be made in both asset and financing approaches to calculating capital along with an appropriate annual depreciation add back to arrive at NOPAT.

As shown in Exhibit 12.5, the equity reserve adjustments to arrive at invested capital include (but are not limited to) the add back of LIFO reserve, accumulated goodwill amortization, capitalized research and development, and cumulative write-off of special items like restructuring and re-engineering costs. Unfortunately, some companies view a write-off of restructuring costs that result in a reduction of capital as an immediate boost to return on invested capital and then profess progress in operations. However, unless there is an outright asset disposal, with proceeds received in the sale or liquidation, then this latter adjustment is critical for objective company benchmarking and analysis. Additionally, the present value of operating leases, if any, would be added to the EVA balance sheet to arrive at a company's overall invested capital.

---

[22] Research estimates on a normal range of cash required for operations vary by industry—such as 0.5% to 2% of net sales. See Copeland, Koller, and Murrin, *Valuation: Measuring and Managing the Value of Companies.*

In the sources of "financing" approach (again, see Exhibit 12.5), the analyst begins with the book value of common equity. To this, he or she adds several "equity equivalent" accounts including preferred stock, minority interest, deferred income tax reserve, and the equity reserve accounts that were listed in the "assets" approach to invested capital. Debt and debt equivalents are then added to arrive at a value-based figure for invested capital. These debt-related accounts include interest bearing short-term debt, long-term debt, and (as before) the present value of operating leases. Either way—the assets or financing approach—we arrive at invested capital for use in calculation of a firm's economic profit.

Caveats

Having introduced the "conventional"[23] accounting adjustments to estimate NOPAT and invested capital, it is important to realize that we have only provided a means to estimate the after-tax return on a company's *existing* assets. This is simply NOPAT divided by invested capital. Estimates of capital returns on future growth assets will of course require similar EVA-based accounting adjustments, but just as importantly, the forecasts themselves can be highly sensitive to unforeseen industry and macroeconomic developments. In other words, an undue focus on all the value-based accounting adjustments that might be made when estimating current economic profit components (such as NOPAT) may cause the manager or investor to miss key valuation and economic profit effects from future growth assets. Moreover, since EVA is NOPAT *less* the dollar cost of capital, the manager or investor needs to consider key economic profit issues that impact the cost of invested capital. We'll highlight some WACC concerns in the context of using CAPM to estimate the cost of equity.[24]

EVA MULTI-FACTOR RISK MODEL

In our calculation of basic EVA, we used the CAPM to estimate the cost of equity; which in turn, is a central component of the overall weighted

---

[23] There are even EVA refinements that can be made to standard accounting adjustments that we cite in the text. For example, the concept of positive *and* negative economic depreciation can be used to improve economic profit estimates—especially the concept of negative depreciation for strategic investments like corporate acquisitions and R&D investments. For further discussion of these "EVA on EVA" refinements, see O'Byrne, "Does Value-Based Management Discourage Investment in Intangibles?"

[24] Further insight on economic profit and the cost of capital can be found in Fabozzi and Grant, "Value-Based Metrics in Financial Theory."

average cost of capital, WACC. While CAPM is a widely used formula for the pricing of investment risk, as explained in Chapter 4, it does not fully capture risks found to systematically impact the return on stocks. This pricing omission has led to the use of multi-factor risk models that include common factors in addition to market risk (the only risk considered by the CAPM). In Chapter 13, a fundamental multi-factor risk model is described. However, currently the common factors used are based on traditional accounting measures discussed in Chapters 10 and 11 rather than on value-based metrics.

As with the CAPM, a multi-factor risk model's output is the expected return for the stock and can therefore be used to estimate the expected return on equity in the cost of capital formula. Here we describe the common factors in addition to beta used in an EVA-based factor model approach employed by Global Asset Management to estimate the required return on common stock (cost of equity). They are size (equity capitalization), NPV-to-Capital ratio, and the standard deviation of economic profit (EVA). The inclusion of the first common factor, namely size, has considerable empirical support and is also found in the fundamental multi-factor risk models.

The second common factor, NPV-to-Capital ratio, captures the risk associated with troubled firms.[25] The NPV-to-Capital ratio is a measure of a company's ability (or lack thereof) to invest in wealth creating projects. It is therefore a measure of company *strength* or resilience. In this context, wealth creators have a high NPV-to-Capital ratio, while wealth destroyers have a low to negative NPV-to-Capital ratio. For troubled or distressed companies, NPV is low or negative due to their fundamental inability to invest in projects that have an after-tax return on invested capital (ROC) that exceeds the WACC. Consequently, it can be argued that investors require high-expected return for investing in the stocks of troubled firms—companies with low to negative NPV– while comparatively low expected return for investing in the stocks of stable and robust firms—namely, companies with attractive NPV. There is empirical support for the inclusion of this factor.[26]

The standard deviation of economic profit is included as a common factor to account for the market-adjusted volatility in a company's eco-

---

[25] We employ the NPV-to-Capital ratio rather than price-to-book value ratio typically used in multi-factor risk models for two reasons: (1) the price/book ratio is plagued by accounting problems due to book value, and, most importantly, (2) NPV is a *direct* measure of wealth creation.

[26] See, James L. Grant, *Foundations of Economic Value Added* (New Hope, PA: Frank J. Fabozzi Associates, 1997) and Ken C. Yook and George M. McCabe, "An Examination of MVA in the Cross-Section of Expected Stock Returns," *Journal of Portfolio Management* (Spring 2001), pp. 75–87.

nomic profit. In practice, the EVA-based factor model estimate of the required return on equity is combined with the after-tax cost of debt to obtain the weighted average cost of capital, WACC. At Global Asset Management, the cost of capital is viewed as a critical input in the estimation and analysis of a company's economic profit and its stock price. Moreover, we believe that EVA factors such as the NPV-to-Capital ratio and the standard deviation of economic profit are important considerations in portfolio construction, risk control, and performance measurement.

CASH FLOW RETURN ON INVESTMENT

There are of course other prominent value-based metrics beyond EVA. In this context, we'll provide some basic insight on another well-known and widely used VBM—namely, Cash Flow Return on Investment (CFROI). While in theory, EVA and CFROI can be used to derive the same result for a company's economic profit, the two VBMs differ in practice in several important ways. Specifically, EVA is a dollar-based measure of economic profit while CFROI is an internal rate of return-type metric that measures the expected rate of return over the average life of a company's existing assets. Unlike EVA, CFROI uses gross cash flow and gross capital investment measures and the resulting IRR is measured in real terms as opposed to nominal terms.

Without getting into all the details, the following *five* steps can be used to estimate a company's CFROI:[27]

- Compute the average life of a company's existing assets
- Compute the gross cash flow
- Compute the gross investment
- Compute the sum of *non*-depreciating assets
- Solve for the CFROI (or internal rate of return)

In the first step, the average life of a company's existing assets can be measured by dividing gross depreciable assets by depreciation expense. Next, gross cash flow is equal to net income adjusted for financing expenses—such as interest expense and operating rental payments—and *non*-cash operating expenses including depreciation and amortization. Gross cash flow also includes the changes in LIFO reserve, deferred income taxes, and other equity reserve accounts.

---

[27] For rigorous explanation and application of CFROI, see Madden, *CFROI Valuation: A Total Systems Approach to Valuing the Firm.*

EXHIBIT 12.6   OK Beverage Company: CFROI

Gross Investment[a] (present value)	$150,000
Gross Cash Flow[b] (payment)	$20,000
Non-Depreciating Assets[c] (future value)	$72,000
Average Asset Life (n)	10 years
Nominal CFROI (IRR)	10.08%

[a] Sum of gross plant and equipment, cumulative equity reserve accounts, present value of operating leases
[b] Sum of net income, changes in equity reserves, interest and rental expense
[c] Sum of net working capital and land

In turn, gross investment includes *gross* plant and equipment and the EVA capital adjustments that we looked at before—including LIFO reserve, capitalized research and development, accumulated goodwill amortization, restructuring charges, and the present value of operating leases (among others). Also, in the CFROI calculation, *non*-depreciating assets include net short-term operating assets (current assets *less* non-interest bearing current liabilities), land, and other *non*-depreciating assets. Following the above-mentioned procedure, managers and investors can estimate a company's (nominal[28]) cash flow return on investment. The resulting CFROI or IRR-based percentage is then compared to the (percentage) cost of capital to determine whether a company's has positive or negative economic profit. Equivalently, a manager or investor, to decide whether a company is a wealth creator or a wealth destroyer, can use the "spread" between CFROI and WACC, just like we explained before using the "EVA spread."

CFROI Application

Before moving on, we'll look at the IRR (internal rate of return) nature of cash flow return on investment. We'll explain this relationship in terms of "OK Beverage Company." Suppose that after making all the necessary accounting adjustments (equity reserve accounts and other adjustments *not* shown for sake of brevity) to estimate CFROI, we obtain the *gross* cash flow and *gross* investment information for the beverage producer shown in Exhibit 12.6. The IRR "keystrokes" are indicated within parentheses.

Based on the five-step procedure to estimate CFROI, we see that OK Beverage Company's CFROI is 10.08%. This figure is equivalent to the estimated after-tax internal rate of return (IRR) earned on the company's existing assets over a useful life of 10 years. Since OK Beverage Company's estimated CFROI just meets the firm's cost of invested capi-

---

[28] For simplicity, we'll look at nominal as opposed to real CFROI.

tal, at 10.2% (calculated before), the firm remains in a position of wealth neutrality. Clearly, OK Beverage still needs a positive growth opportunity (as defined by CFROI *greater than* WACC) so that it can (1) (finally) become a wealth creator, and (2) experience a noticeable improvement in its enterprise value and stock price.

COMPANY SELECTION USING VBM

Now that we have explained the accounting and economic issues that surround value-based metrics such as EVA and CFROI, we'll demonstrate that an economic profit approach to company or security analysis has real world practical merit. In this context, we'll provide an overview of the economic profit (or value-based) approach to company analysis that has been developed by the authors and expanded upon elsewhere.[29] In this context, Exhibit 12.7 shows the "Excess Return on Invested Capital" versus the "Market Value of Invested Capital-to-Replacement Cost of Invested Capital"[30] for a universe of U.S. companies that we track at Global Asset Management.

In Exhibit 12.7, the excess return on invested capital is simply the after-tax return on invested capital (ROC, including the value-based accounting adjustments that we spoke of before) *less* the weighted average cost of capital (WACC). In this exhibit, we show the market value of invested capital (equivalently, the "enterprise value") measured relative to replacement cost of invested capital for consistency with the conventional method of evaluating companies in profitability versus "price-to book" context. There is *no* slippage of EVA focus here because it can be shown that the market value of invested capital-to-replacement cost of invested capital is *directly* related to a company's NPV-to-invested capital.[31]

---

[29] For additional insight on security analysis using EVA, see Grant and Abate, *Focus on Value: A Corporate and Investor Guide to Wealth Creation.*

[30] Note that the "excess return on invested capital" is equivalent to the economic profit-to-capital ratio or the residual return on capital that we spoke of before. This is also referred to as the "EVA spread." Moreover, the use of market value-to-replacement cost of invested capital is really just a scaling of the NPV-to-invested capital ratio.

[31] In principle, the enterprise value-to-invested capital ratio can be written as:

$$V/C = 1 + NPV/C$$

In this expression, V refers to enterprise value (or market value of invested capital) and C is an EVA measure of invested capital. Hence, V/C is greater than one when NPV is positive, while V/C is less than one when NPV is negative. The market value of invested capital-to-replacement cost of invested capital is also a measure of "Tobin's Q."

EXHIBIT 12.7   Excess Returns Relative to Valuation

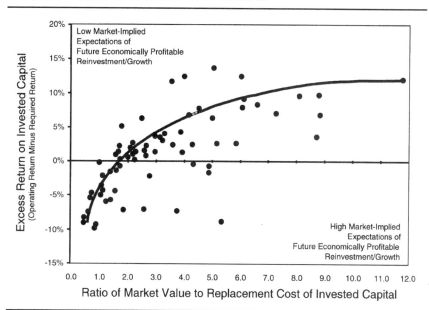

Source: James L. Grant and James A. Abate, *Focus on Value: A Corporate and Investor Guide to Wealth Creation* (New York: John Wiley & Sons, 2001).

Exhibit 12.7 shows a scatter plot of companies measured relative to a curve of "best fit" through the data points. The data points that lie above the curve represent potentially undervalued companies (or stocks), while those data points that fall below the curve represent potentially overvalued companies. For companies that plot above the curve, Exhibit 12.7 suggests that at such excess return on invested capital positions, the companies should command a higher market valuation. If correct, this upward revaluation would be reflected in a rise in the market value of invested capital-to-replacement cost of invested capital ratio. In a more fundamental sense, internal or "warranted" expectation of economic profit growth for companies that plot above the curve is higher than the market implied growth rate of economic profit imbedded in current stock price.

Specifically, while the capital market at large is expecting compression in future economic profit down to the curve for any given market value-to-replacement cost of invested capital ratio, actual internal expectations of economically profitable reinvestment for combinations above the curve imply a noticeably higher valuation for any company's stock. Astute investors can expect to earn potentially positive abnormal return (alpha) on stocks that plot above the curve because of the fortu-itously positive (and presumed consistent) economic profit positions of these companies.

Conversely, for companies that plot below the curve, Exhibit 12.7 implies that these firms should command a lower stock market valua-tion. In this case, internal expectation of economic profit growth is lower than the market implied growth (rate) imbedded in current share price. Here, the capital market incorrectly expects an upward revision in economic profit to the curve for any given market value of invested cap-ital-to-replacement cost of invested capital ratio. However, consistently low to negative expectations of economically profitable reinvestment for companies that fall below the curve implies a lower stock valuation. Active-minded investors should thus look elsewhere if they are restricted to a "long only" position in common stocks. Taken together, we see that the stocks of companies that plot above the curve are poten-tial buy opportunities, while stocks that plot below the curve are poten-tial sell (or short sell) candidates. On a more sophisticated note, the "longs" and "shorts" can be combined into an economic profit approach to long-short investing.

CHAPTER 13

Multi-Factor Equity Risk Models

Frank J. Fabozzi, Ph.D., CFA
Adjunct Professor of Finance
School of Management
Yale University

Frank J. Jones, Ph.D.
Chief Investment Officer
The Guardian Life Insurance Company

Raman Vardharaj
Senior Quantitative Analyst
The Guardian Life Insurance Company of America

In several chapters multi-factor risk models for equity portfolio management were discussed. In Chapter 4, we set forth the theory of asset pricing in terms of risk factors—the arbitrage pricing theory—and mentioned the different types of multi-factor risk models—statistical models, macro models, and fundamental models. In Chapter 8 the different approaches to security analysis are described—traditional fundamental analysis, value-based metric analysis, and fundamental multi-factor risk analysis. In Chapters 9, 10, and 11 traditional fundamental analysis is described and in Chapter 12 value-based metric analysis is covered. In this chapter, we cover fundamental multi-factor risk analysis. Many of the inputs used in a multi-factor risk model are those used in traditional fundamental analysis.

There are several commercially available fundamental multi-factor risk models. There are investment management companies that develop proprietary models. Brokerage firms have developed models that they make available to institutional clients. In this chapter, we will focus on a commercially available model from Barra. (In Chapter 24 where multi-factor risk models for fixed income portfolio management is explained, a model developed by a brokerage firm is illustrated.) While the development of a fundamental multi-factor risk model involves a substantial amount of sophisticated statistical analysis and testing, model development will not be the focus of this chapter. Instead, in this chapter our focus will be explaining how a multi-factor risk model is used in practice to (1) select securities, (2) quantify the risk exposure of a portfolio relative to a benchmark index, (3) construct a portfolio and control risk, and (4) measure performance.

MODEL DESCRIPTION AND ESTIMATION

The basic relationship to be estimated in a multi-factor risk model is

$$R_i - R_f = \beta_{i,F1} R_{F1} + \beta_{i,F2} R_{F2} + \ldots + \beta_{i,FH} R_{FH} + e_i$$

where

R_i = rate of return on stock i
R_f = risk-free rate of return
$\beta_{i,Fj}$ = sensitivity of stock i to risk factor j
R_{Fj} = rate of return on risk factor j
e_i = nonfactor (specific) return on security i

The above function is referred to as a *return generating function*.

Fundamental factor models use company and industry attributes and market data as "descriptors." Examples are price/earnings ratios, book/price ratios, estimated earnings growth, and trading activity. The estimation of a fundamental factor model begins with an analysis of historical stock returns and descriptors about a company. In the Barra model, for example, the process of identifying the risk factors begins with monthly returns for 1,900 companies that the descriptors must explain. Descriptors are not the "risk factors" but instead they are the candidates for risk factors. The descriptors are selected in terms of their ability to explain stock returns. That is, all of the descriptors are potential risk factors but only those that appear to be important in explaining stock returns are used in constructing risk factors.

Once the descriptors that are statistically significant in explaining stock returns are identified, they are grouped into "risk indices" to capture related company attributes. For example, descriptors such as market leverage, book leverage, debt-to-equity ratio, and company's debt rating are combined to obtain a risk index referred to as "leverage." Thus, a risk index is a combination of descriptors that captures a particular attribute of a company.

The Barra fundamental multi-factor risk model, the "E3 model" being the latest version, has 13 risk indices and 55 industry groups. (The descriptors are the same variables that have been consistently found to be important in many well-known academic studies on risk factors.) Exhibit 13.1 lists the 13 risk indices in the Barra model.[1] Also shown in the exhibit are the descriptors used to construct each risk index. The 55 industry classifications are further classified into sectors. For example, the following three industries comprise the energy sector: energy reserves and production, oil refining, and oil services. The consumer noncyclicals sector consists of the following five industries: food and beverages, alcohol, tobacco, home products, and grocery stores. The 13 sectors in the Barra model are basic materials, energy, consumer noncylicals, consumer cyclicals, consumer services, industrials, utility, transport, health care, technology, telecommunications, commercial services, and financial.

Given the risk factors, information about the exposure of every stock to each risk factor (β_{i,F_j}) is estimated using statistical analysis. For a given time period, the rate of return for each risk factor (R_{F_j}) also can be estimated using statistical analysis. The prediction for the expected return can be obtained from equation (1) for any stock. The nonfactor return (e_i) is found by subtracting the actual return for the period for a stock from the return as predicted by the risk factors.

Moving from individual stocks to portfolios, the predicted return for a portfolio can be computed. The exposure to a given risk factor of a portfolio is simply the weighted average of the exposure of each stock in the portfolio to that risk factor. For example, suppose a portfolio has 42 stocks. Suppose further that stocks 1 through 40 are equally weighted in the portfolio at 2.2%, stock 41 is 5% of the portfolio, and stock 42 is 7% of the portfolio. Then the exposure of the portfolio to risk factor j is:

$$0.022\ \beta_{1,F_j} + 0.022\ \beta_{2,F_j} + \ldots + 0.022\ \beta_{40,F_j} + 0.050\ \beta_{41,F_j} + 0.007\ \beta_{42,F_j}$$

The nonfactor error term is measured in the same way as in the case of an individual stock. However, in a well diversified portfolio, the nonfactor error term will be considerably less for the portfolio than for the individual stocks in the portfolio.

---

[1] For a more detailed description of each descriptor, see Appendix A in *Barra, Risk Model Handbook United States Equity: Version 3* (Berkeley, CA: Barra, 1998). A listing of the 55 industry groups is provided in Exhibit 13.9.

EXHIBIT 13.1 Barra E3 Model Risk Definitions

Descriptors in Risk Index	Risk Index
Beta times sigma	Volatility
Daily standard deviation	
High-low price	
Log of stock price	
Cumulative range	
Volume beta	
Serial dependence	
Option-implied standard deviation	
Relative strength	Momentum
Historical alpha	
Log of market capitalization	Size
Cube of log of market capitalization	Size Nonlinearity
Share turnover rate (annual)	Trading Activity
Share turnover rate (quarterly)	
Share turnover rate (monthly)	
Share turnover rate (five years)	
Indicator for forward split	
Volume to variance	
Payout ratio over five years	Growth
Variability in capital structure	
Growth rate in total assets	
Earnings growth rate over the last five years	
Analyst-predicted earnings growth	
Recent earnings change	
Analyst-predicted earnings-to-price	Earnings Yield
Trailing annual earnings-to-price	
Historical earnings-to-price	
Book-to-price ratio	Value
Variability in earnings	Earnings Variability
Variability in cash flows	
Extraordinary items in earnings	
Standard deviation of analyst-predicted earnings-to-price	
Market leverage	Leverage
Book leverage	
Debt to total assets	
Senior debt rating	
Exposure to foreign currencies	Currency Sensitivity
Predicted dividend yield	Dividend Yield
Indicator for firms outside US-E3 estimation universe	Non-Estimation Universe Indicator

Adapted from Table 8-1 in Barra, *Risk Model Handbook United States Equity: Version 3* (Berkeley, CA: Barra, 1998), pp. 71–73. Adapted with permission.

The same analysis can be applied to a stock market index because an index is nothing more than a portfolio of stocks.

RISK DECOMPOSITION

The real usefulness of a linear multi-factor model lies in the ease with which the risk of a portfolio with several assets can be estimated. Consider a portfolio with 100 assets. Risk is commonly defined as the variance of the portfolio's returns. So, in this case, we need to find the variance-covariance matrix of the 100 assets. That would require us to estimate 100 variances (one for each of the 100 assets) and 4,950 covariances among the 100 assets. That is, in all we need to estimate 5,050 values, a very difficult undertaking. Suppose, instead, that we use a 3 factor model to estimate risk. Then, we need to estimate (1) the three factor loadings for each of the 100 assets (i.e., 300 values), (2) the six values of the factor variance-covariance matrix, and (3) the 100 residual variances (one for each asset). That is, in all, we need to estimate only 406 values. This represents a nearly 90% reduction from having to estimate 5,050 values, a huge improvement. Thus, with well-chosen factors, we can substantially reduce the work involved in estimating a portfolio's risk.

Multi-factor risk models allow a manager and a client to decompose risk in order to assess the *potential* performance of a portfolio to the risk factors and to assess the *potential* performance of a portfolio relative to a benchmark. This is the portfolio construction and risk control application of the model. Also, the *actual* performance of a portfolio relative to a benchmark can be assessed. This is the performance attribution analysis application of the model.

Barra suggests that there are various ways that a portfolio's total risk can be decomposed when employing a multi-factor risk model.[2] Each decomposition approach can be useful to managers depending on the equity portfolio management that they pursue. The four approaches are (1) total risk decomposition, (2) systematic-residual risk decomposition, (3) active risk decomposition, and (4) active systematic-active residual risk decomposition. We describe each below and explain how managers pursuing different strategies discussed in Chapter 8 will find the decomposition helpful in portfolio construction and evaluation.

In all of these approaches to risk decomposition, the total return is first divided into the risk-free return and the total excess return. The

---

[2] See Chapter 4 in Barra, *Risk Model Handbook United States Equity: Version 3*. The discussion to follow in this section follows that in the Barra publication.

total excess return is the difference between the *actual* return realized by the portfolio and the risk-free return. The risk associated with the total excess return, called *total excess risk*, is what is further partitioned in the four approaches.

Total Risk Decomposition

There are managers who seek to minimize total risk. For example, a manager pursuing a long-short or market neutral strategy (discussed in Chapter 8), seek to construct a portfolio that minimizes total risk. For such managers, total risk decomposition which breaks down the total excess risk into two components—*common factor risks* (e.g., capitalization and industry exposures) and *specific risk*—is useful. This decomposition is shown in Exhibit 13.2. There is no provision for market risk, only risk attributed to the common factor risks and company-specific influences (i.e., risk unique to a particular company and therefore uncorrelated with the specific risk of other companies). Thus, the market portfolio is not a risk factor considered in this decomposition.

EXHIBIT 13.2   Total Risk Decomposition

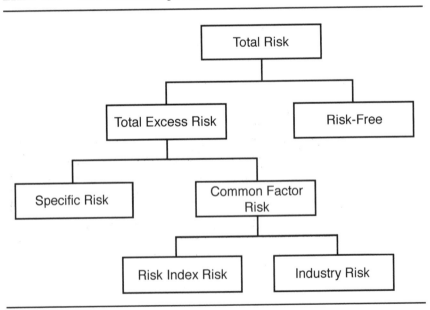

Source: Figure 4.2 in Barra, *Risk Model Handbook United States Equity: Version 3* (Berkeley, CA: Barra, 1998), p. 34. Reprinted with permission.

EXHIBIT 13.3 Systematic-Residual Risk Decomposition

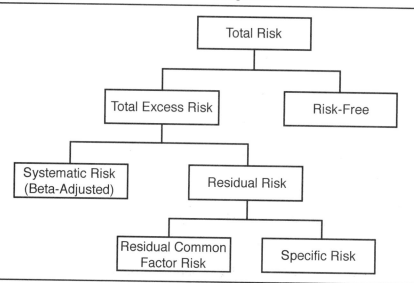

Source: Figure 4.3 in Barra, *Risk Model Handbook United States Equity: Version 3* (Berkeley, CA: Barra, 1998), p. 34. Reprinted with permission.

Systematic-Residual Risk Decomposition

There are managers who seek to time the market or who intentionally make bets to create a different exposure than that of a market portfolio. Such managers would find it useful to decompose total excess risk into systematic risk and residual risk as shown in Exhibit 13.3. Unlike in the total risk decomposition approach just described, this view brings market risk into the analysis. It is the type of decomposition that was described in Chapter 4, where *systematic risk* is the risk related to a portfolio's beta.

Residual risk in the systematic-residual risk decomposition is defined in a different way than residual risk is in the total risk decomposition. In the systematic-residual risk decomposition, residual risk is risk that is uncorrelated with the market portfolio. In turn, residual risk is partitioned into specific risk and common factor risk. Notice that the partitioning of risk described here is different from that in the Arbitrage Pricing Model Theory model described in Chapter 4. In that chapter, all risk factors that could not be diversified away were referred to as "systematic risks." In our discussion here, risk factors that cannot be diversified away are classified as market risk and common factor risk. Residual risk can be diversified to a negligible level.

EXHIBIT 13.4   Active Risk Decomposition

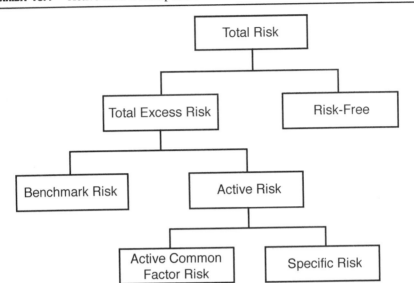

Source: Figure 4.4 in Barra, *Risk Model Handbook United States Equity: Version 3* (Berkeley, CA: Barra, 1998), p. 34. Reprinted with permission.

Active Risk Decomposition

In previous chapters, the need to assess a portfolio's risk exposure and actual performance relative to a benchmark index is explained. The active risk decomposition approach is useful for that purpose. In this type of decomposition, shown in Exhibit 13.4, the total excess return is divided into *benchmark risk* and *active risk*. Benchmark risk is defined as the risk associated with the benchmark portfolio.

Active risk is the risk that results from the manager's attempt to generate a return that will outperform the benchmark. Another name for active risk is *tracking error*, a concept covered in detail in Chapter 7. The active risk is further partitioned into common factor risk and specific risk.

Active Systematic-Active Residual Risk Decomposition

There are managers who overlay a market-timing strategy on their stock selection. That is, they not only try to select stocks they believe will outperform but also try to time the purchase of the acquisition. For a manager who pursues such a strategy, it will be important in evaluating performance to separate market risk from common factor risks. In the active risk decomposition approach just discussed, there is no market risk identified as one of the risk factors.

EXHIBIT 13.5   Active Systematic-Active Residual Risk Decomposition

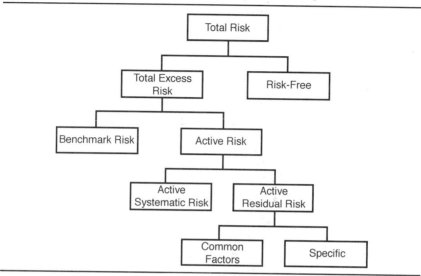

Source: Figure 4.5 in Barra, *Risk Model Handbook United States Equity: Version 3* (Berkeley, CA: Barra, 1998), p. 37. Reprinted with permission.

Since market risk (i.e., systematic risk) is an element of active risk, its inclusion as a source of risk is preferred by managers. When market risk is included, we have the active systematic-active residual risk decomposition approach shown in Exhibit 13.5. Total excess risk is again divided into benchmark risk and active risk. However, active risk is further divided into active systematic risk (i.e., active market risk) and active residual risk. Then active residual risk is divided into common factor risks and specific risk.

Summary of Risk Decomposition

The four approaches to risk decomposition are just different ways of slicing up risk to help a manager in constructing and controlling the risk of a portfolio and for a client to understand how the manager performed. Exhibit 13.6 provides an overview of the four approaches to carving up risk into specific/common factor, systematic/residual, and benchmark/active risks.

APPLICATIONS IN PORTFOLIO CONSTRUCTION AND RISK CONTROL

The power of a multi-factor risk model is that given the risk factors and the risk factor sensitivities, a portfolio's risk exposure profile can be quantified and controlled. The three examples below show how this can be done so that the a manager can avoid making unintended bets. In the examples, we use the Barra E3 factor model.[3]

Assessing the Exposure of a Portfolio

A fundamental multi-factor risk model can be used to assess whether the current portfolio is consistent with a manager's strengths. Exhibit 13.7 is a list of the top 15 holdings of Portfolio ABC as of September 30, 2000. Exhibit 13.8 is a risk-return report for the same portfolio. The portfolio had a total market value of over $3.7 billion, 202 holdings, and a predicted beta of 1.20. The risk report also shows that the portfolio had an active risk of 9.83%. This is its tracking error with respect to the benchmark, the S&P 500. Notice that over 80% of the active risk variance (which is 96.67) comes from the common factor risk variance (which is 81.34), and only a small proportion comes from the stock-specific risk variance (which is 15.33). Clearly, the manager of this portfolio has placed fairly large factor bets.

EXHIBIT 13.6   Risk Decomposition Overview

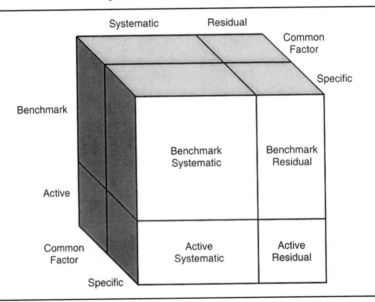

Source: Figure 4.6 in Barra, *Risk Model Handbook United States Equity: Version 3* (Berkeley, CA: Barra, 1998), p. 38. Reprinted with permission.

---

[3] The illustrations were created by the authors based on applications suggested in Chapter VI of *United States Equity Model Handbook* (Berkeley, CA: Barra, 1996).

EXHIBIT 13.7 Portfolio ABC's Holdings (Only the Top 15 Holdings Shown)

Portfolio:	ABC Fund	Benchmark:	S&P500	Model Date:	2000-10-02
Report Date:	2000-10-15	Price Date:	2000-09-29	Model:	U.S. Equity 3

Name	Shares	Price ($)	Weight (%)	Beta	Main Industry Name	Sector
General Elec. Co.	2,751,200	57.81	4.28	0.89	Financial Services	Financial
Citigroup, Inc.	2,554,666	54.06	3.72	0.98	Banks	Financial
Cisco Sys., Inc.	2,164,000	55.25	3.22	1.45	Computer Hardware	Technology
E M C Corp. Mass.	1,053,600	99.50	2.82	1.19	Computer Hardware	Technology
Intel Corp.	2,285,600	41.56	2.56	1.65	Semiconductors	Technology
Nortel Networks Corp. N	1,548,600	60.38	2.52	1.40	Electronic Equipment	Technology
Corning, Inc.	293,200	297.50	2.35	1.31	Electronic Equipment	Technology
International Business	739,000	112.50	2.24	1.05	Computer Software	Technology
Oracle Corp.	955,600	78.75	2.03	1.40	Computer Software	Technology
Sun Microsystems, Inc.	624,700	116.75	1.96	1.30	Computer Hardware	Technology
Lehman Bros. Hldgs. Inc.	394,700	148.63	1.58	1.51	Sec. & Asset Management	Financial
Morgan Stanley Dean Wi.	615,400	91.44	1.52	1.29	Sec. & Asset Management	Financial
Disney Walt Co.	1,276,700	38.25	1.32	0.85	Entertainment	Cnsmr. Services
Coca-Cola Co.	873,900	55.13	1.30	0.68	Food & Beverage	Cnsmr. (non-cyc.)
Microsoft Corp.	762,245	60.31	1.24	1.35	Computer Software	Technology

EXHIBIT 13.8 Portfolio ABC's Risk-Return Decomposition

RISK – RETURN

Number of Assets	202	Total Shares	62,648,570
		Average Share Price	$59.27
Portfolio Beta	1.20	Portfolio Value	$3,713,372,229.96

Risk Decomposition	Variance	Standard Deviation (%)
Active Specific Risk	15.33	3.92
Active Common Factor		
Risk Indices	44.25	6.65
Industries	17.82	4.22
Covariance	19.27	
Total Active Common Factor Risk[a]	81.34	9.02
Total Active[b]	96.67	9.83
Benchmark	247.65	15.74
Total Risk	441.63	21.02

[a] Equal to Risk Indices + Industries + Covariances
[b] Equal to Active Specific Risk + Total Active Common Factor Risk

Exhibit 13.9a assesses the factor risk exposures of Portfolio ABC relative to those of the S&P 500, its benchmark. The first column shows the exposures of the portfolio, and the second column shows the exposures for the benchmark. The last column shows the active exposure, which is the difference between the portfolio exposure and the benchmark exposure. The exposures to the risk index factors are measured in units of standard deviation, while the exposures to the industry factors are measured in percentages. The portfolio has a high active exposure to the momentum risk index factor. That is, the stocks held in the portfolio have significant momentum. The portfolio's stocks were smaller than the benchmark average in terms of market cap. The industry factor exposures reveal that the portfolio had an exceptionally high active exposure to the semiconductor industry and electronic equipment industry. Exhibit 13.9b combines the industry exposures to obtain sector exposures. It shows that Portfolio ABC had a very high active exposure to the Technology sector. Such large bets can expose the portfolio to large swings in returns.

An important use of such risk reports is the identification of portfolio bets, both explicit and implicit. If, for example, the manager of Portfolio ABC did not want to place such a large Technology sector bet or momentum risk index bet, then she can rebalance the portfolio to minimize any such bets.

Risk Control Against a Stock Market Index

In Chapter 8, equity indexing was explained. The objective is to match the performance of some specified stock market index with little tracking error. To do this, the risk profile of the indexed portfolio must match the risk profile of the designated stock market index. Put in other terms, the factor risk exposure of the indexed portfolio must match as closely as possible the exposure of the designated stock market index to the same factors. Any differences in the factor risk exposures result in tracking error. Identification of any differences allows the indexer to rebalance the portfolio to reduce tracking error.

To illustrate this, suppose that an index manager has constructed a portfolio of 50 stocks to match the S&P 500. Exhibit 13.10 shows output of the exposure to the Barra risk indices and industry groups of the 50-stock portfolio and the S&P 500. The last column in the exhibit shows the difference in the exposure. The differences are very small except for the exposures to the size factor and one industry (equity REIT). That is, the 50-stock portfolio has more exposure to the size risk index and equity REIT industry.

EXHIBIT 13.9 Analysis of Portfolio ABC's Exposures
a. Analysis of Risk Exposures to S&P 500

Factor Exposures

Risk Index Exposures (Std. Dev.)

	Mgd.	Bmk.	Act.		Mgd.	Bmk.	Act.
Volatility	0.220	−0.171	0.391	Value	−0.169	−0.034	−0.136
Momentum	0.665	−0.163	0.828	Earnings Variation	0.058	−0.146	0.204
Size	−0.086	0.399	−0.485	Leverage	0.178	−0.149	0.327
Size Non-Linearity	0.031	0.097	−0.067	Currency Sensitivity	0.028	−0.049	0.077
Trading Activity	0.552	−0.083	0.635	Yield	−0.279	0.059	−0.338
Growth	0.227	−0.167	0.395	Non-EST Universe	0.032	0.000	0.032
Earnings Yield	−0.051	0.081	−0.132				

Industry Weights (Percent)

	Mgd.	Bmk.	Act.		Mgd.	Bmk.	Act.
Mining and Metals	0.013	0.375	−0.362	Heavy Machinery	0.000	0.062	−0.062
Gold	0.000	0.119	−0.119	Industrial Parts	0.234	1.086	−0.852
Forestry and Paper	0.198	0.647	−0.449	Electric Utility	1.852	1.967	−0.115
Chemicals	0.439	2.386	−1.947	Gas Utilities	0.370	0.272	0.098
Energy Reserves	2.212	4.589	−2.377	Railroads	0.000	0.211	−0.211
Oil Refining	0.582	0.808	−0.226	Airlines	0.143	0.194	−0.051
Oil Services	2.996	0.592	2.404	Truck/Sea/Air Freight	0.000	0.130	−0.130
Food & Beverages	2.475	3.073	−0.597	Medical Services	1.294	0.354	0.940
Alcohol	0.000	0.467	−0.467	Medical Products	0.469	2.840	−2.370
Tobacco	0.000	0.403	−0.403	Drugs	6.547	8.039	−1.492
Home Products	0.000	1.821	−1.821	Electronic Equipment	11.052	5.192	5.860
Grocery Stores	0.000	0.407	−0.407	Semiconductors	17.622	6.058	11.564
Consumer Durables	0.165	0.125	0.039	Computer Hardware	12.057	9.417	2.640
Motor Vehicles & Parts	0.000	0.714	−0.714	Computer Software	9.374	6.766	2.608
Apparel & Textiles	0.000	0.191	−0.191	Defense & Aerospace	0.014	0.923	−0.909
Clothing Stores	0.177	0.308	−0.131	Telephone	0.907	4.635	−3.728
Specialty Retail	0.445	2.127	−1.681	Wireless Telecom.	0.000	1.277	−1.277
Department Stores	0.000	2.346	−2.346	Information Services	0.372	1.970	−1.598
Constructn. and Real Prop.	0.569	0.204	0.364	Industrial Services	0.000	0.511	−0.511
Publishing	0.014	0.508	−0.494	Life/Health Insurance	0.062	1.105	−1.044
Media	1.460	2.077	−0.617	Property/Casualty Ins.	1.069	2.187	−1.118
Hotels	0.090	0.112	−0.022	Banks	5.633	6.262	−0.630
Restaurants	0.146	0.465	−0.319	Thrifts	1.804	0.237	1.567
Entertainment	1.179	1.277	−0.098	Securities and Asst. Mgmt.	6.132	2.243	3.888
Leisure	0.000	0.247	−0.247	Financial Services	5.050	5.907	−0.857
Environmental Services	0.000	0.117	−0.117	Internet	3.348	1.729	1.618
Heavy Electrical Eqp.	1.438	1.922	−0.483	Equity REIT	0.000	0.000	0.000

Note: Mgd. = Managed; Bmk. = S&P 500 (the benchmark); Act. = Active = Managed − Benchmark

EXHIBIT 13.9 (Continued)
b. Analysis of Sector Exposures Relative to S&P 500

Sector Weights (Percent)

	Mgd.	Bmk.	Act.		Mgd.	Bmk.	Act.
Basic Materials	0.65	3.53	−2.88	Utility	2.22	2.24	−0.02
Mining	0.01	0.38	−0.36	Electric Utility	1.85	1.97	−0.12
Gold	0.00	0.12	−0.12	Gas Utility	0.37	0.27	0.10
Forest	0.20	0.65	−0.45	Transport	0.14	0.54	−0.39
Chemical	0.44	2.39	−1.95	Railroad	0.00	0.21	−0.21
Energy	5.79	5.99	−0.20	Airlines	0.14	0.19	−0.05
Energy Reserves	2.21	4.59	−2.38	Truck Freight	0.00	0.13	−0.13
Oil Refining	0.58	0.81	−0.23	Health Care	8.31	11.23	−2.92
Oil Services	3.00	0.59	2.40	Medical Provider	1.29	0.35	0.94
Cnsmr (non-cyc.)	2.48	6.17	−3.70	Medical Products	0.47	2.84	−2.37
Food/Beverage	2.48	3.07	−0.60	Drugs	6.55	8.04	−1.49
Alcohol	0.00	0.47	−0.47	Technology	53.47	30.09	23.38
Tobacco	0.00	0.40	−0.40	Electronic Equipment	11.05	5.19	5.86
Home Prod.	0.00	1.82	−1.82	Semiconductors	17.62	6.06	11.56
Grocery	0.00	0.41	−0.41	Computer Hardware	12.06	9.42	2.64
Cnsmr. (cyclical)	1.36	6.01	−4.66	Computer Software	9.37	6.77	2.61
Cons. Duarbles	0.17	0.13	0.04	Defense & Aerospace	0.01	0.92	−0.91
Motor Vehicles	0.00	0.71	−0.71	Internet	3.35	1.73	1.62
Apparel	0.00	0.19	−0.19	Telecommunications	0.91	5.91	−5.00
Clothing	0.18	0.31	−0.13	Telephone	0.91	4.63	−3.73
Specialty Retail	0.45	2.13	−1.68	Wireless	0.00	1.28	−1.28
Dept. Store	0.00	2.35	−2.35	Commercial Services	0.37	2.48	−2.11
Construction	0.57	0.20	0.36	Information Services	0.37	1.97	−1.60
Cnsmr Services	2.89	4.69	−1.80	Industrial Services	0.00	0.51	−0.51
Publishing	0.01	0.51	−0.49	Financial	19.75	17.94	1.81
Media	1.46	2.08	−0.62	Life Insurance	0.06	1.11	−1.04
Hotels	0.09	0.11	−0.02	Property Insurance	1.07	2.19	−1.12
Restaurants	0.15	0.47	−0.32	Banks	5.63	6.26	−0.63
Entertainment	1.18	1.28	−0.10	Thrifts	1.80	0.24	1.57
Leisure	0.00	0.25	−0.25	Securities/Asst. Mgmt.	6.13	2.24	3.89
Industrials	1.67	3.19	−1.51	Financial Services	5.05	5.91	−0.86
Env. Services	0.00	0.12	−0.12	Equity REIT	0.00	0.00	0.00
Heavy Electrical	1.44	1.92	−0.48				
Heavy Mach.	0.00	0.06	−0.06				
Industrial Parts	0.23	1.09	−0.85				

Note: Mgd = Managed; Bmk = Benchmark; Act = Active = Managed − Benchmark

The illustration in Exhibit 13.10 uses price data as of December 31, 2001. It demonstrates how a multi-factor risk model can be combined with an optimization model to construct an indexed portfolio when a given number of holdings is sought. Specifically, the portfolio analyzed in Exhibit 13.10 is the result of an application in which the manager wants a portfolio constructed that matches the S&P 500 with only 50 stocks and that minimizes tracking error. Not only is the 50-stock portfolio constructed, but the optimization model combined with the factor model indicates that the tracking error is only 2.19%. Since this is the optimal 50-stock portfolio to replicate the S&P 500 that minimizes tracking error risk, this tells the index manager that if he or she seeks a lower tracking error, more stocks must be held. Note, however, that the optimal portfolio changes as time passes and prices move.

Tilting a Portfolio

Now let's look at how an active manager can construct a portfolio to make intentional bets. Suppose that a portfolio manager seeks to construct a portfolio that generates superior returns relative to the S&P 500 by tilting it toward low P/E stocks. At the same time, the manager does not want to increase tracking error significantly. An obvious approach may seem to be to identify all the stocks in the universe that have a lower than average P/E. The problem with this approach is that it introduces unintentional bets with respect to the other risk indices.

Instead, an optimization method combined with a multi-factor risk model can be used to construct the desired portfolio. The necessary inputs to this process are the tilt exposure sought and the benchmark stock market index. Additional constraints can be placed, for example, on the number of stocks to be included in the portfolio. The Barra optimization model can also handle additional specifications such as forecasts of expected returns or alphas on the individual stocks.

In our illustration, the tilt exposure sought is towards low P/E stocks, that is, towards high earnings yield stocks (since earnings yield is the inverse of P/E). The benchmark is the S&P 500. We seek a portfolio that has an average earnings yield that is at least 0.5 standard deviations more than that of the earnings yield of the benchmark. We do not place any limit on the number of stocks to be included in the portfolio. We also do not want the active exposure to any other risk index factor (other than earnings yield) to be more than 0.1 standard deviations in magnitude. This way we avoid placing unintended bets. While we do not report the holdings of the optimal portfolio here, Exhibit 13.11 provides an analysis of that portfolio by comparing the risk exposure of the 50-stock optimal portfolio to that of the S&P 500.

EXHIBIT 13.10   Factor Exposures of a 50-Stock Portfolio that Optimally Matches the S&P 500

Risk Index Exposures (Std. Dev.)

	Mgd.	Bmk.	Act.		Mgd.	Bmk.	Act.
Volatility	−0.141	−0.084	−0.057	Value	−0.072	−0.070	−0.003
Momentum	−0.057	−0.064	0.007	Earnings Variation	−0.058	−0.088	0.029
Size	0.588	0.370	0.217	Leverage	−0.206	−0.106	−0.100
Size Non-Linearity	0.118	0.106	0.013	Currency Sensitivity	−0.001	−0.012	0.012
Trading Activity	−0.101	−0.005	−0.097	Yield	0.114	0.034	0.080
Growth	−0.008	−0.045	0.037	Non-EST Universe	0.000	0.000	0.000
Earnings Yield	0.103	0.034	0.069				

Industry Weights (Percent)

	Mgd.	Bmk.	Act.		Mgd.	Bmk.	Act.
Mining & Metals	0.000	0.606	−0.606	Heavy Machinery	0.000	0.141	−0.141
Gold	0.000	0.161	−0.161	Industrial Parts	1.124	1.469	−0.345
Forestry and Paper	1.818	0.871	0.947	Electric Utility	0.000	1.956	−1.956
Chemicals	2.360	2.046	0.314	Gas Utilities	0.000	0.456	−0.456
Energy Reserves	5.068	4.297	0.771	Railroads	0.000	0.373	−0.373
Oil Refining	1.985	1.417	0.568	Airlines	0.000	0.206	−0.206
Oil Services	1.164	0.620	0.544	Truck/Sea/Air Freight	0.061	0.162	−0.102
Food & Beverages	2.518	3.780	−1.261	Medical Services	1.280	0.789	0.491
Alcohol	0.193	0.515	−0.322	Medical Products	3.540	3.599	−0.059
Tobacco	1.372	0.732	0.641	Drugs	9.861	10.000	−0.140
Home Products	0.899	2.435	−1.536	Electronic Equipment	0.581	1.985	−1.404
Grocery Stores	0.000	0.511	−0.511	Semiconductors	4.981	4.509	0.472
Consumer Durables	0.000	0.166	−0.166	Computer Hardware	4.635	4.129	0.506
Motor Vehicles & Parts	0.000	0.621	−0.621	Computer Software	6.893	6.256	0.637
Apparel & Textiles	0.000	0.373	−0.373	Defense & Aerospace	1.634	1.336	0.297
Clothing Stores	0.149	0.341	−0.191	Telephone	3.859	3.680	0.180
Specialty Retail	1.965	2.721	−0.756	Wireless Telecom.	1.976	1.565	0.411
Department Stores	4.684	3.606	1.078	Information Services	0.802	2.698	−1.896
Constructn. & Real Prop.	0.542	0.288	0.254	Industrial Services	0.806	0.670	0.136
Publishing	2.492	0.778	1.713	Life/Health Insurance	0.403	0.938	−0.535
Media	1.822	1.498	0.323	Property/Casualty Ins.	2.134	2.541	−0.407
Hotels	1.244	0.209	1.035	Banks	8.369	7.580	0.788
Restaurants	0.371	0.542	−0.171	Thrifts	0.000	0.362	−0.362
Entertainment	2.540	1.630	0.910	Securities & Asst. Mgmt.	2.595	2.017	0.577
Leisure	0.000	0.409	−0.409	Financial Services	6.380	6.321	0.059
Environmental Services	0.000	0.220	−0.220	Internet	0.736	0.725	0.011
Heavy Electrical Eqp.	1.966	1.949	0.017	Equity REIT	2.199	0.193	2.006

Note: Mgd = Managed; Bmk = S&P 500 (the benchmark); Act = Active = Managed − Benchmark

EXHIBIT 13.11 Factor Exposures of a Portfolio Tilted Towards Earnings Yield

Risk Index Exposures (Std. Dev.)

	Mgd.	Bmk.	Act.		Mgd.	Bmk.	Act.
Volatility	−0.126	−0.084	−0.042	Value	0.030	−0.070	0.100
Momentum	0.013	−0.064	0.077	Earnings Variation	−0.028	−0.088	0.060
Size	0.270	0.370	−0.100	Leverage	−0.006	−0.106	0.100
Size Non-Linearity	0.067	0.106	−0.038	Currency Sensitivity	−0.105	−0.012	−0.093
Trading Activity	0.095	−0.005	0.100	Yield	0.134	0.034	0.100
Growth	−0.023	−0.045	0.022	Non-EST Universe	0.000	0.000	0.000
Earnings Yield	0.534	0.034	0.500				

Industry Weights (Percent)

	Mgd.	Bmk.	Act.		Mgd.	Bmk.	Act.
Mining & Metals	0.022	0.606	−0.585	Heavy Machinery	0.000	0.141	−0.141
Gold	0.000	0.161	−0.161	Industrial Parts	1.366	1.469	−0.103
Forestry and Paper	0.000	0.871	−0.871	Electric Utility	4.221	1.956	2.265
Chemicals	1.717	2.046	−0.329	Gas Utilities	0.204	0.456	−0.252
Energy Reserves	4.490	4.297	0.193	Railroads	0.185	0.373	−0.189
Oil Refining	3.770	1.417	2.353	Airlines	0.000	0.206	−0.206
Oil Services	0.977	0.620	0.357	Truck/Sea/Air Freight	0.000	0.162	−0.162
Food & Beverages	0.823	3.780	−2.956	Medical Services	0.000	0.789	−0.789
Alcohol	0.365	0.515	−0.151	Medical Products	1.522	3.599	−2.077
Tobacco	3.197	0.732	2.465	Drugs	7.301	10.000	−2.699
Home Products	0.648	2.435	−1.787	Electronic Equipment	0.525	1.985	−1.460
Grocery Stores	0.636	0.511	0.125	Semiconductors	3.227	4.509	−1.282
Consumer Durables	0.000	0.166	−0.166	Computer Hardware	2.904	4.129	−1.224
Motor Vehicles & Parts	0.454	0.621	−0.167	Computer Software	7.304	6.256	1.048
Apparel & Textiles	0.141	0.373	−0.232	Defense & Aerospace	1.836	1.336	0.499
Clothing Stores	0.374	0.341	0.033	Telephone	6.290	3.680	2.610
Specialty Retail	0.025	2.721	−2.696	Wireless Telecom.	2.144	1.565	0.580
Department Stores	3.375	3.606	−0.231	Information Services	0.921	2.698	−1.777
Constructn. & Real Prop.	9.813	0.288	9.526	Industrial Services	0.230	0.670	−0.440
Publishing	0.326	0.778	−0.452	Life/health Insurance	1.987	0.938	1.048
Media	0.358	1.498	−1.140	Property/Casualty Ins.	4.844	2.541	2.304
Hotels	0.067	0.209	−0.141	Banks	8.724	7.580	1.144
Restaurants	0.000	0.542	−0.542	Thrifts	0.775	0.362	0.413
Entertainment	0.675	1.630	−0.955	Securities & Asst. Mgmt.	3.988	2.017	1.971
Leisure	0.000	0.409	−0.409	Financial Services	5.510	6.321	−0.811
Environmental Services	0.000	0.220	−0.220	Internet	0.434	0.725	−0.291
Heavy Electrical Eqp.	1.303	1.949	−0.647	Equity REIT	0.000	0.193	−0.193

Note: Mgd = Managed; Bmk = S&P 500 (the benchmark); Act = Active = Managed − Benchmark

Fundamental Factor Models and Equity Style Management

In Chapter 8, we covered equity style management. Notice that the risk factors used in fundamental factor models such as the Barra model (see Exhibit 13.1) are the same characteristics used in style management. Since the factors can be used to add value and control risk, this suggests that factor models can be used in style management for the same purposes.

APPLICATION TO PERFORMANCE ATTRIBUTION ANALYSIS

Return attribution is an *ex-post* analysis (an autopsy, so to speak) of the portfolio performance, usually relative to a benchmark. This analysis helps the portfolio manager understand the results of her investment bets, both explicit and implicit. This can point to sources of strengths and weaknesses in the portfolio, and improve the stock-picking and risk-monitoring processes. As a result of this analysis, the manager can, for instance, increase her portfolio exposures in areas where she has demonstrated strengths and reduce them in areas of weaknesses. The results of this analysis can also be used to better communicate the portfolio risk-return trade-offs to investors and other interested parties such as mutual fund board of directors or pension fund trustees.

Style Analysis

One approach to attribution is to use a *returns based style analysis* developed by William Sharpe and described in Chapter 8.[4] Here we regress the portfolio returns against a group of asset class benchmarks and find the sensitivities that best fit the data, as shown below:

$$r_{\text{portfolio}} = \beta_1 A_1 + \beta_2 A_2 + \beta_3 A_3 + \ldots + \beta_n A_n + \varepsilon$$

where $A_1, A_2, \ldots, A_n$ are returns of asset class benchmarks (for example, S&P 500 for large cap stocks, Russell 2000 for small cap stocks, Lehman Aggregate index for investment grade bonds, and so on). The betas are the sensitivities. Once these have been estimated, then we can say that the fund behaves as if it were a weighted combination of the asset classes where the weights are the betas. This combination reflects the fund's style and forms its style benchmark.

---

[4] William F. Sharpe, "Determining a Fund's Effective Asset Mix," *Investment Management Review* (September–October 1988), pp. 16–29.

Assuming the style remains the same going forward, we now calculate whether the fund beat its style benchmark in the following periods. This return in excess of the style benchmark is called the *fund's selection return*. This is the return that active management produced over what could have been obtained passively by holding the weighted combination of the asset class benchmarks (assuming, of course, that these benchmarks are available for passive investment).

$$r_{\text{style benchmark}} = \beta_1 A_1 + \beta_2 A_2 + \beta_3 A_3 + \ldots + \beta_n A_n$$

$$r_{\text{selection}} = r_{\text{portfolio}} - r_{\text{style benchmark}}$$

The advantages of this approach are that it does not require us to know the contents of the portfolio. Also, it is simple and easy to implement. The disadvantages are that the answer depends on how many and what benchmarks are included. Also, consider a situation where the prospectus of an actively managed large cap mutual fund states that it aims to beat the S&P 500, its bogey. Suppose the style analysis indicates that the best fitting style benchmark for the fund is 70% S&P 500, 20% Russell 2000, and 10% Lehman Aggregate bond index. Suppose the fund does beat its style benchmark but does not beat the benchmark mentioned in the prospectus. Does this count as outperformance? After all, the mutual fund's mandate is to beat the S&P 500, not some arbitrary combination of benchmarks that is a result of the manager's past portfolio management activity.

Sector Allocation versus Stock Selection

The sector allocation versus stock selection analysis is a popular approach wherein we assume that a portfolio return in excess of its benchmark is due to (1) its choice of sectors to overweight or underweight and (2) its selection of stocks within each sector.

The percentage allocation by a portfolio manager to an economic sector (such as Technology, Financials, etc.) can be different from the corresponding allocation in the benchmark (e.g., S&P 500) to that sector. This difference may be the result of a "top-down" allocation decision by the manager. In this approach, the manager picks sectors on the basis of their current investment attractiveness. She would overweight sectors on which she is bullish, and underweight the ones on which she is bearish. Alternatively, the difference in sector allocations between the portfolio and its benchmark may be the result of several "bottom-up" decisions. In this approach, the manager focuses on picking stocks through fundamental research, and the sector overweights and underweights would simply be the result of her stock picks. Note that in the first approach, the sector allocations are intentional, while in the second case they may be unintentional or simply byproducts of her stock picking.

In any case, if the portfolio is overweighted in a sector and that sector subsequently has a higher return than the benchmark as a whole, then that would have been a beneficial allocation. This would result in a positive allocation effect for that sector. If, however, that sector subsequently trails the benchmark, then that overweight in the sector would have been a detrimental allocation. This would result in a negative allocation effect for that sector. Similarly, underweighting a sector that subsequently trails the index would result in a positive allocation effect for that sector, and vice versa. The aggregation of the allocation effects across all sectors gives us the overall sector allocation effect.

Within each sector, a portfolio typically would hold only a fraction of the stocks that are present in the benchmark in that sector. The portfolio manager might rely upon fundamental security analysis to pick those stocks within a sector that would outperform the sector as a whole. If the portfolio manager's selections outperform the average return for that sector (on a position-weighted basis), then there would be a positive stock selection effect in that sector. If, however, the stocks held in the portfolio perform poorly or if the stocks not held in the portfolio do better, then there would be a negative stock selection effect in that sector. The aggregation of the selection effects across all sectors gives us the overall stock selection effect.

There is another effect called the "interaction effect," which results from the interaction between the sector allocation effect and the stock selection effect. There is a positive interaction effect if the portfolio manager overweights a sector where she has positive stock selection, and vice versa. This effect is often combined with the stock selection effect to simplify the analysis.

For a given sector,

$$\text{Sector allocation effect} = (r_{B,S} - r_B)\,(w_{P,S} - w_{B,S})$$

$$\text{Stock selection effect} = (r_{P,S} - r_{B,S})\,w_{B,S}$$

$$\text{Interaction effect} = (r_{P,S} - r_{B,S})\,(w_{P,S} - w_{B,S})$$

where

$r_{P,S}$ = portfolio return in sector s
$r_{B,S}$ = benchmark return in sector s

$$w_{B,S} = \text{benchmark weight in sector } s$$
$$w_{P,S} = \text{portfolio weight in sector } s$$
$$r_B = \text{benchmark return}$$

We sum these effects across all sectors to obtain the overall effects for the portfolio.

The above type of analysis can also be used to look at allocation across various market cap segments and selection of stocks within those segments. Similarly, we can look at allocation across segments of any other variable of interest (say, P/E ratio, beta fractiles, etc.) and the choice of stocks within those segments. Exhibits 13.12 and 13.13 show the output of such an analysis for a hypothetical large cap fund, the XYZ fund, benchmarked to the S&P 500. The analysis was performed using returns for the fourth quarter of 2001.

This method of attribution is popular because it is intuitive and easy to interpret. Its chief disadvantage is that it is not based on any underlying risk model. There are no risk factors that drive returns.

Risk Factor Model Based Attribution Analysis

The Barra attribution analysis is based on the same set of factors (risk index factors and industry factors) that go into its multi-factor risk model. The return of a portfolio can be seen as the sum of the risk-free return and the return in excess of the risk-free return. We refer to the latter as the portfolio's "excess return." Similarly, the benchmark has an excess return. The portfolio's excess return can be seen as being composed of two portions, namely (1) the benchmark excess return and (2) the remainder which is called the "active return."

$$r_P = r_{PX} + r_F$$

$$r_B = r_{BX} + r_F$$

$$r_A = r_P - r_B = r_{PX} - r_{BX}$$

where

$$r_P = \text{portfolio return}$$
$$r_{PX} = \text{portfolio excess return}$$
$$r_F = \text{risk-free return}$$
$$r_B = \text{benchmark return}$$
$$r_{BX} = \text{benchmark excess return}$$

EXHIBIT 13.12 Attribution Along Sector Allocation/Stock Selection Dimensions

Economic Sector	XYZ Fund		S&P 500		XYZ less S&P 500		Attribution Analysis		
	Average Weight	Total Return	Average Weight	Total Return	Average Weight	Total Return	Allocation Effect	Selection + Interaction	Total Effect
Consumer Discretionary	9.83	14.67	12.60	19.04	-2.77	-4.37	-0.29	-0.40	-0.69
Consumer Staples	8.17	0.64	8.60	2.49	-0.42	-1.85	0.04	-0.18	-0.14
Energy	8.49	16.11	6.35	4.44	2.13	11.66	-0.36	0.89	0.52
Financials	14.47	5.25	17.84	7.57	-3.38	-2.32	0.09	-0.38	-0.29
Health Care	19.47	-1.76	14.84	1.07	4.63	-2.83	-0.45	-0.57	-1.02
Industrials	7.47	17.35	10.90	16.50	-3.44	0.85	-0.20	0.05	-0.15
Information Technology	16.97	35.88	17.09	34.69	-0.11	1.19	-0.10	0.16	0.06
Materials	0.73	12.18	2.68	12.04	-1.94	0.14	-0.04	-0.03	-0.07
Telecommunication Services	3.53	-13.14	5.77	-10.27	-2.24	-2.87	0.52	-0.12	0.40
Utilities	4.22	4.11	3.27	-3.37	0.95	7.48	-0.16	0.27	0.11
Unassigned	0.13	5.27	0.07	7.88	0.06	-2.61	-0.04	0.01	-0.03
Cash	6.53	0.49	0.00	0.00	6.53	0.49	-0.69	0.00	-0.69
Total	100.00	8.68	100.00	10.65	0.00	-1.98	-1.69	-0.29	-1.98

Figures in columns are in percentages.

EXHIBIT 13.13 Attribution Along Market Cap Allocation/Stock Selection Dimensions

Market Cap Quintile Range ($ millions)	XYZ Fund		S&P 500		XYZ less S&P 500		Attribution Analysis		
	Average Weight	Total Return	Average Weight	Total Return	Average Weight	Total Return	Allocation Effect	Selection + Interaction	Total Effect
Quintile 1: 20,541–369,299	65.06	7.49	71.47	9.02	-6.40	-1.53	0.04	-0.94	-0.90
Quintile 2: 9,042–20,485	8.91	4.55	14.40	10.18	-5.49	-5.63	0.00	-0.54	-0.55
Quintile 3: 5,365–9,006	9.37	21.68	7.76	15.53	1.61	6.14	0.08	0.51	0.59
Quintile 4: 2,719–5,359	8.39	18.51	4.56	23.28	3.83	-4.77	0.39	-0.34	0.06
Quintile 5: 3.4–2,698	1.60	12.83	1.81	30.77	-0.20	-17.94	-0.20	-0.26	-0.46
Unassigned	0.13	5.27	0.00	-4.59	0.13	9.85	-0.03	0.00	-0.03
Cash	6.53	0.49	0.00	0.00	6.53	0.49	-0.69	0.00	-0.69
Total	100.00	8.68	100.00	10.65	0.00	-1.98	-0.42	-1.56	-1.98

Figures in columns are in percentages.

EXHIBIT 13.14 Barra Returns Tree

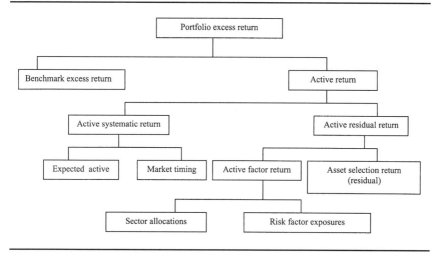

Source: Adapted from the returns tree in "How to Research Active Strategies," Barra Training Course, p. 57. Used with permission.

An index fund would have no active return. An actively managed fund would have an active return due to various reasons such as the following:

- On average, its beta with respect to its benchmark is different from 1 due to a defensive posture (beta less than 1) or an aggressive posture (beta greater than 1).
- Its beta in up markets is different from its beta in down markets, indicating that the fund tries to time the market.
- Its industry/sector allocations are different from those of the benchmark.
- Its risk index factor exposures are different from those of its benchmark.
- It attempts to pick only a subset of the stocks present in the benchmark, and probably holds them in proportions different from the benchmark.

All of these contribute to the active return. The Barra multi-factor risk model helps us estimate the contributions from each of these different sources to the active return. The Barra returns tree is shown in Exhibit 13.14.

Consider the attribution analysis of the same XYZ fund discussed earlier for the same period, namely the fourth quarter of 2001, performed in the context of the Barra multi-factor risk model. This is shown in Exhibit 13.15. Exhibits 13.16 and 13.17 analyze the sector and risk index bets further.

Following the Capital Asset Pricing Model, a portfolio's return depends linearly on its beta, a measure of its sensitivity to the market return. For the XYZ fund, we specify the S&P 500 as both the market and the benchmark. (But, this need not always be the case.) Ideally, a portfolio should have a beta greater than 1 in an up market and a beta less than 1 in a down market. A portfolio with a significant holding of cash would have a beta less than 1, while a portfolio with a significant holding of volatile stocks (such as technology stocks) would have a beta more than 1. Since beta explains a high proportion of the variation in the returns of diversified portfolios with respect to the market returns (i.e., has a high regression R-squared), it is an important measure of market timing bets placed by the portfolio. Barra captures the results of such market timing bets explicitly.

EXHIBIT 13.15   Attribution of XYZ Fund Return During the Fourth Quarter of 2001

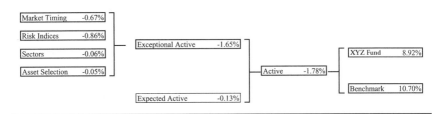

Sources of Return	Contribution (% Return)	Risk (Std. Dev.)	Info. Ratio	T-Stat.
1 Risk Free	0.51	0.00		
2 Benchmark Excess	10.19	14.49		
3 Expected Active	−0.13	0.00		
4 Market Timing	−0.67	1.45	−1.78	−0.89
5 Risk Indices	−0.86	1.17	−2.83	−1.42
6 Sectors	−0.06	1.56	−0.23	−0.11
7 Asset Selection	−0.05	2.02	−0.15	−0.07
8 Total Exceptional Active [4+5+6+7]	−1.65	3.23	−2.03	−1.01
9 Total Active [3+8]	−1.78	3.23	−2.18	−1.09
10 Total Managed [1+2+9]	8.92	13.24		

Info Ratio = Information ratio
T-Stat = T-Statistic

EXHIBIT 13.16 Sector Contributions to Active Return

Source of Return	Avg. Act. Wgt. (%)	Contribution (% Return)	Total Risk (Std. Dev.)	Info. Ratio	T-Stat.
Basic Materials	−1.92	−0.02	0.22	−0.39	−0.20
Energy	3.57	−0.18	0.90	−0.81	−0.40
Consumer (non-cyclical)	0.46	0.02	0.23	0.30	0.15
Consumer (cyclical)	−0.86	−0.01	0.16	−0.32	−0.16
Consumer Services	−0.91	−0.10	0.14	−2.92	−1.46
Industrials	−0.85	0.02	0.09	0.99	0.49
Utility	0.13	−0.01	0.09	−0.27	−0.14
Transport	−0.67	0.00	0.08	0.18	0.09
Health Care	5.25	−0.22	0.68	−1.22	−0.61
Technology	−0.90	0.25	0.46	2.07	1.03
Telecommunications	−1.69	0.24	0.27	3.31	1.65
Commercial Services	1.58	0.10	0.15	2.51	1.25
Financial	−3.20	−0.16	0.43	−1.47	−0.73
Total Sector Contribution		−0.06	1.56	−0.23	−0.11

EXHIBIT 13.17 Risk Index Contributions to Active Return

Source of Return	Average Active Exposure	Contribution (% Return)	Total Risk (Std. Dev.)	Information Ratio	T-Statistic
Volatility	−0.06	−0.58	0.37	−6.02	−3.01
Momentum	0.14	−0.60	1.00	−2.29	−1.15
Size	−0.02	0.11	0.10	4.07	2.04
Size Non-linearity	−0.01	−0.01	0.03	−0.73	−0.37
Trading Activity	0.09	0.04	0.23	0.63	0.32
Growth	0.12	0.05	0.24	0.70	0.35
Earnings Yield	0.02	0.07	0.10	2.58	1.29
Value	−0.10	0.11	0.20	2.02	1.01
Earnings Variation	0.00	0.00	0.03	0.36	0.18
Leverage	−0.02	0.02	0.04	1.56	0.78
Currency Sensitivity	−0.03	0.02	0.07	1.15	0.57
Yield	−0.09	−0.04	0.17	−0.94	−0.47
Non-EST Universe	0.02	−0.04	0.15	−0.99	−0.49
Total Risk Index Contribution		−0.86	1.17	−2.83	−1.42

EXHIBIT 13.18   S&P 500 Sector Betas

	Beta	S&P 500 Weight on 12/31/01	Weight * Beta
Cyclicals			
Technology	1.45	18.9%	0.28
Consumer Services	1.17	5.1%	0.06
Consumer Cyclical	1.00	8.1%	0.08
Financials	0.99	20.0%	0.20
Commercial Services	0.99	3.4%	0.03
Industrials	0.99	3.8%	0.04
Telecommunications	0.94	5.3%	0.05
Transport	0.93	0.7%	0.01
Basic Materials	0.89	3.7%	0.03
Defensive			
Health Care	0.79	14.4%	0.11
Energy	0.76	6.3%	0.05
Consumer Non-Cyclical	0.66	8.0%	0.05
Utilities	0.54	2.4%	0.01
Cash	0.00	0.0%	0.00
Total		100.0%	1.00

Note: The beta for a sector is the forward looking estimate with respect to the S&P 500 as of 12/31/01.
Source: Barra, Inc., Portfolio Manager Applicated. Used with permission.

The active beta of a portfolio is its beta less the market beta (which is 1). Cash has a beta of zero. Suppose a portfolio has 10% cash and 90% diversified stock holdings. Suppose further that the stock portion of the portfolio has a beta of 1. Then, the overall portfolio beta would be 0.9 [= 90% × 1 + 10% × 0]. Its active beta is −0.1 [= 1 − 0.9]. By varying the cash level, the manager can change the portfolio's beta. The portfolio beta is also influenced by sector allocations since the various sectors have different betas, as shown in Exhibit 13.18. The choice of stocks within each sector also influences portfolio beta, though not to the same extent as the sector allocations.

Over the long run, equities have outperformed cash. So, a portfolio that has beta greater than 1 captures more of the equity premium than the benchmark and thus has an expected long-run return advantage component. Note, however, that this return advantage is not likely to occur in every period. It only occurs over the long run. This component of the portfolio active return is termed the "expected active return." If the beta is less than 1, then the expected active return becomes negative.

As mentioned earlier, in the Barra multi-factor risk model, the factors are of two distinct types—risk index factors and industry factors. The industry factors are combined to obtain sectors. Note that sectors themselves are not factors. In the output, though, the industries can be grouped together as sectors to simplify the presentation of results. A combination of active exposures to industry factors gives us the corresponding active exposures to sectors.

Just as the portfolio has active exposures to sectors, it also has active exposures to risk index factors. (As noted before, active exposure is the portfolio exposure less the benchmark exposure.) The manager would maintain overweights on those risk factors that she expects would have returns that exceed the benchmark return and underweights on the risk factors that she forecasts would trail the benchmark. Suppose she has no view on how these risk factors would perform, then she would maintain zero (or close to zero) active exposures to these factors—that is, she would position the portfolio to be risk factor neutral.

Exposures to industry factors (and thus sectors) are measured in percentages, while exposures to risk index factors are measured in units of standard deviations. This is because the descriptors that are combined to form the risk index factors are disparate in nature (such as P/E ratio, leverage, market cap, volatility of returns, etc.) and have different units. So, to facilitate comparisons, each of these is normalized (i.e., converted into a normal curve with zero mean and a standard deviation of 1).

We notice some, but not complete, similarity in the sector allocation results of the earlier approach (shown in Exhibit 13.12) and the sector allocation results of the multi-factor risk approach (shown in Exhibit 13.16). There are two main reasons for the differences, as indicated below:

- *The classification approach*: Barra sectors are not the same as the sectors in other approaches. Companies that fall under a certain Barra sector may fall under a different sector in other classifications. Also, in most classifications, a company can only fall in one sector. In the Barra approach, though, a company can have fractional affiliation to many sectors such that the sum of the fractions is 1. This reflects the fact that some companies have many lines of business not all of which are in the same economic sector (e.g., General Electric Co.).

- *The calculation approach*: Barra removes the effect of beta and risk factors before obtaining the sector allocation results. The approach discussed earlier makes no such adjustment because it has no underlying risk model. The effect of the absence of a risk model can be subtle but important. As an illustration, consider the following example. Barra multi-factor risk model uses a factor called "Value," which tracks the book-to-price ratio. Stocks with low book-to-price ratios would score low on the Value risk factor. Suppose that, among the stocks that have very low book-to-price ratios, most happen to be in the technology sector and the rest happen to be in the telecom sector. Also suppose that during a certain month such stocks do well, but the other stocks in the technology sector (the ones with moderate and high book-to-price ratios) do no better than the overall index. A simple sector allocation/ stock selection type of analysis (discussed in the previous section) would indicate that overweighting the technology sector would have been beneficial during that month. But a Barra attribution analysis would indicate that underweighting the Value risk factor would have been beneficial during that month. After adjusting for the Value risk factor, overweighting the technology sector would probably have had no additional benefit. Underweighting the Value risk factor could have been accomplished by holding the low book-to-price stocks (whether they are in the technology sector or the telecom sector). There may have been no need to overweight the technology sector as a whole. Thus, an attribution based on a risk model would separate the risk factor effects from the sector effects.

The active return due to security selection in the Barra model is simply derived as the residual return after stripping out the active return due to market timing, sector bets, and risk factor bets. The Barra approach does not permit a breakdown of security selection by sector. This is more geared towards a purely quantitative portfolio management process where all security selection is done by a model and not by individual analysts who follow specific sectors.

MULTI-FACTOR RISK MODELS AND TRADITIONAL SECURITY ANALYSIS

As can be seen from the descriptors, a multi-factor risk model uses as its input the same type of information used in traditional security analysis described in Chapters 9, 10, and 11. So, portfolio construction and risk control using multi-factor risk models provides a more formal structure for portfolio analysis, taking into account the correlation or covariance of the risk factors, a drawback that was noted regarding traditional security analysis.

A study by Bruce Jacobs and Kenneth Levy suggests that simple factor models can outperform a dividend discount model (a valuation model used in traditional security analysis as explained in Chapter 11).[5] Specifically, when they compared the contribution of a simple factor model with a traditional dividend discount model they found that less than one-half of 1% of the quarterly average actual returns is explained by the dividend discount model. In contrast, about 43% of the average actual returns is explained by a factor model which includes the dividend discount model and other factors. Thus, in their study the factor model outperformed the dividend discount model hands down.

Some proprietary models developed by investment management companies integrate into a multi-factor risk model the recommendations or projections of equity analysts who base their recommendations on traditional security analysis. For example, a good number of fundamental risk factor models use consensus forecasts for earnings and long-term earnings growth. "Consensus" is defined as the mean of the analysts forecasts for a given company. Analysts use the methodology described in Chapter 11 to obtain their earnings forecasts and long-term growth. Other earnings-related measures are typically incorporated into factor models. In the Barra model, for example, two descriptors used are "net earnings revision" and "earnings torpedo." The former uses I/B/E/S data measuring analysts' optimism of earnings. More specifically, net earnings revision is measured by the percentage of analysts who are feeling more optimistic about earnings in the next period. Earnings torpedo is also based on I/B/E/S data and is a measure of the estimated growth in earnings for a company relative to historical earnings.

As another example, Goldman Sachs Asset Management (GSAM), an investment management subsidiary of Goldman Sachs & Co. (a broker/dealer firm), has a multi-factor risk model that uses the following factors which involve analyst forecasts:[6]

Retained EPS/Price: Year-ahead consensus forecasts of earnings per share less indicated annual dividend divided by price. The one-year forecast of earnings per share is a weighted average of the forecasts for the current and next fiscal years.

Estimate Revisions: For a given company, the number of estimates raised in the past three months, less the number lowered, divided by the total number of estimates.

---

[5] Bruce Jacobs and Kenneth Levy, "On the Value of 'Value'," *Financial Analysts Journal* (July–August 1988), pp. 47–52.
[6] *Select Equity Investment Strategy*, Goldman Sachs Asset Management, February 1997.

Sustainable Growth: The consensus long-term growth forecast of analysts following the company.

There are proprietary models where recommendations based on rankings are incorporated into a risk factor model. Another approach is where recommendations of analysts employing traditional security analysis is used in multi-factor risk models by forcing highly recommended stocks into the solution—that is, constraining the weight on certain stocks in the optimization so that a minimum exposure is realized.

CHAPTER 14

Equity Derivatives I: Features and Valuation

Bruce M.Collins, Ph.D.
CEO
QuantCast LLC

Frank J. Fabozzi, Ph.D., CFA
Adjunct Professor of Finance
School of Management
Yale University

Derivative instruments, or simply derivatives, are contracts that essentially derive their value from the behavior of cash market instruments such as stocks, stock indexes, bonds, currencies, and commodities that underlie the contract. When the underlying for a derivative is a stock or stock index, the contract is called an *equity derivative*. The purpose of this chapter is to explain these instruments, their investment characteristics, and to provide an overview as to how they are priced. In the next chapter we look at how equity derivatives can be used in the management of equity portfolios.

THE ROLE OF DERIVATIVES

Equity derivatives have several properties that provide economic benefits that make them excellent candidates for use in equity portfolio management. These properties are derived from the following four roles that derivatives serve in portfolio management: (1) to modify the risk characteristics of a portfolio (*risk management*); (2) to enhance the expected return of a portfolio (*returns management*); (3) to reduce transaction costs associated with managing a portfolio (*cost management*); and, (4) to achieve efficiency in the presence of legal, tax, or regulatory obstacles (*regulatory management*).

We can further reduce the role of derivatives to the single purpose of risk management and incorporate the other three roles into this one. Thus, one can argue that equity derivatives are used primarily to manage risk or to buy and sell risk at a favorable price. Risk management is a dynamic process that allows portfolio managers to identify, measure, and assess the current risk attributes of a portfolio and to measure the potential benefits from taking the risk. Moreover, risk management involves understanding and managing the factors that can have an adverse impact on the targeted rate of return. The objective is to attain a desired return for a given level of corresponding risk on an after-cost basis. This is consistent with the Markowitz efficient frontier and modern portfolio theory discussed in Chapter 2. The role of equity derivatives in this process is to shift the frontier in favor of the investor by implementing a strategy at a lower cost, lower risk, and higher return or to gain access to an investment that was not available due to some regulatory or other restriction. We can, therefore, regard the management of equity portfolios as a sophisticated exercise in risk management.

Institutional equity investors have the means to accomplish investment objectives with a host of products and product structures. Pension funds, for example, can structure a product to meet their asset allocation targets, to access foreign markets, or to explicitly manage risk. Products that may meet their needs include listed stock index futures, and equity swaps. The choice of an instrument depends on the specific investor needs and circumstances. In each case, the benefits from structuring a derivatives solution to an investment problem either involves cost reduction, risk management, or the management of certain legal or regulatory restrictions.

Equity derivatives give investors more degrees of freedom. In the past, the implementation and management of an investment strategy for pension funds, for example, was a function of management style and was carried out in the cash market. Pension funds managed risk by diversifying among management styles. Prior to the advent of the over-the-counter (OTC) derivatives market in the late 1980s, the first risk management tools available to investors were limited to the listed futures and options markets. Although providing a valuable addition to an investor's risk management tool kit, listed derivatives were limited in application due to their standardized features, limited size, and liquidity constraints. The OTC derivatives market gives investors access to longer-term products that better match their investment horizon and provides flexible structures to meet their exact risk/reward requirements. The number of unique equity derivative structures is essentially unlimited.

EQUITY DERIVATIVES MARKET

The three general categories of derivatives are (1) futures and forwards, (2) options, and (3) swaps. The basic derivative securities are futures/forward contracts and options. Swaps and other derivative structures with more complicated payoffs are regarded as hybrid securities, which can be shown to be nothing more than portfolios of forwards, options, and cash instruments in varying combinations.

Equity derivatives can also be divided into two categories according to whether they are listed or OTC. The listed market consists of options, warrants, and futures contracts. The principal listed options market consists of exchange-traded options with standardized strike prices, expirations, and payout terms traded on individual stocks, equity indexes, and futures contracts on equity indexes. A FLexible EXchange (FLEX) Option was introduced by the CBOE in 1993 that provides the customization feature of the OTC market, but with the guarantee of the exchange. The listed futures market consists of exchange-traded equity index futures and single stock futures with standardized settlement dates and settlement returns.[1] Other equity derivatives might include exchange-traded funds (ETFs), which are index investment products listed and traded on an exchange. ETFs are discussed in Chapter 27.

OTC equity derivatives are not traded on an exchange and have an advantage over listed derivatives because they provide complete flexibility and can be tailored to fit an investment strategy. The OTC equity derivatives market can be divided into three components: OTC options and warrants, equity-linked debt investments, and equity swaps.[2] OTC equity options are customized option contracts that can be applied to any equity index, basket of stocks or an individual stock. OTC options are privately negotiated agreements between an investor and an issuing

---

[1] As of January 2002, single stock futures are in the process of being listed on U.S. exchanges.

[2] A series of equity linked structured products are listed on the American Stock Exchange and the Chicago Board Options Exchange (CBOE), mostly for retail investors. Among these products are the Merrill Lynch Market Index Target-Term Securities[SM] (MITTS) and Salomon Smith Barney TIERS[SM] Principal-Protected Trust Certificates and Targeted Growth Enhanced Terms Securities ("TARGETS[®]"). For a complete listing and description of the products refer to their web sites at www.amex.com and www.cboe.com.

dealer. The structure of the option is completely flexible in terms of strike price, expiration, and payout features.

A fundamental difference between listed and OTC derivatives, however, is that listed options and futures contracts are guaranteed by the exchange, while in the OTC market the derivative is the obligation of a non-exchange entity that is the counterparty. Thus, the investor is subject to credit risk or counterparty risk.

LISTED EQUITY OPTIONS

Equity derivative products are either exchange-traded listed derivatives or over-the-counter derivatives. In this section we will look at listed equity options.

An *option* is a contract in which the option seller grants the option buyer the right to enter into a transaction with the seller to either buy or sell an underlying asset at a specified price on or before a specified date. The specified price is called the *strike price* or *exercise price* and the specified date is called the *expiration date*. The option seller grants this right in exchange for a certain amount of money called the *option premium* or *option price*.

The option seller is also known as the option writer, while the option buyer is the option holder. The asset that is the subject of the option is called the *underlying*. The underlying can be an individual stock, a stock index, or another derivative instrument such as a futures contract or an ETF. The option writer can grant the option holder one of two rights. If the right is to purchase the underlying, the option is a *call option*. If the right is to sell the underlying, the option is a *put option*.

An option can also be categorized according to when it may be exercised by the buyer. This is referred to as the *exercise style*. A *European option* can only be exercised at the expiration date of the contract. An *American option* can be exercised any time on or before the expiration date. A *Bermudan option* is in between an American and a European and can only be exercised on certain dates over the life of the option.

The terms of exchange are represented by the contract unit, which is typically 100 shares for an individual stock and a multiple times an index value for a stock index. The terms of exchange are standard for most contracts. The contract terms for a FLEX option can be customized along four dimensions: underlying, strike price, expiration date, and settlement style. These options are discussed further below.

The option holder enters into the contract with an opening transaction. Subsequently, the option holder then has the choice to exercise or to sell the option. The sale of an existing option by the holder is a closing sale.

Listed versus OTC Equity Options

There are three advantages of listed options relative to OTC options. First, the strike price and expiration dates of the contract are standardized. Second, the direct link between buyer and seller is severed after the order is executed because of the fungible nature of listed options. The Options Clearing Corporation (OCC) serves as the intermediary between buyer and seller. Finally, transaction costs are lower for listed options than their OTC counterparts.

There are many situations in which an institutional investor needs a customized option. Such situations will be identified when we discuss the applications of OTC options in the next chapter. The higher cost of OTC options reflects this customization. However, some OTC exotic option structures may prove to cost less than the closest standardized option because a more specific payout is being bought.

A significant distinction between a listed option and an OTC option is the presence of credit risk or counterparty risk. Only the option buyer is exposed to counterparty risk. Options traded on exchanges and OTC options traded over a network of market makers have different ways of dealing with the problem of credit risk. Organized exchanges reduce counterparty risk by requiring margin, marking to the market daily, imposing size and price limits, and providing an intermediary that takes both sides of a trade. The clearing process provides three levels of protection: (1) the customer's margin, (2) the member firm's guarantee, and (3) the clearinghouse. The OTC market has incorporated a variety of terms into the contractual agreement between counterparties to address the issue of credit risk and these are described when we discuss OTC derivatives.

For listed options, there are no margin requirements for the buyer of an option once the option price has been paid in full. Because the option price is the maximum amount that the option buyer can lose, no matter how adverse the price movement of the underlying, margin is not necessary. The option writer has agreed to transfer the risk inherent in a position in the underlying from the option buyer to itself. The writer, on the other, has certain margin requirements.

Basic Features of Listed Options

The basic features of listed options are summarized in Exhibit 14.1. The exhibit is grouped into four categories with each option category presented in terms of its basic features. These include the type of option, underlying, strike price, settlement information, expiration cycle, exercise style, and some trading rules.

EXHIBIT 14.1 Basic Features of Listed Equity Options

Stock Options

Option Type	Call or Put
Option Category	Equity
Underlying Security	Individual stock or ADR
Contract Value	Equity: 100 shares of common stock or ADRs
Strike Price	2½ points when the strike price is between $5 and $25, 10 points when the strike price is over $200. Strikes are adjusted for splits, recapitalizations, etc.
Settlement and Delivery	100 shares of stock
Exercise Style	American
Expiration Cycle	Two near-term months plus two additional months from the January, February or March quarterly cycles
Transaction Costs	$1–$3 commissions and ⅛ market impact
Position and Size Limits	Large capitalization stocks have an option position limit of 25,000 contracts (with adjustments for splits, recapitalizations, etc.) on the same side of the market; smaller capitalization stocks have an option position limit of 20,000, 10,500, 7,500 or 4,500 contracts (with adjustments for splits, recapitalizations, etc.) on the same side of the market.

Index Options

Option Type	Call or Put
Option Category	Indexes
Underlying Security	Stock index
Contract Value	Multiplier × index price
Strike Price	Five points. 10-point intervals in the far-term month.
Settlement and Delivery	Cash
Exercise Style	American
Expiration Cycle	Four near-term months
Transaction Costs	$1–$3 commissions and ⅛ market impact
Position and Size Limits	150,000 contracts on the same side of the market with no more than 100,000 of such contracts in the near-term series

EXHIBIT 14.1 (Continued)

LEAP Options

Option Type	Call or Put
Option Category	LEAP
Underlying Security	Individual stock or stock index
Contract Value	Equity: 100 shares of common stock or ADRs Index: full or partial value of stock index
Strike Price	Equity: same as equity option Index: Based on full or partial value of index. ⅕ value translates into ⅕ strike price
Settlement and Delivery	Equity: 100 shares of stock or ADR Index: Cash
Exercise Style	American or European
Expiration Cycle	May be up to 39 months from the date of initial listing, January expiration only
Transaction Costs	$1–$3 commissions and ⅛ market impact
Position and Size Limits	Same as equity options and index options

FLEX Options

Option Type	Call, Put, or Cap
Option Category	Equity: E-FLEX option Index: FLEX option
Underlying Security	Individual stock or index
Contract Value	Equity: 100 shares of common stock or ADRs Index: multiplier × index value
Strike Price	Equity: Calls, same as standard calls Puts, any dollar value or percentage Index: Any index value, percentage, or deviation from index value
Settlement and Delivery	Equity: 100 shares of stock Index: Cash
Exercise Style	Equity: American or European Index: American, European, or Cap
Expiration Cycle	Equity: 1 day to 3 years Index: Up to 5 years
Transaction Costs	$1–$3 commissions and ⅛ market impact
Position and Size Limits	Equity: minimum of 250 contracts to create FLEX Index: $10 million minimum to create FLEX No size or position limits

Stock options refer to listed options on individual stocks or American Depository Receipts (ADRs). The underlying is 100 shares of the designated stock. All listed stock options in the United States may be exercised any time before the expiration date; that is, they are American style options.

Index options are options where the underlying is a stock index rather than an individual stock. An index call option gives the option buyer the right to buy the underlying stock index, while a put option gives the option buyer the right to sell the underlying stock index. Unlike stock options where a stock can be delivered if the option is exercised by the option holder, it would be extremely complicated to settle an index option by delivering all the stocks that constitute the index. Instead, index options are cash settlement contracts. This means that if the option is exercised by the option holder, the option writer pays cash to the option buyer. There is no delivery of any stocks.

The most liquid index options are those on the S&P 100 index (OEX) and the S&P 500 index. Both trade on the CBOE. Index options can be listed as American or European. The S&P 500 index option contract is European, while the OEX is American. Both index option contracts have specific standardized features and contract terms. Moreover, both have short expiration cycles. There are almost 100 stock index option contracts listed across 26 separate exchanges and 20 countries. Among the latest arrivals are options traded on the Dow Jones STOXX 50 and the Dow Jones EURO 50 stock indexes. The indexes are comprised of 50 industrial, commercial, and financial European blue chip companies.

The following mechanics should be noted for index options. The dollar value of the stock index underlying an index option is equal to the current cash index value multiplied by the contract's multiple. That is,

$$\text{Dollar value of the underlying index} = \text{Cash index value} \times \text{Contract multiple}$$

For example, if the cash index value for the S&P 100 is 530, then the dollar value of the S&P 100 contract is $530 \times \$100 = \$53,000$.

For a stock option, the price at which the buyer of the option can buy or sell the stock is the strike price. For an index option, the strike index is the index value at which the buyer of the option can buy or sell the underlying stock index. The strike index is converted into a dollar value by multiplying the strike index by the multiple for the contract. For example, if the strike index is 510, the dollar value is $51,000 (510 × $100). If an investor purchases a call option on the S&P 100 with a strike index of 510, and exercises the option when the index value is 530, then the investor has the right to purchase the index for $51,000 when the market value of the index is $53,000. The buyer of the call option would then receive $2,000 from the option writer.

The other two categories listed in Exhibit 14.1, LEAPS and FLEX options, essentially modify an existing feature of either a stock option, an index option, or both. For example, stock option and index option contracts have short expiration cycles. Long-Term Equity Anticipation Securities (LEAPS) are designed to offer options with longer maturities. These contracts are available on individual stocks and some indexes. Stock option LEAPS are comparable to standard stock options except the maturities can range up to 39 months from the origination date. Index options LEAPS differ in size compared with standard index options having a multiplier of 10 rather than 100.

FLEX options allow users to specify the terms of the option contract for either a stock option or an index option. The value of FLEX options is the ability to customize the terms of the contract along four dimensions: underlying, strike price, expiration date, and settlement style. Moreover, the exchange provides a secondary market to offset or alter positions and an independent daily marking of prices. The development of the FLEX option is a response to the growing OTC market. The exchanges seek to make the FLEX option attractive by providing price discovery through a competitive auction market, an active secondary market, daily price valuations, and the virtual elimination of counterparty risk. The FLEX option represents a link between listed options and OTC products.

Risk and Return Characteristics of Options

Now let's illustrate the risk and return characteristics of the four basic option positions—buying a call option (long a call option), selling a call option (short a call option), buying a put option (long a put option), and selling a put option (short a put option). We will use stock options in our example. The illustrations assume that each option position is held to the expiration date. Also, to simplify the illustrations, we assume that the underlying for each option is for 1 share of stock rather than 100 shares and we ignore transaction costs.

Buying Call Options

Assume that there is a call option on stock XYZ that expires in one month and has a strike price of $100. The option price is $3. Suppose that the current or spot price of stock XYZ is $100. (The *spot price* is the cash market price.) The profit and loss will depend on the price of stock XYZ at the expiration date. The buyer of a call option benefits if the price rises above the strike price. If the price of stock XYZ is equal to $103, the buyer of a call option breaks even. The maximum loss is the option price, and there is substantial upside potential if the stock price rises above $103. Exhibit 14.2 shows using a graph the profit/loss profile for the buyer of this call option at the expiration date.

EXHIBIT 14.2   Profit/Loss Profile at Expiration for a Short Call Position and a Long Call Position

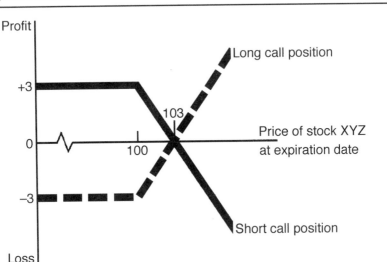

It is worthwhile to compare the profit and loss profile of the call option buyer with that of an investor taking a long position in one share of stock XYZ. The payoff from the position depends on stock XYZ's price at the expiration date. An investor who takes a long position in stock XYZ realizes a profit of $1 for every $1 increase in stock XYZ's price. As stock XYZ's price falls, however, the investor loses, dollar for dollar. If the price drops by more than $3, the long position in stock XYZ results in a loss of more than $3. The long call position, in contrast, limits the loss to only the option price of $3 but retains the upside potential, which will be $3 less than for the long position in stock XYZ. Which alternative is better, buying the call option or buying the stock? The answer depends on what the investor is attempting to achieve.

Writing Call Options

To illustrate the option seller's, or writer's, position, we use the same call option we used to illustrate buying a call option. The profit/loss profile at expiration of the short call position (that is, the position of the call option writer) is the mirror image of the profit and loss profile of the long call position (the position of the call option buyer). That is, the profit of the short call position for any given price for stock XYZ at the expiration date is the same as the loss of the long call position. Consequently, the maximum profit the short call position can produce is the option price. The maximum loss is not limited because it is the highest price reached by stock XYZ on or before the expiration date, less the option price; this price can be indefinitely high. Exhibit 14.2 shows using a graph the profit/loss profile for the seller of this call option at the expiration date.

Buying Put Options

To illustrate a long put option position, we assume a hypothetical put option on one share of stock XYZ with one month to maturity and a strike price of $100. Assume that the put option is selling for $2 and the spot price of stock XYZ is $100. The profit or loss for this position at the expiration date depends on the market price of stock XYZ. The buyer of a put option benefits if the price falls. Exhibit 14.3 shows using a graph the profit/loss profile for the buyer of this put option at the expiration date.

As with all long option positions, the loss is limited to the option price. The profit potential, however, is substantial: The theoretical maximum profit is generated if stock XYZ's price falls to zero. Contrast this profit potential with that of the buyer of a call option. The theoretical maximum profit for a call buyer cannot be determined beforehand because it depends on the highest price that can be reached by stock XYZ before or at the option expiration date.

EXHIBIT 14.3 Profit/Loss Profile at Expiration for a Short Put Position and a Long Put Position

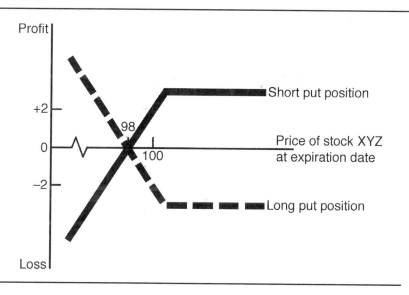

To see how an option alters the risk/return profile for an investor, we again compare it with a position in stock XYZ. The long put position is compared with a short position in stock XYZ because such a position would also benefit if the price of the stock falls. While the investor taking a short stock position faces all the downside risk as well as the upside potential, an investor taking the long put position faces limited downside risk (equal to the option price) while still maintaining upside potential reduced by an amount equal to the option price.

Writing Put Options

The profit and loss profile for a short put option is the mirror image of the long put option. The maximum profit to be realized from this position is the option price. The theoretical maximum loss can be substantial should the price of the underlying fall; if the price were to fall all the way to zero, the loss would be as large as the strike price less the option price the seller received. Exhibit 14.3 shows using a graph the profit/loss profile for the seller of this put option at the expiration date.

The Value of an Option

Now we will look at the basic factors that affect the value of an option and discuss a well-known option pricing model.

Basic Components of the Option Price

The price of an option is a reflection of the option's *intrinsic value* and any additional amount above its intrinsic value. The premium over intrinsic value is often referred to as the *time value*.

Intrinsic Value   The intrinsic value of an option is its economic value if it is exercised immediately. If no positive economic value would result from exercising the option immediately, then the intrinsic value is zero. For a call option, the intrinsic value is positive if the spot price (i.e., cash market price) of the underlying is greater than the strike price. The intrinsic value is then the difference between the two prices. If the strike price of a call option is greater than or equal to the spot price of the underlying, the intrinsic value is zero. For example, if the strike price for a call option is $100 and the spot price of the underlying is $105, the intrinsic value is $5. That is, an option buyer exercising the option and simultaneously selling the underlying would realize $105 from the sale of the underlying, which would be covered by acquiring the underlying from the option writer for $100, thereby netting a $5 gain.

When an option has intrinsic value, it is said to be *in the money* (ITM). When the strike price of a call option exceeds the spot price of the underlying, the call option is said to be *out of the money* (OTM); it has no intrinsic value. An option for which the strike price is equal to the spot price of the underlying is said to be at the money. Both at-the-money and out-of-the-money options have an intrinsic value of zero because they are not profitable to exercise. Our call option with a strike price of $100 would be (1) in the money when the spot price of the underlying is greater than $100, (2) out of the money when the spot price of the underlying is less than $100, and (3) at the money when the spot price of the underlying is equal to $100.

For a put option, the intrinsic value is equal to the amount by which the spot price of the underlying is below the strike price. For example, if the strike price of a put option is $100 and the spot price of the underlying is $92, the intrinsic value is $8. The buyer of the put option who exercises the put option and simultaneously sells the underlying will net $8 by exercising since the underlying will be sold to the writer for $100 and purchased in the market for $92. The intrinsic value is zero if the strike price is less than or equal to the underlying's spot price.

For our put option with a strike price of $100, the option would be (1) in the money when the spot price of the underlying is less than $100, (2) out of the money when the spot price of the underlying exceeds $100, and (3) at the money when the spot price of the underlying is equal to $100.

Time Value   The *time value of an option* is the amount by which the option price exceeds its intrinsic value. The option buyer hopes that, at some time prior to expiration, changes in the market price of the underlying will increase the value of the rights conveyed by the option. For this prospect, the option buyer is willing to pay a premium above the intrinsic value. For example, if the price of a call option with a strike price of $100 is $9 when the spot price of the underlying is $105, the time value of this option is $4 ($9 minus its intrinsic value of $5). Had the current price of the underlying been $90 instead of $105, then the time value of this option would be the entire $9 because the option has no intrinsic value. Other factors being equal, the time value of an option will increase with the amount of time remaining to expiration, since the opportunity for a favorable change in the price of the underlying is greater.

There are two ways in which an option buyer may realize the value of a position taken in an option: the first is to exercise the option, and the second is to sell the option. In the first example above, since the exercise of an option will realize a gain of only $5 and will cause the immediate loss of any time value ($4 in our first example), it is preferable to sell the call. In general, if an option buyer wishes to realize the value of a position, selling will be more economically beneficial than exercising. However, there are circumstances under which it is preferable to exercise prior to the expiration date, depending on whether the total proceeds at the expiration date would be greater by holding the option or by exercising it and reinvesting any cash proceeds received until the expiration date.

Factors that Influence the Option Price

The following six factors influence the option price:

1. Spot price of the underlying
2. Strike price
3. Time to expiration of the option
4. Expected price volatility of the underlying over the life of the option
5. Short-term risk-free rate over the life of the option
6. Anticipated cash dividends on the underlying stock or index over the life of the option

The impact of each of these factors depends on whether (1) the option is a call or a put and (2) the option is an American option or a European option. A summary of the effects of each factor on American put and call option prices is presented in Exhibit 14.4.

Notice how the expected price volatility of the underlying over the life of the option affects the price of both a put and a call option. All other factors being equal, the greater the expected volatility (as measured by the standard deviation or variance) of the price of the underlying, the more an investor would be willing to pay for the option, and the more an option writer would demand for it. This is because the greater the volatility, the greater the probability that the price of the underlying will move in favor of the option buyer at some time before expiration.

EXHIBIT 14.4   Summary of Factors that Effect the Price of an American Option

	Effect of an Increase of Factor on	
Factor	Call Price	Put Price
Spot price of underlying	increase	decrease
Strike price	decrease	increase
Time to expiration of option	increase	increase
Expected price volatility	increase	increase
Short-term rate	increase	decrease
Anticipated cash dividends	decrease	increase

Option Pricing Models

Several models have been developed to determine the theoretical value of an option. The most popular one was developed by Fischer Black and Myron Scholes in 1973 for valuing European call options.[3] Several modifications to their model have followed since then. We discuss this model here to give the reader a feel for the impact of the factors on the price of an option.

By imposing certain assumptions and using arbitrage arguments, the Black-Scholes option pricing model provides the fair (or theoretical) price of a European call option on a non-dividend-paying stock. Basically, the idea behind the arbitrage argument in deriving this and other option pricing models is that if the payoff from owning a call option can be replicated by (1) purchasing the stock underlying the call option and (2) borrowing funds, then the price of the option will be (at most) the cost of creating the replicating strategy.

The formula for the Black-Scholes model is

$$C = SN(d_1) - Xe^{-rt} N(d_2)$$

where

$$d_1 = \frac{\ln(S/K) + (r + 0.5s^2)t}{s\sqrt{t}}$$

d_2 = $d_1 - s\sqrt{t}$
ln = natural logarithm
C = call option price
S = price of the underlying
K = strike price
r = short-term risk-free rate
e = 2.718 (natural antilog of 1)
t = time remaining to the expiration date (measured as a fraction of a year)
s = standard deviation of the change in stock price
$N(.)$ = the cumulative probability density[4]

---

[3] Fischer Black and Myron Scholes, "The Pricing of Corporate Liabilities," *Journal of Political Economy* (May–June 1973), pp. 637–659.
[4] The value for $N(.)$ is obtained from a normal distribution function that is tabulated in most statistics textbooks or from spreadsheets that have this built-in function.

Notice that five of the factors that we said earlier in this chapter influence the price of an option are included in the formula. However, the sixth factor, anticipated cash dividends, is not included because the model is for a non-dividend-paying stock. In the Black-Scholes model, the direction of the influence of each of these factors is the same as stated earlier. Four of the factors—strike price, price of underlying, time to expiration, and risk-free rate—are easily observed. The standard deviation of the price of the underlying must be estimated.

The option price derived from the Black-Scholes model is "fair" in the sense that if any other price existed, it would be possible to earn riskless arbitrage profits by taking an offsetting position in the underlying. That is, if the price of the call option in the market is higher than that derived from the Black-Scholes model, an investor could sell the call option and buy a certain quantity of the underlying. If the reverse is true, that is, the market price of the call option is less than the "fair" price derived from the model, the investor could buy the call option and sell short a certain amount of the underlying. This process of hedging by taking a position in the underlying allows the investor to lock in the riskless arbitrage profit. The number of shares necessary to hedge the position changes as the factors that affect the option price change, so the hedged position must be changed constantly.

To illustrate the Black-Scholes model, assume the following values:

Strike price   = $45
Time remaining to expiration = 183 days
Spot stock price   = $47
Expected price volatility   = standard deviation = 25%
Risk-free rate   = 10%

In terms of the values in the formula:

S = 47
K = 45
t = 0.5 (183 days/365, rounded)
s = 0.25
r = 0.10

Substituting these values into the equations above, we get

$$d_1 = \frac{\ln(47/45) + [0.10 + 0.5(0.25)^2]0.5}{0.25\sqrt{0.5}} = 0.6172$$

$$d_2 = 0.6172 - 0.25\sqrt{0.5} = 0.4404$$

From a normal distribution table:

$$N(0.6172) = 0.7315 \text{ and } N(0.4404) = 0.6702$$

Then:

$$C = 47 \ (0.7315) - 45 \ (e^{-(0.10)(0.5)}) \ (0.6702) = \$5.69$$

Exhibit 14.5 shows the option value as calculated from the Black-Scholes model for different assumptions concerning (1) the standard deviation, (2) the risk-free rate, and (3) the time remaining to expiration. Notice that the option price varies directly with all three factors. That is, (1) the lower (higher) the volatility, the lower (higher) the option price; (2) the lower (higher) the risk-free rate, the lower (higher) the option price; and, (3) the shorter (longer) the time remaining to expiration, the lower (higher) the option price. All of this agrees with what is shown in Exhibit 14.4 about the effect of a change in one of the factors on the price of a call option.

How do we determine the value of put options? There is relationship that shows the relationship among the spot price of the underlying, the call option price, and the put option price. This is called the *put-call parity relationship*. If we can calculate the fair value of a call option, the fair value of a put with the same strike price and expiration on the same stock can be calculated from the put-call parity relationship.

Sensitivity of the Option Price to a Change in Factors

In employing options in investment strategies, a manager would like to know how sensitive the price of an option is to a change in any one of the factors that affect its price. Let's discuss the sensitivity of a call option's price to changes in the price of the underlying, the time to expiration, and expected price volatility.

The Call Option Price and the Price of the Underlying

A manager employing options for risk management wants to know how the option position will change as the price of the underlying changes. Exhibit 14.6 shows the theoretical price of a call option based on the price of the underlying. The horizontal axis is the price of the underlying at any point in time. The vertical axis is the theoretical call option price. The shape of the curve representing the theoretical price of a call option, given the price of the underlying, would be the same regardless of the actual option pricing model used. In particular, the relationship between the price of the underlying and the theoretical call option price is convex.

EXHIBIT 14.5 Comparison of Black-Scholes Call Option Price Varying One Factor at a Time

Base Case
Call option:
Strike price = $45
Time remaining to expiration = 183 days
Current stock price = $47
Expected price volatility = standard deviation = 25%
Risk-free rate = 10%

Holding All Factors Constant Except Expected Price Volatility

Expected Price Volatility	Call Option Price
15%	4.69
20	5.16
25 (base case)	5.69
30	6.25
35	6.83
40	7.42

Holding All Factors Constant Except the Risk-Free Rate

Risk-Free Interest Rate	Call Option Price
7%	5.27
8	5.41
9	5.55
10 (base case)	5.69
11	5.83
12	5.98
13	6.13

Holding All Factors Constant Except Time Remaining to Expiration

Time Remaining to Expiration	Call Option Price
30 days	2.82
60	3.52
91	4.14
183 (base case)	5.69
273	7.00

EXHIBIT 14.6   Theoretical Call Price and Price of Underlying

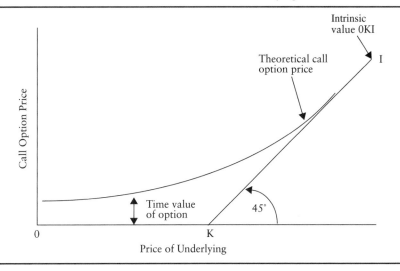

K = Strike price

The line from the origin to the strike price on the horizontal axis in Exhibit 14.6 is the intrinsic value of the call option when the price of the underlying is less than the strike price, since the intrinsic value is zero. The 45-degree line extending from the horizontal axis is the intrinsic value of the call option once the price of the underlying exceeds the strike price. The reason is that the intrinsic value of the call option will increase by the same dollar amount as the increase in the price of the underlying. For example, if the strike price is $100 and the price of the underlying increases from $100 to $101, the intrinsic value will increase by $1. If the price of the underlying increases from $101 to $110, the intrinsic value of the option will increase from $1 to $10. Thus, the slope of the line representing the intrinsic value after the strike price is reached is 1. Since the theoretical call option price is shown by the convex curve, the difference between the theoretical call option price and the intrinsic value at any given price for the underlying is the time value of the option.

Exhibit 14.7 shows the theoretical call option price, but with a tangent line drawn at the price p*. The tangent line in the exhibit can be used to estimate what the new option price will be (and therefore what the change in the option price will be) if the price of the underlying changes. Because of the convexity of the relationship between the option price and the price of the underlying, the tangent line closely approximates the new option price for a small change in the price of the underlying. For large changes, however, the tangent line does not provide as good an approximation of the new option price.

The slope of the tangent line shows how the theoretical call option price will change for small changes in the price of the underlying. The slope of the tangent line is popularly referred to as the *delta* of the option. Specifically,

$$\text{Delta} = \frac{\text{Change in price of call option}}{\text{Change in price of underlying}}$$

For example, a delta of 0.4 means that a \$1 change in the price of the underlying will change the price of the call option by approximately \$0.40.

Exhibit 14.8 shows the curve of the theoretical call option price with three tangent lines drawn. The steeper the slope of the tangent line, the greater the delta. When an option is deep out of the money (that is, the price of the underlying is substantially below the strike price), the tangent line is nearly flat (see line 1 in Exhibit 14.8). This means that delta is close to zero. To understand why, consider a call option with a strike price of \$100 and two months to expiration. If the price of the underlying is \$20, the option price would not increase by much, if anything, should the price of the underlying increase by \$1, from \$20 to \$21.

EXHIBIT 14.7   Estimating the Theoretical Option Price

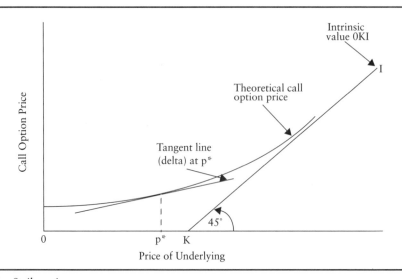

K = Strike price

EXHIBIT 14.8 Theoretical Option Price with Three Tangents

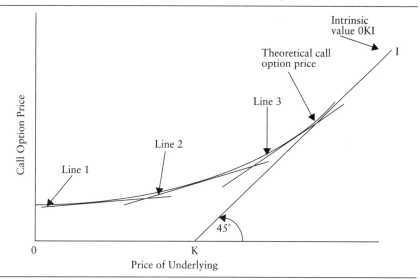

K = Strike price

For a call option that is deep in the money, the delta will be close to 1. That is, the call option price will increase almost dollar for dollar with an increase in the price of the underlying. In Exhibit 14.8, the slope of the tangent line approaches the slope of the intrinsic value line after the strike price. As we stated earlier, the slope of that line is 1.

Thus, the delta for a call option varies from zero (for call options deep out of the money) to 1 (for call options deep in the money). The delta for a call option at the money is approximately 0.5.

The curvature of the convex relationship can also be approximated. This is the rate of change of delta as the price of the underlying changes. The measure is commonly referred to as *gamma* and is defined as follows:

$$\text{Gamma} = \frac{\text{Change in delta}}{\text{Change in price of underlying}}$$

The Call Option Price and Time to Expiration All other factors constant, the longer the time to expiration, the greater the option price. Since each day the option moves closer to the expiration date, the time to expiration decreases. The *theta* of an option measures the change in the option price as the time to expiration decreases, or equivalently, it is a measure of time decay. Theta is measured as follows:

$$\text{Theta} = \frac{\text{Change in price of option}}{\text{Decrease in time to expiration}}$$

Assuming that the price of the underlying does not change (which means that the intrinsic value of the option does not change), theta measures how quickly the time value of the option changes as the option moves toward expiration. Buyers of options prefer a low theta so that the option price does not decline quickly as it moves toward the expiration date. An option writer benefits from an option that has a high theta.

The Call Option Price and Expected Price Volatility   All other factors constant, a change in the expected price volatility will change the option price. The vega (also called kappa) of an option measures the dollar price change in the price of the option for a 1% change in the expected price volatility. That is,

$$\text{Vega} = \frac{\text{Change in option price}}{1\% \text{ change in expected price volatility}}$$

FUTURES CONTRACTS

A *futures contract* is an agreement between two parties, a buyer and a seller, where the parties agree to transact with respect to the underlying at a predetermined price at a specified date. Both parties are obligated to perform over the life of the contract, and neither party charges a fee. Once the two parties have consummated the trade, the exchange where the futures contract is traded becomes the counterparty to the trade, thereby severing the relationship between the initial parties.

Each futures contract is accompanied by an exact description of the terms of the contract, including a description of the underlying, the contract size, settlement cycles, trading specifications, and position limits. The fact is that in the case of futures contracts, delivery is not the objective of either party because the contracts are used primarily to manage risk or costs.

The nature of the futures contract specifies a buyer and a seller who agree to buy or sell a standard quantity of the underlying at a designated future date. However, when we speak of buyers and sellers, we are simply adopting the language of the futures market, which refers to parties of the contract in terms of the future obligation they are committing themselves to. The buyer of a futures contract agrees to take delivery of the underlying and is said to be *long futures*. Long futures positions benefit when the price of the underlying rises. Since futures can be considered a substitute for a subsequent transaction in the cash market, a long futures position is comparable to holding the underlying without the financial cost of purchasing the underlying or the income that comes from holding the underlying. The seller, on the other hand, is said to be *short futures* and benefits when the price of the underlying declines.

The designated price at which the parties agree to transact is called the *futures price*. The designated date at which the parties must transact is the *settlement date* or *delivery date*. Unlike options, no money changes hands between buyer and seller at the contract's inception. However, the futures broker and the futures exchange require initial margin as a "good faith" deposit. In addition, a minimum amount of funds referred to as *maintenance margin* is required to be maintained in the corresponding futures account. The initial margin and the maintenance margin can be held in the form of short-term credit instruments.

Futures are marked-to-the-market on a daily basis. This means that daily gains or losses in the investor's position are accounted for immediately and reflected in his or her account. The daily cash flow from a futures position is called *variation margin* and essentially means that the futures contract is settled daily. Thus, the buyer of the futures contract pays when the price of the underlying falls and the seller pays when the price of the underlying rises. Variation margin differs from other forms of margin because outflows must be met with cash.

Futures contracts have a settlement cycle and there may be several contracts trading simultaneously. The contract with the closest settlement is call the *nearby futures contract* and is usually the most liquid. The next futures contract is the one that settles just after the near contract. The contract with the furthest away settlement is called the *most distant futures contract*.

Differences between Options and Futures

The fundamental difference between futures and options is that buyer of an option (the long position) has the right but not the obligation to enter into a transaction. The option writer is obligated to transact if the buyer so desires. In contrast, both parties are obligated to perform in the case of a futures contract. In addition, to establish a position, the party who is long futures does not pay the party who is short futures. In contrast, the party long an option must make a payment to the party who is short the option in order to establish the position. The price paid is the option price.

The payout structure also differs between a futures contract and an options contract. The price of an option contract represents the cost of eliminating or modifying the risk/reward relationship of the underlying. In contrast, the payout for a futures contract is a dollar-for-dollar gain or loss for the buyer and seller. When the futures price rises, the buyer gains at the expense of the seller, while the buyer suffers a dollar-for-dollar loss when the futures price drops.

Thus, futures payout is symmetrical, while the payout for options is skewed. The maximum loss for the option buyer is the option price. The loss to the futures buyer is the full value of the contract. The option buyer has limited downside losses but retains the benefits of an increase in the value in the position of the underlying. The maximum profit that can be realized by the option writer is the option price, which is offset by significant downside exposure. The losses or gains to the buyer and seller of a futures contract are completely symmetrical. Consequently, futures can be used as a hedge against symmetric risk, while options can be used to hedge asymmetric risk.

Features of Futures

The key elements of a futures contract include the futures price, the amount or quantity of the underlying, and the settlement or delivery date.

Stock Index Futures

The underlying asset of a stock index futures contract is the portfolio of stocks represented by the index.

The value of the underlying portfolio is the value of the index in a specified currency times a number called a *multiplier*. For example, if the current value of the S&P 500 index is 1100, then the seller of a December S&P 500 futures contract is theoretically obligated to deliver in December a portfolio of the 500 stocks that comprise the index. The multiplier for this contract is 500. The portfolio would have to exactly replicate the index with the weights of the stocks equal to their index weights. The current value of one futures contract is $275,000 (= 1100 × 250).

However, because of the problems associated with delivering a portfolio of 500 stocks that exactly replicate the underlying index, stock index futures substitute cash delivery for physical delivery. At final settlement, the futures price equals the spot price and the value of a futures contract is the actual market value of the underlying replicating portfolio that represents the stock index. The contract is marked-to-market based on the settlement price, which is the spot price, and the contract settles.

Exhibit 14.9 provides a list of selected stock index futures traded in the United States.

EXHIBIT 14.9   Selected Equity Futures Contracts Traded in the United States

Index Futures Contract	Index Description	Exchange	Contract Size
Standard & Poor's 500	500 stocks, Cap weighed	CME	Index × $250
Standard & Poor's Mid Cap	400 stocks, Cap weighted	CME	Index × $500
Russell 2000 Index	2000 stocks, Cap weighted	CME	Index × $500
Nikkei 225 Index	225 stocks, Price weighted	CME	Index × $5
Major Market Index	20 stocks, Price weighted	CME	Index × $500
S&P 500/BARRA Growth Index	100+ stocks, Cap weighted	CME	Index × $250
Standard & Poor's BARRA Value	300+ stocks, Cap weighted	CME	Index × $250
NASDAQ 100 Index	100 stocks, Cap weighted	CME	Index × $100
IPC Stock Index	35 stocks, Cap weighted	CME	Futures × $25
NYSE Composite Index	2600+ stocks, Cap weighted	NYFE	Index × $500

Single Stock Futures

A single stock futures (SSF) contract is an agreement between two parties to buy or sell shares of individual companies (as opposed to a stock index in the case of a stock index futures contract) at some time in the future with the terms agreed upon today. The value of traditional futures contracts is captured by SSFs as well because the agreement requires a low capital commitment upfront in the form of initial margin. Two key benefits to investors are that shorting is not constrained by the up tick rule (see Chapter 6) or complicated by stock loans and a simple long or short strategy in the underlying stock can be created.

SSFs currently trade on numerous exchanges around the world including those in Australia, Denmark, Finland, Hong Kong, Hungary, Portugal, South Africa, Sweden, and, most recently, Canada and the UK. As of this writing, there has been modest success for these products. In January 2001 the London International Financial Futures Exchange (LIFFE) introduced SSFs on 30 stocks including seven U.S. companies and the Bourse de Montreal began trading a SSF contract on Nortel Networks. In May, LIFFE expanded the number by 25 contracts to a total of 65 listed SSF contracts on global stocks.

The importance of the LIFFE development is that it is the first time SSFs have been listed on a major global exchange. The contracts are referred to as Universal Stock Futures (USF) and are standardized futures contracts based on shares of European and U.S. companies. In May 2001, Nasdaq and LIFFE announced a partnership, Nasdaq Life Markets LLC, to offer SSF contracts on global stocks.[5]

The standardized features of the contracts for the Nasdaq LIFFE market and the emerging U.S. market include a contract size of 100 shares with quotes in dollars or euros. The minimum tick increment is $0.01 per share or $1 dollar per contract. Settlement calls for the physical delivery of 100 shares (adjusted for corporate events). There is no daily price limits imposed on the contracts, but a position limit of 1,000 contracts or the equivalent to 100,000 shares of the underlying common stock or American Depository Receipt (ADR).

Pricing Stock Index Futures

Futures contracts are priced based on the spot price and cost of carry considerations. For equity contracts these include the cost of financing a position in the underlying asset, the dividend yield on the underlying stocks, and the time to settlement of the futures contract. The theoretical futures price is derived from the spot price adjusted for the cost of carry. This can be confirmed using risk-free arbitrage arguments.

The logic of the pricing model is that the purchase of a futures contract can be looked at as a temporary substitute for a transaction in the cash market at a later date. Moreover, futures contracts are not assets to be purchased and no money changes hands when the agreement is made. Futures contracts are agreements between two parties that establish the terms of a later transaction. It is these facts that lead us to a pricing relationship between futures contracts and the underlying. The seller of a futures contract is ultimately responsible for delivering the underlying and will demand compensation for incurring the cost of holding it. Thus, the futures price will reflect the cost of financing the underlying. However, the buyer of the futures contract does not hold the underlying and therefore does not receive the dividend. The futures price must be adjusted downward to take this into consideration. The adjustment of the yield for the cost of financing is what is called the *net cost of carry*. The futures price is then based on the net cost of carry, which is the cost of financing adjusted for the yield on the underlying. That is,

$$\text{Futures price} = \text{Spot price} + \text{Cost of financing} - \text{Dividend yield}$$

---

[5] More information about these contracts can be found at their websites: www.liffe.com and www.nqlx.com.

The borrowing or financing rate is an interest rate on a money market instrument and the yield in the case of equity futures is the dividend yield on an individual stock or a portfolio of stocks that represent the stock index. The theoretical futures price derived from this process is a model of the fair value of the futures contract. It is the price that defines a no-arbitrage condition. The no-arbitrage condition is the futures price at which sellers are prepared to sell and buyers are prepared to buy, but no risk-free profit is possible.

The theoretical futures price expressed mathematically depends on the treatment of dividends. For individual equities with quarterly dividend payout, the theoretical futures price can be expressed as the spot price adjusted for the present value of expected dividends over the life of the contract and the cost of financing. The expression is given below as:

$$F(t,T) = [S(t) - D] \times [1 + R(t,T)]$$

where

$F(t,T)$ = futures price at time t for a contract that settles in the future at time T

$S(t)$ = current spot price

D = present value of dividends expected to be received over the life of the contract

$R(t,T)$ = borrowing rate for a loan with the same time to maturity as the futures settlement date

For example, if the current price of the S&P 500 stock index is 1175, the borrowing rate is 6%, the time to settlement is 60 days, and the index is expected to yield 2.071%. An annualized dividend yield of 2.071% corresponds to 4 index points when the S&P 500 stock index is 1175:

$$1175 \times [0.02071 \times (60/365)] = 4 \text{ index points}$$

The theoretical futures price can be calculated as follows:

$$D = 4/(1 + 0.06)^{60/365} = 3.96$$

$$R = (1 + 0.06)^{60/365} - 1 = 0.009624 \text{ or } 0.9624\%$$

$$F(t,60) = [1175 - 3.96] \times 1.009624 = 1182.31$$

If the actual futures price is above or below 1182.31, then risk-free arbitrage is possible. For actual futures prices greater than fair value, the futures contract is overvalued. Arbitrageurs will sell the futures contract, borrow enough funds to purchase the underlying stock index, and hold the position until fair value is restored or until the settlement date of the futures contract.

If, for example, we assume the actual futures price is 1188, then the following positions would lead to risk-free arbitrage:

- Sell the overvalued futures at 1188.
- Borrow an amount equivalent to 1175.
- Purchase a stock portfolio that replicates the index for the equivalent of 1175.

The position can be unwound at the settlement date in 60 days at no risk to the arbitrageur. At the settlement date, the futures settlement price equals the spot price. Assume the spot price is unchanged at 1175. Then,

- Collect 4 in dividends.
- Settle the short futures position by delivering the index to the buyer for 1175.
- Repay 1186.31 (1175 × 1.009624) to satisfy the loan (remember the interest rate for the 60 days is 0.9624%).

The net gain is [1188 + 4] − 1186.31 = 5.69. That is, the arbitrageur "earned" 5.69 index points or 48 basis points (5.69/1175) without risk or without making any investment. This activity would continue until the price of the futures converged on fair value.

It does not matter what the settlement price for the index is at the settlement date. This can be clearly shown by treating the futures position and stock position separately. The futures position delivers the difference between the original futures price and the settlement price or 1188 − 1175, which equals 13 index points. The long stock position earned only the dividends and no capital gain. The cost of financing the position in the stock is 11.31 and the net return to the combined short futures and long stock position is 13(futures) + 4(stock) less the 11.31 cost of financing, which is a net return of 5.69. Now consider what happens if the spot price is at any other level at the settlement date. Exhibit 14.10 shows the cash flows associated with the arbitrage. We can see from the results that regardless of the movement of the spot price, the arbitrage profit is preserved.

For actual futures prices less than fair value, the futures contract is undervalued. Arbitrageurs will buy the futures contract, short or sell the underlying, lend the proceeds, and hold the position until fair value is restored or until settlement date of the futures contract. If, for example, we assume the actual futures price is 1180, then the following positions would lead to risk-free arbitrage:

■ Buy the undervalued futures at 1180.
■ Sell or short the stock index at 1175 and collect the proceeds.
■ Lend the proceeds from the stock transaction at 6%.

Once again the position can be unwound at the settlement date at no risk to the arbitrageur. At that time the futures settlement price equals the spot price. Regardless of the settlement price of the index, the arbitrage is preserved in this case as well. Exhibit 14.10 presents a sample of settlement price outcomes. The following process applies to the arbitrage regardless of the direction of the stock market:

■ Settle the short stock position by taking futures delivery of the stock index.
■ Pay the 4 index points in dividends due the index.
■ Receive the proceeds from the loan (remember the term interest rate is 0.9624%).

EXHIBIT 14.10   Arbitrage Cash Flows
Overvalued Futures[a]

Futures Stock Index Settlement Price	Futures Cash Flows	Stock Cash Flows	Costs	Profit
1200	1188 − 1200 = −12	25 + 4 = 29	11.31	5.69
1190	1188 − 1190 = −2	15 + 4 = 19	11.31	5.69
1188	1188 − 1188 = 0	13 + 4 = 17	11.31	5.69
1180	1188 − 1180 = 8	5 + 4 = 9	11.31	5.69
1175	1188 − 1175 = 13	0 + 4 = 4	11.31	5.69
1160	1188 − 1160 = 28	−15 + 4 = −11	11.31	5.69

[a] Short futures at 1188

Undervalued Futures[a]

Futures Stock Index Settlement Price	Futures Cash Flows	Stock Cash Flows	Interest Income	Profit
1200	1200 − 1180 = 20	−25 − 4 = −29	11.31	2.31
1190	1190 − 1180 = 10	−15 − 4 = −19	11.31	2.31
1188	1188 − 1180 = 8	−13 − 4 = −17	11.31	2.31
1180	1180 − 1180 = 0	−5 − 4 = −9	11.31	2.31
1175	1175 − 1180 = −5	0 − 4 = −4	11.31	2.31
1160	1160 − 1180 = −20	15 − 4 = 11	11.31	2.31

[a] Buy futures at 1180

In this example, the arbitrageur "earned" 20 basis points (2.31/1175) or 2.31 index points without risk or without making any investment. This activity would continue until the price of the futures converged on fair value.

The theoretical futures price can also be expressed mathematically based on a security with a known dividend yield. For equities that pay out a constant dividend over the life of a futures contract, this rendition of the model is appropriate. This may apply to stock index futures contracts where the underlying is an equity index of a large number of stocks. Rather than calculating every dividend, the cumulative dividend pay out or the weighted-average dividend produces a constant and known dividend yield. The cost of carry valuation model is modified to reflect the behavior of dividends. This is expressed in the following equation:

$$F(t,T) = S(t) \times [1 + R(t,T) - Y(t,T)]$$

where $Y(t,T)$ is the dividend yield on the underlying over the life of the futures contract and $F(t,T)$, $S(t)$, and $R(t,T)$ are as defined earlier.

For example, if the current price of a stock is 1175, the borrowing rate is 6%, the time to settlement is 60 days, and the annualized dividend yield is 1.38%, the theoretical futures price can be calculated as follows:

$$Y = (1 + 0.0138)^{60/365} - 1 = 0.002256 \text{ or } 0.2256\%$$

$$R = (1 + 0.06)^{60/365} - 1 = 0.009624 \text{ or } 0.9624\%$$

$$F(t,60) = 1175 \times [1 + (0.009624 - 0.002256] = 1183.66$$

In practice, it is important to remember to use the borrowing rate and dividend yield for the term of the contract and not the annual rates. The arbitrage conditions outlined above still hold in this case. The model is specified differently, but the same outcome is possible. When the actual futures price deviates from the theoretical price suggested by the futures pricing model, arbitrage would be possible and likely. The existence of risk-free arbitrage profits will attract arbitrageurs.

In practice, there are several factors that may violate the assumptions of the futures valuation model. Because of these factors, arbitrage must be carried out with some degree of uncertainty and the fair value futures price is not a single price, but actually a range of prices where the upper and lower prices act as boundaries around an arbitrage-free zone. Furthermore, the violation of various assumptions can produce mispricing and risk that reduce arbitrage opportunities.

The futures price ought to gravitate toward fair value when there is a viable and active arbitrage mechanism. Arbitrage activity will only take place beyond the upper and lower limits established by transaction and other costs, uncertain cash flows, and divergent borrowing and lending rates among participants. The variability of the spread between the spot price and futures price, known as the *basis*, is a consequence of mispricing due to changes in the variables that influence the fair value.

The practical aspects of pricing produce a range of prices. This means that the basis can move around without offering a profit motive for arbitrageurs. The perspective of arbitrageurs in the equity futures markets is based on dollar profit but can be viewed in terms of an interest rate. The borrowing or financing rate found in the cost of carry valuation formula assumes borrowing and lending rates are the same. In practice, however, borrowing rates are almost always higher than lending rates. Thus, the model will yield different values depending on the respective borrowing and lending rates facing the user. Every futures price corresponds to an interest rate. We can manipulate the formula and solve for the rate implied by the futures price, which is called the *implied futures rate*. For each market participant there is a theoretical fair value range defined by its respective borrowing and lending rates and transaction costs.

OTC EQUITY DERIVATIVES

An OTC equity derivative can be delivered on a stand-alone basis or as part of a structured product. Structured products involve packaging standard or exotic options, equity swaps, or equity-linked debt into a single product in any combination to meet the risk/return objectives of the investor and may represent an alternative to the cash market even when cash instruments are available.

The three basic components of OTC equity derivatives are OTC options, equity swaps, and equity-linked debt. These components offer an array of product structures that can assist investors in developing and implementing investment strategies that respond to a changing financial world. The rapidly changing investment climate has fundamentally changed investor attitudes toward the use of derivative products. It is no longer a question of what can an investor gain from the use of OTC derivatives, but how much is sacrificed by avoiding this marketplace. OTC derivatives can assist the investor with cost minimization, diversification, hedging, asset allocation, and risk management.

Before we provide a product overview, let's look at counterparty risk. For exchange listed derivative products counterparty or credit risk is minimal because of the clearing house associated with the exchange. However, for OTC products there is counterparty risk. For parties taking a position where performance of both parties is required, both parties are exposed to counterparty risk. The OTC market has incorporated a variety of terms into the contractual agreement between counterparties to address the issue of credit risk. These include netting arrangements, position limits, the use of collateral, recouponing, credit triggers, and the establishment of Derivatives Product Companies (DPCs).

Netting arrangements between counterparties are used in master agreements specifying that in the event of default, the bottom line is the net payment owed across all contractual agreements between the two counterparties. *Position limits* may be imposed on a particular counterparty according to the cumulative nature of their positions and creditworthiness. As the OTC market has grown, the creditworthiness of customers has become more diverse. Consequently, dealers are requiring some counterparties to furnish collateral in the form of a liquid short-term credit instrument. *Recouponing* involves periodically changing the coupon such that the marked-to-market value of the position is zero. For long-term OTC agreements, a *credit trigger provision* allows the dealer to have the position cash settled if the counterparty's credit rating falls below investment grade. Finally, dealers are establishing DPCs as separate business entities to maintain high credit ratings that are crucial in competitively pricing OTC products.

OTC Options

OTC options can be classified as first generation and second generation options. The latter are called *exotic options*. We describe each type of OTC option below.

First Generation of OTC Options

The basic type of first generation OTC options either extends the standardized structure of an existing listed option or created an option on stocks, stock baskets, or stock indexes without listed options or futures. Thus, OTC options were first used to modify one or more of the features of listed options: the strike price, maturity, size, exercise type (American or European), and delivery mechanism. The terms were tailored to the specific needs of the investor. For example, the strike price can be any level, the maturity date at any time, the contract of any size, the exercise type American or European, the underlying can be a stock, a stock portfolio, or an equity index or a foreign equity index, and the settlement can be physical, in cash or a combination.

An example of how OTC options can differ from listed options is exemplified by an Asian option. Listed options are either European or American in structure relating to the timing of exercise. Asian options are options with a payout that is dependent on the average price of the spot price over the life of the option. Due to the averaging process involved, the volatility of the spot price is reduced. Thus, Asian options are cheaper than similar European or American options.

The first generation of OTC options offered flexible solutions to investment situations that listed options did not. For example, hedging strategies using the OTC market allow the investor to achieve customized total risk protection for a specific time horizon. The first generation of OTC options allow investors to fine tune their traditional equity investment strategies through customizing strike prices, and maturities, and choosing any underlying equity security or portfolio of securities. Investors could now improve the management of risk through customized hedging strategies or enhance returns through customized buy writes. In addition, investors could invest in foreign stocks without the need to own them, profit from an industry downturn without the need to short stocks.

Exotics: Second Generation OTC Options

The second generation of OTC equity options includes a set of products that have more complex payoff characteristics than standard American or European call and put options. These second-generation options are sometimes referred to as "exotic" options and are essentially options with specific rules that govern the payoff.[6] Exotic option structures can be created on a stand-alone basis or as part of a broader financing package such as an attachment to a bond issue.

Some OTC option structures are path dependent, which means that the value of the option to some extent depends on the price pattern of the underlying asset over the life of the option. In fact, the survival of some options, such as barrier options, depends on this price pattern. Other examples of path dependent options include Asian options, lookback options, and reset options. Another group of OTC option structures has properties similar to step functions. They have fixed singular payoffs when a particular condition is met. Examples of this include digital or binary options and contingent options. A third group of options is classified as multivariate because the payoff is related to more than one underlying asset. Examples of this group include a general category of rainbow options such as spread options and basket options.

---

[6] For a description of exotic options, see Chapter 10 in Bruce M. Collins and Frank J. Fabozzi, *Derivatives and Equity Portfolio Management* (New Hope, PA: Frank J. Fabozzi Associates, 1999).

Competitive market makers are now prepared to offer investors a broad range of derivative products that satisfy the specific requirements of investors. The fastest growing portion of this market pertaining to equities involves products with option-like characteristics on major stock indexes or stock portfolios.

Equity Swaps

Equity swaps are agreements between two counterparties which provide for the periodic exchange of a schedule of cash flows over a specified time period where at least one of the two payments is linked to the performance of an equity index, a basket of stocks, or a single stock. In a standard or plain vanilla equity swap one counterparty agrees to pay the other the total return to an equity index in exchange for receiving either the total return of another asset or a fixed or floating interest rate. All payments are based on a fixed notional amount and payments are made over a fixed time period.

Equity swap structures are very flexible with maturities ranging from a few months to 10 years. The returns of virtually any asset can be swapped for another without incurring the costs associated with a transaction in the cash market. Payment schedules can be denominated in any currency irrespective of the equity asset and payments can be exchanged monthly, quarterly, annually, or at maturity. The equity asset can be any equity index or portfolio of stocks, and denominated in any currency, hedged or unhedged.

Variations of the plain vanilla equity swap include: international equity swaps where the equity return is linked to an international equity index; currency-hedged swaps where the swap is structured to eliminate currency risk; and call swaps where the equity payment is paid only if the equity index appreciates (depreciation will not result in a payment from the counterparty receiving the equity return to the other counterparty because of call protection).

A basic swap structure is illustrated in Exhibit 14.11. In this case, the investor owns a short-term credit instrument that yields LIBOR plus a spread. The investor then enters into a swap to exchange LIBOR plus the spread for the total return to an equity index. The counterparty pays the total return to the index in exchange for LIBOR plus a spread. Assuming the equity index is the Nikkei 225, a U.S. investor could swap dollar-denominated LIBOR plus a spread for cash flows from the total return to the Nikkei denominated in yen or U.S. dollars. The index could be any foreign or domestic equity index. A swap could also be structured to generate superior returns if the financing instrument in the swap yields a higher return than LIBOR.

EXHIBIT 14.11 Equity Swaps

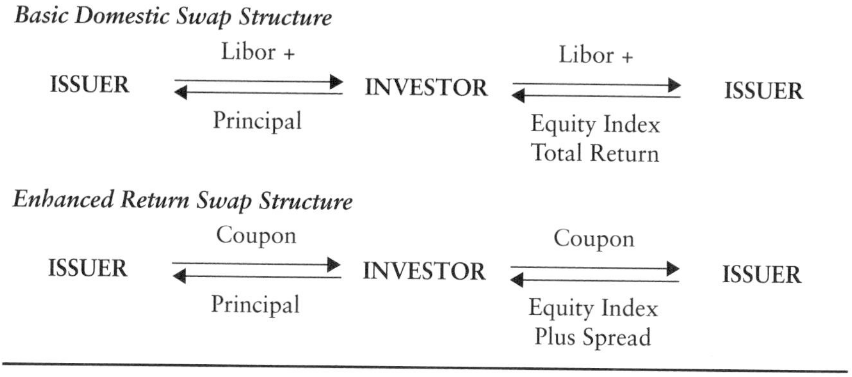

Equity swaps have a wide variety of applications including asset allocation, accessing international markets, enhancing equity returns, hedging equity exposure, and synthetically shorting stocks.

An example of an equity swap is a 1-year agreement where the counterparty agrees to pay the investor the total return to the S&P 500 Index in exchange for dollar-denominated LIBOR on a quarterly basis. The investor would pay LIBOR plus a spread × 91/360 × notional amount. This type of equity swap is the economic equivalent of financing a long position in the S&P 500 Index at a spread to LIBOR. The advantages of using the swap are no transaction costs, no sales or dividend withholding tax, and no tracking error or basis risk versus the index.

The basic mechanics of equity swaps are the same regardless of the structure. However, the rules governing the exchange of payments may differ. For example, a U.S. investor wanting to diversify internationally can enter into a swap and, depending on the investment objective, exchange payments on a currency-hedged basis. If the investment objective is to reduce U.S. equity exposure and increase Japanese equity exposure, for example, a swap could be structured to exchange the total returns to the S&P 500 Index for the total returns to the Nikkei 225 Index. If, however, the investment objective is to gain access to the Japanese equity market, a swap can be structured to exchange LIBOR plus a spread for the total returns to the Nikkei 225 Index. This is an example of diversifying internationally and the cash flows can be denominated in either yen or dollars. The advantages of entering into an equity swap to obtain international diversification are that the investor exposure is devoid of tracking error, and the investor incurs no sales tax, custodial fees, withholding fees, or market impact associated with entering and exiting a market. This swap is the economic equivalent of being long the Nikkei 225 financed at a spread to LIBOR at a fixed exchange rate.

CHAPTER 15

Equity Derivatives II: Portfolio Management Applications

Bruce M.Collins, Ph.D.
CEO
QuantCast LLC

Frank J. Fabozzi, Ph.D., CFA
Adjunct Professor of Finance
School of Management
Yale University

In the previous chapter we described the basic characteristics of the different types of equity derivatives. We identified four primary roles for derivatives: (1) to modify the risk characteristics of an investment portfolio; (2) to enhance the expected return of a portfolio; (3) to reduce transaction costs associated with managing a portfolio; and, (4) to circumvent regulatory obstacles. In this chapter, we will discuss several basic applications of these instruments to equity portfolio management. In addition, because options will change the risk reward characteristics of an investment portfolio, we provide an overview of the relationship between expected returns and risk for strategies employing options.

While forward and futures contracts are time dependent linear derivatives with similar payouts and risk characteristics as the underlying, options are non-linear derivatives that have fundamentally different risk characteristics than the underlying asset. The real value of options in portfolio management regardless of the motivation for their use is that they allow the investor a means of modifying the risk and return characteristics of their investment portfolio. The impact of adding options to an existing portfolio or using options as an investment vehicle is to create skewed distributions that reflect different risks than an investment in the underlying asset.[1] For example, the purchase of a call option rather than a stock changes the payout profile of the investment by capping the losses and thus truncates the probability distribution associated with possible outcomes and necessarily changes the expected return and risk of the investment.[2]

PORTFOLIO APPLICATIONS OF LISTED OPTIONS

Investors can use the listed options market to address a range of investment problems. We'll discuss the use of OTC options later. Advantages of listed options relative to OTC options are that they provide accurate and consistent information about pricing and virtually eliminate credit risk. Moreover, because of these characteristics and the standardization of products, listed options often have low transaction costs and moderate to high liquidity. The issue of transaction costs and liquidity can play an important role in the decision to use derivatives as part of the investment process.

Risk Management Strategies

Risk management in the context of equity portfolio management focuses on price risk. Consequently, the strategies discussed here in some way address the risk of a price decline or a loss due to adverse price movement.

---

[1] The use of options can create so-called "fat tails" in the returns distribution because volatility changes. Options also create an asymmetric or skewed distribution to reflect their contingent payout pattern. The extent of the skewness depends on the option. In addition, the degree of the volatility affects the peakedness or kurtosis of the distribution as well. High volatility conditions, for example, correspond to distributions with thicker tails and low volatility conditions correspond to distributions with higher peaks. For a discussion of these issues see Nassim Taleb, *Dynamic Hedging* (New York: John Wiley & Sons, 1997).

[2] The probability distribution for an option is not normally distributed as the underlying is assumed to be in Black-Scholes option pricing model. However, even in the case when returns are not normally distributed, it is still true that the expected returns and variance of the portfolio can be calculated. The normal distribution assumption of Black-Scholes models allows the mapping to a skewed distribution. The expected returns can be estimated directly from a Taylor expansion, through the use of a factor model (as we do later in the chapter based on CAPM) or through the use of Monte Carlo simulation to generate the probability distribution for the option price.

Options can be used to create asymmetric risk exposures across all or part of the core equity portfolio. This allows the investor to hedge downside risk at a fixed cost with a specific limit to losses should the market turn down.

The most common strategy for risk management is a *protective put buying strategy.* This strategy is used by investors who currently hold a long position in the underlying security or investors who desire upside exposure and downside protection. The motivation is either to hedge some or all of the total risk. Index put options hedge mostly market risk, while put options on an individual stock hedge the total risk associated with a specific stock. This allows portfolio managers to use protective put strategies for separating tactical and strategic strategies. Consider, for example, a manager who is concerned about non-financial events increasing the level of risk in the marketplace. Furthermore, assume the manager is satisfied with the core portfolio holdings and the strategic mix. Put options could be employed as a tactical risk reduction strategy designed to preserve capital and still maintain strategic targets for portfolio returns.

Thus, any investor concerned about downside risk is a candidate for a protective put strategy. Nonetheless, protective put strategies may not be suitable for all investors. The value of protective put strategies, however, is that they provide the investor with the ability to invest in volatile stocks with a degree of desired insurance and unlimited profit potential over the life of the strategy.

The protective put involves the purchase of a put option combined with a long stock position. The put option is comparable to an insurance policy written against the long stock position. The option price is the cost of the insurance premium and the amount the option is out-of-the-money is the deductible. Just as in the case of insurance, the deductible is inversely related to the insurance premium. The deductible is reduced as the strike price increases, which makes the put option more in-the-money or less out-of-the-money. The higher strike price causes the put price to increase and makes the insurance policy more expensive.

Cost Management Strategies

Options can be used to manage the cost of maintaining an equity portfolio in a number of ways. Among the strategies are the use of short put and short call positions to serve as a substitute for a limit order in the cash market. Cash-secured put strategies can be used to purchase stocks at the target price, while covered calls or overwrites can be used to sell stocks at the target price. The target price is the one consistent with the portfolio manager's valuation or technical models and the price intended to produce the desired rate of return.

In addition, synthetic strategies may allow the investor to implement a position at a lower cost than a direct investment in the cash market. For example, foreign investors subject to dividend withholding taxes may find a synthetic long stock position using options an attractive alternative to the cash investment. Moreover, there is always an alternative method of creating a position. Synthetic calls, for example, can be created by borrowing, investing in stock, and buying put options. Likewise, a synthetic protective put strategy can be established by buying call options and discount bonds.

Cash-Secured Put

The motivation behind a *cash-secured put strategy* is to reduce market impact costs associated with the purchase of a stock. The strategy can be used by managers to transact in the cash market without bearing the total cost of the perceived risk to the seller. The demand for the stock may bid up the price of the security regardless of the motivation behind the trade. If, for example, the manager believes that the stock is attractive at or below a particular price, a cash-secured put can be established using a strike price consistent with the target price. If the purchase is not motivated by firm-specific information, but is strategic in nature, part of a passive rebalancing, or based on relative valuation models, then using an option mechanism to purchase the stock may make sense.

The strategy is similar to a limit order in the cash market with two notable differences. First, the option approach pays the buyer a premium, while no such premium exists for a limit order. Second, the limit order can be ended at any time, while the option is only extant over the life of the contract.

A cash market transaction may bid up the price of the stock because sellers believe the trade is motivated by new information. The use of short put options is a means to convey the intent of the buyer. The put seller indicates to the market a willingness to accept the downside risk of a further stock price decline. Consequently, this makes it clear to the market that the interested party does not expect an immediate increase in the stock price. This may reduce the immediacy cost of market impact.

Thus, the short put mechanism of purchasing stock may be appropriate for managers with strategic interest in the stock, but no compelling need for immediate execution. The short put premium provides some downside cushion, which further reduces the effective cost of the stock. If the stock rises over the life of the option and the put expires worthless, then an overvalued stock has become more overvalued. If, on the other hand, the manager wants to own the stock immediately, then a put option strategy is not appropriate.

Naked Calls

Similarly, short calls can be used as a mechanism for selling current holdings at a price consistent with the rate of return objective of the manager. The intention is twofold: (1) to reduce market impact costs and (2) to receive a favorable price for selling the stock shares.

Consider a manager who currently holds a number of stocks based on a quantitative valuation model. The model has created a sell price for each holding based on the investment horizon under consideration. The alternative methods for selling a substantial holding are to work it upstairs through a broker/dealer or establish a short call position with a strike price consistent with investment objectives. The disadvantage of a sizable cash market transaction is that the buyer will interpret the sale as information motivated and adjust the price accordingly. This could result in a meaningful decline in price and lower the return contribution of the stock to the overall portfolio.

A naked call can be written with a strike price as a substitute for a limit order. The investor selling the stock is conveying a clearer message to the market regarding intent. The stock is being sold for reasons other than the possession of adverse information regarding the company's future. The seller's intent is clearer for more aggressive OTM strike prices because it requires a rise in price for exercise. The effect of the overwrite position on portfolio performance is positive for neutral to slightly rising markets and negative for declining markets. The trade will undoubtedly incur transaction costs of some kind in either market. However, the prudent use of options is a useful way to be more specific about the motivation behind the trade.

Return Enhancement Strategies

The most popular return enhancement strategies employing listed options are *covered call strategies*. If the investor currently owns the stock and writes a call on that stock, the strategy has been referred to as an "overwrite." If the strategy is implemented all at once (simultaneously buying the stock and selling the call), it is referred to as a "buy write." The essence of the covered call is to trade price appreciation for income. The strategy is appropriate for slightly bullish investors who don't expect much out of the stock and want to produce additional income. These are investors who are willing either to limit upside appreciation for limited downside protection or to manage the costs of selling the underlying stock. The primary motive is to generate additional income from owning the stock.

Although the call premium provides some limited downside protection, this is not an insurance strategy because it has significant downside risk. Consequently, investors should proceed with caution when considering a covered call strategy.

A covered call is less risky than buying the stock because the call premium lowers the break-even recovery price. The strategy behaves like a long stock position when the stock price is below the strike price. On the other hand, the strategy is insensitive to stock prices above the strike price and is therefore capped on the upside. The maximum profit is given by the call premium and the OTM amount of the call option.

Regulatory Issues

The regulation of derivatives markets and equity markets is quite extensive in the United States. The Securities and Exchange Commission (SEC) is the primary regulator of equity markets and option markets. One focus of the SEC is to protect the investor by making certain that brokers identify the suitability of the investor for trading in options. This has mostly been a problem for smaller investors and not for institutional investors. However, numerous institutional inventors are still subject to a variety of antiquated restrictions that prohibit such investment management choices as short selling. Options can be used to establish a synthetic short position held in lieu of a short position in the cash market. In addition, options can be useful to foreign investors subject to local tax consequences by avoiding a cash market transaction.

PORTFOLIO APPLICATIONS OF STOCK INDEX FUTURES

Now let's look at how stock index futures can work with equity investment strategies. Our focus is on how stock index futures can be used to manage all types of equity strategies more efficiently. We begin by examining how futures can help change equity exposure in order to achieve the desired level of exposure at the lowest possible cost. The two strategies examined are hedging strategies (a special case of risk management) and asset allocation strategies.

Stock index futures contracts are often ideal instruments for managing equity exposure due to their liquidity, flexibility, and low transaction costs. An equity position of comparable dollar value can be managed in the stock index futures market at a fraction of the cost in the cash market. The futures market is also an alternative means of implementing an investment strategy to the cash market.

The choice of whether to use the cash market or the futures market to alter equity exposure depends on the objectives of the manager and the size of the equity exposure. Despite apparent cost advantages, there are limits to the amount of stock index futures available to large institutional investors such as pension funds due to regulatory, size, and liquidity constraints. Nonetheless, stock index futures can still be an effective and valuable tool for portfolio management.

The motivation behind the choice to change equity exposure is important in deciding between the cash market or the stock index futures market. If the decision is a strategic asset allocation decision then it can be viewed as long term. If, on the other hand, the decision is tactical, it is a short-term situation. Stock index futures allow managers to quickly adjust imbalances in their asset allocation positions effectively without the need to purchase individual stocks. This effectively allows portfolio managers to increase or decrease equity exposure without altering the status of their core portfolio or disturbing their long-term investment objectives.

The appropriate way to analyze the cash and futures alternatives is to compare the costs of the two transactions.

Hedging Market Risk

Since stock index futures were first introduced, the most common application is to hedge market risk. Hedging involves the transfer of risk from one party to another. Stock index futures serve as a valuable hedging instrument for both domestic and global equity portfolio managers. The global proliferation of viable futures contracts has brought the capability from the traditional S&P 500 type funds to a broad range of hedging possibilities. The methodology is identical except that hedging foreign equity positions requires currency hedges as well.

Hedging strategies involve cross-hedging when the hedging instrument is not perfectly correlated with the investor's equity portfolio. A perfectly hedged position is one without risk. If the underlying index is the same as the portfolio being hedged, then the hedge is an arbitrage and will generate a certain profit. If the futures contract is fairly priced at the risk-free rate, then the hedge is comparable to a risk-free investment and it will produce the risk-free rate of return. If the portfolio being hedged has some tracking error versus the underlying index, then the rate of return is comparable to a money market instrument with small levels of tracking error.

As a hedging instrument, stock index futures provide investors with a means to manage risk whether holding long or short positions in the equity market. By taking the opposite side of their position, equity managers can insulate the performance of their equity position from market movements. The residual performance is directly related to the level of non-market risk in the portfolio. The most sophisticated hedging techniques do not completely eliminate risk because the gains or losses on the futures side do not precisely offset the gains or losses on the cash equity portfolio. Nonetheless, the hedged position is clearly a low-risk strategy particularly when the equity portfolio is highly correlated with the index underlying the stock index futures contract.

For equity portfolios designed to track known indexes with corresponding futures contracts, tracking error is not a huge problem. However, alternative equity portfolios with low correlations might have significant tracking error versus any particular hedging instrument that will subject the hedge to significant risk. This means that stock index futures can only insulate an equity portfolio from some portion of total risk. If the equity portfolio happens to be a broad market index fund, then S&P 500 index futures can pretty much take care of total risk because non-market risk was eliminated through diversification. However, when this is not the case and the equity portfolio is subject to significant non-market risk, then it exposes the hedging strategy to those same risks.

On the other hand, when the stock index futures contract is based on a broad-market index, it gives managers the ability to hedge systematic risk and take advantage of superior stock selection ability that will produce a positive return even in declining markets. These contracts can be used to isolate the non-market component of total risk. This feature benefits active managers who have the ability to pick high performance stocks, but who do not necessarily like the market. There is no need to stay out of equities. The manager can use stock index futures to remove the market component from the strategy. Over the investment horizon, the returns to the hedged portfolio will include an incremental return to the selected stocks versus the market and any dividends from the stocks.

Hedge Ratios

In order to hedge a position, the amount of the position to be taken in the stock index futures contract must be determined. That is, a risk equivalent position of the cash market portfolio is needed for the stock index futures position in order to hedge the portfolio. The *hedge ratio* indicates the amount of the futures position that must be taken to hedge the cash market portfolio. For example, using the S&P 500 futures contract, a hedge ratio of 1 means that if a manager wants to hedge a $10 million stock portfolio, a $10 S&P 500 futures position must be sold. If the hedge ratio is 0.9, this means that $9 million of S&P 500 futures contracts must be sold to hedge a $10 stock portfolio.

It is tempting to use the portfolio's beta as a hedge ratio because it is an indicator of the sensitivity of the portfolio returns to the stock index returns. It appears, then, to be an ideal sensitivity adjustment. However, applying beta relative to a stock index as a sensitivity adjustment to a stock index futures contract assumes that the index and the futures contract have the same volatility. If futures always sold at their fair value, this would be a reasonable assumption. However, mispricing is an extra element of volatility in a stock index futures contract. Since the stock index futures contract is more volatile than the underlying stock index, using a portfolio beta as a sensitivity measure would result in a portfolio being over-hedged.

The most accurate sensitivity adjustment would be the beta of a portfolio relative to the futures contract. It can be shown that the beta of a portfolio relative to a stock index futures contract is equivalent to the product of the portfolio relative to the underlying index and the beta of the index relative to the futures contract.[3] The beta in each case is estimated using regression analysis in which the data are historical returns for the portfolio to be hedged, the stock index, and the stock index futures contract. The regressions estimated are:

$$r_P = a_P + B_{PI}\, r_I + e_P$$

where

r_P = the return on the portfolio to be hedged
r_I = the return on the stock index
B_{PI} = the beta of the portfolio relative to the stock index
a_P = the intercept of the relationship
e_P = the error term

and

$$r_I = a_I + B_{IF}\, r_F + e_I$$

where

r_F = the return on the stock index futures contract
B_{IF} = the beta of the stock index relative to the stock index futures contract
a_I = the intercept of the relationship
e_I = the error term

Given B_{PI} and B_{IF}, the minimum risk hedge ratio can then be found by:

$$\text{Hedge ratio} = h = B_{PI} \times B_{IF}$$

[3] Edgar Peters, "Hedged Equity Portfolios: Components of Risk and Return," *Advances in Futures and Options Research*, Vol. 1B, 1987, pp. 75–92.

The hedge ratio h in the above expression is referred to as a *minimum risk hedge ratio* (also called an *optimal hedge ratio*) because the ratio minimizes the variance of returns to the hedged position.

There is a special case where the portfolio beta can be used as the hedge ratio. This is the case if the manager can hedge the portfolio until the settlement date. This is because the return to mispricing is no longer an unknown factor when the portfolio can be held to the futures settlement date.

Given the hedge ratio, the manager must determine the number of stock index futures contracts to sell. The number needed can be calculated using the following three steps after B_{PI} and B_{IF} are estimated:

Step 1. Determine the "equivalent market index units" of the market by dividing the market value of the portfolio to be hedged by the current value of the futures contract:

$$\text{Equivalent market indes units} = \frac{\text{Market value of the portfolio to be hedged}}{\text{Current value of the futures contract}}$$

Step 2. Multiply the equivalent market index units by the hedge ratio to obtain the "beta-adjusted equivalent market index units":

$$\text{Beta-adjusted equivalent market index units} = \text{Hedge ratio} \times \text{Equivalent market index units}$$

or,

$$B_{PI} \times B_{IF} \times \text{Equivalent market index units}$$

Step 3. Divide the beta-adjusted equivalent index units by the multiple specified by the stock index futures contract:

$$\text{Number of contracts} = \frac{\text{Beta-adjusted equivalent market index units}}{\text{Multiple of the contract}}$$

Asset Allocation

All investment decisions ultimately are asset allocation decisions. The choice to invest new cash in a domestic index fund instead of a global portfolio or the choice to reduce bond exposure are clear examples. If the decision is a long-term one, then it is a strategic asset allocation decision. Strategic decisions are made with the careful analysis of a client's long-term needs. If, instead, the decision is short-term, it is a tactical asset allocation decision. Tactical asset allocation (TAA) is actually a short-term to intermediate-term timing strategy designed to benefit from identifiable misevaluation in an asset class and seeks to add value to the overall fund performance. TAA could also include a defensive strategy to avoid adverse market movements. The classic example is a shift from equities to bonds or equity to cash in anticipation of a market correction. Asset allocation is not limited to domestic financial assets, but reaches into foreign markets as well.

The mechanics of implementing asset allocation decisions depend upon the investor's choice of an instrument. Whether managers choose to diversify internationally or not, superior security selection may be blown over by the adverse winds of a bear market. There are several ways that managers can respond to tactical asset allocation models that signal a danger of a market reversal. Tactical asset allocation is comparable to dynamic hedging. The choice to reduce or increase exposure to an asset class effectively hedges one risk in favor of another or none. The instruments to hedge market risk are also available for asset allocation decisions.

Managers have a choice of vehicles and methods to implement an asset allocation strategy. The stock index futures solution is available across a number of countries and asset classes, enabling managers to manage the systematic risk of equity portfolios regardless of the country of origin. The derivatives solution to the asset allocation decision allows managers to separate the security selection decision from the market timing or the asset allocation decision. Later in this chapter we discuss the OTC derivatives alternative to stock index futures.

The choice of whether to use cash or futures to accomplish an allocation-related strategy was discussed earlier. Once again the choice comes down to whether the decision is long term or short term.

Creating an Index Fund

An index fund is a portfolio of securities designed to exactly replicate the returns and risk profile of an established index. Equity indexing is an investment strategy that involves investing funds in a stock portfolio designed to track the performance of an established equity index. Index funds were originally developed as a low-cost passive alternative to active management and as part of a strategic asset allocation plan. As such, plain vanilla index funds were created where the benchmark was the most widely accepted stock market proxy—the S&P 500 Index.

To this day, the most common index fund is designed to track the S&P 500 stock index. Recently however, indexing has taken on many different forms and doesn't fit perfectly into the traditional description.

The most obvious development has been the use of numerous new benchmarks to represent more narrowly defined stock indexes and foreign stock indexes. However, it wasn't until the last few years that a global proliferation of stock index futures developed to accompany the new equity benchmark investments.

Traditionally, the only approach to establishing an index fund was to purchase a replicating portfolio in the cash market designed to track the S&P 500. With the arrival of equity index derivatives in the early 1980s, synthetic index funds were created. The return distribution of the S&P 500 Index could be replicated using stock index futures and a money market instrument. The early experience of the S&P 500 Index fund and its synthetic counterpart in the stock index futures market can now be extended to a host of other indexes. Some candidates are indexes with a narrower equity focus and foreign indexes.

As an alternative to holding a cash index fund, a synthetic index fund can be created using stock index futures contracts. The investor purchases stock index futures as a substitute for the cash index and invests the proceeds in a money market instrument. The advantages and disadvantages of using a synthetic index fund versus a cash index fund are the same as those discussed earlier. Based on the assumption of no transaction costs and efficient markets, we know that a synthetic index fund should generate the same returns as a cash index fund. In our next example, however, we relax the assumptions and compare the practical differences between the two applications.

The choice of using the futures market versus the cash market can only be determined by evaluating the trade-offs between costs and risks. The outcome of the synthetic strategy can only match the cash strategy if the following conditions are met:

- The investment amount corresponds to an exact futures amount.
- Interest rates are constant over the investment horizon.
- Expected dividends are realized.
- The futures price is fairly valued when the strategy is initiated.
- All subsequent futures prices are fairly valued.

In practice, these conditions are not exactly met. However, with good estimates of expectations and making the appropriate adjustments to the futures position, under normal market conditions, the risks can be minimized.

The risks of holding a synthetic index fund, for example, must be weighed against the risks of the cash index fund. The two primary sources of risk for using futures are variation margin and price risk. A technique known as "tailing" can be used to minimize the impact of variation margin on returns.[4] Price risk refers to the risk of mispriced futures contracts when the fund is initiated and during times when the position must be rolled into the next settlement cycle. On the other hand, one prominent advantage of a synthetic index fund over a cash index fund is cost. A cash index fund costs 30–40 basis points to initiate, while a synthetic index fund costs 2.5 basis points. The cash index fund is also subject to the cost of periodic rebalancings and to cash drag resulting from a delay in investing new cash.

In practice, many index funds hold a replicating portfolio to represent the benchmark and use stock index futures to manage cost and minimize cash drag. The prudent use of futures can provide the means of achieving the investment objective of matching the returns to the benchmark.

Enhanced Index Funds

An index fund is a passive approach to investing where the objective is to exactly or closely match the performance of an agreed upon benchmark. The most common index fund is a plain vanilla S&P 500 index fund. The index fund manager attempts to match the performance of the S&P 500 index on a total return basis. The purpose of an enhanced index fund is to do better than the benchmark index without incurring additional risk.

It is difficult to outperform a benchmark without incurring tracking error risk. Tracking error risk will usually emerge whenever the replicating portfolio is not an exact replica of the benchmark. However, the incremental returns more than compensate for the small increase in risk. Naturally, over time, the enhanced index fund is expected to perform better than the benchmark on a risk-adjusted basis.

There are three basic approaches to enhanced indexing. The first involves changing the composition of the replicating portfolio in order take advantage of valued-added situations. This may include stock selection, sector selection, or a different weighting scheme. The resulting portfolio is usually constructed to minimize tracking error. The replicating portfolio is "tilted" toward superior performance in some way that is expected to pro-

---

[4] Tailing is a technique designed to minimize the impact of variation margin on returns. The tailing or adjustment factor is applied to the original position such that slightly fewer contracts are bought or sold. The futures position is adjusted by the following formula:.

Tailing factor = 1/Term interest rate

The appropriate interest rate is either the term interest rate until expiration of the futures contract, or the term interest rate until the hedge is lifted. Fund managers prefer not to use tailing because it may put a drag on the strategy when the position is moving favorably.

vide it with the economic fuel to perform better than the benchmark. The replicating portfolio is put on common ground with the benchmark by trying to match its risk characteristics and not its expected return.

Alternatively, the index fund manager can use a stock replacement program to take advantage of misevaluation in the futures market in order to enhance return. The performance of the index fund is "enhanced" through stock index arbitrage and a stock replacement program. The incremental return is the result of futures pricing inefficiencies rather than estimated misevaluation of equities. The index fund has an additional opportunity for incremental return by reversing the arbitrage at a favorable price as well. In fact, some index funds may enter into a stock replacement program aggressively in order to take advantage of opportunities on the other side of the cash/futures swap.

Consequently, plain vanilla indexing can be viewed as an application of futures in the form of cost management. Enhanced indexing by seeking to capitalize on the mispricing between futures and cash is an example of a return enhancing strategy.

The third way to enhance index funds is to use a structured product vehicle that allows the investor to use leverage or fixed income management to deliver returns above an equity benchmark. For example, an equity swap where the investor manages the fixed income portion to obtain a better return than the swap promises can be added to overall performance of the strategy. Also, warrant structures can utilize leverage as well.

Foreign Market Access

As investment strategies have become international in scope, stock index futures have become an effective means of managing equity exposure and risk exposure in a global portfolio. Once a decision is made to develop and maintain a global investment strategy, the equity manager has to decide how to treat currency risk. The choice to invest internationally subjects the equity portfolio to currency risk and market risk in the country where the investment takes place. The manager is now faced with the task of making prudent investment choices and developing an opinion on currency rates. The risk to the portfolio is that the manager's investment decision was correct, but not realized due to an appreciation in the domestic currency.

The use of stock index futures for implementing a global equity investment strategy can reduce currency risk. The reason is that currency risk is confined to initial margin payments and variation margin. These payments are usually much smaller than the initial value of the equity portfolio. Thus, stock index futures are a viable and important alternative for foreign equity investment compared to investing in the foreign stocks themselves.

EXHIBIT 15.1   The Use of OTC Derivatives for Equity Strategies

Equity Strategy	Purpose	Product Candidate
Return-enhancement strategies	Outperform benchmark	Equity Swap
Hedging strategies	Risk management	Exotics, Swaps, Debt*
Spread strategies	Risk management	Equity Swaps, Exotics
Market access strategies	Reduce costs	Swaps, Debt, Warrants,
Changing equity exposure	Reduce costs	Exotics
Index funds	Outperform	Swaps, Debt, Exotics
Standard	benchmark	Swaps, Debt
Enhanced		
Style		
Asset allocation	Risk management	Swaps
Active manager transition	Cost management	Swaps, Exotics

* Debt refers to equity-linked debt products.

The use of stock index futures in a global context shares the same advantages of using stock index futures in a domestic equity investment context. These include high liquidity, rapid execution, low transaction costs, single purchase for broad market exposure, no tracking error, and no custodial costs. A few additional features particularly applicable to foreign investment are that cash settlement avoids the risk of delivery, using stock index futures for country allocation avoids the different settlement periods that may exist between two or more countries, and using futures may avoid withholding taxes. Moreover, in some countries the use of stock index futures allows foreign investors to avoid restrictions on capital movements.

APPLICATIONS OF OTC EQUITY DERIVATIVES

The array of OTC derivative-based equity portfolio management strategies cuts across the two primary categories of investment philosophy—active and passive management. We consider several strategies in this section, which are listed in Exhibit 15.1, together with the purpose of using an OTC derivatives and a product candidate.

Exhibit 15.2 summarizes various OTC equity derivative structures in terms of the role of derivatives for long-term investors and hedgers. A broad spectrum of equity investment activities emanating from the role of derivatives can benefit from these three basic categories of OTC equity derivative structures.

EXHIBIT 15.2 OTC Derivative Structures and Investment Management

Derivative Structure	Investor	Role	Application
OTC Options and Exotics	Long-term Index Funds Style Funds Active Managers Strategic Asset Allocators	Risk Management	Customized protective puts Collar structures Portfolio insurance Currency hedging Asset exposure Probability exposure
		Return Management	Index arbitrage Option writing Volatility forecasting Intra-asset allocation Leverage strategies
		Cost Management	Option writing Market access Valuation estimation Structured products
		Regulatory Management	Foreign market exposure Tax deferral Asset exposure
Equity-Linked Debt	Long-term Index Funds Style Funds Active Managers Strategic Asset Allocators	Risk Management	Customized structures Collar structures Portfolio insurance Currency hedging Asset exposure
		Return Management	Spread premiums
		Cost Management	Foreign market cost avoidance Asset allocation
		Regulatory Management	Asset exposure Foreign market exposure Capital requirement
Equity Swaps	Long-term Index Funds Style Funds Active Managers Strategic Asset Allocators	Risk Management	Diversification Asset allocation Minimize tracking error Currency hedging
		Return Management	Tracking portfolio Spread premium
		Cost Management	Foreign market cost avoidance Asset allocation
		Regulatory Management	Foreign market exposure Tax deferral Asset exposure

Creation of Structured Product Solutions

One of the most important applications of derivative securities is in the creation of structured product solutions to the financial needs or objectives of an institutional investor.[5] Structured products are, like derivative securities, financial products are contractual agreements between two parties—an issuer (the designer or creator of the structure) and a purchaser (the user or holder of the structure). The structure is designed with a linkage to the performance of an existing security or securities. The linkage could be to an equity index or portfolio, an interest rate, an exchange rate, or a commodity price and based on spreads, correlations, convergences, or divergences. The objective could be to protect principal, enhance returns, defer taxes, gain access to difficult markets, manage costs or manage regulatory risks. The process of creating or establishing a structured product is known as "financial engineering" and involves the creation of a structure that meets the specific needs of the client in terms of the objectives listed above. The value of structured products is that they provide great flexibility in design and application.

Typically, structured products are used to provide some form of principal protection while having the potential for upside returns. Thus, a basic structure consists of a fixed income component and a returns generating component. An alternative basic structure offers a leverage factor that can generate a higher magnitude of returns than a traditional investment or a principal protected structure. Examples of structured products include but are not restricted to warrants, principal protection notes, asset-linked notes, various types of swaps, credit linked products, monetization strategies for restricted or concentrated situations, caps and floor products, and securitized cash flows.

Risk Management Strategies

As we have noted, a common use of derivatives is to hedge financial risk. Stock index futures can only insulate an equity portfolio from some portion of total risk. If the equity portfolio happens to be a broad market index fund, then S&P 500 index futures can pretty much take care of total risk because non-market risk was eliminated through diversification. However, when this is not the case and the equity portfolio is subject to significant non-market risk, then it exposes the hedging strategy to those same risks.

Stock index futures contracts in which the underlying is a broad market index allow portfolio managers the ability to hedge systematic

---

[5] For an excellent presentation of structured products see, John C. Braddock, *Derivatives Demystified: Using Structured Financial Products* (New York: John Wiley and Sons, 1997).

risk and take advantage of superior stock selection ability that will produce a positive return even in declining markets. Stock index futures can be used to isolate the non-market component of total risk. This feature benefits active managers who have the ability to pick high performance stocks, but who have little market timing skills. There is no need to stay out of equities during volatile markets. The manager can use stock index futures to hedge market risk.

Consequently, over the investment horizon, the returns to the hedged portfolio will include an incremental return to the selected stocks versus the market and any dividends from the stocks. However, the resulting strategy may go beyond the desired risk-return trade-off. OTC derivative structures can be designed to address all these issues and achieve the exact hedged position desired. All costs can be known upfront with no additional risk to investors, with the exception of some credit risk and market failure risk that accompanies all financial transactions.

Despite the benefits of using stock index futures, listed index futures products do not provide a full range of hedging choices for equity investors. OTC equity derivatives go a long way to fill this gap. Investors can choose among equity swaps, equity-linked debt, and a structured option-like product to hedge with greater precision the specific risk they want to shed and to acquire the risk they want to bear. Exhibit 15.3 provides a list of derivative alternatives for hedging equity portfolios.

With the advent of second-generation "exotic" options, investors can now implement a hedging strategy with the degree of precision they desire. Market risk can be hedged in any country using any derivative structure. Equity swaps can exchange the total return of a portfolio for another less risky asset class. The structure can be designed to hedge currency risk if necessary and desired.

EXHIBIT 15.3   Hedging with Derivatives

	Hedging Instrument	
Hedging Strategy	Listed	OTC
Reduce Market Risk	Stock index futures	Option, swap, debt
Reduce Total Risk	Multiple SIFs contracts	Option, swap, debt
Change Risk Components	Stock index futures	Option, swap, debt
Reduce Currency Risk	Quanto futures	Option, swap, debt
Reduce Interest Rate Risk	Interest rate derivatives	Option, swap, debt
Reduce Inflation Risk	Interest rate derivatives	Option, swap, debt
	Commodity index derivatives	

EXHIBIT 15.4   Alternative Investment Vehicles Global Asset Allocation Strategy

Investment Category	Vehicle	Advantages	Disadvantages
Cash Market	Stock Portfolio	Ownership	Costs and Management
Listed Derivatives	Stock Index Futures	Cost	Managing futures
	Stock Index Options	Listed	Size, Standardization
	FLEX Options	Flexibility, Listed	Size, Tracking Error
OTC Options	Baskets	No tracking error	Cost
	Spread	Any Market	Cost
	Barriers	Low Cost	Volatile Markets
	Compound	Low Cost	Multiple Transactions
Swaps	Equity Swap	Quick, Efficient	Negative Payments
	International Swap		Credit Risk

A structured product using exotics can design a payout that is contingent on certain market activity. For example, a barrier put option can be used to obtain a specific degree of protection without paying extra for outcomes that are not relevant. Ladder options can lock in a market decline, while flexible strike options can ratchet up when the market moves opposite to expectations.

Once again, the bottom line is that structured OTC equity derivative products can overcome the risk inherent in cash or futures market hedging strategies. Investors have the means to hedge all or a specific part of total risk.

Asset Allocation

The mechanics of implementing asset allocation decisions depend upon the investor's choice of an investment vehicle. Exhibit 15.4 presents a list of candidates for a global asset shift which changes foreign equity exposure in the overall asset allocation strategy using listed derivatives and OTC derivatives.

The problem is the same one presented in an earlier discussion of equity investment strategies. The choices unfold similarly. The option-based solution may suffer from high costs due to a highly volatile portfolio or due to significant liquidity risk. However, exotic option structures provide a means to fine-tune the strategy to reflect very precisely forecasted returns. Basket options, such as index options, are cheaper than a portfolio of options. They also provide a portfolio manager with a means of eliminating tracking error between the underlying for the hedging vehicle and the equity portfolio.

Listed options have the additional problem of size limits for standard-ized contracts. FLEX options resolve some but not all of those limita-tions. The stock index futures alternative comes with some administrative issues and risks. The equity swap solution incorporates the asset alloca-tion decision into a single transaction, but necessitates a counterparty and has credit risk. The derivatives solution to the asset allocation deci-sion allows fund managers or portfolio managers to separate the security selection decision from the market timing or the asset allocation deci-sion. The choice of what mechanism to use to accomplish the investment objective depends on whether the decision is long term or short term and the relative costs.

Return Management Strategies

Return management strategies focus on structuring an investment strat-egy to increase returns but not risk. Here we include passive index funds and enhanced index funds because they are investment strategies designed to meet the performance criterion of matching or exceeding a benchmark. We could just as easily think of index funds as a means to match the risk characteristics of a benchmark, which is one of the fea-tures of this strategy. However, once the risk profile is established, the focus of index funds is performance relative to a benchmark.

The modified index fund strategies might also be called return-enhancement strategies. The purpose behind return-enhancement strate-gies is to increase return without an accompanying increase in risk. This means that an "enhanced" index fund ought to do better than the benchmark index without incurring additional risk. However, it may not be an easy task to outperform a benchmark without incurring track-ing error risk. This risk will usually emerge whenever the replicating portfolio does not exactly mimic the composition of the benchmark. Nonetheless, the incremental returns are expected to more than com-pensate for the small increase in risk and, over time, the enhanced index fund is expected to outperform the benchmark on a risk-adjusted basis.

The goal of indexing is to construct a portfolio to exactly match the performance of the benchmark. When this is accomplished, tracking error is zero. In addition to performance reasons, plan sponsors are attracted to index funds because they provide investment diversification and are a means to control costs. Many plan sponsors have combined active and passive management using index funds as a risk management tool. Index funds can also provide a means for market-timing. Thus we see that index funds can fall into return management, risk management, or cost management categories. Part of the reason is that the use of index funds makes performance attribution and cost control more manageable because of the use of an established index as a benchmark. For the plan sponsor, an index fund can represent an entire asset class within the framework of its strategic asset allocation strategy or as part of an intra-asset allocation strategy that mixes active and passive management.

Indexing has taken on many different forms that have broad applications. If we generalize our definition of index funds as a portfolio of stocks designed to match or exceed the returns of a benchmark while maintaining the same risk exposure, then there are many extensions of the original index fund. The many applications of index funds provide a rich landscape for using derivatives to further reduce costs. In fact, the prudent use of equity derivatives can reduce transaction costs to near zero. We regard the reduction of costs as any increase in after-cost return without changing the fundamental composition of the portfolio. This means that the returns are derived from the same sources in the cash market. Thus, it is comparable to getting a better execution in the cash market. Superior execution leads to lower costs, which increases return. The following is a list of index fund applications.

Extended Funds—An *extended funds strategy* involves constructing a portfolio linked to an index that "extends" beyond the traditional S&P 500 index and may include a significantly larger group of stocks. The purpose of this strategy is to gain U.S. equity diversification. The universe of over 5,000 stocks across many sectors is more representative of the U.S. equity market and the U.S. economy. In addition, it provides a means of reducing risk versus a more narrow view represented by the S&P 500 index. No real liquid listed derivatives are available to create a synthetic fund. OTC derivative structures such as equity swaps and equity-linked debt instruments can provide an alternative investment vehicle to an exclusive cash approach.

Non-S&P 500 Index Funds—A non-S&P 500 index funds strategy involves constructing a portfolio linked to a broad-based non-S&P 500 stock index. The strategy underlying these funds is to expand U.S. equity market exposure. Investors who currently have an S&P 500 index fund can combine it with a separate index fund that captures a neglected portion of the market. The end result can effectively be an extended fund with the added advantage of making intra-asset allocation rebalancings when desired. Once we travel outside the plain vanilla index fund, using listed derivatives becomes more difficult. OTC equity derivatives are available for implementing and managing non-S&P 500 index funds.

Foreign or International Index Funds—A foreign or international index funds strategy seeks to design a portfolio that is linked to a foreign or international stock index. Thus, investors who do not invest beyond the borders of the United States are ignoring about half of world equities. The strategy objective of foreign investments is to gain international diversification. Furthermore, as global financial markets continue to deregulate and integrate, emerging markets in other parts of the world will provide additional opportunities. There are, however, direct investment expenses associated with owning foreign securities that exceed similar domestic investments. These may include larger commissions and spreads, stamp taxes, dividend withholding taxes, custody fees, and research fees. Many of these costs can be better managed through the use of OTC index derivatives.

Special-Purpose Index Funds—A portfolio can be constructed to be linked to the performance of a sub-index, such as a market sector, or a portfolio with the same risk profile as a benchmark but with a tilt toward a specific parameter such as yield or price-earnings ratio. This strategy is called a *special-purpose index funds strategy*. Tilted portfolios are designed to enhance the returns to an index fund without assuming additional risk. Sometimes referred to as "enhanced" index funds, this strategy may also involve the use of futures or options to provide incremental return. An enhanced index fund begins with a traditional index fund and then utilizes financing techniques and derivative strategies to enhance return.

Having decided on a passive investment strategy and an appropriate benchmark, the investor's next consideration is how to implement the strategy. A cash market solution needs to address the design and construction of a replicating or tracking portfolio. In the presence of transaction costs, the optimal portfolio may still underperform the benchmark. Thus, in order to overcome the risk of underperformance the investor may have to assume more tracking error risk. The final choice of a replicating portfolio must be made within a cost management framework. The trade-off can be represented by expected tracking error versus expected trading costs. Costs are related to portfolio size and liquidity. Part of the skill of portfolio construction is to find the optimal balance between costs and risk. The marginal trade-off between risk and cost is greater for small sized portfolios.

Earlier we discussed the benefits of using stock index futures to manage an index fund. Synthetic index funds can be created using stock index futures that exactly replicate the returns to the underlying index. Recently, OTC index derivatives have been developed for investors with restrictions on using derivatives. These include equity-linked debt instruments and equity swaps. Equity swaps are important because they are the economic equivalent of financing an equity investment with a fixed-income security, typically a LIBOR-based security.

There are some index funds that use futures almost exclusively. It is not practical for large pension funds to rely exclusively on synthetic index funds due to market constraints. Thus, some combination of the cash market and futures market is appropriate. Index funds can be developed as a more dynamic strategy, and can be used as a risk management tool and a platform for better performance. However, stock index futures have their own administrative considerations and are limited in application because they have a linear pay off.

In order to provide a richer body of choices for implementing and managing index funds over the long haul, the use of OTC derivative structures provides the missing link to more complete and effective global risk management solutions to the investment problem. Equity swaps can be used to create the exact desired equity exposure in a single transaction, which makes them convenient, cost effective, and economically sound.

Return Enhancement Strategies

There are three basic approaches to enhanced indexing which apply to other investment strategies as well. The first approach involves changing the composition of the equity portfolio in order to position the portfolio to take advantage of stocks, stock sectors, some different weighting allotments, or other criteria that the manager believes will cause the portfolio to perform better than a passive benchmark. In the case of index funds, the equity portfolio is the replicating portfolio. Changing the portfolio involves modifying the content of the portfolio and yet maintaining the current level of risk. The resulting portfolio is typically designed to minimize tracking error. For return management strategies, the equity portfolio is designed to match the risk characteristics of a benchmark and not its expected return.

In the second approach, index fund managers can use a stock index futures arbitrage to increase or enhance returns. The strategy is formalized as a stock replacement program, which invests in the less expensive of the cash portfolio or futures. The incremental return is the result of futures pricing inefficiencies rather than estimated mispricing of equities.

OTC equity derivatives can be a useful tool to modify the composition of the portfolio at low cost. The use of derivatives would enter the picture as part of the implementation process. The investor would first establish the necessary rebalancing to achieve the desired exposure to a new set of stocks on either an individual basis, an industry sector basis, or with the intent to modify a portfolio parameter such as price-earnings ratio. In any case, the result in the cash market is a set of sell orders and a set of buy orders. The investor is shedding some risks in favor of others. The rebalanced portfolio represents the right equity exposure to add incremental return necessary to improve performance with no added risk.

As explained earlier, a structured product can be used to enhance returns by providing a means of accessing other sources of additional returns. Various structures are capable of accomplishing these objectives.

Cost Management and Regulatory Management Strategies

We can apply the cost and regulatory management strategies explained earlier using listed options to OTC derivatives as well. The OTC applications extend the benefits further by providing additional flexibility when structuring a strategy. There are also a number of strategies that fall under this category simply because implementing them using derivatives results in lower costs than the cash market alternative. Moreover, in the case of some strategies, implementation in the cash market may have prohibitive regulatory obstacles. An example of both are foreign market access strategies. Derivatives provide investors a means to invest in foreign equities while avoiding some of the costs, tax consequences, and regulatory obstacles simultaneously or separately. This holds true for U.S. investors in equities outside the United States or foreigners investing in U.S. companies.

Here we review some of the listed option strategies discussed earlier in this chapter, but now using OTC derivatives. We explained the use of short puts as a means of buying stocks using derivatives as a substitute for a limit order in the cash market. This strategy is equally applicable to OTC options, which provide the additional advantage of customization to achieve the specific price and time horizon that meet the investor's needs. Similarly, short calls are a means of selling stocks currently held and targeted for sale. The advantages of the OTC market apply here as well.

In addition to these basic applications, OTC structures can be developed as alternatives to cash market transactions that are tailored to reflect very specific investment opinions or forecasts. These may include any structure that is the economic equivalent of a long or short cash position, but does not require the direct purchase or sale of stock. Other applications which could reduce cost involve an array of exotic structures that are priced lower than standard options. Barrier options can be structured to knock-in under conditions that reflect the price targets of the stock. Spread options allow the manager to generate the performance differential between the current situation and the desired situation without actually buying or selling the stock. Basket options can accomplish the result of buying or selling a basket of stocks simultaneously. Equity swaps can achieve the economic equivalent by an exchange of cash flows. OTC derivatives are equally applicable to cost management or regulatory management.

RISK AND EXPECTED RETURN OF OPTION STRATEGIES

Options are like any other risky asset because they compensate investors for assuming systematic risk. Therefore, if options have higher exposure to systematic risk, investors will require and expect higher returns from holding options. Naturally, call options, which pay off in states of the world where the underlying asset's price rises, will have higher expected returns than the underlying asset. In contrast, put options, which pay off in states of the world where the asset's price declines, will have lower expected returns than the risk-free asset that are often negative.[6] Furthermore, adding options to a stock portfolio or writing options against an existing long position will change the risk-return characteristics of the investment and therefore its expected return.

According to the asset pricing framework of Merton and the Black Scholes model, the instantaneous expected return to an option ought to be the same as the return implied by the CAPM.[7] Hence, it can be shown that an option's instantaneous beta is related to the beta of the underlying stock and the elasticity of the option.[8] Rendleman demonstrates that the expected returns and risks for options should be consistent with the principles of risk and return from the CAPM.[9] He shows the impact on expected returns for various investment strategies that use options. One observation is that call options with high positive betas should have high expected returns and put options with negative betas should have low

---

[6] Coval and Tyler find empirical evidence that the returns to option strategies are lower than predicted by the CAPM. They argue that this suggests that other factors besides the market are important for pricing the risk associated with options. (Joshua D. Coval and Tyler Shumway, "Expected Option Returns," *Journal of Finance* (June 2001).

[7] Robert C. Merton, "An Intertemporal Capital Asset Pricing Model," *Econometrica* (September 1973) and Fischer Black and Myron Scholes, "The Pricing of Options and Corporate Liabilities," *Journal of Political Economy* (1973).

[8] That is,

$$\beta_{option} = \beta_{stock} \, (\delta P/\delta S) \, (S/P)$$

where P = price of the option and S = price of the underlying stock.

[9] Richard J. Rendleman, "Option Investing from a Risk-Return Perspective," *Journal of Portfolio Management* (May 1999).

expected returns. The discussion below follows the presentations by Rendlemen and Coval and Shumway.[10]

Expected Returns from Long Calls and Covered Calls

From the CAPM derived by Merton, the expected value of a call can be derived:

$$E[R_{call}] = R_f + \beta_{call} \, [E[R_M] - R_f]$$

The expected return from buying call options is higher than the underlying stock. However, the difference in returns is less the further the option is in-the-money and converges on the stock's expected return for very high stock prices. The reason for this relationship is that the option's beta exceeds that of the underlying stock and in fact can be much higher. For stocks with positive betas, the beta of the option will be higher because of its exposure to greater systematic risk. The fact that an option is a leveraged position in the underlying would also lead to the higher risk and expected returns conclusion. In a portfolio context, adding an option to a diversified portfolio will heighten the systematic risk in the portfolio. Consequently, investors should require a higher rate of return.

For covered calls, which reduce the risk of holding the stock, the expected return ought to be lower than a long stock position. The important behavioral aspect of covered call writing from an expected return perspective is that writing calls on a long stock position reduces risk and consequently will lower expected returns. The fact that covered call strategies are viewed as a means to generate income during flat markets does not change the fact that across the spectrum of possible outcomes, risk is lower, as is expected returns.

Expected Returns from Protective Puts

From the CAPM, if a stock has a positive beta, then a put ought to have a negative beta. This can be demonstrated by viewing the put option as a portfolio of a short position and a discount loan. The expected return must necessarily be below the risk-free rate because the equity risk premium is positive. This can be seen in the following expression.

$$E[R_{put}] = R_f + \beta_{put}[E[R_M] - R_f]$$

---

[10] Rendleman, "Option Investing from a Risk-Return Perspective" and Coval and Shumway, "Expected Option Returns." For a graphical treatment of the expected return and risk for option strategies, see Stoll and Whaley, *Futures and Options: Theory and Applications* (SouthWestern Publishing Co., 1993).

EXHIBIT 15.5 Expected Return and Beta for Option Strategies

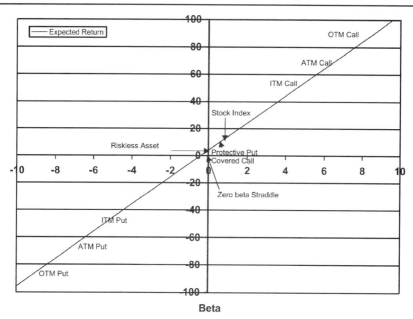

ATM = At-the-money
ITM = In-the-money
OTM = Out-of-the-money

Investors are willing to hold puts because they view it as purchasing insurance. Hence, a put is bought for the same reasons that motivate consumers to buy automobile or homeowner insurance—to hedge against adverse events. In neither case does the consumer expect to generate earnings because the purchase of an insurance policy is basically the purchase of utility in exchange for the expected loss. Consequently, protective put strategies will lower expected returns compared with a long-only strategy.

For more complicated option-based strategies, the outcomes will also result in a different risk-return profile depending on the payout of the strategy. Straddles, for example, with zero betas ought to return the risk-free rate.

The relationship between expected return and beta for the basic option strategies is illustrated in Exhibit 15.5. From the exhibit, we see that the relationship between strike price and expected return shows that the more in-the-money the option, the closer to the risk-return position of the underlying stock. We also observe that the covered call and the protective put strategy both result in lower risk and expected returns versus the long stock position. The riskless asset and the zero-beta straddle ought to be similarly positioned in terms of expected return and beta. On the lower end of the exhibit, we find a similar relationship among put options as call options except with negative betas.

Investing in Fixed-Income Securities

Fixed-Income Securities

Frank J. Fabozzi, Ph.D., CFA
Adjunct Professor of Finance
School of Management
Yale University

In this chapter and the one to follow, we will review the wide range of fixed-income securities. We begin with the general features of fixed-income securities. The risks associated with investing in them is discussed in Chapter 22.

GENERAL FEATURES OF BONDS

We begin our introduction to fixed-income securities or bonds with a description of features common to all of them.

Term to Maturity

The term to maturity of a bond is the number of years over which the issuer has promised to meet the conditions of the obligation. At the maturity date the issuer will pay off any amount the bonds outstanding. The convention is to refer to the "term to maturity" as simply its "maturity" or "term." As we explain later, there may be provisions that allow either the issuer or holder of the debt instrument to alter the term to maturity.

Par Value

The *par value* of a bond is the amount that the issuer agrees to repay the bondholder by the maturity date. This amount is also referred to as the *principal, face value, redemption value,* or *maturity value.* Bonds can have any par value.

Because bonds can have a different par value, the practice is to quote the price of a bond as a percentage of its par value. A value of 100 means 100% of par value. So, for example, if a bond has a par value of $1,000 and is selling for $900, it would be said to be selling at 90. If a bond with a par value of $5,000 is selling for $5,500, the bond is said to be selling for 110. The reason why a bond sells above or below its par value is explained in Chapter 18.

Coupon Rate

The *coupon rate,* also called the *nominal rate* or the *contract rate,* is the interest rate that the issuer/borrower agrees to pay each year. The dollar amount of the payment, referred to as the *coupon interest payment* or simply *interest payment,* is determined by multiplying the coupon rate by the par value of the bond. For example, the interest payment for a bond with a 7% coupon rate and a par value of $1,000 is $70 (7% times $1,000).

The frequency of interest payments varies by the type of bond. In the United States, the usual practice for bonds is for the issuer to pay the coupon in two semiannual installments. Mortgage-backed securities and asset-backed securities typically pay interest monthly. For bonds issued in some markets outside the United States, coupon payments are made only once per year.

Zero-Coupon Bonds

Not all bonds make periodic coupon interest payments. Bonds that are not contracted to make periodic coupon payments are called *zero-coupon bonds.* The investor realizes interest by buying it substantially below its par value. Interest then is paid at the maturity date, with the interest earned by the investor being the difference between the par value and the price paid for the bond. So, for example, if an investor purchases a zero-coupon bond for 70, the interest realized at the maturity date is 30. This is the difference between the par value (100) and the price paid (70).

There is another type of bond that does not pay interest until the maturity date. This type has contractual coupon payments, but those payments are accrued and distributed along with the maturity value at the maturity date. These instruments are called *accrued coupon instruments* or *accrual securities* or *compound interest securities.*

Floating-Rate Securities

The coupon rate on a bond need not be fixed over the its life. *Floating-rate securities,* sometimes called *floaters* or *variable-rate securities,* have coupon payments that reset periodically according to some reference rate. The typical formula for the coupon rate at the dates when the coupon rate is reset is:

$$\text{Reference rate} \pm \text{Quoted margin}$$

The quoted margin is the additional amount that the issuer agrees to pay above the reference rate (if the quoted margin is positive) or the amount less than the reference rate (if the quoted margin is negative). The quoted margin is expressed in terms of *basis points*. A basis point is equal to 0.0001 or 0.01%. Thus, 100 basis points are equal to 1%.

A floating-rate bond may have a restriction on the maximum coupon rate that will be paid at a reset date. The maximum coupon rate is called a *cap*. Because a cap restricts the coupon rate from increasing, a cap is an unattractive feature for the investor. In contrast, there could be a minimum coupon rate specified for a floating-rate security. The minimum coupon rate is called a *floor*. If the coupon reset formula produces a coupon rate that is below the floor, the floor is paid instead. Thus, a floor is an attractive feature for the investor.

Accrued Interest

Bond issuers do not disburse coupon interest payments every day. Instead, typically in the United States coupon interest is paid every six months. In some countries, interest is paid annually. For mortgage-backed and asset-backed securities, interest is usually paid monthly. The coupon interest payment is made to the bondholder of record. Thus, if an investor sells a bond between coupon payments and the buyer holds it until the next coupon payment, then the entire coupon interest earned for the period will be paid to the buyer of the bond since the buyer will be the holder of record. The seller of the bond gives up the interest from the time of the last coupon payment to the time until the bond is sold. The amount of interest over this period that will be received by the buyer even though it was earned by the seller is called *accrued interest*.

In the United States and in many countries, the bond buyer must pay the bond seller the accrued interest. The amount that the buyer pays the seller is the agreed upon price for the bond plus accrued interest. This amount is called the *full price*. The agreed upon bond price without accrued interest is called the *clean price*.

Provisions for Paying Off Bonds

The issuer/borrower of a bond agrees to repay the principal by the stated maturity date. The issuer/borrower can agree to repay the entire amount borrowed in one lump sum payment at the maturity date. That is, the issuer/borrower is not required to make any principal repayments prior to the maturity date. Such bonds are said to have a *bullet maturity*.

There are bonds that have a schedule of principal repayments that are made prior to the final maturity of the instrument. Such bonds are said to be *amortizing instruments*.

There are bonds that have a *call provision*. This provision grants the issuer/borrower an option to retire all or part of the issue prior to the stated maturity date. Some issues specify that the issuer must retire a predetermined amount of the issue periodically. Various types of call provisions are discussed below.

Call and Refunding Provisions

A borrower generally wants the right to retire a bond prior to the stated maturity date because it recognizes that at some time in the future the general level of interest rates may fall sufficiently below the coupon rate so that redeeming the issue and replacing it with another bond with a lower coupon rate would be economically beneficial. This right is a disadvantage to the investor since proceeds received must be reinvested at a lower interest rate. As a result, a borrower who wants to include this right as part of a bond must compensate the investor when the issue is sold by offering a higher coupon rate.

The right of the borrower to retire the issue prior to the stated maturity date is referred to as a "call option." If the borrower exercises this right, the issuer is said to "call" the bond. The price that the borrower must pay to retire the issue is referred to as the *call price*. Typically, there is not one call price but a call schedule, which sets forth a call price based on when the borrower exercises the call option.

When a bond is issued, typically the borrower may not call it for a number of years. That is, the issue is said to have a *deferred call*. The date at which the bond may first be called is referred to as the *first call date*. Bonds can be called in whole (the entire issue) or in part (only a portion).

Noncallable versus Nonrefundable Bonds   If a bond issue does not have any protection against early call, then it is said to be a *currently callable issue*. But most new bond issues, even if currently callable, usually have some restrictions against certain types of early redemption. The most common restriction is prohibiting the refunding of the bonds for a certain number of years. *Refunding* a bond issue means redeeming bonds with funds obtained through the sale of a new bond issue.

Many investors are confused by the terms noncallable and nonrefundable. Call protection is much more absolute than refunding protection.

While there may be certain exceptions to absolute or complete call protection in some cases, it still provides greater assurance against premature and unwanted redemption than does refunding protection. Refunding prohibition merely prevents redemption only from certain sources of funds, namely the proceeds of other debt issues sold at a lower cost of money. The bondholder is only protected if interest rates decline, and the borrower can obtain lower-cost money to pay off the debt.

Sinking Fund Provision

An issuer may be required to retire a specified portion of an issue each year. This is referred to as a *sinking fund requirement*. Generally, the issuer may satisfy the sinking fund requirement by either (1) making a cash payment of the face amount of the bonds to be retired to the trustee, who then calls the bonds for redemption using a lottery, or (2) delivering to the trustee bonds purchased in the open market that have a total par value equal to the amount that must be retired.

Options Granted to Bondholders

There are provisions in bonds that gives either the investor and/or the issuer an option to take some action against the other party. The most common type of option embedded is a call feature, which was discussed earlier. This option is granted to the issuer. There are two options that can be granted to the owner of the bond: the right to put the issue and the right to convert the issue.

A bond with a *put provision* grants the investor the right to sell the bond back to the issuer at a specified price on designated dates. The specified price is called the *put price.*The advantage of the put provision to the investor is that if after the issuance date of the bond market interest rates rise above the bond's coupon rate, the investor can force the issuer to redeem the bond at the put price and then reinvest the proceeds at the prevailing higher rate.

A convertible bond is one that grants the investor the right to convert or exchange the bond for a specified number of shares of common stock. Such a feature allows the investor to take advantage of favorable movements in the price of the issuer's common stock. We will discuss the features of convertible bonds later in this chapter when we cover corporate bonds.

Medium-Term Notes versus Bonds

Medium-term notes (MTNs) differ from bonds only in the manner in which they are distributed to investors when they are initially sold. They are offered continuously to investors by an agent of the issuer. Investors can select from several maturity ranges: 9 months to 1 year, more than 1 year to 18 months, more than 18 months to 2 years, and so on up to 30 years.

The term "medium-term note" to describe this bond is misleading. Traditionally, the term "medium-term" was used to refer to debt issues with a maturity greater than one year but less than 15 years. This is not a characteristic of MTNs since they have been sold with maturities from 9 months to 30 years, and even longer. For example, in July 1993, Walt Disney Corporation issued an MTN with a 100-year maturity.

U.S. TREASURY SECURITIES

U.S. Treasury securities are issued by the U.S. Department of the Treasury. These securities are backed by the full faith and credit of the U.S. government. Therefore, they are viewed as default-free securities. Interest income from Treasury securities is subject to federal income taxes but is exempt from state and local income taxes.

Types of Treasury Securities

There are two types of Treasury securities: discount and coupon securities. Treasury coupon securities come in two forms: fixed-rate and variable-rate securities.

Treasury Bills

Treasuries are issued at a discount to par value, have no coupon rate, and mature at par value. As discount securities, Treasury bills do not pay coupon interest. Instead, Treasury bills are issued at a discount from their maturity value; the return to the investor is the difference between the maturity value and the purchase price. The current practice of the Treasury is to issue all securities with a maturity of one year or less as discount securities. These securities are called *Treasury bills* and are issued on a regular basis with initial maturities of 4 weeks, 3 months, and 6 months. At irregular intervals the Treasury also issues *cash management bills* with maturities ranging from a few days to about 6 months.

Fixed-Rate Treasury Notes and Bonds

All securities with initial maturities of two years or more are issued as coupon securities. Coupon securities are issued at approximately par, have a coupon rate, and mature at par value. Treasury coupon securities issued with original maturities of more than one year and no more than

10 years are called *Treasury notes*. Treasury coupon securities with original maturities greater than 10 years are called *Treasury bonds*. Treasury notes and bonds are referred to as *Treasury coupon securities*. Treasury coupon securities are currently auctioned on a regular basis with initial maturities of 2 years, 5 years, 10 years, and 30 years.

Inflation Protected Treasury Notes and Bonds

The U.S. Department of the Treasury issues notes and bonds that adjust for inflation. These securities are popularly referred to as *Treasury inflation protection securities* (TIPS) or *Treasury inflation indexed securities* (TIIS). The coupon rate on an issue is set at a fixed rate. That rate is determined via the auction process described later. The coupon rate is called the "real rate" since it is the rate that the investor ultimately earns above the inflation rate. The inflation index that the government has decided to use for the inflation adjustment is the non-seasonally adjusted U.S. City Average All Items Consumer Price Index for All Urban Consumers (CPI-U).

Stripped Treasury Securities

While the U.S. Treasury does not issue zero-coupon notes or bonds, brokerage firms have been able to create such products. The procedure is to purchase Treasury coupon securities and issue receipts representing an ownership interest in each coupon payment on the underlying Treasury securities and a receipt on the underlying Treasury securities' maturity value. This process of separating each coupon payment, as well as the principal, to sell securities backed by them is referred to as "coupon stripping."

To illustrate the process, suppose $500 million of a Treasury bond with a 30-year maturity and a coupon rate of 6% is purchased to create zero-coupon Treasury securities. The cash flow from this Treasury bond is 60 semiannual payments of $15 million each ($500 million times 0.06 divided by 2) and the repayment of principal of $500 million 30 years from now. As there are 61 payments to be made by the Treasury, a receipt representing a single payment claim on each payment is issued, which is effectively a zero-coupon bond. The amount of the maturity value for a receipt on a particular payment, whether coupon or principal, depends on the amount of the payment to be made by the U.S. Treasury on the underlying Treasury bond. In our example, 60 coupon receipts each have a maturity value of $15 million, and one receipt, the principal, has a maturity value of $500 million. The maturity dates for the receipts coincide with the corresponding payment dates for the Treasury securities.

These securities are issued under the U.S. Department of the Treasury's *Separate Trading of Registered Interest and Principal Securities* (STRIPS) program and a referred to in the market as "Treasury strips." They are direct obligations of the U.S. government.

Issuance of Treasury Securities

Treasury securities are all issued on an auction basis. For coupon securities, there are monthly 2-year note and 5-year note auctions and quarterly auctions for the 10-year note and 30-year bond. The auctions are conducted on a competitive bid basis. All U.S. Treasury auctions are single-price auctions. In a single-price auction, all bidders are awarded securities at the highest yield of accepted competitive tenders.

The most recently auctioned issue is referred to as the *on-the-run issue* or the *current issue*. Securities that are replaced by the on-the-run issue are called *off-the-run issues*.

FEDERAL AGENCY SECURITIES

Federal agency securities can be classified by the type of issuer, those issued by federally related institutions and those issued by government sponsored enterprises. *Federally related institutions* (also referred to as *government-owned agencies*) are arms of the federal government and generally do not issue securities directly in the marketplace. The major issuers have been the Tennessee Valley Authority (TVA) and the Private Export Funding Corporation. With the exception of securities of the TVA and the Private Export Funding Corporation, the securities are backed by the full faith and credit of the United States government.

Government sponsored enterprises (GSEs) are privately owned, publicly chartered entities. They were created by Congress to reduce the cost of capital for certain borrowing sectors of the economy deemed to be important enough to warrant assistance. The entities in these privileged sectors include farmers, homeowners, and students. Government sponsored enterprises issue securities directly in the marketplace.

Today there are five GSEs that issue securities: Federal Farm Credit System, Federal Home Loan Bank System, Federal National Mortgage Association (Fannie Mae), Federal Home Loan Mortgage Corporation (Freddie Mac), and Student Loan Marketing Association (Sallie Mae). The Federal Farm Credit Bank System is responsible for the credit market in the agricultural sector of the economy. The Federal Home Loan Bank, Freddie Mac, and Fannie Mae are responsible for providing credit to the housing sectors. Sallie Mae provides funds to support higher education. With the exception of the securities issued by the Federal Farm Credit Financial Assistance Corporation, GSE securities are not backed by the full faith and credit of the U.S. government. Consequently, investors purchasing GSEs are exposed to credit risk.

The securities issued by GSEs are one of two types: debentures and mortgage-backed/asset-backed securities. Debentures do not have any specific collateral backing the bond. The ability to repay bondholders depends on the ability of the issuing GSE to generate sufficient cash flows to satisfy the obligation. Several GSEs are frequent issuers of securities and therefore have developed regular programs for securities that they issue. Because of the decline in long-term Treasury bonds as a result of reduced issuance and Treasury buy backs, two GSEs, Fannie Mae and Freddie Mac, are hoping to replace Treasury securities as the benchmark interest rates in the marketplace. Let's take a look at the securities issues by these two GSEs.

Fannie Mae issues short-term debentures, Benchmark Bills, discount notes, medium-term notes, Benchmark Notes, Benchmark Bonds, Callable Benchmark Notes, and global bonds. Benchmark Bills and discount notes are issued at a discount from their maturity value and have maturities of 360 days or less. Benchmark Notes are of 5-year to 10-year maturity and are noncallable. Both Benchmark Notes and Bonds are eligible for stripping. Freddie Mac issues Reference Bills, discount notes, medium-term notes, Reference Notes, Callable Reference Bonds, Reference Notes, and global bonds. Reference Bills and discount notes are issued with maturities of one year or less. Reference Notes and Callable Reference Notes have maturities of 2 to 10 years and are the equivalent to Fannie Mae's Benchmark Notes and Callable Benchmark Notes.

CORPORATE BONDS

As the name indicates, corporate bonds are issued by corporations. Corporate bonds are classified by the type of issuer. The four general classifications used by bond information services are: (1) utilities, (2) transportations, (3) industrials, and (4) banks and finance companies. Finer breakdowns are often made to create more homogeneous groupings. For example, utilities are subdivided into electric power companies, gas distribution companies, water companies, and communication companies. Transportations are divided further into airlines, railroads, and trucking companies. Industrials are the catchall class, and the most heterogeneous of the groupings with respect to investment characteristics. Industrials include all kinds of manufacturing, merchandising, and service companies.

The promises of a corporate bond issuer and the rights of investors are set forth in great detail in a contract called a bond indenture. Failure to pay either the principal or interest when due constitutes legal default and court proceedings can be instituted to enforce the contract. Bondholders, as creditors, have a prior legal claim over preferred and common stockholders as to both income and assets of the corporation for the principal and interest due them.

There are two secondary corporate bond markets: the exchange market (New York Stock Exchange and American Stock Exchange) and the over-the-counter (OTC) market. Most trading takes place in the OTC market which is the market used by institutional investors.

Corporate Bankruptcy and Creditor Rights

The holder of a corporate debt instrument has priority over the equity owners in a bankruptcy proceeding. Moreover, there are creditors who have priority over other creditors. The law governing bankruptcy in the United States is the Bankruptcy Reform Act of 1978. One purpose of the act is to set forth the rules for a corporation to be either liquidated or reorganized. The liquidation of a corporation means that all the assets will be distributed to the holders of claims of the corporation and no corporate entity will survive. In a reorganization, a new corporate entity will result. Some security holders of the bankrupt corporation will receive cash in exchange for their claims, others may receive new securities in the corporation that results from the reorganization, and others may receive a combination of both cash and new securities in the resulting corporation.

Another purpose of the bankruptcy act is to give a corporation time to decide whether to reorganize or liquidate and then the necessary time to formulate a plan to accomplish either a reorganization or liquidation. This is achieved because when a corporation files for bankruptcy, the act grants the corporation protection from creditors who seek to collect their claims. The petition for bankruptcy can be filed either by the company itself, in which case it is called a *voluntary bankruptcy,* or by its creditors, in which case it is called an *involuntary bankruptcy.* A company that files for protection under the bankruptcy act generally becomes a "debtor-in-possession," and continues to operate its business under the supervision of the court.

The bankruptcy act comprises 15 chapters, each chapter covering a particular type of bankruptcy. Chapter 7 deals with the liquidation of a company; Chapter 11 deals with the reorganization of a company. When a company is liquidated, creditors receive distributions based on the *absolute priority rule* to the extent assets are available. The absolute priority rule is the principle that senior creditors are paid in full before junior creditors are paid anything. For secured and unsecured creditors, the absolute priority rule guarantees their seniority to equityholders. In liquidations, the absolute priority rule generally holds. In contrast, studies of actual reorganizations under Chapter 11 have found that the violation of absolute priority is the rule rather than the exception.

Security for Bonds

Either real property or personal property may be pledged to offer security beyond that of the general credit standing of the issuer. With a mortgage bond, the issuer has granted the bondholders a lien against the pledged assets. A lien is a legal right to sell mortgaged property to satisfy unpaid obligations to bondholders. In practice, foreclosure and sale of mortgaged property is unusual. If a default occurs, there is usually a financial reorganization of the issuer in which provision is made for settlement of the debt to bondholders. The mortgage lien is important, though, because it gives the mortgage bondholders a strong bargaining position relative to other creditors in determining the terms of a reorganization.

Some companies do not own fixed assets or other real property and so have nothing on which they can give a mortgage lien to secure bondholders. Instead, they own securities of other companies; they are holding companies and the other companies are subsidiaries. To satisfy the desire of bondholders for security, the issuer grants investors a lien on stocks, notes, bonds or whatever other kind of financial asset they own. Bonds secured by such assets are called *collateral trust bonds*.

Debenture bonds are not secured by a specific pledge of property, but that does not mean that holders have no claim on property of issuers or on their earnings. Debenture bondholders have the claim of general creditors on all assets of the issuer not pledged specifically to secure other debt. And they even have a claim on pledged assets to the extent that these assets generate proceeds in liquidation that are greater than necessary to satisfy secured creditors. *Subordinated debenture bonds* are issues that rank after secured debt, after debenture bonds, and often after some general creditors in their claim on assets and earnings.

It is important to recognize that while a superior legal status will strengthen a bondholder's chance of recovery in case of default, it will not absolutely prevent bondholders from suffering financial loss when the issuer's ability to generate cash flow adequate to pay its obligations is seriously eroded.

Convertible Bonds

A bond issue may give the bondholder the right to convert the security into a predetermined number of shares of common stock of the issuer. An *exchangeable bond* grants the bondholder the right to exchange the security for the common stock of a firm other than the issuer of the security. In our discussion, we use the term convertible bond to refer to both convertible and exchangeable bonds.

The number of shares of common stock that the bondholder will receive from exercising the call option of a convertible bond is called the *conversion ratio*. The conversion privilege may extend for all or only some portion of the bond's life, and the stated conversion ratio may change over time. It is always adjusted proportionately for stock splits and stock dividends. For example, suppose that a corporation issued a convertible bond with a conversion ratio is 25.32 shares. This means that for each $1,000 of par value of this issue the bondholder exchanges for that firm's common stock, he will receive 25.32 shares.

At the time of issuance of a convertible bond, the issuer effectively grants the bondholder the right to purchase the common stock at a price equal to the par value of the convertible bond divided by the conversion ratio. This price is referred to in the prospectus as the *stated conversion price*. The stated conversion price for the hypothetical convertible bond is $1,000/25.32 or $39.49.

Almost all convertible issues are callable by the issuer. Some convertible bonds are putable. Put options can be classified as "hard" puts and "soft" puts. A hard put is one in which the convertible bond must be redeemed by the issuer only for cash. In the case of a soft put, the issuer has the option to redeem the convertible bond for cash, securities, or a combination of the two.

Corporate Bond Ratings

Professional portfolio managers use various techniques to analyze information on companies and bond issues in order to estimate the ability of the issuer to live up to its future contractual obligations. This activity is known as *credit analysis*.

Some large institutional investors and many investment banking firms have their own credit analysis departments. Few individual investors and institutional bond investors, though, do their own analysis. Instead, they rely primarily on nationally recognized statistical rating organizations that perform credit analysis and issue their conclusions in the form of ratings. The three commercial rating companies are Moody's Investors Service, Standard & Poor's Corporation, and Fitch.

Rating Symbols

The rating systems use similar symbols, as shown in Exhibit 16.1. In all systems the term "high grade" means low credit risk, or conversely, high probability of future payments. The highest-grade bonds are designated by Moody's by the symbol Aaa, and by the other two rating systems by the symbol AAA. The next highest grade is denoted by the symbol Aa (Moody's) or AA (the other two rating systems); for the third grade all rating systems use A. The next three grades are Baa or BBB, Ba or BB, and B, respectively. There are also C grades.

Bonds rated triple A (AAA or Aaa) are said to be *prime*; double A (AA or Aa) are of *high quality*; single A issues are called *upper medium grade*; and triple B are *medium grade*. Lower-rated bonds are said to have speculative elements or be distinctly speculative.

EXHIBIT 16.1 Summary of Corporate Bond Rating Systems and Symbols

Fitch	Moody's	S&P	Summary Description
Investment Grade—High Creditworthiness			
AAA	Aaa	AAA	Gilt edge, prime, maximum safety
AA+	Aa1	AA+	
AA	Aa2	AA	High-grade, high-credit quality
AA–	Aa3	AA–	
A+	A1	A+	
A	A2	A	Upper-medium grade
A–	A3	A–	
BBB+	Baa1	BBB+	
BBB	Baa2	BBB	Lower-medium grade
BBB–	Baa3	BBB–	
Speculative—Lower Creditworthiness			
BB+	Ba1	BB+	
BB	Ba2	BB	Low grade, speculative
BB–	Ba3	BB–	
B+	B1		
B	B2	B	Highly speculative
B–	B3		
Predominantly Speculative, Substantial Risk, or in Default			
CCC+		CCC+	
CCC	Caa	CCC	Substantial risk, in poor standing
CC	Ca	CC	May be in default, very speculative
C	C	C	Extremely speculative
		CI	Income bonds—no interest being paid
DDD			
DD			Default
D		D	

All rating agencies use rating modifiers to provide a narrower credit quality breakdown within each rating category. S&P and Fitch use a rating modifier of plus and minus. Moody's uses 1, 2, and 3 as its rating modifiers.

Bond issues that are assigned a rating in the top four categories are referred to as *investment-grade bonds*. Issues that carry a rating below the top four categories are referred to as *noninvestment-grade bonds* or *speculative bonds*, or more popularly as *high-yield bonds* or *junk bonds*. Thus, the corporate bond market can be divided into two sectors: the investment-grade and non-investment-grade markets.

The Rating Process

The rating process involves the analysis of a multitude of quantitative and qualitative factors over the past, present, and future. The past and present are introductions to what the future may hold. Ratings should be prospective because future operations should provide the wherewithal to repay the debt. The ratings apply to the particular issue, not the issuer. While bond analysts rely on numbers and calculate many ratios to get a picture of the company's debt-servicing capacity, a rating is only an opinion or judgment of an issuer's ability to meet all of its obligations when due, whether during prosperity or during times of stress. The purpose of ratings is to rank issues in terms of the probability of default, taking into account the special features of the issue, the relationship to other obligations of the issuer, and current and prospective financial condition and operating performance.

In conducting its examination, the rating agencies consider the four Cs of credit—character, capacity, collateral, and covenants. The first of the Cs stands for *character of management*, the foundation of sound credit. In assessing management quality, the analysts at Moody's, for example, try to understand the business strategies and policies formulated by management. Following are factors that are considered: strategic direction, financial philosophy, conservatism, track record, succession planning, and control systems.

The next C is *capacity* or the ability of an issuer to repay its obligations. In assessing the ability of an issuer to pay, an analysis of the financial statements is undertaken. In addition to management quality, the factors examined by Moody's, for example, are industry trends, the regulatory environment, basic operating and competitive position, financial position and sources of liquidity, company structure (including structural subordination and priority of claim), parent company support agreements, and special event risk.

The third C, *collateral*, is looked at not only in the traditional sense of assets pledged to secure the debt, but also to the quality and value of those unpledged assets controlled by the issuer. In both senses the collateral is capable of supplying additional aid, comfort, and support to the debt and the debtholder. Assets form the basis for the generation of cash flow that services the debt in good times as well as bad.

The final C is for *covenants*, the terms and conditions of the lending agreement. Covenants lay down restrictions on how management operates the company and conducts its financial affairs. Covenants can restrict management's discretion. A default or violation of any covenant may provide a meaningful early warning alarm enabling investors to take positive and corrective action before the situation deteriorates further. Covenants have value because they play an important part in minimizing risk to creditors. They help prevent the unconscionable transfer of wealth from debtholders to equityholders.

Changes in Bond Ratings

Ratings of bonds change over time. Issuers are upgraded when their likelihood of default (as assessed by the rating company) decreases, and downgraded when their likelihood of default (as assessed by the rating company) increases. The rating companies publish the issues that they are reviewing for possible rating change.

To help investors understand how ratings change over time, the rating agencies publish this information periodically in the form of a table. This table is called a *rating transition matrix*. The table is useful for investors to assess potential downgrades and upgrades. A rating transition matrix is available for different holding periods.

MUNICIPAL SECURITIES

Bonds are issued by state and local governments and by entities that they establish. Local government units include municipalities, counties, towns and townships, school districts, and special service system districts. Included in the category of municipalities are cities, villages, boroughs, and incorporated towns that received a special state charter. Counties are geographical subdivisions of states whose functions are law enforcement, judicial administration, and construction and maintenance of roads. As with counties, towns and townships are geographical subdivisions of states and perform similar functions as counties. A special purpose service system district, or simply special district, is a political subdivision created to foster economic development or related services to a geographical area. Special districts provide public utility services (water, sewers, and drainage) and fire protection services. Public

INVESTING IN FIXED-INCOME SECURITIES

agencies or instrumentalities include authorities and commissions. Municipal securities expose investors to credit risk and are rated by the nationally recognized rating organizations.

These securities are popularly referred to as municipal securities, despite the fact that they are also issued by states and public agencies and their instruments. An *official statement* describing the issue and the issuer is prepared for new offerings.

There are both tax-exempt and taxable municipal securities. "Tax-exempt" means that interest on a municipal security is exempt from federal income taxation. The tax-exemption of municipal securities applies to interest income, not capital gains. The exemption may or may not extend to taxation at the state and local levels. Each state has its own rules as to how interest on municipal securities is taxed. Most municipal securities that have been issued are tax-exempt. Municipal securities are commonly referred to as "tax-exempt securities" despite the fact that there are taxable municipal securities that have been issued and are traded in the market.

Types of Municipal Securities

There are basically two types of municipal security structures: tax-backed debt and revenue bonds. We describe each type below, as well as variants.

Tax-Backed Debt

Tax-backed bonds are instruments issued by states, counties, special districts, cities, towns, and school districts that are secured by some form of tax revenue. Tax-backed debt includes general obligation debt, appropriation-backed obligations, bonds supported by public credit enhancement programs, and dedicated tax-backed obligations. We discuss each below.

The broadest type of tax-backed debt is general obligation debt. There are two types of general obligation pledges: unlimited and limited. An *unlimited tax general obligation debt* is the stronger form of general obligation pledge because it is secured by the issuer's unlimited taxing power. The tax revenue sources include corporate and individual income taxes, sales taxes, and property taxes. Unlimited tax general obligation debt is said to be secured by the full faith and credit of the issuer. A *limited tax general obligation debt* is a limited tax pledge because for such debt there is a statutory limit on tax rates that the issuer may levy to service the debt.

Agencies or authorities of several states have issued bonds that carry a potential state liability for making up shortfalls in the issuing entity's obligation. The appropriation of funds from the state's general tax revenue must be approved by the state legislature. However, the state's pledge is not binding. Bonds with this nonbinding pledge of tax revenue are called *moral obligation bonds*. Because a moral obligation bond requires legislative approval to appropriate the funds, it is classified as an appropriation-backed obligation. The purpose of the moral obligation pledge is to enhance the creditworthiness of the issuing entity.

While a moral obligation is a form of credit enhancement provided by a state, it is not a legally enforceable or legally binding obligation of the state. There are entities that have issued debt that carries some form of public credit enhancement that is legally enforceable. This occurs when there is a guarantee by the state or a federal agency or when there is an obligation to automatically withhold and deploy state aid to pay any defaulted debt service by the issuing entity. Typically, the latter form of public credit enhancement is used for bonds of a state's school systems.

In recent years, states and local governments have issued increasing amounts of bonds where the debt service is to be paid from so-called "dedicated" revenues such as sales taxes, tobacco settlement payments, fees, and penalty payments. Many are structured to mimic the asset-backed securities discussed later.

Revenue Bonds

The second basic type of security structure is found in a revenue bond. Revenue bonds are issued for enterprise financings that are secured by the revenues generated by the completed projects themselves, or for general public-purpose financings in which the issuers pledge to the bondholders the tax and revenue resources that were previously part of the general fund.

Revenue bonds can be classified by the type of financing. These include utility revenue bonds, transportation revenue bonds, housing revenue bonds, higher education revenue bonds, health care revenue bonds, sports complex and convention center revenue bonds, seaport revenue bonds, and industrial revenue bonds.

Special Bond Structures

Some municipal securities have special security structures. These include insured bonds, bank-backed municipal bonds, and refunded bonds.

Insured bonds, in addition to being secured by the issuer's revenue, are also backed by insurance policies written by commercial insurance companies. Insurance on a municipal bond is an agreement by an insurance company to pay the bondholder any bond principal and/or coupon interest that is due on a stated maturity date but that has not been paid by the bond issuer. Once issued, municipal bond insurance usually extends for the term of the bond issue, and it cannot be canceled by the insurance company.

Municipal securities have been increasingly supported by various types of credit facilities provided by commercial banks. The support is in addition to the issuer's cash flow revenues. There are three basic types of bank support: letter of credit, irrevocable line of credit, and revolving line of credit. A letter-of-credit is the strongest type of support available from a commercial bank. Under this arrangement, the bank is required to advance funds to the trustee if a default has occurred. An irrevocable line of credit is not a guarantee of the bond issue though it does provide a level of security. A revolving line of credit is a liquidity-type credit facility that provides a source of liquidity for payment of maturing debt in the event no other funds of the issuer are currently available. Because a bank can cancel a revolving line of credit without notice if the issuer fails to meet certain covenants, bond security depends entirely on the creditworthiness of the municipal issuer.

Although originally issued as either revenue or general obligation bonds, municipals are sometimes refunded. A refunding usually occurs when the original bonds are escrowed or collateralized by direct obligations guaranteed by the U.S. government. By this it is meant that a portfolio of securities guaranteed by the U.S. government is placed in a trust. The portfolio of securities is assembled such that the cash flows from the securities match the obligations that the issuer must pay. Once this portfolio of securities whose cash flows match those of the municipality's obligation is in place, the refunded bonds are no longer secured as either general obligation or revenue bonds. The bonds are now supported by cash flows from the portfolio of securities held in an escrow fund. Such bonds, if escrowed with securities guaranteed by the U.S. government, have little, if any, credit risk. They are the safest municipal bonds available. The escrow fund for a refunded municipal bond can be structured so that the refunded bonds are to be called at the first possible call date or a subsequent call date established in the original bond indenture. Such bonds are known as *prerefunded municipal bonds*. While refunded bonds are usually retired at their first or subsequent call date, some are structured to match the bond to the retirement date. Such bonds are known as *escrowed-to-maturity bonds*.

ASSET-BACKED SECURITIES

An asset-backed security (ABS) is a security backed by a pool of loans or receivables. A special category of ABSs are securities backed by real estate property, both residential and commercial. We will postpone our discussion of real estate backed securities until the next chapter.

Asset-backed securities are issued by corporations. This form of raising debt is an alternative to bond issuance. For an issuer that has an opportunity to issuer an ABS or a bond, the decision as to which to issue depends on what the cost is. All other factors constant, an issuer will select the funding source that is less expensive.

The key to structuring an ABS is a third-party entity known as the *special purpose vehicle* (SPV). It is this entity that legally buys the pool of loans or receivables from the company seeking to raise funds and then issues the securities.

Features of ABS

The collateral for an ABS can be classified as either amortizing or non-amortizing assets. *Amortizing assets* are loans in which the borrower's periodic payment consists of scheduled principal and interest payments over the life of the loan. The schedule for the repayment of the principal is called an *amortization schedule* and we will give an example in the next chapter when we discuss the standard residential mortgage loan. Auto loans are amortizing assets. *Prepayments* are any excess payment over the scheduled principal payment. Furthermore, prepayments are classified as either voluntary or involuntary. An *involuntary prepayment* occurs when the borrower has defaulted and the asset is repossessed and sold.

In contrast to amortizing assets, *non-amortizing assets* do not have a schedule for the periodic payments that the individual borrower must make. Instead, a non-amortizing asset is one in which the borrower must make a minimum periodic payment. If that payment is less than the interest on the outstanding loan balance, the shortfall is added to the outstanding loan balance. If the periodic payment is greater than the interest on the outstanding loan balance, then the difference is applied to the reduction of the outstanding loan balance. There is no schedule of principal payments (i.e., no amortization schedule) for a non-amortizing asset. Consequently, the concept of a prepayment does not apply. A credit card receivable described later is an example of a non-amortizing asset.

For an amortizing asset, projection of the cash flows requires projecting prepayments. One factor that may affect prepayments is the prevailing level of interest rates relative to the interest rate on the loan. In projecting prepayments it is critical to determine the extent to which borrowers take advantage of a decline in interest rates below the loan rate in order to refinance the loan. As we will see when we discuss valuation modeling in Chapter 20, whether or not borrowers will take advantage of refinancing when interest rates decline will determine the valuation methodology. In addition, modeling defaults for the collateral is critical in estimating the cash flows of an ABS. Projecting prepayments for amortizing assets requires an assumption about the default rate and the recovery rate. For a non-amortizing asset, while the concept of a prepayment does not exist, a projection of defaults is still necessary to project how much will be recovered and when.

The maturity of an ABS is not a meaningful parameter. Instead, the "average life" of the security is calculated. This measure will be explained in the next chapter.

Servicer

All loans must be serviced. Servicing involves collecting payments from borrowers, notifying borrowers who may be delinquent, and, when necessary, recovering and disposing of the collateral if the borrower does not make loan repayments by a specified time. These responsibilities are fulfilled by a third-party to an ABS transaction, the *servicer*. Moreover, while still viewed as a "third party" in many asset-backed securities transactions, the servicer is likely to be the originator of the loans used as the collateral. The role of the servicer is critical in an ABS transaction. Therefore, rating agencies look at the ability of a servicer to perform all the activities that a servicer will be responsible for before they assign a rating to the bonds in a transaction.

Credit Enhancements

ABS are credit enhanced. That means that credit support is provided for one or more bondholders in the structure. Typically a double A or triple A rating is sought for the most senior bondholder in a deal. The amount of credit enhancement necessary depends on rating agency requirements. There are two general types of credit enhancement structures: external and internal.

External Credit Enhancements

External credit enhancements come in the form of third-party guarantees that provide for first loss protection against losses up to a specified level, for example, 10%. The most common forms of external credit enhancement are (1) a corporate guarantee, (2) a letter of credit, and (3) bond insurance. Bond insurance provides the same function as in municipal bond structures. Typically, bond insurance is not used as the primary protection but to supplement other forms of credit enhancement. An ABS with external credit support is subject to the credit risk of the third-party guarantor. If the third-party guarantor is downgraded, the issue itself could be subject to downgrade.

Internal Credit Enhancements

Internal credit enhancements come in more complicated forms than external credit enhancements. The most common forms of internal credit enhancements are reserve funds, overcollateralization, and senior-subordinated structures.

Reserve Funds   Reserve funds come in two forms: cash reserve funds and excess servicing spread. *Cash reserve funds* are straight deposits of cash generated from issuance proceeds. In this case, part of the underwriting profits from the deal are deposited into a fund.

Excess servicing spread accounts involve the allocation of excess spread or cash into a separate reserve account after paying out the net coupon, servicing fee, and all other expenses on a monthly basis. For example, suppose that the gross weighted average coupon of the collateral is 8%. This means that the collateral is paying about 8%. Payments must be made to bondholders and the servicer and other fees. Suppose that the servicing and other fees are 0.50% and that the net weighted average coupon is 7.25%. The net weighted average coupon is just the rate that is paid to all the bondholders in the structure. Therefore, the amount being paid out is 7.75% (7.25% + 0.50%). Hence, 8% is coming in from the collateral and 7.75% is being paid out, leaving a spread of 0.25% or 25 basis points. This amount is referred to the *excess servicing spread* and this amount can be paid into a reserve account. The amount in this excess servicing spread account will gradually increase and can be used to pay for possible future losses.

Overcollateralization   The total par value of the tranches is the liability of the structure. So, if a structure has two tranches with a par value of $300 million, then that is the amount of the liability. The amount of the collateral backing the structure must be at least equal to the amount of the liability. If the amount of the collateral exceeds the amount of the liability of the structure, the deal is said to be *overcollateralized*. The amount of overcollateralization represents a form of internal credit enhancement because it can be used to absorb losses. For example, if the liability of the structure is $300 million and the collateral's value is $320 million, then the structure is overcollateralized by $20 million. Thus, the first $20 million of losses will not result in a loss to any of the tranches.

Senior-Subordinated Structure   In a senior-subordinated structure there is a senior bondholder, also referred to as the "senior tranche," and at least one subordinated bondholder, also called the "subordinated tranche."

For example, suppose an ABS deal has $300 million as collateral (i.e., a pool of loans). The structure may look as follows:

senior tranche	$270 million
subordinated tranche	$30 million

This means that the first $30 million of losses are absorbed by the subordinated tranche.

The structure can have more than one subordinated tranche. For example, the structure could be as follows:

senior tranche	$270 million
subordinated tranche 1	$22 million
subordinated tranche 2	$8 million

In this structure, the subordinated tranches 1 and 2 are called the *non-senior tranches*. The senior tranche still has protection up to $30 million as in the previous structure with only one subordinated tranche. In the second structure, the first $8 million of losses is absorbed by the subordinated tranche 2. Hence, this tranche is referred to as the *first-loss tranche*. Subordinated tranche 1 has protection of up to $8 million in losses, the protection provided by the first-loss tranche.

Passthrough versus Paythrough Structures

A pool of loans or receivables is used as collateral and certificates (securities) are issued with each certificate entitled to a pro rata share of the cash flow from the collateral. So, if a $100 million loan pool is the collateral for an ABS and 10,000 certificates are issued, then the holder of one certificate is entitled to 1/10,000 of the cash flow from the collateral. This type of structure is called a *passthrough structure*.

As explained above, for credit enhancement an ABS deal can be structured as a senior-subordinated structure as follows:

senior tranche	$280 million	10,000 certificates issued
subordinated tranche	$20 million	1,000 certificates issued

This structure is called a *passthrough structure* because each certificate holder (senior or subordinate tranche) is entitled to a pro rata share of the cash flow from the collateral. That is, each certificate holder of the senior tranche is entitled to receive 1/10,000 of the cash flow to be paid to the senior tranche from the collateral. Each certificate holder of the subordinated tranche is entitled to receive 1/1,000 of the cash flow to be paid to the subordinated tranche from the collateral.

It common to create a structure such that the senior tranches are carved up into different tranches. This type of ABS structure is referred to as a *paythrough structure*. In this structure, each tranche created will receive the cash flow from the collateral based on a set of rules set forth in the prospectus as to how the priority of the distribution of interest and principal will be distributed to each of the senior tranches. This will be made clear in the next chapter when we discuss a security called a collateralized mortgage obligation.

Major Non-Real Estate-Backed ABS Types

ABS can be classified as real estate- and non-real estate-backed securities. Real estate-backed securities are the subject of the next chapter. Next we review the major non-real estate-backed ABS types.

Auto Loan-Backed Securities

Auto loan-backed securities are issued by the financial subsidiaries of auto manufacturers (domestic and foreign), commercial banks, independent finance companies, and small financial institutions specializing in auto loans. There are auto loan-backed deals that are passthrough structures and paythrough structures.

The cash flow for auto loan-backed securities consists of regularly scheduled monthly loan payments (interest and scheduled principal repayments) and any prepayments. For securities backed by auto loans, prepayments result from (1) sales and trade-ins requiring full payoff of the loan, (2) repossession and subsequent resale of the vehicle, (3) loss or destruction of the vehicle, (4) payoff of the loan with cash to save on the interest cost, and (5) refinancing of the loan at a lower interest cost. Prepayments due to repossession and subsequent resale are sensitive to the economic cycle. In recessionary economic periods, prepayments due to this factor increase. Refinancings are of minor importance for automobile loans.

Student Loan-Backed Securities

Student loans are made to cover college cost (undergraduate, graduate, and professional programs such as medical and law schools) and tuition for a wide range of vocational and trade schools. Securities backed by student loans are popularly referred to as SLABS (student loan asset-backed securities). The major issuer of SLABS is the Student Loan Marketing Association (Sallie Mae), a GSE.

The student loans that have been most commonly securitized are those that are made under the Federal Family Education Loan Program (FFELP). Under this program, the government makes loans to students via private lenders. The decision by private lenders to extend a loan to a student is not based on the applicant's ability to repay the loan. If a default of a loan occurs and the loan has been properly serviced, then the government will guarantee up to 98% of the principal plus accrued interest. Alternative loans are loans that are not part of a government guarantee program. These loans are basically consumer loans and the lender's decision to extend an alternative loan will be based on the ability of the applicant to repay the loan. Alternative loans have been securitized.

SBA Loan-Backed Securities

The Small Business Administration (SBA) is an agency of the U.S. government empowered to guarantee loans made by approved SBA lenders to qualified borrowers. The monthly cash flow that the investor in an SBA-backed security receives consists of (1) the coupon interest based on the coupon rate set for the period, (2) the scheduled principal repayment (i.e., scheduled amortization), and (3) prepayments.

Credit Card Receivable-Backed Securities

Credit card receivable-backed securities are backed by credit card receivables. Credit cards are issued by banks (e.g., Visa and MasterCard), retailers (e.g., JC Penney and Sears), and travel and entertainment companies (e.g., American Express). For a pool of credit card receivables, the cash flow consists of finance charges collected, fees, and principal. Finance charges collected represent the periodic interest the credit card borrower is charged based on the unpaid balance after the grace period. Fees include late payment fees and any annual membership fees. Interest to security holders is paid periodically (e.g, monthly, quarterly, or semiannually). The interest rate may be fixed or floating.

A credit card receivable-backed security is a nonamortizing security. For a specified period of time, referred to as the *lockout period* or *revolving period*, the principal payments made by credit card borrowers comprising the pool are reinvested in additional receivables to maintain the size of the pool. The lockout period can vary from 18 months to 10 years. So, during the lockout period, the cash flow that is paid out to security holders is based on finance charges collected and fees. After the lockout period, the principal is no longer reinvested but paid to investors. This period is referred to as the *principal-amortization period*.

Collateralized Debt Obligations

A collateralized debt obligation (CDO) is an asset-backed security backed by a diversified pool of one or more of the following types of debt obligations: (1) non-investment grade (i.e., high yield) corporate bonds, (2) emerging market bonds, and (3) bank loans to corporate entities. When a CDO is backed only by bonds, it is referred to as a *collateralized bond obligation* (CBO). If the collateral is only bank loans, it is referred to as a *collateralized loan obligation* (CDO).

The typical structure of a CDO is as follows. There is (1) a senior tranche, (2) different layers of subordinate tranches, and (3) an equity tranche. In a CDO there is an asset manager responsible for managing the portfolio of debt obligations.

There are three phases in the life of a CDO. The first phase is a startup phase or ramp phase. In this phase, which is one or two months, the asset manager assembles the portfolio with the proceeds received from the sale of the CDO tranches. Once the portfolio is assembled, the manager monitors the portfolio and is responsible for reinvesting any principal repayments due to any calls or proceeds received from any defaulted issues. This phase is called the *reinvestment phase*. This phase varies from 3 years to 5 years. Finally, principal payments to the senior and junior tranches must be made over the balance of the CDO's life. This phase is called the *pay down phase*.

Because the cash flows from the structure are designed to accomplish the objective for each tranche, restrictions are imposed on the asset managers. The asset manager is not free to buy and sell bonds. The conditions for disposing of issues held are specified and are usually driven by credit risk management. Also, in assembling the portfolio during the start-up phase, the asset manager must meet certain requirements set forth by the rating agency or agencies that rate the deal. These requirements have to do with constructing a diversified portfolio and minimum ratings for the issues acquired. The asset manager during the reinvestment and pay down phases must monitor the collateral to ensure that certain tests or covenants are being met.

CHAPTER 17

Real Estate-Backed Securities

Frank J. Fabozzi, Ph.D., CFA
Adjunct Professor of Finance
School of Management
Yale University

Real estate-backed securities are securities backed by a pool (collection) of mortgage loans. Residential or commercial properties can be used as collateral for such securities. Real estate backed securities backed by residential mortgage loans include mortgage passthrough securities, stripped mortgage-backed securities, and collateralized mortgage obligations. In this chapter we describe these securities as well as securities backed by commercial mortgage loans.

MORTGAGES

We begin our discussion with the raw material for a mortgage-backed security (MBS)—the mortgage loan. A mortgage loan, or simply mortgage, is a loan secured by the collateral of some specified real estate property, which obliges the borrower to make a predetermined series of payments. The mortgage gives the lender the right if the borrower defaults (i.e., fails to make the contracted payments) to "foreclose" on the loan and seize the property in order to ensure that the debt is paid off. The interest rate on the mortgage loan is called the mortgage rate or contract rate. Here our focus is on residential mortgage loans.

An individual who wants to borrow funds to purchase a home will apply for a loan from a mortgage originator. The individual who seeks funds completes an application form that provides personal financial information, and pays an application fee; then the mortgage originator performs a credit evaluation of the applicant. The two primary factors in determining whether the funds will be lent are the (1) payment-to-income (PTI) ratio, and (2) the loan-to-value (LTV) ratio. The former is the ratio of monthly payments to monthly income and is a measure of the ability of the applicant to make monthly payments (both mortgage and real estate tax payments). The lower this ratio, the greater the likelihood that the applicant will be able to meet the required payments.

LTV is the ratio of the amount of the loan to the market (or appraised) value of the property. The lower this ratio, the greater the protection the lender has if the applicant defaults on the payments and the lender must repossess and sell the property. For example, if an applicant wants to borrow $150,000 on property with an appraised value of $200,000, the LTV is 75%. Suppose the applicant subsequently defaults on the mortgage. The lender can then repossess the property and sell it to recover the amount owed. But the amount that will be received by the lender depends on the market value of the property. In our example, even if conditions in the housing market are weak, the lender will still be able to recover the proceeds lent if the value of the property declines by $50,000. Suppose instead that the applicant wanted to borrow $180,000 for the same property. The LTV would then be 90%. If the lender had to sell the property because the applicant defaults, there is less protection for the lender.

When the lender makes the loan based on the credit of the borrower and on the collateral for the mortgage, the mortgage is said to be a *conventional mortgage*. The lender also may take out mortgage insurance to guarantee the fulfillment of the borrower's obligation. Some borrowers can qualify for mortgage insurance guaranteed by one of three U.S. government agencies: the Federal Housing Administration (FHA), the Veteran's Administration (VA), and the Rural Housing Service (RHS). There are also private mortgage insurers.

There are many types of mortgage designs available in the United States. A mortgage design is a specification of the interest rate, term of the mortgage, and manner in which the borrowed funds are repaid. Here we will discuss the major one: the fixed-rate, level-payment, fully amortized mortgage. With an understanding of the features of this mortgage, securities backed by mortgages can be understood.

Fixed-Rate, Level-Payment, Fully Amortized Mortgage

The basic idea behind the design of the fixed-rate, level-payment, fully amortized mortgage is that the borrower pays interest and repays principal in equal installments over an agreed-upon period of time, called the maturity or term of the mortgage. The frequency of payment is typically monthly. Each monthly mortgage payment for this mortgage design is due on the first of each month and consists of:

1. Interest of $\frac{1}{12}$th of the annual interest rate times the amount of the outstanding mortgage balance at the beginning of the previous month, and
2. A repayment of a portion of the outstanding mortgage balance (principal).

The difference between the monthly mortgage payment and the portion of the payment that represents interest equals the amount that is applied to reduce the outstanding mortgage balance. The monthly mortgage payment is designed so that after the last scheduled monthly payment of the loan is made, the amount of the outstanding mortgage balance is zero (i.e., the mortgage is fully repaid or amortized).

To illustrate this mortgage design, consider a 30-year (360-month) $100,000 mortgage with a mortgage rate of 8.125%. The monthly mortgage payment would be $742.50. Exhibit 17.1 shows for selected months how each monthly mortgage payment is divided between interest and repayment of principal. At the beginning of month 1, the mortgage balance is $100,000, the amount of the original loan. The mortgage payment for month 1 includes interest on the $100,000 borrowed for the month. Since the interest rate is 8.125%, the monthly interest rate is 0.0067708 (0.08125 divided by 12). Interest for month 1 is therefore $677.08 ($100,000 times 0.0067708). The $65.42 difference between the monthly mortgage payment of $742.50 and the interest of $677.08 is the portion of the monthly mortgage payment that represents repayment of principal. The $65.42 in month 1 reduces the mortgage balance. Notice that the last mortgage payment in month 360 is sufficient to pay off the remaining mortgage balance.

As Exhibit 17.1 clearly shows, the portion of the monthly mortgage payment applied to interest declines each month, and the portion applied to reducing the mortgage balance increases. The reason for this is that as the mortgage balance is reduced with each monthly mortgage payment, the interest on the mortgage balance declines. Since the monthly mortgage payment is fixed, an increasingly larger portion of the monthly payment is applied to reduce the principal in each subsequent month.

The monthly mortgage payment made by the borrower is not what the investor receives. This is because the mortgage must be serviced. We discussed servicing in the previous chapter. The servicing fee is a portion of the mortgage rate. If the mortgage rate is 8.125% and the servicing fee is 50 basis points, then the investor receives interest of 7.625%. The interest rate that the investor receives is said to be the *net interest* or *net coupon*.

EXHIBIT 17.1   Amortization Schedule for a Fixed-Rate, Level-Payment,
Fully Amortized Mortgage
Mortgage loan: $100,000
Mortgage rate: 8.125%
Monthly payment: $742.50
Term of loan: 30 years (360 months)

Month	Beginning Mortgage Balance ($)	Monthly Payment ($)	Monthly Interest ($)	Scheduled Principal Repayment ($)	Ending Mortgage Balance ($)
1	100,000.00	742.50	677.08	65.42	99,934.58
2	99,934.58	742.50	676.64	65.86	99,868.72
3	99,868.72	742.50	676.19	66.31	99,802.41
25	98,301.53	742.50	665.58	76.91	98,224.62
26	98,224.62	742.50	665.06	77.43	98,147.19
27	98,147.19	742.50	664.54	77.96	98,069.23
74	93,849.98	742.50	635.44	107.05	93,742.93
75	93,742.93	742.50	634.72	107.78	93,635.15
76	93,635.15	742.50	633.99	108.51	93,526.64
141	84,811.77	742.50	574.25	168.25	84,643.52
142	84,643.52	742.50	573.11	169.39	84,474.13
143	84,474.13	742.50	571.96	170.54	84,303.59
184	76,446.29	742.50	517.61	224.89	76,221.40
185	76,221.40	742.50	516.08	226.41	75,994.99
186	75,994.99	742.50	514.55	227.95	75,767.04
233	63,430.19	742.50	429.48	313.02	63,117.17
234	63,117.17	742.50	427.36	315.14	62,802.03
235	62,802.03	742.50	425.22	317.28	62,484.75
289	42,200.92	742.50	285.74	456.76	41,744.15
290	41,744.15	742.50	282.64	459.85	41,284.30
291	41,284.30	742.50	279.53	462.97	40,821.33
321	25,941.42	742.50	175.65	566.85	25,374.57
322	25,374.57	742.50	171.81	570.69	24,803.88
323	24,803.88	742.50	167.94	574.55	24,229.32
358	2,197.66	742.50	14.88	727.62	1,470.05
359	1,470.05	742.50	9.95	732.54	737.50
360	737.50	742.50	4.99	737.50	0.00

Prepayments and Cash Flow Uncertainty

Our illustration of the cash flows from a fixed-rate, level-payment, fully amortized mortgage assumes that the homeowner does not pay off any portion of the mortgage balance prior to the scheduled due date. But homeowners do pay off all or part of their mortgage balance prior to the maturity date. Payments made in excess of the scheduled principal repayments are called *prepayments*. Later we will discuss factors that affect prepayments.

The effect of prepayments is that the amount and timing of the cash flows from a mortgage are not known with certainty. This risk is referred to as *prepayment risk*. For example, all that the investor in a $100,000, 8.125% 30-year mortgage knows is that as long as the loan is outstanding and the borrower does not default, interest will be received and the principal will be repaid at the scheduled date each month; then at the end of the 30 years, the investor would have received $100,000 in principal payments. What the investor does not know—the uncertainty—is for how long the loan will be outstanding, and therefore what the timing of the principal payments will be. This is true for all mortgage loans, not just fixed-rate, level-payment, fully amortized mortgages.

The majority of mortgages outstanding do not penalize the borrower for prepaying any part or all of the outstanding mortgage balance. In recent years, *prepayment penalty mortgages* (PPMs) have been originated. In a PPM there is a specified time period, called the "lockout period," where prepayments above a specified amount will result in a prepayment penalty. After the lockout period there are no penalties for prepayment. The motivation for the PPM is that it reduces prepayment risk for the lender during the lockout period. It does so by effectively making it more costly for the borrower to prepay in order to take advantage of a decline in mortgage rates. In exchange for this reduction in prepayment risk, the lender will offer a mortgage rate that is less than that of an otherwise comparable mortgage loan without a prepayment penalty.

MORTGAGE PASSTHROUGH SECURITIES

Investing in mortgages exposes an investor to default risk and prepayment risk. A more efficient way is to invest in a mortgage passthrough security. This is a security created when one or more holders of mortgages form a pool of mortgages and sell shares or participation certificates in the pool. A pool may consist of several thousand or only a few mortgages. When a mortgage is included in a pool of mortgages that is used as collateral for a mortgage passthrough security, the mortgage is said to be "securitized."

The cash flows of a mortgage passthrough security depend on the cash flows of the underlying mortgages. The cash flows consist of monthly mortgage payments representing interest, the scheduled repayment of principal, and any prepayments for all the mortgages in the pool.

Payments are made to securityholders each month. Neither the amount nor the timing, however, of the cash flows from the pool of mortgages is identical to that of the cash flows passed through to investors. The monthly cash flows for a passthrough are less than the monthly cash flows of the underlying mortgages by an amount equal to servicing and other fees. The other fees are those charged by the issuer or guarantor of the passthrough for guaranteeing the issue. The coupon rate on a passthrough, called the *passthrough coupon rate*, is less than the mortgage rate on the underlying pool of mortgage loans by an amount equal to the servicing fee and guarantee fee. Consequently, if there are 10,000 certificates issued, then the holder of one certificate is entitled to 1/10,000 of the cash flow from the pool of mortgages after adjusting for all fees.

The timing of the cash flows is also different. The monthly mortgage payment is due from each mortgagor on the first day of each month, but there is a delay in passing through the corresponding monthly cash flow to the securityholders. The length of the delay varies by the type of passthrough security.

Not all of the mortgages that are included in a pool of mortgages that are securitized have the same mortgage rate and the same maturity. Consequently, when describing a passthrough security, a weighted average coupon rate and a weighted average maturity are determined. A *weighted average coupon rate*, or WAC, is found by weighting the mortgage rate of each mortgage loan in the pool by the amount of the mortgage balance outstanding. A *weighted average maturity*, or WAM, is found by weighting the remaining number of months to maturity for each mortgage loan in the pool by the amount of the mortgage balance outstanding.

Other features of mortgage passthrough securities vary by issuer. The key features of a passthrough will have an impact on its investment characteristics (particularly its prepayment characteristics). These features include (1) the type of guarantee, (2) the mortgage design of the underlying pool of loans, and (3) the characteristics of the mortgage loans in a pool.

Agency Passthroughs

Mortgage passthroughs are classified into Government National Mortgage Association (Ginnie Mae) mortgage passthroughs, Federal National Mortgage Association (Fannie Mae) mortgage passthroughs, Federal Home Loan Mortgage Corporation (Freddie Mac) mortgage passthroughs, and private entity mortgage passthroughs. The first three issuers are federal agencies which were described in the previous chapter. Ginnie Mae is a federally related institution while Fannie Mae and Freddie Mac are government sponsored enterprises (GSEs).

There are several practices in the market in referring to the mortgage passthroughs issued by these entities. Some market participants simply refer to them as "agency passthroughs." Other market participants refer to the mortgage passthroughs issued by Ginnie Mae as "agency passthroughs" and those issued by the two GSEs as "conventional passthroughs" and then all three are referred to as "agency/conventional passthroughs." In this chapter mortgage passthroughs issued by Ginnie Mae, Fannie Mae, and Freddie Mac will be referred to as agency passthroughs.

For a mortgage to be included in the pool of mortgages that is the collateral for an agency passthrough, the loans must meet the criteria established by the agency. These criteria are referred to as "underwriting standards." A mortgage that meets the underwriting standards is referred to as a "conforming loan" and obviously a loan that fails the underwriting standards is called a "nonconforming loan."

Private entities are issuers of mortgage passthroughs that are not one of the federal agencies. They include commercial bank, savings and loan associations, investment banking firms, finance companies, and mortgage companies. The mortgage passthrough securities issued by private entities are referred to as "nonagency passthroughs." The mortgages that back nonagency passthrough securities are nonconforming loans. We will discuss some of the underwriting standards later in this chapter because as will be seen, the mortgages underlying nonagency passthrough securities are mortgages that fail one particular underwriting standard.

Default Risk

A Ginnie Mae passthrough—referred to by as a *Ginnie Mae mortgage-backed security (MBS)*—is guaranteed by the full faith and credit of the U.S. government. That is, the investor will receive timely payment of interest and principal when it is due even if borrowers default on their loans. Thus, a Ginnie Mae MBS is viewed as risk-free in terms of default risk, just like Treasury securities.

Because Fannie Mae and Freddie Mac are GSEs, a mortgage passthrough that they issue is not guaranteed by the full faith and credit of the U.S. government. Market participants, however, view their mortgage passthroughs as having minimal credit risk. A passthrough issued by Fannie Mae—called a *Fannie Mae mortgage-backed security (MBS)*—is guaranteed with respect to the timely payment of interest and principal. A Freddie Mac passthrough—called a *Freddie Mac participation certificate* (PC)—can have one of two guarantees. One type of guarantee is where Freddie Mac guarantees the timely payment of interest and the eventual payment of principal. By "eventual" it is meant that the principal due will be paid when it is collected, but in no circumstance later than one year. The second type of guarantee is one in which Freddie Mac guarantees the timely payment of both interest and principal. Freddie Mac now only issues this type of PC.

For nonagency passthroughs, there is no explicit or implicit government guarantee. Instead, a private entity must credit enhance the issue. The mechanisms for credit enhancement (internal and external) were explained in the previous chapter.

Prepayment Conventions and Cash Flows

In order to value a passthrough security, it is necessary to project its cash flows. The difficulty is that the cash flows are unknown because of prepayments. The only way to project cash flows is to make some assumptions about the prepayment rate over the life of the underlying mortgage pool. The prepayment rate is sometimes referred to as the *speed*. Two conventions have been used as a benchmark for prepayment rates: conditional prepayment rate and Public Securities Association prepayment benchmark.

Conditional Prepayment Rate   One convention for projecting prepayments and the cash flows of a passthrough assumes that some fraction of the remaining principal in the pool is prepaid each month for the remaining term of the mortgage. The prepayment rate assumed for a pool, called the *conditional prepayment rate* (CPR), is based on the characteristics of the pool (including its historical prepayment experience) and the current and expected future economic environment.

The CPR is an annual prepayment rate. To estimate monthly prepayments, the CPR must be converted into a monthly prepayment rate, commonly referred to as the *single-monthly mortality rate* (SMM). A formula can be used to determine the SMM for a given CPR:

$$SMM = 1 - (1 - CPR)^{1/12}$$

Suppose that the CPR used to estimate prepayments is 6%. The corresponding SMM is:

$$SMM = 1 - (1 - 0.06)^{1/12} = 1 - (0.94)^{0.08333} = 0.005143$$

An SMM of $w\%$ means that approximately $w\%$ of the remaining mortgage balance at the beginning of the month, less the scheduled principal payment, will prepay that month. That is,

Prepayment for month t
= SMM × (Beginning mortgage balance for month t
– Scheduled principal payment for month t)

For example, suppose that an investor owns a passthrough in which the remaining mortgage balance at the beginning of some month is $290 million. Assuming that the SMM is 0.5143% and the scheduled principal payment is $3 million, the estimated prepayment for the month is:

$$0.005143 \times (\$290,000,000 - \$3,000,000) = \$1,476,041$$

PSA Prepayment Benchmark   The Public Securities Association (PSA) prepayment benchmark is expressed as a monthly series of CPRs. The PSA benchmark assumes that prepayment rates are low for newly originated mortgages and then will speed up as the mortgages become seasoned.

The PSA benchmark assumes the following prepayment rates for 30-year mortgages:

1. A CPR of 0.2% for the first month, increased by 0.2% per year per month for the next 30 months when it reaches 6% per year, and
2. A 6% CPR for the remaining years

This benchmark, referred to as "100% PSA" or simply "100 PSA." and mathematically is expressed as follows:

if $t \le 30$ then CPR = 6% $t/30$
if $t > 30$ then CPR = 6%

where t is the number of months since the mortgage originated.

Slower or faster speeds are then referred to as some percentage of PSA. For example, 50 PSA means one-half the CPR of the PSA benchmark prepayment rate; 150 PSA means 1.5 times the CPR of the PSA benchmark prepayment rate; 300 PSA means three times the CPR of the benchmark prepayment rate. A prepayment rate of 0 PSA means that no prepayments are assumed.

The CPR is converted to an SMM using the formula given above. For example, assuming 165 PSA the SMMs for month 20 after the mortgage is originated is calculated as follows:

$$CPR = 6\% \ (20/30) = 4\% = 0.04$$

$$165 \ PSA = 1.65 \ (0.04) = 0.066$$

$$SMM = 1 - (1 - 0.066)^{1/12} = 0.005674$$

Notice that the SMM assuming 165 PSA is not just 1.65 times the SMM assuming 100 PSA. It is the CPR that is a multiple of the CPR assuming 100 PSA.

For months 31 to 360, the CPR is 6% at 100 PSA and the CPR and SMM for each month for 165 PSA is:

$$165 \ PSA = 1.65 \ (0.06) = 0.099$$

$$SMM = 1 - (1 - 0.099))^{1/12} = 0.00865$$

Illustration of Monthly Cash Flow Construction   We now show how to construct a monthly cash flow for a hypothetical passthrough given a PSA assumption. For the purpose of this illustration, the underlying mortgages for this hypothetical passthrough are assumed to be fixed-rate, level-payment, fully amortized mortgages with a WAC of 8.125%. It will be assumed that the passthrough rate is 7.5% with a WAM of 357 months.

Exhibit 17.2 shows the cash flow for selected months assuming 165 PSA. The cash flow is broken down into three components: (1) interest (based on the passthrough rate), (2) the regularly scheduled principal repayment, and (3) prepayments based on 165 PSA.

Column (2) gives the outstanding mortgage balance at the beginning of the month. It is equal to the outstanding balance at the beginning of the previous month reduced by the total principal payment in the previous month. Column (3) shows the SMM for 165 PSA. Two things should be noted in this column. First, for month 1, the SMM is for a passthrough that has been seasoned 3 months because the WAM is 357. The total monthly mortgage payment is shown in Column (4). Notice that the total monthly mortgage payment declines over time as prepayments reduce the mortgage balance outstanding. There is a formula to determine what the monthly mortgage balance will be for each month given prepayments, but we will not present that formula here. Column (6) gives the regularly scheduled principal repayment. This is the difference between the total monthly mortgage payment [the amount shown in Column (4)] and the gross coupon interest for the month. The gross coupon interest is 8.125% multiplied by the outstanding mortgage balance at the beginning of the month, then divided by 12.

EXHIBIT 17.2 Monthly Cash Flow for a $400 Million Passthrough with a 7.5% Passthrough Rate, a WAC of 8.125%, and a WAM of 357 Months Assuming 165 PSA

(1)	(2)	(3)	(4)	(5)	(6)	(7)	(8)	(9)
Month	Outstanding Balance	SMM	Mortgage Payment	Net Interest	Scheduled Principal	Prepayment	Total Principal	Cash Flow
1	$400,000,000	0.00111	$2,975,868	$2,500,000	$267,535	$442,389	$709,923	$3,209,923
2	399,290,077	0.00139	2,972,575	2,495,563	269,048	552,847	821,896	3,317,459
3	398,468,181	0.00167	2,968,456	2,490,426	270,495	663,065	933,560	3,423,986
4	397,534,621	0.00195	2,963,513	2,484,591	271,873	772,949	1,044,822	3,529,413
5	396,489,799	0.00223	2,957,747	2,478,061	273,181	882,405	1,155,586	3,633,647
26	350,540,672	0.00835	2,656,123	2,190,879	282,671	2,923,885	3,206,556	5,397,435
27	347,334,116	0.00865	2,633,950	2,170,838	282,209	3,001,955	3,284,164	5,455,002
28	344,049,952	0.00865	2,611,167	2,150,312	281,662	2,973,553	3,255,215	5,405,527
29	340,794,737	0.00865	2,588,581	2,129,967	281,116	2,945,400	3,226,516	5,356,483
30	337,568,221	0.00865	2,566,190	2,109,801	280,572	2,917,496	3,198,067	5,307,869
100	170,142,350	0.00865	1,396,958	1,063,390	244,953	1,469,591	1,714,544	2,777,933
101	168,427,806	0.00865	1,384,875	1,052,674	244,478	1,454,765	1,699,243	2,751,916
102	66,728,563	0.00865	1,372,896	1,042,054	244,004	1,440,071	1,684,075	2,726,128
103	165,044,489	0.00865	1,361,020	1,031,528	243,531	1,425,508	1,669,039	2,700,567
200	56,746,664	0.00865	585,990	354,667	201,767	489,106	690,874	1,045,540
201	56,055,790	0.00865	580,921	350,349	201,377	483,134	684,510	1,034,859
202	55,371,280	0.00865	575,896	346,070	200,986	477,216	678,202	1,024,273
203	54,693,077	0.00865	570,915	341,832	200,597	471,353	671,950	1,013,782
204	54,021,127	0.00865	565,976	337,632	200,208	465,544	665,752	1,003,384
205	53,355,375	0.00865	561,081	333,471	199,820	459,789	659,609	993,080
353	760,027	0.00865	155,107	4,750	149,961	5,277	155,238	159,988
354	604,789	0.00865	153,765	3,780	149,670	3,937	153,607	157,387
355	451,182	0.00865	152,435	2,820	149,380	2,611	151,991	154,811
356	299,191	0.00865	151,117	1,870	149,091	1,298	150,389	152,259
357	148,802	0.00865	149,809	930	148,802	0	148,802	149,732

Note: Since the WAM is 357 months, the underlying mortgage pool is seasoned an average of 3 months. Therefore, the CPR for month 27 is 1.65 × 6%.

The prepayment for the month is reported in Column (7). The prepayment is found using the formula given in the previous section. For example, in month 100, the beginning mortgage balance is $170,142,350, the scheduled principal payment is $244,953, and the SMM at 165 PSA is 0.00865. Therefore, the prepayment is:

$$0.00865 \times (\$170,142,350 - \$244,953) = \$1,469,612$$

The difference between $1,469,591 shown in Column (7) and the prepayment of $1,469,612 computed here is simply due to the rounding of the SMM shown in the exhibit to save space.

The total principal payment reported in Column (8) is the sum of Columns (6) and (7). Finally, the projected monthly cash flow for this passthrough is shown in Column (9). The monthly cash flow is the sum of the interest paid to the passthrough investor [Column (5)] and the total principal payments for the month [Column (8)].

Factors Affecting Prepayment Behavior

A prepayment model is a statistical model that is used to forecast prepayments. It begins by modeling the statistical relationships among the factors that are expected to affect prepayments. The four factors that affect prepayment behavior are (1) prevailing mortgage rate, (2) characteristics of the underlying mortgage pool, (3) seasonal factors, and (4) general economic activity. We discuss these factors in the following sections.

Prevailing Mortgage Rate   The single most important factor affecting prepayments because of refinancing is the current level of mortgage rates relative to the borrower's contract rate. The more the contract rate exceeds the prevailing mortgage rate, the greater the incentive to refinance the mortgage loan. For refinancing to make economic sense, the interest savings must be greater than the costs associated with refinancing the mortgage. These costs include legal expenses, origination fees, title insurance, and the value of the time associated with obtaining another mortgage loan. Some of these costs, such as title insurance and origination points, will vary proportionately with the amount to be financed. Other costs, such as the application fee and legal expenses, are typically fixed.

Historically, it has been observed that when mortgage rates fall to more than 200 basis points below the contract rate, prepayment rates increase. However, the creativity of mortgage originators in designing mortgage loans such that the refinancing costs are folded into the amount borrowed has changed the view that mortgage rates must drop dramatically below the contract rate to make refinancing economical. Moreover, mortgage originators now do an effective job of advertising to make homeowners cognizant of the economic benefits of refinancing.

The historical pattern of prepayments and economic theory suggests that it is not only the level of mortgage rates that affects prepayment behavior but also the path that mortgage rates take to get to the current level. To illustrate why, suppose the underlying contract rate for a pool of mortgage loans is 11% and that 3 years after origination, the prevailing mortgage rate declines to 8%. Let's consider two possible paths of the mortgage rate in getting to the 8% level. In the first path, the mortgage rate declines to 8% at the end of the first year, then rises to 13% at the end of the second year, and then falls to 8% at the end of the third year. In the second path, the mortgage rate rises to 12% at the end of the first year, continues its rise to 13% at the end of the second year, and then falls to 8% at the end of the third year.

If the mortgage rate follows the first path, those who can benefit from refinancing will more than likely take advantage of this opportunity when the mortgage rate drops to 8% in the first year. When the mortgage rate drops again to 8% at the end of the third year, the likelihood is that prepayments because of refinancing will not surge; those who can benefit by taking advantage of the refinancing opportunity will have done so already when the mortgage rate declined the first time. This prepayment behavior is referred to as *refinancing burnout* (or simply, burnout).

In contrast, the expected prepayment behavior when the mortgage rate follows the second path is quite different. Prepayment rates are expected to be low in the first 2 years. When the mortgage rate declines to 8% in the third year, refinancing activity, and therefore prepayments, are expected to surge. Consequently, burnout is related to the path of mortgage rates.

Our focus so far has been on the factors that affect prepayments caused by refinancing. Prepayments also occur because of housing turnover. The level of mortgage rates affects housing turnover to the extent that a lower rate increases the affordability of homes.

Characteristics of the Underlying Mortgage Loans The following characteristics of the underlying mortgage loans affect prepayments: (1) the contract rate, (2) whether the loans are FHA/VA-guaranteed or noninsured loans, (3) the amount of seasoning, (4) the type of loan (e.g. fixed rate versus adjustable rate and 15-year maturity versus 30-year maturity), and (4) the geographical location of the underlying properties.

Seasonality There is a well-documented seasonal pattern in prepayments. This pattern is related to activity in the primary housing market, with home buying increasing in the spring and gradually reaching a peak in the late summer. Home buying declines in the fall and winter. Mirroring this activity are the prepayments that result from the turnover of housing as home buyers sell their existing homes and purchase new ones. Prepayments are low in the winter months and begin to rise in the spring, reaching a peak in the summer months. However, probably because of delays in passing through prepayments, the peak may not be observed until early fall.

Macroeconomic Factors Economic theory would suggest that general economic activity affects prepayment behavior through its effect on housing turnover. The link is as follows: A growing economy results in a rise in personal income and in opportunities for worker migration; this increases family mobility and as a result increases housing turnover. The opposite holds for a weak economy.

Average Life

The stated maturity of a mortgage passthrough is an inappropriate measure because of principal repayments over time. Instead, market participants calculate an *average life* which is the average time to receipt of principal payments (scheduled principal payments and projected prepayments), weighted by the amount of principal expected. Specifically, the average life is found by first calculating:

$$
\begin{array}{l}
1 \times (\text{Projected principal received in month 1}) \\
+\ 2 \times (\text{Projected principal received in month 2}) \\
+\ 3 \times (\text{Projected principal received in month 3}) \\
\qquad \cdots \\
\underline{+\ T \times (\text{Projected principal received in month } T)} \\
\text{Weighted monthly average of principal received}
\end{array}
$$

where T is the last month that principal is expected to be received. Then the average life is found as follows:

$$
\text{Average life} = \frac{\text{Weighted monthly average of principal received}}{12 \times (\text{Total principal to be received})}
$$

The average life of a passthrough depends on the PSA prepayment assumption. To see this, the average life is shown below for different prepayment speeds for the passthrough used to illustrate the cash flows in Exhibit 17.2:

PSA speed	50	100	165	200	300	400	500	600	700
Average life	15.11	11.66	8.76	7.68	5.63	4.44	3.68	3.16	2.78

Contraction Risk and Extension Risk

An investor who owns passthrough securities does not know what the cash flows will be because that depends on prepayments. As noted earlier, this risk is called prepayment risk. However, prepayment risk can be divided into two risks, contraction risk and extension risk. We will explain these two risks by means of an example.

Suppose an investor buys a 10% coupon mortgage passthrough at a time when the prevailing mortgage rate is 10%. Suppose further that the expected average life for this mortgage passthrough is 9 years based on a prepayment rate of 110 PSA. Let's consider what will happen to prepayments if mortgage rates decline to, say, 6%. The borrower will have an incentive to prepay all or part of the mortgage resulting in a shortening of the average life of the security from what it was expected to be when the security was purchased. For example, the market might expect that the prepayment speed will increase to 200 PSA resulting in a decrease in the average life to 6 years. The disadvantage to the investor is that the funds received from the prepayments will have to be reinvested at lower interest rates. This risk that the average life of the security will be shortened forcing the investor to reinvest at lower interest rates is referred to as *contraction risk*.

Now let's look at what happens if mortgage rates rise to 14%. Prepayments can be expected to slow down because homeowners will not refinance or partially prepay their mortgages, resulting in an increase in the expected average life. For example, the market might expect the prepayment rate to decrease to 75 PSA that would result in an average life of 12 years. Unfortunately, it is in a rising interest rate environment when investors want prepayments to speed up so that they can reinvest the principal received at the higher market interest rate. This adverse consequence of rising mortgage rates is called *extension risk*.

Therefore, prepayment risk encompasses contraction risk and extension risk. Prepayment risk makes passthrough securities unattractive for certain individuals and financial institutions to hold for purposes of accomplishing their investment objectives. Some individuals and institutional investors are concerned with extension risk and others with contraction risk when they purchase a passthrough security. Is it possible to alter the cash flows of a passthrough to reduce the contraction risk and extension risk for institutional investors? This can be done as we will see when we discuss collateralized mortgage obligations.

STRIPPED MORTGAGE-BACKED SECURITIES

A mortgage passthrough distributes the cash flow from the underlying pool of mortgages on a pro rata basis to the securityholders. A *stripped mortgage-backed security* (stripped MBS) is created by altering that distribution of principal and interest from a pro rata distribution to an unequal distribution. In the most common type of stripped MBS, all the interest is allocated to one class—the *interest only class*—and all the principal to the other class—the *principal-only class*.

Principal-Only Securities

A principal-only security, also a called the *PO* or a *principal-only mortgage strip*, is purchased at a substantial discount from par value. The return an investor realizes depends on the speed at which prepayments are made. The faster the prepayments, the higher the investor's return. For example, suppose there is a mortgage pool consisting only of 30-year mortgages, with $400 million in principal, and that investors can purchase POs backed by this mortgage pool for $175 million. The dollar return on this investment will be $225 million. How quickly that dollar return is recovered by PO investors determines the actual return that will be realized. In the extreme case, if all homeowners in the underlying mortgage pool decide to prepay their mortgage loans immediately, PO investors will realize the $225 million immediately. At the other extreme, if all homeowners decide to remain in their homes for 30 years and make no prepayments, the $225 million will be spread out over 30 years, which would result in a lower return for PO investors.

Let's look at how the price of the PO would be expected to change as mortgage rates in the market change. When mortgage rates decline below the contract rate, prepayments are expected to speed up, accelerating payments to the PO holder. Thus, the cash flow of a PO improves (in the sense that principal repayments are received earlier). The cash flow will be discounted at a lower interest rate because the mortgage rate in the market has declined. The result is that the PO price will increase when mortgage rates decline. When mortgage rates rise above the contract rate, prepayments are expected to slow down. The cash flow deteriorates (in the sense that it takes longer to recover principal repayments). Couple this with a higher discount rate, and the price of a PO will fall when mortgage rates rise.

Interest-Only Securities

An interest-only class, also called an *IO* or an *interest-only mortgage strip*, has no par value. In contrast to the PO investor, the IO investor wants prepayments to be slow because the IO investor receives interest only on the amount of the principal outstanding. When prepayments are made, less dollar interest will be received as the outstanding principal declines. In fact, if prepayments are too fast, the IO investor may not recover the amount paid for the IO even if the security is held to maturity.

Let's look at the expected price response of an IO to changes in mortgage rates. If mortgage rates decline below the contract rate, prepayments are expected to accelerate. This would result in a deterioration of the expected cash flow for an IO. While the cash flow will be discounted at a lower rate, the net effect typically is a decline in the price of an IO. If mortgage rates rise above the contract rate, the expected cash flow improves, but the cash flow is discounted at a higher interest rate. The net effect may be either a rise or fall for the IO.

Thus, we see an interesting characteristic of an IO: Its price tends to move in the same direction as the change in mortgage rates (1) when mortgage rates fall below the contract rate and (2) for some range of mortgage rates above the contract rate. Both POs and IOs exhibit substantial price volatility when mortgage rates change. The greater price volatility of the IO and PO compared to the passthrough from which they were created is because the combined price volatility of the IO and PO must be equal to the price volatility of the passthrough.

An average life for a PO can be calculated based on some prepayment assumption. However, an IO receives no principal payments, so technically an average life cannot be computed. Instead, for an IO a "cash flow average life" is computed, using the projected interest payments in the average life formula instead of principal.

AGENCY COLLATERALIZED MORTGAGE OBLIGATIONS

Some institutional investors are concerned with extension risk and others with contraction risk when they invest in a mortgage passthrough. This problem can be mitigated by redirecting the cash flows of mortgage passthrough securities to different bond classes, called *tranches*, so as to create securities that have different exposure to prepayment risk and, therefore, different risk/return patterns than the passthrough securities from which the tranches were created. As explained in the previous chapter, an asset-backed security can be either a passthrough structure or a paythrough structure. A CMO is an example of a paythrough structure.

When the cash flows of pools of mortgage passthrough securities are redistributed to different bond classes, the resulting securities are called *collateralized mortgage obligations* (CMOs). The creation of a CMO cannot eliminate prepayment risk; it can only distribute the various forms of this risk among different classes of bondholders. The CMO's major financial innovation is that the securities created more closely satisfy the asset/liability needs of institutional investors and thus broaden the appeal of mortgage-backed products to bond investors.

Rather than list the different types of tranches that can be created in a CMO structure, we will show how the tranches can be created. This will provide an excellent illustration of financial engineering. Although there are many different types of CMOs that have been created, we will only look at three of the key innovations in the CMO market: sequential-pay tranches, accrual tranches, and planned amortization tranches. Two other important tranches that are not illustrated here are the floating-rate tranche and the inverse floating-rate tranche.

Sequential-Pay CMOs

A *sequential-pay* CMO is structured so that each class of bond (i.e., tranche) is retired sequentially. To illustrate a sequential-pay CMO, we discuss CMO-1, a hypothetical deal made up to illustrate the basic features of the structure. The collateral for this hypothetical CMO is a hypothetical mortgage passthrough with a total par value of $400 million and the following characteristics: (1) the security's coupon rate is 7.5%, (2) the WAC is 8.125%, and (3) the WAM is 357 months. This is the same mortgage passthrough that we used earlier in this chapter to describe the cash flow of a passthrough based on some PSA assumption.

From this $400 million of collateral, four tranches are created. Their characteristics are summarized in Exhibit 17.3. The total par value of the four tranches is equal to the par value of the collateral (i.e., the mortgage passthrough). In this simple structure, the coupon rate is the same for each tranche and also the same as the coupon rate on the collateral. There is no reason why this must be so, and, in fact, typically the coupon rate varies by tranche.

EXHIBIT 17.3   CMO-1: A Hypothetical Four-Tranche Sequential-Pay Structure

Tranche	Par Amount	Coupon Rate (%)
A	$194,500,000	7.5
B	36,000,000	7.5
C	96,500,000	7.5
D	73,000,000	7.5
Total	$400,000,000	

Payment rules:
1. *For payment of periodic coupon interest:* Disburse periodic coupon interest to each tranche on the basis of the amount of principal outstanding at the beginning of the period.
2. *For disbursement of principal payments:* Disburse principal payments to tranche A until it is completely paid off. After tranche A is completely paid off, disburse principal payments to tranche B until it is completely paid off. After tranche B is completely paid off, disburse principal payments to tranche C until it is completely paid off. After tranche C is completely paid off, disburse principal payments to tranche D until it is completely paid off.

Now remember that a CMO is created by redistributing the cash flow—interest and principal—to the different tranches based on a set of payment rules. The payment rules at the bottom of Exhibit 17.3 describe how the cash flow from the passthrough (i.e., collateral) is to be distributed to the four tranches. There are separate rules for the payment of the coupon interest and the payment of principal, the principal being the total of the regularly scheduled principal payment and any prepayments.

In CMO-1, each tranche receives periodic coupon interest payments based on the amount of the outstanding balance at the beginning of the month. The disbursement of the principal, however, is made in a special way. A tranche is not entitled to receive principal until the entire principal of the tranche has been paid off. More specifically, tranche A receives all the principal payments until the entire principal amount owed to that tranche, $194,500,000, is paid off; then tranche B begins to receive principal and continues to do so until it is paid the entire $36,000,000. Tranche C then receives principal, and when it is paid off, tranche D starts receiving principal payments.

Although the priority rules for the disbursement of the principal payments are known, the precise amount of the principal in each period is not. This will depend on the cash flow and, therefore, on the principal payments of the collateral, which will depend on the actual prepayment rate of the collateral. An assumed PSA speed allows the cash flow to be projected. Exhibit 17.2 shows the cash flow (interest, regularly scheduled principal repayment, and prepayments) assuming 165 PSA. Assuming that the collateral does prepay at 165 PSA, the cash flow available to all four tranches of CMO-1 will be precisely the cash flow shown in Exhibit 17.2.

To demonstrate how the priority rules for CMO-1 work, Exhibit 17.4 shows the cash flow for selected months assuming the collateral prepays at 165 PSA. For each tranche the exhibit shows: (1) the balance at the end of the month, (2) the principal paid down (regularly scheduled principal repayment plus prepayments), and (3) interest. In month 1, the cash flow for the collateral consists of principal payment of $709,923 and interest of $2.5 million (0.075 times $400 million divided by 12). The interest payment is distributed to the four tranches based on the amount of the par value outstanding. So, for example, tranche A receives $1,215,625 (0.075 times $194,500,000 divided by 12) of the $2.5 million. The principal, however, is all distributed to tranche A. Therefore, the cash flow for tranche A in month 1 is $1,925,548. The principal balance at the end of month 1 for tranche A is $193,790,076 (the original principal balance of $194,500,000 less the principal payment of $709,923). No principal payment is distributed to the three other tranches because there is still a principal balance outstanding for tranche A. This will be true for months 2 through 80.

EXHIBIT 17.4 Monthly Cash Flow for Selected Months for
CMO-1 Assuming 165 PSA

Month	Tranche A			Tranche B		
	Balance	Principal	Interest	Balance	Principal	Interest
1	194,500,000	709,923	1,215,625	36,000,000	0	225,000
2	193,790,077	821,896	1,211,188	36,000,000	0	225,000
3	192,968,181	933,560	1,206,051	36,000,000	0	225,000
4	192,034,621	1,044,822	1,200,216	36,000,000	0	225,000
5	190,989,799	1,155,586	1,193,686	36,000,000	0	225,000
6	189,834,213	1,265,759	1,186,464	36,000,000	0	225,000
7	188,568,454	1,375,246	1,178,553	36,000,000	0	225,000
8	187,193,208	1,483,954	1,169,958	36,000,000	0	225,000
9	185,709,254	1,591,789	1,160,683	36,000,000	0	225,000
10	184,117,464	1,698,659	1,150,734	36,000,000	0	225,000
11	182,418,805	1,804,473	1,140,118	36,000,000	0	225,000
12	180,614,332	1,909,139	1,128,840	36,000,000	0	225,000
75	12,893,479	2,143,974	80,584	36,000,000	0	225,000
76	10,749,504	2,124,935	67,184	36,000,000	0	225,000
77	8,624,569	2,106,062	53,904	36,000,000	0	225,000
78	6,518,507	2,087,353	40,741	36,000,000	0	225,000
79	4,431,154	2,068,807	27,695	36,000,000	0	225,000
80	2,362,347	2,050,422	14,765	36,000,000	0	225,000
81	311,926	311,926	1,950	36,000,000	1,720,271	225,000
82	0	0	0	34,279,729	2,014,130	214,248
83	0	0	0	32,265,599	1,996,221	201,660
84	0	0	0	30,269,378	1,978,468	189,184
85	0	0	0	28,290,911	1,960,869	176,818
95	0	0	0	9,449,331	1,793,089	59,058
96	0	0	0	7,656,242	1,777,104	47,852
97	0	0	0	5,879,138	1,761,258	36,745
98	0	0	0	4,117,880	1,745,550	25,737
99	0	0	0	2,372,329	1,729,979	14,827
100	0	0	0	642,350	642,350	4,015
101	0	0	0	0	0	0
102	0	0	0	0	0	0
103	0	0	0	0	0	0
104	0	0	0	0	0	0
105	0	0	0	0	0	0

EXHIBIT 17.4 (Continued)

	Tranche C			Tranche D		
Month	Balance	Principal	Interest	Balance	Principal	Interest
1	96,500,000	0	603,125	73,000,000	0	456,250
2	96,500,000	0	603,125	73,000,000	0	456,250
3	96,500,000	0	603,125	73,000,000	0	456,250
4	96,500,000	0	603,125	73,000,000	0	456,250
5	96,500,000	0	603,125	73,000,000	0	456,250
6	96,500,000	0	603,125	73,000,000	0	456,250
7	96,500,000	0	603,125	73,000,000	0	456,250
8	96,500,000	0	603,125	73,000,000	0	456,250
9	96,500,000	0	603,125	73,000,000	0	456,250
10	96,500,000	0	603,125	73,000,000	0	456,250
11	96,500,000	0	603,125	73,000,000	0	456,250
12	96,500,000	0	603,125	73,000,000	0	456,250
95	96,500,000	0	603,125	73,000,000	0	456,250
96	96,500,000	0	603,125	73,000,000	0	456,250
97	96,500,000	0	603,125	73,000,000	0	456,250
98	96,500,000	0	603,125	73,000,000	0	456,250
99	96,500,000	0	603,125	73,000,000	0	456,250
100	96,500,000	1,072,194	603,125	73,000,000	0	456,250
101	95,427,806	1,699,243	596,424	73,000,000	0	456,250
102	93,728,563	1,684,075	585,804	73,000,000	0	456,250
103	92,044,489	1,669,039	575,278	73,000,000	0	456,250
104	90,375,450	1,654,134	564,847	73,000,000	0	456,250
105	88,721,315	1,639,359	554,508	73,000,000	0	456,250
175	3,260,287	869,602	20,377	73,000,000	0	456,250
176	2,390,685	861,673	14,942	73,000,000	0	456,250
177	1,529,013	853,813	9,556	73,000,000	0	456,250
178	675,199	675,199	4,220	73,000,000	170,824	456,250
179	0	0	0	72,829,176	838,300	455,182
180	0	0	0	71,990,876	830,646	449,943
181	0	0	0	71,160,230	823,058	444,751
182	0	0	0	70,337,173	815,536	439,607
183	0	0	0	69,521,637	808,081	434,510
184	0	0	0	68,713,556	800,690	429,460
185	0	0	0	67,912,866	793,365	424,455
350	0	0	0	1,235,674	160,220	7,723
351	0	0	0	1,075,454	158,544	6,722
352	0	0	0	916,910	156,883	5,731
353	0	0	0	760,027	155,238	4,750
354	0	0	0	604,789	153,607	3,780
355	0	0	0	451,182	151,991	2,820
356	0	0	0	299,191	150,389	1,870
357	0	0	0	148,802	148,802	930

After month 81, the principal balance will be zero for tranche A. For the collateral, the cash flow in month 81 is $3,318,521, consisting of a principal payment of $2,032,196 and interest of $1,286,325. At the beginning of month 81 (end of month 80), the principal balance for tranche A is $311,926. Therefore, $311,926 of the $2,032,196 of the principal payment from the collateral will be disbursed to tranche A. After this payment is made, no additional principal payments are made to this tranche as the principal balance is zero. The remaining principal payment from the collateral $1,720,271, is disbursed to tranche B. According to the assumed prepayment speed of 165 PSA, tranche B then begins receiving principal payments in month 81.

Exhibit 17.4 shows that tranche B is fully paid off by month 100, when tranche C now begins to receive principal payments. Tranche C is not fully paid off until month 178, at which time tranche D begins receiving the remaining principal payments. The maturity (i.e., the time until the principal is fully paid off) for these four tranches assuming 165 PSA would be 81 months for tranche A, 100 months for tranche B, 178 months for tranche C, and 357 months for tranche D.

Let's look at what has been accomplished by creating the CMO. First, as shown earlier in this chapter, the average life for the mortgage passthrough is 8.76 years, assuming a prepayment speed of 165 PSA. Below is the average life of the collateral and the four tranches assuming different prepayment speeds:

Prepayment Speed (PSA)	Average Life for				
	Collateral	Tranche A	Tranche B	Tranche C	Tranche D
50	15.11	7.48	15.98	21.02	27.24
100	11.66	4.90	10.86	15.78	24.58
165	8.76	3.48	7.49	11.19	20.27
200	7.68	3.05	6.42	9.60	18.11
300	5.63	2.32	4.64	6.81	13.36
400	4.44	1.94	3.70	5.31	10.34
500	3.68	1.69	3.12	4.38	8.35
600	3.16	1.51	2.74	3.75	6.96
700	2.78	1.38	2.47	3.30	5.95

Notice that the four tranches have average lives that are both shorter and longer than the collateral, thereby attracting investors who have a preference for an average life different from that of the collateral.

There is still a major problem: There is considerable variability of the average life for the tranches. We'll see how this can be tackled later on. However, there is some protection provided for each tranche against prepayment risk. This is because prioritizing the distribution of principal (i.e., establishing the payment rules for principal) effectively protects the shorter-term tranche A in this structure against extension risk. This protection must come from somewhere, so it comes from the three other tranches. Similarly, tranches C and D provide protection against extension risk for tranches A and B. At the same time, tranches C and D benefit because they are provided protection against contraction risk, the protection coming from tranches A and B.

Accrual Bonds

In CMO-1, the payment rules for interest provide for all tranches to be paid interest each month. In many sequential-pay CMO structures, at least one tranche does not receive current interest. Instead, the interest for that tranche would accrue and be added to the principal balance. Such a bond class is commonly referred to as an *accrual tranche*, or a *Z bond* (because the bond is similar to a zero-coupon bond). The interest that would have been paid to the accrual tranche is then used to speed up paying down the principal balance of earlier tranches.

To see this, consider CMO-2, a hypothetical CMO structure with the same collateral as CMO-1 and with four tranches, each with a coupon rate of 7.5%. The structure is shown in Exhibit 17.5. The difference is in the last tranche, Z, which is an accrual tranche.

Let's look at month 1 for CMO-2 and compare it to month 1 in CMO-1 shown in Exhibit 17.4 based on 165 PSA. The principal payment from the collateral is $709,923. In CMO-1, this is the principal paydown for tranche A. In CMO-2, the interest for tranche Z, $456,250, is not paid to that tranche but instead is used to pay down the principal of tranche A. So, the principal payment to tranche A is $1,166,173, the collateral's principal payment of $709,923 plus the interest of $456,250 that was diverted from tranche Z.

The inclusion of the accrual tranche results in a shortening of the expected final maturity for tranches A, B, and C. The final payout for tranche A is 64 months rather than 81 months, for tranche B it is 77 months rather than 100 months, and for tranche C it is 112 rather than 178 months. The average lives for tranches A, B, and C are shorter in CMO-2 compared to CMO-1 because of the inclusion of the accrual bond. For example, at 165 PSA, the average lives are as follows:

Structure	Tranche A	Tranche B	Tranche C
CMO-2	2.90	5.86	7.87
CMO-1	3.48	7.49	11.19

EXHIBIT 17.5   CMO-2: A Hypothetical Four-Tranche
Sequential-Pay Structure with an Accrual Bond Class

Tranche	Par Amount	Coupon Rate (%)
A	$194,500,000	7.5
B	36,000,000	7.5
C	96,500,000	7.5
Z (Accrual)	73,000,000	7.5
Total	$400,000,000	

Payment rules:
1. *For payment of periodic coupon interest:* Disburse periodic coupon interest to
tranches A, B, and C on the basis of the amount of principal outstanding at the beginning of the period. For tranche Z, accrue the interest based on the principal plus
accrued interest in the previous period. The interest for tranche Z is to be paid to the
earlier tranches as a principal pay down.
2. *For disbursement of principal payments:* Disburse principal payments to tranche
A until it is completely paid off. After tranche A is completely paid off, disburse principal payments to tranche B until it is completely paid off. After tranche B is completely paid off, disburse principal payments to tranche C until it is completely paid
off. After tranche C is completely paid off, disburse principal payments to tranche Z
until the original principal balance plus accrued interest is completely paid off.

The reason for the shortening of the nonaccrual tranches is that the
interest that would be paid to the accrual bond is being allocated to the
other tranches. Tranche Z in CMO-2 will have a longer average life
than tranche D in CMO-1. Thus, shorter-term tranches and a longer-
term tranche are created by including an accrual bond. The accrual
bond appeals to investors who are concerned with reinvestment risk.
Since there are no coupon payments to reinvest, reinvestment risk is
eliminated until all the other tranches are paid off.

Planned Amortization Class Tranches

In a *planned amortization class* (PAC) CMO structure, if prepayments
are within a specified range, the cash flow pattern is known for some of
the tranches in the structure, particularly those tranches identified as
PAC tranches. The greater predictability of the cash flow for these
tranches occurs because there is a principal repayment schedule that
must be satisfied. PAC tranches have priority over all other tranches in
the CMO structure in receiving principal payments from the underlying
collateral. The greater certainty of the cash flow for the PAC tranches
comes at the expense of the non-PAC classes, called the *support tranches*

or *companion tranches*. It is the support tranches that absorb the pre-payment risk.

To illustrate how to create a PAC bond, we will use as collateral the $400 million mortgage passthrough with a coupon rate of 7.5%, a WAC of 8.125%, and a WAM of 357 months. The second column of Exhibit 17.6 shows the principal payment (regularly scheduled principal repayment plus prepayments) for selected months assuming a prepayment speed of 90 PSA, and the next column shows the principal payments for selected months assuming that the mortgage passthrough prepays at 300 PSA.

The last column of Exhibit 17.6 gives the minimum principal payment if the collateral speed is 90 PSA or 300 PSA for months 1 to 349. (After month 349, the outstanding principal balance will be paid off if the prepayment speed is between 90 PSA and 300 PSA.) For example, in the first month, the principal payment would be $508,169.52 if the collateral prepays at 90 PSA and $1,075,931.20 if the collateral prepays at 300 PSA. Thus, the minimum principal payment is $508,169.52, as reported in the last column of Exhibit 17.6. In month 103, the minimum principal payment is also the amount if the prepayment speed is 90 PSA, $1,446,761, compared to $1,458,618.04 for 300 PSA. In month 104, however, a prepayment speed of 300 PSA would produce a principal payment of $1,433,539.23, which is less than the principal payment of $1,440,825.55 assuming 90 PSA. So, $1,433,539.23 is reported in the last column of Exhibit 17.6. In fact, from month 104 on, the minimum principal payment is the one that would result assuming a prepayment speed of 300 PSA.

In fact, if the collateral prepays at any speed between 90 PSA and 300 PSA, the minimum principal payment would be the amount reported in the last column of Exhibit 17.6. For example, if we had included principal payment figures assuming a prepayment speed of 200 PSA, the minimum principal payment would not change: From month 11 through month 103, the minimum principal payment is that generated from 90 PSA, but from month 104 on, the minimum principal payment is that generated from 300 PSA.

This characteristic of the collateral allows for the creation of a PAC tranche, assuming that the collateral prepays over its life at a constant speed between 90 PSA and 300 PSA. A schedule of principal repayments that the PAC bondholders are entitled to receive before any other tranche in the CMO is specified. The monthly schedule of principal repayments is as specified in the last column of Exhibit 17.6, which shows the minimum principal payment. Although there is no assurance that the collateral will prepay between these two speeds, a PAC bond can be structured assuming that it will.

EXHIBIT 17.6   Monthly Principal Payment for $400 Million Par
7.5% Coupon Passthrough with an 8.125% WAC and a
357 WAM Assuming Prepayment Rates of 90 PSA and 300 PSA

	Principal Payment		Minimum Principal Payment
Month	At 90% PSA	At 300% PSA	PAC Schedule
1	$508,169.52	$1,075,931.20	$508,169.52
2	569,843.43	1,279,412.11	569,843.43
3	631,377.11	1,482,194.45	631,377.11
4	692,741.89	1,683,966.17	692,741.89
5	753,909.12	1,884,414.62	753,909.12
6	814,850.22	2,083,227.31	814,850.22
7	875,536.68	2,280,092.68	875,536.68
8	935,940.10	2,474,700.92	935,940.10
9	996,032.19	2,666,744.77	996,032.19
10	1,055,784.82	2,855,920.32	1,055,784.82
11	1,115,170.01	3,041,927.81	1,115,170.01
12	1,174,160.00	3,224,472.44	1,174,160.00
13	1,232,727.22	3,403,265.17	1,232,727.22
14	1,290,844.32	3,578,023.49	1,290,844.32
15	1,348,484.24	3,748,472.23	1,348,484.24
16	1,405,620.17	3,914,344.26	1,405,620.17
17	1,462,225.60	4,075,381.29	1,462,225.60
18	1,518,274.36	4,231,334.57	1,518,274.36
101	1,458,719.34	1,510,072.17	1,458,719.34
102	1,452,725.55	1,484,126.59	1,452,725.55
103	1,446,761.00	1,458,618.04	1,446,761.00
104	1,440,825.55	1,433,539.23	1,433,539.23
105	1,434,919.07	1,408,883.01	1,408,883.01
211	949,482.58	213,309.00	213,309.00
212	946,033.34	209,409.09	209,409.09
213	942,601.99	205,577.05	205,577.05
346	618,684.59	13,269.17	13,269.17
347	617,071.58	12,944.51	12,944.51
348	615,468.65	12,626.21	12,626.21
349	613,875.77	12,314.16	3,432.32
350	612,292.88	12,008.25	0
351	610,719.96	11,708.38	0
352	609,156.96	11,414.42	0
353	607,603.84	11,126.28	0
354	606,060.57	10,843.85	0
355	604,527.09	10,567.02	0
356	603,003.38	10,295.70	0
357	601,489.39	10,029.78	0

EXHIBIT 17.7 CMO-3: CMO Structure with One PAC Tranche and One Support Tranche

Tranche	Par Amount	Coupon Rate (%)
P (PAC)	$243,800,000	7.5
S (Support)	156,200,000	7.5
Total	$400,000,000	

Payment rules:

1. *For payment of periodic coupon interest:* Disburse periodic coupon interest to each tranche on the basis of the amount of principal outstanding at the beginning of the period.

2. *For disbursement of principal payments:* Disburse principal payments to tranche P based on its schedule of principal repayments. Tranche P has priority with respect to current and future principal payments to satisfy the schedule. Any excess principal payments in a month over the amount necessary to satisfy the schedule for tranche P are paid to tranche S. When tranche S is completely paid off, all principal payments are to be made to tranche P regardless of the schedule.

Exhibit 17.7 shows a CMO structure, CMO-3, created from the $400 million, 7.5% coupon mortgage passthrough with a WAC of 8.125% and a WAM of 357 months. There are just two tranches in this structure: a 7.5% coupon PAC tranche created assuming 90 to 300 PSA with a par value of $243.8 million, and a support bond with a par value of $156.2 million.

The average life for the PAC tranche and the support tranche in CMO-3 assuming various actual prepayment speeds is shown below:

Prepayment Rate (PSA)	PAC Tranche (P)	Support Tranche (S)
0	15.97	27.26
50	9.44	24.00
90	7.26	18.56
100	7.26	18.56
150	7.26	12.57
165	7.26	11.16
200	7.26	8.38
250	7.26	5.37
300	7.26	3.13
350	6.56	2.51
400	5.92	2.17
450	5.38	1.94
500	4.93	1.77
700	3.70	1.37

Notice that between 90 PSA and 300 PSA, the average life for the PAC tranche is stable at 7.26 years. However, at slower or faster PSA speeds, the schedule is broken, and the average life changes, lengthening when the prepayment speed is less than 90 PSA and shortening when it is greater than 300 PSA. Even so, there is much greater variability for the average life of the support tranche. The average life for the support tranche is substantial.

Most CMO structures that have a PAC typically have more than one PAC tranche. The tranches are created by carving up a PAC tranche into a series of sequential-pay PAC tranches.

NONAGENCY MORTGAGE-BACKED SECURITIES

Mortgage loans used as collateral for an agency security are conforming loans. That is, they must meet the underwriting standards of the agency. The collateral for a nonagency MBS consists of nonconforming loans (i.e., loans that do not conform to the underwriting standards of the agency).

In this section we will discuss nonagency MBS. Some of the securities in this sector are considered part of the mortgage-backed securities market and others as part of the asset-backed securities market. There are deals in which the underlying collateral is mixed with various types of mortgage-related loans. That is, the collateral backing that a deal may include is a combination of first-lien mortgages, home equity loans, and manufactured housing loans—loan products that we describe later. The Securities Data Corporation (SDC) has established criteria for classifying a mortgage product with mixed collateral as either a "nonagency MBS" or an "asset-backed security" (ABS). The purpose of the classification is not to aid in the analysis of these securities, but rather to construct the so-called league tables for ranking investment banking firms by deal type. The SDC's rules for classifying a deal as either a nonagency MBS or an ABS are as follows. If, at issuance, more than 50% of a deal consists of either manufactured housing loans, home equity loans, second mortgage loans, or home improvement loans, then the deal is classified as an ABS. For deals in which more than 50% of the loans are first liens, the SDC uses a size test to classify the deal. If more than 50% of the aggregate principal balance of the loans have a loan balance of more than $200,000, the deal is classified as a nonagency MBS. A deal in which 50% of the loans are first liens, but more than 50% of the aggregate principal balance of the loans is less than $200,000, is classified as an ABS.

Collateral for a Nonagency Mortgage

A loan may be nonconforming for one or more of the following reasons:

1. The mortgage balance exceeds the amount permitted by the agency.
2. The borrower characteristics fail to meet the underwriting standards established by the agency.
3. The loan characteristics fail to meet the underwriting standards established by the agency.
4. The applicant fails to provide full documentation as required by the agency.

There are alternative lending programs for borrowers seeking nonconforming loans for any of the aforementioned reasons. A mortgage loan that is nonconforming merely because the mortgage balance exceeds the maximum permitted by the agency guideline is called a *jumbo loan*.

With respect to the characteristics of the borrower, a loan may fail to qualify because the borrower's credit history does not meet the underwriting standards or the payment-to-income (PTI) ratio exceeds the maximum permitted. Borrowers who do satisfy the underwriting standards with respect to borrower characteristics are referred to as *A credit borrowers* or *prime borrowers*. *Alternative A loans (Alt-A loans)* are made to borrowers whose qualifying mortgage characteristics do not conform to the underwriting criteria established by the agencies but whose borrower characteristics do. For instance, the borrower may be self-employed and may not be able to provide all the necessary documentation for income verification. In such respects, Alt-A loans allow reduced or alternate forms of documentation to qualify for the loan. An Alt-A loan borrower, however, should not be confused with borrowers with blemished credits (discussed next). The typical Alt-A borrower will have an excellent credit rating—referred to as an "A" rating, and hence the loan is referred to as an Alt-A loan—which is especially important to the originator since the credit quality of the borrower must compensate for the lack of other necessary documentation. What is appealing to borrowers about the Alt-A program is the flexibility that the program offers in terms of documentation, and borrowers are willing to pay a premium for the privilege. Typically, rates on Alt-A loans range between 75 to 125 basis points above the rate on otherwise comparable standard mortgage rates.

B and C borrowers or *subprime borrowers* are borrowers who fail to satisfy the underwriting standards of the agencies because of borrower characteristics. These characteristics include credit history and maximum PTI. Borrowers who apply for subprime loans vary from those who have or had credit problems due to difficulties in repayment of debt brought on by an adverse event, such as job loss or medical emergencies, to those that continue to mismanage their debt and finances. The distinguishing feature of a subprime mortgage is that the potential universe of subprime mortgagors can be divided into various risk grades, ranging from B through D. The risk gradation is a function of past credit history and the magnitude of credit blemishes existing in the history. (The loans are actually scaled by originators from B to D. Every originator establishes its own profiles for classifying a loan into a risk category.) Additionally, some of the higher grades in this loan category have also been labeled as "fallen angels" to indicate the fact that the creditworthiness of such borrowers was hampered by a life event, such as job loss or illness. Since such borrowers tend to pose greater credit risk, subprime mortgages command a pricing premium over standard mortgages.

A *home equity loan* (HEL) is a loan backed by residential property. It is often a first lien on property where the borrower has either an impaired credit history and/or the payment-to-income ratio is too high for the loan to qualify as a conforming loan. Typically, the borrower uses a home equity loan to consolidate consumer debt using the current home as collateral rather than to obtain funds to purchase a new home. Home equity loans can be either closed end or open end. Most home equity loan-backed deals have been backed by closed-end HELs. A closed-end HEL is designed the same way as a fully amortizing residential mortgage loan. That is, it has a fixed maturity and the payments are structured to fully amortize the loan by the maturity date. There are both fixed-rate and variable-rate closed-end HELs.

A characteristic that may result in a loan failing to meet the underwriting standards is that the loan-to-value (LTV) ratio exceeds the maximum established by the agency or the loan is not a first-mortgage lien. There are lenders who specialize in loans that exceed the maximum LTV. These lending programs are sometimes referred to as *high LTV programs* or *125 LTV programs* because the lender may be willing to lend up to 125% of the appraised or market value of the property. Basically, the lender is making a consumer loan based on the credit of the borrower to the extent that the loan amount exceeds the appraised or market value. For this reason, lenders with high LTV programs have limited these loans to A credit borrowers.

Manufactured housing-backed securities are backed by loans for manufactured homes. In contrast to site-built homes, manufactured homes are built at a factory and then transported to a manufactured home community or private land. The loan may be either a mortgage loan (for both the land and the home) or a consumer retail installment loan. The typical loan for a manufactured home is 15 to 20 years. The loan repayment is structured to fully amortize the amount borrowed.

Prepayments

Nonagency MBS are exposed to prepayment risk. Prepayments are of two types: voluntary and involuntary. Involuntary prepayments are due to defaults. If a borrower fails to make payments and the property is seized and sold, the proceeds received from the sale after all expenses are paid is paid to the investor. This amount is a voluntary prepayment. Thus, in investing in nonagency MBS it is necessary to project involuntary prepayments. In turn, projecting involuntary prepayments requires a projection of the default rate and a recovery rate (i.e., how much will be recovered as a percentage of the loan amount).

Dealers involved in the underwriting and market making of nonagency MBS have developed prepayment models for these loans. Several firms have found that the key difference between the prepayment behavior of borrowers of nonconforming mortgages and conforming mortgages is the important role played by the credit characteristics of the borrower. Borrower characteristics and the seasoning process must be kept in mind when trying to assess prepayments for a particular deal.

In the prospectus of an offering, a base-case prepayment assumption is made—the initial speed and the amount of time until the collateral is seasoned. Thus, the prepayment benchmark is issuer specific. The benchmark speed in the prospectus is called the *prospectus prepayment curve* or PPC. As with the PSA benchmark described earlier in this chapter, slower or faster prepayment speeds are a multiple of the PPC. For example, the PPC for a particular nonagency deal might state the following:

> . . . a 100% Prepayment Assumption assumes conditional prepayment rates of 1.5% per annum of the then-outstanding principal balance of the mortgage loans in the first month of the life of the loans and an additional 0.5% per annum in each month thereafter until month 20. Beginning in month 20, 100% Prepayment Assumption assumes a conditional prepayment rate of 11% per annum each month.

For this deal, 100% PPC, 80% PPC, and 150% PPC would then be as follows for selected months:

Month	100% PPC (%)	80% PPC (%)	150% PPC (%)
1	1.5	1.2	2.3
2	2.0	1.6	3.0
3	2.5	2.0	3.8
. . .	. . .	. . .	. . .
18	10.0	8.0	15.0
19	10.5	8.4	15.8
20	11.0	8.8	16.5

Unlike the PSA prepayment benchmark, the PPC is not generic. By this it is meant that the PPC is issuer specific. In contrast, the PSA prepayment benchmark applies to any type of collateral issued by an agency for any type of loan design. This feature of the PPC is important for an investor to keep in mind when comparing the prepayment characteristics and investment characteristics of the collateral between issuers and issues (new and seasoned).

PSA Standard Default Assumption Benchmark

With the increase in nonagency security issuance, a standardized benchmark for default rates was introduced by the then Public Securities Association (now called the Bond Market Association). The PSA standard default assumption (SDA) benchmark gives the annual default rate for a mortgage pool as a function of the seasoning of the mortgages. The PSA SDA benchmark, or 100 SDA, specifies the following:

1. The default rate in month 1 is 0.02% and increases by 0.02% up to month 30 so that in month 30 the default rate is 0.60%.
2. From month 30 to month 60, the default rate remains at 0.60%.
3. From month 61 to month 120, the default rate declines from 0.60% to 0.03%.
4. From month 120 on, the default rate remains constant at 0.03%.

As with the PSA prepayment benchmark, multiples of the benchmark are found by multiplying the default rate by the assumed multiple. A "0 SDA" means that no defaults are assumed.

Credit Enhancements

All nonagency securities are credit enhanced. That means that credit support is provided for one or more bondholders in the structure. Typically a double A or triple A rating is sought for the most senior tranche in a deal. The amount of credit enhancement necessary depends on rating agency requirements. We discussed the various forms of credit enhancement—internal and external—in the previous chapter when ABS was covered. So, we won't repeat them here. However, there are two forms of credit enhancement that are found in nonagency deals that were not discussed in the previous and we will review them here—pool insurance and shifting interest mechanism.

Pool Insurance

Pool insurance policies cover losses resulting from defaults and foreclosures. Policies are typically written for a dollar amount of coverage that continues in force throughout the life of the pool. However, some policies are written so that the dollar amount of coverage declines as the pool seasons as long as two conditions are met: (1) the credit performance is better than expected, and (2) the rating agencies that rated the issue approve. Since only defaults and foreclosures are covered, additional insurance must be obtained to cover losses resulting from bankruptcy (i.e., court-mandated modification of mortgage debt—"cramdown"), fraud arising in the origination process, and special hazards (i.e., losses resulting from events not covered by a standard homeowner's insurance policy). Pool insurance is a form of external credit enhancement.

Shifting Interest Mechanism

As explained in the previous chapter, in a senior-subordinated structure there is a senior tranche and at least one subordinated tranche. For example, suppose a deal has $300 million as collateral (i.e., a pool of loans). The basic concern in the senior-subordinated structure is that while the subordinated tranches provide a certain level of credit protection for the senior tranche at the closing of the deal, the level of protection changes over time due to prepayments. The objective after the deal closes is to distribute any prepayments such that the credit protection for the senior tranche does not deteriorate over time.

The mechanism used to address this concern called the *shifting interest mechanism*. Here is how it works. The percentage of the principal balance of the subordinated tranche to that of the principal balance for the entire deal is called the *level of subordination* or the *subordinate interest*. The higher the percentage, the greater the level of protection for the senior tranches. The subordinate interest changes after the deal is closed due to prepayments. That is, the subordinate interest shifts (hence the term "shifting interest"). The purpose of a shifting interest mechanism is to allocate prepayments so that the subordinate interest is maintained at an acceptable level to protect the senior tranche. In effect, by paying down the senior tranche more quickly, the amount of subordination is maintained at the desired level.

Special Structures: NAS and PAC Tranches

Tranches have been structured to give some senior tranches greater prepayment protection than other senior tranches. The two types of structures that do this are the planned amortization class (PAC) tranche, discussed earlier in this chapter, and the *nonaccelerating senior* (NAS) tranche. A NAS tranche receives principal payments according to a schedule. The schedule is not a dollar amount. Rather, it is a principal schedule that shows for a given month the share of pro rata principal that must be distributed to the NAS tranche. A typical principal schedule for a NAS tranche is as follows:

Months	Share of Pro Rata Principal (%)
1 through 36	0
37 through 60	45
61 through 72	80
73 through 84	100
After month 84	300

The average life for the NAS tranche is stable for a large range of prepayments because for the first 3 years all prepayments are made to the other senior tranches. This reduces the risk of the NAS tranche contracting (i.e., shortening) due to fast prepayments. After month 84, 300% of its pro rata share is paid to the NAS tranche, thereby reducing its extension risk.

COMMERCIAL MORTGAGE-BACKED SECURITIES

Commercial mortgage-backed securities (CMBSs) are backed by a pool of commercial mortgage loans on income-producing property—multifamily properties (i.e., apartment buildings), office buildings, industrial properties (including warehouses), shopping centers, hotels, and health care facilities (i.e., senior housing care facilities). The basic building block of the CMBS transaction is a commercial loan that was originated either to finance a commercial purchase or to refinance a prior mortgage obligation.

Unlike residential mortgage loans where the lender relies on the ability of the borrower to repay and has recourse to the borrower if the payment terms are not satisfied, commercial mortgage loans are nonrecourse loans. This means that the lender can only look to the income-producing property backing the loan for interest and principal repayment. If there is a default, the lender looks to the proceeds from the sale of the property for repayment and has no recourse to the borrower for any unpaid balance. Basically, this means that the lender must view each property as a stand-alone business and evaluate each property using measures that have been found useful in assessing credit risk.

Regardless of the property type, the two measures that have been found to be key indicators of the potential credit performance are the debt-to-service coverage ratio and the loan-to-value (LTV) ratio. The *debt-to-service coverage* (DSC) ratio is the ratio of the property's net operating income (NOI) divided by the debt service. The NOI is defined as the rental income reduced by cash operating expenses (adjusted for a replacement reserve). A ratio greater than 1 means that the cash flow from the property is sufficient to cover debt servicing. The higher the ratio, the more likely that the borrower will be able to meet debt servicing from the property's cash flow. In computing the LTV, "value" in the ratio is either market value or appraised value. In valuing commercial property, there can be considerable variation in the estimates of the property's market value. The lower the LTV, the greater the protection afforded the lender.

Another characteristic of the underlying loans that is used in gauging the quality of a CMBS deal is the prepayment protection provisions. We review these provisions later. Finally, there are characteristics of the property that affect quality. Specifically, investors and rating agencies look at the concentration of loans by property type and by geographical location.

There are three types of CMBS deal structures that have been of interest to bond investors: (1) liquidating trusts, (2) multiproperty single borrower, and (3) multiproperty conduit. The liquidating or nonperforming trusts are a small segment of the CMBS market. This segment, as the name implies, represents CMBS deals backed by nonperforming mortgage loans. The fastest growing segment of the CMBS is conduit-originated transactions. Conduits are commercial-lending entities that are established for the sole purpose of generating collateral to securitize.

As with any securitization transaction, the rating agencies will determine the level of credit enhancement to achieve a desired rating level for each tranche in the structure. For example, if certain DSC and LTV ratios are needed, and these ratios cannot be met at the loan level, then subordination is used to achieve these levels.

Call Protection

The degree of call protection available to a CMBS investor is a function of the following two characteristics: (1) call protection available at the loan level and (2) call protection afforded from the actual CMBS structure. At the commercial loan level, call protection can take the following forms: (1) prepayment lockout, (2) defeasance, (3) prepayment penalty points, and (4) yield maintenance charges.

A prepayment lockout is a contractual agreement that prohibits any prepayments during a specified period of time, called the lockout period. The lockout period at issuance can be from 2 to 5 years. After the lockout period, call protection comes in the form of either prepayment penalty points or yield maintenance charges. Prepayment lockout and defeasance are the strongest forms of prepayment protection.

With defeasance, rather than prepaying a loan, the borrower provides sufficient funds for the servicer to invest in a portfolio of Treasury securities that replicates the cash flows that would exist in the absence of prepayments. The substitution of the cash flow of a Treasury portfolio for that of the borrower improves the credit quality of the CMBS deal.

Prepayment penalty points are predetermined penalties that must be paid by the borrower if the borrower wishes to refinance. For example, 5-4-3-2-1 is a common prepayment penalty point structure. That is, if the borrower wishes to prepay during the first year, he must pay a 5% penalty for a total of $105 rather than $100 (which is the norm in the residential market). Likewise, during the second year, a 4% penalty would apply, and so on.

Yield maintenance charge, in its simplest terms, is designed to make the lender indifferent as to the timing of prepayments. The yield maintenance charge, also called the *make-whole charge*, makes it uneconomical to refinance solely to get a lower mortgage rate. Several methods have been used in practice to compute the yield maintenance charge.

The other type of call protection available in CMBS transactions is structural. That is, because the CMBS bond structures are sequential-pay (by rating), the AA-rated tranche cannot pay down until the AAA is completely retired, and the AA-rated bonds must be paid off before the A-rated bonds, and so on. However, principal losses due to defaults are impacted from the bottom of the structure upward.

Balloon Maturity Provisions

Many commercial loans backing CMBS transactions are balloon loans that require substantial principal payment at the end of the term of the loan. If the borrower fails to make the balloon payment, the borrower is in default. The lender may extend the loan, and in so doing may modify the original loan terms. During the workout period for the loan, a higher interest rate will be charged, the "default interest rate."

The risk that a borrower will not be able to make the balloon payment, because either the borrower cannot arrange for refinancing at the balloon payment date or cannot sell the property to generate sufficient funds to pay off the balloon balance, is called *balloon risk*. Since the term of the loan will be extended by the lender during the workout period, balloon risk is also referred to as *extension risk*.

CHAPTER 18

General Principles of
Bond Valuation

Frank J. Fabozzi, Ph.D., CFA
Adjunct Professor of Finance
School of Management
Yale University

Steven V. Mann, Ph.D.
Professor of Finance
The Moore School of Business
University of South Carolina

Valuation is the process of determining the fair value of a financial asset. In this chapter, we will explain the general principles of bond valuation. Our focus will be on how to value option-free bonds. In Chapter 20 we will see how more complex bond structures—that is, bonds that are callable and/or putable and mortgage-backed and certain asset-backed securities—are valued.

GENERAL PRINCIPLES OF BOND VALUATION

The fundamental principle of valuation is that the value of any financial asset is equal to the present value of its expected future cash flows. This principle holds for any financial asset from zero-coupon bonds to interest rate swaps. Thus, the valuation of a financial asset involves the following three steps:

Step 1: Estimate the expected future cash flows.

Step 2: Determine the appropriate interest rate or interest rates that should be used to discount the cash flows.

Step 3: Calculate the present value of the expected future cash flows found in Step 1 by the appropriate interest rate or interest rates determined in Step 2.[1]

Estimating Cash Flows

Cash flow is simply the cash that is expected to be received in the future from owning a financial asset. For a fixed-income security, it does not matter whether the cash flow is interest income or repayment of principal. A security's *cash flows* represent the sum of each period's expected cash flow. Even if we disregard default, the cash flows for only a few fixed-income securities are simple to forecast accurately. Noncallable U.S. Treasury securities possess this feature since they have known cash flows.[2] For Treasury coupon securities, the cash flows consist of the coupon interest payments every six months up to and including the maturity date and the principal repayment at the maturity date.

Many fixed-income securities have features that make estimating their cash flows problematic. These features may include one or more of the following:

1. The issuer or the investor has the option to change the contractual due date of the repayment of the principal.
2. The coupon and/or principal payment is reset periodically based on a formula that depends on one or more market variables (e.g., interest rates, inflation rates, exchange rates, etc.).
3. The investor has the choice to convert or exchange the security into common stock or some other financial asset.

---

[1] The careful reader will note that according to the Capital Asset Pricing Model (CAPM) an investor only requires compensation for the covariance of a security's return with the market portfolio. However, CAPM is not rich enough to price all financial assets sufficiently well to be of practical use in the fixed-income area. The reason is that CAPM is a single-period model of equilibrium expected returns in a highly idealized setting (no taxes, no transaction costs, etc.) that abstracts from liquidity risk and even default risk. The only bond assumed in the CAPM is a riskless one, exogenous to the model. Proponents of the CAPM argue that it can be effectively applied in equity valuation because even relatively small portfolios of equities remove nearly all risks except the covariance with the market.

[2] While the probability of default of the U.S. government is not zero, it is close enough to that threshold to be safely ignored. Besides, if the U.S. government ever does default, we will have other things to worry about than valuing bonds.

Callable bonds, putable bonds, mortgage-backed securities, and asset-backed securities are examples of (1). Floating-rate securities and Treasury Inflation Protected Securities (TIPs) are examples of (2). Convertible bonds and exchangeable bonds are examples of (3).

For securities that fall into the first category, a key factor determining whether the owner of the option (either the issuer of the security or the investor) will exercise the option to alter the security's cash flows is the level of interest rates in the future relative to the security's coupon rate. In order to estimate the cash flows for these types of securities, we must determine how the size and timing of their expected cash flows will change in the future. For example, when estimating the future cash flows of a callable bond, we must account for the fact that when interest rates change, the expected cash flows change. As we will see in Chapter 20, this introduces an additional layer of complexity to the valuation process. For bonds with embedded options, estimating cash flows is accomplished by introducing a parameter that reflects the expected volatility of interest rates.

Determining the Appropriate Interest Rate or Rates

Once we estimate the cash flows for a fixed-income security, the next step is to determine the appropriate interest rate for discounting each cash flow. Before proceeding, we pause here to note that we will once again use the terms "interest rate," "discount rate," and "required yield" interchangeably throughout the chapter. The interest rate used to discount a particular security's cash flows will depend on three basic factors: (1) the level of benchmark interest rates (i.e., U.S. Treasury rates); (2) the risks that the market perceives the securityholder is exposed to; and (3) the compensation the market expects to receive for these risks.[3]

The minimum interest rate that an investor should require is the yield available in the marketplace on a default-free cash flow. For bonds with dollar-denominated cash flows, yields on U.S. Treasury securities serve as benchmarks for default-free interest rates. For now, we can think of the minimum interest rate that investors require as the yield on a comparable maturity Treasury security.

The additional compensation or spread over the yield on the Treasury issue that investors will require reflects the additional risks the investor faces by acquiring a security that is not issued by the U.S. government. These risks include default risk, liquidity risk, and the risks associated with any embedded options. These yield spreads (discussed in more detail in Chapter 19) will depend not only on the risks an individ-

---

[3] As explained in footnote 1, the CAPM cannot handle these risks.

ual issue is exposed to but also on the level of Treasury yields, the market's risk aversion, the business cycle, and so forth.

For each cash flow estimated, the same interest rate can be used to calculate the present value. This is the traditional approach to valuation and it serves as a useful starting point for our discussion. We discuss the traditional approach in the next section and use a single interest rate to determine present values. By doing this, however, we are implicitly assuming that the yield curve is flat. Since the yield curve is almost never flat and a coupon bond can be thought of as a package of zero-coupon bonds, it is more appropriate to value each cash flow using an interest rate specific to that cash flow. After the traditional approach to valuation is discussed, we will explain the proper approach to valuation using multiple interest rates and demonstrate why this must be the case.

Discounting the Expected Cash Flows

Once the expected (estimated) cash flows and the appropriate interest rate or interest rates that should be used to discount the cash flows are determined, the final step in the valuation process is to value the cash flows. The present value of an expected cash flow to be received t years from now using a discount rate i is:

$$\text{present value}_t = \frac{\text{expected cash flow in period } t}{(1 + i)^t}$$

The value of a financial asset is then the sum of the present value of all the expected cash flows. Specifically, assuming that there are N expected cash flows:

$$\text{value} = \text{present value}_1 + \text{present value}_2 + \dots + \text{present value}_N$$

Determining a Bond's Value

Determining a bond's value involves computing the present value of the expected future cash flows using a discount rate that reflects market interest rates and the bond's risks. A bond's cash flows come in two forms—coupon interest payments and the repayment of principal at maturity. In practice, many bonds deliver semiannual cash flows. Fortunately, this does not introduce any complexities into the calculation. Two simple adjustments are needed. First, we adjust the coupon payments by dividing the annual coupon payment by 2. Second, we adjust the discount rate by dividing the annual discount rate by 2. The time period t in the present value expression is treated in terms of 6-month periods as opposed to years.

To illustrate the process, let's value a 4-year, 6% coupon bond with a maturity value of $100. The coupon payments are $3 ($0.06 \times $100/2$) every six months for the next eight periods. In addition, on the maturity date, the investor receives the repayment of principal ($100). The value of a non-amortizing bond can be divided in two components: (1) the present value of the coupon payments (i.e., an annuity) and (2) the present value of the maturity value (i.e., a lump sum). Therefore, when a single discount rate is employed, a bond's value can be thought of as the sum of two presents values—an annuity and a lump sum

The adjustment for the discount rate is easy to accomplish but tricky to interpret. For example, if an annual discount rate of 6% is used, how do we obtain the semiannual discount rate? We will simply use one-half the annual rate, 3.0% (6%/2). How can this be? A 3.0% semiannual rate is not a 6% effective annual rate. As we will see later in this chapter, the convention in the bond market is to quote annual interest rates that are just double the semiannual rates. This convention will be explained more fully later when we discuss yield to maturity. For now, accept on faith that one-half the discount rate is used as a semiannual discount rate in the balance of the chapter.

We now have everything in place to value a semiannual coupon-paying bond. Recall, the present value of an annuity is equal to:

$$\text{annuity payment} \times \left[\frac{1 - \dfrac{1}{(1+r)^{\text{no. of years}}}}{r} \right]$$

where r is the *annual* discount rate.

Applying this formula to a semiannual-pay bond, the annuity payment is one half the annual coupon payment and the number of periods is double the number of years to maturity. Accordingly, the present value of the coupon payments can be expressed as:

$$\text{semiannual coupon payment} \times \left[\frac{1 - \dfrac{1}{(1+i)^{\text{no. of years} \times 2}}}{i} \right]$$

where i is the *semiannual* discount rate $(r/2)$. Notice that in the formula, for the number of periods we use the number of years multiplied by 2 since a period in our illustration is six months.

The present value of the maturity value is just the present value of a lump sum and is equal to:

$$\text{present value of the maturity value} = \frac{\$100}{(1+i)^{\text{no. of years} \times 2}}$$

We will illustrate the calculation by valuing our 4-year, 6% coupon bond assuming that the relevant discount rate is 7%. The data are summarized below:

semiannual coupon payment = $3 (per $100 of par value)
semiannual discount rate (i) = 3.5% (7%/2)
number of years to maturity = 4

The present value of the coupon payments is:

$$\$3 \times \left[\frac{1 - \dfrac{1}{(1.035)^{4 \times 2}}}{0.035} \right] = \$20.6219$$

This number tells us that the coupon payments contribute $20.6219 to the bond's value.

The present value of the maturity value is:

$$\text{present value of the maturity value} = \frac{\$100}{(1.035)^{4 \times 2}} = \$75.9412$$

This number ($75.9412) tells us how much the maturity value contributes to the bond's value. The bond's value is then $96.5631 ($20.6219 + $75.9412). The price is less than par value and the bond is said to be trading at a *discount*. This will occur when the fixed coupon rate a bond offers (6%) is less than the required yield demanded by the market (the 7% discount rate). A discount bond has an inferior coupon rate relative to new comparable bonds being issued at par so its price must drop so as to bid up to the required yield of 7%. If the discount bond is held to maturity, the investor will experience a capital gain that just offsets the

lower the current coupon rate so that it appears equally attractive to new comparable bonds issued at par.

Suppose instead of a 7% discount rate, a 5% discount rate is used. This discount rate is less than the coupon rate on the bond (6%). It can be shown that the present value of the coupon payments is $21.5104 and the present value of the maturity value is $82.0747. Thus, the bond's value in this case is $103.5851. That is, the price is greater than par value and the bond is said to be trading at a *premium*. This will occur when the fixed coupon rate a bond offers (6%) is greater than the required yield demanded by the market (the 5% discount rate). Accordingly, a premium bond carries a higher coupon rate than new bonds (otherwise the same) being issued today at par so the price will be bid up and the required yield will fall until it equals 5%. If the premium bond is held to maturity, the investor will experience a capital loss that just offsets the benefits of the higher coupon rate so that it will appear equally attractive to new comparable bonds issued at par.

Finally, let's suppose that the discount rate is equal to the coupon rate. That is, suppose that the discount rate is 6%. It can be shown that the present value of the coupon payments is $21.0591 and the present value of the maturity value is $78.9409. Thus, the bond's value in this case is $100 or par value. Thus, when a bond's coupon rate is equal to the discount rate, the bond will trade at par value.

Valuing a Zero-Coupon Bond

For a zero-coupon bond, there is only one cash flow—the repayment of principal at maturity. The value of a zero-coupon bond that matures N years from now is:

$$\frac{\text{Maturity value}}{(1 + i)^{\text{no. of years} \times 2}}$$

where i is the semiannual discount rate.

The expression presented above states that the price of a zero-coupon bond is simply the present value of the maturity value. In the present value computation, why is the number of periods used for discounting rather than the number of years to the bond's maturity when there are no semiannual coupon payments? We do this in order to make the valuation of a zero-coupon bond consistent with the valuation of a coupon bond. In other words, both coupon and zero-coupon bonds are valued using semiannual compounding.

To illustrate, the value of a 10-year zero-coupon bond with a maturity value of $100 discounted at a 6.4% interest rate is $53.2606, as presented below:

$$i = 032 = (0.064/2)$$

$$N = 10$$

$$\frac{\$100}{(1.032)^{10 \times 2}} = \$53.2606$$

Valuing a Bond Between Coupon Payments

In our discussion of bond valuation to this point, we have assumed that the bonds are valued on their coupon payment dates (i.e., the next coupon payment is one full period away). For bonds with semiannual coupon payments, this occurs only twice a year. Our task now is to describe how bonds are valued on the other 363 or 364 days of the year.

In order to value a bond with the settlement date between coupon payments, we must answer three questions. First, how many days are there until the next coupon payment date? The answer depends on the day count convention for the bond being valued. Second, how should we compute the present value of the cash flows received over the fractional period? Third, how much must the buyer compensate the seller for the coupon earned over the fractional period? This amount is accrued interest. Below we will answer these three questions in order to determine the full price and the clean price of a coupon bond.

Computing the Full Price   When valuing a bond purchased with a settlement date between coupon payment dates, the first step is to determine the fractional periods between the settlement date and the next coupon date. Using the appropriate day count convention, this is determined as follows:

$$w \text{ periods} = \frac{\text{days between settlement date and next coupon payment date}}{\text{days in the coupon period}}$$

Then the present value of each expected future cash flow to be received t periods from now using a discount rate i assuming the next coupon payment is w periods from now (settlement date) is:

$$\text{present value}_t = \frac{\text{expected cash flow}}{(1 + i)^{t - 1 + w}}$$

Note for the first coupon payment subsequent to the settlement date, $t = 1$ so the exponent is just w. This procedure for calculating the present value when a bond is purchased between coupon payments is called the "Street method." In the Street method, as can be seen in the previous expression, coupon interest is compounded over the fractional period w.[4]

To illustrate this calculation, suppose that a U.S. Treasury note maturing June 15, 2001 is purchased with a settlement date of January 27, 2000. This note's coupon rate is 5.5% and it has coupon payment dates of June 15 and December 15. As a result, the next coupon payment is June 15, 2000, while the previous coupon payment was December 15, 1999. There are three cash flows remaining—June 15, 2000, December 15, 2000, and June 15, 2001. The final cash flow represents the last coupon payment and the maturity value of $100. Also assume the following:

1. actual/actual day count convention
2. 140 days between the settlement date and the next coupon payment date
3. 183 days in the coupon period

Then w is 0.7659 periods (140/183). The present value of each cash flow assuming that each is discounted at a 6.1% annual discount rate is

$$\textit{Period 1: present value}_1 = \frac{\$2.75}{(1.0305)^{0.7650}} = \$2.6875$$

$$\textit{Period 2: present value}_2 = \frac{\$2.75}{(1.0305)^{1.7650}} = \$2.6080$$

$$\textit{Period 3: present value}_3 = \frac{\$102.75}{(1.0305)^{2.7650}} = \$94.5593$$

The sum of the present values of the cash flows is $99.8548. This price is referred to as the *full price* (or the *dirty price*).

It is the full price the bond's buyer pays the seller at delivery. However, the very next cash flow received and included in the present value calculation was not earned by the bond's buyer. A portion of the next coupon payment is the *accrued interest*. Accrued interest is the portion of a bond's next coupon payment that the bond's seller is entitled to depending on the amount of time the bond was held by the seller. Recall, the buyer recovers the accrued interest when the next coupon payment is delivered.

---

[4] The "Treasury method" treats coupon interest over the fractional period as simple interest.

Computing the Accrued Interest and the Clean Price   The last step in this process is to find the bond's value without accrued interest (called the *clean price* or simply *price*). To do this, the accrued interest must be computed. The first step is to determine the number of days in the accrued interest period (i.e., the number of days between the last coupon payment date and the settlement date) using the appropriate day count convention. For ease of exposition, we will assume in the example that follows that the actual/actual calendar is used. We will also assume there are only two bondholders in a given coupon period—the buyer and the seller.

As an illustration, we return to the previous example with the 5.5% coupon Treasury note. Since there are 183 days in the coupon period and 140 days from the settlement date to the next coupon period, there are 43 days (183 − 140) in the accrued interest period. Therefore, the percentage of the next coupon payment that is accrued interest is:

$$\frac{43}{183} = 0.2350 = 23.50\%$$

Of course, this is the same percentage found by simply subtracting w from 1. In our example, w was 0.7650. Then, 1 − 0.7650 = 0.2350.

Given the value of w, the amount of accrued interest (AI) is equal to:

$$AI = \text{semiannual coupon payment} \times (1 - w)$$

Accordingly, using a 5.5% Treasury note with a settlement date of January 27, 2000, the portion of the next coupon payment that is accrued interest is:

$$\$2.75 \times (1 - 0.7650) = \$0.64625 \text{ (per \$100 of par value)}$$

Once we know the full price and the accrued interest, we can determine the clean price. The clean price is the price quoted in the market and represents the bond's value to the new bondholder. The clean price is computed as follows:

$$\text{clean price} = \text{full price} - \text{accrued interest}$$

In our illustration, the clean price is:

$$99.2086 = \$99.8548 - \$0.64625$$

Note that in computing the full price, the present value of the next coupon payment is computed. However, the buyer pays the seller the accrued interest now despite the fact that it will not be recovered until the next coupon payment date. To make this concrete, suppose one sells a bond such that the settlement date is halfway between the coupon payment dates. In this case $w = 0.50$. Accordingly, the seller will be entitled to one-half of the next coupon payment which would not otherwise be received for another three months. Thus, when calculating the clean price, we subtract "too much" accrued interest—one-half the coupon payment rather than the present value of one-half the coupon payment. Of course, this is the market convention for calculating accrued interest but it does introduce a curious twist in bond valuation.

The Price/Discount Rate Relationship

An important general property of present value is then the higher (lower) the discount rate, the lower (higher) the present value. Since the value of a security is the present value of the expected future cash flows, this property carries over to the value of a security: The higher (lower) the discount rate, the lower (higher) a security's value. We can summarize the relationship between the coupon rate, the required market yield, and the bond's price relative to its par value as follows:

coupon rate = yield required by market ⇒ price = par value
coupon rate < yield required by market ⇒ price < par value (discount)
coupon rate > yield required by market ⇒ price > par value (premium)

This agrees with what we found for the 4-year, 6% coupon bond:

Coupon Rate	Yield Required by Market	Price	Bond Trading at
6%	7%	$96.5631	discount
6%	5%	$103.5851	premium
6%	6%	$100.0000	par

Exhibit 18.1 depicts this inverse relationship between an option-free bond's price and its discount rate (i.e., required yield). There are two things to infer from the price/discount rate relationship depicted in the exhibit. First, the relationship is downward sloping. This is simply the inverse relationship between present values and discount rates at work. Second, the relationship is represented as a curve rather than a straight line. In fact, the shape of the curve in Exhibit 18.1 is referred to as *convex*. By convex, it simply means the curve is "bowed in" relative to the origin. This second observation raises two questions about the convex or curved shape of the price/discount rate relationship. First, why is it curved? Second, what is the import of the curvature?

EXHIBIT 18.1   Price/Discount Rate Relationship for an Option-Free Bond

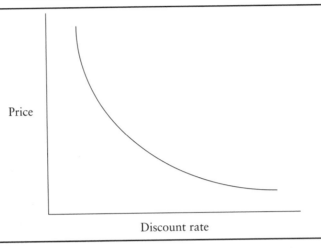

The answer to the first question is mathematical. The answer lies in the denominator of the bond pricing formula. Since we are raising one plus the discount rate to powers greater than one, it should not be surprising that the relationship between the level of the price and the level of the discount rate is not linear.

As for the importance of the curvature to bond investors, let's consider what happens to bond prices in both falling and rising interest rate environments. First, what happens to bond prices as interest rates fall? The answer is obvious—bond prices rise. How about the rate at which they rise? If the price/discount rate relationship was linear, as interest rates fell, bond prices would rise at a constant rate. However, the relationship is not linear, it is curved and curved inward. Accordingly, when interest rates fall, bond prices *increase* at an *increasing* rate. Now, let's consider what happens when interest rates rise. Of course, bond prices fall. How about the rate at which bond prices fall? Once again, if the price/discount rate relationship were linear, as interest rates rose, bond prices would fall at a constant rate. Since it curved inward, when interest rates rise, bond prices *decrease* at a *decreasing* rate. In Chapter 21, we will explore more fully the implications of the curvature or convexity of the price/discount rate relationship.

Time Path of Bond

As a bond moves towards its maturity date, its value changes. More specifically, assuming that the discount rate does not change, a bond's value:

1. Decreases over time if the bond is selling at a premium
2. Increases over time if the bond is selling at a discount
3. Is unchanged if the bond is selling at par value[5]

At the maturity date, the bond's value is equal to its par or maturity value. So, as a bond's maturity approaches, the price of a discount bond will rise to its par value and a premium bond will fall to its par value—a characteristic sometimes referred to as "pull to par value."

ARBITRAGE-FREE BOND VALUATION

The traditional approach to valuation is to discount every cash flow of a fixed-income security using the same interest or discount rate. The fundamental flaw of this approach is that it views each security as the same package of cash flows. For example, consider a 5-year U.S. Treasury note with a 6% coupon rate. The cash flows per $100 of par value would be 9 payments of $3 every six months and $103 ten 6-month periods from now. The traditional practice would discount every cash flow using the same discount rate regardless of when the cash flows are delivered in time and the shape of the yield curve. Finance theory tells us that any security should be thought of as a package or portfolio of zero-coupon bonds.

The proper way to view the 5-year 6% coupon Treasury note is as a package of zero-coupon instruments whose maturity value is the amount of the cash flow and whose maturity date coincides with the date the cash flow is to be received. Thus, the 5-year 6% coupon Treasury issue should be viewed as a package of 10 zero-coupon instruments that mature every six months for the next five years. This approach to valuation does not allow a market participant to realize an arbitrage profit by breaking apart or "stripping" a bond and selling the individual cash flows (i.e., stripped securities) at a higher aggregate value than it would cost to purchase the security in the market. Simply put, arbitrage profits are possible when the sum of the parts is worth more than the whole or vice versa. We described the process of stripping Treasuries in Chapter 16. Because this approach to valuation precludes arbitrage profits, we refer to it as the *arbitrage-free valuation approach*.

By viewing any security as a package of zero-coupon bonds, a consistent valuation framework can be developed. Viewing a security as a pack-

---

[5] We are assuming the bond is valued on its coupon anniversary dates. We will relax this assumption shortly and consider what happens to a par bond between coupon payment dates.

age of zero-coupon bonds means that two bonds with the same maturity and different coupon rates are viewed as different packages of zero-coupon bonds and valued accordingly. Moreover, two cash flows that have identical risk delivered at the same time will be valued using the same discount rate even though they are attached to two different bonds.

To implement the arbitrage-free approach it is necessary to determine the theoretical rate that the U.S. Treasury would have to pay on a zero-coupon Treasury security for each maturity. We say "theoretical" because other than U.S. Treasury bills, the Treasury does not issue zero-coupon bonds. Zero-coupon Treasuries are, however, created by dealer firms. The name given to the zero-coupon Treasury rate is the *Treasury spot rate*. Our next task is to explain how the Treasury spot rate can be calculated.

Theoretical Spot Rates

The theoretical spot rates for Treasury securities represent the appropriate set of interest or discount rates that should be used to value default-free cash flows. A default-free theoretical spot rate can be constructed from the observed Treasury yield curve or par curve. We will begin our quest of how to estimate spot rates with the par curve.

Par Rates

The raw material for all yield curve analysis is the set of yields on the most recently issued (i.e., on-the-run) Treasury securities. The U.S. Treasury routinely issues six securities—the 1-month, 3-month, and 6-month bills and the 2-, 5-, and 10-year notes. These on-the-run Treasury issues are default risk-free and trade in one of the most liquid and efficient secondary markets in the world. Because of these characteristics, historically Treasury yields serve as a reference benchmark for risk-free rates which are used for pricing other securities.

In practice, however, the observed yields for the on-the-run Treasury coupon issues are not usually used directly. Instead, the coupon rate is adjusted so that the price of the issue would be the par value. Accordingly, the par yield curve is the adjusted on-the-run Treasury yield curve where coupon issues are at par value and the coupon rate is therefore equal to the yield to maturity. The exception is for the 6-month Treasury bills; the bond-equivalent yield for this issue is already the spot rate.

Deriving a par curve from a set of five points starting with the yield on the 6-month bill and ending the yield on the 10-year bond is not a trivial matter. The end result is a curve that tells us "if the Treasury were to issue a security today with a maturity equal to say 12 years, what coupon rate would the security have to pay in order to sell at par?" Some analysts contend that estimating the par curve with only the yields of the on-the-run Treasuries uses too little information that is available from the market. In particular, one must estimate the back-end of the yield curve with only one security, i.e., the 10-year note. Some analysts prefer to use the on-the-run Treasuries and selected off-the-run Treasuries.

In summary, a par rate is the average discount rate of many cash flows (those of a par bond) over many periods. This begs the question, "the average of what?" As we will see, par rates are complicated averages of the implied spot rates. Thus, in order to uncover the spot rates, we must find a method to "break apart" the par rates. There are several approaches that are used in practice. The approach that we describe below for creating a theoretical spot rate curve is called *bootstrapping*.

Bootstrapping the Spot Rate Curve

Bootstrapping begins with the par curve. To illustrate bootstrapping, we will use the Treasury par curve shown in Exhibit 18.2. The par yield curve shown extends only out to 10 years. Our objective is to show how the values in the last column of the exhibit (labeled "Spot Rate") are obtained. Throughout the analysis and illustrations to come, it is important to remember the basic principle is that the value of the Treasury coupon security should be equal to the value of the package of zero-coupon Treasury securities that duplicates the coupon bond's cash flows.

The key to this process is the existence of the Treasury strips market that we described in Chapter 16. A government securities dealer has the ability to take apart the cash flows of a Treasury coupon security (i.e., strip the security) and create zero-coupon securities. These zero-coupon securities, which are called Treasury strips, can be sold to investors. At what interest rate or yield can these Treasury strips be sold to investors? The answer is they can be sold at the Treasury spot rates. If the market price of a Treasury security is less than its value after discounting with spot rates (i.e., the sum of the parts is worth more than the whole), than a dealer can buy the Treasury security, strip it, and sell off the Treasury strips so as to generate greater proceeds than the cost of purchasing the Treasury security. The resulting profit is an arbitrage profit.

Before we proceed to our illustration of bootstrapping, a very sensible question must be addressed. Specifically, if Treasury strips are in effect zero-coupon Treasury securities, why not use strip rates (i.e., the rates on Treasury strips) as our spot rates? In other words, why must we estimate theoretical spot rates via bootstrapping using yields from Treasury bills, notes, and bonds when we already have strip rates conveniently available? There are three major reasons. First, although Treasury strips are actively traded, they are not as liquid as on-the-run Treasury bills, notes, and bonds. As a result, Treasury strips have some liquidity risk for which investors will demand some compensation in the form of higher yields. Second, the tax treatment of strips is different from that of Treasury coupon securities. Specifically, the accrued interest on strips is taxed even though no cash is received by the investor. Thus they are negative cash flow securities to taxable entities, and, as a result, their yield reflects this tax disadvantage. Finally, there are maturity sectors where non-U.S. investors find it advantageous to trade off yield for tax advantages associated with a strip. Specifically, certain non-U.S. tax authorities allow their citizens to treat the difference between the maturity value and the purchase price as a capital gain and tax this gain at a favorable tax rate. Some will grant this favorable treatment only when the strip is created from the principal rather than the coupon. For this reason, those who use Treasury strips to represent theoretical spot rates restrict the issues included to coupon strips.

EXHIBIT 18.2   Hypothetical Treasury Par Yield Curve

Period	Years	Annual Yield to Maturity (BEY) (%)[*]	Price	Spot Rate (BEY) (%)[*]
1	0.5	3.00	—	3.0000
2	1.0	3.30	—	3.3000
3	1.5	3.50	100.00	3.5053
4	2.0	3.90	100.00	3.9164
5	2.5	4.40	100.00	4.4376
6	3.0	4.70	100.00	4.7520
7	3.5	4.90	100.00	4.9622
8	4.0	5.00	100.00	5.0650
9	4.5	5.10	100.00	5.1701
10	5.0	5.20	100.00	5.2772
11	5.5	5.30	100.00	5.3864
12	6.0	5.40	100.00	5.4976
13	6.5	5.50	100.00	5.6108
14	7.0	5.55	100.00	5.6643
15	7.5	5.60	100.00	5.7193
16	8.0	5.65	100.00	5.7755
17	8.5	5.70	100.00	5.8331
18	9.0	5.80	100.00	5.9584
19	9.5	5.90	100.00	6.0863
20	10.0	6.00	100.00	6.2169

[*] The yield to maturity and the spot rate are annual rates. They are reported as bond-equivalent yields. To obtain the semiannual yield or rate, one half the annual yield or annual rate is used.

Now let's see how to generate the spot rates. Consider the 6-month Treasury security in Exhibit 18.2. This security is a Treasury bill and is issued as a zero-coupon instrument. Therefore, the annualized bond-equivalent yield (not the bank discount yield) of 3.00% for the 6-month Treasury security is equal to the 6-month spot rate. Market participants can do a fairly decent job of estimating the 1-year Treasury rate. Suppose the cited yield of 3.30% is a good estimate of the 1-year spot rate. Given these two spot rates, we can compute the spot rate for a theoretical 1.5-year zero-coupon Treasury. The value of a theoretical 1.5-year Treasury should equal the present value of the three cash flows from the 1.5-year coupon Treasury, where the yield used for discounting is the spot rate corresponding to the time of receipt of the cash flow. Since all the coupon bonds are selling at par, as explained in the previous section, the yield to maturity for each bond is the coupon rate. Using $100 as par, the cash flows for the 1.5-year coupon Treasury are:

0.5 year	$0.035 \times \$100 \times 0.5$	$= \$\ \ 1.75$
1.0 year	$0.035 \times \$100 \times 0.5$	$= \$\ \ 1.75$
1.5 years	$0.035 \times \$100 \times 0.5 + 100$	$= \$101.75$

The present value of the cash flows is then:

$$\frac{1.75}{(1+z_1)^1} + \frac{1.75}{(1+z_2)^2} + \frac{101.75}{(1+z_3)^3}$$

where

z_1 = one-half the annualized 6-month theoretical spot rate
z_2 = one-half the 1-year theoretical spot rate
z_3 = one-half the 1.5-year theoretical spot rate

Since the 6-month spot rate is 3% and the 1-year spot rate is 3.30%, we know that:

$$z_1 = 0.0150 \text{ and } z_2 = 0.0165$$

We can compute the present value of the 1.5-year coupon Treasury security as:

$$\frac{1.75}{(1+z_1)^1} + \frac{1.75}{(1+z_2)^2} + \frac{101.75}{(1+z_3)^3} = \frac{1.75}{(1.015)^1} + \frac{1.75}{(1.0165)^2} + \frac{101.75}{(1+z_3)^3}$$

Since the price of the 1.5-year coupon Treasury security is equal to its par value (see Exhibit 18.2), the following relationship must hold:[6]

$$\frac{1.75}{(1.015)^1} + \frac{1.75}{(1.0165)^2} + \frac{101.75}{(1+z_3)^3} = 100$$

Note we are treating the 1.5 year par bond as if it were a portfolio of three zero-coupon bonds. Moreover, each cash flow has its own discount rate that depends on when the cash flow is delivered in the future and the shape of the yield curve. This is in sharp contrast to the traditional valuation approach that forces each cash flow to have the same discount rate.

We can solve for the theoretical 1.5-year spot rate as follows:

$$1.7241 + 1.6936 + \frac{101.75}{(1+z_3)^3} = 100$$

$$\frac{101.75}{(1+z_3)^3} = 96.5822$$

$$(1+z_3)^3 = \frac{101.75}{96.5822}$$

$$(1+z_3)^3 = 1.05351$$

$$z_3 = 0.017527$$

$$= 1.7527\%$$

Doubling this yield we obtain the bond-equivalent yield of 3.5053%, which is the theoretical 1.5-year spot rate. This is the rate that the market would apply to a 1.5-year zero-coupon Treasury security if, in fact, such a security existed. In other words, all Treasury cash flows to be received 1.5 years from now should be valued (i.e., discounted) at 3.5053%.

Given the theoretical 1.5-year spot rate, we can obtain the theoretical 2-year spot rate. The cash flows for the 2-year coupon Treasury in Exhibit 18.2 are:

0.5 year	$0.039 \times \$100 \times 0.5$	=	\$ 1.95
1.0 year	$0.039 \times \$100 \times 0.5$	=	\$ 1.95
1.5 years	$0.039 \times \$100 \times 0.5$	=	\$ 1.95
2.0 years	$0.039 \times \$100 \times 0.5 + 100$	=	\$101.95

---

[6] If we had not been working with a par yield curve, the equation would have been set to the market price for the 1.5-year issue rather than par value.

The present value of the cash flows is then:

$$\frac{1.95}{(1+z_1)^1} + \frac{1.95}{(1+z_2)^2} + \frac{1.95}{(1+z_3)^3} + \frac{101.95}{(1+z_4)^4}$$

where z_4 = one-half of the 2-year theoretical spot rate.

Since the 6-month spot rate, 1-year spot rate, and 1.5-year spot rate are 3.00%, 3.30%, and 3.5053%, respectively, then:

$$z_1 = 0.0150 \quad z_2 = 0.0165 \quad z_3 = 0.017527$$

Therefore, the present value of the 2-year coupon Treasury security is:

$$\frac{1.95}{(1.0150)^1} + \frac{1.95}{(1.0165)^2} + \frac{1.95}{(1.017527)^3} + \frac{101.95}{(1+z_4)^4}$$

Since the price of the 2-year coupon Treasury security is equal to par, the following relationship must hold:

$$\frac{1.95}{(1.0150)^1} + \frac{1.95}{(1.0165)^2} + \frac{1.95}{(1.017527)^3} + \frac{101.95}{(1+z_4)^4} = 100$$

We can solve for the theoretical 2-year spot rate as follows:

$$\frac{101.95}{(1+z_4)^4} = 94.3407$$

$$(1+z_4)^4 = \frac{101.95}{94.3407}$$

$$z_4 = 0.019582 = 1.9582\%$$

Doubling this yield, we obtain the theoretical 2-year spot rate bond-equivalent yield of 3.9164%.

One can follow this approach sequentially to derive the theoretical 2.5-year spot rate from the calculated values of z_1, z_2, z_3, and z_4 (the 6-month-, 1-year-, 1.5-year-, and 2-year rates), and the price and coupon of the 2.5-year bond in Exhibit 18.2. Further, one could derive theoretical spot rates for the remaining 15 half-yearly rates. The spot rates thus obtained are shown in the last column of Exhibit 18.2. They represent the term structure of default-free spot rate for maturities up to 10 years at the particular time to which the bond price quotations refer.

EXHIBIT 18.3   Determination of the Arbitrage-Free Value of an
8% 10-Year Treasury and Arbitrage Opportunity

					Arbitrage-Free Value	Abitrage Opportunity		
Period	Years	Cash Flow ($)	Spot Rate (%)	Present Value ($)	Sell for	Buy for	Arbitrage Profit	
1	0.5	4	6.05	3.8826	3.8836	3.8632	0.0193	
2	1.0	4	6.15	3.7649	3.7649	3.7312	0.0337	
3	1.5	4	6.21	3.6494	3.6494	3.6036	0.0458	
4	2.0	4	6.26	3.5361	3.5361	3.4804	0.0557	
5	2.5	4	6.29	3.4263	3.4263	3.3614	0.6486	
6	3.0	4	6.37	3.3141	3.3141	3.2465	0.0676	
7	3.5	4	6.38	3.2107	3.3107	3.1355	0.0752	
8	4.0	4	6.40	3.1090	3.1090	3.0283	0.0807	
9	4.5	4	6.41	3.0113	3.0113	2.9247	0.0866	
10	5.0	4	6.48	2.9079	2.9079	2.8247	0.0832	
11	5.5	4	6.49	2.8151	2.8151	2.7282	0.0867	
12	6.0	4	6.53	2.7203	2.7203	2.6349	0.0854	
13	6.5	4	6.63	2.6178	2.6178	2.5448	0.0730	
14	7.0	4	6.78	2.5082	2.5082	2.4578	0.0504	
15	7.5	4	6.79	2.4242	2.4242	2.3738	0.0504	
16	8.0	4	6.81	2.3410	2.3410	2.2926	0.0484	
17	8.5	4	6.84	2.2583	2.2583	2.2142	0.0441	
18	9.0	4	6.93	2.1666	2.1666	2.1385	0.0281	
19	9.5	4	7.05	2.0711	2.0711	2.0654	0.0057	
20	10.0	104	7.20	51.2670	51.2670	51.8645	−0.5975	
			Total	107.0018	107.0018	106.5141	0.4877	

Let us summarize to this point. We started with the par curve which is constructed using the adjusted yields from the on-the-run Treasuries. A par rate is the average discount rate of many cash flows over many periods. Specifically, par rates are complicated averages of spot rates. The spot rates are uncovered from par rates via bootstrapping. A spot rate is the average discount rate of a single cash flow over many periods. It appears that spot rates are also averages. As we will see later in this chapter, spot rates are averages of one or more forward rates.

Valuation Using Treasury Spot Rates

To illustrate how Treasury spot rates are used to compute the arbitrage-free value of a Treasury security, we will use the hypothetical Treasury spot rates shown in the fourth column of Exhibit 18.3 to value an 8%, 10-year Treasury security. The present value of each period's cash flow is shown in the fifth column. The sum of the present values is the arbitrage-free value for the Treasury security. For the 8%, 10-year Treasury it is $107.0018.

Reason for Using Treasury Spot Rates

Thus far, we have simply asserted that the value of a Treasury security should be based on discounting each cash flow using the corresponding Treasury spot rate. But what if market participants value a security using just the yield for the on-the-run Treasury with a maturity equal to the maturity of the Treasury security being valued? Let's see why the value of a Treasury security should trade close to its arbitrage-free value.

Stripping and Arbitrage-Free Valuation

The key to the arbitrage-free valuation approach is the existence of the Treasury strips market. A dealer has the ability to take apart the cash flows of a Treasury coupon security (i.e., strip the security) and create zero-coupon securities. These zero-coupon securities, which we called *Treasury strips*, can be sold to investors. At what interest rate or yield can these Treasury strips be sold to investors? They can be sold at the Treasury spot rates. If the market price of a Treasury security is less than its value using the arbitrage-free valuation approach, then a dealer can buy the Treasury security, strip it, and sell off the individual Treasury strips so as to generate greater proceeds than the cost of purchasing the Treasury security. The resulting profit is an *arbitrage profit*. Since, as we will see, the value determined by using the Treasury spot rates does not allow for the generation of an arbitrage profit, this is referred to as an "arbitrage-free" approach.

To illustrate this, suppose that the yield for the on-the-run 10-year Treasury issue is 7.08%. Suppose that the 8% coupon 10-year Treasury issue is valued using the traditional approach based on 7.08%. The value based on discounting all the cash flows at 7.08% is $106.5141.

Consider what would happen if the market priced the security at $106.5141. The value based on the Treasury spot rates (Exhibit 18.3) is $107.0018. What can the dealer do? The dealer can buy the 8% 10-year issue for $106.5141, strip it, and sell the Treasury strips at the spot rates shown in Exhibit 18.3. By doing so, the proceeds that will be received by the dealer are $107.0018. This results in an arbitrage profit (ignoring transaction costs) of $0.4877 (= $107.0018 − $106.5141). Dealers recognizing this arbitrage opportunity will bid up the price of the 8% 10-year Treasury issue in order to acquire it and strip it. At what point will the arbitrage profit disappear? When the security is priced at $107.0018, the value that we said is the arbitrage-free value.

To understand in more detail where this arbitrage profit is coming from, look at the last three columns in Exhibit 18.3. The sixth column shows how much each cash flow can be sold for by the dealer if it is stripped. The values in this column are just those in the fifth column. The next-to-last column shows how much the dealer is effectively purchasing the cash flow for if each cash flow is discounted at 7.08%. The sum of the arbitrage profit from each stripped cash flow is the total arbitrage profit and is contained in the last column.

We have just demonstrated how coupon stripping of a Treasury issue will force the market value to be close to the value as determined by the arbitrage-free valuation approach when the market price is less than the arbitrage-free value (i.e., the whole is worth less than the sum of the parts). What happens when a Treasury issue's market price is greater than the arbitrage-free value? Obviously, a dealer will not want to strip the Treasury issue since the proceeds generated from stripping will be less than the cost of purchasing the issue.

When such situations occur, the dealer can purchase a package of Treasury strips so as to create a synthetic Treasury coupon security that is worth more than the same maturity and same coupon Treasury issue. This process is called *reconstitution*.

The process of stripping and reconstitution assures that the price of a Treasury issue will not depart materially (depending on transaction costs) from its arbitrage-free value.

Credit Spreads and the Valuation of Non-Treasury Securities

The Treasury spot rates can be used to value any default-free security. For a non-Treasury security, the theoretical value is not as easy to determine. The value of a non-Treasury security is found by discounting the cash flows by the Treasury spot rates plus a yield spread which reflects the additional risks (e.g., default risk, liquidity risks, the risk associated with any embedded options, and so on).

The spot rate used to discount the cash flow of a non-Treasury security can be the Treasury spot rate plus a constant credit spread. For example, suppose the 6-month Treasury spot rate is 6.05% and the 10-year Treasury spot rate is 7.20%. Also suppose that a suitable credit spread is 100 basis points. Then a 7.05% spot rate is used to discount a 6-month cash flow of a non-Treasury bond and a 8.20% discount rate is used to discount a 10-year cash flow. (Remember that when each semiannual cash flow is discounted, the discount rate used is one-half the spot rate: 3.525% for the 6-month spot rate and 4.10% for the 10-year spot rate.)

The drawback of this approach is that there is no reason to expect the credit spread to be the same regardless of when the cash flow is expected to be received. Consequently, the credit spread may vary with a bond's term to maturity. In other words, there is a *term structure of credit spreads*. Generally, credit spreads increase with maturity. This is a typical shape for the term structure of credit spreads. Moreover, the shape of the term structure is not the same for all credit ratings. Typically, the lower the credit rating, the steeper the term structure of credit spreads.

Dealer firms typically estimate the term structure of credit spreads for each credit rating and market sector. Typically, the credit spread increases with maturity. In addition, the shape of the term structure is not the same for all credit ratings. Typically, the lower the credit rating, the steeper the term structure of credit spreads.

When the relevant credit spreads for a given credit rating and market sector are added to the Treasury spot rates, the resulting term structure is used to value the bonds of issuers with that credit rating in that market sector. This term structure is referred to as the *benchmark spot rate curve* or *benchmark zero-coupon rate curve*.

For example, Exhibit 18.4 reproduces the Treasury spot rate curve in Exhibit 18.3. Also shown in the exhibit is a hypothetical term structure of credit spread for a non-Treasury security. The resulting benchmark spot rate curve is in the next-to-the-last column. Like before, it is this spot rate curve that is used to value the securities of issuers that have the same credit rating and are in the same market sector. This is done in Exhibit 18.4 for a hypothetical 8% 10-year issue. The arbitrage-free value is $101.763. Notice that the theoretical value is less than that for an otherwise comparable Treasury security. The arbitrage-free value for an 8% 10-year Treasury is $107.0018 (see Exhibit 18.3).

EXHIBIT 18.4   Calculation of Arbitrage-Free Value of a Hypothetical
8% 10-Year Non-Treasury Security Using Benchmark Spot Rate Curve

Period	Years	Cash Flow ($)	Treasury Spot Rate (%)	Credit Spread (%)	Benchmark Spot (%)	Present Value ($)
1	0.5	4	6.05	0.30	6.35	3.8769
2	1.0	4	6.15	0.33	6.48	3.7529
3	1.5	4	6.21	0.34	6.55	3.6314
4	2.0	4	6.26	0.37	6.63	3.5108
5	2.5	4	6.29	0.42	6.71	3.3916
6	3.0	4	6.37	0.43	6.80	3.2729
7	3.5	4	6.38	0.44	6.82	3.1632
8	4.0	4	6.40	0.45	6.85	3.0553
9	4.5	4	6.41	0.46	6.87	2.9516
10	5.0	4	6.48	0.52	7.00	2.8357
11	5.5	4	6.49	0.53	7.02	2.7369
12	6.0	4	6.53	0.55	7.08	2.6349
13	6.5	4	6.63	0.58	7.21	2.5241
14	7.0	4	6.78	0.59	7.37	2.4101
15	7.5	4	6.79	0.63	7.42	2.3161
16	8.0	4	6.81	0.64	7.45	2.2281
17	8.5	4	6.84	0.69	7.53	2.1340
18	9.0	4	6.93	0.73	7.66	2.0335
19	9.5	4	7.05	0.77	7.82	1.9301
20	10.0	104	7.20	0.82	8.02	47.3731
					Total	101.763

CHAPTER 19

Yield Measures and Forward Rates

Frank J. Fabozzi, Ph.D., CFA
Adjunct Professor of Finance
School of Management
Yale University

Steven V. Mann, Ph.D.
Professor of Finance
The Moore School of Business
University of South Carolina

A bond's yield is a measure of its *potential* return. Market participants commonly assess a security's relative value by calculating a yield and some yield spread. There are a number of yield measures that are quoted in the market. These measures are based on certain assumptions which result in limiting the usefulness of the yield measure in gauging relative value. In this chapter, we will explain the various yield and yield spread measures as well as document their limitations. At the end of this chapter we will explain what forward rates are and their relationship to spot rates discussed in the previous chapter.

SOURCES OF RETURN

The dollar return an investor expects to receive comes from three potential sources:

1. The periodic interest payments made by the issuer (i.e., coupon payments)
2. Any capital gain (or capital loss, which is a negative dollar return) when the bond matures, is sold by the investor, or is called by the issuer
3. Income earned from reinvestment of the bond's interim cash flows (i.e., coupon payments and principal repayments.)

In order to be a useful indicator of a bond's potential return, a yield measure should account for all three of these potential sources of dollar return in a reasonable way. We will begin our discussion by examining the three return sources in more detail.

We will illustrate the sources of dollar returns using an example. On the afternoon of July 5, 2000, the on-the-run 5-year Treasury note was trading at 102-20+ assuming next day settlement (i.e., $102.6406 per $100 of par value). This note carries a coupon rate of 6.75% and matures on May 15, 2005. Coupon payments are delivered on May 15 and November 15. Suppose the $1 million of par value of these 5-year notes are purchased on July 5, 2000. If this position is held to maturity, what are the three sources of dollar returns?

Periodic Interest Payments

The most obvious source of dollar return is the periodic coupon interest payments. For the $1 million par value of this 5-year note, the semiannual coupon payments consist of 10 payments of $33,750 with the first occurring on November 15, 2000. Since this note has a settlement date between coupon periods, the buyer pays the seller accrued interest. There are 52 days between the date the bond was issued (May 15, 2000) and the bond's settlement date of July 6, 2000. In addition, there are 184 days in the coupon period. At settlement, the buyer will pay the seller $9,538.04 (per $1 million in par value) in accrued interest which is calculated as follows:

$$\$33,750 \times (52/184) = \$9,538.04$$

For a zero-coupon bond, there are no interim coupon payments so the return from this source is zero. This is true even though the investor is effectively receiving interest by purchasing the instrument at a discount to its par value and realizing interest at the maturity date when the investor receives the repayment of principal.

Capital Gain or Loss[1]

The investor's tenure as a bond's owner ends as a result of one of the following circumstances. First, the investor may simply sell the bond and will receive the bond's prevailing market price plus accrued interest. Next, the issuer may call the bond in which case the investor receives the call price plus accrued interest or the investor may put the bond and receive the put price plus accrued interest. Lastly, if the bond matures, the investor will receive the maturity value plus the final coupon payment. Regardless of the reason, if the proceeds received are greater than the investor's initial purchase price, a capital gain is generated which is an additional source of dollar return. Similarly, if the proceeds received are less than the investor's initial purchase price, a capital loss is generated which is a negative dollar return. For the 5-year note described above, the purchase price is $1,035,944.29 (i.e., the clean price plus accrued interest). Thus, if the investor holds this note until the maturity date of May 15, 2005, the investor will generate a capital loss of $35,944.29 ($1,000,000 − $1,035,944.29).

Reinvestment Income

The source of dollar return called *reinvestment income* represents the interest earned from reinvesting the bond's interim cash flows (interest and/or principal payments) until the bond is removed from the investor's portfolio. With the exception of zero-coupon bonds, fixed income securities deliver coupon payments that can be reinvested. Moreover, amortizing securities (e.g., mortgage-backed and asset-backed securities) make periodic principal repayments which can also be invested.

As an example, if $1 million of the 5-year note is held to maturity, the investor will receive $337,500 in coupon payments over the next 10 semiannual periods. Suppose an investor can reinvest each of these 10 coupon payments at say 6.111% compounded semiannually. The reinvestment income can be determined using the future value of an ordinary annuity formula. The general formula for the future value of an ordinary annuity when payments occur m times per year is:

$$FV_n = A\left[\frac{(1+i)^n - 1}{i}\right]$$

where

---

[1] The definition of capital gain or loss here is different from that defined for tax purposes.

A = Amount of the annuity ($)
i = Periodic interest rate which is the annual interest rate divided by m (in decimal form)
n = $N \times m$

Accordingly, the future value of 10 semiannual payments of $33,750 to be received plus the interest earned by investing the payments at 6.111% compounded semiannually is found as follows:

A = 33,750
m = 2
i = 0.030555 (0.06111/2)
N = 5
n = 10 (5 × 2)

therefore,

$$FV_{10} = \$33,750 \left[\frac{(1.030555)^{10} - 1}{0.030555} \right]$$

$$= \$33,750(11.49322) = \$387,896.30$$

Thus, the coupon payments and reinvestment income together are $387,896.30. The reinvestment income alone is $50,396.30 which is found by subtracting the total coupon payments ($387,896.30 – $337,500).

TRADITIONAL YIELD MEASURES

There are several yield measures commonly quoted by dealers and traders in the bond market. Among the more prominent are *current yield*, *yield to maturity*, *yield to call*, *yield to put*, *yield to worst*, and *cash flow yield*. Here we will demonstrate how to compute various yield measures for a bond given its price. We will also highlight their limitations as measures of potential return. This discussion will pave the way for a more useful yield measure for determining the potential return from investing in a bond, total return, which will be discussed in Chapter 22.

Current Yield

The current yield of a bond is calculated by dividing the security's annual dollar coupon payment by the market price. The formula for the current yield is:

$$\text{Current yield} = \frac{\text{Annual dollar coupon payment}}{\text{Price}}$$

To illustrate the calculation, consider a 7.45% coupon bond issued by Ford Motor Co. in July 1999 that matures on July 16, 2031. The market price of this bond on July 10, 2000, was 94.697251. The current yield is 7.867% as shown below:

Annual dollar coupon payment = $100 × 0.0745 = $7.45

$$\text{Current yield} = \frac{\$7.45}{\$94.697251} = 0.07867 = 7.867\%$$

Current yield possesses a number of drawbacks as a potential return measure. Current yield considers only coupon interest and no other source of return that will affect an investor's yield. That is, current yield ignores the capital gain that the investor will realize if the bond is held to maturity as well as any reinvestment income.

Yield to Maturity

The most common measure of yield in the bond market is the *yield to maturity*. The yield to maturity is simply a bond's internal rate of return. Specifically, the yield to maturity is the interest rate that will make the present value of the bond's cash flows equal to its market price plus accrued interest (i.e., the full price). To find the yield to maturity, we must first determine the bond's expected future cash flows. Then we search by trial and error for the interest rate that will make the present value of the bond's cash flows equal to the market price plus accrued interest.

To illustrate, consider once again the 7.45% coupon Ford Motor Company bond. The clean price for this bond was $946,972.51 for $1 million par value and the accrued interest was $36,008.33. Accordingly, the full price is $982,980.84 per $1 million par value. The cash flows of the bond are (1) 63 payments every six months of $37,250 and (2) a payment of $1,000,000 63 six-month periods from now. The interest rate that makes the present value of these cash flows equal to $982,980.84 is 3.995%. Hence, 3.995% is the semiannual yield to maturity.

The *market convention* adopted to annualize the semiannual yield to maturity is to double it and call the resulting number the yield to maturity. Thus, the yield to maturity for the Ford Motor Company bond is 7.911% (2 × 3.995%). The yield to maturity computed using this convention— doubling the semiannual yield—is called a *bond-equivalent yield.*

Important Relationships

In Chapter 19, we explained the relationship between the coupon rate, the required yield, and a bond's price relative to its par value (i.e., discount, premium, or par value). If a bond is held to maturity, we know that the yield to maturity is the required yield. We restate these relationships substituting yield to maturity for required yield as shown below:

Bond Selling at	Relationship
Par	coupon rate = yield to maturity
Discount	coupon rate < yield to maturity
Premium	coupon rate > yield to maturity

The following relationships between the price of a bond (relative to par), coupon rate, current yield, and yield to maturity also hold:

Bond Price Selling at	Relationship
Par	coupon rate = current yield = yield to maturity
Discount	coupon rate < current yield < yield to maturity
Premium	coupon rate > current yield > yield to maturity

A quick example will illustrate these relationships. For a 10-year 7% coupon and a $100 maturity value, it is easy to verify that when the bond is selling at $100, the coupon rate, current yield, and yield to maturity are all 7%. If the bond is selling at $93.2048, the yield to maturity is 8%. The current yield is 7.5103% ($7/93.2048) and is less than the yield to maturity because it ignores the built-in capital gain if the bond is held to maturity. The coupon rate is 7% which is the lowest of the three measures for this bond. Conversely, if the bond is selling at $107.4387, the yield to maturity is 6%. The current yield of 6.5153% ($7/107.4387) is higher than the yield to maturity because it ignores the built-in capital loss if the bond is held to maturity. The coupon rate is 7% which is higher than the current yield.

Limitations of the Yield to Maturity Measure

At first blush, the yield to maturity appears to be an informative measure of a bond's potential return. It considers not only the coupon income but any capital gain or loss that will be realized by holding the bond to maturity. The yield to maturity recognizes the timing of the cash flows. It also considers the third source of dollar return that we discussed at the beginning of the chapter—reinvestment income. However, when calculating yield to maturity, we are implicitly assuming that the coupon payments can be reinvested at an interest equal to the semiannual yield to maturity.[2]

The following example demonstrates this. In what follows, the analysis will be cast in terms of dollars. Be sure to keep in mind the distinction between *total future dollars* which are equal to all dollars that the bond investor expects to receive (including the recovery of the principal) and the *total dollar return* which is equal to the dollars the investor expects to realize from the three sources of return, namely, coupon payments, capital gain/loss, and reinvestment income.

Let's illustrate the distinction between total future dollars and total dollar return with a simple example. Suppose one invested $100 for ten years at 7% compounded semiannually (i.e., 3.5% every six months). What is the total future dollars that will result from this investment? This is nothing more than asking for the future value of a single cash flow invested at 3.5% for 20 six-month periods. The total future dollars generated are $198.98, as shown below:

$$\text{Total future dollars} = \$100(1.035)^{20} = \$198.98$$

The total future dollars of this investment ($198.98) are comprised of the return of principal $100 and the total interest of $98.98. If we subtract the amount invested ($100) from the total future dollars, the difference is $98.98, which is the total dollar return.

Consider a hypothetical 10-year bond selling at par ($100) with a coupon rate of 7%. Assume the bond delivers coupon payments semiannually. The yield to maturity for this bond is 7%. Suppose an investor buys this bond, holds it to maturity, and receives the maturity value of $100. In addition, the investor receives 20 semiannual coupon payments of $3.50 and can reinvest them every six months that they received at a semiannual rate of 3.5%. What are the total future dollars assuming a 7% reinvestment rate? As demonstrated above, an investment of $100 must generate $198.98 in order to generate a yield of 7% compounded semiannually. Alternatively, the bond investment of $100 must deliver a total dollar return of $98.98.

Let us partition the total dollar return for this bond into its three components: coupon payments, capital gain/loss, and reinvestment income. The coupon payments contribute $70 ($3.5 × 20) of the total

---

[2] This assumes that the bond in question pays semiannual cash flows. If the bond pays annual cash flows, the cash flows must be reinvested at the annual yield to maturity.

dollar return. The capital gain/loss component is zero because the bond is purchased at par and held to maturity. Lastly, the remainder of the total dollar return ($28.98) must be due to reinvestment income.

To verify this, this par bond's total dollar return of $98.98 is driven by two sources of dollar return—coupon payments and reinvestment income. Recall from the beginning of the chapter, the reinvestment income can be determined using the future value of an ordinary annuity formula given earlier. Accordingly, the future value of 20 semiannual payments of $3.50 to be received plus the interest earned by investing the payments at 7% compounded semiannually is found as follows:

A = $3.50
m = 2
i = 0.035 (0.07/2)
N = 10
n = 20 (10 × 2)

therefore,

$$FV_{20} = \$3.50\left[\frac{(1.035)^{20} - 1}{0.035}\right]$$
$$= \$3.50(27.27968) = \$98.98$$

Thus, the coupon payments and reinvestment income together are $98.98 which agrees with total dollar return from our earlier calculation. The reinvestment income alone is $28.28 ($98.98 − $70).

To summarize, in order to generate at 7% return over the 10 years until maturity, an investor must generate a total dollar return of $98.98. How plausible is this? If the bond does not default, the investor will receive all the coupon payments ($70) and the repayment of principal at maturity ($0 capital gain). How about the reinvestment income of $28.28? Of course, obtaining this amount depends on being able to reinvest at a 7% rate compounded semiannually all coupon payments over the next 10 years.

Clearly, the investor will only realize the yield to maturity that is computed at the time of purchase if the following two assumptions hold:

Assumption 1: The coupon payments can be reinvested at the yield to maturity.
Assumption 2: The bond is held to maturity.

With respect to the first assumption, the risk that an investor faces is that future interest rates will be less than the yield to maturity at the time the bond is purchased. This risk is called *reinvestment risk*. As for the second assumption, if the bond is not held to maturity, it may have to be sold for less than its purchase price, resulting in a return that is less than the yield to maturity. This risk is called *interest rate risk*.

Factors Affecting Reinvestment Risk

There are two characteristics of a bond that affect the degree of reinvestment risk. First, for a given yield to maturity and a given non-zero coupon rate, the longer the maturity the more the bond's total return is dependent on reinvestment income to realize the yield to maturity at the time of purchase. The implication is that the yield to maturity measure for long-term coupon bonds tells us little about the potential return an investor may realize if the bond is held to maturity. For long-term bonds, the reinvestment income component will be the most important source of total dollar return.

The second bond characteristic that affects reinvestment income is the coupon rate. For a coupon bond of a given maturity and yield to maturity, the higher the coupon rate, the more dependent the bond's total dollar return will be on the reinvestment of the coupon payments in order to produce the yield to maturity at the time of purchase. In other words, holding maturity and yield to maturity constant, a bond selling at a premium will be more dependent on reinvestment income than a bond selling at par. This is true because the reinvestment income must offset the capital loss realized by holding the premium bond to maturity. Conversely, a bond selling at a discount depends less on reinvestment income than a bond selling at par because a portion of the return is derived from the capital gain that is realized from maturing the bond. For a zero-coupon bond, none of the bond's total dollar return is dependent on reinvestment income. Hence, a zero-coupon bond has no reinvestment risk if held to maturity.

Yield to Call

For callable bonds, the market convention is to calculate a yield to call in addition to a yield to maturity. A callable bond may be called at more than one price and these prices are specified in a call price schedule. The yield to call assumes that the issuer will call the bond at some call date and the call price is then specified in the call schedule.

The procedure for calculating the yield to call is the same as that for the yield to maturity: Determine the interest rate that will make the present value of the expected cash flows equal to the market price plus accrued interest. The expected cash flows are the coupon payments to a particular call date in the future and the call price. There are various yield to call measures—yield to custom, yield to next call, and yield to refunding.

Yield to custom computes a yield to call for a call date and a price specified by the user. Typically, a bond does not have one call price but a call schedule which sets forth the call price based on when the issuer can exercise the call option. The call price according to the call schedule for the particular date selected will be used in the yield calculation. *Yield to next call* is the yield to call for the next call date after the current settlement date.

Yield to refunding is employed when bonds are currently callable but have some restrictions on the source of funds used to buy back the debt when a call is exercised. Namely, if a debt issue contains some refunding protection, bonds cannot be called for a certain period of time with the proceeds of other debt issues sold at a lower cost of money. As a result, the bondholder is afforded some protection if interest rates decline and the issuer can obtain lower cost funds to pay off the debt. It should be stressed that the bonds can be called with funds derived from other sources (e.g., cash on hand) during the refunded-protected period. The refunding date is the first date the bond can be called using lower cost debt. Given this backdrop, the yield to refunding is the discount rate (appropriately annualized) that discounts the cash flows to the first refunding date back to the bond's market price.

Yield to Put

When a bond is putable, the yield to the first put date is calculated and called the yield to put. This yield is the interest rate that will make the present value of the bond's cash flows to the first put date equal to the clean price plus accrued interest. As with all yield measures that are internal rates of return (e.g., yield to maturity and yield to call), yield to put assumes that any interim coupon payments can be reinvested at the calculated yield. Moreover, the yield to put assumes that the put will be exercised on the first possible date; that is the investor will put the bond back to the issuer and receive the put price plus the accrued interest.

For example, suppose that a 7% coupon bond maturing in five years is putable at par in two years and the bond's price is $103.39. The cash flows for this bond if the put is exercised in two years are: (1) 4 coupon payments of $3.50 every six months and (2) the $100 put price in four 6-month periods from now. The semiannual interest rate that will make the present value of the cash flows equal to the price of $103.39 is

2.5968%. Therefore, 2.5968% is the semiannual yield to put and 5.1968% is the yield to put on a bond-equivalent basis.

Yield to Worst

A yield can be calculated for every possible call and put date. Additionally, a yield to maturity can be calculated. The lowest of all these possible yields is called the *yield to worst*.

Cash Flow Yield

As discussed in Chapters 16 and 17, mortgage-backed and asset-backed securities are backed by a pool of loans or receivables. For example, mortgage-backed securities are backed by a pool of mortgage loans. The cash flows for these securities include principal repayment as well as interest. Uncertainty in the cash flows arises because the individual borrowers whose loans comprise the pool usually have the option to prepay the loan in whole or in part usually without penalty prior to the scheduled principal repayment date. Thus, a mortgaged-backed or asset-backed security has an embedded short position in a prepayment option. Owing to this prepayment option, it is necessary to assume the rate at which prepayments will occur in order to project the security's cash flows. The assumed rate is called the *prepayment rate* or *prepayment speed*.

A yield can be calculated given the projected cash flows based on an assumed prepayment rate. The yield is the interest rate that will make the present value of the assumed cash flows equal to the clean price plus accrued interest. A yield calculated in this manner is called a *cash flow yield*.

The cash flows for mortgaged-backed and asset-backed securities are often delivered monthly rather than semiannually. Accordingly, the interest rate that will make the present value of the assumed cash flows (interest and principal payments) equal to the market price plus accrued interest is a monthly yield. This monthly yield is then annualized using the following convention.

First, the semiannual effective yield is computed from the monthly yield by compounding it for six months as follows:

$$\text{effective semiannual yield} = (1 + \text{monthly yield})^6 - 1$$

Second, the effective semiannual yield is doubled to obtain the annual cash flow yield on a bond-equivalent basis. Specifically,

$$
\begin{aligned}
\text{cash flow yield} &= 2 \times \text{effective semiannual yield} \\
&= 2[(1 + \text{monthly yield})^6 - 1]
\end{aligned}
$$

For example, if the monthly yield is 0.63%, then:

$$\text{cash flow yield} = 2[(1.0063)^6 - 1] = 7.6801\%$$

Thus, the cash flow yield on a bond-equivalent basis is 7.6801%.

Although it is commonly quoted by market participants, the cash flow yield suffers from limitations similar to the yield to maturity. These shortcomings include: (1) the projected cash flows assume that the prepayment speed will be realized, (2) the projected cash flows are assumed to be reinvested at the cash flow yield, and (3) the mortgage-backed or asset-backed security is assumed to be held until the final payoff of all the loans in the pool based on some prepayment assumption. If the cash flows are reinvested at rate lower than the cash flow yield (i.e., reinvestment risk) or if actual prepayments differ from those projected, then the cash flow yield will not be realized. Mortgage-backed and asset-backed securities are particularly sensitive to reinvestment risk since payments are usually monthly and include principal repayments as well as interest.

Portfolio Yield Measures

The yield on a portfolio of bonds is the discount rate that makes the present value of the portfolio's expected future cash flows equal to the portfolio's total market value. Thus, in principle, we calculate the portfolio yield in the same manner as the yield to maturity on a single bond. In other words, the portfolio yield is the portfolio's internal rate of return. This calculation begins by first forecasting the cash flows for all the bonds that comprise the portfolio. The next step is to find the interest rate that will make the present value of the cash flows equal to the portfolio market value.

To illustrate how to calculate a portfolio's internal rate of return, we will use the following three-bond portfolio:

Bond	Coupon Rate (%)	Maturity (in Years)	Par Value (in Dollars)	Market Value (in Dollars)	Yield to Maturity (%)
A	6.00%	5	$20,000,000	$19,578,880	6.5%
B	5.25%	2	$10,000,000	$9,860,609	6.0%
C	5.50%	4	$30,000,000	$29,266,032	6.2%

The cash flows for each bond in the portfolio and for the entire portfolio are as follows:

Period	Bond A ($)	Bond B ($)	Bond C ($)	Portfolio ($)
1	600,000	262,500	825,000	1,687,500
2	600,000	262,500	825,000	1,687,500
3	600,000	262,500	825,000	1,687,500
4	600,000	10,262,500	825,000	11,687,500
5	600,000		825,000	1,425,000
6	600,000		825,000	1,425,000
7	600,000		825,000	1,425,000
8	600,000		30,825,000	31,425,000
9	600,000			600,000
10	20,600,000			20,600,000

Suppose the total market value of this portfolio is $58,705,521. The internal rate of return for this three-bond portfolio is found via iteration and is the interest rate that makes the present value of the portfolio's cash flows shown in the last column of the table above equal to $58,705,521. If the semiannual interest rate of 3.1522% is used, the present value of the portfolio's cash flows equals $56,511,509. The portfolio's internal rate of return on a bond-equivalent basis is found by doubling 3.1522% which is 6.3044%.

The portfolio's internal rate of return carries the same baggage as yield to maturity which we discussed earlier. Namely, the portfolio's cash flows can be reinvested at the internal rate of return and the investor will hold the portfolio until the maturity date of the longest bond in the portfolio.

YIELD SPREAD MEASURES

Traditional yield spread analysis for a non-Treasury security involves calculating the difference between the risky bond's yield and the yield on a comparable maturity benchmark Treasury security. As an illustration, let's use the 7.45% coupon Ford Motor Company bond whose yield to maturity of 7.91% we calculated earlier. Using a settlement date of July 10, 2000, the appropriate Treasury bond was the 6.25% coupon with a maturity date of May 15, 2030 which had a yield to maturity of 5.86%. The traditional yield spread is simply the difference between the yields to maturity of these two bonds 205 basis points (7.91% − 5.86%). This yield spread measure is referred to as the *nominal spread*.

The nominal spread measure has several drawbacks. For now, the most important is that the nominal spread fails to account for the term structure of spot rates for both bonds. Moreover, as we will see in the next chapter when we discuss the valuation of bonds with embedded options (e.g., callable bonds), the nominal spread does not take into consideration the fact that expected interest rate volatility may alter the non-Treasury bond's expected future cash flows. We will focus here only on the first drawback and pose an alternative spread measure that incorporates the spot rate curve. In the next chapter we will discuss another spread measure, the option-adjusted spread (OAS), for bonds with embedded options.

Zero-Volatility Spread

The *zero-volatility spread*, also referred to as the *Z-spread* or *static spread,* is a measure of the spread that the investor would realize over the entire Treasury spot rate curve if the bond were held to maturity. Unlike the nominal spread, it is not a spread at one point on the yield curve. The Z-spread is the spread that will make the present value of the cash flows from the non-Treasury bond, when discounted at the Treasury rate plus the spread, equal to the non-Treasury bond's market price plus accrued interest. A trial-and-error procedure is used to compute the Z-spread.

To illustrate how this is done, consider the following two 5-year bonds:

Issue	Coupon	Price	Yield to Maturity
Treasury	5.055%	100.0000	5.0550%
Non-Treasury	7.000%	101.9576	6.5348%

The nominal spread for the non-Treasury bond is 147.98 basis points. Let's use the information presented in Exhibit 19.1 to determine the Z-spread. The third column in the exhibit shows the cash flows for the 7% 5-year non-Treasury issue. The fourth column is a hypothetical Treasury spot rate curve that we will employ in this example. The goal is to determine the spread that, when added to all the Treasury spot rates, will produce a present value for the non-Treasury bond equal to its market price of $101.9576.

Suppose we select a spread of 100 basis points. To each Treasury spot rate shown in the fourth column of Exhibit 19.1, 100 basis points are added. So, for example, the 1-year (period 2) spot rate is 5.33% (4.33% plus 1%). The spot rate plus 100 basis points is used to calculate the present values as shown in the fifth column.[3] The total present value in the fifth column is $104.110. Because the present value is not equal to the non-Treasury issue's price of ($101.9576), the Z-spread is not 100 basis points. If a spread of 120 basis points is tried, it can be seen from the next-to-the-last column of Exhibit 19.1 that the present

---

[3] The discount rate used to compute the present value of each cash flow in the third column is found by adding the assumed spread to the spot rate and then dividing by 2.

value is $103.243; again, because this is not equal to the non-Treasury issue's price, 120 basis points is not the Z-spread. The last column of Exhibit 19.1 shows the present value when a 150 basis point spread is used. The present value of the cash flows is equal to the non-Treasury issue's price. Accordingly, 150 basis points is the Z-spread, compared to the nominal spread of 147.98 basis points.

What does the Z-spread represent for this non-Treasury security? Since the Z-spread is relative to the benchmark Treasury spot rate curve, it represents a spread required by the market to compensate for all the risks of holding the non-Treasury bond versus a Treasury security with the same maturity. These risks include the non-Treasury's credit risk, liquidity risk, and the risks associated with any embedded options.

Divergence Between Z-Spread and Nominal Spread

Generally, the divergence is a function of the term structure's shape and the security's characteristics. Among the relevant security characteristics are coupon rate, term to maturity, and type of principal repayment provision—non-amortizing versus amortizing. The steeper the term structure, the greater will be the divergence. For standard coupon-paying bonds with a bullet maturity (i.e., a single payment of principal), the Z-spread and the nominal spread will usually not differ significantly. For monthly-pay amortizing securities the divergence can be substantial in a steep yield curve environment.

EXHIBIT 19.1   Determination of the Z-Spread for an 7% 5-Year Non-Treasury Issue Selling at $101.9576 to Yield 6.5347%

Period	Years	Cash Flow ($)	Spot Rate (%)	Present Value ($) Assuming a Spread of		
				100 bp	120 bp	150 bp
1	0.5	3.50	4.20	3.4113	3.4080	3.4030
2	1.0	3.50	4.33	3.3207	3.3142	3.3045
3	1.5	3.50	4.39	3.2793	3.2222	3.2081
4	2.0	3.50	4.44	3.1438	3.1315	3.1133
5	2.5	3.50	4.51	3.0553	3.0405	3.0184
6	3.0	3.50	4.54	2.9708	2.9535	2.9278
7	3.5	3.50	4.58	2.8868	2.8672	2.8381
8	4.0	3.50	4.73	2.7921	2.7705	2.7384
9	4.5	3.50	4.90	2.6942	2.6708	2.6360
10	5.0	103.50	5.11	76.6037	75.8643	74.7699
			Total	104.110	103.243	101.958

Z-Spread Relative to Any Benchmark

A Z-spread can be calculated relative to any benchmark spot rate curve in the same manner. The question arises: What does the Z-spread mean when the benchmark is not the Treasury spot rate curve (i.e., default-free spot rate curve)? This is especially true in Europe where swap curves are commonly used as a benchmark for pricing.[4] When the Treasury spot rate curve is the benchmark, we indicated that the Z-spread for non-Treasury issues captured credit risk, liquidity risk, and any option risks. When the benchmark is the spot rate curve for the issuer, for example, the Z-spread reflects the spread attributable to the issue's liquidity risk and any option risks.

Accordingly, when a Z-spread is cited, it must be cited relative to some benchmark spot rate curve. This is essential because it indicates the credit and sector risks that are being considered when the Z-spread is calculated. While Z-spreads are typically calculated in the United States using Treasury securities as the benchmark interest rates, this is usually not the case elsewhere.

FORWARD RATES

We have just described how a default-free theoretical spot rate curve can be extrapolated from the Treasury yield curve. Additional information useful to market participants can be extrapolated from the default-free theoretical spot rate curve: forward rates. A forward rate is the fundamental unit of yield curve analysis. Forward rates are the building blocks of interest rates just as atoms are the building blocks of solid matter in physics. A forward rate is the discount rate of a single cash flow over a single period. Under certain assumptions, these rates can be viewed as the market's consensus of future interest rates.[5]

Examples of forward rates that can be calculated from the default-free theoretical spot rate curve are the:

- 6-month forward rate six months from now
- 6-month forward rate three years from now
- 1-year forward rate one year from now
- 3-year forward rate two years from now
- 5-year forward rates three years from now

---

[4] Swaps and swap rates are discussed in Chapter 25.
[5] See, Antti Illmanen, "Market's Rate Expectations and Forward Rates," Part 2, *Understanding the Yield Curve* (New York: Salomon Brothers, 1995).

Since the forward rates are implicitly extrapolated from the default-free theoretical spot rate curve, these rates are sometimes referred to as *implicit forward rates*. Recall, spot rates are averages of implied forward rates so it should not be surprising that we "break apart" spot rates to uncover forward rates. We begin by showing how to compute the 6-month forward rates. Then we explain how to compute any forward rate between any two periods in the future.

Deriving 6-Month Forward Rates

To illustrate the process of extrapolating 6-month forward rates, we will use the yield curve and the corresponding spot rate curve from Exhibit 18.5 of Chapter 18. We will use a very simple no arbitrage principle as we did earlier when deriving the spot rates in Chapter 18. Namely, the "law of one price" says that if two goods are perfect substitutes they must sell for the same price. Specifically, if two investments produce the same expected cash flows and have the same risk, they should have the same value.

Suppose an investor has a 1-year anticipated investment horizon. In general, an investor has three basic ways to satisfy this maturity preference. First, an investor can purchase a security having a maturity that matches the investment horizon. For example, an investor can buy a 1-year zero coupon bond and hold it to maturity. We will call this a "buy and hold" strategy. Second, an investor can invest in a series of short-term securities (e.g., buy a 6-month zero-coupon bond today, hold it to maturity, and reinvest the proceeds into another 6-month zero-coupon bond six months from now.) We will call this a "rollover" strategy. Finally, an investor can invest in a security with a maturity greater than the anticipated holding period and sell it at the appropriate time (e.g., buy a 2-year zero coupon bond and selling it after one year). If the yield curve is upward-sloping, this strategy is called "riding the yield curve."

For simplicity, let's consider an investor who has a 1-year investment horizon and is faced with the following two alternatives (we will return to the riding the yield curve strategy shortly):

- Buy a 1-year Treasury bill (buy-and-hold strategy), or
- Buy a 6-month Treasury bill, and when it matures in six months buy another 6-month Treasury bill (rollover strategy).

The investor will be indifferent between the two alternatives if they produce the same expected return over the 1-year investment horizon. The investor knows the spot rates that are available on the 6-month Treasury bill and the 1-year Treasury bill. However, she does not know what yield will be available on a 6-month Treasury bill that will be purchased six months from now (i.e., the second leg of the rollover strategy). That is, she does not know the 6-month forward rate six months from now. Given the spot rates for the 6-month Treasury bill and the 1-year Treasury bill, the forward rate on a 6-month Treasury bill is the rate that equalizes the expected dollar return between the two alternatives.

To see how that rate can be determined, suppose that an investor purchased a 6-month Treasury bill for $X. At the end of six months, the value of this investment would be:

$$X(1 + z_1)$$

where z_1 is one-half the bond-equivalent yield (BEY) of the theoretical 6-month spot rate. Intuitively, this product tells us how much money the investor will have available to reinvest in the second 6-month bill, six months from now.

Let f represent one-half the forward rate (expressed as a BEY) on a 6-month Treasury bill available six months from now. If the investor were to rollover her investment by purchasing that bill at that time, then the future dollars available at the end of one year from the $X investment would be:

$$X(1 + z_1)(1 + f)$$

Note we cannot calculate this expression because we do not know f as of yet.

Now consider the buy-and-hold strategy. Namely, buying the 1-year Treasury bill and maturing it. If we let z_2 represent one-half the BEY of the theoretical 1-year spot rate, then the future dollars available at the end of one year from the $X investment would be:

$$X(1 + z_2)^2$$

The reason that the squared term appears is that the amount invested is being compounded for two periods at one-half the 1-year spot rate due to semiannual compounding.

Now we are prepared to analyze the investor's choices and what this tells us about forward rates. The investor will be indifferent between the two alternatives confronting her if she makes the same dollar investment ($X) and expects to receive the same future dollars from both alternatives at the end of one year. That is, the investor will be indifferent if:

$$X(1 + z_1)(1 + f) = X(1 + z_2)^2$$

Dividing both sides by X (the initial investment) leaves the following:

$$(1 + z_1)(1 + f) = (1 + z_2)^2$$

We can interpret the left-side of this expression as the expected holding-period return of the rollover strategy. Likewise, the right-hand side is the expected holding-period return of the buy-and-hold strategy. Given that z_1 and z_2 are known, what does f have to be six months hence for these two strategies to have the same holding-period returns? In simple words, f is the value that makes the right side equal the left side. Note this result is courtesy of the no-arbitrage condition. Solving for f, we get:

$$f = \frac{(1 + z_2)^2}{(1 + z_1)} - 1$$

Doubling f gives the BEY for the 6-month forward rate six months from now.

We can illustrate the use of this formula with the theoretical spot rates shown in543rom that exhibit, we know that:

6-month bill spot rate = 0.030, therefore $z_1 = 0.0150$
1-year bill spot rate = 0.033, therefore $z_2 = 0.0165$

Substituting into the formula, we have:

$$f = \frac{(1.0165)^2}{(1.0150)} - 1 = 0.0180 = 1.8\%$$

Therefore, the 6-month forward rate six months from now is 3.6% (1.8% × 2) BEY.

Let's confirm our results. If X is invested in the 6-month Treasury bill at 1.5% and the proceeds then reinvested for six months at the 6-month forward rate of 1.8%, the total proceeds from this alternative would be:

$$X(1.015)(1.018) = 1.03327\ X$$

Investment of X in the 1-year Treasury bill at one-half the 1-year rate, 1.65%, would produce the following proceeds at the end of one year:

$$X(1.0165)^2 = 1.03327\ X$$

Both alternatives deliver the same payoff if the 6-month Treasury bill yield six months from now is 1.8% (3.6% on a BEY). This means that, if an investor is guaranteed a 1.8% yield (3.6% BEY) on a 6-month Treasury bill six months from now, she will be indifferent between the two alternatives.

It is quite helpful to think of forward rates as break-even rates. In our example, the yield curve is upward-sloping. As a result, an investor picks up additional yield by investing in the 1-year bill rather than the 6-month bill. The 6-month forward rate tells us how much the 6-month spot rate must rise six months from now so that an investor buying the 6-month bill and intending to rollover the proceeds into another 6-month bill will earn the same 1-year holding-period return. Obviously, the 6-month spot needs to rise over the next six months to offset the 1-year bill's yield advantage. As we have seen, if the 6-month spot rate is 3.6% six months from now, an investor will be indifferent between the two strategies. Simply put, forward rates tell us how much the spot curve needs to change over the next period so that all Treasury securities earn the same holding-period return.

The same line of reasoning can be used to obtain the 6-month forward rate beginning at any time period in the future. For example, the following can be determined:

■ The 6-month forward rate three years from now
■ The 6-month forward rate five years from now

The notation that we use to indicate 6-month forward rates is $_1f_m$ where the subscript 1 indicates a 1-period (six months in our illustration) rate and the subscript m indicates the period beginning m periods from now. When m is equal to zero, this means the current rate. Thus, the first 6-month forward rate is simply the current 6-month spot rate. That is, $_1f_0 = z_1$.

The general formula for determining a 6-month forward rate is:

$$_1f_m = \frac{(1 + z_{m+1})^{m+1}}{(1 + z_m)^m} - 1$$

This expression tells us if the $m + 1$-period and m-period spot rates are known, the 1-period forward rate between periods m and $m+1$ is computed by dividing $m+1$-period zero-coupon bond's holding-period return by the m-period zero-coupon bond's holding-period return.

For example, suppose that the 6-month forward rate four years (eight 6-month periods) from now is sought. In terms of our notation, m is 8 and we seek $_1f_8$. The formula is then:

$$_1f_8 = \frac{(1+z_9)^9}{(1+z_8)^8} - 1$$

From Exhibit 18.2 in Chapter 18, since the 4-year spot rate is 5.065% and the 4.5-year spot rate is 5.1701%, z_8 is 2.5325% and z_9 is 2.58505%. Then,

$$_1f_8 = \frac{(1.0258505)^9}{(1.025325)^8} - 1 = 3.0064\%$$

Doubling this rate gives a 6-month forward rate four years from now of 6.01%.

The 6-month forward rates for the Treasury yield curve and corresponding spot rate curve shown in Exhibit 18.2 in Chapter 18 are shown below (annualized rates on a bond-equivalent basis):

Notation	Forward Rate
$_1f_0$	3.00
$_1f_1$	3.60
$_1f_2$	3.92
$_1f_3$	5.15
$_1f_4$	6.54
$_1f_5$	6.33
$_1f_6$	6.23
$_1f_7$	5.79
$_1f_8$	6.01
$_1f_9$	6.24
$_1f_{10}$	6.48
$_1f_{11}$	6.72
$_1f_{12}$	6.97
$_1f_{13}$	6.36
$_1f_{14}$	6.49
$_1f_{15}$	6.62
$_1f_{16}$	6.76
$_1f_{17}$	8.10
$_1f_{18}$	8.40
$_1f_{19}$	8.72

The set of these forward rates is called the *short-term forward-rate curve*.

Relationship between Spot Rates and Short-Term Forward Rates

Suppose an investor invests $\$X$ in a 3-year zero-coupon Treasury security. The total proceeds three years (six periods) from now would be:

$$X(1 + z_6)^6$$

Alternatively, the investor could buy a 6-month Treasury bill and reinvest the proceeds every six months for three years. The future dollars or dollar return will depend on the 6-month forward rates. Suppose that the investor can actually reinvest the proceeds maturing every six months at the calculated 6-month forward rates shown above. At the end of three years, an investment of $\$X$ would generate the following proceeds:

$$X(1 + z_1)(1 + {}_1f_1)(1 + {}_1f_2)(1 + {}_1f_3)(1 + {}_1f_4)(1 + {}_1f_5)$$

Since the two investments must generate the same proceeds at the end of three years, the two previous equations are set equal to one another:

$$X(1 + z_6)^6 = X(1 + z_1)(1 + {}_1f_1)(1 + {}_1f_2)(1 + {}_1f_3)(1 + {}_1f_4)(1 + {}_1f_5)$$

Solving for the 3-year (6-period) spot rate, we have:

$$z_6 = [(1 + z_1)(1 + {}_1f_1)(1 + {}_1f_2)(1 + {}_1f_3)(1 + {}_1f_4)(1 + {}_1f_5)]^{\frac{1}{6}} - 1$$

This equation tells us that the 3-year spot rate depends on the current 6-month spot rate and the five 6-month forward rates. Earlier we described a spot rate as the average discount rate of a single cash flow over many periods. We can see now that long-term spot rates are averages of the current single period spot rate and the implied forward rates. In fact, the right-hand side of this equation is a *geometric* average of the current 6-month spot rate and the five 6-month forward rates.

Let's use the values in Exhibit 18.2 in Chapter 18 to confirm this result. Since the 6-month spot rate in Exhibit 18.2 in Chapter 18 is 3%, z_1 is 1.5% and therefore:

$$z_6 = [(1.015)(1.018)(1.0196)(1.02577)(1.0327)(1.03165)]^{\frac{1}{6}} - 1$$
$$= 0.023761 = 2.3761\%$$

Doubling this rate gives 4.7522%. This agrees with the 3-year spot rate shown in Exhibit 18.2 in Chapter 18.

In general, the relationship among a T-period spot rate, the current 6-month spot rate, and the 6-month forward rates is as follows:

$$z_T = [(1 + z_1)(1 + {}_1f_1)(1 + {}_1f_2) ... (1 + {}_1f_{T(1)})]^{1/T} - 1$$

Therefore, discounting at the forward rates will give the same present value as discounting at the spot rates. For example, suppose we have a single default-free cash flow to be delivered three years from today. There are two equivalent ways to discount this cash flow back to time zero. First, discount the cash flow back six periods at one-half the 3-year spot rate. Second, discount the cash flow back one period at a time using the appropriate forward rate each period. So, it does not matter whether one discounts cash flows by spot rates or forward rates, the value is the same. The same principle applies with equal force for coupon-paying bonds.

Forward Rates as the Market's Expectation of Future Rates

There are two questions about forward rates that are of interest to portfolio managers. First, are implied forward rates the market's expectation of future spot rates? Second, how well do implied forward rates do at predicting future interest rates? We will answer each question in turn.

According to the *pure expectations theory of interest rates*, forward rates exclusively represent expected future spot rates. Thus, the entire yield curve at a given time reflects the market's expectations of the family of future short-term rates. Under this view, an upward-sloping yield curve indicates that the market expects short-term rates to rise throughout the relevant future. Similarly, a flat yield curve reflects an expectation that future short-term rates will be mostly constant, while a downward-sloping yield curve must reflect an expectation that future short-term rates will decline. Of course, there are factors that influence the yield curve other than the market's expectations of future interest rates.

The statement that forward rates reflect the market's consensus of future interest rates is strictly true only if investors do not demand an additional risk premium for holding bonds with longer maturities and if investors' preference for positive convexity (explained in Chapter 21) does not influence the yield curve's shape. Antti Illmanen states in series of articles called *Understanding the Yield Curve*, "Whenever the spot rate curve is upward sloping, the forwards imply rising rates. That is, rising rates are needed to offset long-term bonds' yield advantage. However, it does not necessarily follow that the market expects rising rates."[6] In certain circumstances, risk premiums and the convexity bias can exert considerable influence on yields.

In response to the second question, several empirical studies suggest that forward rates do a poor job in predicting future spot rates.[7] For example, Michele Kreisler and Richard Worley present evidence that suggests there is little or no relationship between the yield curve's slope and subsequent interest rate movements. In other words, increases in rates are as likely to follow positively-sloped yield curves as flat or inverted yield curves.[8]

Why then should fixed-income practitioners care about implied forward rates? As we have noted, forward rates should be interpreted as break-even levels for future spot rates. By definition, if forward rates are subsequently realized, all government bonds (regardless of maturity) will earn the same 1-period return. Given this property, forward rates serve as benchmarks to which we compare our subjective expectations of future interest rates. It is not enough to say "interest rates will rise over the next six months. This is an empty statement—rise relative to what? The "to what" is the implied forward rate. If the yield curve is upward-sloping and one believes spot rates will rise more than suggested by the implied forward rates, then a rollover strategy dominates a buy-and-hold. Conversely, if one believes spot rates will rise by less than the implied forward rates suggest, then the reverse is true.

[6] Antti Illmanen, "Market's Rate Expectations and Forward Rate," *Understanding the Yield Curve: Part II* (New York: Salomon Brothers, 1995).
[7] See, for example, John Y. Campbell, Andrew W. Lo and Craig MacKinlay, *The Econometrics of Financial Markets* (Princeton, NJ: Princeton University Press, 1997).
[8] Michele A. Kreisler and Richard B. Worley, "Value Measures for Managing Interest-Rate Risk," Chapter 3 in Frank J. Fabozzi (ed.), *Managing Fixed-Income Portfolios* (New Hope, PA: Frank J. Fabozzi Associates, 1997)

CHAPTER 20

Valuation of Bonds with Embedded Options

Frank J. Fabozzi, Ph.D., CFA
Adjunct Professor of Finance
School of Management
Yale University

Steven V. Mann, Ph.D.
Professor of Finance
The Moore School of Business
University of South Carolina

The valuation of option-free bonds was explained in Chapter 18. In this chapter we will explain the models used to value bonds with embedded options. For non-mortgage-backed securities, the lattice model is used. For mortgage-backed securities and some asset-backed securities, the Monte Carlo simulation model is used.

OVERVIEW OF THE VALUATION OF BONDS WITH EMBEDDED OPTIONS

To develop an analytical framework for valuing a bond with an embedded option, it is necessary to decompose a bond into its component parts. Consider, for example, the most common bond with an embedded option, a callable bond. A callable bond is a bond in which the bondholder has sold the issuer an option (more specifically, a call option) that allows the issuer to repurchase the contractual cash flows of the bond from the time of the bond's first call date until the maturity date.

Consider the following two bonds: (1) a callable bond with an 8% coupon, 20 years to maturity, and callable in five years at 104 and (2) a 10-year 9% coupon bond callable immediately at par. For the first bond, the bondholder owns a 5-year option-free bond and has sold a call option granting the issuer the right to call away from the bondholder 15 years of cash flows five years from now for a price of 104. The investor who owns the second bond has a 10-year option-free bond and has sold a call option granting the issuer the right to immediately call the entire 10-year contractual cash flows, or any cash flows remaining at the time the issue is called, for 100.

Effectively, the owner of a callable bond is entering into two separate transactions. First, the investor buys an option-free bond from the issuer for which he pays some price. Then, the investor sells the issuer a call option for which he/she receives the option price. Therefore, we can summarize the position of a callable bondholder as follows:

long a callable bond = long an option-free bond + sold a call option

In terms of value, the value of a callable bond is therefore equal to the value of the two component parts. That is,

value of a callable bond
= value of an option-free bond − value of a call option

The reason the call option's value is subtracted from the value of the option-free bond is that when the bondholder sells a call option, he/she receives the option price. Actually, the position is more complicated than we just described. The issuer may be entitled to call the bond at the first call date and anytime thereafter, or at the first call date and any subsequent coupon anniversary date. Thus the investor has effectively sold an American-type call option to the issuer, but the call price may vary with the date the call option is exercised. This is because the call schedule for a bond may have a different call price depending on the call date. Moreover, the underlying bond for the call option is the remaining coupon payments that would have been made by the issuer had the bond not been called. For exposition purposes, it is easier to understand the principles associated with the investment characteristics of callable bonds by describing the investor's position as long an option-free bond and short a call option.

The same logic applies to putable bonds. In the case of a putable bond, the bondholder has the right to sell the bond to the issuer at a designated price and time. A putable bond can be broken into two separate transactions. First, the investor buys an option-free bond. Second, the investor buys a put option from the issuer that allows the investor to sell the bond to the issuer. Therefore, the position of a putable bond-holder can be described as:

long a putable bond = long an option-free bond + long a put option

In terms of value,

value of a putable bond
= value of an option-free bond + value of a put option

Option-Adjusted Spread and Option Cost

Before presenting the valuation models, we will discuss two measures that are derived from a valuation model—option-adjusted spread and option cost.

Option-Adjusted Spread

What an investor seeks to do is to buy a security whose value is greater than its price. A valuation model such as the two described later in this chapter allows an investor to estimate the theoretical value of a security, which at this point would be sufficient to determine the fairness of the price of the security. That is, the investor can say that this bond is 1 point cheap or 2 points cheap, and so on.

A valuation model need not stop here, however. Instead, it can convert the divergence between the security's price observed in the market and the theoretical value derived from the model into a yield spread measure. This step is necessary because many market participants find it more convenient to think in terms of yield spread than price differences.

The *option-adjusted spread* (OAS) was developed as a yield spread measure to convert dollar differences between value and price. Thus, basically, the OAS is used to reconcile value with market price. But what is it a "spread" over? As we shall see when we describe the two valuation methodologies, the OAS is a spread over some benchmark curve. The benchmark curve itself is not a single curve, but a series of curves that allow for changes in interest rates.

The reason that the resulting spread is referred to as "option-adjusted" is because the cash flows of the security whose value we seek are adjusted to reflect any embedded options. In contrast, as explained in the previous chapter, the zero-volatility spread does not consider how the cash flows will change when interest rates change in the future. That is, the zero-volatility spread assumes that interest rate volatility is zero. Consequently, the zero-volatility spread is also referred to as the *static spread*.

While the product of a valuation model is the OAS, the process can be worked in reverse. For a specified OAS, the valuation model can determine the theoretical value of the security that is consistent with that OAS.

Option Cost

The implied cost of the option embedded in any security can be obtained by calculating the difference between the OAS at the assumed volatility of interest rates and the zero-volatility spread. That is,

option cost = zero-volatility spread − option-adjusted spread

The reason that the option cost is measured in this way is as follows. In an environment of no interest rate changes, the investor would earn the zero-volatility spread. When future interest rates are uncertain, the spread is different because of the embedded option; the OAS reflects the spread after adjusting for this option. Therefore, the option cost is the difference between the spread that would be earned in a static interest rate environment (the zero-volatility spread) and the spread after adjusting for the option (the OAS).

For callable bonds and mortgage passthrough securities, the option cost is positive. This is because the borrower's ability to alter the cash flow will result in an OAS that is less than the zero-volatility spread. In the case of a putable bond, the OAS is greater than the zero-volatility spread so that the option cost is negative. This occurs because of the investor's ability to alter the cash flow.

In general, when the option cost is positive, this means that the investor has sold or is short an option. This is true for callable bonds and mortgage passthrough securities. A negative value for the option cost means that the investor has purchased or is long an option. A putable bond is an example of a security with a negative option cost. There are certain securities in the mortgage-backed securities market that also have an option cost that is negative.

While the option cost as described above is measured in basis points, it can be translated into a dollar price.

LATTICE MODEL

There are several models that have been proposed to value bonds with embedded options. Of interest to us are those models that provide an "arbitrage-free value" for a security. In Chapter 18 we saw that an arbitrage-free value for an option-free bond was obtained by first generating the spot rates (or forward rates). The spot rates are the rates that would produce a value for each on-the-run Treasury issue that is equal to its observed market price. In developing the interest rates that should be used to value a bond with an embedded option, the same principle applies. That is, no matter how complex the valuation model, when each on-the-run Treasury issue is valued using the model, the value produced should be equal to the on-the-run issue's market price. This is because it is assumed that the on-the-run issues are fairly priced.

The first complication in building a model to value bonds with embedded options is that the future cash flows will depend on what happens to interest rates in the future. This means that future interest rates must be considered. This is incorporated into a valuation model by considering how interest rates can change based on some assumed interest rate volatility. Given the assumed interest rate volatility, an interest rate "tree" representing possible future interest rates consistent with the volatility assumption can be constructed. Since the interest rate tree looks like a lattice, these valuation models are commonly referred to as *lattice models*. It is from the interest rate tree (or lattice) that two important elements in the valuation process are obtained. First, the interest rates on the tree are used to generate the cash flows taking into account the embedded option. Second, the interest rates on the tree are used to compute the present value of the cash flows.

For a given interest rate volatility, there are several interest rate models that have been used in practice to construct an interest rate tree. An *interest rate model* is a probabilistic description of how interest rates can change over the life of the bond. An interest rate model does this by making an assumption about the relationship between the level of short-term interest rates and the interest rate volatility as measured by the standard deviation. A discussion of the various interest rate models that have been suggested in the finance literature and that are used by practitioners in developing valuation models is beyond the scope of this chapter. What is important to understand is that the interest rate models commonly used are based on how short-term interest rates can evolve (i.e., change) over time. Consequently, these interest rate models are referred to as *one-factor models*, where "factor" means only one interest rate is being modeled over time. More complex models consider how more than one interest rate changes over time. For example, an interest rate model can specify how the short-term interest rate and the long-term interest rate can change over time. Such a model is called a *two-factor model.*

Given an interest rate model and an interest rate volatility assumption, it can be assumed that interest rates can realize one of two possible rates in the next period. A valuation model that makes this assumption in creating an interest rate tree is called a *binomial lattice model*, or simply *binomial model*. There are valuation models that assume that interest rates can take on three possible rates in the next period and these models are called *trinomial lattice models*, or simply *trinomial models*. There are even more complex models that assume in creating an interest rate tree that more than three possible rates in the next period can be realized. Regardless of the assumption about how many possible rates can be realized in the next period, the interest rate tree generated must produce a value for the on-the-run Treasury issue that is equal to its observed market price—that is, it must produce an arbitrage-free value. Moreover, the intuition and the methodology for using the interest rate tree (i.e., the backward induction methodology described later) are the same.

Once an interest rate tree is generated that (1) is consistent with both the interest rate volatility assumption and the interest rate model, and (2) generates the observed market price for each on-the-run issue, the next step is to use the interest rate tree to value a bond with an embedded option. The complexity here is that a set of rules must be introduced to determine, for any period, when the embedded option will be exercised. For a callable bond, these rules are called the "call rules." The rules vary from model builder to model builder.

At this stage, all of this sounds terribly complicated. While the building of a model to value bonds with embedded options is more complex than building a model to value option-free bonds, the basic principles are the same. In the case of valuing an option-free bond, the model that is built is simply a set of spot rates that are used to value cash flows. The spot rates will produce an arbitrage-free value. For a model to value a bond with embedded options, the interest rate tree is used to value future cash flows and the interest rate tree is combined with the call rules to generate the future cash flows. Again, the interest rate tree will produce an arbitrage-free value.

Let's move from theory to practice. Only a few practitioners will develop their own model to value bonds with embedded options. Instead, it is typical for a portfolio manager or analyst to use a model developed by either a dealer firm or a vendor of analytical systems. A fair question is then: Why bother covering a valuation model that is readily available from a third party? The answer is that a valuation model should not be a black box to portfolio managers and analysts. The models in practice share all of the principles described in this chapter, but differ with respect to certain assumptions that can produce quite different results. The reasons for these differences in valuation must be understood. Moreover, third-party models give the user a choice of changing the assumptions. A user who has not "walked through" a valuation model has no appreciation of the significance of these assumptions and therefore of how to assess the impact of these assumptions on the value produced by the model. There is always "modeling risk" when we use the output of a valuation model. This is the risk that the underlying assumptions of a model may be incorrect. Understanding a valuation model permits the user to effectively determine the significance of an assumption.

An example of understanding the assumptions of a model is the volatility used. Suppose that the market price of a bond is $89. Suppose further that a valuation model produces a value for a bond with an embedded option of $90 based on a 12% interest rate volatility assumption. Then, according to the valuation model, this bond is cheap by 1 point. However, suppose that the same model produces a value of $87 if a 15% volatility is assumed. This tells the portfolio manager or analyst that the bond is 2 points rich. Which is correct?

Below we will use the binomial model to demonstrate all of the issues and assumptions associated with valuing a bond with embedded options. Specifically, it is used to value agency debentures, corporates, and municipal bond structures with embedded options. The reason it is not used to value mortgage-backed securities and certain types of asset-backed securities will be explained when we describe the Monte Carlo simulation valuation model later in this chapter.

BINOMIAL MODEL

To illustrate the binomial valuation methodology, we start with the on-the-run yield curve for the particular issuer whose bonds we want to value. The starting point is the Treasury's on-the-run yield curve. To obtain a particular issuer's on-the-run yield curve, an appropriate credit spread is added to each on-the-run Treasury issue. The credit spread need not be constant for all maturities.

In our illustration, we use the hypothetical on-the-run issues for an issuer shown in Exhibit 20.1. Each bond is trading at par value (100) so the coupon rate is equal to the yield to maturity. We will simplify the illustration by assuming annual-pay bonds. Using the bootstrapping methodology explained in Chapter 18, the spot rates are those shown in the last column of Exhibit 20.1.

EXHIBIT 20.1   On-the-Run Yield Curve and Spot Rates for an Issuer

Maturity (Years)	Yield to Maturity (%)	Market Price ($)	Spot Rate (%)
1	3.5	100	3.5000
2	4.2	100	4.2147
3	4.7	100	4.7345
4	5.2	100	5.2707

EXHIBIT 20.2   Four-Year Binomial Interest Rate Tree

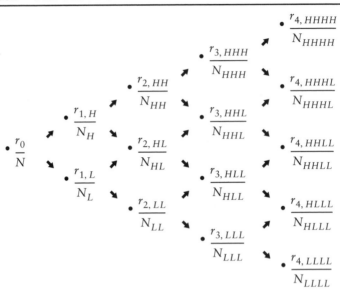

| Today | Year 1 | Year 2 | Year 3 | Year 4 |

Binomial Interest Rate Tree[1]

Once we allow for embedded options, consideration must be given to interest rate volatility. This can be done by introducing a *binomial interest rate tree*. This tree is nothing more than a graphical depiction of the 1-period or short rates over time based on some assumption about interest rate volatility. How this tree is constructed is illustrated here.

Exhibit 20.2 provides an example of a binomial interest rate tree. In this tree, each node (bold circle) represents a time period that is equal to one year from the node to its left. Each node is labeled with an N, representing node, and a subscript that indicates the path that the 1-year rate took to get to that node. L represents the lower of the two 1-year rates and H represents the higher of the two 1-year rates. For example, node N_{HH} means to get to that node the following path for 1-year rates occurred: The 1-year rate realized is the higher of the two rates in the first year and then the higher of the 1-year rates in the second year.[2]

---

[1] The model described in this section was presented in Andrew J. Kalotay, George O. Williams, and Frank J. Fabozzi, "A Model for the Valuation of Bonds and Embedded Options," *Financial Analysts Journal* (May–June 1993), pp. 35–46.

[2] Note that N_{HL} is equivalent to N_{LH} in the second year and that in the third year N_{HHL} is equivalent to N_{HLH} and N_{LHH} and that N_{HLL} is equivalent to N_{LLH}. We have simply selected one label for a node rather than clutter up the exhibit.

Look first at the point denoted by just N in Exhibit 20.2. This is the root of the tree and is nothing more than the current 1-year spot rate, or equivalently the current 1-year rate, which we denote by r_0. What we have assumed in creating this tree is that the 1-year rate can take on two possible rates the next period and the two rates have the same probability of occurring. One rate will be higher than the other. It is assumed that the 1-year rate can evolve over time based on a random process called a lognormal random walk with a certain volatility.

We use the following notation to describe the tree in Year 1. Let

σ = assumed volatility of the 1-year rate
$r_{1,L}$ = the lower 1-year rate one year from now
$r_{1,H}$ = the higher 1-year rate one year from now

The relationship between $r_{1,L}$ and $r_{1,H}$ is as follows:

$$r_{1,H} = r_{1,L}(e^{2\sigma})$$

where e is the base of the natural logarithm 2.71828.

For example, suppose that $r_{1,L}$ is 4.4448% and σ is 10% per year, then:

$$r_{1,H} = 4.4448\%(e^{2\times0.10}) = 5.4289\%$$

In Year 2, there are three possible values for the 1-year rate, which we will denote as follows:

$r_{2,LL}$ = 1-year rate in Year 2 assuming the lower rate in Year 1 and the lower rate in Year 2
$r_{2,HH}$ = 1-year rate in Year 2 assuming the higher rate in Year 1 and the higher rate in Year 2
$r_{2,HL}$ = 1-year rate in Year 2 assuming the higher rate in Year 1 and the lower rate in Year 2 or equivalently the lower rate in Year 1 and the higher rate in Year 2

The relationship between $r_{2,LL}$ and the other two 1-year rates is as follows:

$$r_{2,HH} = r_{2,LL}(e^{4\sigma}) \text{ and } r_{2,HL} = r_{2,LL}(e^{2\sigma})$$

So, for example, if $r_{2,LL}$ is 4.6958%, then assuming once again that σ is 10%, then:

$$r_{2,HH} = 4.6958\%(e^{4\times0.10}) = 7.0053\%$$

and,

$$r_{2,HL} = 4.6958\%(e^{4\times0.10}) = 5.7354\%$$

In Year 3, there are four possible values for the 1-year rate, which are denoted as follows: $r_{3,HHH}$, $r_{3,HHL}$, $r_{3,HLL}$, and $r_{3,LLL}$, and whose first three rates are related to the last as follows:

$$r_{3,HHH} = (e^{6\sigma})\, r_{3,LLL}$$
$$r_{3,HHL} = (e^{4\sigma})\, r_{3,LLL}$$
$$r_{3,HLL} = (e^{2\sigma})\, r_{3,LLL}$$

Exhibit 20.2 shows the notation for a 4-year binomial interest rate tree. We can simplify the notation by letting r_t be the 1-year rate t years from now for the lower rate since all the other short rates t years from now depend on that rate.

Before we go on to show how to use this binomial interest rate tree to value bonds, let's focus on two issues here. First, what does the volatility parameter σ represent? Second, how do we find the value of the bond at each node?

Volatility and the Standard Deviation

It can be shown that the standard deviation of the 1-year rate is equal to $r_0\sigma$.[3] The standard deviation is a statistical measure of volatility. In Chapter 2 we explain how it is estimated. It is important to see that the process that we assumed generates the binomial interest rate tree (or equivalently the short rates), implies that volatility is measured relative to the current level of rates. For example, if σ is 10% and the 1-year rate (r_0) is 4%, then the standard deviation of the 1-year rate is 4% × 10% = 0.4% or 40 basis points. However, if the current 1-year rate is 12%, the standard deviation of the 1-year rate would be 12% × 10% or 120 basis points.

Determining the Value at a Node

To find the value of the bond at a node, we first calculate the bond's value at the two nodes to the right of the node we are interested in. For example, in Exhibit 20.2, suppose we want to determine the bond's value at node

---

[3] This can be seen by noting that $e^{2\sigma} \approx 1 + 2\sigma$. Then the standard deviation of the 1-year rate is

$$\frac{re^{2\sigma} - r}{2} \approx \frac{r + 2\sigma r - r}{2} = \sigma r$$

N_H. The bond's value at node N_{HH} and N_{HL} must be determined. Hold aside for now how we get these two values because as we will see, the process involves starting from the last year in the tree and working backwards to get the final solution we want, so these two values will be known.

Effectively what we are saying is that if we are at some node, then the value at that node will depend on the future cash flows. In turn, the future cash flows depend on (1) the bond's value one year from now and (2) the coupon payment one year from now. The latter is known. The former depends on whether the 1-year rate is the higher or lower rate. The bond's value depending on whether the rate is the higher or lower rate is reported at the two nodes to the right of the node that is the focus of our attention. So, the cash flow at a node will be either (1) the bond's value if the short rate is the higher rate plus the coupon payment, or (2) the bond's value if the short rate is the lower rate plus the coupon payment. For example, suppose that we are interested in the bond's value at N_H. The cash flow will be either the bond's value at N_{HH} plus the coupon payment, or the bond's value at N_{HL} plus the coupon payment.

To get the bond's value at a node we follow the fundamental rule for valuation: The value is the present value of the expected cash flows. The appropriate discount rate to use is the 1-year rate at the node. Now there are two present values in this case: the present value if the 1-year rate is the higher rate and one if it is the lower rate. Since it is assumed that the probability of both outcomes is equal, an average of the two present values is computed. The computation is as follows. For any node assuming that the 1-year rate is r_* at the node where the valuation is sought and letting:

$$V_H = \text{the bond's value for the higher 1-year rate}$$
$$V_L = \text{the bond's value for the lower 1-year rate}$$
$$C = \text{coupon payment}$$

then the cash flow at a node is either:

$$V_H + C \text{ for the higher 1-year rate}$$

$$V_L + C \text{ for the lower 1-year rate}$$

The present value of these two cash flows using the 1-year rate at the node, r_*, is:

$$\frac{V_H + C}{(1 + r_*)} = \text{present value for the higher 1-year rate}$$

$$\frac{V_L + C}{(1 + r_*)} = \text{present value for the lower 1-year rate}$$

Then, the value of the bond at the node is found as follows:

$$\text{value at a node} = \frac{1}{2}\left[\frac{V_H + C}{(1 + r_*)} + \frac{V_L + C}{(1 + r_*)}\right]$$

Constructing the Binomial Interest Rate Tree

To see how to construct the binomial interest rate tree, let's use the assumed on-the-run yields in Exhibit 20.1. We will assume that volatility, σ, is 10% and construct a 2-year tree using the 2-year bond with a coupon rate of 4.2%.

Exhibit 20.3 shows a more detailed binomial interest rate with the cash flow shown at each node. We'll see how all the values reported in the exhibit are obtained. The root rate for the tree, r_0, is simply the current 1-year rate, 3.5%.

In the first year there are two possible 1-year rates, the higher rate and the lower rate. What we want to find is the two 1-year rates that will be consistent with the volatility assumption, the process that is assumed to generate the short rates, and the observed market value of the bond. There is no simple formula for this. It must be found by an iterative process (i.e., trial-and-error). The steps are described and illustrated below.

Step 1: Select a value for r_1. Recall that r_1 is the lower 1-year rate. In this first trial, we *arbitrarily* selected a value of 4.75%.

EXHIBIT 20.3   The 1-Year Rates for Year 1 Using the 2-Year 4.2% On-the-Run Issue: First Trial

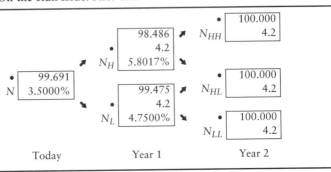

Step 2: Determine the corresponding value for the higher 1-year rate. As explained earlier, this rate is related to the lower 1-year rate as follows: $r_1 e^{2\sigma}$. Since r_1 is 4.75%, the higher 1-year rate is 5.8017% (= 4.75% $e^{2\times0.10}$). This value is reported in Exhibit 20.3 at node N_H

Step 3: Compute the bond value's in Year 1. This value is determined as follows:

3*a.* Determine the bond's value in Year 2. In our example, this is simple. Since we are using a 2-year bond, the bond's value is its maturity value ($100) plus its final coupon payment ($4.2). Thus, it is $104.2.

3*b.* Calculate the present value of the bond's value found in 3a for the higher rate in Year 2. The appropriate discount rate is the higher 1-year rate, 5.8017% in our example. The present value is $98.486 (= $104.2/1.058017). This is the value of V_H that we referred to earlier.

3*c.* Calculate the present value of the bond's value found in 3a for the lower rate. The discount rate assumed for the lower 1-year rate is 4.75%. The present value is $99.475 (= $104.2/1.0475) and is the value of V_L.

3*d.* Add the coupon to both V_H and V_L to get the cash flow at N_H and N_L, respectively. In our example we have $102.686 for the higher rate and $103.675 for the lower rate.

3*e.* Calculate the present value of the two values using the 1-year rate r_*. At this point in the valuation, r_* is the root rate, 3.50%. Therefore,

$$\frac{V_H + C}{1 + r_*} = \frac{\$102.686}{1.035} = \$99.213$$

and

$$\frac{V_L + C}{1 + r_*} = \frac{\$103.675}{1.035} = \$100.169$$

Step 4: Calculate the average present value of the two cash flows in Step 3. This is the value we referred to earlier as

$$\text{value at a node} = \frac{1}{2}\left[\frac{V_H + C}{(1 + r_*)} + \frac{V_L + C}{(1 + r_*)}\right]$$

In our example, we have

$$\text{value at a node} = \frac{1}{2}(\$99.213 + \$100.169) = \$99.691$$

Step 5: Compare the value in Step 4 to the bond's market value. If the two values are the same, then the r_1 used in this trial is the one we seek. This is the 1-year rate that would then be used in the binomial interest rate tree for the lower rate and to obtain the corresponding higher rate. If, instead, the value found in Step 4 is not equal to the market value of the bond, this means that the value r_1 in this trial is not the 1-year rate that is consistent with (1) the volatility assumption, (2) the process assumed to generate the 1-year rate, and (3) the observed market value of the bond. In this case, the five steps are repeated with a different value for r_1.

When r_1 is 4.75%, a value of $99.691 results in Step 4 which is less than the observed market price of $100. Therefore, 4.75% is too high and the five steps must be repeated trying a lower rate for r_1.

Let's jump right to the correct rate for r_1 in this example and rework Steps 1 through 5. This occurs when r_1 is 4.4448%. The corresponding binomial interest rate tree is shown in Exhibit 20.4.

Step 1: In this trial we select a value of 4.4448% for r_1, the lower 1-year rate.

Step 2: The corresponding value for the higher 1-year rate is 5.4289% ($= 4.4448\% \; e^{2 \times 0.10}$).

EXHIBIT 20.4   The 1-Year Rates for Year 1 Using the 2-Year 4.2% On-the-Run Issue

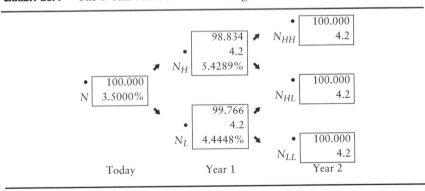

Step 3: The bond's value in Year 1 is determined as follows:

3a. The bond's value in Year 2 is $104.2, just as in the first trial.

3b. The present value of the bond's value found in 3a for the higher 1-year rate, V_H, is $98.834 (= $104.2/1.054289).

3c. The present value of the bond's value found in 3a for the lower 1-year rate, V_L, is $99.766 (= $104.2/1.044448).

3d. Adding the coupon to V_H and V_L, we get $103.034 as the cash flow for the higher rate and $103.966 as the cash flow for the lower rate.

3e. The present value of the two cash flows using the 1-year rate at the node to the left, 3.5%, gives:

$$\frac{V_H + C}{1 + r_*} = \frac{\$103.034}{1.035} = \$99.550$$

and,

$$\frac{V_L + C}{1 + r_*} = \frac{\$103.966}{1.035} = \$100.450$$

Step 4: The average present value is $100, which is the value at the node.

Step 5: Since the average present value is equal to the observed market price of $100, r_1 or $r_{1,L}$ is 4.4448% and $r_{1,H}$ is 5.4289%.

We can "grow" this tree for one more year by determining r_2. Now we will use the 3-year on-the-run issue, the 4.7% coupon bond, to get r_2. The same five steps are used in an iterative process to find the 1-year rates in the tree in Year 2. Our objective is now to find the value of r_2 that will produce a bond value of $100 (since the 3-year on-the-run issue has a market price of $100) and is consistent with (1) a volatility assumption of 10%, (2) a current 1-year rate of 3.5%, and (3) the two rates one year from now of 4.4448% (the lower rate) and 5.4289% (the higher rate).

We explain how this is done using Exhibit 20.5. Let's look at how we get the information in the exhibit. The maturity value and coupon payment are shown in the boxes at the four nodes at Year 3. Since the 3-year on-the-run issue has a maturity value of $100 and a coupon payment of $4.7, these values are the same in the box shown at each node. For the three nodes at Year 2 the coupon payment of $4.7 is shown.

Unknown at these three nodes are (1) the three rates in Year 2 and (2) the value of the bond at Year 2. For the two nodes in Year 1, the coupon payment is known, as are the 1-year rates. These are the rates found earlier. The value of the bond, which depends on the bond values at the nodes to the right, is unknown at these two nodes. All of the unknown values are indicated by a question mark.

Exhibit 20.6 is the same as Exhibit 20.5 but complete with the values previously unknown. As can be seen from Exhibit 20.6, the value of r_2, or equivalently $r_{2,LL}$, which will produce the desired result is 4.6958%. We showed earlier that the corresponding rates $r_{2,HL}$ and $r_{2,HH}$ would be 5.7354% and 7.0053%, respectively. To verify that these are the 1-year rates in Year 2, work backwards from the four nodes at Year 3 of the tree in Exhibit 20.6. For example, the value in the box at N_{HH} is found by taking the value of $104.7 at the two nodes to its right and discounting at 7.0053%. The value is $97.846. (Since it is the same value for both nodes to the right, it is also the average value.) Similarly, the value in the box at N_{HL} is found by discounting $104.70 by 5.7354% and at N_{LL} by discounting at 4.6958%. The same procedure used in Exhibits 20.3 and 20.4 is used to get the values at the other nodes.

Valuing an Option-Free Bond with the Tree

Now consider an option-free bond with four years remaining to maturity and a coupon rate of 6.5%. The value of this bond can be calculated by discounting the cash flow at the spot rates in Exhibit 20.1 as shown in the following calculation:

EXHIBIT 20.5   Information for Deriving the 1-Year Rates for Year 2 Using the 3-Year 4.7% On-the-Run Issue

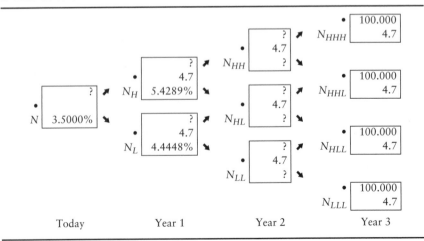

EXHIBIT 20.6   The 1-Year Rates for Year 2 Using the 3-Year 4.7%
On-the-Run Issue

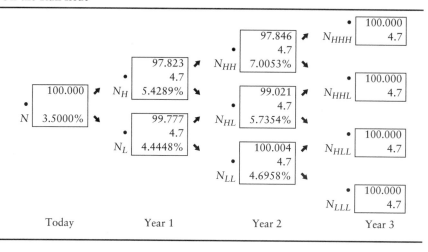

$$\frac{\$6.5}{(1.035)^1} + \frac{\$6.5}{(1.042147)^2} + \frac{\$6.5}{(1.047345)^3} + \frac{\$100 + \$6.5}{(1.052707)^4} = \$104.643$$

An option-free bond that is valued using the binomial interest rate tree should have the same value as discounting by the spot rates.

Exhibit 20.7 shows the 1-year rates or binomial interest rate tree that can then be used to value any bond for this issuer with a maturity up to four years. To illustrate how to use the binomial interest rate tree, consider once again the 6.5% option-free bond with three years remaining to maturity. Also assume that the issuer's on-the-run yield curve is the one in Exhibit 20.1, hence the appropriate binomial interest rate tree is the one in Exhibit 20.7. Exhibit 20.8 shows the various values in the discounting process, and produces a bond value of $104.643.

This value is identical to the bond value found when we discounted at the spot rates. This clearly demonstrates that the valuation model is consistent with the standard valuation model for an option-free bond.

Valuing a Callable Bond

Now we will demonstrate how the binomial interest rate tree can be applied to value a callable bond. The valuation process proceeds in the same fashion as in the case of an option-free bond, but with one exception: When the call option may be exercised by the issuer, the bond value at a node must be changed to reflect the lesser of its values if it is not called (i.e., the value obtained by applying the recursive valuation formula described above) and the call price.

EXHIBIT 20.7 Binomial Interest Rate Tree for Valuing Up to a 4-Year Bond for Issuer (10% Volatility Assumed)

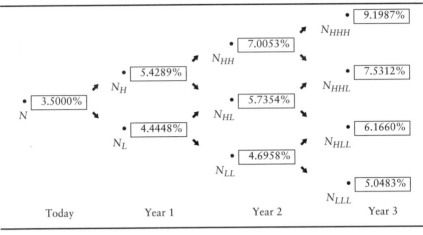

EXHIBIT 20.8 Valuing an Option-Free Bond with Four Years to Maturity and a Coupon Rate of 6.5% (10% Volatility Assumed)

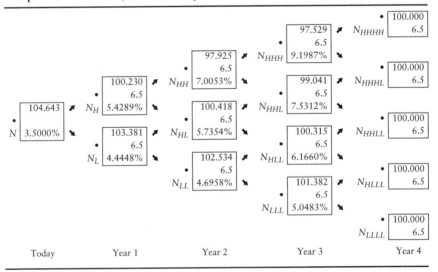

For example, consider a 6.5% corporate bond with four years remaining to maturity that is callable in one year at $100. Exhibit 20.9 shows two values at each node of the binomial interest rate tree. The discounting process explained above is used to calculate the first of the two values at each node. The second value is the value based on whether the issue will be called. For simplicity, let's assume that this issuer calls the issue if it exceeds the call price. Then, in Exhibit 20.9 at nodes N_L, N_H, N_{LL}, N_{HL},

N_{LLL}, and N_{HLL} the values from the recursive valuation formula are 101.968, 100.032, 101.723, 100.270, 101.382, and 100.315, respectively. These values exceed the assumed call price ($100) and therefore the second value is $100 rather than the calculated value. It is the second value that is used in subsequent calculations. The root of the tree indicates that the value for this callable bond is $102.899.

The question that we have not addressed in our illustration, which is nonetheless important, is the circumstances under which the issuer will call the bond. A detailed explanation of the call rule is beyond the scope of this chapter. Basically, it involves determining when it would be economic for the issuer, on an after-tax basis, to call the issue.

Determining the Call Option Value

The value of a callable bond is equal to the value of an option-free bond minus the value of the call option. This means that:

value of a call option
= value of an option-free bond – value of a callable bond

EXHIBIT 20.9 Valuing a Callable Bond with Four Years to Maturity, a Coupon Rate of 6.5%, and Callable in One Year at 100 (10% Volatility Assumed)

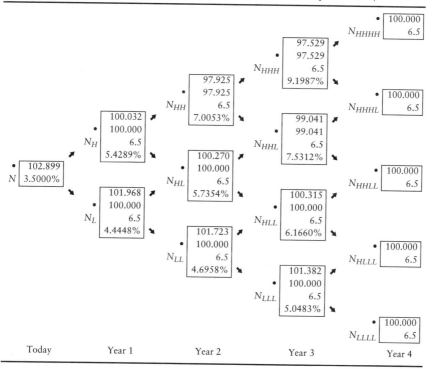

We have just seen how the value of an option-free bond and the value of a callable bond can be determined. The difference between the two values is, therefore, the value of the call option.

In our illustration, the value of the option-free bond is $104.643. If the call price is $100 in each year, the value of the callable bond is $102.899. Therefore, the value of the call option is $1.744 (= $104.634 − $102.899).

Extension to Other Embedded Options

The bond valuation framework presented here can be used to analyze other embedded options such as put options, caps and floors on floating-rate notes, and the optional accelerated redemption granted to an issuer in fulfilling its sinking fund requirement.

For example, let's consider a putable bond. Suppose that a 6.5% coupon bond with four years remaining to maturity is putable in one year at par ($100). Also assume that the appropriate binomial interest rate tree for this issuer is the one in Exhibit 20.7. It can be demonstrated that the value of this putable bond is $105.327.

Since the value of a putable bond can be expressed as the value of an option-free bond plus the value of a put option on that bond, this means that:

> value of a put option
> = value of an option-free bond − value of a putable bond

In our example, since the value of the putable bond is $105.327 and the value of the corresponding option-free bond is $104.643, the value of the put option is −$0.684. The negative sign indicates the issuer has sold the option, or equivalently, the investor has purchased the option.

The framework can also be used to value a bond with multiple or interrelated embedded options. The bond values at each node are altered based on whether one of the options is exercised.

Volatility and the Theoretical Value

In our example, interest rate volatility was assumed to be 10%. The volatility assumption has an important impact on the theoretical value. More specifically, the higher the expected volatility, the higher the value of an option. The same is true for an option embedded in a bond. Correspondingly, this affects the value of the bond with an embedded option.

For example, for a callable bond, a higher interest rate volatility assumption means that the value of the call option increases and, since the value of the option-free bond is not affected, the value of the callable bond must be lower. For a putable bond, higher interest rate volatility means that its value will be higher.

To illustrate this, suppose that a 20% volatility is assumed rather than 10%. The value of the hypothetical callable bond is $102.108 if volatility is assumed to be 20% compared to $102.899 if volatility is assumed to be 10%. The hypothetical putable bond at 20% volatility has a value of $106.010 compared to $105.327 at 10% volatility.

In the construction of the binomial interest rate, it was assumed that volatility is the same for each year. The methodology can be extended to incorporate a term structure of volatility.

Option-Adjusted Spread

Suppose the market price of the 4-year 6.5% callable bond is $102.218 and the theoretical value assuming 10% volatility is $102.899. This means that this bond is cheap by $0.681 according to the valuation model. The option-adjusted spread is the constant spread that, when added to all the 1-year rates on the binomial interest rate tree, will make the arbitrage-free value (i.e., the value produced by the binomial model) equal to the market price.

In our illustration, if the market price is $102.218, the OAS would be the constant spread added to every rate in Exhibit 20.9 that will make the arbitrage-free value equal to $102.218. The solution in this case would be 35 basis points.

As with the value of a bond with an embedded option, the OAS will depend on the volatility assumption. For a given bond price, the higher the interest rate volatility assumed, the lower the OAS for a callable bond. For example, if volatility is 20% rather than 10%, the OAS would be −6 basis points. This illustration clearly demonstrates the importance of the volatility assumption. Assuming volatility of 10%, the OAS is 35 basis points. At 20% volatility, the OAS declines and in this case is negative and therefore the bond is overvalued relative to the model.

How do we interpret the OAS? In general, a nominal spread between two yields reflects differences in the:

1. Credit risk of the two issues
2. Liquidity risk of the two issues
3. Option risk of the two issues

For example, if one of the issues is a non-U.S. Treasury issue with an embedded option and the benchmark interest rates are the rates for the U.S. Treasury on-the-run securities, then the nominal spread is a measure of the difference due to the:

1. Credit risk of the non-Treasury issue
2. Liquidity risk associated with the non-Treasury issue
3. Option risk associated with the non-Treasury issue that is not present in Treasury issues

What the OAS seeks to do is remove from the nominal spread the amount that is due to the option risk. The measure is called an OAS because (1) it is a spread and (2) it adjusts the cash flows for the option when computing the spread to the benchmark interest rates. The second point can be seen from Exhibits 20.8 and 20.9. Notice that at each node the value obtained from the backward induction method is adjusted based on the call option and the call rule. Thus, the resulting spread is "option adjusted."

Consequently, if the Treasury on-the-run issues are used as the benchmark, because the call option has been taken into account, the OAS is measuring the compensation for the:

1. Credit risk of the non-Treasury issue
2. Liquidity risk associated with the non-Treasury issue

So, for example, an OAS of 160 basis points for a callable BBB industrial issue would mean that based on the valuation model (including the volatility assumption), the OAS is compensation for the credit risk and the lower liquidity of the industrial issue relative to the Treasury benchmark issues. The OAS has removed the compensation for the call feature present in the industrial issue that is not present in the Treasury benchmark interest rates.

However, suppose that the benchmark interest rates are the on-the-run interest rates for the issuer, as in our illustration of how to use the binomial model to value a bond with an embedded option. Then there is no difference in the credit risk between the benchmark interest rates and the non-Treasury issue. That is, the OAS reflects only the difference in the liquidity of an issue relative to the on-the-run issues. The valuation has removed the spread due to the option risk and using the issuer's own benchmark interest rates removes the credit risk.

Suppose instead that the benchmark interest rates used are not of that particular issuer but the on-the-run issues for issuers in the same sector of the bond market and the same credit rating of the issue being analyzed. For example, suppose that the callable bond issue being analyzed is that issued by the XYZ Manufacturing Company, a BBB industrial company. An on-the-run yield curve can be estimated for the XYZ Manufacturing Company. Using that on-the-run yield curve, the OAS reflects the difference in the liquidity risk between the particular callable bond of the XYZ Manufacturing Company analyzed and the on-the-run issues of the XYZ Manufacturing Company. However, if instead the benchmark interest rates used to value the callable bond of the XYZ Manufacturing Company are those of a generic BBB industrial company, the OAS reflects (1) the difference between the liquidity risk of the XYZ Manufacturing Company's callable bond and that of a generic BBB industrial company and (2) differences between event risk/credit risk specific to XYZ Manufacturing Company's issue beyond generic BBB credit risk.

Consequently, we know that an OAS is a spread after adjusting for the embedded option. But we know nothing else until the benchmark interest rates are identified. Without knowing the benchmark used—Treasury on-the-run yield curve, an issuer's on-the-run yield curve, or a generic on-the-run yield curve for issuers in the same sector of the bond market and of the same credit rating—we cannot interpret what the OAS is providing compensation for. Some market participants might view this as unrealistic since most of the time the on-the-run Treasury yield curve is used and therefore the OAS reflects credit risk and liquidity risk. However, vendors of analytical systems and most dealer models allow an investor to specify the benchmark interest rates to be used. The default feature in these systems (i.e., what the model uses as the benchmark interest rates if the investor does not specify the benchmark) is the Treasury on-the-run yield curve.

So, once an investor is told what the OAS of a particular bond is, the first question should be: Relative to what benchmark interest rates? This is particularly important in non-U.S. markets where the OAS concept is beginning to be used with greater frequency. It also means that comparing OAS values across global markets is difficult because different benchmark interest rates are being used and therefore the OAS is capturing different risks.

VALUATION OF MBS AND ABS

Now we will demonstrate how to value mortgage-backed and asset-backed securities. We begin by reviewing the conventional framework—static cash flow yield analysis—and its limitations. Then we discuss a more advanced technology, the Monte Carlo valuation model and a byproduct of the model, the option-adjusted spread analysis. The static cash flow yield methodology is the simplest of the two valuation technologies to apply, although it may offer little insight into the relative value of a mortgage-backed or asset-backed security. The option-adjusted spread technology while far superior in valuation is based on assumptions that must be recognized by an investor and the sensitivity of the security's value to changes in those assumptions must be tested.

Static Cash Flow Yield Analysis

As explained in the previous chapter, the yield on any financial instrument is the interest rate that makes the present value of the expected cash flow equal to its market price plus accrued interest. For mortgage-backed and asset-backed securities, the yield calculated is called a *cash flow yield*. The problem in calculating the cash flow yield of a mortgage-backed and asset-backed security is that because of prepayments (voluntary and involuntary) the cash flow is unknown. Consequently, to determine a cash flow yield some assumption about the prepayment rate must be made.

The cash flow for a mortgage-backed and asset-backed security is typically monthly. The convention is to compare the yield on a mortgage-backed security to that of a Treasury coupon security by calculating the MBS's bond-equivalent yield. As explained in the previous chapter, the bond-equivalent yield for a Treasury coupon security is found by doubling the semiannual yield. However, it is incorrect to follow that convention for mortgage-backed and asset-backed securities because the investor has the opportunity to generate greater interest by reinvesting the more frequent cash flows. The market practice/convention is to calculate a yield so as to make it comparable to the yield to maturity on a bond-equivalent yield basis. The formula for annualizing the monthly cash flow yield for a mortgage-backed security is as follows:

$$\text{bond-equivalent yield} = 2[(1 + i_M)^6 - 1]$$

where i_M is the monthly interest rate that will equate the present value of the projected monthly cash flow to the market price (plus accrued interest) of the security.

As we explained in the previous chapter, all yield measures suffer from problems that limit their use in assessing a security's potential return. The yield to maturity has two major shortcomings as a measure of a bond's potential return. To realize the stated yield to maturity, the investor must: (1) reinvest the coupon payments at a rate equal to the yield to maturity, and (2) hold the bond to the maturity date. The reinvestment of the coupon payments is critical and for long-term bonds can be as much as 80% of the bond's return. The risk of having to reinvest the interest payments at less than the computed yield is called *reinvestment risk*. The risk associated with having to sell the security prior to the maturity date is called *interest rate risk*.

These shortcomings are equally applicable to the cash flow yield measure: (1) the projected cash flows are assumed to be reinvested at the cash flow yield, and (2) the mortgage-backed and asset-backed security is assumed to be held until the final payout based on some prepayment assumption. The importance of reinvestment risk, the risk that the cash flow will have to be reinvested at a rate lower than the cash flow yield, is particularly important for mortgage-backed and asset-backed securities because payments are monthly and both interest and principal (regularly scheduled repayments and prepayments) must be reinvested. Moreover, an additional assumption is that the projected cash flow is actually realized. If the prepayment experience is different from the prepayment rate assumed, the cash flow yield will not be realized.

Given the computed cash flow yield and the average life for a mortgage-backed or asset-backed security based on some prepayment assumption, the next step is to compare the yield to the yield for a comparable Treasury security. "Comparable" is typically defined as a Treasury security with the same maturity as the average life of the security. The difference between the cash flow yield and the yield on a comparable Treasury security is called a *nominal spread*. We described this measure in the previous chapter.

Unfortunately, it is the nominal spread that some investors will use as a measure of relative value. However, this spread masks the fact that a portion of the nominal spread is compensation for accepting prepayment risk. For example, CMO support tranches are offered at large nominal spreads. However, the spread embodies the substantial prepayment risk associated with support tranches. An investor who buys solely on the basis of nominal spread—dubbed a "yield hog"—fails to determine whether that nominal spread offers potential compensation given the substantial prepayment risk faced by the holder of a support tranche.

Instead of nominal spread, investors need a measure that indicates the potential compensation after adjusting for prepayment risk. This measure is called the *option-adjusted spread* (OAS). Earlier in this chapter we demonstrated how this measure is computed within the context of the lattice model. Below we will explain how this measure is computed using the model employed for mortgage-backed securities and certain types of asset-backed securities.

Monte Carlo Simulation

In fixed income valuation modeling, there are two methodologies commonly used to value securities with embedded options—the lattice model and the Monte Carlo model. The lattice model was explained earlier in the chapter. The Monte Carlo simulation model involves simulating a sufficiently large number of potential interest rate paths in order to assess the value of a security along these different paths. This model is the most flexible of the two valuation methodologies for valuing interest rate sensitive instruments where the history of interest rates is important. Mortgage-backed and some asset-backed securities are commonly valued using this model. As explained below, a byproduct of a valuation model is the OAS.

Interest Rate History and Path-Dependent Cash Flows

For some fixed income securities and derivative instruments, the periodic cash flows are *path-dependent*. This means that the cash flow received in one period is determined not only by the current interest rate level, but also by the path that interest rates took to get to the current level.

In the case of mortgage passthrough securities (or simply, passthroughs), prepayments are path-dependent because this month's prepayment rate depends on whether there have been prior opportunities to refinance since the underlying mortgages were originated. Unlike passthroughs, the decision as to whether a corporate issuer will elect to refund an issue when the current rate is below the issue's coupon rate is not dependent on how rates evolved over time to reach the current level.

Moreover, in the case of securities backed by adjustable-rate mortgages (ARMs), prepayments are not only path-dependent but the periodic coupon rate depends on the history of the reference rate upon which the coupon rate is determined. This is because ARMs have periodic caps and floors as well as a lifetime cap and floor. For example, an ARM whose coupon rate resets annually could have the following restriction on the coupon rate: (1) the rate cannot change by more than 200 basis points each year and (2) the rate cannot be more than 500 basis points from the initial coupon rate.

Pools of passthroughs are used as collateral for the creation of collateralized mortgage obligations (CMOs) as discussed in the previous chapter. Consequently, for CMOs there are typically two sources of path dependency in a tranche's cash flows. First, the collateral prepayments are path-dependent as discussed above. Second, the cash flow to be received in the current month by a tranche depends on the outstanding balances of the other tranches in the deal. Thus, we need the history of prepayments to calculate these balances.

Valuing Mortgage-Backed Securities[4]

Conceptually, the valuation of passthroughs using the Monte Carlo method is simple. In practice, however, it is very complex. The simulation

---

[4] Portions of the material in this section and the one to follow are adapted from Frank J. Fabozzi, Scott F. Richard, and David S. Horowitz, "Valuation of CMOs," Chapter 6 in Frank J. Fabozzi (ed.), *Advances in the Valuation and Management of Mortgage-Backed Securities* (New Hope, PA: Frank J. Fabozzi Associates, 1998).

involves generating a set of cash flows based on simulated future mortgage refinancing rates, which in turn imply simulated prepayment rates.

Valuation modeling for CMOs is similar to valuation modeling for passthroughs, although the difficulties are amplified because the issuer has sliced and diced both the prepayment and interest rate risk into smaller pieces and distributed these risks among the tranches. The sensitivity of the passthroughs comprising the collateral to these two risks is not transmitted equally to every tranche. Some of the tranches wind up more sensitive to prepayment and interest rate risk than the collateral, while some of them are much less sensitive.

Using Simulation to Generate Interest Rate Paths and Cash Flows   The typical model that Wall Street firms and commercial vendors use to generate random interest rate paths takes as input today's term structure of interest rates and a volatility assumption. The term structure of interest rates is the theoretical spot rate (or zero coupon) curve implied by today's Treasury securities which serve as a benchmark. The volatility assumption determines the dispersion of future interest rates in the simulation. The simulations should be calibrated to the market so that the average simulated price of a zero-coupon Treasury bond equals today's actual price.

Each model has its own model of the evolution of future interest rates and its own volatility assumptions. Typically, there are no important differences in the interest rate models of dealer firms and vendors, although their volatility assumptions can be significantly different.

The random paths of interest rates should be generated from an arbitrage-free model of the future term structure of interest rates. By arbitrage-free it is meant that the model replicates today's term structure of interest rates, an input of the model, and that for all future dates there is no possible arbitrage within the model.

The simulation works by generating many scenarios of future interest rate paths. In each month of the scenario, a monthly interest rate and a mortgage refinancing rate are generated. The monthly interest rates are used to discount the projected cash flows in the scenario. The mortgage refinancing rate is needed to determine the cash flow because it represents the opportunity cost the mortgagor is facing at that time.

If the refinancing rates are high relative to the mortgagor's original coupon rate (i.e., the rate on the mortgagor's loan), the mortgagor will have less incentive to refinance, or even a positive disincentive (i.e., the homeowner will avoid moving in order to avoid refinancing). If the refinancing rate is low relative to the mortgagor's original coupon rate, the mortgagor has an incentive to refinance.

Prepayments (voluntary and involuntary) are projected by feeding the refinancing rate and loan characteristics, such as age, into a prepayment model. Given the projected prepayments, the cash flow along an interest rate path can be determined.

To make this process more concrete, consider a newly issued mortgage passthrough security with a maturity of 360 months. Exhibit 20.10 shows N simulated interest rate path scenarios. Each scenario consists of a path of 360 simulated 1-month future interest rates. Just how many paths should be generated is explained later. Exhibit 20.11 shows the paths of simulated mortgage refinancing rates corresponding to the scenarios shown in Exhibit 20.10. Assuming these mortgage refinancing rates, the cash flow for each scenario path is shown in Exhibit 20.12.

Calculating the Present Value for a Scenario Interest Rate Path   Given the cash flow on an interest rate path, its present value can be calculated. The discount rate for determining the present value is the simulated spot rate for each month on the interest rate path plus an appropriate spread. The spot rate on a path can be determined from the simulated future monthly rates in Exhibit 20.12. The relationship that holds between the simulated spot rate for month T on path n and the simulated future 1-month rates is:[5]

$$z_T(n) = \{[1 + f_1(n)][1 + f_2(n)]...[1 + f_T(n)]\}^{1/T} - 1$$

EXHIBIT 20.10   Simulated Paths of 1-Month Future Interest Rates

Month	Interest Rate Path Number						
	1	2	3	...	n	...	N
1	$f_1(1)$	$f_1(2)$	$f_1(3)$	...	$f_1(n)$	...	$f_1(N)$
2	$f_2(1)$	$f_2(2)$	$f_2(3)$	...	$f_2(n)$	...	$f_2(N)$
3	$f_3(1)$	$f_3(2)$	$f_3(3)$	...	$f_3(n)$	...	$f_3(N)$
t	$f_t(1)$	$f_t(2)$	$f_t(3)$	...	$f_t(n)$	...	$f_t(N)$
358	$f_{358}(1)$	$f_{358}(2)$	$f_{358}(3)$	...	$f_{358}(n)$	...	$f_{358}(N)$
359	$f_{359}(1)$	$f_{359}(2)$	$f_{359}(3)$	...	$f_{359}(n)$	...	$f_{359}(N)$
360	$f_{360}(1)$	$f_{360}(2)$	$f_{360}(3)$	...	$f_{360}(n)$	...	$f_{360}(N)$

Notation:
$f_t(n)$ = 1-month future interest rate for month t on path n
N = total number of interest rate paths

[5] This is the same equation we saw in Chapter 19 when we examined the relationship between long-term spot rates and short-term forward rates.

EXHIBIT 20.11 Simulated Paths of Mortgage Refinancing Rates

| Month | Interest Rate Path Number | | | | | | |
	1	2	3	...	n	...	N
1	$r_1(1)$	$r_1(2)$	$r_1(3)$	...	$r_1(n)$	...	$r_1(N)$
2	$r_2(1)$	$r_2(2)$	$r_2(3)$	...	$r_2(n)$	...	$r_2(N)$
3	$r_3(1)$	$r_3(2)$	$r_3(3)$	...	$r_3(n)$	...	$r_3(N)$
t	$r_t(1)$	$r_t(2)$	$r_t(3)$	...	$r_t(n)$	...	$r_t(N)$
358	$r_{358}(1)$	$r_{358}(2)$	$r_{358}(3)$	...	$r_{358}(n)$	...	$r_{358}(N)$
359	$r_{359}(1)$	$r_{359}(2)$	$r_{359}(3)$	...	$r_{359}(n)$	...	$r_{359}(N)$
360	$r_{360}(1)$	$r_{360}(2)$	$r_{360}(3)$	...	$r_{360}(n)$	...	$r_{360}(N)$

Notation:

$r_t(n)$ = mortgage refinancing rate for month t on path n

N = total number of interest rate paths

EXHIBIT 20.12 Simulated Cash Flow on Each of the Interest Rate Paths

| Month | Interest Rate Path Number | | | | | | |
	1	2	3	...	n	...	N
1	$C_1(1)$	$C_1(2)$	$C_1(3)$	...	$C_1(n)$	...	$C_1(N)$
2	$C_2(1)$	$C_2(2)$	$C_2(3)$	...	$C_2(n)$	...	$C_2(N)$
3	$C_3(1)$	$C_3(2)$	$C_3(3)$	...	$C_3(n)$	...	$C_3(N)$
t	$C_t(1)$	$C_t(2)$	$C_t(3)$	...	$C_t(n)$	...	$C_t(N)$
358	$C_{358}(1)$	$C_{358}(2)$	$C_{358}(3)$	...	$C_{358}(n)$	...	$C_{358}(N)$
359	$C_{359}(1)$	$C_{359}(2)$	$C_{359}(3)$	...	$C_{359}(n)$	...	$C_{359}(N)$
360	$C_{360}(1)$	$C_{360}(2)$	$C_{360}(3)$	...	$C_{360}(n)$	...	$C_{360}(N)$

Notation:

$C_t(n)$ = cash flow for month t on path n

N = total number of interest rate paths

where

$z_T(n)$ = simulated spot rate for month T on path n

$f_j(n)$ = simulated future 1-month rate for month j on path n

EXHIBIT 20.13   Simulated Paths of Monthly Spot Rates

Month	Interest Rate Path Number						
	1	2	3	...	n	...	N
1	$z_1(1)$	$z_1(2)$	$z_1(3)$	...	$z_1(n)$	...	$z_1(N)$
2	$z_2(1)$	$z_2(2)$	$z_2(3)$	...	$z_2(n)$	...	$z_2(N)$
3	$z_3(1)$	$z_3(2)$	$z_3(3)$	...	$z_3(n)$	...	$z_3(N)$
t	$z_t(1)$	$z_t(2)$	$z_t(3)$	...	$z_t(n)$	...	$z_t(N)$
358	$z_{358}(1)$	$z_{358}(2)$	$z_{358}(3)$	...	$z_{358}(n)$	...	$z_{358}(N)$
359	$z_{359}(1)$	$z_{359}(2)$	$z_{359}(3)$	...	$z_{359}(n)$	...	$z_{359}(N)$
360	$z_{360}(1)$	$z_{360}(2)$	$z_{360}(3)$	...	$z_{360}(n)$	...	$z_{360}(N)$

Notation:

$z_t(n)$ = spot rate for month t on path n
N   = total number of interest rate paths

Consequently, the interest rate path for the simulated future 1-month rates can be converted to the interest rate path for the simulated monthly spot rates as shown in Exhibit 20.13.

Therefore, the present value of the cash flow for month T on interest rate path n discounted at the simulated spot rate for month T plus some spread is:

$$PV[C_T(n)] = \frac{C_T(n)}{[1 + z_T(n) + K]^{1/T}}$$

where

$PV[C_T(n)]$ = present value of cash flow for month T on path n
$C_T(n)$ = cash flow for month T on path n
$z_T(n)$ = spot rate for month T on path n
K = spread

The present value for path n is the sum of the present values of the cash flows for each month on path n. That is,

$$PV[\text{Path}(n)] = PV[C_1(n)] + PV[C_2(n)] + ... + PV[C_{360}(n)]$$

where $PV[\text{Path}(n)]$ is the present value of interest rate path n.

Determining the Theoretical Value

The present value of a given interest rate path is the theoretical value of a passthrough if that path was actually realized. The theoretical value of the passthrough can be determined by calculating the average of the theoretical values of all the interest rate paths. That is,

$$\text{Theoretical value} = \frac{PV[\text{Path}(1)] + PV[\text{Path}(2)] + \ldots + PV[\text{Path}(N)]}{N}$$

where N is the number of interest rate paths.

This procedure for valuing a passthrough is also followed for a CMO tranche. The cash flow for each month on each interest rate path is found according to the principal repayment and interest distribution rules of the deal. In order to do this, a model for reverse engineering a CMO deal is needed.

Option-Adjusted Spread

In the Monte Carlo model, the *option-adjusted spread* (OAS) is the spread that, when added to all the spot rates on all interest rate paths, will make the average present value of the paths equal to the observed market price (plus accrued interest). Mathematically, OAS is the value for K (the spread) that will satisfy the following condition:

$$\frac{PV[Path(1)] + PV[Path(2)] + \ldots + PV[Path(N)]}{N} = \text{market price}$$

where N is the number of interest rate paths. The left-hand side of the above equation looks identical to that of the equation for the theoretical value. The difference is that the objective is to determine what spread, K, will make the model produce a theoretical value equal to the market price.

Special Considerations in Valuing Asset-Backed Securities

The model that should be used for valuing an asset-backed security (ABS) depends on the characteristic of the loans or receivables backing the deal. An ABS can have one of the following three characteristics:

Characteristic 1: The ABS does not have a prepayment option.
Characteristic 2: The ABS has a prepayment option but borrowers do not exhibit a tendency to prepay when refinancing rates fall below the loan rate.
Characteristic 3: The ABS has a prepayment option and borrowers are expected to prepay when refinancing rates fall below the loan rate.

An example of a Characteristic 1 type ABS is a security backed by credit card receivables. An example of a Characteristic 2 type ABS is a security backed by automobile loans. A security backed by closed-end home equity loans where the borrowers are of high quality (i.e., prime borrowers) is an example of a Characteristic 3 type ABS. There are some real-estate backed ABS where the verdict is still out as to the degree to which borrowers take advantage of refinancing opportunities. Specifically, these include securities backed by manufactured housing loans and securities backed by closed-end home equity loans to borrowers classified as low quality borrowers.

There are two possible approaches to valuing an ABS. They are the

1. Zero-volatility spread (Z-spread) approach
2. Option-adjusted spread (OAS) approach

For the Z-spread approach (discussed in the previous chapter) the interest rates used to discount the cash flows are the spot rates plus the zero-volatility spread. The value of an ABS is then the present value of the cash flows based on these discount rates. The Z-spread approach does not consider the prepayment option. Consequently, the Z-spread approach should be used to value Characteristic 1 type ABS. (In terms of the relationship between the Z-spread, OAS, and option cost discussed earlier in this chapter, this means that the value of the option is zero and therefore the Z-spread is equal to the OAS.) Since the Z-spread is equal to the OAS, the Z-spread approach to valuation can be used.

The Z-spread approach can also be used to value Characteristic 2 type ABS because while the borrowers do have a prepayment option, the option is not typically exercised when rates decline below the loan rate. Thus, as with Characteristic 1 type ABS, the Z-spread is equal to the OAS.

The OAS approach—which is considerably more computationally extensive than the Z-spread approach—is used to value securities where there is an embedded option and there is an expectation that the option will be exercised if it makes economic sense for the borrower to do so. Consequently, the OAS approach is used to value Characteristic 3 type ABS. The choice is then whether to use the lattice model or the Monte Carlo simulation model. Since typically the cash flow for an ABS with a prepayment option is interest rate path dependent—as with a mortgage-backed security—the Monte Carlo simulation model is used.

When the Monte Carlo model must be employed for an ABS, then there are some modifications to the model relative to its application for valuing agency mortgage-backed securities. First, instead of the mortgage refinancing rate, the appropriate rate is the borrowing rate for comparable loans of the underlying loan pool. Moreover, an assumption must be made about the relationship between the relevant borrowing rate and the Treasury rate. Second, given the refinancing rates, the collateral's cash flows on each interest rate path can be generated. This requires a prepayment and default/recovery model to project involuntary prepayments.

CHAPTER 21

Measuring Interest Rate Risk

Frank J. Fabozzi, Ph.D., CFA
Adjunct Professor of Finance
School of Management
Yale University

Steven V. Mann, Ph.D.
Professor of Finance
The Moore School of Business
University of South Carolina

A general principle of valuation is the present value of an expected future cash flow changes in the opposite direction from changes in the interest rate used to discount the cash flows. We observed this principle at work when we discussed the price/yield relationship for option-free bonds in Chapter 18. This inverse relationship lies at the heart of the major risk faced by fixed-income investors—*interest rate risk*. Interest rate risk involves the possibility that the value of a bond position or a bond portfolio's value will decline due to an adverse interest rate movement. Specifically, a long bond position's value will decline if interest rates rise, resulting in a loss. Conversely, for a short bond position, a loss will be realized if interest rates fall. To effectively control interest rate risk, a portfolio manager must be able to quantify the portfolio's interest rate risk exposure. The purpose of this chapter is to understand the dimensions of interest rate risk and explain how it is measured.

PRICE VOLATILITY CHARACTERISTICS OF BONDS

There are four characteristics of a bond that affect its price volatility: (1) term to maturity, (2) coupon rate, (3) the level of yields, and (4) the presence of embedded options. In this section, we will examine each of these price volatility characteristics.

Price Volatility Characteristics of Option-Free Bonds

Let's begin by focusing on option-free bonds (i.e., bonds that do not have embedded options). A fundamental characteristic of an option-free bond is that the price of the bond changes in the opposite direction from a change in the bond's required yield. When the price/yield relationship for any hypothetical option-free bond is graphed, it exhibits the basic shape shown in Exhibit 18.1 in Chapter 18. As the required yield decreases, the price of an option-free bond increases. Conversely, as the required yield decreases, the price of an option-free bond increases. In other words, the price/yield relationship is negatively sloped. In addition, the price/yield relationship is not linear (i.e., not a straight line). The shape of the price/yield relationship for any option-free bond is referred to as *convex*. The price/yield relationship is for an instantaneous change in the required yield.

Exhibit 21.1 shows the price/yield for the U.S. Treasury principal strip with a market price of 18.2645 and matures on May 15, 2030. On a settlement date of October 11, 2000, the yield is 5.828%. To construct the graph, the principal strip was repriced using increments and decrements of 10 basis points from 7.828% to 3.828%. Exhibit 21.2 shows the two price/yield relationships for the 6% coupon, 2-year Treasury note and 6.25% coupon, 30-year Treasury bond. The 6%, 2-year note yielded 5.939% on October 11, 2000 and matures on September 30, 2002. This note delivers coupon payments on March 30 and September 30. Correspondingly, the 6.25%, 30-year bond yielded 5.817% on October 11, 2000 and matures on May 15, 2030. This bond delivers coupon payments on May 15 and November 15. Note the Treasury bond's price/yield relationship is more steeply sloped and more curved than the price/yield relationship for the 2-year Treasury note. The reasons for these differences will be discussed shortly.

The price sensitivity of a bond to changes in the required yield can be measured in terms of the dollar price change or the percentage price change. Exhibit 21.3 uses four hypothetical bonds to show the percentage change in each bond's price for various changes in yield, assuming that the initial yield for all four bonds is 7%. An examination of Exhibit 21.3 reveals the following properties concerning the price volatility of an option-free bond:

EXHIBIT 21.1 Price/Yield Relationship for a Treasury Principal Strip*

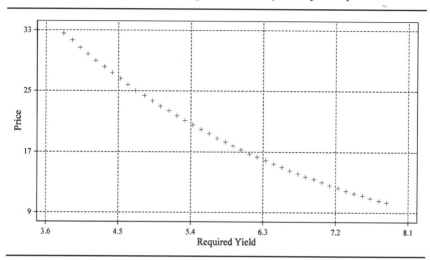

* Priced with a settlement date of 10/11/00.

EXHIBIT 21.2 Price/Yield Relationships for a 6% 2-Year Treasury Note and a 6.25% 30-Year Treasury Bond*

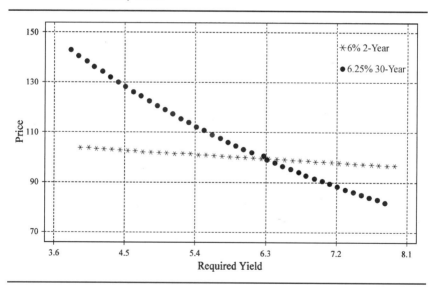

* Both bonds are priced with a settlement date of 10/11/00.

EXHIBIT 21.3   Instantaneous Percentage Price Change for
Four Hypothetical Bonds (Initial Yield for All Four Bonds is 7%)

Yield (%)	Price ($)			
	7%, 10-Year	7%, 30-Year	9%, 10-Year	9%, 30-Year
5.00	15.5892	30.9087	14.8547	29.5111
6.00	7.4387	13.8378	7.0954	13.2607
6.50	3.6368	6.5634	3.4688	6.3007
6.90	0.7138	1.2599	0.6815	1.2111
6.99	0.0711	0.1248	0.0679	0.1201
7.00	0.0000	0.0000	0.0000	0.0000
7.01	−0.0710	−0.1246	−0.0679	−0.1200
7.10	−0.0707	−1.2350	−0.6750	−1.1880
7.50	−3.4740	−5.9350	−3.3190	−5.7160
8.00	−6.7950	−11.3120	−6.4940	−10.9110
9.00	−13.0080	−20.6380	−12.4440	−19.9650

Property 1: Although the price moves in the opposite direction from the change in required yield, the percentage price change is not the same for all bonds.

Property 2: For small changes in the required yield, the percentage price change for a given bond is roughly the same, whether the required yield increases or decreases.

Property 3: For large changes in required yield, the percentage price change is not the same for an increase in required yield as it is for a decrease in required yield.

Property 4: For a given large change in basis points in the required yield, the percentage price increase is greater than the percentage price decrease.

    While the properties are expressed in terms of percentage price change, they also hold for dollar price changes.

    The implication of Property 4 is that if an investor is long a bond, the price appreciation that will be realized if the required yield decreases is greater than the capital loss that will be realized if the required yield increases by the same number of basis points. For an investor who is short a bond, the reverse is true: The potential capital loss is greater than the potential capital gain if the yield changes by a given number of basis points.

Price Volatility Characteristics of Bonds with Embedded Options

Now let's turn to the price volatility characteristics of bonds with embedded options. As explained in previous chapters, the price of a bond with an embedded option is comprised of two components. The first is the value of the same bond if it had no embedded option. That is, the price if the bond is option free. The second component is the value of the embedded option.

The two most common types of embedded options are call (or pre-pay) options and put options. As interest rates in the market decline, the issuer may call or prepay the debt obligation prior to the scheduled principal repayment date. The other type of option is a put option. This option gives the investor the right to require the issuer to purchase the bond at a specified price. Below we will examine the price/yield relationship for bonds with both types of embedded options (calls and puts) and implications for price volatility.

Bonds with Call and Prepay Options

In the discussion below, we will refer to a bond that may be called or is prepayable as a callable bond. Exhibit 21.4 shows the price/yield relationship for an option-free bond and a callable bond. The convex curve given by $a–a'$ is the price/yield relationship for an option-free bond. The unusual shaped curve denoted by $a–b$ in the exhibit is the price/yield relationship for the callable bond.

EXHIBIT 21.4   Price/Yield Relationship for a Callable Bond and an Option-Free Bond

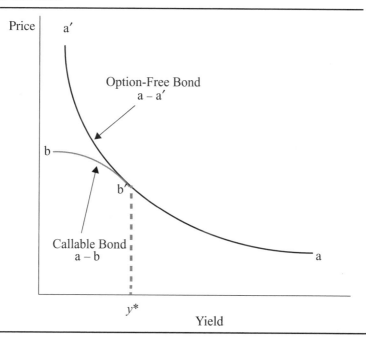

The reason for the price/yield relationship for a callable bond is as follows. When the prevailing market yield for comparable bonds is higher than the coupon rate on the callable bond, it is unlikely that the issuer will call the issue. For example, if the coupon rate on a bond is 7% and the prevailing market yield on comparable bonds is 12%, it is highly unlikely that the issuer will call a 7% coupon bond so that it can issue a 12% coupon bond. Since the bond is unlikely to be called, the callable bond will have a similar price/yield relationship as an otherwise comparable option-free bond. Consequently, the callable bond is going to be valued as if it is an option-free bond. However, since there is still some value to the call option, the bond will not trade exactly like an option-free bond.

As yields in the market decline, the concern is that the issuer will call the bond. The issuer will not necessarily exercise the call option as soon as the market yield drops below the coupon rate. Yet, the value of the embedded call option increases as yields approach the coupon rate from higher yield levels. For example, if the coupon rate on a bond is 7% and the market yield declines to 7.5%, the issuer will most likely not call the issue. However, market yields are at a level at which the investor is concerned that the issue may eventually be called if market yields decline further. Cast in terms of the value of the embedded call option, that option becomes more valuable to the issuer and therefore it reduces the price relative to an otherwise comparable option-free bond.[1] In Exhibit 21.4, the value of the embedded call option at a given yield can be measured by the difference between the price of an option-free bond (the price shown on the curve a–a') and the price on the curve a–b. Notice that at low yield levels (below y^* on the horizontal axis), the value of the embedded call option is high.

Let's look at the difference in the price volatility properties relative to an option-free bond given the price/yield relationship for a callable bond shown in Exhibit 21.4. Exhibit 21.5 blows up the portion of the price/yield relationship for the callable bond where the two curves in Exhibit 21.4 depart (segment b–b' in Exhibit 21.4). We know from our discussion of the price/yield relationship that for a large change in yield of a given number of basis points, the price of an option-free bond increases by more than it decreases (Property 4 above). Is that what happens for a callable bond in the region of the price/yield relationship shown in Exhibit 21.5? No, it is not. In fact, as can be seen in the exhibit, the opposite is true! That is, for a given large change in yield, the price appreciation is less than the price decline.

---

[1] In terms of option theory, discussed in Chapter 14, this characteristic means that when the coupon rate for the issue is below the market yield, the embedded call option is said to be "out-of-the-money." When the coupon rate for the issue is above the market yield, the embedded call option is said to be "in-the-the money."

EXHIBIT 21.5 Negative Convexity Region of the Price/Yield Relationship for a Callable Bond

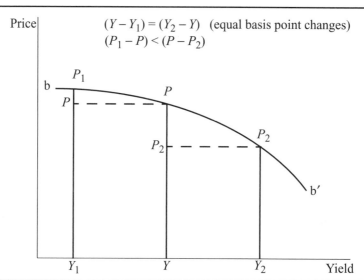

The price volatility characteristic of a callable bond is important to understand. The characteristic of a callable bond—that its price appreciation is less than its price decline when rates change by a large number of basis points—is referred to as *negative convexity*. But notice from Exhibit 21.4 that callable bonds do not exhibit this characteristic at every yield level. When yields are high (relative to the issue's coupon rate), the bond exhibits the same price/yield relationship as an option-free bond and therefore at high yield levels it also has the characteristic that the gain is greater than the loss. Because market participants have referred to the shape of the price/yield relationship shown in Exhibit 21.5 as negative convexity, market participants refer to the relationship for an option-free bond as *positive convexity*. Consequently, a callable bond exhibits negative convexity at low yield levels and positive convexity at high yield levels.

As can be seen from the exhibits, when a bond exhibits negative convexity, the bond compresses in price as rates decline. That is, at a certain yield level there is very little price appreciation when rates decline. When a bond enters this region, the bond is said to exhibit "price compression."

Bonds with Embedded Put Options

Putable bonds may be redeemed by the bondholder on the dates and at the put price specified in the indenture. Typically, the put price is par value. The advantage to the investor is that if yields rise such that the bond's value falls below the put price, the investor will exercise the put option. If the put price is par value, this means that if market yields rise above the coupon rate, the bond's value will fall below par and the investor will then exercise the put option.

The value of a putable bond is equal to the value of an option-free bond plus the value of the put option. Thus, the difference between the value of a putable bond and the value of an otherwise comparable option-free bond is the value of the embedded put option. At low yield levels (low relative to the issue's coupon rate), the price of the putable bond is basically the same as the price of the option-free bond because the value of the put option is small. As rates rise, the price of the putable bond declines, but the price decline is less than that for an option-free bond. The divergence in the price of the putable bond and an otherwise comparable option-free bond at a given yield level is the value of the put option. When yields rise to a level where the bond's price would fall below the put price, the price at these levels is the put price.

DURATION

Given the background about a bond's price volatility characteristics, we can now turn our attention to an alternate approach to full valuation: the duration/convexity approach. Simply put, *duration* is a measure of the approximate sensitivity of a bond's value to rate changes. More specifically, *duration is the approximate percentage change in value for a 100 basis point change in rates*. We will see in this section that duration is the first approximation (i.e., linear) of the percentage price change. To improve the estimate obtained using duration, a measure called "convexity" can be used. Hence, using duration and convexity together to estimate a bond's percentage price change resulting from interest rate changes is called the *duration/convexity approach*.

Calculating Duration

The duration of a bond is estimated as follows:

$$\frac{\text{price if yields decline} - \text{price if yields rise}}{2(\text{initial price})(\text{change in yield in decimal})}$$

If we let

Δy = change in yield in decimal

V_0 = initial price
V_- = price if yields decline by Δy
V_+ = price if yields increase by Δy

then duration can be expressed as:

$$\text{duration} = \frac{V_- - V_+}{2(V_0)(\Delta y)} \tag{1}$$

For example, consider the 6.25% coupon, 30-year Treasury discussed earlier that matures on May 15, 2030 and on a settlement date of October 11, 2000 is priced to yield 5.817% with a full price of 108.6034 since it is between coupon payment dates. Let's change (i.e., shock) the yield down and up by 20 basis points and determine what the new prices will be in the numerator of equation (1). If yield were decreased by 20 basis points from 5.817% to 5.617%, the bond's full price would increase to 111.6060. If the yield increases by 20 basis points, the full price would decrease to 105.7259. Thus,

$\Delta y = 0.002$ $V_0 = 108.6034$ $V_- = 111.6060$ $V_+ = 105.7259$

then,

$$\text{duration} = \frac{111.6060 - 105.7259}{2 \times (108.6034) \times (0.002)} = 13.536$$

Duration is interpreted as the approximate percentage change in price for a 100 basis point change in rates. Consequently, a duration of 13.536 means that the approximate change in price for this bond is 13.536% for a 100 basis point change in rates. A common question raised about this interpretation is the consistency between the yield change that is used to compute duration using equation (1) and the interpretation of duration. For example, recall that in computing the duration of the 30-year Treasury bond, we used a 20 basis point yield change to obtain the two prices to use in the numerator of equation (1). Yet, we interpret the duration computed as the approximate percentage price change for a 100 basis point change in yield. The reason is that regardless of the yield change used to estimate duration in equation (1), the interpretation is unchanged. If we used a 30 basis point change in yield to compute the prices used in the numerator of equation (1), the resulting duration measure is interpreted as the approximate percentage price change for a 100 basis point change in yield. Shortly, we will use different changes in yield to illustrate the sensitivity of the computed duration using equation (1).

Approximating the Percentage Price Change Using Duration

In order to approximate the percentage price change for a given change in yield and a given duration, we employ the following formula:

$$\text{approximate percentage price change} = -\text{duration} \times \Delta y \times 100 \qquad (2)$$

The reason for the negative sign on the right-hand side of equation (2) is due to the inverse relationship between price change and yield change.

For example, consider the 6.25% coupon, 30-year U.S. Treasury bond trading at a full price of 108.6034 whose duration we just showed is 13.536. The approximate percentage price change for a 10 basis point increase in yield (i.e., $\Delta y = +0.001$) is:

$$\text{approximate percentage price change}$$
$$= -13.536 \times (+0.001) \times 100 = -1.3536\%$$

How good is this approximation? The actual percentage price change is −1.339% (= 107.1494 − 108.6034)/108.6034). Duration, in this case, did an excellent job of estimating the percentage price change. We would come to the same conclusion if we used duration to estimate the percentage price change if the yield declined by 10 basis points (i.e., $\Delta y = +0.001$). In this case, the approximate percentage price change would be +1.3536% (i.e., the direction of the estimated price change is the reverse but the magnitude of the change is the same.)

In terms of estimating the new price, let's see how duration performed. The initial full price is 108.6034. For a 10 basis point increase in yield, duration estimates that the price will decline by −1.3536%. Thus, the full price will decline to 107.1333 (found by multiplying 108.6034 by one minus 0.013536). The actual price if the yield increases by 10 basis points is 107.1494. Thus, the price estimated using duration is very close to the actual price. For a 10 basis point decrease in yield, the actual full price is 110.0887 and the estimated price using duration is 110.0735 (a price increase of 1.3536%).

Now let us examine how well duration does in estimating the percentage price change when the yield increases by 200 basis points instead of 10 basis points. In this case, Δy is equal to +0.02. Substituting into equation (2) we have:

$$\text{approximate percentage price change}$$
$$= -13.536 \times (+0.02) \times 100 = -27.072$$

How good is this estimate? The actual percentage price change when the yield increases by 200 basis points (5.817% to 7.817%) is −22.15%. Thus, the estimate is not as accurate as when we used duration to approximate the percentage price change for a change in yield of only 10 basis points. If we use duration to approximate the percentage price change when the yield decreases by 200 basis points, the approximate percentage price change in this scenario is +27.072. The actual percentage price change is +33.93%.

As before, let's examine the use of duration in terms of estimating the new price. Since the initial full price is 108.6034 and a 200 basis point increase in yield will decrease the price by −27.072%, the estimated new price using duration is 79.20 (found by multiplying 100.2907 by one minus 0.27072). The actual full price if the yield rises by 200 basis points (5.939% to 7.939%) is 84.5475. Consequently, the estimate is not as accurate as the estimate for a 10 basis point change in yield. The estimated new price using duration for a 200 basis point decrease in yield is 138.01 compared to the actual price of 145.4489. Once again, the estimation of the price using duration is not as accurate as for a 10 basis point change. Notice that whether the yield is increased or decreased by 200 basis points, duration underestimates what the new price will be. We will discover why shortly. Here is a summary of what we found in our application to approximate the 30-year U.S. Treasury bond's percentage price change.

Yield Change (bp)	Initial Price	New Price Based on Duration	New Price Actual	Percent Price Change Based on Duration	Percent Price Change Actual	Comment
+10	108.6034	107.1333	107.1494	−1.3536	−1.3390	estimated price close to new price
−10	108.6034	110.0735	110.0887	+1.3536	+1.3676	estimated price close to new price
+200	108.6034	79.2000	84.5475	−27.0720	−22.1500	underestimates new price
−200	108.6034	138.0100	145.4489	+27.0720	+33.9300	underestimates new price

This result should come as no surprise to careful readers of the last section on price volatility characteristics of bonds. Specifically equation (2) is somewhat at odds with the properties of the price/yield relationship.

Graphical Depiction of Using Duration to Estimate Price Changes

Earlier we used the graph of the price/yield relationship to demonstrate the price volatility properties of bonds. We can use graphs to illustrate what we observed in our examples about how duration estimates the percentage price change, as well as some other noteworthy points.

EXHIBIT 21.6   Estimating the New Price Using a Tangent Line

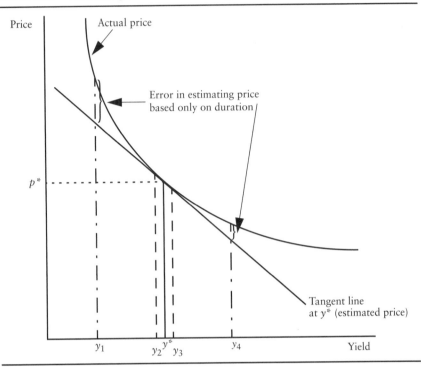

The shape of the price/yield relationship for an option-free bond is convex. Exhibit 21.6 shows this relationship. In the exhibit a tangent line is drawn to the price/yield relationship at yield y^*. (For those unfamiliar with the concept of a tangent line, it is a straight line that just touches a curve at one point within a relevant (local) range. In Exhibit 21.6, the tangent line touches the curve at the point where the yield is equal to y^* and the price is equal to p^*.) The tangent line is used to *estimate* the new price if the yield changes. If we draw a vertical line from any yield (on the horizontal axis), as in Exhibit 21.6, the distance between the horizontal axis and the tangent line represents the price approximated by using duration starting with the initial yield y^*.

Now how is the tangent line, used to approximate what the new price will be if yields change, related to duration? The tangent line tells us the approximate new price of a bond if the yield changes. Given (1) the initial price and (2) the new price of a bond if the yield changes using the tangent line, the approximate percentage price change can be computed for a given change in yield. But this is precisely what duration [using equation (2)] gives us: the approximate percentage change for a given change in yield. Thus, using the tangent line one obtains the same approximate percentage price change as using equation (2).

This helps us understand why duration did an effective job of estimating the percentage price change, or equivalently the new price, when the yield changes by a small number of basis points. Look again at Exhibit 21.6. Notice that for a small change in yield, the tangent line does not depart much from the price/yield relationship. Hence, when the yield changes up or down by 10 basis points, the tangent line does a good job of estimating the new price, as we found in our earlier numerical illustration.

Exhibit 21.6 also shows what happens to the estimate using the tangent line when the yield changes by a large number of basis points. Notice that the error in the estimate gets larger the further one moves from the initial yield. The estimate is less accurate the more convex the bond.

Also note that regardless of the magnitude of the yield change, the tangent line always underestimates what the new price will be for an option-free bond because the tangent line is below the price/yield relationship. This explains why we found in our illustration that when using duration we underestimated what the actual price will be.

Rate Shocks and Duration Estimate

In calculating duration using equation (1), it is necessary to shock interest rates (yields) up and down by the same number of basis points to obtain the values for V_- and V_+. In our illustration, 20 basis points was arbitrarily selected. But how large should the shock be? That is, how many basis points should be used to shock the rate? Looking at equation (1) it is relatively easy to discern why the size of the interest rate shock should not matter too much. Specifically, the choice of Δy has two effects on equation (1). In the numerator, the choice of Δy affects the spread between V_- and V_+ in that the larger the interest rate shock, the larger the spread between the two prices. In the denominator, the choice of Δy appears directly and the denominator is larger for larger values of Δy. The two effects should largely neutralize each other, unless the price/yield relationship is highly convex (i.e., curved).

In Exhibit 21.7, the duration estimate for our three U.S. Treasury securities from Exhibits 21.1 and 21.2 using equation (1) for rate shocks of 1 basis point to 100 basis points is reported. The duration estimates for the 2-year note are unaffected by the size of the shock. The duration estimates for the 30-year bond are affected only slightly even though a 30-year bond will have higher positive convexity (i.e., a price/yield relationship that is more curved) than a 2-year note. Lastly, if the duration estimates are ever going to be affected by the size of the interest rate shock, this should be evident when this exercise is performed on a 30-year principal strip from Exhibit 21.1, which has very large positive convexity (i.e., a price/yield relationship that is very curved). However, even in this case, the duration estimates are affected only marginally. It would appear that the size of the interest rate shock is unimportant for approximating the duration of *option-free bonds* using equation (1).

When we deal with more complicated securities, small rate shocks that do not reflect the types of rate changes that may occur in the market do not permit the determination of how prices can change because expected cash flows may change when dealing with bonds with embedded options. In comparison, if large rate shocks are used, we encounter the asymmetry caused by convexity. Moreover, large rate shocks may cause dramatic changes in the expected cash flows for bonds with embedded options that may be far different from how the expected cash flows will change for smaller rate shocks.

There is another potential problem with using small rate shocks for complicated securities. The prices that are inserted into the duration formula as given by equation (1) are derived from a valuation model. These valuation models and their underlying assumptions are discussed in Chapter 20. The duration measure depends crucially on a valuation model. If the rate shock is small and the valuation model used to obtain the prices for equation (1) is poor, dividing poor price estimates by a small shock in rates in the denominator will have a significant affect on the duration estimate.

What is done in practice by dealers and vendors of analytical systems? Each system developer uses rate shocks that they have found to be realistic based on historical rate changes.

EXHIBIT 21.7   Duration Estimates for Different Rate Shocks

Assumptions: All of these bonds are priced with a settlement date of 10/11/00. The initial yields for the note, bond and principal strip are 5.939%, 5.817%, and 5.828% respectively.

Bond	1 bp	10 bps	20 bps	50 bps	100 bps
2-year, 6% coupon U.S. Treasury note maturing 9/30/02	1.83	1.83	1.83	1.83	1.83
30-year, 6.25% coupon U.S. Treasury bond maturing 5/15/30	13.53	13.53	13.54	13.56	13.65
30-year U.S. Treasury principal strip maturing 5/15/30	28.74	28.76	28.78	28.86	29.18

Modified Duration versus Effective Duration

One form of duration that is cited by practitioners is *modified duration*. Modified duration is the approximate percentage change in a bond's price for a 100 basis point change in yield *assuming that the bond's expected cash flows do not change when the yield changes*. What this means is that in calculating the values of V_- and V_+ in equation (1), the same cash flows used to calculate V_0 are used. Therefore, the change in the bond's price when the yield is changed is due solely to discounting cash flows at the new yield level.

The assumption that the cash flows will not change when the yield is changed makes sense for option-free bonds such as noncallable Treasury securities. This is because the payments made by the U.S. Department of the Treasury to holders of its obligations do not change when interest rates change. However, the same cannot be said for bonds with embedded options (i.e., callable and putable bonds and mortgage-backed securities). For these securities, a change in yield may significantly alter the expected cash flows.

Earlier in the chapter, we presented the price/yield relationship for callable and prepayable bonds. Failure to recognize how changes in yield can alter the expected cash flows will produce two values used in the numerator of equation (1) that are not good estimates of how the price will actually change. The duration is then not a good number to use to estimate how the price will change.

When we discussed valuation models for bonds with embedded options in Chapter 20, we learned how these models (lattice models and Monte Carlo simulation) take into account how changes in yield will affect the expected cash flows. Thus, when V_- and V_+ are the values produced from these valuation models, the resulting duration takes into account both the discounting at different interest rates and how the expected cash flows may change. When duration is calculated in this manner, it is referred to as *effective duration* or *option-adjusted duration* or *OAS duration*.

Macaulay Duration and Modified Duration

It is worth comparing the relationship between modified duration to another duration measure. Modified duration can also be written as:[2]

$$\frac{1}{(1+\text{yield}/k)}\left[\frac{1 \times \text{PVCF}_1 + 2 \times \text{PVCF}_2 + \dots + n \times \text{PVCF}_n}{k \times \text{Price}}\right]$$

---

[2] More specifically, this is the formula for the modified duration of a bond on a coupon anniversary date.

where

k	=	number of periods, or payments, per year (e.g., $k = 2$ for semiannual-pay bonds and $k = 12$ for monthly-pay bonds)
n	=	number of periods until maturity (i.e., number of years to maturity times k)
yield	=	yield to maturity of the bond
$PVCF_t$	=	present value of the cash flow in period t discounted at the yield to maturity where $t = 1, 2, \ldots, n$

The expression in the brackets of the modified duration formula given by equation (3) is a measure formulated in 1938 by Frederick Macaulay.[3] This measure is popularly referred to as *Macaulay duration*. Thus, modified duration is commonly expressed as:

$$\text{Modified duration} = \frac{\text{Macaulay duration}}{(1 + \text{yield}/k)}$$

The general formulation for duration as given by equation (1) provides a short-cut procedure for determining a bond's modified duration. Because it is easier to calculate the modified duration using the short-cut procedure, most vendors of analytical software will use equation (1) rather than equation (3) to reduce computation time.

However, it must be clearly understood that modified duration is a flawed measure of a bond's price sensitivity to interest rate changes for a bond with an embedded option and therefore so is Macaulay duration. The use of the formula for duration given by equation (3) *misleads* the user because it masks the fact that changes in the expected cash flows must be recognized for bonds with embedded options. Although equation (3) will give the same estimate of percent price change for an option-free bond as equation (1), equation (1) is still better because it acknowledges that cash flows and thus value can change due to yield changes.

Portfolio Duration

A portfolio's duration can be obtained by calculating the weighted average of the duration of the bonds in the portfolio. The weight is the proportion of the portfolio that a security comprises. Mathematically, a portfolio's duration can be calculated as follows:

$$w_1 D_1 + w_2 D_2 + w_3 D_3 + \ldots + w_K D_K$$

---

[3] Frederick Macaulay, *Some Theoretical Problems Suggested by the Movement of Interest Rates, Bond Yields, and Stock Prices in the U.S. Since 1856* (New York: National Bureau of Economic Research, 1938).

EXHIBIT 21.8 Summary of a 3-Treasury Bond Portfolio

Bond	Full Price ($)	Yield (%)	Par Amount Owned ($)	Market Value ($)	Duration
2-year, 6% coupon U.S. Treasury note maturing 9/30/02	100.2907	5.939	5,000,000	5,014,535	1.83
30-year, 6.25% coupon U.S. Treasury bond maturing 5/15/30	108.6034	5.817	4,000,000	4,344,136	13.53
30-year U.S. Treasury principal strip maturing 5/15/30	18.2645	5.828	2,000,000	365,290	28.76

where

w_i = market value of bond i/market value of the portfolio
D_i = duration of bond i
K = number of bonds in the portfolio

To illustrate the calculation, consider the following 3-bond portfolio in which all three bonds are U.S. Treasuries from Exhibits 21.1 and 21.2. Exhibit 21.8 presents the full price per $100 of par value for each bond, its yield, the par amount owned, the market value, and its duration.

In this illustration, the 2-year note and the 30-year bond are priced with a settlement date between coupon payments dates so the market prices reported are full prices. The market value for the portfolio is $9,723,961. Since each bond is option-free, modified duration can be used.

In this illustration, K is equal to 3 and:

w_1 = $5,014,535/$9,723,961 = 0.516 D_1 = 1.83
w_2 = $4,344,136/$9,723,961 = 0.447 D_2 = 13.53
w_3 = $365,290/$9,723,961   = 0.037 D_3 = 28.76

The portfolio's duration is:

$$0.516(1.83) + 0.447(13.53) + 0.037(28.76) = 8.056$$

A portfolio duration of 8.056 means that for a 100 basis point change in the yield for each of the three bonds, the portfolio's market value will change by approximately 8.056%. It is paramount to keep in mind that it is assumed that the yield for each of the three bonds must change by 100 basis points. This is a critical assumption and its importance cannot be overemphasized. Portfolio managers will find it necessary to be able to measure a portfolio's exposure to shifts in the yield curve. We will examine one popular method for doing this later in the chapter when we discuss *key rate duration*.

An alternative procedure for calculating a portfolio's duration is to calculate the dollar price change for a given number of basis points for each security in the portfolio and then add up all the changes in market value. Dividing the total of the changes in market value by the portfolio's initial market value produces a percentage change in market value that can be adjusted to obtain the portfolio's duration.

For example, consider the 3-bond portfolio given in Exhibit 21.8. Suppose that we calculate the dollar change in market value for each bond in the portfolio based on its respective duration for a 50 basis point change in yield. We would then have:

U.S. Treasury Security	Market Value ($)	Duration	Change in Value for 50 bp Yield Change ($)
2-year, 6% note maturing 9/30/02	5,014,535	1.83	45,882
30-year, 6.25% bond maturing 5/15/30	4,344,136	13.53	293,881
30-year principal strip maturing 5/15/30	365,290	28.76	52,529
Total			392,292

Thus, a 50 basis point change in all rates changes the market value of the 3-bond portfolio by $392,292. Since the market value of the portfolio is $9,723,961, a 50 basis point change produced a change in value of 4.034% ($393,292 divided by $9,723,961). Since duration is the approximate percentage change for a 100 basis point change in rates, this means that the portfolio duration is 8.068 (found by doubling 4.034). This is virtually the same value for the portfolio's duration as found earlier.

Contribution to Portfolio Duration

Some portfolio managers view their exposure to a particular issue or to a sector in terms of the percentage of that issue or sector in the portfolio. A better measure of exposure of an individual issue or sector to changes in interest rates is in terms of its *contribution to the portfolio duration*. Contribution to portfolio duration is computed by multiplying the percentage that the individual issues comprises of the portfolio by the duration of the individual issue or sector. Specifically,

$$\text{contribution to portfolio duration} = \frac{\text{market value of issue or sector}}{\text{market value of portfolio}} \times \text{duration of issue or sector}$$

This exposure can also be cast in terms of dollar exposure. To accomplish this, the dollar duration of the issue or sector is used instead of the duration of the issue or sector.

A portfolio manager who desires to determine the contribution to a portfolio of a sector relative to the contribution of the same sector in a broad-based market index can compute the difference between these two contributions.

SPREAD DURATION

As we have seen, duration is a measure of the change in a bond's value when interest rates change. The interest rate that is assumed to shift is the Treasury rate which serves as the benchmark interest rate. However, for non-Treasury instruments, the yield is equal to the Treasury yield plus a spread to the Treasury yield curve. This is why non-Treasury securities are often called "spread products." Of course, the price of a bond exposed to credit risk can change even though Treasury yields are unchanged because the spread required by the market changes. A measure of how a non-Treasury security's price will change if the spread sought by the market changes is called *spread duration*.

The problem is, what spread is assumed to change? There are three measures that are commonly used for fixed-rate bonds: nominal spread, zero-volatility spread, and option-adjusted spread. Each of these spread measures were described in Chapter 19.

The nominal spread is the traditional spread measure. The nominal spread is simply the difference between the yield on a non-Treasury issue and the yield on a comparable maturity Treasury. When the spread is taken to be the nominal spread, spread duration indicates the approximate percentage change in price for a 100 basis point change in the nominal spread holding the Treasury yield constant.

The zero-volatility or static spread is the spread that when added to the Treasury spot rate curve will make the present value of the cash flows equal to the bond's price plus accrued interest. When spread is defined in this way, spread duration is the approximate percentage change in price for a 100 basis point change in the zero-volatility spread holding the Treasury spot rate curve constant.

Finally, the option-adjusted spread (OAS) is the constant spread that, when added to all the rates on the interest rate tree, will make the theoretical value equal to the market price. Spread duration based on OAS can be interpreted as the approximate percentage change in price of a non-Treasury for a 100 basis point change in the OAS, holding the Treasury rate constant.

A sensible question arises: How do you know whether a spread duration for a fixed-rate bond is a spread based on the nominal spread, zero-volatility spread or the OAS? The simple answer is you do not know! You must ask the broker/dealer or vendor of the analytical system. To add further to the confusion surrounding spread duration, consider the term "OAS duration" that is referred to by some market participants. What does it mean? On the one hand, it could mean simply the spread duration that we just described. On the other hand, many market participants use the term "OAS duration" interchangeably with the term "effective duration." Once again, the only way to know what OAS is measuring is to ask the broker/dealer or vendor.

Just as a contribution to duration can be computed for an issue or a sector, one can compute a contribution to spread duration.

KEY RATE DURATIONS

Duration measures the sensitivity of a bond's price to a given change in yield. The traditional formulation is derived under the assumption that the reference yield curve is flat and moves in parallel shifts. Simply put, all bond yields are the same regardless of when the cash flows are delivered across time and changes in yields are perfectly correlated. Several recent attempts have been made to address this inadequacy and develop interest rate risk measures that allow for more realistic changes in the yield curve's shape.

One approach to measuring the sensitivity of a bond to changes in the shape of the yield curve is to change the yield for a particular maturity of the yield curve and determine the sensitivity of a security or portfolio to this change holding all other yields constant. The sensitivity of the bond's value to a particular change in yield is called *rate duration*. There is a rate duration for every point on the yield curve. Consequently, there is not one rate duration but a vector of rate durations representing each maturity on the yield curve. The total change in value if all rates move by the same number of basis points is simply the duration of a security or portfolio to a parallel shift in rates.

The most popular version of this approach was developed by Thomas Ho in 1992.[4] This approach examines how changes in Treasury yields at different points on the spot curve affect the value of a bond portfolio. Ho's methodology has three basic steps. The first step is to select several key maturities or "key rates" of the spot rate curve. Ho's

---

[4] Thomas S. Y. Ho, "Key Rate Durations: Measures of Interest Rate Risk," *The Journal of Fixed Income* (September 1992), pp. 29–44.

approach focuses on 11 key maturities on the spot rate curve. These rate durations are called *key rate durations*. The specific maturities on the spot rate curve for which a key rate duration is measured are 3 months, 1 year, 2 years, 3 years, 5 years, 7 years, 10 years, 15 years, 20 years, 25 years, and 30 years. However, in order to illustrate Ho's methodology, we will select only three key rates: 1 year, 10 years, and 30 years.

The next step is to specify how other rates on the spot curve change in response to key rate changes. Ho's rule is that a key rate's effect on neighboring rates declines linearly and reaches zero at the adjacent key rates. For example, suppose the 10-year key rate increases by 40 basis points. All spot rates between 10 years and 30 years will increase but the amount each changes will be different and the magnitude of the change diminishes linearly. Specifically, there are 40 semiannual periods between 10 and 30 years. Each spot rate starting with 10.5 years increases by 1 basis point less than the spot rate to its immediate left (i.e., 39 basis points) and so forth. The 30-year rate which is the adjacent key rate is assumed to be unchanged. Thus, only one key rate changes at a time. Spot rates between 1 year and 10 years change in an analogous manner such that all rates change but by differing amounts. Changes in the 1-year key rate affect spot rates between 1 and 10 years while spot rates 10 years and beyond are assumed to be unaffected by changes in the 1-year spot rate. In a similar vein, changes in the 30-year key rate affect all spot rates between 30 years and 10 years while spot rates shorter than 10 years are assumed to be unaffected by the change in the 30-year rate. This process is illustrated in Exhibit 21.9. Note that if we add the three rate changes together we obtain a parallel yield curve shift of 40 basis points.

The third and final step is to calculate the percentage change in the bond's portfolio value when each key rate and neighboring spot rates are changed. There will be as many key rate durations as there are preselected key rates. Let's illustrate this process by calculating the key rate duration for a coupon bond. Our hypothetical 6% coupon bond has a maturity value of $100 and matures in 5 years. The bond delivers coupon payments semiannually. Valuation is accomplished by discounting each cash flow using the appropriate spot rate. The bond's current value is $107.32 and the process is illustrated in Exhibit 21.10. The initial hypothetical (and short) spot curve is contained in column (3).[5] The present values of each of the bond's cash flows is presented in the last column.

---

[5] The spot rates are annual rates and are reported as bond-equivalent yields. When present values are computed, we use the appropriate semiannual rates which are taken to be one half the annual rate.

EXHIBIT 21.9   Graph of How Spot Rates Change When Key Rates Change

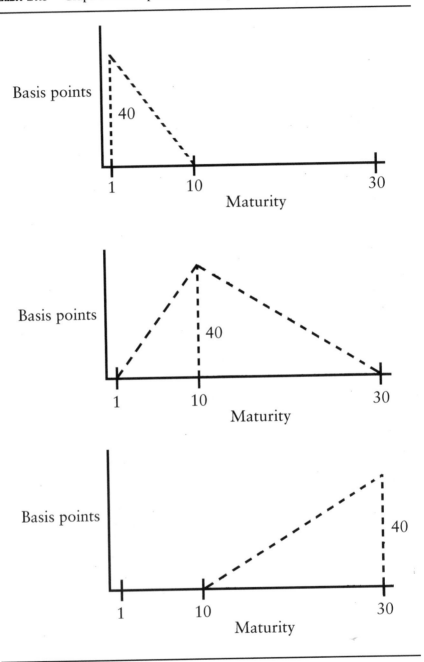

EXHIBIT 21.10 Valuation of the 5-Year 6% Coupon Bond to Compute Key Rate Duration

Years	Period	Cash Flow ($)	Initial Spot Rates[a]		After 0.5-Yr Key Rate[b]		After 3-Yr Key Rate[c]		After 5-Yr Key Rate[d]	
			Spot Rate (%)	Present Value ($)	Spot Rate (%)	Present Value ($)	Spot Rate (%)	Present Value ($)	Spot Rate (%)	Present Value ($)
0.5	1	3	3.00	2.96	3.20	2.95	3.00	2.96	3.00	2.96
1.0	2	3	3.25	2.90	3.41	2.90	3.29	2.90	3.25	2.90
1.5	3	3	3.50	2.85	3.62	2.84	3.58	2.84	3.50	2.85
2.0	4	3	3.75	2.79	3.83	2.78	3.87	2.78	3.75	2.79
2.5	5	3	4.00	2.72	4.04	2.71	4.16	2.71	4.00	2.72
3.0	6	3	4.10	2.66	4.10	2.66	4.30	2.64	4.10	2.66
3.5	7	3	4.20	2.59	4.20	2.59	4.35	2.58	4.25	2.59
4.0	8	3	4.30	2.53	4.30	2.53	4.40	2.52	4.40	2.52
4.5	9	3	4.35	2.47	4.35	2.47	4.40	2.47	4.50	2.46
5.0	10	103	4.40	82.86	4.40	82.86	4.40	82.86	4.60	82.05
		Total		107.32		107.30		107.25		106.48

a. Valuation using initial spot rates.
b. Valuation after 0.5-year key rate and neighboring spot rate change.
c. Valuation after 3-year key rate and neighboring spot rate change.
d. Valuation after 5-year key rate and neighboring spot rate change.

To compute the key rate duration of the 5-year bond, we must select some key rates. We assume the key rates are 0.5, 3, and 5 years. To compute the 0.5-year key rate duration, we shift the 0.5-year rate upwards by 20 basis points and adjust the neighboring spot rates between 0.5 and 3 years as described earlier. (The choice of 20 basis points is arbitrary.) The next step is to compute the bond's new value as a result of the shift. This calculation is shown in Exhibit 21.10. The bond's value subsequent to the shift is $107.30. To estimate the 0.5-year key rate duration, we divide the percentage change in the bond's price as a result of the shift in the spot curve by the change in the 0.5-year key rate. Accordingly, we employ the following formula:

$$\text{key rate duration} = -\frac{P_0 - P_1}{P_0 \Delta y}$$

where

P_1 = the bond's value after the shift in the spot curve
P_0 = the bond's value using the initial spot curve
Δy = shift in the key rate (in decimal)

Substituting in numbers from our illustration presented above, we can compute the 0.5-year key rate duration as follows:

$$0.5\text{-year key rate duration} = \frac{107.32 - 107.30}{107.32(0.002)} = 0.0932$$

To compute the 3-year key rate duration, we repeat this process. We shift the 3-year rate by 20 basis points and adjust the neighboring spot rates as described earlier. The spot rates after the 3-year key rate and neighboring rates are shifted are shown in Exhibit 21.10. Note that in this case the only two spot rates that do not change are the 0.5-year and the 5-year key rates. Then, we compute the bond's new value as a result of the shift. The bond's post-shift value is $107.25 and the calculation appears in Exhibit 21.10. Accordingly, the 3-year key rate duration is computed as follows:

$$3\text{-year key rate duration} = \frac{107.32 - 107.25}{107.32(0.002)} = 0.3261$$

The final step is to compute the 5-year key duration. We shift the 5-year rate by 20 basis points and adjust the neighboring spot rates. The spot rates after the 5-year key rate and neighboring rates are shifted are shown in Exhibit 21.10. The bond's post-shift value is $106.48 and the calculation appears in Exhibit 21.10. Accordingly, the 5-year key rate duration is computed as follows:

$$5\text{-year key rate duration} = \frac{107.32 - 106.48}{107.32(0.002)} = 3.9135$$

What information can be gleaned from these key rate durations? Each key rate duration by itself means relatively little. However, the distribution of the bond's key rate durations helps us assess its exposure to yield curve risk. Intuitively, the sum of the key rate durations is approximately equal to a bond's duration.[6] As a result, it is useful to think of a set of key rate durations as a decomposition of duration into sensitivities to various portions of the yield curve. In our illustration, it is not surprising that the lion's share of the yield curve risk exposure of the coupon bond in our illustration is due to the bond's terminal cash flow, so the 5-year key rate duration is the largest of the three. Simply put, the 5-years bond's value is more sensitive to movements in longer spot rates and less sensitive to movements in shorter spot rates.

---

[6] The reason it is only approximate is because modified duration assumes a flat yield curve whereas key rate duration takes the spot curve as given.

Key rate durations are most useful when comparing two (or more) bond portfolios that have approximately the same duration. If the spot curve is flat and experiences a parallel shift, these two bond portfolios can be expected to experience approximately the same percentage change in value. However, the performance of the two portfolios will generally not be the same for a nonparallel shift in the spot curve. The key rate duration profile of each portfolio will give the portfolio manager some clues about the relative performance of the two portfolios when the yield curve changes shape and slope.

CONVEXITY

The duration measure indicates that regardless of whether interest rates increase or decrease, the approximate percentage price change is the same. However, as we noted earlier, this is not consistent with Property 3 of a bond's price volatility. Specifically, while for small changes in yield the percentage price change will be the same for an increase or decrease in yield, for large changes in yield this is not true. This suggests that duration is only a good approximation of the percentage price change for small changes in yield.

We demonstrated this property earlier using a 6.25% 30-year Treasury bond priced to yield 5.817% with a duration of 13.53. For a 10 basis point change in yield, the estimate was accurate for both an increase and decrease in yield. However, for a 200 basis point change in yield the approximate percentage price change was off considerably.

The reason for this result is that duration is in fact a first (linear) approximation for a small change in yield.[7] The approximation can be improved by using a second approximation. This approximation is referred to as "convexity." *The use of this term in the industry is unfortunate since the term convexity is also used to describe the shape or curvature of the price/yield relationship.* The convexity measure of a security can be used to approximate the change in price that is not explained by duration.

Convexity Measure

The convexity measure of a bond is approximated using the following formula:

---

[7] The reason it is a linear approximation can be seen in Exhibit 21.6 where the tangent line is used to estimate the new price. That is, a straight line is being used to approximate a non-linear (i.e., convex) relationship.

$$\text{Convexity measure} = \frac{V_+ + V_- - 2V_0}{2V_0(\Delta y)^2} \tag{3}$$

where the notation is the same as used earlier for duration as given by equation (4).

For the 6.25%, 30-year Treasury bond priced to yield 5.817% with a settlement date of October 11, 2000, we know that for a 20 basis point change in yield ($\Delta y = 0.002$):

$$V_0 = 108.6034, \ V_- = 111.6060, \text{ and } V_+ = 105.7259$$

Recall from our earlier discussion, that the 30-year bond from Exhibit 21.2 makes coupon payments on May 15 and November 15. Note that the settlement date of October 11, 2000 is between coupon payment dates. As a result, we will use full prices (flat price plus the accrued interest) in the calculation. Substituting these values into the convexity measure given by equation (3):

$$\text{Convexity measure} = \frac{105.7259 + 111.6060 - 2(108.6034)}{2(108.6037)(0.002)^2} = 143.99$$

We'll see how to use this convexity measure shortly. Before doing so, there are three points that should be noted. First, there is no simple interpretation of the convexity measure as there is for duration. Second, it is more common for market participants to refer to the value computed in equation (4) as the "convexity of a bond" rather than the "convexity measure of a bond." Finally, the convexity measure reported by dealers and vendors will differ for an option-free bond. The reason is that the value obtained from equation (4) is often scaled for the reason explained after we demonstrate how to use the convexity measure.

Convexity Adjustment to Percentage Price Change

Given the convexity measure, the approximate percentage price change adjustment due to the bond's convexity (i.e., the percentage price change not explained by duration) is:

$$\text{Convexity adjustment to percentage price change}$$
$$= \text{Convexity measure} \times (\Delta y)^2 \times 100 \tag{4}$$

For example, for the 6.25% 30-year Treasury bond, the convexity adjustment to the percentage price change based on duration if the yield increases from 5.817% to 7.817% is

$$143.99 \times (0.02)^2 \times 100 = 5.76\%$$

If the yield decreases from 5.817% to 3.817%, the convexity adjustment to the approximate percentage price change based on duration would also be 5.76%.

The approximate percentage price change based on duration and the convexity adjustment is found by summing the two estimates. So, for example, if yields change from 5.817% to 7.817%, the estimated percentage price change would be:

Estimated change using duration alone	=	−27.06
Convexity adjustment	=	+5.76
Total estimated percentage price change	=	−21.30

The actual percentage price change is −22.15.

For a decrease of 200 basis points, from 5.817% to 3.817%, the approximate percentage price change would be as follows:

Estimated change using duration alone	=	+27.06
Convexity adjustment	=	+5.76
Total estimated percentage price change	=	+32.82%

The actual percentage price change is +33.93%. Thus, duration combined with the convexity adjustment does a much better job of estimating the sensitivity of a bond's price to large changes in yield.

Notice that when the convexity measure is positive, we have the situation described earlier that the gain is greater than the loss for a given large change in rates. That is, the bond exhibits positive convexity. We can see this in the example above. However, if the convexity measure is negative, we have the situation where the loss will be greater than the gain. For example, suppose that a callable bond has an effective duration of 4 and a convexity measure of −30. This means that the approximate percentage price change for a 200 basis point change is 8%. The convexity adjustment for a 200 basis point change in rates is then:

$$-30 \times (0.02)^2 \times 100 = -1.2$$

The convexity adjustment is −1.2% and therefore the bond exhibits the negative convexity property illustrated in Exhibit 21.4. The approximate percentage price change after adjusting for convexity is:

Estimated change using duration	=	−8.0%
Convexity adjustment	=	−1.2%
Total estimated percentage price change	=	−9.2%

For a decrease of 200 basis points, the approximate percentage price change would be as follows:

Estimated change using duration	=	+8.0%
Convexity adjustment	=	−1.2%
Total estimated percentage price change	=	+6.8%

Notice that the loss is greater than the gain—a property called *negative convexity* that we discussed earlier.

Scaling the Convexity Measure

The convexity measure as given by equation (3) means nothing in isolation. It is the substitution of the computed convexity measure into equation (4) that provides the estimated adjustment for convexity that is meaningful. Therefore, it is possible to scale the convexity measure in any way as long as the same convexity adjustment is obtained.

For example, in some books the convexity measure is defined as follows:

$$\text{Convexity measure} = \frac{V_+ + V_- - 2V_0}{V_0(\Delta y)^2} \tag{5}$$

Equation (5) differs from equation (3) since it does not include 2 in the denominator. Thus, the convexity measure computed using equation (5) will be double the convexity measure using equation (3). So, for our earlier illustration, since the convexity measure using equation (3) is 143.99, the convexity measure using equation (5) would be 287.98.

Which is correct, 143.99 or 287.98? The answer is both. The reason is that the corresponding equation for computing the convexity adjustment would not be given by equation (4) if the convexity measure is obtained from equation (5). Instead, the corresponding convexity adjustment formula would be:

$$\begin{aligned} &\text{Convexity adjustment to percentage price change} \\ &= (\text{Convexity measure}/2) \times (\Delta y)^2 \times 100 \end{aligned} \tag{6}$$

Equation (6) differs from equation (4) in that the convexity measure is divided by 2. Thus, the convexity adjustment will be the same whether one uses equation (3) to get the convexity measure and equation (4) to get the convexity adjustment or one uses equation (5) to compute the convexity measure and equation (6) to determine the convexity adjustment.

Some dealers and vendors scale the convexity measure in different ways. It is the convexity adjustment that is important—not the convexity measure in isolation. This is also important to understand when comparing the convexity measures reported by dealers and vendors.

Modified Convexity and Effective Convexity

The prices used in equation (3) to calculate convexity can be obtained by either assuming that when the yield changes the expected cash flows either do not change or they do change. In the former case, the resulting convexity is referred to as *modified convexity*. (Actually, in the industry, convexity is not qualified by the adjective "modified.") In contrast, *effective convexity* assumes that the cash flows do change when yields change. This is the same distinction made for duration.

As with duration, there is little difference between modified convexity and effective convexity for option-free bonds. However, for bonds with embedded options there can be quite a difference between the calculated modified convexity and effective convexity measures. In fact, for all option-free bonds, either convexity measure will have a positive value. For bonds with embedded options, the calculated effective convexity measure can be negative when the calculated modified convexity measure is positive.

PRICE VALUE OF A BASIS POINT

Some managers use another measure of the price volatility of a bond to quantify interest rate risk—the *price value of a basis point* (PVBP). This measure, also called the *dollar value of an 01* (DV01), is the absolute value of the change in the price of a bond for a 1 basis point change in yield. That is,

$$\text{PVBP} = |\text{ initial price} - \text{price if yield is changed by 1 basis point }|$$

Does it make a difference if the yield is increased or decreased by 1 basis point? It does not because of Property 2—the change will be about the same for a small change in basis points.

To illustrate the computation, let's examine a 5.75% coupon, 10-year U.S. Treasury note that matures on August 15, 2010. If the bond is priced to yield 5.778% on a settlement date of October 11, 2000, we can compute the PVBP by using the prices for either the yield at 5.768 or 5.788. The bond's initial full price at 5.778% is 100.6739. If the yield is decreased by 1 basis point to 5.768%, the PVBP is 0.0742 (|100.7481 – 100.6739|). If the yield is increased by 1 basis point to 5.788%, the PVBP is 0.0742 (|100.5997 – 100.6739|).

The PVBP is related to duration. In fact, PVBP is simply a special case of a measure called *dollar duration*. Dollar duration is the approximate dollar price change for a 100 basis point change in yield. We know that a bond's duration is the approximate percentage price change for a 100 basis point change in interest rates. We also know how to compute the approximate percentage price change for any number of basis points given a bond's duration using equation (2). Given the initial price and the approximate percentage price change for 1 basis point, we can compute the change in price for a 1 basis point change in rates.

For example, consider the 5.75% coupon, 10-year Treasury note. The duration is 7.371. Using equation (2), the approximate percentage price change for a 1 basis point increase in interest rates (i.e., $\Delta y = 0.0001$) ignoring the negative sign in equation (2) is:

$$7.371 \times (0.0001) \times 100 = 0.07371\%$$

Given the initial full price of 100.6739, the dollar price change estimated using duration is:

$$0.07371\% \times 100.6739 = \$0.0742$$

This is the same price change as shown above for a PVBP for this bond.

THE IMPORTANCE OF YIELD VOLATILITY

What we have not considered thus far is the volatility of interest rates. For example, as we explained earlier, all other factors equal, the higher the coupon rate, the lower the price volatility of a bond to changes in interest rates. In addition, the higher the level of yields, the lower the price volatility of a bond to changes in interest rates.

This can also be cast in terms of duration properties: The higher the coupon, the lower the duration; and the higher the yield level the lower the duration. Given these two properties, a 10-year non-investment grade bond has a lower duration than a current coupon 10-year Treasury note since the former has a higher coupon rate and trades at a higher yield level. Does this mean that a 10-year non-investment grade bond has less interest rate risk than a current coupon 10-year Treasury note? The missing link is the relative volatility of rates which we shall refer to as *yield volatility* or *interest rate volatility*. The greater the expected yield volatility, the greater the interest rate risk for a given duration and current value of a position.

Consequently, to measure the exposure of a portfolio or position to rate changes, it is necessary to measure yield volatility. This requires an understanding of the fundamental principles of probability distributions. The measure of yield volatility is the standard deviation of yield changes.

CHAPTER 22

Fixed-Income Portfolio Strategies

Frank J. Fabozzi, Ph.D., CFA
Adjunct Professor of Finance
School of Management
Yale University

In this chapter various fixed-income portfolio strategies are covered. We begin with a discussion of the risks associated with investing in fixed-income securities. Then a framework is presented that can be used to assess the potential performance of a trade or a current or revised portfolio. After this framework is provided, strategies for managing a portfolio relative to a bond market index and those for managing a portfolio relative to liabilities are explained.

RISKS ASSOCIATED WITH INVESTING IN FIXED-INCOME SECURITIES

Fixed-income securities may expose an investor to one or more of the following risks: (1) interest rate risk; (2) yield curve risk; (3) call and prepayment risk; (4) credit risk; (5) liquidity risk; and (6) exchange rate or currency risk. In previous chapters we discussed several of these risks. In this section, we summarize these risks. Later in this chapter, we discuss other types of risks that are associated with managing funds against a bond market index.

Interest Rate Risk

The price of a typical fixed-income security will change in the opposite direction from a change in interest rates. That is, when interest rates

615

rise, a fixed-income security's price will fall; when interest rates fall, a fixed-income security's price will rise. This relationship was demonstrated in Chapter 21. This risk is referred to as *interest rate risk*. Fortunately, this risk can be quantified. As explained in Chapter 21, duration measures the price sensitivity of a fixed-income security to changes in the level of interest rates. The appropriate measure of duration that should be used is effective duration. A measure of convexity can be used to improve the estimate of the price sensitivity that is not explained by duration.

Yield Curve Risk

A portfolio of fixed-income securities is not only exposed to a change in the level of interest rates, but also to changes in the shape of the yield curve. This risk is called *yield curve risk*. Various measures have been suggested to quantify yield curve risk. One such measure was described in Chapter 21, key rate duration. Another way is to look at the distribution of the present value of the portfolio's cash flows.

Call and Prepayment Risk

A fixed-income security may include a provision that allows the issuer to retire or call all or part of the issue before the maturity date. From the investor's perspective, there are three disadvantages associated with call provisions. First, the cash flow pattern of a callable bond is not known with certainty. Second, because the issuer will call the bonds when interest rates have dropped, the investor is exposed to reinvestment risk (i.e., the investor will have to reinvest the proceeds when the bond is called at relatively lower interest rates). Finally, the capital appreciation potential of a bond will be reduced because the price of a callable bond may not rise much above the price at which the issuer will call the bond. Because of these disadvantages faced by the investor, a callable bond is said to expose the investor to *call risk*. The same disadvantages apply to mortgage-backed and asset-backed securities that can prepay. In this case the risk is referred to as *prepayment risk*.

There are ways of approximating this risk for a portfolio which are discussed in Chapter 24. These measures draw from measures used in option pricing theory.

Credit Risk

Investors in non-Treasury U.S. securities are exposed to credit risk. There are three types of credit risk: (1) default risk, (2) credit spread risk, and (3) downgrade risk.

Default Risk

Traditionally, credit risk is defined as the risk that the issuer will fail to satisfy the terms of the obligation with respect to the timely payment of interest and repayment of the amount borrowed. This form of credit risk is called *default risk*. This risk is gauged by market participants based on the credit rating assigned to an issue.

Credit Spread Risk

Even in the absence of default, an investor is concerned that the market value of a bond will decline and/or the price performance of that bond will be worse than that of other bonds against which the investor is compared. To understand this, recall that the price of a bond changes in the opposite direction to the change in the yield required by the market. Thus, if yields in the economy increase, the price of a bond declines, and vice versa.

The yield on a bond is made up of two components: (1) the yield on a similar default-free bond issue and (2) a premium above the yield on a default-free bond issue necessary to compensate for the risks associated with the bond. The risk premium is referred to as a *spread*. In the United States, Treasury issues are the benchmark yields because they are believed to be default free, they are highly liquid, and Treasury issues are not callable (with the exception of some old issues). The part of the risk premium or spread attributable to default risk is called the *credit spread*.

The price performance of a non-Treasury bond issue and the return that the investor will realize by holding that issue over some time period will depend on how the credit spread changes. If the credit spread increases—investors say that the spread has "widened"—the market price of the bond issue will decline (assuming Treasury rates have not changed). The risk that an issuer's debt obligation will decline due to an increase in the credit spread is called *credit spread risk*.

Downgrade Risk

While there are investors who seek to allocate funds among different sectors of the bond market to capitalize on anticipated changes in credit spreads, an investor investigating the credit quality of an individual issue is concerned with the prospects of the credit spread increasing for that particular issue. While market participants gauge the default risk of an issue by looking at the credit ratings assigned to issues by the rating agencies, a credit rating assigned to an issue can be changed since an issue is purchased.

An improvement in the credit quality of an issue or issuer is rewarded with a better credit rating, referred to as an *upgrade*; a deterioration in the credit rating of an issue or issuer is penalized by the assignment of an inferior credit rating, referred to as a *downgrade*. An unanticipated downgrading of an issue or issuer increases the credit spread and results in a decline in the price of the issue or the issuer's bonds. This risk is referred to as *downgrade risk* and is closely related to credit spread risk. To estimate this risk, an investor can use the rating transition matrix produced periodically by rating agencies. A rating transition matrix indicates that over a specified period of time (e.g., one year or three years), the percentage of issues with a certain rating at the beginning of the time period that were downgraded by the end of the time period.

Occasionally, the ability of an issuer to make interest and principal payments changes dramatically and unexpectedly because of factors including a natural disaster (such as an earthquake or hurricane) or an industrial accident that impairs an issuer's ability to meet its obligations or a takeover or corporate restructuring that impairs an issuer's ability to meet its obligations. These events can result in a downgrading of an issue. A downgrade due to such events is referred to as *event risk*.

Liquidity Risk

When an investor wants to sell a bond prior to the maturity date, he or she is concerned whether the price that can be obtained from dealers is close to the true value of the issue. For example, if recent trades in the market for a particular issue have been between 97.25 and 97.75 and market conditions have not changed, an investor would expect to sell the bond somewhere in the 97.25 to 97.75 area.

Liquidity risk is the risk that the investor will have to sell a bond below its true value where the true value is indicated by recent transactions. The primary measure of liquidity is the size of the spread between the bid price (the price at which a dealer is willing to buy a security) and the ask price (the price at which a dealer is willing to sell a security). The wider the bid-ask spread, the greater the liquidity risk.

A liquid market can generally be defined by in terms of two properties: (1) small bid-ask spreads and (2) spreads that do not materially increase for large transactions. Bid-ask spreads change over time and therefore liquidity risk changes over time.

For investors who plan to hold a bond until maturity and need not mark a position to market, liquidity risk is not a major concern. An institutional investor that plans to hold an issue to maturity but is periodically marked to market is concerned with liquidity risk. By marking a position to market, it is meant that the security is revalued in the portfolio based on its current market price. For example, mutual funds are required to mark to market at the end of each day the holdings in their portfolio in order to compute the net asset value (NAV). While other institutional investors may not mark to market as frequently as mutual funds, they are marked to market when reports are periodically sent to clients or the board of directors or trustees.

Exchange Rate or Currency Risk

For a U.S. investor, a bond whose payments occur in a foreign currency (referred to a nondollar-denominated bond) has unknown U.S. dollar cash flows. The dollar cash flows are dependent on the exchange rate at the time the payments are received. For example, suppose an investor purchases a bond whose payments are in Japanese yen. If the yen depreciates relative to the U.S. dollar, then fewer dollars will be received. The risk of this occurring is referred to as *exchange rate* or *currency risk*. Of course, should the yen appreciate relative to the U.S. dollar, the investor will benefit by receiving more dollars.

TOTAL RETURN FRAMEWORK

A portfolio manager is evaluated in terms of performance. Performance may be relative to a bond market index or liabilities. Regardless of the benchmark, performance is measured in terms of total return. This measure relates the total cash flow from an investment to the amount invested. Shortly, we will be more specific as to how total return is calculated.

Total return is used in two contexts. When a manager is constructing a portfolio, he wants to know the potential total return that can be realized based on assumptions of how factors that affect the portfolio's performance will change. Total return used in this way is a forward looking measure and is referred to as a *potential total return*.

The other context in which total return is used is to assess the *realized* performance of a portfolio over some time. This is backward looking measure, also referred to as a *realized total return* or *historical total return* or *actual total return*. In Chapter 5, the procedure for calculating the realized total return and the issues associated with the calculation are explained. It is the realized total return that is used in evaluating the actual performance of a manager based on return attribution analysis, a methodology described later in this chapter.

In this section we will describe how potential total return is computed. This measure can be computed for an individual bond or for a portfolio. The potential total return provides a measure that can be used to assess not only the potential performance of a portfolio but also the potential performance of a trade that is being contemplated by a manager. We begin with the calculation of the potential total return for an individual bond.

Potential Total Return of a Bond

An investor who purchases a bond can expect to receive a dollar return from one or more of the following sources: (1) the coupon interest payments made by the issuer; (2) any capital gain (or capital loss—negative dollar return) when the bond matures, is called, is put, is refunded, or is sold; and (3) income from reinvestment of the coupon interest payments and interim principal payments. Any measure of the potential return from holding a bond over some investment horizon should consider these three sources of return. In Chapter 19, we explained why yield measures are limited with respect to assessing potential performance over some investment horizon.

If yield measures offer little insight into the potential performance of a bond, what measure can be used? The proper measure is one that considers all three sources of potential dollar return over the investor's investment horizon. The potential total return is precisely that measure. It is the interest rate that will make the proceeds (i.e., price plus accrued interest) invested grow to the projected total dollar return at the end of the investment horizon. Below we simply refer to the potential total return as total return.

The total return requires that the investor specify (1) an investment horizon, (2) a reinvestment rate, and (3) a selling price for the bond at the end of the investment horizon (which depends on the assumed yield to maturity for the bond at the end of the investment horizon). More formally, the steps for computing a total return over some investment horizon for a bond that pays coupon interest semiannually and is non-amortizing are as follows:

Step 1: Compute the total coupon payments plus the reinvestment income based on an assumed reinvestment rate. The reinvestment rate is one-half the annual interest rate that the investor assumes can be earned on the reinvestment of coupon interest payments.

Step 2: Determine the projected sale price at the end of the investment horizon. We refer to this as the *horizon price*. In Chapters 18 and 20 we explained how the value of a bond is determined based on the term structure of default-free interest rates (i.e., the Treasury spot rate curve) and the term structure of credit spreads. Moreover, for bonds with embedded options, the price will depend on the option-adjusted spread (OAS). So, to determine the horizon price in the total return analysis it is necessary to use at the horizon date an assumed Treasury spot rate curve, term structure of credit spreads, and OAS. Obviously, the assumed values reflect changes in interest rates and spreads from the beginning to the end of the investment horizon. We shall refer to these rates as the structure of rates at the horizon date.

However, in the illustrations to follow, to simplify we will assume a single yield to price a security at the horizon date. This yield would reflect the Treasury rate plus a spread and we will refer to it as the *horizon yield*.

Step 3: Add the values computed in Steps 1 and 2. Reduce this value by any borrowing cost to obtain the total future dollars that will be received from the investment given the assumed reinvestment rate and projected structure of rates at the horizon date (or horizon yield in our illustrations to follow).

Step 4: Compute the semiannual total return using the following formula:

$$\left(\frac{\text{total future dollars}}{\text{full price of bond}} \right)^{1/h} - 1$$

where the full price is the price plus accrued interest and h is the number of semiannual periods in the investment horizon.

Step 5: For semiannual-pay bonds, double the interest rate found in Step 4. The resulting interest rate is the total return expressed on a bond-equivalent basis. Instead, the total return can be expressed on an effective rate basis by using the following formula:

$$(1 + \text{semiannual total return})^2 - 1$$

The decision as to whether to calculate the total return on a bond-equivalent basis or an effective rate basis depends on the situation. If the total return is being compared to a benchmark index that is calculated on a bond-equivalent basis, then the total return should be calculated in that way. However, if the bond is being used to satisfy liabilities that are calculated on an effective rate basis, then the total return should be calculated in that way.

To illustrate the computation of the total return, suppose that an investor with a 1-year investment horizon is considering the purchase of a 20-year 6% corporate bond. The issue is selling for $86.4365 for a yield of 7.3%. The issue will be purchased for cash (i.e., no funds will be borrowed). Assume that the yield curve is flat (i.e., the yield for all maturities is the same) and the yield for the on-the-run 20-year Treasury issue is 6.5%. This means that the nominal spread over the on-the-Treasury issue for this corporate bond is 80 basis points. The investor expects that:

- He can reinvest the coupon payments (there will be two of them over the 1-year investment horizon) at 6%.
- The Treasury yield curve will shift down by 25 basis points and remains flat at the end of 1 year, so that the yield for the 19-year Treasury issue is 6.25% (6.5% minus 25 basis points).
- The spread to the 19-year Treasury issue is unchanged at 80 basis points so the horizon yield is 7.05% (6.25% plus 80 basis points).

The calculations are as shown below.

Step 1: Compute the total coupon payments plus the reinvestment income assuming an annual reinvestment rate of 6% or 3% every six months. The semiannual coupon payments are $3. The future value of an annuity can be used or because the investment horizon is only one year, it can be computed as follows:

First coupon payment reinvested for six months = $3 (1.03)   = $3.09
Second coupon payment not reinvested since at horizon date = $3.00
Total   = $6.09

Step 2: The horizon price at the end of the 1-year investment horizon is determined as follows. The horizon yield is 7.05% by assumption. The 6% coupon 20-year corporate bond now has 19 years to maturity. The price of this bond when discounted at a flat 7.05% yield (the yield curve is assumed to be flat) is $89.0992.

Step 3: Adding the amounts in Steps 2 and 3 gives the total future dollars of $95.1892.

Step 4: Compute the following (*h* is 2 in our illustration):

$$\left(\frac{\$95.1892}{\$86.4365}\right)^{1/2} - 1 = 4.94\%$$

Step 5: The total return on a bond-equivalent basis and on an effective rate basis are shown as follows:

$2 \times 4.94\% = 9.88\%$ (BEY)

$(1.0494)^2 - 1 = 10.13\%$ (effective rate basis)

Calculating the Total Return for a MBS and ABS

The calculation of the total return illustrated thus far was for a bond that pays interest semiannually. In calculating total return of mortgage-backed and asset-backed securities, the total return calculation must give recognition to the fact that there will be principal repayments (scheduled and prepayments) that are received before the end of the investment horizon. Therefore, the total future dollars will depend on (1) the projected principal repayment (scheduled plus projected prepayments) and (2) the interest earned on reinvestment of the projected interest payments and the projected principal payments. Moreover, to obtain the total future dollars, a prepayment rate over the investment horizon must be assumed in order to obtain the projected prepayments.

In addition, since typically MBS and ABS pay monthly, the monthly total return is then found using the formula:

$$\text{monthly total return} = \left(\frac{\text{total future dollars}}{\text{full price}} \right)^{\frac{1}{\text{number of months in horizon}}} - 1$$

The monthly total return can be annualized on a bond-equivalent yield basis as follows:

$$\text{bond-equivalent annual return} = 2[(1 + \text{monthly total return})^6 - 1]$$

or, by computing the effective annual return as follows:

$$\text{effective annual return} = (1 + \text{monthly total return})^{12} - 1$$

OAS-Total Return

In Chapter 19, the OAS was described. The OAS can be incorporated into a total return analysis to determine the horizon price. This requires a valuation model. At the end of the investment horizon, it is necessary to specify how the OAS is expected to change. The horizon price can be "backed out" of a valuation model. This technique can be extended to the total return framework by making assumptions about the required variables at the horizon date.

Assumptions about the OAS value at the investment horizon reflect the expectations of the portfolio manager. It is common to assume that the OAS at the horizon date will be the same as the OAS at the time of purchase. A total return calculated using this assumption is referred to as a *constant-OAS total return*. Alternatively, active managers will make bets on how the OAS will change—either widening or tightening. The total return framework can be used to assess how sensitive the performance of a bond with an embedded option is to changes in the OAS.

Portfolio Total Return

The appropriate measure for assessing the potential performance of a portfolio is total return. This is determined by first calculating the total future dollars of each bond in the portfolio under a given scenario considering horizon yields, reinvestment rates, spreads, and, if applicable, prepayment rates. The sum of all the total future dollars for each bond in the portfolio is then calculated. The portfolio total return is then found as explained earlier for a given bond: It is the interest rate that will make the market value of the portfolio today grow to the portfolio's total future dollars.

Total Return Analysis for Multiple Scenarios

The obvious problem with total return as we have presented it thus far is that it is based on one set of underlying assumptions regarding the factors that affect return over some investment horizon. In practice, more than one scenario for the factors that impact the total return are analyzed. There are two approaches used: scenario analysis and Monte Carlo simulation analysis.

Scenario Analysis

To test the sensitivity of the total return to the underlying assumptions, a technique called *scenario analysis* is used. This technique involves evaluating the total return under different scenarios defined by the manager. Scenario analysis can be used to assess potential trades. For each scenario, one or more trades can be assessed relative to each other or some other benchmark (such as a funding cost or a bond market index). Regulators also require certain institutions to perform scenario analysis based on assumptions specified by regulations.

As an illustration of scenario analysis for a single bond, FHLMC (Freddie Mac) 1407-PF was analyzed on 8/31/98 using the analytics of Capital Management Sciences. The tranche was a planned amortization class (PAC) tranche trading at 99.697.[1] (For this PAC tranche the support tranches had been paid off, so it was called a "busted" PAC.) The OAS was 75 basis points and the average life was 0.67 years.

---

[1] PAC tranches are explained in Chapter 17.

Exhibit 22.1 shows the total return based on the assumptions shown in the exhibit. Note the assumption regarding the reinvestment rate (4.618%). The investment horizon is three months. The assumed change in yield is shown in the first column and the corresponding 3-month total return is reported in the second column. The price at the investment horizon is shown in the third column. Notice that the price is based on the PSA assumption shown in the fourth column. The base case (i.e., zero yield change) is 500 PSA. Prepayments are assumed to be faster when rates decline and slower when rates increase. The bottom of Exhibit 22.1 shows a graph of the total return.

Exhibit 22.2 shows the results of a total return analysis for a scenario in which the Treasury rates decrease and the OAS on the PAC tranche being analyzed widens. Specifically, the top panel of the exhibit shows the Treasury yield curve at the beginning of the horizon and the assumed curve at the end of the horizon, three months later. The spread on the collateral and the spread on the PAC tranche are assumed to increase by 15 basis points at the end of the horizon. The 3-month total return shown in the exhibit is 0.79%. The lower panel of the exhibit shows the composition of the total return for the assumed scenario. The major source of return is the income (0.96). The total return was reduced by rolling down the yield curve ("yield curve roll") which resulted in a reduction of 22 basis points.

Monte Carlo Simulation Analysis

The total return of a bond portfolio depends on the outcome of a number of factors. For example, a portfolio's total return will depend on the magnitude of the change in Treasury rates, the spread between non-Treasury and Treasury securities, changes in the shape of the yield curve, changes in the quality rating of individual corporate bond issues, and actual prepayment speeds in the case of mortgage-backed securities. Each variable may have a substantial number of possible outcomes. Consequently, to evaluate all possible combinations of outcomes in order to assess the risks associated with a portfolio may be impractical.

For example, suppose that a portfolio manager wants to assess the potential performance of a portfolio over a 1-year investment horizon. Suppose further that the portfolio's performance will be determined by the actual outcome for each of nine variables and that each of the nine variables has seven possible outcomes for the return. There would then be 4,782,969 (9^7) possible outcomes representing all possible combinations of the nine variables. Furthermore, each of the 4,782,969 outcomes will not have the same probability of occurrence.

EXHIBIT 22.1   Total Return for a FHLMC 1407 PF
Pricing Date 8/31/98

Horizon:	3 months	Issuer:	FHLMC 1407-PF	
Reinv. Rate	4.618	Coupon:	6.250%	
		Maturity:	10/15/16	
		Yield:	6.369%	

			PSA Speed (%)		
Yield Change	Return (%)	Price($)	Lifetime	12 Month	CPR[a]
−300	1.44	99.801	650	969	39.00
−250	1.46	99.764	650	969	39.00
−200	1.47	99.721	650	969	39.00
−150	1.49	99.672	647	965	38.82
−100	1.50	99.642	644	960	38.64
−50	1.51	99.641	597	890	35.83
0	1.45	99.596	500	729	30.00
50	1.28	99.429	355	472	21.30
100	0.97	99.115	223	240	13.38
150	0.52	98.657	160	147	9.57
200	−0.03	98.112	141	137	8.46
250	−0.60	97.538	131	130	7.87
300	−1.18	96.954	122	117	7.32

[a] Conditional prepayment rate

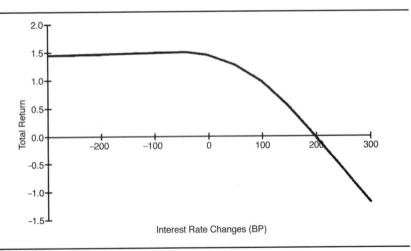

Source: Illustration provided by Capital Management Sciences.

EXHIBIT 22.2 Scenario Analysis for FHLMC 1407-PF Assuming a Downward Shift in the Yield

Scenario assumptions:

3-month investment horizon

4.618% reinvestment rate

Treasury yield curve shift:

Maturity	Initial Yield	Horizon Yield
6 months	4.595%	4.095%
1 year	4.595	4.102
2 years	5.532	4.052
3 years	5.539	4.073
5 years	4.555	4.116
7 years	4.570	4.158
10 years	4.578	4.207
20 years	5.279	5.043
30 years	5.246	5.146

Change in spread of agency collateral to Treasuries: 15 basis points
Change in spread of PACs: 15 basis points

Total return analysis: 3-month return = 0.79%

Composition of return:

Income	0.96%
Price change due to:	
Change in parallel rates	−0.03%
Change in slope	0.08%
Yield curve roll	−0.21%
Change in mortgage spreads	−0.01%

Source: Illustration provided by Capital Management Sciences, Inc.

At the other extreme, a portfolio manager can take the "best guess" for the value of each variable and determine the impact on return. The best-guess value of each variable is usually the expected value of the variable. There are serious problems with this shortcut approach. To understand the shortcomings of the best-guess approach, suppose the probability associated with the best guess for each variable is 75%. If the probability distribution for each variable is independently distributed, then the probability of occurrence for the best-guess result would be only 7.5% (0.75^9). A portfolio manager should not place a great deal of confidence in this best-guess result.

EXHIBIT 22.3   Total Return Distributions: FHLMC 151C versus U.S. Treasury
Benchmark

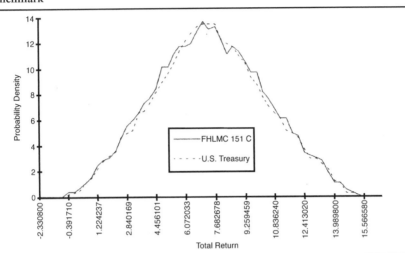

Between the extremes of enumerating and evaluating all possible combinations and the best-guess approach is the simulation approach. Simulation is more of a procedure than a model. The solutions obtained will not generate an optimal solution to a problem. Rather, simulation provides information about the problem so that a portfolio manager can assess the risks of a particular course of action.

There are many types of simulation techniques. When probability distributions are assigned to the variables, the simulation technique is known as a *Monte Carlo simulation*. By employing Monte Carlo simulation, a portfolio manager can determine the statistical properties of a problem that he or she faces. Using this information, a portfolio manager can select the most prudent course of action.

To illustrate the application of simulation, we use a total return simulation based on an investment horizon of two years and assuming interim cash flows are reinvested in Treasury strips that mature at the horizon date. The total return for each trial is calculated assuming a constant OAS. There are 200 trials for each simulation. The illustration involves comparing a FHLMC 151 C tranche (a PAC tranche) to a U.S. Treasury benchmark consisting of a combination of 3-year and 5-year on-the-run Treasuries.[2] The coupon rate for the tranche and the passthrough coupon

---

[2] This illustration is from David E. Canuel and Charles F. Melchreit, "Total Return Analysis in CMO Portfolio Management," Chapter 4 in Frank J. Fabozzi (ed.), *Advances in the Valuation and Management of Mortgage-Backed Securities* (New Hope, PA: Frank J. Fabozzi Associates, 1998).

rate are both 9%. Exhibit 22.3 graphs the results of the simulation, a total return distribution for the tranche versus the U.S. Treasury benchmark. The PAC tranche has a total return distribution similar to that of the Treasury benchmark because of the high degree of prepayment protection at the time of issuance (an initial PAC collar of 90 to 270 PSA).

Exhibit 22.4 shows the distribution for the spread between the tranche's total return and the Treasury benchmark's total return for each trial. This exhibit provides further insight into the relative performance of the tranche and the Treasury benchmark that is not evident from Exhibit 22.3. The distribution has a tail to the left, which reduces the mean of the distribution significantly. The mean of the PAC distribution is 59 basis points above that of the Treasury distribution, while the spread in the total return of the PAC was 75 basis points.

MANAGING VERSUS A BOND MARKET INDEX

When the benchmark is a bond market index, the first step that the manager must undertake is to understand that index. We shall refer to the bond market index as the "benchmark index." So, we begin our discussion with a review of the various types of bond market indexes.

Bond Market Indexes

Bond market indexes are classified as broad-based U.S. bond market indexes, specialized U.S. bond market indexes, and global and international bond market indexes.

EXHIBIT 22.4   Total Return Differences: FHLMC 151C versus U.S. Treasury Benchmark

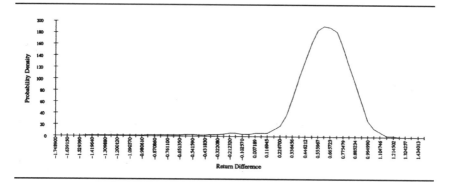

EXHIBIT 22.5 Percentage Composition of Lehman Brothers U.S. Aggregate Index as of September 31, 2001

Sector	Percent of Market Value
Treasury	23.44%
Agency	11.27
Mortgage Passthroughs	34.76
Commercial Mortgage-Backed Securities	1.95
Asset-Backed Securities	1.75
Credit	26.83
Total	100.00%

Source: Lehman Brothers, *Global Relative Value,* Fixed Income Research, September 4, 2001, p. 2.

Broad-Based U.S. Bond Market Indexes

The three broad-based U.S. bond market indexes most commonly used by institutional investors are the Lehman Brothers U.S. Aggregate Index, the Salomon Smith Barney (SSB) Broad Investment-Grade Bond Index (BIG), and the Merrill Lynch Domestic Market Index. There are more than 5,500 issues in each index. Each index is broken into sectors. The Lehman index, for example, is divided into the following six sectors: (1) Treasury sector, (2) agency sector, (3) mortgage passthrough sector, (4) commercial mortgage-backed securities sector, (5) asset-backed securities sector, and (6) credit sector. Exhibit 22.5 shows the percentage composition of the index as of August 31, 2001.

The agency sector includes agency debentures, not mortgage-backed or asset-backed securities issued by federal agencies. The mortgage passthrough sector includes agency passthrough securities—Ginnie Mae, Fannie Mae, and Freddie Mac passthrough securities. Thus, agency collateralized mortgage obligations and agency stripped mortgage-backed securities are not included. These mortgage derivatives products are not included because it would be double counting since they are created from agency passthroughs. In constructing the index for the mortgage sector for the Lehman index, for example, Lehman groups more than 800,000 individual mortgage pools with a fixed-rate coupon into generic aggregates. These generic aggregates are defined in terms of agency (i.e., Ginnie Mae, Fannie Mae, and Freddie Mac), program type (i.e., 30-year, 15-year, balloon mortgages, etc.), coupon rate for the passthrough, and the year the passthrough was originated (i.e., vintage).

The credit sector in the Lehman Brothers index includes corporate issues. In the other two U.S. broad-based bond market indexes, this sector is referred to as the corporate sector. All issues included in the credit sector, as well as the ABS and CMBS sector, are those that have an investment-grade rating (i.e., at least BBB–).

Specialized U.S. Bond Market Indexes

The specialized U.S. bond market indexes focus on one sector of the bond market or a subsector of the bond market. Indexes on sectors of the market are published by the three firms that produce the broad-based U.S. bond market indexes. Nonbrokerage firms have created specialized indexes for sectors. For example, the three that have created the broad-based indexes and the firms of CS First Boston and Donaldson Lufkin and Jenrette have created indexes for the high-yield bond sector (i.e., issues rates below BBB–).

Global and International Bond Market Indexes

The growth in non-U.S. bond investing has resulted in a proliferation of international bond market indexes. Three types of indexes are available that include non-U.S. bonds. The first is an index that includes both U.S. and non-U.S. bonds. Such indexes are referred to as *global bond indexes*. The second type includes only non-U.S. bonds and is commonly referred to as *ex-U.S. bond indexes*. Finally, there are specialized bond indexes for particular non-U.S. bond sectors. Indexes can be reported on a hedged currency basis and/or an unhedged currency basis.

The Spectrum of Strategies

A good way to understand the spectrum of bond portfolio strategies for managing versus a benchmark index and the key elements of each strategy is in terms of the benchmark established by the client. This is depicted in Exhibit 22.6. The exhibit, developed by Kenneth Volpert of the Vanguard Group, shows the risk and return of a strategy versus a benchmark. Volpert classifies the strategies as follows:

1. Pure bond index matching
2. Enhanced indexing/ matching primary risk factors
3. Enhanced indexing/minor risk factor mismatches
4. Active management/larger risk factor mismatches
5. Active management/full-blown active

We discuss each of these strategies in the following sections.

The key is the match or mismatch of a portfolio's risk exposure relative to the risk exposure of a benchmark index. The risk of a benchmark index can be decomposed into several major or primary risks.

Most of these are the risk discussed earlier in this chapter. However, there are other risks associated with managing a portfolio relative to a benchmark index. These risks result from the difference in the exposure of portfolio relative to the same risk in the benchmark index. The difference between indexing and active management is the extent to which the portfolio can deviate from the primary or major risk factors associated with the benchmark index.

The primary risk factors associated with a benchmark index are:

1. The duration of the index
2. The present value distribution of the cash flows
3. Percent in sector and quality
4. Duration contribution of sector[3]
5. Duration contribution of credit quality
6. Sector/coupon/maturity cell weights
7. Issuer exposure control

EXHIBIT 22.6   Bond Management Risk Spectrum

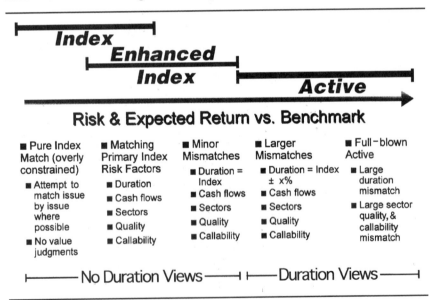

Source: Exhibit 1 in Kenneth E. Volpert, "Managing Indexed and Enhanced Indexed Bond Portfolios," Chapter 4 in Frank J. Fabozzi (ed.), *Fixed Income Readings for the Chartered Financial Analysts Program* (New Hope, PA: Frank J. Fabozzi Associates, 2000).

---

[3] Duration contribution of a sector is explained in Chapter 21.

Pure Bond Indexing Strategy

In terms of risk and return, a pure bond index matching strategy involves the least risk of underperforming the benchmark index. Several factors explain the popularity of bond indexing. First, the empirical evidence suggests that historically the overall performance of active bond managers has been poor. The second factor is the lower advisory management fees charged for an indexed portfolio compared to active management advisory fees. Advisory fees charged by active managers typically range from 15 to 50 basis points. The range for indexed portfolios, in contrast, is 1 to 20 basis points (with the upper range representing the fees for enhanced indexing discussed later). Some pension plan sponsors have decided to do away with advisory fees and to manage some or all of their funds in-house following an indexing strategy. Lower nonadvisory fees, such as custodial fees, is the third explanation for the popularity of bond indexing.

Critics of indexing point out that while an indexing strategy matches the performance of some bond market index, the performance of that index does not necessarily represent optimal performance. Moreover, matching an index does not mean that the manager will satisfy a client's return requirement objective. For example, if the objective of a life insurance company or a pension fund is to have sufficient funds to satisfy a predetermined liability, indexing only reduces the likelihood that performance will not be materially worse than the index. The return on the index is not necessarily related to the liability.

The pure bond indexing strategy involves creating a portfolio so as to replicate the issues comprising the benchmark index. This means that the indexed portfolio is a mirror image of the index. However, a manager pursuing this strategy will encounter several logistical problems in constructing an indexed portfolio. First of all, the prices for each issue used by the organization that publishes the index may not be execution prices available to the manager. In fact, they may be materially different from the prices offered by some dealers. In addition, the prices used by organizations reporting the value of indexes are based on bid prices. Dealer ask prices, however, are the ones that the manager would have to transact at when constructing or rebalancing the indexed portfolio. Thus there will be a bias between the performance of the index and the indexed portfolio that is equal to the bid-ask spread.

Furthermore, there are logistical problems unique to certain sectors in the bond market. Consider first the corporate bond market. There are more than 4,000 issues in the corporate bond sector of a broad-based bond market index. Because of the illiquidity for many of the issues, not only may the prices used by the organization that publishes the index be unreliable, but also many of the issues may not even be available. Next, consider the mortgage sector. There are over 800,000 agency passthrough issues. As explained earlier, the organizations that publish indexes aggregate all these issues into a few hundred generic issues. The manager is then faced with the difficult task of finding passthrough securities with the same risk/return profile of these hypothetical generic issues.

How does a manager construct a portfolio to replicate a benchmark index? Two approaches for doing so are the cell approach and the multi-factor risk model approach. Both approaches are discussed in Chapter 23. Each approach assumes that the performance of an individual bond depends on a number of systematic factors that affect the performance of all bonds and on a factor unique to the individual issue. This last risk is *diversifiable risk*. The objective of the two approaches is to construct an indexed portfolio that eliminates this diversifiable risk.

Enhanced Indexing/Matching Primary Risk Factors Approach

An enhanced indexing strategy can be pursued so as to construct a portfolio to match the primary risk factors without acquiring each issue in the index. This is a common strategy used by smaller funds because of the difficulties of acquiring all of the issues comprising the index. While in the spectrum of strategies defined by Volpert this strategy is called an "enhanced indexing strategy," some investors refer to this as simply an indexing strategy.

Enhanced Indexing/Minor Risk Factor Mismatches

Another enhanced indexing strategy is one where the portfolio is constructed so as to have minor deviations from the risk factors that affect the performance of the benchmark index. For example, there might be a slight overweighting of issues or sectors where the manager believes there is relative value. However, it is important to point out that the duration of the constructed portfolio is matched to the duration of the index. This is depicted in Exhibit 22.6 which shows that there are no duration bets for the pure indexing strategy and the two enhanced indexing strategies.

Active Management/Larger Risk Factor Mismatches

Active bond strategies are those that attempt to outperform the market by intentionally constructing a portfolio that will have a greater index mismatch than in the case of enhanced indexing. The decision to pursue an active strategy or to engage a client to request a manager to pursue an active strategy must be based on the belief that there is some type of gain from such costly efforts; for there to be a gain, pricing inefficiencies must exist. The particular strategy chosen depends on why the manager believes this is the case.

Volpert classifies two types of active strategies. In the more conservative of the two active strategies, the manager makes larger mismatches relative to the benchmark index in terms of risk factors. This includes minor mismatches of duration. Typically, there will be a limitation as to the degree of duration mismatch. For example, the manager may be constrained to be within +1 of the duration of the benchmark index. So, if the duration of the benchmark index is 4, the manager may have a duration between 3 and 5. To take advantage of anticipated reshaping of the yield curve, there can be significant differences in the cash flow distribution between the benchmark index and the portfolio constructed by the manager. As another example, if the manager believes that within the corporate sector A rated issues will outperform AA rated issues, the manager may overweight the A rated issues and underweight AA rated issues.

Active Management/Full-Blown Active

In the full-blown active management case, the manager is permitted to make a significant duration bet without any constraint. The manager can have a duration of zero (i.e., be all in cash) or can leverage the portfolio to a high multiple of the duration of the index. The manager can decide not to invest in only one or more of the major sectors of the broad-based bond market indexes. The manager can make a significant allocation to sectors not included in the index. For example, there can be a substantial allocation to nonagency mortgage-backed securities.

We will discuss various strategies used in active portfolio management in the next section.

Value Added Strategies

Active portfolio strategies and enhanced indexing/minor risk factor mismatch strategies seek to generate additional return after adjusting for risk. We shall refer to these strategies as *value added strategies*. These strategies can be classified as strategic strategies and tactical strategies.

Strategic strategies, sometimes referred to as *top-down value added strategies*, involve the following:

1. Interest rate expectations strategies
2. Yield curve strategies
3. Inter- and intra-sector allocation strategies

Tactical strategies, sometimes referred to as *relative value strategies*, are short-term trading strategies. They include:

1. Strategies based on rich/cheap analysis

2. Yield curve trading strategies
3. Return enhancing strategies employing futures and options

Below we discuss the first two strategies. Strategies involving futures and options for adding incremental return are basically the same as those used by common stock portfolio managers using equity derivatives. These strategies are discussed in Chapter 15.

Interest Rate Expectations Strategies

A manager who believes that he can accurately forecast the future level of interest rates will alter the portfolio's duration based on his forecast. As duration is a measure of interest rate sensitivity, this involves increasing a portfolio's duration if interest rates are expected to fall and reducing duration if interest rates are expected to rise. For those managers whose benchmark is a bond market index, this means increasing the portfolio duration relative to the benchmark index if interest rates are expected to fall and reducing it if interest rates are expected to rise. The degree to which the duration of the managed portfolio is permitted to diverge from that of the benchmark index may be limited by the client. Interest rate expectations strategies are commonly referred to as *duration strategies*.

A portfolio's duration may be altered in the cash market by swapping (or exchanging) bonds in the portfolio for new bonds that will achieve the target portfolio duration. Alternatively, a more efficient means for altering the duration of a bond portfolio is to use interest rate futures contracts. As we explain in Chapter 25, buying futures increases a portfolio's duration, while selling futures decreases it.

The key to this active strategy is, of course, an ability to forecast the direction of future interest rates. The academic literature does not support the view that interest rates can be forecasted so that risk-adjusted excess returns can be consistently realized. It is doubtful whether betting on future interest rates will provide a consistently superior return.

Yield Curve Strategies

The yield curve for U.S. Treasury securities shows the relationship between maturity and yield. The shape of the yield curve changes over time. A shift in the yield curve refers to the relative change in the yield for each Treasury maturity. A parallel shift in the yield curve refers to a shift in which the change in the yield for all maturities is the same. A nonparallel shift in the yield curve means that the yield for every maturity does not change by the same number of basis points.

Top-down yield curve strategies involve positioning a portfolio to capitalize on expected changes in the shape of the Treasury yield curve. There are three yield curve strategies: (1) bullet strategies, (2) barbell strategies, and (3) ladder strategies. In a *bullet strategy*, the portfolio is constructed so that the maturity of the bonds in the portfolio are highly concentrated at one point on the yield curve. In a *barbell strategy*, the maturity of the bonds included in the portfolio is concentrated at two short-term and long-term maturities. Actually, in practice when managers refer to a barbell strategy it is relative to a bullet strategy. For example, a bullet strategy might be to create a portfolio with maturities concentrated around 10 years while a corresponding barbell strategy might be a portfolio with 5-year and 20-year maturities. In a ladder strategy the portfolio is constructed to have approximately equal amounts of each maturity. So, for example, a portfolio might have equal amounts of bonds with one year to maturity, two years to maturity, etc.

Each of these strategies will result in different performance when the yield curve shifts. The actual performance will depend on both the type of shift and the magnitude of the shift. When this strategy is applied by a manager whose benchmark is a broad-based bond market index, there is a mismatching of maturities relative to the benchmark index in one or more of the maturity sectors.

Inter- and Intra-Sector Allocation Strategies

A manager can allocate funds among the major bond sectors that is different from that the allocation in the benchark index. This is referred to as an *inter-sector allocation strategy* and results in *sector spread risk*. Several duration measures that we discussed in Chapter 21 provide information about the level of exposure to sector spread risk. First is the difference in the spread duration between the benchmark index and the portfolio. The second is the difference in the contribution to spread duration for each sector in the benchmark index and the corresponding sector in the portfolio.

In making inter- and intra-sector allocations, a manager is anticipating how spreads will change. Spreads reflect differences in credit risk, call risk (or prepayment risk), and liquidity risk. When the spread for a particular sector or subsector is expected to decline or "narrow," a manager may decide to overweight that particular sector or subsector. It will be underweighted if the manager expects the spread to increase or "widen."

Credit or quality spreads change because of expected changes in economic prospects. Credit spreads between Treasury and non-Treasury issues widen in a declining or contracting economy and narrow during economic expansion. The economic rationale is that in a declining or contracting economy, corporations experience a decline in revenue and cash flow, making it difficult for corporate issuers to service their contractual debt obligations. To induce investors to hold non-Treasury securities, the yield spread relative to Treasury securities must widen. The converse is that during economic expansion and brisk economic activity, revenue and cash flow pick up, increasing the likelihood that corporate issuers will have the capacity to service their contractual debt obligations.

A manager therefore can use economic forecasts of the economy in developing forecasts of credit spreads. Also, some managers base forecasts on historical credit spreads. The underlying principle is that there is a "normal" credit spread relationship that exists. If the current credit spread in the market differs materially from that "normal" credit spread, then the manager should position the portfolio so as to benefit from a return to the "normal" credit spread. The assumption is that the "normal" credit spread is some type of average or mean value and that mean reversion will occur. If, in fact, there has been a structural shift in the marketplace, this may not occur as the normal spread may change.

A manager will also look at technical factors to assess relative value. For example, a manager may analyze the prospective supply and demand for new issues on spreads in individual sectors or issuers to determine whether they should be overweighted or underweighted. This commonly used tactical strategy is referred to as *primary market analysis*.

Now let's look at spreads due to call or prepayment risk. Expectations about how these spreads will change will affect the inter-sector allocation decision between Treasury securities and spread products that have call risk. Corporate and agency bonds have callable and noncallable issue, all mortgages are prepayable, and asset-backed securities have products that are callable but borrowers may be unlikely to exercise the call. Consequently, with sectors having different degrees of call risk, expectations about how spreads will change also affect intra-allocation decisions. They affect (1) the allocation between callable and noncallable bonds within the corporate bond sector and (2) within the agency, corporate, mortgage, and ABS sectors the allocation among premium (i.e., high coupon), par, and discount (i.e., low coupon) bonds.

Spreads due to call risk will change as a result of expected changes in (1) the direction of the change in interest rates and (2) interest rate volatility. An expected drop in the level of interest rates will widen the yield spread between callable bonds and noncallable bonds as the prospects that the issuer will exercise the call option increase. The reverse is true: The spread narrows if interest rates are expected to rise. An increase in interest rate volatility increases the value of the embedded call option, and thereby increases the spread between (1) callable bonds and noncallable bonds and (2) premium and discount bonds.

EXHIBIT 22.7 Total Return Scenario Analysis for Various Degrees of Leverage

Assumed Yield 6 Months From Now (%)	Annual Return for $1 Million of Equity and Debt of $X Million					
	$0	$1	$2	$4	$5	$11
10.00	−29.8%	−68.5%	−107.3%	−146.0%	−223.6%	−456.1%
9.50	−21.5	−52.1	−82.6	−113.2	174.2	−357.5
9.00	−12.6	−34.1	−55.7	−77.2	120.4	−249.7
8.50	−2.8	−14.5	−26.3	−38.0	61.6	−132.1
8.00	8.0	7.0	6.0	5.0	3.0	−3.0
7.50	19.8	30.6	41.5	52.3	73.9	138.8
7.00	32.8	56.6	80.5	104.3	151.9	294.8
6.50	47.2	85.3	123.5	161.6	238.0	466.9
6.00	63.0	117.0	171.1	225.1	333.1	657.2

Leveraging Strategies

The investment principle of borrowing funds in the hope of earning a return in excess of the cost of funds is called *leveraging*. The attractive feature of leveraging is that it magnifies the return that will be realized from investment in a security for a given change in the price of that security. That's the good news. The bad news is that leveraging also magnifies any loss.

To illustrate this point, consider an investor who wants to purchase a 30-year U.S. Treasury bond in anticipation of a decline in interest rates 6 months from now. Suppose that the investor has $1 million to invest. The $1 million is referred to as the investor's equity. Assuming that the coupon rate for the 30-year Treasury bond is 8% with the next coupon payment 6 months from now and the bond can be purchased at par value, then the investor can purchase $1 million of par value of an 8% coupon 30-year Treasury bond with the equity available.

The second column in Exhibit 22.7 shows a total return scenario analysis for various yields 6 months from now at which the 8% coupon 30-year Treasury bond will trade. The dollar return consists of the coupon payment 6 months from now and the change in the value of the 30-year Treasury bond. At the end of 6 months, the 30-year Treasury bond is a 29.5-year Treasury bond. The total return is found by dividing the dollar return by the $1 million equity investment and then annualizing by simply multiplying by 2. Notice that the range for the total return based on the assumed yields 6 months from now ranges from −29.8% to +63.0%.

In our illustration, the investor did not borrow any funds. Hence, the strategy is referred to as an "unleveraged strategy." Now let's suppose that the investor can borrow $1 million to purchase an additional $1 million of par value of the 30-year 8% coupon Treasury bond. Assume further that the loan agreement specifies that: (1) the maturity of the loan is 6 months, (2) the annual interest rate is 9%, and (3) $2 million par value of the 30-year 8% coupon Treasury bond is used as collateral. Therefore, the loan is a collateralized loan. The collateral for this loan is the $1 million par value of the 30-year 8% Treasury bond purchased by the investor. The $2 million invested comes from the $1 million of equity and $1 million of borrowed funds. In this strategy, the investor is using leverage. The third column in Exhibit 22.7 shows the total return for this leveraged strategy assuming different yields at the end of 6 months. The total return is measured relative to the $1 million equity investment made by the investor, not the $2 million. The dollar return on the $1 million of equity invested adjusts for the cost of the borrowing. By using borrowed funds, the range for the total return is wider (–68.5% to +117.0%) than in the case where no funds are borrowed (–29.8% to 63.0%).

This example clearly shows how leveraging is a two-edged sword— it can magnify the total return both up and down. Notice that by not borrowing, if the market yield does not change at the end of 6 months, then the unleveraged strategy would have generated an 8% total return. In contrast, the leveraging strategy would produce only a 7% total return because while the value of the 30-year Treasury bond did not change, it cost the investor $45,000 to borrow $1 million for 6 months but only earned coupon interest of $40,000 on the $1 million.

Exhibit 22.7 also shows the total return for different amounts borrowed (i.e., for different degrees of leveraging). Effectively, what is leveraging doing? By leveraging, an investor is increasing the duration of a position. That is, the unleveraged position has a lower duration than a leveraged position. The greater amount borrowed, the greater the duration. Consequently, when interest rates rise, losses are magnified by the higher duration resulting from leveraging but when interest rates decline the opposite occurs.

Borrowing in the Bond Market

In the bond market, an investor can borrow funds to purchase a bond via collateralized borrowing. This means that funds are borrowed where the collateral for the loan is the bond purchased with the borrowed funds. This can be done by buying a bond on margin and the procedure is identical to the one described in Chapter 6 for buying stock on margin. However, institutional investors typically do not borrow funds using that mechanism. Rather, institutional investors borrow via another form of collateralized borrowing called a *repurchase agreement* or simply *repo*. The advantage to the investor of using the repo market for borrowing on a short-term basis is that the borrowing rate is lower than the cost of bank financing.

A repo is the sale of a security with a commitment by the seller to buy the same security back from the purchaser at a specified price at a designated future date. The price at which the seller must subsequently repurchase the security is called the *repurchase price*, and the date that the security must be repurchased is called the *repurchase date*.

To illustrate a repo agreement, suppose an investor wants to purchase $5 million of a particular Treasury security on a leveraged basis. In the repo market, the investor can use the $5 million of the Treasury security as collateral for a loan. The term of the loan and the interest rate that the dealer agrees to pay are specified. The interest rate is called the *repo rate*. When the term of the loan is 1 day, it is called an *overnight repo*; a loan for more than one day is called a *term repo*. The transaction is referred to as a repurchase agreement because it calls for the sale of the security and its repurchase at a future date. Both the sale price and the purchase price are specified in the agreement. The difference between the purchase (repurchase) price and the sale price is the dollar interest cost of the loan.[4]

Although there may be high-quality collateral underlying a repo transaction, both parties to the transaction are exposed to credit risk. Why does credit risk occur in a repo transaction? Consider our initial example where an investor uses $5 million of a Treasury security as collateral to borrow. If the investor cannot repurchase the security, the lender may keep the collateral; if interest rates increase subsequent to the repo transaction, however, the market value of the Treasury security will decline, and the lender will own securities with a market value less than the amount it lent to the investor. If the market value of the security rises instead because interest rates have declined, the investor will be concerned with the return of the collateral, which then has a market value higher than the loan.

Repos are carefully structured to reduce credit risk exposure. The amount lent is less than the market value of the security used as collateral, thereby providing the lender with some cushion in case the market

---

[4] In practice, the terminology about a repo is confusing. The entity loaning the funds is effectively making a short-term loan. The investor borrowing the funds is creating a leveraged position in the security. The convention in the industry is if the borrower is dealer firm trying to create a leveraged position, the repo is referred to as simply a repo. However, if a non-dealer firm is borrowing funds, then the repo is referred to as a "reverse repo."

value of the security declines. The amount by which the market value of the security used as collateral exceeds the value of the loan is called *repo margin* or simply margin. Margin is also referred to as the "haircut." Repo margin is generally between 1% and 3%. For borrowers of lower creditworthiness and/or when less liquid securities are used as collateral, the repo margin can be 10% or more. Another practice to limit credit risk is to mark the collateral to market on a regular basis. (Marking a position to market means recording the value of a position at its market value.) This practice assures that the market value of the collateral will be maintained at the necessary level. If the collateral's market value falls below the minimum amount, the investor will be required to post additional funds or securities. If the additional funds are not provided by the investor, the lender will sell the collateral to recover the amount lent. Consequently, when employing a leveraging strategy using repos, an investor must be prepared to put up additional funds.

Performance Attribution Analysis

As explained in Chapter 1, the assessment of the performance of a manager should be done using a methodology called *performance attribution analysis*. In Chapter 13, it is shown how the methodology is applied to assess the performance of common stock portfolio managers. We will illustrate a fixed income performance attribution model here.[5] The model used is that of a commercial vendor, Global Advanced Technology (G.A.T.) which was acquired by BARRA. This commercially available model decomposes a portfolio's total return into the following return factors: (1) static return, (2) interest sensitive returns, (3) spread change returns, and (4) trading return. The difference between the total return and the sum of the four factors is called the *residual* (or residual error). Each of the return factors can be further decomposed as described in this section.

The *static return* is the portion of a portfolio's total return that is attributable to "rolling down the yield curve." This return calculates how much is earned assuming a static (meaning zero volatility) world defined as one in which the yield curve evolves to its implied forward curve.[6] In turn, the static return can further be decomposed into two components: (1) *risk-free return* and (2) *accrual of OAS return*. The risk-free return is based on the assumption that the portfolio consists of only Treasury strips. The risk-free return is then calculated based on the rolling down of the yield curve. The accrual of OAS return is also calcu-

---

[5] This illustration is taken from Frank J. Jones and Leonard J. Peltzman, "Fixed Income Attribution Analysis," Chapter 28 in Frank J. Fabozzi (ed.), *Managing Fixed Income Portfolios* (New Hope, PA: Frank J. Fabozzi Associates, 1997).
[6] Implied forward rates are explained in Chapter 19.

lated from rolling down the yield curve. However, it is based on investment spread products.

The *interest sensitive return* is that portion of a portfolio's return attributable to changes in the level, slope, and shape of the entire yield curve. In turn, this return is decomposed into two components: (1) *effective duration return* and (2) *convexity return.* As explained in Chapter 21, key rate durations can be used to measure the sensitivity of a portfolio to changes in the shape of the yield curve. The effective duration return is the sum of returns attributable to each key rate duration. The convexity return is the return due to a change in the portfolio's duration over the evaluation period.

The *spread change return* is the portion of a portfolio's return that is due to changes in both (1) sector spreads and (2) individual security richness/cheapness. The portion of the spread return attributable to changes in the sector's OAS is called the *delta OAS return* and the spread return due to a widening or tightening of a specific issue's spread is called the *delta rich/cheap return.*

The portion of a portfolio's total return that is attributable to changes in the composition of the portfolio is called the *trading return.* This return allows for the identification of a manager's value added by changing the composition of the portfolio as opposed to a simple buy-and-hold strategy.

In the illustration, an attribution analysis is performed on a portfolio of corporate securities. We will refer to this portfolio as Portfolio A. The evaluation period is the month of September 1996, a month when the yield curve shifted downward. The shift was almost a parallel shift. The effective duration for Portfolio A was 7.09. The benchmark index is the Merrill Lynch Corporate Index. The effective duration for the index is 5.76. Thus, Portfolio A had a larger duration than the benchmark index (7.09 versus 5.76).

Exhibit 22.8 presents the results of the attribution analysis for the portfolio and by sector. Exhibit 22.9 provides a summary of the analysis. The return on Portfolio A was 2.187% while that on the benchmark index was 1.954%. Thus, Portfolio A outperformed the index by 23 bps during September.

Because the yield curve shifted downward in an almost parallel fashion, Portfolio A would be expected to outperform the benchmark index because of the portfolio's larger duration. This is captured in the interest sensitive return. Exhibit 22.9 indicates that holding all other factors constant, the outperformance would have been 37.9 basis points. The reason why Portfolio A did not outperform by that much was due to the spread change return which was −18.5 basis points. The static return and the trading return were minimal.

EXHIBIT 22.8 Performance Attribution Analysis Example

Portfolio A: $3.0 billion corporate bond portfolio with an effective duration of 7.09

Merrill Corporate Index: Benchmark index with a duration of 5.76

	% of Portfolio	Total Return	Static Return	Interest Sensitive Return	Spread Change Return	Trading Return	Residual
Portfolio Totals							
Portfolio A	100.000	2.187	0.453	1.813	−0.087	−0.003	0.011
Merrill Corporate	100.000	1.954	0.452	1.433	0.098	0.000	−0.029
Difference	0.000	0.233	0.001	0.379	−0.185	−0.003	0.040
Sector Analysis*							
Agencies							
Portfolio A	0.000	0.000	0.000	0.000	0.000	0.000	0.000
Merrill Corporate	12.044	2.083	0.476	1.918	−0.118	0.000	−0.193
Difference	−12.044	−2.083	−0.476	−1.918	−0.118	0.000	0.193
Industrials							
Portfolio A	31.480	2.325	0.459	1.924	−0.026	−0.059	0.027
Merrill Corporate	26.769	2.121	0.460	1.606	0.108	0.000	−0.053
Difference	7.711	0.204	−0.001	0.318	−0.134	−0.059	0.080
Financials							
Portfolio A	15.580	2.023	0.439	1.560	0.077	−0.057	0.004
Merrill Corporate	37.363	1.707	0.444	1.210	0.060	0.000	−0.008
Difference	−21.783	0.316	−0.006	0.350	0.017	−0.057	0.012
Utilities							
Portfolio A	15.900	0.310	0.528	−0.090	0.540	0.042	−0.711
Merrill Corporate	7.385	2.167	0.469	1.564	0.185	0.000	−0.051
Difference	8.515	−1.857	0.060	−1.654	0.356	0.042	−0.660
Telephones							
Portfolio A	17.080	2.439	0.439	1.843	0.027	0.144	−0.014
Merrill Corporate	4.440	2.331	0.447	1.723	0.201	0.000	−0.040
Difference	12.640	0.108	−0.008	0.120	−0.174	0.144	0.026
Oil							
Portfolio A	4.940	0.562	0.467	2.035	−1.939	0.000	0.000
Merrill Corporate	1.670	2.123	0.462	1.513	0.194	0.000	−0.047
Difference	3.270	−1.561	0.004	0.522	−2.133	0.000	−0.047
Internationals							
Portfolio A	14.180	2.264	0.443	1.891	−0.079	0.021	−0.011
Merrill Corporate	10.022	2.118	0.446	1.597	0.095	0.000	−0.021
Difference	4.158	0.147	−0.004	0.294	−0.174	0.021	0.010
Miscellaneous							
Portfolio A	0.000	0.000	0.000	0.000	0.000	0.000	0.000
Merrill Corporate	0.308	0.796	0.416	0.384	−0.025	0.000	0.021
Difference	0.308	−0.796	−0.416	−0.384	0.025	0.000	−0.021

* In the sector analyses, we are comparing the constituents of Portfolio A that fall into a particular sector to the constituents of the benchmark that fall into the same sector. For example, the industrials from Portfolio A are being evaluated against the industrials from the Merrill Corporate Index.

EXHIBIT 22.9 Summary of Performance Attribution Analysis

Risk Factor	Portfolio A Returns (bps)	Merrill Corporate Index Returns (bps)	Difference	% of Total Return Difference
Static Return	45.3	45.2	0.1	0.4%
Interest Sensitive Return	181.3	143.3	37.9	162.7%
Spread Change Return	−8.7	9.8	−18.5	−79.4%
Trading Return	−0.3	0.0	−0.3	−1.3%
Residual	0.1	−2.9	4.0	17.2%
Total	218.7	195.4	23.3	100%

Exhibit 22.8 provides information about the sector bets that the manager made (i.e., underweighting or overweighting). It shows how the allocation paid off for each sector.

MANAGING FUNDS AGAINST LIABILITIES

When the manager faces liabilities, using a bond market index as the benchmark is inappropriate. Instead, the liabilities themselves are the benchmark. In this section we discuss two strategies for managing funds where the benchmark is a single liability payment or a series of liability payments. The two strategies are immunization and cash flow matching. Immunization is a hybrid strategy having elements of both active and passive strategies. It is used to minimize the risk of reinvestment over a specified investment horizon. Immunization can be employed to structure a portfolio designed to fund a single liability or multiple liabilities. Cash flow matching is used to construct a portfolio designed to fund a schedule of liabilities from portfolio return and asset value, with the portfolio's value diminishing to zero after payment of the last liability.

Immunization

Classical immunization is defined as the process by which a fixed income portfolio is created having an assured return for a specific time horizon irrespective of interest rate changes.[7] In a concise form, the fol-

---

[7] The classical theory of immunization was set forth in F. M. Reddington, "Review of the Principles of Life Insurance Valuations," *Journal of the Institute of Actuaries*, 1952; and Lawrence Fisher and Roman Weil, "Coping with Risk of Interest Rate Fluctuations: Returns to Bondholders from Naive and Optimal Strategies," *Journal of Business* (October 1971), pp. 408–431.

lowing are the important characteristics: (1) a specified time horizon; (2) an assured rate of return during the holding period to a fixed horizon date; and (3) insulation from the effects of potential adverse interest rate changes on the portfolio value at the horizon date.

General Principle

The fundamental mechanism underlying immunization is a portfolio structure that balances the change in the value of the portfolio at the end of the investment horizon with the return from the reinvestment of portfolio cash flows (coupon payments and maturing securities). That is, immunization requires offsetting interest rate risk and reinvestment risk. To accomplish this balancing act requires controlling duration. By setting the duration of the portfolio equal to the desired portfolio time horizon, the offsetting of positive and negative incremental return sources can be assured. (That is, if the investment horizon is 5 years, the duration is initially set at 5.) This is a necessary condition for effectively immunized portfolios. Exhibit 22.10 summarizes the general principles of classical immunization.

EXHIBIT 22.10   General Principles of Classical Immunization

> *Goal:* Lock in a minimum target return and target investment value regardless of how interest rates change over the investment horizon.
>
> *Risk when interest rates change:* (1) reinvestment risk and (2) interest rate or price risk
>
> Principle:
>
> *Scenario 1:* Interest rates increase
> Implications:
> 1. Reinvestment income increases
> 2. Value of bonds in the portfolio with a maturity greater than the investment horizon declines
>
> *Goal:* Gain in reinvestment income ≥ loss in portfolio value
>
> *Scenario 2:* Interest rates decline
> Implications:
> 1. Reinvestment income decreases
> 2. Value of bonds in the portfolio with a maturity greater than the investment horizon increases
>
> *Goal:* Loss in reinvestment income ≤ gain in portfolio value
>
> *Assumption:* Parallel shift in the yield curve (i.e., all yields rise and fall uniformly)

How often should the portfolio be rebalanced to adjust its duration? On the one hand, the more frequent rebalancing increases transaction costs, thereby reducing the likelihood of achieving the target return. On the other hand, less frequent rebalancing will result in the portfolio's duration wandering from the target duration, which will also reduce the likelihood of achieving the target return. Thus the manager faces a trade-off: Some transaction costs must be accepted to prevent the portfolio duration from wandering too far from its target, but some maladjustment in the portfolio duration must be lived with, or transaction costs will become prohibitively high.

In the actual process leading to the construction of an immunized portfolio, the selection of the universe is extremely important. The lower the credit quality of the securities considered, the higher the potential risk and return. Immunization theory assumes there will be no defaults and that securities will be responsive only to overall changes in interest rates. The lower the credit quality of securities permitted in the immunized portfolio, the greater the possibility that these assumptions will not be met. Further, securities with embedded options such as call features or mortgage-backed prepayments complicate and may even prevent the accurate measure of cash flows and hence duration, frustrating the basic requirements of immunization. Finally, liquidity is a consideration for immunized portfolios because, as just noted, the portfolio must be rebalanced over time.

Immunization Risk

Perhaps the most critical assumption of the classical immunization strategy concerns the type of interest rate change. A property of a classically immunized portfolio is that the target value of the investment is the lower limit of the value of the portfolio at the horizon date if there is a parallel shift in the yield curve.[8] This would appear to be an unrealistic assumption. According to the theory, if there is a change in interest rates that does not correspond to this shape preserving shift, matching the duration to the investment horizon no longer assures immunization.

A natural extension of classical immunization theory is a technique for modifying the assumption of parallel shifts in the yield curve. One approach is a strategy that can handle any arbitrary interest rate change so that it is not necessary to specify an alternative duration measure. This approach establishes a measure of immunization risk against any arbitrary interest rate change.[9] In constructing a portfolio, this immunization

---

[8] Fisher and Weil, "Coping with Risk of Interest Rate Fluctuations."

[9] H. Gifford Fong and Oldrich A. Vasicek, "A Risk Minimizing Strategy for Portfolio Immunization," *Journal of Finance* (December 1984), pp. 1541–1546.

risk measure can be minimized subject to the constraint that the duration of the portfolio be equal to the investment horizon. This will result in a portfolio with minimum exposure to any interest rate movements.

One way of minimizing immunization risk is shown in Exhibit 22.11. The spikes in the two panels of the exhibit represent actual portfolio cash flows. The taller spikes depict the actual cash flows generated by matured securities while the smaller spikes represent coupon payments. Both portfolio A and portfolio B are composed of two bonds with a duration equal to the investment horizon. Portfolio A is, in effect, a barbell portfolio—a portfolio comprising short and long maturities and interim coupon payments. For portfolio B, the two bonds mature very close to the investment horizon and the coupon payments are nominal over the investment horizon. As explained earlier in this chapter, a portfolio with this characteristic is called a bullet portfolio.

It is not difficult to see why the barbell portfolio should be riskier than the bullet portfolio. Assume that both portfolios have durations equal to the horizon length, so that both portfolios are immune to parallel rate changes. This immunity is attained as a consequence of balancing the effect of changes in reinvestment rates on payments received during the investment horizon against the effect of changes in market value of the portion of the portfolio still outstanding at the end of the investment horizon. When interest rates change in an arbitrary nonparallel way, however, the effect on the two portfolios is very different. Suppose, for instance, that short rates decline while long rates go up. Both portfolios would realize a decline of the portfolio value at the end of the investment horizon below the target investment value, since they experience a capital loss in addition to lower reinvestment rates. The decline, however, would be substantially higher for the barbell portfolio for two reasons. First, the lower reinvestment rates are experienced on the barbell portfolio for longer time intervals than on the bullet portfolio, so that the opportunity loss is much greater. Second, the portion of the barbell portfolio still outstanding at the end of the investment horizon is much longer than that of the bullet portfolio, which means that the same interest rate increase at the end of the investment horizon would result in a much greater capital loss. Thus the bullet portfolio has less exposure to whatever the change in the interest rate structure may be than the barbell portfolio.

It should be clear from the foregoing discussion that immunization risk is the risk of reinvestment. The portfolio that has the least reinvestment risk will have the least immunization risk. When there is a high dispersion of cash flows around the horizon date, as in the barbell portfolio, the portfolio is exposed to higher reinvestment risk. However, when the cash flows are concentrated around the horizon date, as in the bullet portfolio, the portfolio is subject to minimum reinvestment risk.

EXHIBIT 22.11   Immunization Risk Measure

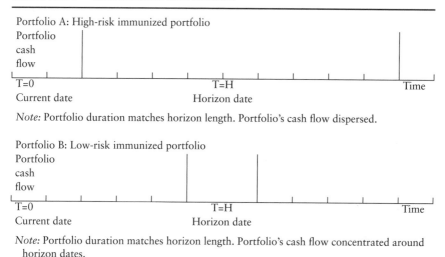

Portfolio A: High-risk immunized portfolio

Portfolio cash flow

T=0
Current date

T=H
Horizon date

Time

Note: Portfolio duration matches horizon length. Portfolio's cash flow dispersed.

Portfolio B: Low-risk immunized portfolio

Portfolio cash flow

T=0
Current date

T=H
Horizon date

Time

Note: Portfolio duration matches horizon length. Portfolio's cash flow concentrated around horizon dates.

Contingent Immunization

There are variants of the classical immunization strategy. A *contingent immunization strategy* involves the identification of both the available immunization target rate and a lower safety net level return with which the client would be minimally satisfied. The manager can continue to pursue an active strategy until an adverse investment experience drives the then-available potential return—combined active return (from actual past experience) and immunized return (from expected future experience)—down to the safety net level; at such time the manager would be obligated to completely immunize the portfolio and lock in the safety net level return. As long as this safety net is not violated, the manager can continue to actively manage the portfolio. Once the immunization mode is activated because the safety net is violated, the manager can no longer return to the active mode unless, of course, the contingent immunization plan is abandoned.

The key considerations in implementing a contingent immunization strategy are (1) establishing accurate immunized initial and ongoing available target returns, (2) identifying a suitable and immunizable safety net, and (3) implementing an effective monitoring procedure to ensure that the safety net is not violated.

Cash Flow Matching

The immunization strategy described previously is used to immunize a portfolio created to satisfy a single liability in the future against adverse interest rate movements. However, it is more common in situations to have multiple future liabilities. One example is the liability structure of defined benefit pension plans. Another example is a life insurance annuity contract. When there are multiple future liabilities, it is possible to extend the principles of immunization to such situations. However, it is more common in practice to use a *cash flow matching strategy.* This strategy is used to construct a portfolio designed to fund a schedule of liabilities from portfolio return and asset value, with the portfolio's value diminishing to zero after payment of the last liability.

A cash flow matching strategy can be described intuitively as follows. A bond is selected with a maturity that matches the last liability. An amount of principal equal to the amount of the last liability is then invested in this bond. The remaining elements of the liability stream are then reduced by the coupon payments on this bond, and another bond is chosen for the next-to-last liability, adjusted for any coupon payments of the first bond selected. Going backward in time, this sequence is continued until all liabilities have been matched by payments on the securities selected for the portfolio. Exhibit 22.12 provides a simple illustration of this process for a 5-year liability stream. Optimization techniques are employed to construct a least-cost cash flow matching portfolio from an acceptable universe of bonds.

EXHIBIT 22.12   Illustration of Cash Flow Matching Process

Assume: 5-year liability stream
Cash flow from bonds are annual.

Step 1:
Cash flow from Bond A selected to satisfy L_5
        Coupons = A_c; Principal = A_p and $A_c + A_p = L_5$
Unfunded liabilities remaining:

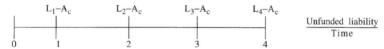

Step 2:
Cash flow from Bond B selected to satisfy L_4
        Unfunded liability = $L_4 - A_c$
        Coupons = B_c; Principal = B_p and $B_c + B_p = L_4 - A_c$
Unfunded liabilities remaining:

Step 3:
Cash flow from Bond C selected to satisfy L_3
        Unfunded liability = $L_3 - A_c - B_c$
        Coupons = C_c; Principal = C_p and $C_c + C_p = L_3 - A_c - B_c$
Unfunded liabilities remaining:

Step 4:
Cash flow from Bond D selected to satisfy L_2
        Unfunded liability = $L_2 - A_c - B_c - C_c$
        Coupons = D_c; Principal = D_p and $D_c + D_p = L_2 - A_c - B_c - C_c$
Unfunded liabilities remaining:

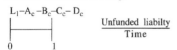

Step 5:
Select Bond E with a cash flow of $L_1 - A_c - B_c - C_c - D_c$

CHAPTER 23

Bond Portfolio Analysis Relative to a Benchmark

Lev Dynkin
Managing Director
Lehman Brothers

Jay Hyman
Senior Vice President
Lehman Brothers

Vadim Konstantinovsky, CFA
Senior Vice President
Lehman Brothers

The selection of investment guidelines and an appropriate benchmark marks the beginning of the portfolio management process. Once a portfolio is established, investors must continually monitor its positioning relative to the benchmark. Periodic transactions are needed to maintain desired exposures (e.g., +0.5 longer in duration or overexposed to corporates by 10%) and to express changes in market outlook. In a typical investment cycle, forward-looking analytics are applied at the start of each period to position the portfolio according to the investor's view.[1]

To illustrate these techniques, we will take as a case study the government/credit portfolio of the Invest-Rite Asset Management Com-

---

[1] At the end of the period, ex-post analysis is used to review the achieved performance. This process is called attribution analysis and is discussed in Chapter 13.

pany. This hypothetical portfolio is benchmarked against the Lehman Brothers Gov/Credit Index, but deviates from the benchmark in both term structure and sector allocations. We follow this portfolio through a full monthly investment cycle and show how these deviations are analyzed and how their effect on performance is quantified.

ANALYZING PORTFOLIO AND BENCHMARK COMPOSITION: A CELL-BASED APPROACH

Market structure analysis is a structural comparison of the portfolio and benchmark. The two sets of bonds are compared by partitioning them into a matrix of cells. Different choices of partition variables focus on different aspects of portfolio composition. Corporate portfolios, for example, can be divided along a hierarchy of industry categories (e.g., basic industry, consumer cyclical, or energy). Segmenting by duration highlights the yield curve exposures. Segmenting by duration and sector shows how yield curve views are implemented using various asset classes (e.g., a yield-curve barbell achieved by combining MBS at the short end with long corporates). The amount of information a portfolio manager derives from a market structure report depends on the proper selection of risk dimensions and output fields. More information can be derived by analyzing the projected returns under various interest rate and credit spread scenarios within each cell.

Exhibit 23.1 shows a market structure comparison of the Invest-Rite portfolio and the Gov/Credit Index. Contributions of a given cell to both risk and return of the overall portfolio or benchmark are functions of the weight of the cell. Contribution is defined as the percentage allocated to a cell times the cell average (e.g., contribution to duration equals percentage allocation times duration and is proportional to dollar duration). To be risk-neutral to the benchmark, a portfolio should match contributions to duration within each cell. Our example portfolio strongly underweights the long and short portions of the index, with over 95% of its market value in the 3 to 7 duration range. The portfolio is short duration relative to the benchmark by 0.25. This difference can be broken down in terms of either sector (long by 0.67 to corporates, short by −0.92 to governments) or term structure (long by 3.07 in the 3 to 7 duration range, short in all the others).

Another analytical approach to comparing a portfolio with a benchmark is to generate and compare their cash flow profiles. Cash flows may be represented on a discounted or non-discounted basis, in absolute (dollar) terms or as percentages of the total present value.

They can be projected by month, quarter, year, or another frequency. This analysis can be followed by a more detailed market structure analysis to identify the sources and implications of cash flow differences. For a portfolio of bullet securities, this is equivalent to key rate durations analysis.[2] Exhibit 23.2 plots the differences in cash flow distribution (in percentages of present value) between the Invest-Rite portfolio and the Gov/Credit Index. The butterfly-type pattern in this graph reveals significant exposure to non-parallel yield curve movements. As will become apparent in scenario analysis, these exposures reflect a view that the yield curve will steepen.

The portfolio profiling described here is useful alongside any sophisticated quantitative model of risk and return because it represents the basic intuitive view of portfolio exposures relative to the benchmark.

EXHIBIT 23.1   Invest-Rite Portfolio versus Gov/Credit Index: Market Structure Report, October 31, 1999

Dur. Range		% of Market Value			Adjusted Duration			Contrib. to Duration		
		Govt.	Corp.	Total	Govt.	Corp.	Total	Govt.	Corp.	Total
0–3	Portfolio	0.8	0.0	0.8	2.71	0.00	2.71	0.02	0.00	0.02
	Index	26.4	7.1	33.5	1.80	2.06	1.85	0.47	0.15	0.62
	Diff.	−25.6	−7.1	−32.7	0.92	−2.06	0.86	−0.45	−0.15	−0.60
3–7	Portfolio	46.2	49.7	95.8	5.00	5.20	5.10	2.31	2.59	4.89
	Index	21.4	16.6	38.0	4.59	5.05	4.79	0.98	0.84	1.82
	Diff.	24.7	33.1	57.8	0.41	0.16	0.31	1.32	1.75	3.07
7–10	Portfolio	3.1	0.2	3.3	7.02	7.02	7.02	0.22	0.02	0.23
	Index	6.5	4.7	11.2	8.68	8.42	8.57	0.56	0.40	0.96
	Diff.	−3.4	−4.5	−7.9	−1.67	−1.39	−1.55	−0.34	−0.38	−0.72
10+	Portfolio	0.0	0.0	0.0	0.00	0.00	0.00	0.00	0.00	0.00
	Index	12.4	4.9	17.3	11.64	11.26	11.53	1.44	0.55	2.00
	Diff.	−12.4	−4.9	−17.3	−11.64	−11.26	−11.53	−1.44	−0.55	−2.00
Total	Portfolio	50.1	49.9	100.0	5.08	5.21	5.15	2.55	2.60	5.15
	Index	66.7	33.3	100.0	5.19	5.80	5.40	3.46	1.93	5.40
	Diff.	−16.6	16.6	0.0	−0.11	−0.59	−0.25	−0.92	0.67	−0.25

---

[2] Key rate duration is explained in Chapter 21.

EXHIBIT 23.2 Invest-Rite Portfolio versus Gov/Credit Index: Cash Flow Distribution, October 31, 1999

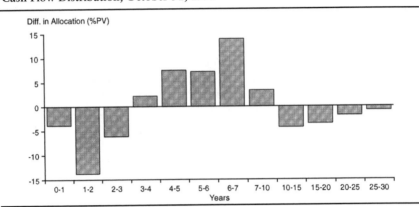

QUANTIFYING PORTFOLIO RISK RELATIVE TO A BENCHMARK: THE MULTI-FACTOR APPROACH

Managers must monitor portfolio exposures versus the benchmark along many dimensions simultaneously. They may choose to express a market view by over-weighting a particular part of the yield curve, sector, or quality. They also need to be aware of any unintentional exposures. Any difference between portfolio and benchmark composition represents a potential for return deviations.

The qualitative cell-based comparison by allocations to different market segments has two shortcomings. First, it does not indicate which mismatches are likely to contribute the most to return deviations between portfolio and benchmark. The biggest mismatches do not necessarily carry the most risk. For example, a spread duration[3] mismatch in the AA–industrial cell is not nearly as risky as a mismatch of the same magnitude in the BAA–Yankee cell. Second, it ignores correlations that might exist among different risk axes.

One approach to quantifying the expected return deviation between portfolio and benchmark is to attribute most of the individual security return variance to a small set of systematic market influences, or risk factors. This method, known as *multi-factor risk analysis*, is based on a comparison of sensitivities of the portfolio and benchmark to each of the risk factors. The analysis of positions consisting of thousands of bonds is reduced to a comparison of a few risk exposures. Based on the historical

---

[3] Spread duration is explained in Chapter 21.

volatilities and correlations of the risk factors, the model quantifies the net risk due to these exposures.

In Chapter 24, we explain and illustrate the Lehman Brothers multifactor risk model. The model uses risk factors representing exposures to term structure, agency and corporate sectors, credit quality, coupon, optionality, MBS prepayments, MBS volatility, and MBS spreads. The risk factors are explanatory variables in a statistical analysis of historical returns for individual securities.

Common market risk factors do not always explain the entire return variance of a security. Credit events associated with individual issuers can pose significant risk to a portfolio that is not sufficiently diversified. Because the model is based on historical returns of individual bonds, it is able to quantify non-systematic (diversifiable) risk. Parts of each bond's return unexplained by the systematic risk factors are used to model non-systematic risk.

To measure risk, the model computes sensitivities of each bond in the portfolio and in the index to all risk factors and aggregates them by percentage of market value. The difference between the resulting aggregate sensitivities of the portfolio and benchmark is used to produce the magnitude of systematic risk. In addition, the model measures the differences in concentration of the portfolio and benchmark by issue and issuer to estimate non-systematic risk. The two measures of risk are then combined to compute the total tracking error, the projected standard deviation of the difference between the portfolio and benchmark returns.

The systematic tracking error can be reduced by restructuring the portfolio so that its risk characteristics match the index more closely. The non-systematic component can be reduced through diversification.

The risk model, relying on historical volatilities and correlations, interprets the structural differences between the portfolio and benchmark to produce a more accurate picture of portfolio risk. Simple "eyeballing" of the market structure report shown in Exhibit 23.1 might leave some doubt as to the relative importance of the different types of risk the Invest-Rite portfolio faces. The magnitude of the overweight to corporates (measured by difference in contribution to duration) is 0.67, while the overall duration difference is only –0.25. This might lead one to overemphasize the sector risk and underestimate the term structure risk. As shown in Exhibit 23.3, the tracking error for this portfolio is due predominantly to the term structure exposure. This is because yields are more volatile than credit spreads and because the overall duration difference is not a sufficient measure of yield curve risk for this portfolio. The extent to which the long and short exposures to different parts of the curve offset each other is closely related to the correlation between the movement of long and short Treasury yields. The risk model evaluates all these effects simultaneously when projecting tracking error.

PROJECTING RETURNS: SCENARIO ANALYSIS

Another perspective on risk involves comparing projected portfolio and benchmark returns under various yield curve and spread scenarios. A manager can focus on the set of scenarios that he considers most likely or those he considers most dangerous. This type of analysis complements the multi-factor risk model in that it allows a manager to stress-test benchmarked portfolios by subjecting both portfolio and benchmark to extreme scenarios not consistent with the history underlying the risk model. While extreme scenarios are unlikely, they often highlight potential sources of return deviations that may not manifest themselves under normal circumstances.

EXHIBIT 23.3   Invest-Rite Portfolio versus Gov/Credit Index:
Risk Analysis Report, October 31, 1999

	Tracking Error		Incremental
	Isolated	Cumulative	Change
Systematic Tracking Error Breakdown (% per year)			
Due to:			
Term Structure	0.663	0.663	0.663
Non-Term Structure	0.300		
Sector	0.165	0.673	0.010
Quality	0.136	0.694	0.021
Optionality	0.075	0.707	0.013
Coupon	0.041	0.721	0.014
MBS Sector	0.000	0.721	0.000
MBS Volatility	0.000	0.721	0.000
MBS Prepayments	0.000	0.721	0.000
Total Systematic			0.721
Non-Systematic Tracking Error Breakdown (% per year)			
Issuer-Specific			0.108
Issue-Specific			0.108
Total Non-Systematic			0.108
Total Tracking Error			0.729

EXHIBIT 23.4 Invest-Rite Portfolio versus Gov/Credit Index: Scenario Stress-Testing, Horizon Date: November 30, 1999

	Duration	Convexity
Portfolio:	5.15	0.26
Index:	5.40	0.56
Total Systematic Tracking Error (bp/mo):		20.8
Term Structure		19.1
Non-Term Structure		8.7

Scenario	Portfolio Return (%)	Index Return (%)	Difference (bp)	Multiple of Tracking Error
No Change	0.58	0.55	3	0.1
Parallel Shift				
Up 25 bp	−0.66	−0.76	9	0.5
Down 25 bp	1.85	1.89	−4	0.2
Up 250 bp	−11.15	−10.83	−32	1.5
Down 250 bp	13.76	15.46	−170	8.2
Twisting Movement				
10 bp Flattening	0.45	0.55	−10	0.5
10 bp Steepening	0.71	0.55	16	0.8
100 bp Flattening	−0.79	0.49	−129	6.2
100 bp Steepening	1.99	0.66	133	6.4

Exhibit 23.4 shows several scenario performance projections for the Invest-Rite portfolio, some of them likely and some extreme. The portfolio's duration view (shorter than the benchmark) is apparent in the performance under moderate parallel shift scenarios; the steepening and flattening scenarios highlight its bullet-versus-barbell term structure exposure. As Exhibit 23.4 shows, extreme scenarios can lead to one-month performance differences as far as eight tracking errors apart and produce surprising results. For instance, the portfolio underperforms in the "up 250 bp" parallel shift scenario, despite being short duration. This is the effect of the portfolio's much lower convexity relative to the benchmark.

ANALYZING PORTFOLIO PERFORMANCE

The identification of sources of relative performance helps measure the effects of various allocation decisions within the overall portfolio management process. Careful analysis of return surprises may point out unintended portfolio characteristics that should be corrected in the future.

There are two main approaches to analyzing achieved returns. The first, that is somewhat similar to the multi-factor approach to risk modeling, ascribes portions of each security's price return to common market factors such as passage of time, yield curve movements, and changes in volatilities and spreads. Security-level results are aggregated to analyze the portfolio and benchmark performance in isolation and in comparison with each other. Return subcomponents should correspond to exposures commonly taken by portfolio managers. For example, if a portfolio is barbelled to express a yield curve flattening view, the anticipated outperformance should result from twist return.

The second method can be likened to the asset allocation approach to modeling risk. Outperformance is attributed to portfolio-level allocation differences relative to the benchmark. The allocation dimensions should be selected and prioritized to reflect the portfolio manager's decision process. Unlike the first method, this approach explains return differences between a portfolio and a benchmark, rather than returns themselves. Performance attribution can thus be performed only in a context of comparison to a benchmark and cannot be applied to a portfolio in isolation.

An illustration of performance atribution analysis is presented in Chapter 24.

INDEX REPLICATION STRATEGIES

Many investors manage portfolios (or parts of portfolios) to match index returns. Even active managers may fall back to passive index tracking in times when they have no definite views. The simplest way to replicate an index is to buy most of the securities in the index in the proper proportions. However, this method is practical only for the largest index funds. For smaller portfolios, maintaining the necessary proportions of a large number of bonds would necessitate buying odd lots and lead to overwhelming transaction costs. Furthermore, this strategy is appropriate only for portfolios that are to remain neutral to the index over a long period of time. Investors with smaller portfolios often build index proxies, portfolios that contain only a small number of securities yet deviate minimally from the returns of much larger target indices.

Investors sometimes use *proxy portfolios* for modeling purposes, rather than for direct investment. Any mathematical model used in a portfolio management context becomes more valuable if it can be applied consistently to both the portfolio and the benchmark. In some cases, though, it is not feasible to include the entire benchmark in an analysis, due to either constraints on processing time or data availability. Proxy portfolios are often used in such settings to stand in for the actual benchmark and speed up the analysis.

There are several different techniques for constructing proxy portfolios as well as other methods of tracking index returns, such as replication with futures contracts or swaps. These techniques may be more appropriate for investors who wish to maintain a passive position for only a limited time or for those who seek index returns on a fund with frequent inflows and outflows.

There are two basic approaches to index replication, presented below in this order: cell matching (stratified sampling) and tracking error minimization with a multi-factor risk model. They can be viewed as complementary.

Sampling techniques are the "common sense" approach. To replicate an index, one has to represent its every important component with a few securities. The holdings of securities in a particular cell are usually computed to match that cell's contribution to overall duration. The problem with this approach is that a mismatch to the benchmark in any cell appears to be equally important. In reality, matching some cells is more critical than matching others because the return (or spread) volatility associated with them is higher. Sampling techniques also ignore correlations among cells that sometimes cause risk from an overweight in one cell to be canceled with an overweight in another.

Risk models allow managers to replicate indices by creating minimum tracking error portfolios. These models rely on historical volatilities and correlations between returns of different asset classes or different risk factors in the market. So the factor model's "knowledge" is limited to the historical experience observed over the calibration period. Such model may ignore a significant structural mismatch that historically did not result in returns volatility. For example, in replicating an index of 3,000 corporate bonds with a portfolio of 30 bonds, the risk model may ignore allocations to AAA/AA credit qualities because, historically, the volatility of their spreads was comparatively low. The model will deploy these 30 bonds where it believes it matters the most from a historical risk perspective. At the same time, experienced portfolio managers may be alerted to this mismatch by stratified sampling analysis and may wish to take corrective measures based on their expectations that are not necessarily reflective of history.

There is another approach to index replication (not described here)— simulation of portfolio and benchmark returns across a sufficiently complete set of stochastic scenarios. This is an alternative to the history-based approach employed by the risk model. The portfolio is optimized to have an average return that is as close as possible to the benchmark, as well as a similar distribution of returns over the set of scenarios. The number of bonds in such portfolios will be proportional to the tightness of the imposed constraints. Scenarios have to include all likely interest rate, spread, and volatility changes to capture all risk dimensions (and align the respective sensitivities) relevant to the particular portfolio and the benchmark.

The replicating portfolio does not necessarily consist of securities sampled out of the index being replicated. A very practical alternative is using futures and swaps—liquid market instruments with return characteristics similar to many of the index securities. We provide a brief account of our methodology of index replication with these derivatives. This is popular with investors engaged in "portable alpha" strategies (structuring liquid derivatives baskets to replicate index returns and investing cash outside of the index to gain alpha).[4]

Replication by Stratified Sampling

The market structure analysis described above profiles indices or portfolios to show allocations and exposures along arbitrary risk dimensions. Some useful grids include sector by quality, sector by duration, and weighted average coupon (WAC) by weighted average maturity (WAM).

This form of profiling a benchmark can be applied to establish and maintain a proxy portfolio via a cell-matching technique. A portfolio manager can map a benchmark onto an arbitrary grid and then set portfolio allocations to each cell that match those of the benchmark. To improve tracking further, the manager may target characteristics of each individual cell such as duration, convexity, or quality when selecting and purchasing securities to represent the cell. The more securities are selected in each cell, the more closely the resulting portfolio tracks the index.

We have used this approach successfully to replicate the Lehman Brothers MBS index on a monthly basis. The index is broken down along three dimensions: program (GNMA 30-year, conventional 30-year, all 15-year, and balloons), seasoning (TBA, moderately seasoned, seasoned) and price (premium, cusp coupon, discount). The proxy portfolio is the result of an optimization. A similar optimization framework was used to replicate a far more diversified benchmark—the Lehman Brothers High Yield Index.

Tracking Error Minimization

Investors often look for "optimal" index proxies: portfolios that best track index returns using a given number of securities. The risk model described earlier and in more detail in Chapter 24 has been successfully applied (using its tracking error minimization feature) to construct proxies for several popular Lehman Brothers indices: Government, Credit, and MBS. This

---

[4] Alpha is the excess return over a benchmark.

approach has been particularly successful in the homogeneous MBS passthrough market, in which systematic risks (interest rates, volatility, and prepayment) dominate.[5] Yet even for the highly diverse Credit Index, a sufficiently high level of tracking can be achieved with relatively few securities.

Exhibit 23.5 shows the annualized tracking errors of a Credit Index proxy as a function of the number of bonds. Exhibit 23.6 summarizes the observed performance of the Treasury, credit, and MBS proxies over twenty months and shows that the observed return deviations are well within the predicted ranges.

EXHIBIT 23.5   Effect of Diversification on Tracking the Lehman Brothers Credit Index

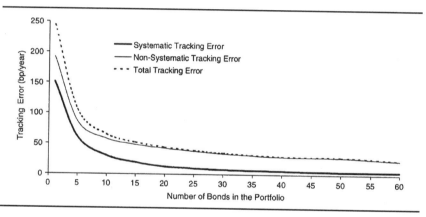

EXHIBIT 23.6   Effectiveness of the Risk Model—Observed Performance of Proxy Portfolios
January 1997–December 1998, bp/month

	Index		
	Treasury	Corporate	MBS
Predicted Tracking Error	6.6	13.5	4.3
Observed Tracking Error	3.2	12.5	1.9
Average Return Difference	0.0	6.6	−0.3
Minimum Return Difference	−6.1	−11.8	−3.4
Maximum Return Difference	6.0	38.0	3.4

[5] Lev Dynkin, Vadim Konstantinovsky, and Bruce Phelps, "Replicating MBS Index Returns with TBAs and Large Pools," in Frank J. Fabozzi (ed.), *Professional Perspectives on Fixed Income Portfolio Management: Volume 3* (New York: John Wiley & Sons, 2002).

Replication with Futures and Swaps

In Chapter 25, fixed-income derivatives are discussed. Derivatives can play an important role in reducing the dimensionality of the portfolio management problem. Liquid futures and swaps contracts facilitate rapid asset allocation shifts between currencies and yield curves. In a portfolio with large cash inflows, futures and swaps can be used to match index risk sensitivities temporarily until suitable active investment opportunities are found. Similarly, when a fund has to keep a significant amount of cash on hand for redemptions it may experience substantial deviations from index returns. Futures and swaps require essentially zero cash outlays up front and can be used to replicate index returns for the amount of the cash holdings. Finally, replication with derivatives can be useful in the start-up phase, when diversified cash investments in tradable sizes are not feasible, particularly in less liquid markets.

Futures and swaps, coupled with some aggressive ways of investing cash, can also be part of active strategies to outperform a benchmark. The cash left after the initial margin and some reserve for future variation margin can be invested in sectors where the manager has strong expertise (e.g., short-term high yield product or ABS). The return on the cash investment plus any over- or underperformance of the tracking derivatives portfolio determines the total performance versus the benchmark. This style of active management is sometimes called "portable alpha," because the replicating basket of futures or swaps allows managers to transfer performance alpha from their areas of expertise and apply it to an arbitrary benchmark.

CHAPTER 24

Multi-Factor Fixed-Income Risk Models and Their Applications*

Lev Dynkin
Managing Director
Lehman Brothers

Jay Hyman
Senior Vice President
Lehman Brothers

In Chapter 4, multi-factor risk models were described and in Chapter 13 a fundamental risk factor model was explained and applied for common stock. In this chapter we discuss a risk model developed for fixed-income portfolio management. A multi-factor risk model estimates the risk from owning a particular bond based not on the historical performance of that bond, but on historical returns of all bonds with characteristics similar to those currently pertaining to the bond. We present the risk model by way of example. In each of the following sections, a numerical example of the model's application motivates the discussion of a particular feature. The benchmark used in the example is the Lehman Aggregate Index.

* Wei Wu coauthored the original version of the paper from which this chapter is derived. The authors would like to thank Jack Malvey for his substantial contribution to this chapter and Ravi Mattu, George Williams, Ivan Gruhl, Amitabh Arora, Vadim Konstantinovsky, Peter Lindner, and Jonathan Carmel for their valuable comments.

QUANTIFYING RISK

Given our premise that the least-risky portfolio is the one that exactly replicates the benchmark, we proceed to compare the composition of a fixed-income portfolio to that of its benchmark. Are they similar in exposures to changes in the term structure of interest rates, in allocations to different asset classes within the benchmark, and in allocations to different quality ratings? Such portfolio versus benchmark comparisons form the foundation for modern fixed-income portfolio management. Techniques such as "stratified sampling" or "cell-matching" have been used to construct portfolios that are similar to their benchmarks in many components (i.e., duration, quality etc.). However, these techniques can not answer quantitative questions concerning portfolio risk. How much risk is there? Is portfolio A more or less risky than portfolio B? Will a given transaction increase or decrease risk? To best decrease risk relative to the benchmark, should the focus be on better aligning term structure exposures or sector allocations? How do we weigh these different types of risk against each other? What actions can be taken to mitigate the overall risk exposure? Any quantitative model of risk must account for the magnitude of a particular event as well as its likelihood. When multiple risks are modeled simultaneously, the issue of correlation also must be addressed.

The risk model we present in this chapter provides quantitative answers to such questions. This multi-factor model compares portfolio and benchmark exposures along all dimensions of risk, such as yield curve movement, changes in sector spreads, and changes in implied volatility. Exposures to each *risk factor* are calculated on a bond-by-bond basis and aggregated to obtain the exposures of the portfolio and the benchmark.

As explained in Chapter 7, *tracking error*, which quantifies the risk of performance difference (projected standard deviation of the return difference) between the portfolio and the benchmark, is projected based on the differences in risk factor exposures. This calculation of overall risk incorporates historical information about the volatility of each risk factor and the correlations among them.[1]

---

[1] The volatilities and correlations of all the risk factors are stored in a covariance matrix, which is calibrated based on monthly returns of individual bonds in the Lehman Brothers Aggregate Index dating back to 1987. The model is updated monthly with historical information. The choice of risk factors has been reviewed periodically since the model's introduction in 1990. The model covers U.S. dollar-denominated securities in most Lehman Brothers domestic fixed-rate bond indices (Aggregate, High Yield, Eurobond). The effect of non-index securities on portfolio risk is measured by mapping onto index risk categories. The net effect of all risk factors is known as systematic risk.

The model is based on historical returns of individual securities and its risk projections are a function of portfolio and benchmark positions in individual securities. This approach allows us to quantify residual return volatility of each security after all systematic risk factors have been applied. As a result, we can measure non-systematic risk of a portfolio relative to the benchmark based on differences in their diversification. This form of risk, also known as *concentration risk* or *security-specific risk*, is the result of a portfolio's exposure to individual bonds or issuers. Non-systematic risk can represent a significant portion of the overall risk, particularly for portfolios containing relatively few securities, even for assets without any credit risk.

PORTFOLIO MANAGEMENT WITH THE RISK MODEL

Passive portfolio managers, or "indexers," seek to replicate the returns of a broad market index. They can use the risk model to help keep the portfolio closely aligned with the index along all risk dimensions. Active portfolio managers attempt to outperform the benchmark by positioning the portfolio to capitalize on market views. They can use the risk model to quantify the risk entailed in a particular portfolio position relative to the market. This information is often incorporated into the performance review process, where returns achieved by a particular strategy are weighed against the risk taken. Enhanced indexers express views against the index, but limit the amount of risk assumed. They can use the model to keep risk within acceptable limits and to highlight unanticipated market exposures that might arise as the portfolio and index change over time. These management styles can be associated with approximate ranges of tracking errors. Passive managers typically seek tracking errors of 5 to 25 basis points per year. Tracking errors for enhanced indexers range from 25 to 75 bp, and those of active managers are even higher.

THE RISK REPORT

For illustration, we apply the risk model to a sample portfolio of 57 bonds benchmarked against the Lehman Brothers Aggregate Index. The model produces two important outputs: a tracking error summary report and a set of risk sensitivities reports that compare the portfolio composition to that of the benchmark. These various comparative reports form the basis of our risk analysis, by identifying structural differences between the two. Of themselves, however, they fail to quantify the risk due to these mismatches. The model's anchor is therefore the tracking error report, which quantifies the risks associated with each cross-sectional comparison. Taken together, the various reports produced by the model provide a complete understanding of the risk of this portfolio versus its benchmark.

From the overall statistical summary shown in Exhibit 24.1, it can be seen that the portfolio has a significant term structure exposure, as its duration (4.82) is longer than that of the benchmark (4.29). In addition, the portfolio is over-exposed to corporate bonds and under-exposed to Treasuries. We will see this explicitly in the sector report later; it is reflected in the statistics in Exhibit 24.1 by a higher average yield and coupon. The overall annualized tracking error, shown at the bottom of the statistics report, is 52 bp. Tracking error is defined as one standard deviation of the difference between the portfolio and benchmark annualized returns. In simple terms, this means that with a probability of about 68% the portfolio return over the next year will be within ±52 bp of the benchmark return.[2]

EXHIBIT 24.1   Top-Level Statistics Comparison Sample Portfolio versus Aggregate Index, 9/30/98

	Portfolio	Benchmark
Number of Issues	57	6,932
Average Maturity/Average Life (years)	9.57	8.47
Internal Rate of Return (%)	5.76	5.54
Average Yield to Maturity (%)	5.59	5.46
Average Yield to Worst (%)	5.53	5.37
Average Option-Adjusted Convexity	0.04	−0.22
Average OAS to Maturity (bp)	74	61
Average OAS to Worst (bp)	74	61
Portfolio Mod. Adjusted Duration	4.82	4.29
Portfolio Average Price	108.45	107.70
Portfolio Average Coupon (%)	7.33	6.98
Risk Characteristics		
Estimated Total Tracking Error (bp/year)	52	
Portfolio Beta	1.05	

[2] This interpretation requires several simplifying assumptions. The 68% confidence interval assumes that returns are normally distributed, which may not be the case. Second, this presentation ignores differences in the expected returns of portfolio and benchmark (due, for example, to a higher portfolio yield). Strictly speaking, the confidence interval should be drawn around the expected outperformance.

EXHIBIT 24.2   Tracking Error Breakdown for Sample Portfolio
Sample Portfolio versus Aggregate Index, 9/30/98

	Tracking Error (Basis Points Per Year)		
	Isolated	Cumulative	Change in Cumulative*
Tracking Error Term Structure	36.3	36.3	36.3
Non-Term Structure	39.5		
Tracking Error Sector	32.0	38.3	2.0
Tracking Error Quality	14.7	44.1	5.8
Tracking Error Optionality	1.6	44.0	−0.1
Tracking Error Coupon	3.2	45.5	1.5
Tracking Error MBS Sector	4.9	43.8	−1.7
Tracking Error MBS Volatility	7.2	44.5	0.7
Tracking Error MBS Prepayment	2.5	45.0	0.4
Total Systematic Tracking Error			45.0
Non-Systematic Tracking Error			
Issuer-specific	25.9		
Issue-specific	26.4		
Total	26.1		
Total Tracking Error			52

	Systematic	Non-Systematic	Total
Benchmark Return Standard Deviation	417	4	417
Portfolio Return Standard Deviation	440	27	440

* Isolated Tracking Error is the projected deviation between the portfolio and benchmark return due to a single category of systematic risk. Cumulative Tracking Error shows the combined effect of all risk categories from the first one in the table to current.

Sources of Systematic Tracking Error

What are the main sources of this tracking error? The model identifies market forces influencing all securities in a certain category as *systematic risk factors*. Exhibit 24.2 divides the tracking error into components corresponding to different categories of risk. Looking down the first column, we see that the largest sources of systematic tracking error between this portfolio and its benchmark are the differences in sensitivity to term structure movements (36.3 bp) and to changes in credit spreads by sector (32 bp) and credit quality (14.7 bp). The components of systematic tracking error correspond directly to the groups of risk factors. A detailed report of the differences in portfolio and benchmark exposures (sensitivities) to the relevant set of risk factors illustrates the origin of each component of systematic risk.

Sensitivities to risk factors are called *factor loadings*. They are expressed in units that depend on the definition of each particular risk factor. For example, for risk factors representing volatility of corporate spreads factor loadings are given by spread durations, for risk factors measuring volatility of prepayment speed (in units of PSA) factor loadings are given by "PSA Duration."[3] The factor loadings of a portfolio or an index are calculated as a market-value weighted average over all constituent securities. Differences between portfolio and benchmark factor loadings form a vector of *active portfolio exposures*. A quick comparison of the magnitudes of the different components of tracking error highlights the most significant mismatches.

Term Structure Risk

Because the largest component of tracking error is due to term structure, let us examine the term structure risk in our example. Risk factors associated with term structure movements are represented by the fixed set of points on the theoretical Treasury spot curve shown in Exhibit 24.3. Each of these risk factors exhibits a certain historical return volatility. The extent to which the portfolio and the benchmark returns are affected by this volatility is measured by factor loadings (exposures). These exposures are computed as percentages of the total present value of the portfolio and benchmark cash flows allocated to each point on the curve. The risk of the portfolio performing differently from the benchmark due to term structure movements is due to the differences in the portfolio and benchmark exposures to these risk factors and to their volatilities and correlations. Exhibit 24.3 compares the term structure exposures of the portfolio and benchmark for our example. The "Difference" column shows the portfolio to be overweighted in the 2-year section of the curve, underweighted in the 3- to 10-year range, and overweighted at the long end. This makes the portfolio longer than the benchmark and more barbelled.[4]

The tracking error is calculated from this vector of differences between portfolio and benchmark exposures. However, mismatches at different points are not treated equally. Exposures to factors with higher volatilities have a larger effect on tracking error. In this example, the risk exposure with the largest contribution to tracking error is the over-

---

[3] A discussion of prepayments and the PSA (Public Securities Association) prepayment benchmark are explained in Chapter 17.
[4] A barbell portfolio structure is explained in Chapter 22.

weight of 1.45% to the 25-year point on the curve. While other vertices have larger mismatches (e.g., –2.07% at 7 years), their overall effect on risk is not as strong because the longer duration of a 25-year zero causes it to have a higher return volatility.

It should also be noted that the risk caused by overweighting one segment of the yield curve can sometimes be offset by underweighting another. Exhibit 24.3 shows the portfolio to be underexposed to the 1.50-year point on the yield curve by –2.82% and overexposed to the 2.00-year point on the curve by +2.34%. Those are largely offsetting positions in terms of risk because these two adjacent points on the curve are highly correlated and almost always move together. To eliminate completely the tracking error due to term structure, differences in exposures to each term structure risk factor need to be reduced to zero. To lower term structure risk, it is most important to focus first on reducing exposures at the long end of the curve, particularly those that are not offset by opposing positions in nearby points.

EXHIBIT 24.3   Term Structure Report
Sample Portfolio versus Aggregate Index, 9/30/98

| Year | Cash Flows | | Difference |
	Portfolio	Benchmark	
0.00	1.45%	1.85%	–0.40%
0.25	3.89	4.25	–0.36
0.50	4.69	4.25	0.45
0.75	4.34	3.76	0.58
1.00	8.90	7.37	1.53
1.50	7.47	10.29	–2.82
2.00	10.43	8.09	2.34
2.50	8.63	6.42	2.20
3.00	4.28	5.50	–1.23
3.50	3.90	4.81	–0.92
4.00	6.74	7.19	–0.46
5.00	6.13	6.96	–0.83
6.00	3.63	4.67	–1.04
7.00	5.77	7.84	–2.07
10.00	7.16	7.37	–0.21
15.00	4.63	3.88	0.75
20.00	3.52	3.04	0.48
25.00	3.18	1.73	1.45
30.00	1.22	0.68	0.54
40.00	0.08	0.07	0.01

Sector Risk

The tracking error due to sector exposures is explained by the detailed sector report shown in Exhibit 24.4. This report shows the sector allocations of the portfolio and the benchmark in two ways. In addition to reporting the percentage of market value allocated to each sector, it shows the contribution of each sector to the overall spread duration.[5] These contributions are computed as the product of the percentage allocations to a sector and the market-weighted average spread duration of the holdings in that sector.

Contributions to spread duration (factor loadings) measure the sensitivity of return to systematic changes in particular sector spreads (risk factors) and are a better measure of risk than simple market allocations.[6] The rightmost column in this report, the difference between portfolio and benchmark contributions to spread duration in each sector, is the exposure vector that is used to compute tracking error due to sector. A quick look down this column shows that the largest exposures in our example are an underweight of 0.77 to Treasuries and an overweight of 1.00 to consumer non-cyclicals in the industrial sector.[7] Note that the units of risk factors and factor loadings for sector risk differ from those used to model the term structure risk.

Credit Quality Risk

The analysis of credit quality risk shown in Exhibit 24.5 follows the same approach. Portfolio and benchmark allocations to different credit rating levels are compared in terms of contributions to spread duration. Once again we see the effect of the overweighting of corporates: There is an overweight of 0.80 to single As and an underweight of −0.57 in AAAs (U.S. government debt). The risk represented by tracking error due to quality corresponds to a systematic widening or tightening of spreads for a particular credit rating, uniformly across all industry groups.

---

[5] Just as traditional duration can be defined as the sensitivity of bond price to a change in yield, spread duration is defined as the sensitivity of bond price to a change in spread. While this distinction is largely academic for bullet bonds, it can be significant for other securities, such as bonds with embedded options and floating-rate securities. The sensitivity to spread change is the correct measure of sector risk. An explanation of spread duration is provided in Chapter 21.

[6] An explanation of contribution to duration is provided in Chapter 21.

[7] The fine-grained breakdown of the corporate market into industry groups corresponds to the second tier of the Lehman Brothers hierarchical industry classification scheme.

EXHIBIT 24.4 Detailed Sector Report
Sample Portfolio versus Aggregate Index, 9/30/98

Detailed Sector	Portfolio % of Portf.	Adj. Dur.	Contrib. to Adj. Dur.	Benchmark % of Portf.	Adj. Dur.	Contrib. to Adj. Dur.	Difference % of Portf.	Contrib. to Adj. Dur.
Treasury								
Coupon	27.09	5.37	1.45	39.82	5.58	2.22	−12.73	−0.77
Strip	0.00	0.00	0.00	0.00	0.00	0.00	0.00	0.00
Agencies								
FNMA	4.13	3.40	0.14	3.56	3.44	0.12	0.57	0.02
FHLB	0.00	0.00	0.00	1.21	2.32	0.03	−1.21	−0.03
FHLMC	0.00	0.00	0.00	0.91	3.24	0.03	−0.91	−0.03
REFCORP	3.51	11.22	0.39	0.83	12.18	0.10	2.68	0.29
Other Agencies	0.00	0.00	0.00	1.31	5.58	0.07	−1.31	−0.07
Financial Inst.								
Banking	1.91	5.31	0.10	2.02	5.55	0.11	−0.11	−0.01
Brokerage	1.35	3.52	0.05	0.81	4.14	0.03	0.53	0.01
Financial Cos.	1.88	2.92	0.06	2.11	3.78	0.08	−0.23	−0.02
Insurance	0.00	0.00	0.00	0.52	7.47	0.04	−0.52	−0.04
Other	0.00	0.00	0.00	0.28	5.76	0.02	−0.28	−0.02
Industrials								
Basic	0.63	6.68	0.04	0.89	6.39	0.06	−0.26	−0.01
Capital Goods	4.43	5.35	0.24	1.16	6.94	0.08	3.26	0.16
Consumer Cycl.	2.01	8.37	0.17	2.28	7.10	0.16	−0.27	0.01
Consum. Non-cycl.	8.88	12.54	1.11	1.66	6.84	0.11	7.22	1.00
Energy	1.50	6.82	0.10	0.69	6.89	0.05	0.81	0.05
Technology	1.55	1.58	0.02	0.42	7.39	0.03	1.13	−0.01
Transportation	0.71	12.22	0.09	0.57	7.41	0.04	0.14	0.04
Utilities								
Electric	0.47	3.36	0.02	1.39	5.02	0.07	−0.93	−0.05
Telephone	9.18	2.08	0.19	1.54	6.58	0.10	7.64	0.09
Natural Gas	0.80	5.53	0.04	0.49	6.50	0.03	0.31	0.01
Water	0.00	0.00	0.00	0.00	0.00	0.00	0.00	0.00
Yankee								
Canadians	1.45	7.87	0.11	1.06	6.67	0.07	0.38	0.04
Corporates	0.49	3.34	0.02	1.79	6.06	0.11	−1.30	−0.09
Supranational	1.00	6.76	0.07	0.38	6.33	0.02	0.62	0.04
Sovereigns	0.00	0.00	0.00	0.66	5.95	0.04	−0.66	−0.04
Hypothetical	0.00	0.00	0.00	0.00	0.00	0.00	0.00	0.00
Cash	0.00	0.00	0.00	0.00	0.00	0.00	0.00	0.00

EXHIBIT 24.4   (Continued)

	Portfolio			Benchmark			Difference	
Detailed Sector	% of Portf.	Adj. Dur.	Contrib. to Adj. Dur.	% of Portf.	Adj. Dur.	Contrib. to Adj. Dur.	% of Portf.	Contrib. to Adj. Dur.
Mortgage								
Conventnl. 30-yr.	12.96	1.52	0.20	16.60	1.42	0.24	−3.64	−0.04
GNMA 30-yr.	7.53	1.23	0.09	7.70	1.12	0.09	−0.16	0.01
MBS 15-yr.	3.52	1.95	0.07	5.59	1.63	0.09	−2.06	−0.02
Balloons	3.03	1.69	0.05	0.78	1.02	0.01	2.25	0.04
OTM	0.00	0.00	0.00	0.00	0.00	0.00	0.00	0.00
European & International								
Eurobonds	0.00	0.00	0.00	0.00	0.00	0.00	0.00	0.00
International	0.00	0.00	0.00	0.00	0.00	0.00	0.00	0.00
Asset Backed	0.00	0.00	0.00	0.96	3.14	0.03	−0.96	−0.03
CMO	0.00	0.00	0.00	0.00	0.00	0.00	0.00	0.00
Other	0.00	0.00	0.00	0.00	0.00	0.00	0.00	0.00
Totals	100.00		4.82	100.00		4.29	0.00	0.54

EXHIBIT 24.5   Quality Report
Sample Portfolio versus Aggregate Index, 9/30/98

	Portfolio			Benchmark			Difference	
Quality	% of Portf.	Adj. Dur.	Cntrb. to Adj. Dur.	% of Portf.	Adj. Dur.	Cntrb. to Adj. Dur.	% of Portf.	Cntrb. to Adj. Dur.
Aaa+	34.72	5.72	1.99	47.32	5.41	2.56	−12.60	−0.57
MBS	27.04	1.51	0.41	30.67	1.37	0.42	−3.62	−0.01
Aaa	1.00	6.76	0.07	2.33	4.84	0.11	−1.33	−0.05
Aa	5.54	5.67	0.31	4.19	5.32	0.22	1.35	0.09
A	17.82	7.65	1.36	9.09	6.23	0.57	8.73	0.80
Baa	13.89	4.92	0.68	6.42	6.28	0.40	7.47	0.28
Ba	0.00	0.00	0.00	0.00	0.00	0.00	0.00	0.00
B	0.00	0.00	0.00	0.00	0.00	0.00	0.00	0.00
Caa	0.00	0.00	0.00	0.00	0.00	0.00	0.00	0.00
Ca or lower	0.00	0.00	0.00	0.00	0.00	0.00	0.00	0.00
NR	0.00	0.00	0.00	0.00	0.00	0.00	0.00	0.00
Totals	100.00		4.82	100.00		4.29	0.00	0.54

EXHIBIT 24.6   Optionality Report
Sample Portfolio versus Aggregate Index, 9/30/98

	Option Delta Analysis							
	Portfolio			Benchmark			Difference	
Option Delta	% of Portf.	Delta	Cntrb. to Delta	% of Portf.	Delta	Cntrb. to Delta	% of Portf.	Cntrb. to Delta
Bullet	63.95	0.000	0.000	57.53	0.000	0.000	6.43	0.000
Callable Traded to Matur.	4.74	0.000	0.000	2.66	0.057	0.002	2.08	−0.002
Callable Traded to Call	4.26	0.474	0.020	7.06	0.584	0.041	−2.80	−0.021
Putable Traded to Matur.	0.00	0.000	0.000	0.35	0.129	0.001	−0.35	−0.001
Putable Traded to Put	0.00	0.000	0.000	0.78	0.507	0.004	−0.78	−0.004
Totals	72.96		0.020	68.38		0.047	4.58	−0.027

	Option Gamma Analysis							
	Portfolio			Benchmark			Difference	
Option Gamma	% of Portf.	Delta	Cntrb. to Delta	% of Portf.	Delta	Cntrb. to Delta	% of Portf.	Cntrb. to Delta
Bullet	63.95	0.0000	0.0000	57.53	0.0000	0.0000	6.43	0.0000
Callable Traded to Matur.	4.74	0.0000	0.0000	2.66	0.0024	0.0001	2.08	−0.0001
Callable Traded to Call	4.26	0.0059	0.0002	7.06	0.0125	0.0009	−2.80	−0.0006
Putable Traded to Matur.	0.00	0.0000	0.0000	0.35	−0.0029	−0.0000	−0.35	0.0000
Putable Traded to Put	0.00	0.0000	0.0000	0.78	−0.0008	−0.0000	−0.78	0.0000
Totals	72.96		0.0002	68.38		0.0009	4.58	−0.0007

As we saw in Exhibit 24.2, the largest sources of systematic risk in our sample portfolio are term structure, sector, and quality. We have therefore directed our attention first to the reports that address these risk components; we will return to them later. Next we examine the reports explaining optionality risk and mortgage risk, even though these risks do not contribute significantly to the risk of this particular portfolio.

Optionality Risk

Exhibit 24.6 shows the optionality report. The model looks at price sensitivity measures that are commonly used in the option area—option delta and gamma. These measures are discussed in Chapter 14.

MBS Risk

The risks particular to mortgage-backed securities consist of spread risk, prepayment risk, and convexity risk.[8] The underpinnings for MBS sector spread risk, like those for corporate sectors, are found in the detailed sector report shown in the mortgage part of Exhibit 24.4. Mortgage-backed securities are divided into four broad sectors based on a combination of originating agency and product: conventional 30-year; GNMA 30-year; all 15-year; and all balloons. The contributions of these four sectors to the portfolio and benchmark spread durations form the factor loadings for mortgage sector risk.

Exposures to prepayments are shown in Exhibit 24.7. This group of risk factors corresponds to systematic changes in prepayment speeds by sector. Thus, the factor loadings represent the sensitivities of mortgage prices to changes in prepayment speeds (PSA durations). Premium mortgages will show negative prepayment sensitivities (i.e., prices will decrease with increasing prepayment speed), while those of discount mortgages will be positive. To curtail the exposure to sudden changes in prepayment rates, the portfolio should match the benchmark contributions to prepayment sensitivity in each mortgage sector.

The third mortgage-specific component of tracking error is due to MBS volatility. As explained in Chapter 20, convexity is used as a measure of volatility sensitivity because volatility shocks will have the strongest impact on prices of those mortgages whose prepayment options are at the money (current coupons). These securities tend to have the most negative convexity. Exhibit 24.8 shows the comparison of portfolio and benchmark contributions to convexity in each mortgage sector, which forms the basis for this component of tracking error.

Sources of Non-Systematic Tracking Error

In addition to the various sources of systematic risk, Exhibit 24.2 indicates that the sample portfolio has 26 bp of non-systematic tracking error, or special risk. This risk stems from portfolio concentrations in individual securities or issuers. The portfolio report in Exhibit 24.9 helps elucidate this risk.

---

[8] Mortgage-backed securities and the risks associated with investing in them are described in Chapter 17.

EXHIBIT 24.7 MBS Prepayment Sensitivity Report
Sample Portfolio versus Aggregate Index, 9/30/98

MBS Sector	Portfolio			Benchmark			Difference	
	% of Portfolio	PSA Sens.	Cntrb. to PSA Sens.	% of Portfolio	PSA Sens.	Cntrb. to PSA Sens.	% of Portfolio	Cntrb. to PSA Sens.
COUPON < 6.0%								
Conventional	0.00	0.00	0.00	0.00	1.28	0.00	0.00	0.00
GNMA 30-yr.	0.00	0.00	0.00	0.00	1.03	0.00	0.00	0.00
15-year MBS	0.00	0.00	0.00	0.14	0.01	0.00	−0.14	0.00
Balloon	0.00	0.00	0.00	0.05	−0.08	0.00	−0.05	0.00
6.0% ≤ COUPON < 7.0%								
Conventional	2.90	−1.14	−0.03	5.37	−1.05	−0.06	−2.48	0.02
GNMA 30 yr.	0.76	−1.19	−0.01	1.30	−1.11	−0.01	−0.53	0.01
15-year MBS	3.52	−0.86	−0.03	3.26	−0.88	−0.03	0.26	0.00
Balloon	3.03	−0.54	−0.02	0.48	−0.73	0.00	2.55	−0.01
7.0% ≤ COUPON < 8.0%								
Conventional	4.93	−2.10	−0.10	8.32	−2.79	−0.23	−3.39	0.13
GNMA 30-yr.	4.66	−3.20	−0.15	3.90	−2.82	−0.11	0.76	−0.04
15-year MBS	0.00	0.00	0.00	1.83	−1.92	−0.04	−1.83	0.04
Balloon	0.00	0.00	0.00	0.25	−1.98	−0.01	−0.25	0.01
8.0% ≤ COUPON < 9.0%								
Conventional	5.14	−3.91	−0.20	2.26	−4.27	−0.10	2.87	−0.10
GNMA 30-yr.	0.00	0.00	0.00	1.71	−4.71	−0.08	−1.71	0.08
15-year MBS	0.00	0.00	0.00	0.31	−2.16	−0.01	−0.31	0.01
Balloon	0.00	0.00	0.00	0.00	−2.38	0.00	0.00	0.00
9.0% ≤ COUPON < 10.0%								
Conventional	0.00	0.00	0.00	0.54	−6.64	−0.04	−0.54	0.04
GNMA 30-yr.	2.11	−7.24	−0.15	0.62	−6.05	−0.04	1.49	−0.12
15-year MBS	0.00	0.00	0.00	0.04	−1.61	0.00	−0.04	0.00
Balloon	0.00	0.00	0.00	0.00	0.00	0.00	0.00	0.00
COUPON ≥ 10.0%								
Conventional	0.00	0.00	0.00	0.10	−8.14	−0.01	−0.10	0.01
GNMA 30-yr.	0.00	0.00	0.00	0.17	−7.49	−0.01	−0.17	0.01
15-year MBS	0.00	0.00	0.00	0.00	0.00	0.00	0.00	0.00
Balloon	0.00	0.00	0.00	0.00	0.00	0.00	0.00	0.00
Subtotals								
Conventional	12.96		−0.34	16.6		−0.43	−3.64	0.09
GNMA 30-yr.	7.53		−0.31	7.70		−0.26	−0.16	−0.06
15-year MBS	3.52		−0.03	5.59		−0.07	−2.06	0.04
Balloon	3.03		−0.02	0.78		−0.01	2.25	−0.01
Totals	27.04		−0.70	30.67		−0.76	−3.62	0.07

EXHIBIT 24.8 MBS Convexity Analysis
Sample Portfolio versus Aggregate Index, 9/30/98

MBS Sector	Portfolio			Benchmark			Difference	
	% of Portfolio	Con-vexity	Cntrb. to Convexity	% of Portfolio	Con-vexity	Cntrb. to Convexity	% of Portfolio	Cntrb. to Convexity
COUPON < 6.0%								
Conventional	0.00	0.00	0.00	0.00	−0.56	0.00	0.00	0.00
GNMA 30-yr.	0.00	0.00	0.00	0.00	−0.85	0.00	0.00	0.00
15-year MBS	0.00	0.00	0.00	0.14	−0.88	0.00	−0.14	0.00
Balloon	0.00	0.00	0.00	0.05	−0.48	0.00	−0.05	0.00
6.0% ≤ COUPON < 7.0%								
Conventional	2.90	−3.52	−0.10	5.37	−3.19	−0.17	−2.48	0.07
GNMA 30-yr.	0.76	−3.65	−0.03	1.30	−3.13	−0.04	−0.53	0.01
15-year MBS	3.52	−1.78	−0.06	3.26	−2.06	−0.07	0.26	0.00
Balloon	3.03	−1.50	−0.05	0.48	−1.11	−0.01	2.55	−0.04
7.0% ≤ COUPON < 8.0%								
Conventional	4.93	−3.39	−0.17	8.32	−2.60	−0.22	−3.39	0.05
GNMA 30-yr.	4.66	−2.40	−0.11	3.90	−2.88	−0.11	0.76	0.00
15-year MBS	0.00	0.00	0.00	1.83	−1.56	−0.03	−1.83	0.03
Balloon	0.00	0.00	0.00	0.25	−0.97	0.00	−0.25	0.00
8.0% ≤ COUPON < 9.0%								
Conventional	5.14	−1.27	−0.07	2.26	−1.01	−0.02	2.87	−0.04
GNMA 30-yr.	0.00	0.00	0.00	1.71	−0.56	−0.01	−1.71	0.01
15-year MBS	0.00	0.00	0.00	0.31	−0.93	0.00	−0.31	0.00
Balloon	0.00	0.00	0.00	0.00	−0.96	0.00	0.00	0.00
9.0% ≤ COUPON < 10.0%								
Conventional	0.00	0.00	0.00	0.54	−0.80	0.00	−0.54	0.00
GNMA 30-yr.	2.11	−0.34	−0.01	0.62	−0.36	0.00	1.49	−0.01
15-year MBS	0.00	0.00	0.00	0.04	−0.52	0.00	−0.04	0.00
Balloon	0.00	0.00	0.00	0.00	0.00	0.00	0.00	0.00
COUPON ≥ 10.0%								
Conventional	0.00	0.00	0.00	0.10	−0.61	0.00	−0.10	0.00
GNMA 30-yr.	0.00	0.00	0.00	0.17	−0.21	0.00	−0.17	0.00
15-year MBS	0.00	0.00	0.00	0.00	0.00	0.00	0.00	0.00
Balloon	0.00	0.00	0.00	0.00	0.00	0.00	0.00	0.00
Subtotals								
Conventional	12.96		−0.33	16.6		−0.42	−3.64	0.08
GNMA 30-yr.	7.53		−0.15	7.70		−0.16	−0.16	0.02
15-year MBS	3.52		−0.06	5.59		−0.10	−2.06	0.04
Balloon	3.03		−0.05	0.78		−0.01	2.25	−0.04
Totals	27.04		−0.59	30.67		−0.69	−3.62	0.10

EXHIBIT 24.9 Portfolio Report: Composition of Sample Portfolio, 9/30/98

IssuerName	Coup.	Maturity	Moody	S&P	Sect.	Adj. Dur.	Par Val.	%
Baker Hughes	8.000	05/15/04	A2	A	IND	4.47	5,000	0.87
Boeing Co.	6.350	06/15/03	Aa3	AA	IND	3.98	10,000	1.58
Coca-Cola Enterprises I	6.950	11/15/26	A3	A+	IND	12.37	50,000	8.06
Eli Lilly Co.	6.770	01/01/36	Aa3	AA	IND	14.18	5,000	0.83
ENRON Corp.	6.625	11/15/05	Baa2	BBB+	UTL	5.53	5,000	0.80
Federal Natl. Mtg. Assn.	5.625	03/15/01	Aaa+	AAA+	USA	2.27	10,000	1.53
Federal Natl. Mtg. Assn.-G	7.400	07/01/04	Aaa+	AAA+	USA	4.66	8,000	1.37
FHLM Gold 7-Years Balloon	6.000	04/01/26	Aaa+	AAA+	FHg	1.69	20,000	3.03
FHLM Gold Guar Single F.	6.500	08/01/08	Aaa+	AAA+	FHd	1.95	23,000	3.52
FHLM Gold Guar Single F.	7.000	01/01/28	Aaa+	AAA+	FHb	1.33	32,000	4.93
FHLM Gold Guar Single F.	6.500	02/01/28	Aaa+	AAA+	FHb	2.83	19,000	2.90
First Bank System	6.875	09/15/07	A2	A–	FIN	6.73	4,000	0.65
Fleet Mortgage Group	6.500	09/15/99	A2	A+	FIN	0.92	4,000	0.60
FNMA Conventional Long T.	8.000	05/01/21	Aaa+	AAA+	FNa	0.96	33,000	5.14
FNMA MTN	6.420	02/12/08	Aaa+	AAA+	USA	3.40	8,000	1.23
Ford Motor Credit	7.500	01/15/03	A1	A	FIN	3.62	4,000	0.65
Fort James Corp.	6.875	09/15/07	Baa2	BBB–	IND	6.68	4,000	0.63
GNMA I Single Family	9.500	10/01/19	Aaa+	AAA+	GNa	1.60	13,000	2.11
GNMA I Single Family	7.500	07/01/22	Aaa+	AAA+	GNa	0.75	30,000	4.66
GNMA I Single Family	6.500	02/01/28	Aaa+	AAA+	GNa	3.14	5,000	0.76
GTE Corp.	9.375	12/01/00	Baa1	A	TEL	1.91	50,000	8.32
Int-American Dev. Bank-G	6.375	10/22/07	Aaa	AAA	SUP	6.76	6,000	1.00
Intl Business Machines	6.375	06/15/00	A1	A+	IND	1.58	10,000	1.55
Lehman Brothers Inc.	7.125	07/15/02	Baa1	A	FIN	3.20	4,000	0.59
Lockheed Martin	6.550	05/15/99	A3	BBB+	IND	0.59	10,000	1.53
Manitoba Prov. Canada	8.875	09/15/21	A1	AA–	CAN	11.34	4,000	0.79
Mcdonalds Corp.	5.950	01/15/08	Aa2	AA	IND	7.05	4,000	0.63
Merrill Lynch & Co.-GLO	6.000	02/12/03	Aa3	AA–	FIN	3.77	5,000	0.76
Nationsbank Corp.	5.750	03/15/01	Aa2	A+	FIN	2.26	3,000	0.45
New York Telephone	9.375	07/15/31	A2	A+	TEL	3.66	5,000	0.86
Nike Inc.	6.375	12/01/03	A1	A+	IND	4.30	3,000	0.48
Norfolk Southern Corp.	7.800	05/15/27	Baa1	BBB+	IND	12.22	4,000	0.71
Norwest Financial Inc.	6.125	08/01/03	Aa3	AA–	FIN	4.12	4,000	0.62
Ont. Prov. Canada-global	7.375	01/27/03	Aa3	AA–	CAN	3.67	4,000	0.65
Pub. Svc. Electric + Gas	6.125	08/01/02	A3	A–	ELU	3.36	3,000	0.47
Raytheon Co.	7.200	08/15/27	Baa1	BBB	IND	12.61	8,000	1.31
Resolution Funding Corp.	8.125	10/15/19	Aaa+	AAA+	USA	11.22	17,000	3.51
Time Warner Ent.	8.375	03/15/23	Baa2	BBB–	IND	11.45	5,000	0.90
Ultramar Diamond Sham.	7.200	10/15/17	Baa2	BBB	IND	10.06	4,000	0.63
US Treasury Bonds	10.375	11/15/12	Aaa+	AAA+	UST	6.38	10,000	2.17
US Treasury Bonds	10.625	08/15/15	Aaa+	AAA+	UST	9.68	14,000	3.43
US Treasury Bonds	6.250	08/15/23	Aaa+	AAA+	UST	13.26	30,000	5.14
US Treasury Notes	8.875	02/15/99	Aaa+	AAA+	UST	0.37	9,000	1.38
US Treasury Notes	6.375	07/15/99	Aaa+	AAA+	UST	0.76	4,000	0.61
US Treasury Notes	7.125	09/30/99	Aaa+	AAA+	UST	0.96	17,000	2.59
US Treasury Notes	5.875	11/15/99	Aaa+	AAA+	UST	1.06	17,000	2.62
US Treasury Notes	6.875	03/31/00	Aaa+	AAA+	UST	1.42	8,000	1.23
US Treasury Notes	6.000	08/15/00	Aaa+	AAA+	UST	1.75	11,000	1.70
US Treasury Notes	8.000	05/15/01	Aaa+	AAA+	UST	2.31	9,000	1.50
US Treasury Notes	7.500	11/15/01	Aaa+	AAA+	UST	2.72	10,000	1.67
US Treasury Notes	6.625	03/31/02	Aaa+	AAA+	UST	3.12	6,000	0.96
US Treasury Notes	6.250	08/31/02	Aaa+	AAA+	UST	3.45	10,000	1.60
US Treasury Notes	5.750	08/15/03	Aaa+	AAA+	UST	4.22	1,000	0.16
US Treasury Notes	6.500	05/15/05	Aaa+	AAA+	UST	5.33	1,000	0.17
US Treasury Notes	6.125	08/15/07	Aaa+	AAA+	UST	6.90	1,000	0.17
Wells Fargo + Co.	6.875	04/01/06	A2	A–	FIN	5.89	5,000	0.80
Westpac Banking Corp.	7.875	10/15/02	A1	A+	FOC	3.34	3,000	0.49

EXHIBIT 24.10   Calculation of Variance Due to Special Risk (Issue-Specific Model)*

	Portfolio Weights	Benchmark Weights	Contribution to Issue-Specific Risk
Issue 1	w_{P_1}	w_{B_1}	$(w_{P_1} - w_{B_1})^2 \sigma_{\varepsilon_1}^2$
Issue 2	w_{P_2}	w_{B_2}	$(w_{P_2} - w_{B_2})^2 \sigma_{\varepsilon_2}^2$
...			
Issue $N-1$	$w_{P_{N-1}}$	$w_{B_{N-1}}$	$(w_{P_{N-1}} - w_{B_{N-1}})^2 \sigma_{\varepsilon_{N-1}}^2$
Issue N	w_{P_N}	w_{B_N}	$(w_{P_N} - w_{B_N})^2 \sigma_{\varepsilon_N}^2$
Total Issue-Specific Risk			$\displaystyle\sum_{i=1}^{N} (w_{P_i} - w_{B_i})^2 \sigma_{\varepsilon_i}^2$

* w_{P_i} and w_{B_i} are weights of security i in the portfolio and in the benchmark as a percentage of total market value. $\sigma_{\varepsilon_i}^2$ is the variance of residual returns for security i. It is obtained from historical volatility of security-specific residual returns unexplained by the combination of all systematic risk factors.

The rightmost column of the exhibit shows the percentage of the portfolio's market value invested in each security. As the portfolio is relatively small, each bond makes up a noticeable fraction. In particular, there are two extremely large positions in corporate bonds, issued by GTE Corp. and Coca-Cola. With $50 million apiece, each of these two bonds represents more than 8% of the portfolio. A negative credit event associated with either of these firms (i.e., a downgrade) would cause large losses in the portfolio, while hardly affecting the highly diversified benchmark. The Aggregate Index consisted of almost 7,000 securities as of September 30, 1998, so that the largest U.S. Treasury issue accounts for less than 1%, and most corporate issues contribute less than 0.01% of the index market value. Thus, any large position in a corporate issue represents a material difference between portfolio and benchmark exposures that must be considered in a full treatment of risk.

    The magnitude of the return variance that the risk model associates with a mismatch in allocations to a particular issue is proportional to the square of the allocation difference and to the residual return variance estimated for the issue. This calculation is shown in schematic form in Exhibit 24.10 and illustrated numerically for our sample portfolio in Exhibit 24.11.

EXHIBIT 24.11   Illustration of the Calculation of Non-Systematic Tracking Error

Issuer	Coupon	Maturity	Spec. Risk Vol. (bp/mo.)	% of Portf.	% of Bnchmrk.	Diff.	Contrib. Tracking Error (bp/mo.)
Boeing Co.	6.350	06/15/03	44	1.58	0.01	1.58	2
Coca-Cola Enterprises Inc.	6.950	11/15/26	77	8.06	0.01	8.05	21
GTE Corp.	9.375	12/01/00	37	8.32	0.01	8.31	11
Eli Lilly Co.	6.770	01/01/36	78	0.83	0.01	0.82	2
Manitoba Prov. Canada	8.875	09/15/21	73	0.79	0.01	0.79	2
Norfolk Southern Corp.	7.800	05/15/27	84	0.71	0.02	0.70	2
Raytheon Co.	7.200	08/15/27	85	1.31	0.01	1.30	4
Resolution Funding Corp.	8.125	10/15/19	19	3.51	0.12	3.39	2
Time Warner Ent.	8.375	03/15/23	80	0.90	0.02	0.88	2
U.S. Treasury Bonds	10.625	08/15/15	17	3.43	0.18	3.25	2
U.S. Treasury Bonds	8.875	02/15/19	18	0.00	0.49	−0.49	0
U.S. Treasury Bonds	8.125	08/15/19	18	0.00	0.47	−0.47	0
U.S. Treasury Bonds	8.750	08/15/20	18	0.00	0.54	−0.54	0
U.S. Treasury Bonds	8.000	11/15/21	17	0.00	0.81	−0.81	0
U.S. Treasury Bonds	6.250	08/15/23	19	5.14	0.46	4.68	3
U.S. Treasury Bonds	6.125	11/15/27	20	0.00	0.44	−0.44	0
FHLM Gold Guar. Single Fam. 30-yr.	7.000	04/01/27	16	0.00	0.56	−0.56	0
FHLM Gold Guar. Single Fam. 30-yr.	7.000	01/01/28	15	4.93	0.46	4.47	2
FNMA Conventional Long T. 30-yr.	6.500	03/01/28	15	0.00	1.16	−1.16	1
FNMA Conventional Long T. 30-yr.	7.000	07/01/22	16	0.00	0.65	−0.65	0
FNMA Conventional Long T. 30-yr.	7.000	05/01/27	16	0.00	0.69	−0.69	0
FNMA Conventional Long T. 30-yr.	8.000	05/01/21	17	5.14	0.24	4.90	3
GNMA I Single Fam. 30-yr.	7.500	07/01/22	16	4.66	0.30	4.36	2

With the return variance based on the square of the market weight, it is dominated by the largest positions in the portfolio. The set of bonds shown includes those with the greatest allocations in the portfolio and in the benchmark. The large position in the Coca-Cola bond contributes 21 bp of the total non-systematic risk of 26 bp. This is due to the 8.05% overweighting of this bond relative to its position in the index and the 77 bp monthly volatility of non-systematic return that the model has estimated for this bond.[9] The contribution to the annualized tracking error is then given by:

$$\sqrt{12 \times (0.0805 \times 77)^2} = 21$$

While the overweighting to GTE is larger in terms of percentage of market value, the estimated risk is lower due to the much smaller non-

---

[9] This estimate is based on bond characteristics such as sector, quality, duration, age, and amount outstanding.

systematic return volatility (37 bp). This is mainly because the GTE issue has a much shorter maturity (12/2000) than the Coca-Cola issue (11/2026). For bonds of similar maturities, the model tends to assign higher special risk volatilities to lower-rated issues. Thus, mismatches in low-quality bonds with long duration will be the biggest contributors to non-systematic tracking error.

We assume independence of the risk from individual bonds, so the overall non-systematic risk is computed as the sum of the contributions to variance from each security. Note that mismatches also arise due to bonds that are underweighted in the portfolio. Most bonds in the index do not appear in the portfolio, and each missing bond contributes to tracking error. However, the percentage of the index each bond represents is usually very small. Besides, their contributions to return variance are squared in the calculation of tracking error. Thus, the impact of bonds not included in the portfolio is usually insignificant. The largest contribution to tracking error stemming from an underweighting to a security is due to the 1998 issuance of FNMA 30-year 6.5% pass-throughs, which represents 1.16% of the benchmark. Even this relatively large mismatch contributes only a scant 1 bp to tracking error.

Combining Components of Tracking Error

Given the origins of each component of tracking error shown in Exhibit 24.2, we can address the question of how these components combine to form the overall tracking error. Of the 52 bp of overall tracking error (TE), 45 bp correspond to systematic TE and 26 bp to non-systematic TE. The net result of these two sources of tracking error does not equal their sum. Rather, the squares of these two numbers (which represent variances) sum to the variance of the result. Next we take its square root to obtain the overall TE ($[45.0^2 + 26.1^2]^{0.5} = 52.0$). This illustrates the risk-reducing benefits of diversification from combining independent (zero correlation) sources of risk.

When components of risk are not assumed to be independent, correlations must be considered. At the top of Exhibit 24.2, we see that the systematic risk is composed of 36.3 bp of term structure risk and 39.5 bp from all other forms of systematic risk combined (non-term structure risk). If these two were independent, they would combine to a systematic tracking error of 53.6 bp ($[36.3^2 + 39.5^2]^{0.5} = 53.6$). The combined systematic tracking error of only 45 bp reflects negative correlations among certain risk factors in the two groups.

The tracking error breakdown report in Exhibit 24.2 shows the sub-components of tracking error due to sector, quality, etc. These sub-components are calculated in two different ways. In the first column, we estimate the isolated tracking error due to the effect of each group of related risk factors considered alone. The tracking error due to term structure, for example, reflects only the portfolio/benchmark mismatches in exposures along the yield curve, as well as the volatilities of each of these risk factors and the correlations among them.

Similarly, the tracking error due to sector reflects only the mismatches in sector exposures, the volatilities of these risk factors, and the correlations among them. However, the correlations between the risk factors due to term structure and those due to sector do not participate in either of these calculations. Exhibit 24.12 depicts an idealized covariance matrix containing just three groups of risk factors relating to the yield curve (Y), sector spreads (S), and quality spreads (Q). Exhibit 24.12a illustrates how the covariance matrix is used to calculate the sub-components of tracking error in the isolated mode. The three shaded blocks represent the parts of the matrix that pertain to: movements of the various points along the yield curve and the correlations among them ($Y \times Y$); movements of sector spreads and the correlations among them ($S \times S$); and movements of quality spreads and the correlations among them ($Q \times Q$). The unshaded portions of the matrix, which deal with the correlations among different sets of risk factors, do not contribute to any of the partial tracking errors.

EXHIBIT 24.12 Illustration of "Isolated" and "Cumulative" Calculations of Tracking Error Subcomponents*

a. Isolated Calculation of Tracking Error Components

$Y \times Y$	$Y \times S$	$Y \times Q$
$S \times Y$	$S \times S$	$S \times Q$
$Q \times Y$	$Q \times S$	$Q \times Q$

b. Cumulative Calculation of Tracking Error Components

$Y \times Y$	$Y \times S$	$Y \times Q$
$S \times Y$	$S \times S$	$S \times Q$
$Q \times Y$	$Q \times S$	$Q \times Q$

* Y – Yield curve risk factors; S – Sector spread risk factors; Q – Credit Quality spread risk factors.

The next two columns of Exhibit 24.12 represent a different way of subdividing tracking error. The middle column shows the *cumulative tracking error*, which incrementally introduces one group of risk factors at a time to the tracking error calculation. In the first row, we find 36.3 bp of tracking error due to term structure. In the second, we see that if term structure and sector risk are considered together, while all other risks are ignored, the tracking error increases to 38.3 bp. The rightmost column shows that the resulting "change in tracking error" due to the incremental inclusion of sector risk is 2.0 bp. As additional groups of risk factors are included, the calculation converges toward the total systematic tracking error, which is obtained with the use of the entire matrix. Exhibit 24.12b illustrates the rectangular section of the covariance matrix that is used at each stage of the calculation. The incremental tracking error due to sector reflects not only the effect of the $S \times S$ box in the diagram, but the $S \times Y$ and $Y \times S$ cross terms as well. That is, the partial tracking error due to sector takes into account the correlations between sector risk and yield curve risk. It answers the question, "Given the exposure to yield curve risk, how much more risk is introduced by the exposure to sector risk?"

The incremental approach is intuitively pleasing because the partial tracking errors (the "Change in Tracking Error" column of Exhibit 24.2) add up to the total systematic tracking error. Of course, the order in which the various partial tracking errors are considered will affect the magnitude of the corresponding terms. Also, note that some of the partial tracking errors computed in this way are negative. This reflects negative correlations among certain groups of risk factors. For example, in Exhibit 24.2, the incremental risk due to the MBS Sector is –1.7 bp.

The two methods used to subdivide tracking error into different components are complementary and serve different purposes. The isolated calculation is ideal for comparing the magnitudes of different types of risk to highlight the most significant exposures. The cumulative approach produces a set of tracking error sub-components that sum to the total systematic tracking error and reflect the effect of correlations among different groups of risk factors. The major drawback of the cumulative approach is that results are highly dependent on the order in which they are computed. The order currently used by the model was selected based on the significance of each type of risk; it may not be optimal for every portfolio/benchmark combination.

Other Risk Model Outputs

The model's analysis of portfolio and benchmark risk is not limited to the calculation of tracking error. The model also calculates the absolute return volatilities (sigmas) of portfolio and benchmark.[10] *Portfolio sigma* is calculated in the same fashion as tracking error, but is based on the factor loadings (sensitivities to market factors) of the portfolio, rather than on the differences from the benchmark. Sigma represents the volatility of portfolio returns, just as tracking error represents the volatility of the return difference between portfolio and benchmark. Also like tracking error, sigma consists of systematic and non-systematic components, and the volatility of the benchmark return is calculated in the same way.

Both portfolio and benchmark sigmas appear at the bottom of the tracking error report (Exhibit 24.2). Note that the tracking error of 52 bp (the annualized volatility of return difference) is greater than the difference between the return volatilities (sigmas) of the portfolio and the benchmark (440 bp – 417 bp = 23 bp). It is easy to see why this should be so. Assume a benchmark of Treasury bonds, whose entire risk is due to term structure. A portfolio of short term, high-yield corporate bonds could be constructed such that the overall return volatility would match that of the Treasury benchmark. The magnitude of the credit risk in this portfolio might match the magnitude of the term structure risk in the benchmark, but the two would certainly not cancel each other out. The tracking error in this case might be larger than the sigma of either the portfolio or the benchmark.

In our example, the portfolio sigma is greater than that of the benchmark. Thus, we can say that the portfolio is "more risky" than the benchmark—its longer duration makes it more susceptible to a rise in interest rates. What if the portfolio was shorter than the benchmark and had a lower sigma? In this sense, we could consider the portfolio to be less risky. However, tracking error could be just as big given its capture of the risk of a yield curve rally in which the portfolio would lag. To reduce the risk of underperformance (tracking error), it is necessary to match the risk exposures of the portfolio and benchmark. Thus, the reduction of tracking error will typically result in bringing portfolio sigma nearer to that of the benchmark; but sigma can be changed in many ways that will not necessarily improve the tracking error.

It is interesting to compare the non-systematic components of portfolio and benchmark risk. The first thing to notice is that, when viewed in the context of the overall return volatility, the effect of non-systematic risk is negligible. To the precision shown, for both the portfolio and benchmark, the overall sigma is equal to its systematic part. The portfolio-level risk due to individual credit events is very small when compared to the

---

[10] The reason the term sigma is used is that the practice in statistics is to use the Greek symbol "sigma" to represent the standard deviation of a variable. In investment management, sigma is used to represent the standard deviation or volatility of returns.

total volatility of returns, which includes the entire exposure to all systematic risks, notably yield changes. The portfolio also has significantly more non-systematic risk (27 bp) than does the benchmark (4 bp), because the latter is much more diversified. In fact, because the benchmark exposures to any individual issuer are so close to zero, the non-systematic tracking error (26 bp) is almost the same as the non-systematic part of portfolio sigma. Notice that the non-systematic risk can form a significant component of the tracking error (26.1 bp out of a total of 52 bp) even as it is a negligible part of the absolute return volatility.

Another quantity calculated by the model is *beta*, which measures the risk of the portfolio relative to that of the benchmark. The beta for our sample portfolio is 1.05, as shown at the bottom of Exhibit 24.1. This means that the portfolio is more risky (volatile) than the benchmark. For every 100 bp of benchmark return (positive or negative), we would expect to see 105 bp for the portfolio. It is common to compare the beta produced by the risk model with the ratio of portfolio and benchmark durations. In this case, the duration ratio is 4.82/4.29 = 1.12, which is somewhat larger than the risk model beta. This is because the duration-based approach considers only term structure risk (and only parallel shift risk at that), while the risk model includes the combined effects of all relevant forms of risk, along with the correlations among them.

RISK MODEL APPLICATIONS

In this section we explore several applications of the model to portfolio management.[11]

Quantifying Risk Associated with a View

The risk model is primarily a diagnostic tool. Whatever position a portfolio manager has taken relative to the benchmark, the risk model will quantify how much risk has been assumed. This helps measure the risk of the exposures taken to express a market view. It also points out the potential unintended risks in the portfolio.

Many firms use risk-adjusted measures to evaluate portfolio performance. A high return achieved by a series of successful but risky market plays may not please a conservative pension plan sponsor. A more modest return, achieved while maintaining much lower risk versus the

---

[11] Additional applications are provided in Lev Dynkin, Jay Hyman, and Wei Wu, "Multi-Factor Risk Models and Their Applications," in Frank J. Fabozzi (ed.), *Professional Perspectives on Fixed Income Portfolio Management*, Volume 2, 2001, pp. 101–145.

benchmark, might be seen as a healthier approach over the long term. This point of view can be reflected either by adjusting performance by the amount of risk taken or by specifying in advance the acceptable level of risk for the portfolio. In any case, the portfolio manager should be cognizant of the risk inherent in a particular market view and weigh it against the anticipated gain. The increasing popularity of risk-adjusted performance evaluation is evident in the frequent use of the concept of an *information ratio*—portfolio outperformance of the benchmark per unit of standard deviation of observed outperformance.[12]

Projecting the Effect of Proposed Transactions on Tracking Error

Proposed trades are often analyzed in the context of a 1-for-1 (substitution) swap. Selling a security and using the proceeds to buy another may earn a few additional basis points of yield. The risk model allows analysis of such a trade in the context of the portfolio and its benchmark. By comparing the current portfolio versus benchmark risk and the pro forma risk after the proposed trade, an asset manager can evaluate how well the trade fits the portfolio. Our portfolio analytics platform offers an interactive mode to allow portfolio modifications and immediately see the effect on tracking error.

For example, having noticed that our sample portfolio has an extremely large position in the Coca-Cola issue, we might decide to cut the size of this position in half. To avoid making any significant changes to the systematic risk profile of the portfolio, we might look for a bond with similar maturity, credit rating, and sector. Exhibit 24.13 shows an example of such a swap. Half the position in the Coca-Cola 30-year bond is replaced by a 30-year issue from Anheuser-Busch, another single-A rated issuer in the beverage sector. As shown later, this transaction reduces non-systematic tracking error from 26 bp to 22 bp. While we have unwittingly produced a 1 bp increase in the systematic risk (the durations of the two bonds were not identical), the overall effect was a decrease in tracking error from 52 bp to 51 bp.

EXHIBIT 24.13   A Simple Diversification Trade: Cut the Size of the Largest Position in Half

Issuer	Coupon	Maturity	Par Value ($000s)	MV ($000s)	Sector	Quality	Dur. Adj.
Sell: Coca-Cola Enterprises Inc.	6.95	11/15/2026	25000	27053	IND	A3	12.37
Buy: Anheuser-Busch Co., Inc.	6.75	12/15/2027	25000	26941	IND	A1	12.86

---

[12] An explanation of the information ratio is provided in Chapter 7.

Optimization

For many portfolio managers, the risk model acts not only as a measurement tool but plays a major role in the portfolio construction process. The model has a unique optimization feature that guides investors to transactions that reduce portfolio risk. The types of questions it addresses are: What single transaction can reduce the risk of the portfolio relative to the benchmark the most? How could the tracking error be reduced with minimum turnover? The portfolio manager is given an opportunity to intervene at each step in the optimization process and select transactions that lead to the desired changes in the risk profile of the portfolio and are practical at the same time.

As in any portfolio optimization procedure, the first step is to choose the set of assets that may be purchased. The composition of this investable universe, or bond swap pool, is critical. This universe should be large enough to provide flexibility in matching all benchmark risk exposures, yet it should contain only securities that are acceptable candidates for purchase. This universe may be created by querying a bond database (selecting, for instance, all corporate bonds with more than $500 million outstanding that were issued in the last three years) or by providing a list of securities available for purchase.

Once the investable universe has been selected, the optimizer begins an iterative process (known as *gradient descent*), searching for 1-for-1 bond swap transactions that will achieve the investor's objective. In the simplest case, the objective is to minimize the tracking error. The bonds in the swap pool are ranked in terms of reduction in tracking error per unit of each bond purchased. The system indicates which bond, if purchased, will lead to the steepest decline in tracking error, but leaves the ultimate choice of the security to the investor. Once a bond has been selected for purchase, the optimizer offers a list of possible market-value-neutral swaps of this security against various issues in the portfolio (with the optimal transaction size for each pair of bonds), sorted in order of possible reduction in tracking error. Investors are free to adjust the model's recommendations, either selecting different bonds to sell or adjusting (e.g., rounding off) recommended trade amounts.

Exhibit 24.14 shows how this optimization process is used to minimize the tracking error of the sample portfolio. A close look at the sequence of trades suggested by the optimizer reveals that several types of risk are reduced simultaneously. In the first trade, the majority of the large position in the Coca-Cola 30-year bond is swapped for a 3-year Treasury. This trade simultaneously changes systematic exposures to term structure, sector, and quality; it also cuts one of the largest issuer exposures, reducing non-systematic risk. This one trade brings the overall tracking error down from 52 bp to 29 bp. As risk declines and the portfolio risk profile approaches the benchmark, there is less room for such drastic improvements. Transaction sizes become smaller, and the improvement in tracking error with each trade slows. The second and third transactions continue to adjust the sector and quality exposures and fine-tune the risk exposures along the curve. The fourth transaction addresses the other large corporate exposure, cutting the position in GTE by two-thirds. The first five trades reduce the tracking error to 16 bp, creating an essentially passive portfolio.

EXHIBIT 24.14 Sequence of Transactions Selected by Optimizer Showing Progressively Smaller Tracking Error, $000s, Initial Tracking Error: 52.0 bp

Transaction # 1		
Sold:	31000 of COCA-COLA ENTERPRISES	6.950 2026/11/15
Bought:	30000 of U.S. TREASURY NOTES	8.000 2001/05/15
Cash Left Over:	−17.10	
New Tracking Error:	29.4 bp	
Cost of this Transaction:	152.500	
Cumulative Cost:	152.500	
Transaction # 2		
Sold:	10000 of LOCKHEED MARTIN	6.550 1999/05/15
Bought:	9000 of U.S. TREASURY NOTES	6.125 2007/08/15
Cash Left Over:	132.84	
New Tracking Error:	25.5 bp	
Cost of this Transaction:	47.500	
Cumulative Cost:	200.000	
Transaction # 3		
Sold:	4000 of NORFOLK SOUTHERN CORP.	7.800 2027/05/15
Bought:	3000 of U.S. TREASURY BONDS	10.625 2015/08/15
Cash Left Over:	−8.12	
New Tracking Error:	23.1 bp	
Cost of this Transaction:	17.500	
Cumulative Cost:	217.500	
Transaction # 4		
Sold:	33000 of GTE CORP.	9.375 2000/12/01
Bought:	34000 of U.S. TREASURY NOTES	6.625 2002/03/31
Cash Left Over:	412.18	
New Tracking Error:	19.8 bp	
Cost of this Transaction:	167.500	
Cumulative Cost:	385.000	
Transaction # 5		
Sold:	7000 of COCA-COLA ENTERPRISES	6.950 2026/11/15
Bought:	8000 of U.S. TREASURY NOTES	6.000 2000/08/15
Cash Left Over:	−304.17	
New Tracking Error:	16.4 bp	
Cost of this Transaction:	37.500	
Cumulative Cost:	422.500	

EXHIBIT 24.15   Tracking Error Summary
Passive Portfolio versus Aggregate Index, 9/30/98

	Tracking Error (bp/year)		
	Isolated	Cumulative	Change
Tracking Error Term Structure	7.0	7.0	7.0
Non-Term Structure	9.6		
Tracking Error Sector	7.4	10.5	3.5
Tracking Error Quality	2.1	11.2	0.7
Tracking Error Optionality	1.6	11.5	0.3
Tracking Error Coupon	2.0	12.3	0.8
Tracking Error MBS Sector	4.9	10.2	−2.1
Tracking Error MBS Volatility	7.2	11.1	0.9
Tracking Error MBS Prepayment	2.5	10.3	−0.8
Total Systematic Tracking Error		10.3	
Non-Systematic Tracking Error			
Issuer-Specific	12.4		
Issue-Specific	3.0		
Total	12.7		
Total Tracking Error Return		16	

	Systematic	Non-Systematic	Total
Benchmark Sigma	417	4	417
Portfolio Sigma	413	13	413

An analysis of the tracking error for this passive portfolio is shown in Exhibit 24.15. The systematic tracking error has been reduced to just 10 bp and the non-systematic risk to 13 bp. Once systematic risk drops below non-systematic risk, the latter becomes the limiting factor. In turn, further tracking error reduction by just a few transactions becomes much less likely. When there are exceptionally large positions, like the two mentioned in the above example, non-systematic risk can be reduced quickly. Upon completion of such risk reduction transactions, further reduction of tracking error requires a major diversification effort. The critical factor that determines non-systematic risk is the percentage of the portfolio in any single issue. On average, a portfolio of 50 bonds has 2% allocated to each position. To reduce this average allocation to 1%, the number of bonds would need to be doubled.

EXHIBIT 24.16   Term Structure Risk Report for Passive Portfolio, 9/30/98

| Year | Cash Flows | | Difference (%) |
	Portfolio (%)	Benchmark (%)	
0.00	1.33	1.85	−0.52
0.25	3.75	4.25	−0.50
0.50	4.05	4.25	−0.19
0.75	3.50	3.76	−0.27
1.00	8.96	7.37	1.59
1.50	7.75	10.29	−2.54
2.00	8.30	8.09	0.21
2.50	10.30	6.42	3.87
3.00	5.32	5.50	−0.19
3.50	8.24	4.81	3.43
4.00	6.56	7.19	−0.63
5.00	5.91	6.96	−1.05
6.00	3.42	4.67	−1.24
7.00	5.75	7.84	−2.10
10.00	6.99	7.37	−0.38
15.00	4.00	3.88	0.12
20.00	2.98	3.04	−0.05
25.00	2.37	1.73	0.64
30.00	0.47	0.68	−0.21
40.00	0.08	0.07	0.01

The risk exposures of the resulting passive portfolio match the benchmark much better than the initial portfolio. Exhibit 24.16 details the term structure risk of the passive portfolio. Compared with Exhibit 24.3, the overweight at the long end is reduced significantly. The overweight at the 25-year vertex has gone down from 1.45% to 0.64%, and (perhaps more importantly) it is now offset partially by underweights at the adjacent 20- and 30-year vertices. Exhibit 24.17 presents the sector risk report for the passive portfolio. The underweight to Treasuries (in contribution to duration) has been reduced from −0.77% to −0.29% relative to the initial portfolio (Exhibit 24.4), and the largest corporate overweight, to consumer non-cyclicals, has come down from +1.00% to +0.24%.

EXHIBIT 24.17 Sector Risk Report for Passive Portfolio, 9/30/98

Detailed Sector	Portfolio % of Port.	Portfolio Adj. Dur.	Portfolio Contrib. to Adj. Dur.	Benchmark % of Port.	Benchmark Adj. Dur.	Benchmark Contrib. to Adj. Dur.	Difference % of Port.	Difference Contrib. to Adj. Dur.
Treasury								
Coupon	40.98	4.72	1.94	39.82	5.58	2.22	1.16	−0.29
Strip	0.00	0.00	0.00	0.00	0.00	0.00	0.00	0.00
Agencies								
FNMA	4.12	3.40	0.14	3.56	3.44	0.12	0.56	0.02
FHLB	0.00	0.00	0.00	1.21	2.32	0.03	−1.21	−0.03
FHLMC	0.00	0.00	0.00	0.91	3.24	0.03	−0.91	−0.03
REFCORP	3.50	11.22	0.39	0.83	12.18	0.10	2.68	0.29
Other Agencies	0.00	0.00	0.00	1.31	5.58	0.07	−1.31	−0.07
Financial Institutions								
Banking	1.91	5.31	0.10	2.02	5.55	0.11	−0.11	−0.01
Brokerage	1.35	3.52	0.05	0.81	4.14	0.03	0.53	0.01
Financial Cos.	1.88	2.92	0.05	2.11	3.78	0.08	−0.23	−0.02
Insurance	0.00	0.00	0.00	0.52	7.47	0.04	−0.52	−0.04
Other	0.00	0.00	0.00	0.28	5.76	0.02	−0.28	−0.02
Industrials								
Basic	0.63	6.68	0.04	0.89	6.39	0.06	−0.26	−0.01
Capital Goods	2.89	7.88	0.23	1.16	6.94	0.08	1.73	0.15
Consumer Cycl.	2.01	8.37	0.17	2.28	7.10	0.16	−0.27	0.01
Consum. Non-cycl.	2.76	12.91	0.36	1.66	6.84	0.11	1.10	0.24
Energy	1.50	6.82	0.10	0.69	6.89	0.05	0.81	0.05
Technology	1.55	1.58	0.02	0.42	7.39	0.03	1.13	−0.01
Transportation	0.00	0.00	0.00	0.57	7.41	0.04	−0.57	−0.04
Utilities								
Electric	0.47	3.36	0.02	1.39	5.02	0.07	−0.93	−0.05
Telephone	3.69	2.32	0.09	1.54	6.58	0.10	2.15	−0.02
Natural Gas	0.80	5.53	0.04	0.49	6.50	0.03	0.31	0.01
Water	0.00	0.00	0.00	0.00	0.00	0.00	0.00	0.00
Yankee								
Canadians	1.45	7.87	0.11	1.06	6.67	0.07	0.38	0.04
Corporates	0.49	3.34	0.02	1.79	6.06	0.11	−1.30	−0.09
Supranational	1.00	6.76	0.07	0.38	6.33	0.02	0.62	0.04
Sovereigns	0.00	0.00	0.00	0.66	5.95	0.04	−0.66	−0.04
Hypothetical	0.00	0.00	0.00	0.00	0.00	0.00	0.00	0.00
Cash	0.00	0.00	0.00	0.00	0.00	0.00	0.00	0.00
Mortgage								
Conventional 30-yr.	12.96	1.52	0.20	16.60	1.42	0.24	−3.64	−0.04
GNMA 30-yr.	7.53	1.23	0.09	7.70	1.12	0.09	−0.17	0.01
MBS 15-yr.	3.52	1.95	0.07	5.59	1.63	0.09	−2.07	−0.02
Balloons	3.02	1.69	0.05	0.78	1.02	0.01	2.24	0.04
OTM	0.00	0.00	0.00	0.00	0.00	0.00	0.00	0.00
European & International								
Eurobonds	0.00	0.00	0.00	0.00	0.00	0.00	0.00	0.00
International	0.00	0.00	0.00	0.00	0.00	0.00	0.00	0.00
Asset Backed	0.00	0.00	0.00	0.96	3.14	0.03	−0.96	−0.03
CMO	0.00	0.00	0.00	0.00	0.00	0.00	0.00	0.00
Other	0.00	0.00	0.00	0.00	0.00	0.00	0.00	0.00
Totals	100.00		4.35	100.00		4.29	0.00	0.00

Minimization of tracking error, illustrated above, is the most basic application of the optimizer. This is ideal for passive investors who want their portfolios to track the benchmark as closely as possible. This method also aids investors who hope to outperform the benchmark mainly on the basis of security selection, without expressing views on sector or yield curve. Given a carefully selected universe of securities from a set of favored issuers, the optimizer can help build security picks into a portfolio with no significant systematic exposures relative to the benchmark.

For more active portfolios, the objective is no longer minimization of tracking error. When minimizing tracking error, the optimizer tries to reduce the largest differences between the portfolio and benchmark. But what if the portfolio is meant to be long duration or overweighted in a particular sector to express a market view? These views certainly should not be "optimized" away. However, unintended exposures need to be minimized, while keeping the intentional ones.

For instance, assume in the original sample portfolio that the sector exposure is intentional but the portfolio should be neutral to the benchmark for all other sources of risk, especially term structure. The risk model allows the investor to keep exposures to one or more sets of risk factors (in this case, sector) and optimize to reduce the components of tracking error due to all other risk factors. This is equivalent to reducing all components of tracking error but the ones to be preserved. The model introduces a significant penalty for changing the risk profile of the portfolio in the risk categories designated for preservation.

Exhibit 24.18 shows the transactions suggested by the optimizer in this case.[13] At first glance, the logic behind the selection of the proposed transactions is not as clear as before. We see a sequence of fairly small transactions, mostly trading up in coupon. Although this is one way to change the term structure exposure of a portfolio, it is usually not the most obvious or effective method. The reason for this lies in the very limited choices we offered the optimizer for this illustration. As in the example of tracking error minimization, the investable universe was limited to securities already in the portfolio. That is, only rebalancing trades were permitted. Because the most needed cash flows are at vertices where the portfolio has no maturing securities, the only way to increase those flows is through higher coupon payments. In a more realistic optimization exercise, we would include a wider range of maturity

---

[13] Tracking error does not decrease with each transaction. This is possible because the optimizer does not minimize the tracking error itself in this case, but rather a function that includes the tracking error due to all factors but sector, as well as a penalty term for changing sector exposures.

dates (and possibly a set of zero-coupon securities as well) in the investable universe to give the optimizer more flexibility in adjusting portfolio cash flows. Despite these self-imposed limitations, the optimizer succeeds in bringing down the term structure risk while leaving the sector risk almost unchanged. Exhibit 24.19 shows the tracking error breakdown for the resulting portfolio. The term structure risk has been reduced from 36 bp to 12 bp, while the sector risk remains almost unchanged at 30 bp.

EXHIBIT 24.18   Sequence of Transactions Selected by Optimizer, Keeping Exposures to Sector, $000s, Initial Tracking Error: 52.0 bp

Transaction # 1		
Sold:	2000 of COCA-COLA ENTERPRISES	6.950 2026/11/15
Bought:	2000 of NORFOLK SOUTHERN CORP.	7.800 2027/05/15
Cash Left Over:	−235.19	
New Tracking Error:	52.1 bp	
Cost of this Transaction:	10.000	
Cumulative Cost:	10.000	
Transaction # 2		
Sold:	2000 of COCA-COLA ENTERPRISES	6.950 2026/11/15
Bought:	2000 of NEW YORK TELEPHONE	9.375 2031/07/15
Cash Left Over:	−389.36	
New Tracking Error:	50.1 bp	
Cost of this Transaction:	10.000	
Cumulative Cost:	20.000	
Transaction # 3		
Sold:	10000 of U.S. TREASURY BONDS	6.250 2023/08/15
Bought:	10000 of NEW YORK TELEPHONE	9.375 2031/07/15
Cash Left Over:	−468.14	
New Tracking Error:	47.4 bp	
Cost of this Transaction:	50.000	
Cumulative Cost:	70.000	
Transaction # 4		
Sold:	2000 of COCA-COLA ENTERPRISES	6.950 2026/11/15
Bought:	2000 of FHLM Gold Guar. Single Fam.	7.000 2028/01/01
Cash Left Over:	−373.47	
New Tracking Error:	46.0 bp	
Cost of this Transaction:	10.000	
Cumulative Cost:	80.000	

EXHIBIT 24.18 (Continued)

Transaction # 5		
Sold:	6000 of U.S. TREASURY BONDS	6.250 2023/08/15
Bought:	6000 of GNMA I Single Fam.	7.500 2022/07/01
Cash Left Over:	272.43	
New Tracking Error:	47.2 bp	
Cost of this Transaction:	30.000	
Cumulative Cost:	110.000	
Transaction # 6		
Sold:	1000 of NORFOLK SOUTHERN CORP.	7.800 2027/05/15
Bought:	1000 of U.S. TREASURY NOTES	6.125 2007/08/15
Cash Left Over:	343.44	
New Tracking Error:	46.4 bp	
Cost of this Transaction:	5.000	
Cumulative Cost:	115.000	
Transaction # 7		
Sold:	2000 of NORFOLK SOUTHERN CORP.	7.800 2027/05/15
Bought:	2000 of ANHEUSER-BUSCH CO., INC.	6.750 2027/12/15
Cash Left Over:	587.60	
New Tracking Error:	45.7 bp	
Cost of this Transaction:	10.000	
Cumulative Cost:	125.000	

EXHIBIT 24.19 Summary of Tracking Error Breakdown for Sample Portfolios

Tracking Error Due to:	Original Portfolio	Swapped Coca-Cola	Passive	Keep Sector Exposures
Term Structure	36	37	7	12
Sector	32	32	7	30
Systematic Risk	45	46	10	39
Non-Systematic	26	22	13	24
Total	52	51	16	46

SUMMARY

Fixed-income portfolio managers are increasingly using multi-factor risk models. Such models quantify expected deviation in performance ("tracking error") between a portfolio of fixed-income securities and a benchmark. The benchmark is often an index representing the market, such as the Lehman Brothers Aggregate Index.

The forecast of the return deviation is based on specific mismatches between the sensitivities of the portfolio and the benchmark to major market forces ("risk factors") that drive security returns. The model uses historical variances and correlations of the risk factors to translate the structural differences of the portfolio and the index into an expected tracking error. The model quantifies not only this systematic market risk, but security-specific (non-systematic) risk as well.

Using an illustrative portfolio, we demonstrated the implementation of the model. We showed how each component of tracking error can be traced back to the corresponding difference between the portfolio and benchmark risk exposures. We described the methodology for the minimization of tracking error and discussed several portfolio management applications—quantifying risk associated with a view, risk budgeting, projecting the effect of proposed transactions on tracking error, and optimization.

In this chapter, we described a risk model for dollar-denominated government, corporate, and mortgage-backed securities. The model quantifies expected deviation in performance ("tracking error") between a portfolio of fixed-income securities and an index representing the market, such as the Lehman Brothers Aggregate, Corporate, or High Yield Index.

The forecast of the return deviation is based on specific mismatches between the sensitivities of the portfolio and the benchmark to major market forces ("risk factors") that drive security returns. The model uses historical variances and correlations of the risk factors to translate the structural differences of the portfolio and the index into an expected tracking error. The model quantifies not only this systematic market risk, but security-specific (non-systematic) risk as well.

Using an illustrative portfolio, we demonstrated the implementation of the model. We showed how each component of tracking error can be traced back to the corresponding difference between the portfolio and benchmark risk exposures. We described the methodology for the minimization of tracking error and discussed a variety of portfolio management applications.

CHAPTER 25

Fixed-Income Derivatives and Risk Control

Frank J. Fabozzi, Ph.D., CFA
Adjunct Professor of Finance
School of Management
Yale University

In Chapters 14 and 15, equity derivatives and their application to equity portfolio management were discussed. In this chapter we look at the various types of fixed-income derivatives and how they are used in fixed-income portfolio management. There are two general types of fixed-income derivatives: interest rate derivatives and credit derivatives. Interest rate derivatives play an important role in managing the interest rate risk of a portfolio or institution. Credit derivatives are used to control a portfolio's credit risk exposure.

INTEREST RATE FUTURES AND FORWARD CONTRACTS

A futures contract is an agreement that requires a party to the agreement either to buy or sell something at a designated future date at a predetermined price. The buyer of a futures contract is said to be long the contract. The seller of a futures contract is said to be short the contract. The risk/return feature of futures contracts and the mechanics of trading them are covered in Chapter 14 and will not be repeated here. Instead, we will focus on specific contract features, the special considerations in pricing them, and several portfolio applications.

Futures versus Forward Contracts

A forward contract, just like a futures contract, is an agreement for the future delivery of something at a specified price at the end of a designated period of time. Futures contracts are standardized agreements as to the delivery date (or month) and quality of the deliverable, and are traded on organized exchanges. A forward contract differs in that it is usually non-standardized (that is, the terms of each contract are negotiated individually between buyer and seller), there is no clearinghouse, and secondary markets are often non-existent or extremely thin. Unlike a futures contract, which is an exchange-traded product, a forward contract is an over-the-counter instrument.

Futures contracts are marked to market at the end of each trading day. Consequently, futures contracts are subject to interim cash flows as additional margin may be required in the case of adverse price movements, or as cash is withdrawn in the case of favorable price movements. A forward contract may or may not be marked to market, depending on the wishes of the two parties. For a forward contract that is not marked to market, there are no interim cash flow effects because no additional margin is required.

Finally, the parties in a forward contract are exposed to credit risk because either party may default on its obligation. This risk is called *counterparty risk*. This risk is minimal in the case of futures contracts because the clearinghouse associated with the exchange guarantees the other side of the transaction. In the case of a forward contract, both parties face counterparty risk. Thus, there exists bilateral counterparty risk.

Other than these differences, most of what we say about futures contracts applies equally to forward contracts.

Exchange-Traded Interest Rate Futures Contracts

Interest rate futures contracts can be classified by the maturity of their underlying security. Short-term interest rate futures contracts have an underlying security that matures in one year or less. The maturity of the underlying security of long-term futures contracts exceeds one year. Examples of the former are futures contracts in which the underlying is a 3-month Treasury bill and a 3-month Eurodollar certificate of deposit (CD). Examples of the latter are futures contracts in which the underlying is a Treasury coupon security and an Agency note. In the following sections, we describe the Treasury futures contracts, the Agency note futures contracts, and Eurodollar CD futures contract.

Treasury Bond Futures

The Treasury bond futures contract is traded on the Chicago Board of Trade (CBOT). The underlying instrument for a Treasury bond futures contract is $100,000 par value of a hypothetical 20-year coupon bond. The coupon rate on the hypothetical bond, called the *notional coupon*, is 6%.

The futures price is quoted in terms of par being 100. Quotes are in 32nds of 1%. Thus a quote for a Treasury bond futures contract of 97-16 means 97 and ¹⁶⁄₃₂ or 97.50. So, if a buyer and seller agree on a futures price of 97-16, this means that the buyer agrees to accept delivery of the hypothetical underlying Treasury bond and pay 97.50% of par value and the seller agrees to accept 97.50% of par value. Since the par value is $100,000, the futures price that the buyer and seller agree to for this hypothetical Treasury bond is $97,500.

We have been referring to the underlying as a hypothetical Treasury bond. The seller of a Treasury bond futures contract who decides to make delivery rather than liquidate his position by buying the contract prior to the settlement date must deliver some Treasury bond. But what Treasury bond? The CBOT allows the seller to deliver one of several Treasury bonds that the CBOT specifies are acceptable for delivery. Exhibit 25.1 shows the 30 Treasury bond issues that the seller could have selected from to deliver to the buyer of the September 2002 futures contract, the December 2002 futures contract, and the March 2003 futures contract. The CBOT makes its determination of the Treasury issues that are acceptable for delivery from all outstanding Treasury issues that have at least 15 years to maturity from the first day of the delivery month.

It is important to remember that while the underlying Treasury bond for this contract is a hypothetical issue and therefore cannot itself be delivered into the futures contract, the contract is not a cash settlement contract as is the equity futures contracts described in Chapter 14. The only way to close out a Treasury bond futures contract is to either initiate an offsetting futures position, or to deliver a Treasury issue that is acceptable for delivery.

Conversion Factors The delivery process for the Treasury bond futures contract makes the contract interesting. At the settlement date, the seller of a futures contract (the short) is required to deliver to the buyer (the long) $100,000 par value of a 6% 20-year Treasury bond. Since no such bond exists, the seller must choose from one of the acceptable deliverable Treasury bonds that the CBOT has specified. Suppose the seller is entitled to deliver $100,000 of a 5% 20-year Treasury bond to settle the futures contract. The value of this bond is less than the value of a 6% 20-year bond. If the seller delivers the 5% 20-year bond, this would be unfair to the buyer of the futures contract who contracted to receive $100,000 of a 6% 20-year Treasury bond. Alternatively, suppose the seller delivers $100,000 of a 7% 20-year Treasury bond. The value of a 7% 20-year Treasury bond is greater than that of a 6% 20-year Treasury bond, so this would be a disadvantage to the seller.

EXHIBIT 25.1 Eligible Issues for the September 2002, December 2002, and March 2002 Treasury Futures Contract (as of December 27, 2001)

Coupon	Maturity Date	Conversion Factor for		
		Sep. 2002	Dec. 2002	Mar. 2003
5¼	11/15/28	0.9019	0.9022	0.9027
5¼	02/15/29	0.9014	0.9019	0.9022
5⅜	02/15/31	0.9153	0.9157	0.9159
5½	08/15/28	0.9347	0.9351	0.9353
6	02/15/26	0.9999	1.0000	0.9999
6⅛	11/15/27	1.0161	1.0159	1.0159
6⅛	08/15/29	1.0164	1.0165	1.0163
6¼	08/15/23	1.0293	1.0293	1.0290
6¼	05/15/30	1.0335	1.0332	1.0332
6⅜	08/15/27	1.0479	1.0478	1.0475
6½	11/15/26	1.0632	1.0627	1.0626
6⅝	02/15/27	1.0792	1.0790	1.0785
6¾	08/15/26	1.0942	1.0938	1.0933
6⅞	08/15/25	1.1077	1.1073	1.1066
7⅛	02/15/23	1.1307	1.1300	1.1290
7¼	08/15/22	1.1434	1.1426	1.1414
7½	11/15/24	1.1819	1.1808	1.1799
7⅝	11/15/22	1.1878	1.1864	1.1853
7⅝	02/15/25	1.1980	1.1971	1.1958
7⅞	02/15/21	1.2061	1.2047	1.2029
8	11/15/21	1.2249	1.2232	1.2217
8⅛	08/15/19	1.2224	1.2206	1.2185
8⅛	05/15/21	1.2355	1.2336	1.2320
8⅛	08/15/21	1.2371	1.2355	1.2336
8½	02/15/20	1.2662	1.2641	1.2617
8¾	05/15/20	1.2954	1.2929	1.2906
8¾	08/15/20	1.2977	1.2954	1.2929
8⅞	02/15/19	1.2957	1.2931	1.2902
9	11/15/18	1.3058	1.3028	1.3000
9⅛	05/15/18	1.3125	1.3092	1.3063

Source: Chicago Board of Trade

How can this problem be resolved? To make delivery equitable to both parties, the CBOT uses conversion factors for adjusting the price of each Treasury issue that can be delivered to satisfy the Treasury bond futures contract. Exhibit 25.1 shows for each of the acceptable Treasury issues for the September 2002, December 2002, and March 2003 futures contract the corresponding conversion factor. The conversion factor is constant throughout the life of a given futures contract (i.e., a given settlement date) but differs from contract to contract.

Given the conversion factor for an issue and the futures price, the adjusted price is found by multiplying the conversion factor by the futures price. The adjusted price is called the *converted price.*

The price that the buyer must pay the seller when a Treasury bond is delivered is called the *invoice price.* The invoice price is the futures settlement price plus accrued interest. However, as just noted, the seller can deliver one of several acceptable Treasury issues and to make delivery fair to both parties, the invoice price must be adjusted based on the actual Treasury issue delivered. It is the conversion factor that is used to adjust the invoice price. The invoice price is:

$$\text{invoice price} = \text{contract size} \times \text{futures settlement price} \\ \times \text{conversion factor} + \text{accrued interest}$$

Suppose a Treasury bond futures contract settles at 118-16. This means 118.5% of par value or 1.185 times par value. Suppose also that the conversion factor for this issue is 1.2370. Since the contract size is $100,000, the invoice price the buyer pays the seller is:

$$\$100,000 \times 1.185 \times 1.2370 + \text{accrued interest} \\ = \$146,584.50 + \text{accrued interest}$$

Cheapest-to-Deliver Issue In Chapter 14 the pricing of an equity futures contract is discussed and illustrated using a cash and carry transaction. In that discussion the *implied futures rate* is explained. For the seller of a futures contract (the short), the implied futures rate is an effective lending rate; that is, it is a rate at which funds can be lent or invested. For the buyer of a futures contract (the long), the implied futures rate is an effective borrowing rate. Rather than using the term implied future rate, participants in the interest rate futures area refer to this rate as the *implied repo rate.*

The seller of the futures contract (the short) has the choice of which of the eligible Treasury bonds to deliver to the long to settle the contract. For each eligible Treasury bond issue, the short can calculate an implied repo rate. That is, for each of the eligible 30 Treasury bond issues shown in Exhibit 25.1, for a given contract, the short can calculate an implied repo rate. Remember that the implied repo rate is the rate at which the short is lending funds or, in other words, the rate at which the short is earning on a short-term investment.

This short-term investment comes about by buying a Treasury bond issue and selling the Treasury bond futures contract. The sale of the Treasury bond futures contract locks in a price for the Treasury bond issue purchased at the futures settlement date. Suppose that the futures settlement date is 60 days from now. The short would know the price that will be received in 60 days, which is the converted price specified by the Treasury bond futures contract sold, and the coupon interest earned plus the estimated reinvestment income from reinvesting the coupon interest received over the 60 days. Given the price paid for the Treasury bond issue, a return can be obtained. This is the implied repo rate.

Therefore, in selecting the issue to be delivered, the seller of the futures contract will select from among all the eligible issues the one that will give the highest implied repo rate. The issue that gives the highest implied repo rate is called the *cheapest-to-deliver issue*.

Other Delivery Options   In addition to the choice of which acceptable Treasury issue to deliver—sometimes referred to as the *quality option* or *swap option*—the short has at least two more options granted under CBOT delivery guidelines. The short is permitted to decide when in the delivery month delivery actually will take place. This is called the *timing option*. The other option is the right of the short to give notice of intent to deliver up to 8:00 p.m. Chicago time after the closing of the exchange (3:15 p.m. Chicago time) on the date when the futures settlement price has been fixed. This option is referred to as the *wild card option*. The presence of the quality option, the timing option, and the wild card option—in sum referred to as the *delivery options*—means that the long position can never be sure which Treasury bond will be delivered or when it will be delivered.

Delivery Procedure   For a short who wants to deliver, the delivery procedure involves three days. The first day is the *position day*. On this day, the short notifies the CBOT that it intends to deliver. The short has until 8:00 p.m. central standard time to do so. The second day is the *notice day*. On this day, the short specifies which particular issue will be delivered. The short has until 2:00 p.m. central standard time to make this declaration. (On the last possible notice day in the delivery month, the short has until 3:00 p.m.) The CBOT then selects the long to whom delivery will be made. This is the long position that has been outstanding for the longest period of time. The long is then notified by 4:00 p.m. that delivery will be made. The third day is the *delivery day*. By 10:00 a.m. on this day the short must have in its account the Treasury issue that it specified on the notice day and by 1:00 p.m. must deliver that bond to the long that was assigned by the CBOT to accept delivery. The long pays the short the invoice price upon receipt of the bond.

Pricing of the Treasury Bond Futures Contract   In Chapter 14, it was demonstrated based on a cost of carry model that the theoretical futures price for an equity futures contact is:

$$\text{Futures price} = \text{Spot price} + \text{Cost of financing} - \text{Dividend yield}$$

In the case of a fixed income security, the relationship changes to:

$$\text{Futures price} = \text{Spot price} + \text{Cost of financing} - \text{Interest earned}$$

The interest earned is the accrued interest on the underlying fixed income instrument.

To derive the theoretical futures price using the arbitrage argument presented for the equity futures contract presented in Chapter 14 (the cost of carry model), we made several assumptions. Below we look at the implications of these assumptions for the pricing of the Treasury bond futures contract.

First, in the cost of carry model, no *interim* cash flows due to variation margin or coupon interest payments (dividend payments in the case of equity futures) were assumed. However, we know that interim cash flows can occur for both of these reasons. Because we assumed no initial margin and variation margin, the price derived is technically the theoretical price for a forward contract that is not marked-to-market. Incorporating interim coupon payments into the pricing model is not difficult. However, the value of the coupon payments at the settlement date will depend on the interest rate at which they can be reinvested. The shorter the maturity of the futures contract and the lower the coupon rate, the less important the reinvestment income is in determining the futures price.

Second, in deriving the theoretical futures price it is assumed that the borrowing and lending rates are equal. Typically, however, the borrowing rate is higher than the lending rate. This was noted in the discussion of equity futures. As a result, there is not one theoretical futures price, but a boundary or range for the futures price where it can be priced such that there is no arbitrage opportunity.

Third, the arbitrage arguments used to derive the theoretical futures price assumes that only one instrument or a package of securities (as in the case of an equity index futures contract) is deliverable. But as just explained, the Treasury bond futures—as well as the Treasury note and Agency note futures contract reviewed later—are designed to allow the short the choice of delivering one of a number of deliverable issues (the quality or swap option). Because there may be more than one deliverable, market participants track the price of each deliverable bond and determine which issue is the cheapest to deliver. The futures price will then trade in relation to the cheapest-to-deliver issue.

There is the risk that while an issue may be the cheapest to deliver at the time a position in the futures contract is taken, it may not be the cheapest to deliver after that time. A change in the cheapest-to-deliver issue can dramatically alter the futures price. What are the implications of the quality (swap) option on the futures price? Because the swap option is an option granted by the long to the short, the long will want to pay less for the futures contract than indicated above. Therefore, as a result of the quality option, the theoretical futures price must be adjusted as follows:

$$\text{Futures price} = \text{Spot price} + \text{Cost of financing} - \text{Interest earned}$$
$$- \text{Value of quality option}$$

Market participants have employed theoretical models in attempting to estimate the fair value of the quality option. A discussion of these models is beyond the scope of this chapter.

Finally, in the cost of carry model, a known delivery date is assumed. For Treasury bond and note futures contracts, the short has a timing and wild card option, so the long does not know when the security will be delivered. The effect of the timing and wild card options on the theoretical futures price is the same as with the quality option. These delivery options result in a theoretical futures price that is lower than the one suggested earlier, as shown:

$$\text{Futures price} = \text{Spot price} + \text{Cost of financing} - \text{Interest earned}$$
$$- \text{Value of quality option} - \text{Value of timing option}$$
$$- \text{Value of wildcard option}$$

or alternatively,

$$\text{Futures price} = \text{Spot price} + \text{Cost of financing} - \text{Interest earned}$$
$$- \text{Delivery options}$$

Market participants attempt to value the delivery options, but a discussion of these models is beyond the scope of this chapter.

Treasury Note Futures

There are three Treasury note futures contracts: 10-year, 5-year, and 2-year. All three contracts are modeled after the Treasury bond futures contract and are traded on the CBOT. There are eligible issues that can be delivered. The delivery options granted to the short position are the same as for the Treasury bond futures contract.

Agency Note Futures Contract

The CBOT and the Chicago Mercantile Exchange (CME) have a futures contract in which the underlying is a Fannie Mae or Freddie Mac agency debenture. The underlying for the CBOT 10-year Agency note futures contract is a Fannie Mae Benchmark Note or Freddie Mac Reference Note having a par value of $100,000 and a notional coupon of 6%. The 10-year Agency note futures contract of the CME is similar to that of the CBOT, but has a notional coupon of 6.5% instead of 6%. The CBOT and the CME also have a 5-year Agency note futures contract. Again, the CBOT's underlying is a 6% notional coupon and the CME's is a 6.5% notional coupon.

As a result, of the many issues that are deliverable, there is a cheapest-to-deliver issue. This issue is found in exactly the same way as with the Treasury futures contract.

Eurodollar CD Futures Contracts

The contracts discussed thus far have been for underlying instruments with a maturity greater than one year. The most important futures contract based on a money market instrument is the Eurodollar CD futures contract. Eurodollar CDs are denominated in dollars but represent the liabilities of banks outside the United States. The contracts are traded on both the International Monetary Market of the Chicago Mercantile Exchange and the London International Financial Futures Exchange. The rate paid on Eurodollar CDs is the London interbank offered rate (LIBOR).

The 3-month Eurodollar CD is the underlying instrument for the Eurodollar CD futures contract. The contract is for $1 million of face value and is traded on an index price basis. The index price basis in which the contract is quoted is equal to 100 minus the product of the annualized LIBOR futures rate in decimal and 100. For example, a Eurodollar CD futures price of 94.00 means a 3-month LIBOR futures rate of 6% (100 minus 0.06×100).

The Eurodollar CD futures contract is a cash settlement contract. That is, the parties settle in cash for the value of a Eurodollar CD based on LIBOR at the settlement date.

The Eurodollar CD futures contract allows the buyer of the contract to lock in the rate on 3-month LIBOR today for a future 3-month period. For example, suppose that on May 1, 2002 an investor purchases a Eurodollar CD futures contract that settles in June 2002. Assume that the LIBOR futures rate for this contract is 4%. This means that the investor has agreed to invest in a 3-month Eurodollar CD that pays a rate of 4%. Specifically, the investor has locked in a rate for a 3-month investment of 4% beginning June 2002. If the investor on May 1, 2002 purchased a contract that settles in September 2002 and the LIBOR futures rate is 4.4%, the investor has locked in the rate on a 3-month investment beginning September 2002.

From the perspective of the seller of a Eurodollar CD futures contract, the seller is agreeing to lend funds for three months at some future date at the LIBOR futures rate. For example, suppose on May 1, 2002 a bank sells a Eurodollar CD futures contract that settles in June 2002 and the LIBOR futures rate is 4%. The bank locks in a borrowing rate of 4% for three months beginning in June 2002. If the settlement date is September 2002 and the LIBOR futures rate is 4.4%, the bank is locking in a borrowing rate of 5.4% for the 3-month period beginning September 2002.

The key point here is that the Eurodollar CD futures contract allows a participant in the financial market to lock in a 3-month rate on an investment or a 3-month borrowing rate. The 3-month period begins in the month that the contract settles.

Controlling Interest Rate Risk with Futures

A key use of interest rate futures is to control a portfolio's interest rate risk. The price of an interest rate futures contract moves in the opposite direction from the change in interest rates: When rates rise, the futures price will fall; when rates fall, the futures price will rise. By buying a futures contract, a portfolio's exposure to a rate increase is increased. That is, the portfolio's duration increases. By selling a futures contract, a portfolio's exposure to a rate increase is decreased. Equivalently, this means that the portfolio's duration is reduced.

A manager with strong expectations about the direction of the future course of interest rates will adjust a portfolio's duration so as to capitalize on those expectations. A manager who wants to position a portfolio in anticipation that rates will rise can sell interest rate futures to reduce duration. A manager who wants to position a portfolio in anticipation of a fall in rates can buy interest rate futures to increase duration.

Before interest rate futures were available, investors who wanted to speculate on interest rates did so with long-term Treasury bonds; they shorted bonds if they expected rates to rise, and they bought them if they expected rates to fall. Using interest rate futures instead of trading long-term Treasuries themselves has three advantages. First, transaction costs for trading futures are lower than trading in the cash market. Second, margin requirements are lower for futures than for Treasury securities; using futures thus permits greater leverage. Finally, it is easier to sell short in the futures market than in the Treasury market. Consequently, while managers can alter the duration of their portfolios with cash market instruments, a quick and inexpensive means for doing so (on either a temporary or permanent basis) is to use futures contracts.

General Principle

The general principle in controlling interest rate risk with futures is to combine the dollar exposure of the current portfolio and that of a futures position so that it is equal to the target dollar exposure. This means that the manager must be able to accurately measure the dollar exposure of both the current portfolio and the futures contract employed to alter the exposure.

As explained in Chapter 21, there are two commonly used measures for approximating the change in the value of a bond or bond portfolio to changes in interest rates: price value of a basis point (PVBP) and duration. PVBP is the dollar price change resulting from a one-basis-point change in yield. Duration is the approximate percentage change in price for a 100 basis point change in rates. There are two measures of duration: modified and effective. As explained in Chapter 21, effective duration is the appropriate measure that should be used for bonds with embedded options. In the foregoing discussion, when we refer to duration, we mean effective duration. Moreover, since the manager is interested in dollar price exposure, it is the effective dollar duration that should be used. For a one basis point change in rates, PVBP is equal to the effective dollar duration for a one basis point change in rates.

As emphasized in Chapter 21, to estimate the effective dollar duration, it is necessary to have a good valuation model. It is the valuation model that is used to determine what the new values for the bonds in the portfolio will be if rates change. The difference between the current values of the bonds in the portfolio and the new values estimated by the valuation model when rates are changed is the dollar price exposure. Consequently, the starting point in controlling interest rate risk is the development of a reliable valuation model and this model is also needed to value the derivative contracts that the manager wants to use to control interest rate exposure.

Suppose that a manager seeks a target duration for the portfolio based on either expectations of interest rates or client-specified exposure. Given the target duration, a target dollar duration for a small basis point change in interest rates can be obtained. For a 50 basis point change in interest rates, for example, the target dollar duration can be found by multiplying the dollar value of the portfolio by the target duration and then dividing by 200. For example, suppose that the manager of a $500 million portfolio wants a target duration of 6. This means that the manager seeks a 3% change in the value of the portfolio for a 50 basis point change in rates (assuming a parallel shift in rates of all maturities). Multiplying the target duration of 6 by $500 million and dividing by 200 gives a target dollar duration of $15 million.

The manager must then determine the dollar duration of the current portfolio. The current dollar duration for a 50 basis point change in interest rates is found by multiplying the current duration by the dollar value of the portfolio and dividing by 200. So, for our $500 million portfolio, suppose that the current duration is 4. The current dollar duration is then $10 million (4 times $500 million divided by 200).

The target dollar duration is then compared to the current dollar duration. The difference between the two dollar durations is the dollar exposure that must be provided by a position in the futures contract. If the target dollar duration exceeds the current dollar duration, a futures position must increase the dollar exposure by the difference. To increase the dollar exposure, an appropriate number of futures contracts must be purchased. If the target dollar duration is less than the current dollar duration, an appropriate number of futures contracts must be sold. That is,

If target dollar duration − current dollar duration > 0, buy futures
If target dollar duration − current dollar duration < 0, sell futures

Once a futures position is taken, the portfolio's dollar duration is equal to the current dollar duration without futures plus the dollar duration of the futures position. That is,

portfolio's dollar return = current dollar duration without futures
+ dollar duration of futures position

The objective is to control the portfolio's interest rate risk by establishing a futures position such that the portfolio's dollar duration is equal to the target dollar duration. Thus,

Portfolio's dollar duration = Target dollar duration

Or, equivalently,

target dollar duration = current dollar duration without futures
+ dollar duration of futures position   (1)

Over time, the portfolio's dollar duration will move away from the target dollar duration. The manager can alter the futures position to adjust the portfolio's dollar duration to the target dollar duration.

Determining the Number of Contracts

Each futures contract calls for a specified amount of the underlying instrument. When interest rates change, the value of the underlying instrument changes, and therefore the value of the futures contract changes. How much the futures dollar value will change when interest rates change must be estimated. This amount is called the dollar duration per futures contract. For example, suppose the futures price of an interest rate futures contract is 70 and that the underlying instrument has a par value of $100,000. Thus, the futures delivery price is $70,000 (0.70 times $100,000). Suppose that a change in interest rates of 50 basis points results in the futures price changing by about 3 points. Then the dollar duration per futures contract is $2,100 (0.03 times $70,000).

The dollar duration of a futures position is then the number of futures contracts multiplied by the dollar duration per futures contract. That is,

dollar duration of futures position
= number of futures contracts × dollar duration per futures contract   (2)

How many futures contracts are needed to obtain the target dollar duration? Substituting equation (2) into equation (1), we get

number of futures contracts × dollar duration per futures contract
= target dollar duration − current dollar duration without futures   (3)

Solving for the number of futures contracts we have:

number of futures contracts
$$= \frac{\text{target dollar duration} - \text{current dollar duration without futures}}{\text{dollar duration per futures contract}} \quad (4)$$

Equation (4) gives the approximate number of futures contracts that are necessary to adjust the portfolio's dollar duration to the target dollar duration. A positive number means that the futures contract must be purchased; a negative number means that the futures contract must be sold. Notice that if the target dollar duration is greater than the current dollar duration without futures, the numerator is positive and therefore futures contracts are purchased. If the target dollar duration is less than the current dollar duration without futures, the numerator is negative and therefore futures contracts are sold.

Dollar Duration for a Futures Position

Now we turn to how to measure the dollar duration and duration of a bond futures position. Keep in mind what the goal is: It is to measure the sensitivity of a bond futures position to changes in rates.

The general methodology for computing the dollar duration of a futures position for a given change in interest rates is straightforward given a valuation model. The procedure is the same as for computing the dollar duration of any cash market instrument—shock (change) interest rates up and down by the same number of basis points and determine the average dollar price change.

An adjustment is needed for the Treasury bond and note futures contracts. As explained earlier, the pricing of the futures contract depends on the cheapest-to-deliver issue (CTD). The calculation of the dollar duration of a Treasury bond or note futures contract requires determining the effect a change in interest rates will have on the price of the CTD issue, which in turn affects how the futures price will change. The dollar duration of a Treasury bond and note futures contract is determined as follows:

$$\text{dollar duration of futures contract} = \text{dollar duration of the CTD issue} \times \frac{\text{dollar duration of futures contract}}{\text{dollar duration of CTD issue}}$$

Recall that there is a conversion factor for each issue that is acceptable for delivery for the futures contract. The conversion factor makes delivery equitable to both the buyer and seller of the futures contract. For each deliverable issue, the product of the futures price and the conversion factor is the converted price. Relating this to the equation above, the second ratio is approximately equal to the conversion factor of the cheapest-to-deliver issue. Thus, we can write:

$$\text{dollar duration of futures contract} = \text{dollar duration of the CTD issue} \times \text{conversion factor for the CTD issue}$$

Hedging with Interest Rate Futures

Hedging with futures calls for taking a futures position as a temporary substitute for transactions to be made in the cash market at a later date. If cash and futures prices move together, any loss realized by the hedger from one position (whether cash or futures) will be offset by a profit on the other position. Hedging is a special case of controlling interest rate risk. In a hedge, the manager seeks a target duration or target dollar duration of zero.

A *short* (or sell) *hedge* is used to protect against a decline in the cash price of a bond. To execute a short hedge, futures contracts are sold. By establishing a short hedge, the manager has fixed the future cash price and transferred the price risk of ownership to the buyer of the futures contract.

INTEREST RATE SWAPS

In an interest rate swap, two parties agree to exchange periodic interest payments. The dollar amount of the interest payments exchanged is based on some predetermined dollar principal, which is called the *notional principal*. The dollar amount each counterparty pays to the other is the agreed-upon periodic interest rate times the notional principal. The only dollars that are exchanged between the parties are the interest payments, not the notional principal. In the most common type of swap, one party agrees to pay the other party fixed interest payments at designated dates for the life of the contract. This party is referred to as the *fixed-rate payer*. The other party, who agrees to make interest rate payments that float with some reference rate, is referred to as the *floating-rate payer*.

The reference rates that have been used for the floating rate in an interest rate swap are those on various money market instruments: Treasury bills, the London interbank offered rate, commercial paper, bankers acceptances, certificates of deposit, the federal funds rate, and the prime rate. The most common is the London interbank offered rate (LIBOR). LIBOR is the rate at which prime banks offer to pay on Eurodollar deposits available to other prime banks for a given maturity. Basically, it is viewed as the global cost of bank borrowing. There is not just one rate but a rate for different maturities. For example, there is a 1-month LIBOR, 3-month LIBOR, 6-month LIBOR, etc.

To illustrate an interest rate swap, suppose that for the next five years party X agrees to pay party Y 10% per year, while party Y agrees to pay party X 6-month LIBOR (the reference rate). Party X is a fixed-rate payer/floating-rate receiver, while party Y is a floating-rate payer/fixed-rate receiver. Assume that the notional principal is $50 million, and that payments are exchanged every six months for the next five years. This means that every six months, party X (the fixed-rate payer/floating-rate receiver) will pay party Y $2.5 million (10% times $50 million divided by 2). The amount that party Y (the floating-rate payer/fixed-rate receiver) will pay party X will be 6-month LIBOR times $50 million divided by 2. If 6-month LIBOR is 7%, party Y will pay party X $1.75 million (7% times $50 million divided by 2). Note that we divide by two because one-half year's interest is being paid.

The convention that has evolved for quoting swaps levels is that a swap dealer sets the floating rate equal to the reference rate and then quotes the fixed rate that will apply. The fixed rate is some spread above the Treasury yield curve with the same term to maturity as the swap.

Interest rate swaps are over-the-counter instruments. This means that they are not traded on an exchange. An institutional investor wishing to enter into a swap transaction can do so through either a securities firm or a commercial bank that transacts in swaps. The risk that the two parties take on when they enter into a swap is that the other party will fail to fulfill its obligations as set forth in the swap agreement. That is, each party faces default risk and therefore there is bilateral counterparty risk.

Risk/Return Characteristics of an Interest Rate Swap

The value of an interest rate swap will fluctuate with market interest rates. To see how, let's consider our hypothetical swap. Suppose that interest rates change immediately after parties X and Y enter into the swap. First, consider what would happen if the market demanded that in any 5-year swap the fixed-rate payer must pay 11% in order to receive 6-month LIBOR. If party X (the fixed-rate payer) wants to sell the position to party A, then party A will benefit by having to pay only 10% (the original swap rate agreed upon) rather than 11% (the current swap rate) to receive 6-month LIBOR. Party X will want compensation for this benefit. Consequently, the value of party X's position has increased. Thus, if interest rates increase, the fixed-rate payer will realize a profit and the floating-rate payer will realize a loss.

Next, consider what would happen if interest rates decline to, say, 6%. Now a 5-year swap would require a new fixed-rate payer to pay 6% rather than 10% to receive 6-month LIBOR. If party X wants to sell the position to party B, the latter would demand compensation to take over the position. In other words, if interest rates decline, the fixed-rate payer will realize a loss, while the floating-rate payer will realize a profit.

Interpreting a Swap Position

There are two ways that a swap position can be interpreted: (1) a package of forward/futures contracts, and (2) a package of cash flows from buying and selling cash market instruments.

Package of Forward Contracts

Contrast the position of the counterparties in an interest rate swap summarized above to the position of the long and short interest rate futures (forward) contract. The long futures position gains if interest rates decline and loses if interest rates rise—this is similar to the risk/return profile for a floating-rate payer. The risk/return profile for a fixed-rate payer is similar to that of the short futures position: a gain if interest rates increase and a loss if interest rates decrease. By taking a closer look at the interest rate swap we can understand why the risk/return relationships are similar.

Consider party X's position in our previous swap illustration. Party X has agreed to pay 10% and receive 6-month LIBOR. More specifically, assuming a $50 million notional principal, X has agreed to buy a commodity called "6-month LIBOR" for $2.5 million. This is effectively a 6-month forward contract where X agrees to pay $2.5 million in exchange for delivery of 6-month LIBOR. If interest rates increase to 11%, the price of that commodity (6-month LIBOR) is higher, resulting in a gain for the fixed-rate payer, who is effectively long a 6-month forward contract on 6-month LIBOR. The floating-rate payer is effectively short a 6-month forward contract on 6-month LIBOR. There is therefore an implicit forward contract corresponding to each exchange date.

Now we can see why there is a similarity between the risk/return relationship for an interest rate swap and a forward contract. If interest rates increase to, say, 11%, the price of that commodity (6-month LIBOR) increases to $2.75 million (11% times $50 million divided by 2). The long forward position (the fixed-rate payer) gains, and the short forward position (the floating-rate payer) loses. If interest rates decline to, say, 9%, the price of our commodity decreases to $2.25 million (9% times $50 million divided by 2). The short forward position (the floating-rate payer) gains, and the long forward position (the fixed-rate payer) loses.

Consequently, interest rate swaps can be viewed as a package of more basic interest rate derivatives, such as forwards. The pricing of an interest rate swap will then depend on the price of a package of forward contracts with the same settlement dates in which the underlying for the forward contract is the same reference rate.

Package of Cash Market Instruments

To understand why a swap can be interpreted as a package of cash market instruments, consider an investor who enters into the transaction below:

- Buy $50 million par of a 5-year floating-rate bond that pays 6-month LIBOR every six months
- Finance the purchase by borrowing $50 million for five years on terms requiring a 10% annual interest rate paid every six months

The cash flows for this transaction are as follows (the subscript for LIBOR indicates the 6-month LIBOR as per the terms of the floating-rate bond at time t).

| Six Month | Cash Flow (in Millions of Dollars) From: | | |
Period	Floating-Rate Bond	Borrowing Cost	Net
0	$-\$50$	$+\$50.0$	$\$0$
1–9	$+(LIBOR_t/2) \times 50$	-2.5	$+(LIBOR_t/2) \times 50 - 2.5$
10	$+(LIBOR_{10}/2) \times 50 + 50$	-52.5	$+(LIBOR_{10}/2) \times 50 - 2.5$

The second column shows the cash flow from purchasing the 5-year floating-rate bond. There is a $50 million cash outlay and then ten cash inflows. The amount of the cash inflows is uncertain because they depend on future LIBOR. The next column shows the cash flow from borrowing $50 million on a fixed-rate basis. The last column shows the net cash flow from the entire transaction. As the last column indicates, there is no initial cash flow (no cash inflow or cash outlay). In all ten 6-month periods, the net position results in a cash inflow of LIBOR and a cash outlay of $2.5 million. This net position, however, is identical to the position of a fixed-rate payer/floating-rate receiver.

It can be seen from the net cash flow that a fixed-rate payer has a cash market position that is equivalent to a long position in a floating-rate bond and a short position in a fixed-rate bond—the short position being the equivalent of borrowing by issuing a fixed-rate bond.

What about the position of a floating-rate payer? It can be easily demonstrated that the position of a floating-rate payer is equivalent to purchasing a fixed-rate bond and financing that purchase at a floating rate, where the floating rate is the reference rate for the swap. That is, the position of a floating-rate payer is equivalent to a long position in a fixed-rate bond and a short position in a floating-rate bond.

Swaptions

There are options on interest rate swaps. These derivative contracts are called *swaptions* and grant the option buyer the right to enter into an interest rate swap at a future date. The time until expiration of the swap, the term of the swap, and the swap rate are specified. The swap rate is the strike rate for the option.

A *payer's swaption* entitles the option buyer to enter into an interest rate swap in which the buyer of the option pays a fixed rate and receives a floating rate. Suppose that the strike rate is 6.5%, the term of the swap is three years, and the swaption expires in two years. This means that the buyer of this option some time over the next two years has the right to enter into a 3-year interest rate swap where the buyer pays 6.5% (the swap rate which is equal to the strike rate) and receives the reference rate.

In a *receiver's swaption* the buyer of the option has the right to enter into an interest rate swap to pay a floating rate and receive a fixed rate. For example, if the strike rate is 7%, the swap term is five years, and the option expires in one year, the buyer of a receiver's swaption has the right some time over the next year to enter into a 5-year interest rate swap in which the buyer receives a swap rate of 7% (i.e., the strike rate) and pays the reference rate.

Controlling Interest Rate Risk with Swaps

Effectively, a position in an interest rate swap is a leveraged position. This agrees with both of the economic interpretations of an interest rate swap explained earlier—it is a leveraged position involving either buying a fixed-rate bond and financing on a floating-rate basis (i.e., floating-rate payer position) or buying a floating-rate bond on a fixed-rate basis (i.e., fixed-rate payer position). So, we would expect that the dollar duration of a swap is a multiple of the bond that effectively underlies the swap.

Using this economic leveraged cash position interpretation of a swap, we can calculate a swap's dollar duration. From the perspective of the floating-rate payer, the position can be viewed as follows:

> long a fixed-rate bond + short a floating-rate bond

This means that the dollar duration of an interest rate swap from the perspective of a floating-rate payer is just the difference between the dollar duration of the two bond positions that comprise the swap. That is,

dollar duration of a swap for a floating-rate payer
= dollar duration of a fixed-rate bond − dollar duration of a floating-rate bond

Most of the interest rate sensitivity of a swap will result from the dollar duration of the fixed-rate bond since the dollar duration of the floating-rate bond will be small because as interest rates change, the reference rate on a floating-rate bond changes. The dollar duration of a floating-rate bond is smaller the closer the swap is to its reset date. If the dollar duration of the floating-rate bond is close to zero then:

> dollar duration of a swap for a floating-rate payer
> = dollar duration of a fixed-rate bond

Thus, adding an interest rate swap to a portfolio in which the manager pays a floating-rate and receives a fixed-rate increases the dollar duration of the portfolio by roughly the dollar duration of the underlying fixed-rate bond. This is because it effectively involves buying a fixed-rate bond on a leveraged basis.

From the perspective of a fixed-rate payer, the dollar duration can be found as follows:

dollar duration of a swap for a fixed-rate payer
= dollar duration of a floating-rate bond − dollar duration of a fixed-rate bond

Again, assuming that the dollar duration of the floater is small, we have

dollar duration of a swap for a fixed-rate payer
= −dollar duration of a fixed-rate bond

Consequently, a manager who adds a swap to a portfolio involving paying fixed and receiving floating decreases the dollar duration of the portfolio by an amount roughly equal to the dollar duration of the fixed-rate bond.

The dollar duration of a portfolio that includes a swap is:

dollar duration of assets − dollar duration of liabilities
+ dollar duration of a swap position

INTEREST RATE OPTIONS

An option is a contract in which the writer of the option grants the buyer of the option the right, but not the obligation, to purchase from or sell to the writer something at a specified price within a specified period of time (or at a specified date). The risk/return characteristics of an option are explained in Chapter 14, along with the differences between options and futures and the pricing of options.

Exchange-traded interest rate options can be written on a fixed income security or an interest rate futures contract. The former options are called *options on physicals*. *Options on interest rate futures*, called *futures options*, have been far more popular than options on physicals.

Exchange-Traded Futures Options

There are futures options on all the interest rate futures contracts. An option on a futures contract gives the buyer the right to buy from or sell to the writer a designated futures contract at the strike price at any time during the life of the option. If the futures option is a call option, the buyer has the right to purchase one designated futures contract at the strike price. That is, the buyer has the right to acquire a long futures position in the underlying futures contract. If the buyer exercises the call option, the writer acquires a corresponding short position in the futures contract.

A put option on a futures contract grants the buyer the right to sell one designated futures contract to the writer at the strike price. That is, the option buyer has the right to acquire a short position in the designated futures contract. If the put option is exercised, the writer acquires a corresponding long position in the designated futures contract.

As the parties to the futures option will realize a position in a futures contract when the option is exercised, the question is: What will the futures price be? That is, at what futures price will the long be required to pay for the instrument underlying the futures contract, and at what futures price will the short be required to sell the instrument underlying the futures contract?

Upon exercise, the futures price for the futures contract will be set equal to the strike price. The position of the two parties is then immediately marked-to-market in terms of the then-current futures price. Thus, the futures position of the two parties will be at the prevailing futures price. At the same time, the option buyer will receive from the option seller the economic benefit from exercising. In the case of a call futures option, the option writer must pay the difference between the current futures price and the strike price to the buyer of the option. In the case of a put futures option, the option writer must pay the option buyer the difference between the strike price and the current futures price.

For example, suppose an investor buys a call option on some futures contract in which the strike price is 85. Assume also that the futures price is 95 and that the buyer exercises the call option. Upon exercise, the call buyer is given a long position in the futures contract at 85 and the call writer is assigned the corresponding short position in the futures contract at 85. The futures positions of the buyer and the writer are immediately marked-to-market by the exchange. Because the prevailing futures price is 95 and the strike price is 85, the long futures position (the position of the call buyer) realizes a gain of 10, while the short futures position (the position of the call writer) realizes a loss of 10. The call writer pays the exchange 10 and the call buyer receives from the exchange 10. The call buyer, who now has a long futures position at 95, can either liquidate the futures position at 95 or maintain a long futures position. If the former course of action is taken, the call buyer sells a futures contract at the prevailing futures price of 95. There is no gain or loss from liquidating the position. Overall, the call buyer realizes a gain of 10. The call buyer who elects to hold the long futures position will face the same risk and reward of holding such a position, but still realizes a gain of 10 from the exercise of the call option.

Suppose instead that the futures option is a put rather than a call, and the current futures price is 60 rather than 95. Then if the buyer of this put option exercises it, the buyer would have a short position in the futures contract at 85; the option writer would have a long position in the futures contract at 85. The exchange then marks the position to market at the then-current futures price of 60, resulting in a gain to the put buyer of 25 and a loss to the put writer of the same amount. The put buyer who now has a short futures position at 60 can either liquidate the short futures position by buying a futures contract at the prevailing futures price of 60 or maintain the short futures position. In either case the put buyer realizes a gain of 25 from exercising the put option.

Over-the-Counter Options

Over-the-counter options, also called *dealer options*, are purchased by institutional investors who want to hedge the risk associated with a specific security. Typically, the maturity of the option coincides with the time period over which the buyer of the option wants to hedge, so the buyer is not concerned with the option's liquidity.

The parties to any over-the-counter contract are exposed to counterparty risk. In the case of forward contracts where both parties are obligated to perform, both parties face counterparty risk. In contrast, in the case of an option, once the option buyer pays the option price, it has satisfied its obligation. It is only the seller that must perform if the option is exercised. Thus, the option buyer is exposed to counterparty risk—the risk that the option seller will fail to perform.

Pricing Interest Rate Options

There are two option pricing models that have been used in pricing interest rate options—the Black-Scholes mode and the binomial model.

Black-Scholes Option Pricing Model

As explained in Chapter 14, the most popular model for the pricing of equity options is the Black-Scholes option pricing model. Because the basic Black-Scholes formula is for a non-cash paying security, let's apply it to a zero-coupon bond with three years to maturity. Assume the following values:

Strike price	= $88.00
Time remaining to expiration	= 2 years
Current price	= $83.96
Expected price volatility	= standard deviation = 10%
Risk-free rate	= 6%

Note that the current price of $83.96 is the present value of the maturity value of $100 discounted at 6% (assuming a flat yield curve). The Black-Scholes option pricing model would produce a value of $8.116.

There is no reason to suspect that this estimated value of $8.116 is unreasonable. However, let's change the problem slightly. Instead of a strike price of $88, let's make the strike price $100.25. The Black-Scholes option pricing model would produce a value of $2.79. Is there any reason to believe this is unreasonable? Well, consider that this is a call option on a zero-coupon bond that will never have a value greater than its maturity value of $100. Consequently, a call option with a strike price of $100.25 must have a value of zero. Yet, the Black-Scholes option pricing model tells us that the value is $2.79! In fact, with a higher volatility assumption, the model would give an even greater value for the call option.

Why is the Black-Scholes model off by so much in our example? The answer lies in its underlying assumptions. Specifically, there are three assumptions underlying the Black-Scholes model that limit its use in pricing options on fixed-income instruments.

First, the probability distribution for the prices assumed by the Black-Scholes model permits some probability—no matter how small—that the price can take on any positive value. But in the case of a zero-coupon bond, the price cannot take on a value above $100. In the case of a coupon bond, we know that the price cannot exceed the sum of the coupon payments plus the maturity value. For example, for a 5-year 10% coupon bond with a maturity value of $100, the price cannot be greater than $150 (five coupon payments of $10 plus the maturity value of $100). Thus, unlike stock prices, bond prices have a maximum value. The only way that a bond's price can exceed the maximum value is if negative interest rates are permitted. This is not likely to occur, so any probability distribution for prices assumed by an option pricing model that permits bond prices to be higher than the maximum bond value could generate nonsensical option prices. The Black-Scholes model does allow bond prices to exceed the maximum bond value (or, equivalently, allows negative interest rates).

The second assumption of the Black-Scholes model is that the short-term interest rate is constant over the life of the option. Yet the price of an interest rate option will change as interest rates change. A change in the short-term interest rate changes the rates along the yield curve. Therefore, to assume that the short-term rate will be constant is inappropriate for interest rate options. The third assumption is that the variance of prices is constant over the life of the option. As a bond moves closer to maturity its price volatility declines. Therefore, the assumption that price variance is constant over the life of the option is inappropriate.

Arbitrage-Free Lattice Model

The proper way to value options on bonds is to use an arbitrage-free model that takes into account the yield curve. We have already developed the basic principles for employing this model. In Chapter 20, we explained how to construct a lattice interest rate tree such that the tree would be arbitrage free. The interest rate tree is used to value bonds (both option-free and bonds with embedded options). The same tree can be used to value a stand-alone option on a bond.

INTEREST RATE AGREEMENTS (CAPS AND FLOORS)

An *interest rate agreement* is an agreement between two parties whereby one party, for an upfront premium, agrees to compensate the other at specific time periods if the reference rate is different from a predetermined level. When one party agrees to pay the other when the reference rate exceeds a predetermined level, the agreement is referred to as an *interest rate cap* or *ceiling*. The agreement is referred to as an *interest rate floor* when one party agrees to pay the other when the reference rate falls below a predetermined level. The predetermined level is called the *strike rate*.

The terms of an interest rate agreement include:

1. The reference rate
2. The strike rate that sets the ceiling or floor
3. The length of the agreement
4. The frequency of settlement
5. The notional principal

For example, suppose that C buys an interest rate cap from D with terms as follows:

1. The reference rate is 3-month LIBOR.
2. The strike rate is 6%.
3. The agreement is for four years.
4. Settlement is every three months.
5. The notional principal is $20 million.

Under this agreement, every three months for the next four years, D will pay C whenever 3-month LIBOR exceeds 6% at a settlement date. The payment will equal the dollar value of the difference between 3-month LIBOR and 6% times the notional principal divided by 4. For example, if three months from now 3-month LIBOR on a settlement date is 8%, then D will pay C 2% (8% minus 6%) times $20 million divided by 4, or $100,000. If 3-month LIBOR is 6% or less, D does not have to pay anything to C.

In the case of an interest rate floor, assume the same terms as the interest rate cap we just illustrated. In this case, if 3-month LIBOR is 8%, C receives nothing from D, but if 3-month LIBOR is less than 6%, D compensates C for the difference. For example, if 3-month LIBOR is 5%, D will pay C $50,000 (6% minus 5% times $20 million divided by 4).

CREDIT DERIVATIVES

The derivatives we have discussed thus far are interest rate derivatives. Treasury futures contracts can be used to control interest rate risk with respect to changes in the level of interest rates (as measured by Treasury yields). However, there are also changes in the spread that must be controlled for non-Treasury securities or, as they are more popularly referred to, *spread products*. What has developed in the over-the-counter or dealer market are derivative products that provide protection against credit risk. These products are referred to as *credit derivatives*. There are three main types of credit derivatives that we will describe: credit options, credit forwards, and credit swaps.

Credit Options

There are two types of credit options. The first type is a credit option written on an underlying issue. For this type of credit option the payout is determined based on whether a default occurs for the underlying issue. The amount of the payout is a fixed amount determined at the time the option is purchased. If a default does not occur by the option's expiration date, there is no payout.

The same type of credit option can also be written where the payoff is based upon whether or not the issue is downgraded. Then the payoff is specified by the amount of the loss expected if there is a downgrade. Credit options can also be written in which a default is defined in broader terms than simply failure to meet an interest or principal payment. For example, the event that could trigger a payoff can be defined in terms of whether some financial measure is above or below a certain value. For example, a minimum net worth can be specified. This form of a credit option can specify that if the issuer's book value falls below $150 million, for example, then there is a payoff.

For the second type of credit option, the payoff is determined by the level of the credit spread over a referenced security, typically a Treasury security. The strike is specified in terms of the level of the credit spread. The payoff can specify that if the credit spread for the issue is greater than the strike spread, there is a payoff. For example, suppose that the referenced issue is a bond of company XYZ. Suppose the current spread is 200 basis points. The strike spread can be specified as 250 basis points and that if the credit spread by the expiration date exceeds that strike spread there is a payoff. Alternatively, the payoff can specify that if the credit spread is less than the strike, there is a payoff.

The tricky part of the payoff for an option written on a credit spread is the determination of the payoff. Remember that if interest rates in general increase, the price of the issue underlying the option will decline, and vice versa. What the payoff must do is separate the change in the price of the underlying issue due to a change in the general level of rates and the change in the credit spread. This is done by having the payoff based on the difference in the actual credit spread and the strike spread multiplied by a specified notional amount and by a risk factor. The risk factor is a quantitative measure that is derived from a bond's duration and convexity. For purposes of our discussion, it is not necessary to understand how the risk factor is computed. Instead, let's see how the payoff is determined. The payoff function is determined as follows if the credit option is based on the credit spread being greater than the strike spread:

$$\text{(credit spread} - \text{strike spread)} \times \text{notional amount} \times \text{risk factor}$$

where the credit spread and the strike spread are expressed in decimal form.

For example, suppose that for the issue of company XYZ the strike spread is 250 basis points and that the notional amount of the credit option is $10 million. Suppose also that the risk factor for this issue is 5. If at the expiration date of this option the credit spread for this issue is 300 basis points, then the payoff is:

$$(0.030 - 0.025) \times \$10,000,000 \times 5 = \$250,000$$

If the credit spread at the expiration date is 250 basis points or less, then there is no payoff.

If the credit spread option had a payoff based on the credit spread narrowing, then the payoff function would be:

$$\text{(strike spread} - \text{credit spread)} \times \text{notional amount} \times \text{risk factor}$$

Credit Forward Contracts

The underlying for a credit forward contract is the credit spread. The payoff depends on the credit spread at the settlement date of the contract. The payoff is positive (i.e., the party receives cash) if the credit spread moves in favor of the party at the settlement date. The party makes a payment if the credit spread moves against the party at the settlement date.

For example, suppose that a manager has a view that the credit spread will increase (i.e., widen) to more than the current 250 basis points in one year for an issue of company XYZ. Then the payoff function for this credit forward contract would be:

(credit spread at settlement date − 250) × notional amount × risk factor

Assuming that the notional amount is $10 million and the risk factor is 5, then if the credit spread at the settlement date is 325 basis points, the amount that will be received by the manager is:

$$(0.0325 - 0.025) \times \$10,000,000 \times 5 = \$375,000$$

Instead, suppose that the credit spread at the settlement date decreased to 190 basis points, then the manager would have to pay out $300,000 as shown below:

$$(0.019 - 0.025) \times \$10,000,000 \times 5 = -\$300,000$$

In general, if a manager takes a position in a credit forward contract to benefit from an increase in the credit spread, then the payoff would be as follows:

(credit spread at settlement date − credit spread in contract)
× notional amount × risk factor

For a manager taking a position that the credit spread will decrease, the payoff is:

(credit spread in contract − credit spread at settlement date)
× notional amount × risk factor

Credit Swaps

There are two different types of credit swaps: credit default swaps and total return swaps. *Credit default swaps* are used by a manager to shift credit exposure to a credit protection seller. A *total return swap* is used by a manager to increase credit exposure.

Credit default swaps come in two forms: credit insurance and swapping risky credit payments for certain fixed payments. With credit insurance, the buyer pays a fee to enter into a credit default swap. The buyer receives a payment every period for the life of the contract if a referenced credit defaults on a payment. While this contract is called a "swap," it is basically a package of credit options. Rather than a payment being contingent on an individual referenced credit, the referenced credit can be a portfolio of bonds. The second form of credit default swap is one in which a manager agrees to exchange the total return on a credit risky asset for known periodic payments from the counterparty. The payments are exchanged based on what happens to the value of the credit risky asset. If it declines in value, the manager receives a payment to compensate for the decline in value plus a periodic payment from the counterparty.

With a total return credit swap, the manager agrees to pay all cash flows from the referenced asset or assets including the change in the value of the referenced asset or assets. The manager receives in exchange a floating rate plus any depreciation of the referenced asset from the credit swap seller.

Investment Companies and Exchange-Traded Funds

Investment Companies

Frank J. Jones, Ph.D.
Chief Investment Officer
The Guardian Life Insurance Company of America

Frank J. Fabozzi, Ph.D., CFA
Adjunct Professor of Finance
School of Management
Yale University

Investment companies are entities that sell shares to the public and invest the proceeds in a diversified portfolio of securities. Each share sold represents a proportional interest in the portfolio of securities managed by the investment company on behalf of its shareholders. The type of securities purchased depends on the company's investment objective.

TYPES OF INVESTMENT COMPANIES

There are three types of investment companies: open-end funds, closed-end funds, and unit trusts.

Open-End Funds (Mutual Funds)

Open-end funds, commonly referred to simply as *mutual funds*, are portfolios of securities, mainly stocks, bonds, and money market instruments. There are several important aspects of mutual funds. First, investors in mutual funds own a pro rata share of the overall portfolio. Second, the investment manager of the mutual fund actively manages

727

the portfolio, that is buys some securities and sells others (this characteristic is unlike unit investment trusts, discussed later).

Third, the value or price of each share of the portfolio, called the *net asset value* (NAV), equals the market value of the portfolio minus the liabilities of the mutual fund divided by the number of shares owned by the mutual fund investors. That is,

$$\text{NAV} = \frac{\text{Market value of portfolio} - \text{Liabilities}}{\text{Number of shares outstanding}}$$

For example, suppose that a mutual fund with 10 million shares outstanding has a portfolio with a market value of $215 million and liabilities of $15 million. The NAV is:

$$\text{NAV} = \frac{\$215,000,000 - \$15,000,000}{\$10,000,000} = \$20$$

Fourth, the NAV or price of the fund is determined only once each day, at the close of the day. For example, the NAV for a stock mutual fund is determined from the closing stock prices for the day. Business publications provide the NAV each day in their mutual fund tables. The published NAV's are the closing NAV's. Fifth, and very importantly, all new investments into the fund or withdrawals from the fund during a day are priced at the closing NAV (investments after the end of the day or on a non-business day are priced at the next day's closing NAV).

The total number of shares in the fund increases if there are more investments than withdrawals during the day, and vice versa. For example, assume that at the beginning of a day a mutual fund portfolio has a value of $1 million, there are no liabilities, and there are 10,000 shares outstanding. Thus, the NAV of the fund is $100. Assume that during the day $5,000 is deposited into the fund, $1,000 is withdrawn, and the prices of all the securities in the portfolio remain constant. This means that 50 shares were issued for the $5,000 deposited (since each share is $100) and 10 shares redeemed for $1,000 (again, since each share is $100). The net number of new shares issued is then 40. Therefore, at the end of the day there will be 10,040 shares and the total value of the fund will be $1,004,000. The NAV will remain at $100.

If, instead, the prices of the securities in the portfolio change, both the total size of the portfolio and, therefore, the NAV will change. In the previous example, assume that during the day the value of the portfolio doubles to $2 million. Since deposits and withdrawals are priced at the end-of-day NAV, which is now $200 after the doubling of the portfolio's value, the $5,000 deposit will be credited with 25 shares ($5,000/$200) and the $1,000 withdrawn will reduce the number of shares by 5 shares ($1,000/$200). Thus, at the end of the day there will be 10,020 shares (25 − 5) in the fund with an NAV of $200, and the value of the fund will be $2,004,000. (Note that 10,020 shares × $200 NAV equals $2,004,000, the portfolio value).

Overall, the NAV of a mutual fund will increase or decrease due to an increase or decrease in the prices of the securities in the portfolio. The number of shares in the fund will increase or decrease due to the net deposits into or withdrawals from the fund. And the total value of the fund will increase or decrease for both reasons.

Closed-End Funds

The shares of a *closed-end fund* are very similar to the shares of common stock of a corporation. The new shares of a closed-end fund are initially issued by an underwriter for the fund. And after the new issue, the number of shares remains constant. After the initial issue, there are no sales or purchases of fund shares by the fund company as there are for open-end funds. The shares are traded on a secondary market, either on an exchange or in the over-the-counter market.

Investors can buy shares either at the time of the initial issue (as discussed below), or in the secondary market. Shares are sold only on the secondary market. The price of the shares of a closed-end fund are determined by the supply and demand in the market in which these funds are traded. Thus, investors who transact closed-end fund shares must pay a brokerage commission at the time of purchase and at the time of sale.

The NAV of closed-end funds is calculated in the same way as for open-end funds. However, the price of a share in a closed-end fund is determined by supply and demand, so the price can fall below or rise above the net asset value per share. Shares selling below NAV are said to be "trading at a discount," while shares trading above NAV are "trading at a premium." Newspapers list quotations of the prices of these shares under the heading "Closed-End Funds."

Consequently, there are two important differences between open-end funds and closed-end funds. First, the number of shares of an open-end fund varies because the fund sponsor will sell new shares to investors and buy existing shares from shareholders. Second, by doing so, the share price is always the NAV of the fund. In contrast, closed-end funds have a constant number of shares outstanding because the fund sponsor does not redeem shares and sell new shares to investors (except at the time of a new underwriting). Thus, the price of the fund shares will be determined by supply and demand in the market and may be above or below NAV, as discussed above.

Although the divergence of the price from NAV is often puzzling, in some cases the reasons for the premium or discount are easily understood. For example, a share's price may be below the NAV because the fund has a large built-in tax liabilities and investors are discounting the share's price for that future tax liability.[1] (We'll discuss this tax liability issue later in this chapter.) A fund's leverage and resulting risk may be another reason for the share's price trading below NAV. A fund's shares may trade at a premium to the NAV because the fund offers relatively cheap access to, and professional management of, stocks in another country about which information is not readily available to small investors.

Under the Investment Company Act of 1940, closed-end funds are capitalized only once. They make an initial IPO (initial public offering) and then their shares are traded on the secondary market, just like any corporate stock, as discussed previously. The number of shares is fixed at the IPO; closed-end funds cannot issue more shares. In fact, many closed-end funds become leveraged to raise more funds without issuing more shares.

An important feature of closed-end funds is that the initial investors bear the substantial cost of underwriting the issuance of the funds' shares. The proceeds that the managers of the fund have to invest equals the total paid by initial buyers of the shares minus all costs of issuance. These costs, which average around 7.5% of the total amount paid for the issue, normally include selling fees or commissions paid to the retail brokerage firms that distribute them to the public. The high commissions are strong incentives for retail brokers to recommend these shares to their retail customers, and also for investors to avoid buying these shares on their initial offering.

The relatively new exchange traded funds (EFTs) which are discussed Chapter 27, pose a threat to both mutual funds and closed-end funds. ETFs are essentially hybrid closed-end vehicles, which trade on exchanges but which typically trade very close to NAV.

Since closed-end funds are traded like stocks, the cost to any investor of buying or selling a closed-end fund is the same as that of a stock. The obvious charge is the stock broker's commission. The bid/offer spread of the market on which the stock is traded is also a cost.

---

[1] Harold Bierman, Jr. and Bhaskaran Swaminathan, "Managing a Closed-End Investment Fund," *Journal of Portfolio Management* (Summer 2000), p. 49.

Unit Trusts

A *unit trust* is similar to a closed-end fund in that the number of unit certificates is fixed. Unit trusts typically invest in bonds. They differ in several ways from both mutual funds and closed-end funds that specialize in bonds. First, there is no active trading of the bonds in the portfolio of the unit trust. Once the unit trust is assembled by the sponsor (usually a brokerage firm or bond underwriter) and turned over to a trustee, the trustee holds all the bonds until they are redeemed by the issuer. Typically, the only time the trustee can sell an issue in the portfolio is if there is a dramatic decline in the issuer's credit quality. As a result, the cost of operating the trust will be considerably less than costs incurred by either a mutual fund or a closed-end fund. Second, unit trusts have a fixed termination date, while mutual funds and closed-end funds do not.[2] Third, unlike the mutual fund and closed-end fund investor, the unit trust investor knows that the portfolio consists of a specific portfolio of bonds and has no concern that the trustee will alter the portfolio. While unit trusts are common in Europe, they are not common in the United States.

All unit trusts charge a sales commission. The initial sales charge for a unit trust ranges from 3.5% to 5.5%. In addition to these costs, there is the cost incurred by the sponsor to purchase the bonds for the trust that an investor indirectly pays. That is, when the brokerage firm or bond-underwriting firm assembles the unit trust, the price of each bond to the trust also includes the dealer's spread. There is also often a commission if the units are sold.

In the remainder of this chapter our primary focus is on open-end (mutual) funds.

FUND SALES CHARGES AND ANNUAL OPERATING EXPENSES

There are two types of costs borne by investors in mutual funds. The first is the *shareholder fee*, usually called the *sales charge*. This cost is a "one-time" charge debited to the investor for a specific transaction, such as a purchase, redemption or exchange. The type of charge is related to the way the fund is sold or distributed. The second cost is the annual fund operating expense, usually called the *expense ratio*, which covers the funds' expenses, the largest of which is for investment management. This charge is imposed annually. This cost occurs on all funds and for all types of distribution. We discuss each cost below.

---

[2] The are, however, exceptions. Target term closed-end funds have a fixed termination date.

Sales Charge

Sales charges on mutual funds are related to their method of distribution. The current menu of sales charges and distribution mechanisms has evolved significantly and is now much more diverse than it was a decade ago. To understand the current diversity and the evolution of distribution mechanisms, consider initially the circumstances of a decade ago. At that time, there were two basic methods of distribution, two types of sales charges, and the type of the distribution was directly related to the type of sales charge.

The two types of distribution were sales-force (or wholesale) and direct. *Sales-force (wholesale) distribution* occurred via an intermediary, that is via an agent, a stockbroker, insurance agent, or other entity who provided investment advice and incentive to the client, actively "made the sale," and provided subsequent service. The distribution approach is active, that is the fund is typically sold, not bought.

The other approach is *direct* (from the fund company to the investor), whereby there is no intermediary or salesperson to actively approach the client, provide investment advice and service, or make the sale. Rather, the client approaches the mutual fund company, most likely by a "1-800" telephone contact, in response to media advertisements or general information, and opens the account. Little or no investment counsel or service is provided either initially or subsequently. With respect to the mutual fund sale, this is a *passive* approach, although these mutual funds may be quite active in their advertising and other marketing activities. Funds provided by the direct approach are bought, not sold.

There is a *quid pro quo*, however, for the service provided in the sales-force distribution method. The *quid pro quo* is a sales charge borne by the customer and paid to the agent. The sales charge for the agent-distributed fund is called a *load*. The traditional type of load is called a *front-end load*, since the load is deducted initially or "up-front." That is, the load is deducted from the amount invested by the client and paid to the agent/distributor. The remainder is the net amount invested in the fund in the client's name. For example, if the load on the mutual fund is 5% and the investor invests $100, the $5 load is paid to the agent and the remaining $95 is the net amount invested in the mutual fund at NAV. Importantly, only $95, not $100, is invested in the fund. The fund is, thus, said to be "purchased above NAV" (i.e., the investor pays $100 for $95 of the fund). The $5 load compensates the sales agent for the investment advice and service provided to the client by the agent. The load to the client, of course, represents income to the agent.

Let's contrast this with directly placed mutual funds. There is no sales agent and, therefore, there is no need for a sales charge. Funds with no sales charges are called *no-load mutual funds*. In this case, if the client provides $100 to the mutual fund, $100 is invested in the fund in the client's name. This approach to buying the fund is called buying the fund "at NAV," that is the whole amount provided by the investor is invested in the fund.

A decade ago, many observers speculated that load funds would become obsolete and no-load funds would dominate because of the sales charge. Increasingly financially sophisticated individuals, the reasoning went, would make their own investment decisions and not need to compensate agents for their advice and service. But, as discussed below, the actual trend has been quite different.

Why has there not been a trend away from the more costly agent distributed funds as many expected? There are two reasons. First, many investors have remained dependent on the investment counsel and service, and perhaps more importantly, the initiative of the sales agent. Second, sales-force distributed funds have shown considerable ingenuity and flexibility in imposing sales charges, which both compensate the distributors and appear attractive to the clients. Among the recent adaptations of the sales load are *back-end loads* and *level loads*. While the front-end load is imposed at the time of the purchase of the fund, the back-end load is imposed at the time fund shares are sold or redeemed. Level loads are imposed uniformly each year. These two alternative methods both provide ways to compensate the agent. However, unlike with the front-end load, both of these distribution mechanisms permit the client to buy a fund at NAV—that is, not have any of their initial investment debited as a sales charge before it is invested in their account.

The most common type of back-end load currently is the *contingent deferred sales charge* (CDSC). This approach imposes a gradually declining load on withdrawal. For example, a common "3,3,2,2,1,1,0" CDSC approach imposes a 3% load on the amount withdrawn after one year, 3% after the second year, 2% after the third year, etc. There is no sales charge for withdrawals after the seventh year.

The third type of load is neither a front-end load at the time of investment nor a (gradually declining) back-end load at the time of withdrawal, but a constant load each year (e.g., a 1% load every year). This approach is called a *level load*. This type of load appeals to the types of financial planners who charge annual fees (called *fee-based* financial planners) rather than commissions, such as sales charges (called *commission-based* financial planners).

Many mutual fund families often offer their funds with all three types of loads—that is, front end loads (usually called "A shares"); back-end loads (often called "B shares"); and level loads (often called "C shares") and permit the distributor and its client to select the type of load they prefer.[3]

According to the National Association of Securities Dealers (NASD), the maximum allowable sales charge is 8.5%, although most funds impose lower charges.

The sales charge for a fund applies to most, even very small, investments (although there is typically a minimum initial investment). For large investments, however, the sales charge may be reduced. For example, a fund with a 4.5% front-end load may reduce this load to 3.0% for investments over $1 million. There may be in addition further reductions in the sales charge at greater investments. The amount of investment needed to obtain a reduction in the sales charge is called a *breakpoint*—the breakpoint is $1 million in this example. There are also mechanisms whereby the total amount of the investment necessary to qualify for the breakpoint does not need to be invested up front, but only over time (according to a "letter of intent" signed by the investor).[4]

The sales charge is, in effect, paid by the client to the distributor. How does the fund family, typically called the *sponsor* or manufacturer of the fund, cover its costs and make a profit? That is the topic of the second type of "cost" to the investor, the fund annual operating expense.

Annual Operating Expenses (Expense Ratio)

The *operating expense*, also called the *expense ratio*, is debited annually from the investor's fund balance by the fund sponsor. The three main categories of annual operating expenses are the management fee, distribution fee, and other expenses.

The *management fee*, also called the *investment advisory fee* is the fee charged by the investment advisor for managing a fund's portfolio. If the investment advisor is part of a company separate from the fund sponsor, some or all of this investment advisory fee is passed on to the investment advisor by the fund sponsor. In this case, the fund manager is called a *subadvisor*. The management fee varies by the type of fund, specifically by the difficulty of managing the fund. For example, the management fee may increase from money market funds to bond funds, to U.S. growth stock funds, to emerging market stock funds, as illustrated by the examples to follow.

---

[3] Edward S. O'Neal, "Mutual Fund Share Classes and Broker Incentives," *Financial Analysts Journal* (September/October 1999), pp. 76–87.

[4] Daniel C. Inro, Christine X. Jaing, Michael Y. Ho, Wayne Y. Lee, "Mutual Fund Performance: Does Fund Size Matter?" *Financial Analysts Journal* (May/June 1999), pp. 74–87.

EXHIBIT 26.1   Annual Operating Expenses for Three Mutual Funds

Type of Expense	Fidelity: Magellan	Vanguard: S&P 500 Index	American: Income Fund of America-A
Management Fee	0.57%	0.16%	0.28%
Distribution and/or Service (12b-1) Fees	0.00%	0.00%	0.24%
Other Expenses	0.18%	0.02%	0.07%
Total	0.75%	0.18%	0.59%

In 1980, the SEC approved the imposition of a fixed annual fee, called *the 12b-1 fee*, which is, in general, intended to cover *distribution costs*, including continuing agent compensation and manufacturer marketing and advertising expenses. Such 12b-1 fees are now imposed by many mutual funds. By law, 12b-1 fees cannot exceed 1% of the fund's assets per year. The 12b-1 fee may include a service fee of up to 0.25% of assets per year to compensate sales professionals for providing services or maintaining shareholder accounts. The major rationale for the component of the 12b-1 fee which accrues to the selling agent is to provide an incentive to selling agents to continue to service their accounts after having received a transaction-based fee such as a front-end load. As a result, a 12b-1 fee of this type is consistent with sales-force sold, load funds, not with directly sold, no-load funds. The rationale for the component of the 12b-1 fee which accrues to the manufacturer of the fund is to give incentive to and compensate for continuing advertising and marketing costs.

Other expenses include primarily the costs of (1) custody (holding the cash and securities of the fund), (2) the transfer agent (transferring cash and securities among buyers and sellers of securities and the fund distributions, etc.), (3) independent public accountant fees, and (4) directors' fees.

The sum of the annual management fee, the annual distribution fee, and other annual expenses is called the *expense ratio*. All the cost information on a fund, including selling charges and annual expenses, are included in the fund prospectus.

Exhibit 26.1 shows the expense ratios from the current prospectuses of the three largest mutual funds—the Fidelity Magellan Fund, the Vanguard S&P 500 Index Fund, and the American Income Fund of America Fund. The first two are direct funds and the third is a sales-force fund. The Fidelity Magellan and Vanguard S&P 500 Index funds are directly sold and, thus, have no 12b-1 distribution expenses. The American Income Fund of America, on the other hand, is sales-force sold and has a distribution or 12b-1 fee. With respect to the management fee, index funds are easier to manage and, thus, the Vanguard S&P 500 Index fund has the lowest management fee. The Fidelity Magellan is a very actively managed pure stock fund, which is difficult to manage, and has the highest management fee.

As we explained earlier, many agent-distributed funds are provided in different forms, typically the following: (1) A shares: front-end load; (2) B shares: back-end load (contingent deferred sales charge); and, (3) C shares: level load. These different forms of the same fund are called share *classes*. Exhibit 26.2 provides an example of hypothetical sales charges and annual expenses of funds of different classes for an agent distributed stock mutual fund. The sales charge accrues to the distributor. The management fee accrues to the mutual fund manager. Other expenses, including custody and transfer fees and the fees of managing the fund company, accrue to the fund sponsor to cover expenses.

Multiple Share Classes

Share classes were first offered in 1989 following the SEC's approval of multiple share class. Initially share classes were used primarily by sales-force funds to offer alternatives to the front-end load as a means of compensating brokers. Later, some of these funds used additional share classes as a means of offering the same fund or portfolio through alternative distribution channels in which some fund expenses varied by channel. Offering new share classes was more efficient and less costly than setting up two separate funds.[5] By the end of the 1990s, the average long-term sales-force fund offered nearly three share classes. Direct market funds tended to continue to offer only one share class.

EXHIBIT 26.2   Hypothetical Sales Charges and Annual Expenses of Funds of Different Classes for an Agent Distributed Stock Mutual Fund

				Annual Operating Expenses			
	Sales Charge			Management Fee	Distribution (12b-1 Fee)	Other Expenses	Expense Ratio
	Front	Back	Level				
A	4.5%	0	0%	0.90%	0.00%	0.15%	1.05%
B	0	a	0%	0.90%	0.75%	0.15%	1.80%
C	0	0	1%	0.90%	0.75%	0.15%	1.80%

[a] 3%, 3%, 2%, 2%, 1%, 0%

[5] Brian Reid, *The 1990's: A Decade of Expansion and Changes in the U.S. Mutual Fund Industry*, Investment Company Institute, p. 15.

ADVANTAGES OF INVESTING IN MUTUAL FUNDS

There are several advantages of the indirect ownership of securities by investing in mutual funds. The first is risk reduction through diversification. By investing in a fund, an investor can obtain broad-based ownership of a sufficient number of securities to reduce portfolio risk. While an individual investor may be able to acquire a broad-based portfolio of securities, the degree of diversification will be limited by the amount available to invest. By investing in an investment company, however, the investor can effectively achieve the benefits of diversification at a lower cost even if the amount of money available to invest is not large.

The second advantage is the reduced cost of contracting and processing information because an investor purchases the services of a presumably skilled financial advisor at less cost than if the investor directly and individually negotiated with such an advisor. The advisory fee is lower because of the larger size of assets managed, as well as the reduced costs of searching for an investment manager and obtaining information about the securities. Also, the costs of transacting in the securities are reduced because a fund is better able to negotiate transactions costs; and custodial fees and record keeping costs are less for a fund than for an individual investor. For these reasons, there are said to be economies of scale in investment management.

Third, and related to the first two advantages, is the advantage of the professional management of the mutual fund. Fourth is the advantage of liquidity. Mutual funds can be bought or liquidated any day at the closing NAV. Fifth is the advantage of the variety of funds available, in general, and even in one particular funds family, as discussed below.

Finally, money market funds and some other types of funds provide payment services by allowing investors to write checks drawn on the fund, although this facility may be limited in various ways.

TYPES OF FUNDS BY INVESTMENT OBJECTIVE

Mutual funds have been provided to satisfy the various investment objectives of investors. In general, there are stock funds, bond funds, money market funds, and others. Within each of these categories, there are several sub-categories of funds. There are also U.S.-only funds, international funds (no U.S. securities), and global funds (both U.S. and international securities). There are also passive and active funds. Passive (or indexed) funds are designed to replicate an index, such as: the S&P 500 Stock Index; the Lehman Aggregate Bond Index; or the Morgan Stanley Capital International EAFE Index (Europe, Australasia, and the Far East). Active funds, on the other hand, attempt to outperform an index and other funds by actively trading the fund portfolio. There are also many other categories of funds, as discussed below. Each fund's objective is stated in its prospectus, as required by the SEC and the "1940 Act," as discussed later.

Stock funds differ by:

- The average market capitalization ("market cap;" large, mid, and small) of the stocks in the portfolio;
- Style (growth, value, and blend); and
- Sector—"sector funds" specialize in one particular sector or industry, such as technology, healthcare or utilities.

The categories for market cap, while not fixed over time, were as of late 2000 approximately:

- Small—$0 to $2 billion;
- Mid—$2 billion to $12 billion; and
- Large—over $12 billion.

With respect to style, stocks with high price-to-book and price-to-earnings ratios are considered "growth stocks," and stocks with low price-to-book and price-to-earnings ratios are considered value stocks, although other variables are also considered. There are also blend stocks with respect to style.

Bond funds differ by the creditworthiness of the issuers of the bonds in the portfolio (for example, U.S. government, investment grade corporate, and high yield corporate) and by the maturity (or duration) of the bonds (long, intermediate, and short.) There is also a category of bond funds called municipal bond funds whose coupon interest is tax exempt. Municipal funds may also be single state (that is, all the bonds in the portfolio were issued by issuers in the same state) or multi-state.

There are also other categories of funds such as asset allocation, hybrid, or balanced funds (all of which hold both stocks and bonds), and convertible bond funds.

There is also a category of money market funds (maturities of one year or less) that provide protection against interest rate fluctuations. These funds may have some degree of credit risk (except for the U.S. government money market category). Many of these funds offer check-writing privileges. In addition to taxable money market funds, there are also tax exempt municipal money market funds.

Among the other fund offerings are *index funds* and *funds of funds*. Index funds, as discussed above, attempt to passively replicate an index. With respect to index funds, the number of index funds rose from 15 in

1990 to 193 in 1999 with $383 billion in total assets. The variety of index funds also expanded, domestically and internationally. Equity funds are the most common type of index funds, accounting for about 88% of these funds and $357 billion in assets.

Funds of funds invest in other funds not in individual securities. A fund of funds is a fund that invests in other mutual funds. In 1990, there were only 16 fund of funds with $1.4 billion in assets. By 1999, there were 213 fund of funds with $48 billion in assets.[6]

Mutual fund data are provided by the Investment Company Institute, the national association for mutual funds. Most investors, however, use data on mutual funds provided by other organizations. The most popular ones are Morningstar and Lipper. These firms provide data on fund expenses, portfolio managers, fund sizes, and fund holdings. But perhaps most importantly, they provide performance (that is, rate of return) data and rankings among funds based on performances and other factors.

The problem with comparing funds is that is that fund managers can pursue different styles. In Chapter 8, the different styles for equity funds are explained. Morningstar and Lipper divide mutual funds into several categories which are intended to be fairly homogeneous by investment objective or more specifically in terms of style. The categories provided by these two organizations are similar but not identical and are shown and compared in Exhibit 26.3. Thus, the performance of one Morningstar "large cap blend" fund can be meaningfully compared with another fund in the same category, but not with a "small cap value" fund. Morningstar's ranking system whereby each fund is rated from one-star (the worst) to five-stars (the best) relative to the other funds in its category is well known.

It is not always simple to classify a mutual fund manager into any one of the generic investment style categories that Morningstar or Lipper use. Consequently, as an alternative to these categories, William Sharpe has suggested a statistical framework for identifying mutual fund manager benchmarks. Specifically, the benchmark can be constructed using multiple regression analysis from various specialized market indexes.[7] That is, a benchmark can be statistically created that adjusts for a manager's index-like tendencies. Such a benchmark is called a *Sharpe benchmark*.

---

[6] Reid, *The 1990's: A Decade of Expansion and Changes in the U.S. Mutual Fund Industry*, pp. 14–15.

[7] See William F. Sharpe, "Determining a Fund's Effective Asset Mix," *Investment Management Review* (September/October 1988), pp. 16–29 and William F. Sharpe, "Asset Allocation: Management Style and Performance Measurement," *Journal of Portfolio Management* (Winter 1992).

EXHIBIT 26.3   Fund Categories: Morningstar versus Lipper

Morningstar		Lipper	
LG	Large Growth	LG	Large-Cap Growth
LV	Large Value	LV	Large-Cap Value
LB	Large Blend	LC	Large-Cap Core
MG	Mid-Cap Growth	MG	Mid-Cap Growth
MV	Mid-Cap Value	MV	Mid-Cap Value
MB	Mid-Cap Blend	MC	Mid-Cap Core
		XG	Multi-Cap Growth
		XC	Multi-Cap Core
		XV	Multi-Cap Value
SG	Small Growth	SG	Small-Cap Growth
SV	Small Value	SV	Small-Cap Value
SB	Small Blend	SC	Small-Cap Core
DH	Domestic Hybrid	EI	Equity Income
		BL	Balanced
FS	Foreign Stock	IL	International Stock (non US)
WS	World Stock	GL	Global Stock (incl. US)
ES	Europe Stock	EU	European Region
EM	Diversified Emerging Mkt	EM	Emerging Markets
DP	Diversified Pacific Asia	PR	Pacific Region
PJ	Pacific Asia ex-Japan		
JS	Japan Stock		
LS	Latin America Stock	LT	Latin American
IH	International Hybrid	SE	Sector
		SQ	Specialty Equity
ST	Technology	TK	Science & Technology
SU	Utilities	UT	Utility
SH	Health	HB	Health & Biotech
SC	Communication		
SF	Financial		
SN	Natural Resources	NR	Natural Resources
SP	Precious Metals		
SR	Real Estate		

EXHIBIT 26.3 (Continued)

Morningstar		Lipper	
CS	Short-Term Bond	SB	Short-Term Bond
GS	Short Government	SU	Short Term U.S.
GI	Interm. Government	IG	Intmdt. U.S. Govt.
CI	Inter-Term Bond	IB	Intermediate Bond
MT	Mortgage		
CL	Long-Term Bond	AB	Long-Term Bond
GL	Long Government	LU	Long-Term U.S. Funds
		GT	General U.S. Taxable
CV	Convertibles		
UB	Ultrashort Bond		
HY	High-Yield Bond	HC	High-Yield Taxable
MO	Multisector Bond		
IB	International Bond	WB	World Bond
EB	Emerging Bond		
		GM	General Muni Debt
ML	Muni National Long		
MI	Muni National Interm	IM	Intmdt. Muni Debt
		SM	Short-Term Muni
		HM	High-Yield Muni
		NM	Insured Muni
SL	Muni Single St. Long	SS	Single State Muni Debt
SI	Muni Single St. Interm.		
MS	Muni Single St. Short		
MY	Muni New York Long		
MC	Muni California Long		
MN	Muni New York Interm		
MF	Muni California Interm		

THE CONCEPT OF A FAMILY OF FUNDS

A concept that revolutionized the fund industry and benefitted many investors is what the mutual fund industry calls *a family of funds*, a group of funds or a complex of funds. That is, many fund management companies offer investors a choice of numerous funds with different investment objectives in the same fund family. In many cases, investors may move their assets from one fund to another within the family at little or no cost, and with only a phone call. Of course, if these funds are in a taxable account, there may be tax consequences to the sale. While the same policies regarding loads and other costs may apply to all the members of the family, a management company may have different fee structures for transfers among different funds under its control.

Large fund families usually include money market funds, U.S. bond funds of several types, global stock and bond funds, broadly diversified U.S. stock funds, U.S. stock funds which specialize by market capitalization and style, and stock funds devoted to particular sectors such as healthcare, technology or gold companies. Well-known management companies, such as Fidelity, Vanguard, and American Funds, the three largest fund families, sponsor and manage varied types of funds in a family. Fund families may also use external investment advisors along with their internal advisors in their fund families. The number of family funds has grown from 123 in 1980 to 433 in 1999.

Fund data provided in newspapers group the various funds according to their families. For example, all the Fidelity funds are listed under the Fidelity heading, all the Vanguard funds are listed under their name, and so on.

TAXATION OF MUTUAL FUNDS

Mutual funds must distribute at least 90% of their net investment income earned (bond coupons and stock dividends) exclusive of realized capital gains or losses to shareholders (along with meeting other criteria) to be considered a *regulated investment company* (RIC) and, thus, not be required to pay taxes at the fund level prior to distributions to shareholders. Consequently, funds make these distributions. Taxes, if this criterion is met, are then paid on distributions, only at the investor level, not the fund level. Even though many mutual fund investors choose to reinvest these distributions, the distributions are taxable to the investor, either as ordinary income or capital gains (long term or short term), whichever is relevant.

Capital gains distributions must occur annually, and typically occur late during the calendar year. The capital gains distributions may be either long-term or short-term capital gains, depending on whether the fund held the security for a year or more. Mutual fund investors have no control over the size of these distributions and, as a result, the timing and amount of the taxes paid on their fund holdings is largely out of their control. In particular, withdrawals by some investors may necessitate sales in the fund, which in turn cause realized capital gains and a tax liability to accrue to investors who maintain their holding.

New investors in the fund may assume a tax liability even though they have no gains. That is, all shareholders as of the date of record receive a full year's worth of dividends and capital gains distributions, even if they have owned shares for only one day. This lack of control over capital gains taxes is regarded as a major limitation of mutual funds. In fact, this adverse tax consequence is one of the reasons suggested for a closed-end company's price selling below par value. Also, this adverse tax consequence is one of the reasons for the popularity of exchange-traded funds to be discussed later.

Of course, the investor must also pay ordinary income taxes on distributions of income. Finally, when the fund investors sell the fund, they will have long-term or short-term capital gains, taxes on the gains, or losses, depending on whether they held the fund for a year or not.

REGULATION OF FUNDS

There are four major laws or Acts which relate either indirectly or directly to mutual funds. The first is the Securities Act of 1933 ("the '33 Act") which provides purchasers of new issues of securities with information regarding the issuer and, thus, helps prevent fraud. Because open-end investment companies issue new shares on a continuous basis, mutual funds must comply with the '33 Act. The Securities Act of 1934 ("the '34 Act") is concerned with the trading of securities once they have been issued, with the regulation of exchanges, and with the regulation of broker-dealers. Mutual fund portfolio managers must comply with the '34 Act in their transactions.

All investment companies with 100 or more shareholders must register with the SEC according to the Investment Company Act of 1940 ("the '40 Act"). The primary purposes of the '40 Act are to reduce investment company selling abuses and to ensure that investors receive sufficient and accurate information. Investment companies must provide periodic financial reports and disclose their investment policies to investors. The '40 Act prohibits changes in the nature of an investment company's fundamental investment policies without the approval of shareholders. This Act also provides some tax advantages for eligible Regulated Investment Companies (RIC), as indicated below. The purchase and sale of mutual fund shares must meet the requirements of fair dealing that the SEC '40 Act and the NASD (National Association of Securities Dealers), a self-regulatory organization, have established for all securities transactions in the United States.

Finally, the Investment Advisors Act of 1940 specifies the registration requirements and practices of companies and individuals who provide investment advisory services. This Act deals with Registered Investment Advisors (RIAs).

Overall, while an investment company must comply with all aspects of the '40 Act, it is also subject to the '33 Act, the '34 Act, and the Investment Advisors Act of 1940.

The SEC also extended the '34 Act in 1988 to provide protections such that advertisements and claims by mutual funds would not be inaccurate or misleading to investors. New regulations aimed at potential self-dealing were established in the Insider Trading and Securities Fraud Enforcement Act of 1988, which requires mutual fund investment advisors to institute and enforce procedures that reduce the chances of insider trading.

An important feature of the '40 Act exempts any company that qualifies as a "regulated investment company" from taxation on its gains, either from income or capital appreciation, as indicated above. To qualify as an RIC, the fund must distribute to its shareholders 90% of its net income excluding realized capital gains each year. Furthermore, the fund must follow certain rules about the diversification and liquidity of its investments, and the degree of short-term trading and short-term capital gains.

Fees charged by mutual funds are also, as noted previously, subject to regulation. The foundation of this regulatory power is the government's de facto role as arbiter of costs of transactions regarding securities in general. For example, the SEC and the NASD have established rules as part of the overall guide to fair dealing with customers about the markups dealers can charge financial institutions on the sale of financial assets. The SEC set a limit of 8.5% on a fund's load but allows the fund to pass through certain expenses under the 12b-1 rule, as indicated below. Effective July 1, 1993, the SEC has amended the rule to set a maximum of 8.5% on the total of all fees, inclusive of front-end and back-end loads as well as expenses such as advertising.

Some funds charge a *12b-1 fee*, as authorized in the '40 Act. The 12b-1 fee may be divided into two parts. The first component is a *distri-*

bution fee, which can be used for fund marketing and distribution costs. The maximum distribution fee is 0.75% (of net assets per year). The second is a *service fee* (or *trail commission*), which is used to compensate the sales professionals for their ongoing services. The maximum service fee is 0.25%. Thus, the maximum 12b-1 fee is 1%. While no-load funds can have 12b-1 fees, the practice has been that in order to call itself a no-load funds, its 12b-1 fee must be at most 0.25% (all of which would be a distribution fee.) In general, the distribution fee component of the 12b-1 fee is used to develop new customers while the service fee is used for servicing existing customers.

A rule called "prospectus simplification" or "Plain English Disclosure" was enacted on October 1, 1998 to improve the readability of the fund prospectus and other fund documents. According to the SEC, prospectuses and other documents were written by lawyers for other lawyers and not for the typical mutual fund investor. This initiative mandated that prospectuses and other document be written in "plain English" for individual investors.

Among the recent SEC priorities which directly affect mutual funds are:

1. *Reporting after-tax fund returns.* This requires funds to display the pre-liquidation and post-liquidation impact of taxes on 1-, 5-, and 10-year returns both in the fund's prospectus and in annual reports. Such reporting could increase the popularity of tax–managed funds (funds with a high tax efficiency).
2. More complete reporting of fees, including fees in dollars and cents terms as well as in percentage terms.
3. More accurate and consistent reporting of investment performance.
4. Requiring fund investment practices to be more consistent with the name of a fund to more accurately reflect their investment objectives. The SEC is considering requiring that 80% of a fund's assets be invested in the type of security that its name implies (e.g. healthcare stocks). The requirement is currently 65%.
5. Disclosing portfolio practices such as "window dressing" (buying or selling stocks at the end of a reporting period to include desired stocks or eliminate undesired stocks from the reports at the end of the period in order to improve the appeared composition of the portfolio), or "portfolio pumping" (buying shares of stocks already held at the end of a reporting period to improve performance during the period).
6. Requiring fund managers to list their security holdings more frequently than the current twice a year.
7. Various rules to increase the effectiveness of independent fund boards.

STRUCTURE OF A FUND

A mutual fund organization is structured as follows:

1. A *board of directors* (also called the *fund trustees*), which represents the *shareholders* who are the owners of the mutual fund.
2. The mutual fund, which is an entity based on the Investment Company Act of 1940.
3. An *investment advisor*, who manages the fund's portfolios and is a registered investment advisor (RIA) according to the Investment Advisor's Act of 1940.
4. A *distributor* or broker/dealer, who is registered under the Securities Act of 1934.
5. Other service providers, both external to the fund (the independent public accountant, custodian, and transfer agent) and internal to the fund (marketing, legal, reporting, etc.).

The role of the board of directors is to represent the fund shareholders. The board is composed of both "interested" (or "inside") directors who are affiliated with the investment company (current or previous management) and "independent" (or "outside") directors who have no affiliation with the investment company. The practice is changing such that a majority of the board must be outside directors.

The mutual fund enters into a contract with an investment advisor to manage the fund's portfolios. The investment advisor can be an affiliate of a brokerage firm, an insurance company, a bank, an investment management firm, or an unrelated company.

The distributor, which may or may not be affiliated with the mutual fund or investment advisor, is a broker-dealer.

The role of the custodian is to hold the fund assets, segregating them from other accounts to protect the shareholders' interests. The transfer agent processes orders to buy and redeem fund shares, transfers the securities and cash, collects dividends and coupons, and makes distributions. The independent public accountant audits the fund's financial statements.

CHAPTER 27

Exchange-Traded Funds

Gary L. Gastineau
Managing Director
ETF Advisors, LLC

Exchange-traded funds (ETFs) are the most important—and potentially the most versatile—financial instruments introduced since the debut of financial futures 30 years ago. We begin this chapter by explaining the origins of ETFs and some of their important features like intra-day trading on a stock exchange, creation and redemption of fund shares "in-kind," and tax efficiency. We also compare the recently popular open-end ETFs to competitive products like closed-end funds, conventional mutual funds, HOLDRs, and Folios in terms of costs, and applications. Advocates of conventional mutual funds, ETFs, and separate stock portfolios (including HOLDRs and Folios) have engaged in extensive discussions about the relative tax-efficiency of their respective approaches to equity portfolio management.[1]

THE HISTORY AND STRUCTURE OF ETFS AND SOME COMPETITORS[2]

Exchange-traded funds, referred to by friends and foes alike as "ETFs," are outstanding examples of step-by-step evolution of new financial

---

[1] For a discussion of the principal tax-efficiency issues, see Chapter 4 in Gary L. Gastineau, *The Exchange-Traded Funds Manual* (New York: John Wiley & Sons, 2002).

[2] A more detailed discussion appears in Gary L. Gastineau, "Exchange-Traded Funds—An Introduction," *The Journal of Portfolio Management* (Spring 2001), pp. 88–96.

instruments starting with a series of proto-products that led in a natural progression to the current generation of exchange-traded funds and set the stage for products yet to come.

Portfolio Trading

The basic idea of trading an entire portfolio in a single transaction did not originate with the TIPS or SPDRS, which are the earliest successful examples of the modern portfolio-traded-as-a-share structure. The idea originated with what has come to be known as "portfolio trading" or "program trading." In the late 1970s and early 1980s, program trading was the then revolutionary ability to trade an entire portfolio, often a portfolio consisting of all the S&P 500 stocks, with a single order placed at a major brokerage firm. Some modest advances in electronic order entry technology at the NYSE and the Amex and the availability of large order desks at some major investment banking firms made these early portfolio or program trades possible. At about the same time, the introduction of S&P 500 index futures contracts at the Chicago Mercantile Exchange provided an arbitrage link between the futures contracts and the traded portfolios of stocks. It even became possible, in a trade called an *exchange of futures for physicals* (EFP) to exchange a stock portfolio position, long or short, for a stock index futures position, long or short. The effect of these developments was to make portfolio trading either in cash or futures markets an attractive activity for many trading desks and for many institutional investors. -

As a logical consequence of these developments affecting large investors, there arose interest—one might even say insistent demand—for a readily tradable portfolio or basket product for smaller institutions and the individual investor. Before the introduction of "mini" contracts, futures contracts were relatively large in notional size. Even with "mini" contracts, the variation margin requirements for carrying a futures contract are cumbersome and relatively expensive for a small investor. Perhaps even more important, there are approximately ten times as many securities salespeople as futures salespeople. The need for a security—that is, an SEC-regulated portfolio product—that could be used by individual investors was apparent. An important predecessor came from Canada.

Toronto Stock Exchange Index Participations (TIPs)

TIPs were a warehouse receipt-based instrument designed to track the TSE-35 index and a later product tracked the TSE-100 index as well. The TSE-100 product was initially called HIPs. These products traded actively and attracted substantial investment from Canadians and from international indexing investors. TIPs were unique in their expense ratio. The ability of the trustee (State Street Bank) to loan out the stock in the TIPs portfolio and frequent demand for stock loans on shares of large companies in Canada led to what was, in effect, a negative expense ratio at times.

The TIPs were a victim of their own success. They proved costly for the Exchange and for some of its members who were unable to recover their costs from investors. Early in 2000, the Toronto Stock Exchange decided to get out of the portfolio share business and TIPs positions were liquidated or rolled into a Barclays Global Investors (BGI) 60 stock index share at the option of the TIPs holder. The BGI fund was relatively low cost, but not as low cost as the TIPs, so a large fraction of the TIPs shares were liquidated.

Standard & Poor's Depository Receipts (SPDRS)

SPDRS (pronounced "spiders"), developed by the American Stock Exchange (Amex), are the shares of a unit trust which holds an S&P 500 portfolio that, unlike the portfolios of most U.S. unit trusts, can be changed as the index changes. The reason for the selection of the unit trust structure was the Amex's concern for simplicity and costs. A mutual fund must pay the costs of a board of directors, even if the fund is very small. The Amex was uncertain of the demand for SPDRs and did not want to build a more costly infrastructure than was necessary. SPDRs traded reasonably well on the Amex in their earlier years, but only in the late 1990s did SPDRs asset growth become truly exponential. Investors began to look past the somewhat esoteric in-kind share creation and redemption process (used by market makers and large investors to acquire and redeem SPDRs in large blocks) and focused on the investment characteristics and tax efficiency of the SPDRs shares.

Today, the S&P 500 SPDRs have more assets than any other index fund except the Vanguard 500 mutual fund. The SPDRs account for more than one-third of ETF assets in the United States. Interestingly, however, from 70% to 90% of traditional U.S. index fund money goes into S&P 500 portfolios. Clearly, the interest in ETFs based on indexes other than the S&P 500 suggests that there is more to ETFs than an alternative to conventional index funds.[3]

World Equity Benchmark Shares (WEBS)— Renamed iShares MSCI Series

The WEBS, originally developed by Morgan Stanley, are important for two reasons. First, they are foreign index funds. More precisely, they are

---

[3] For specific analysis of the 500 SPDRs see Edwin J. Elton, Martin J. Gruber, George Comer, and Kai Li, "Where Are the Bugs?" *Journal of Business* (June 2002).

U.S.-based funds holding stocks issued by non-U.S.-based firms. Second, they are one of the earliest exchange-traded index products to use a mutual fund as opposed to a unit trust structure. The mutual fund structure has more investment flexibility and there are some other differences in dividend reinvestment and stock lending, but most of these differences are in the process of being eliminated. We would expect most new funds to use the mutual fund structure.

In addition to WEBS, a variety of additional ETF products are now available. The Mid-Cap SPDRs (a unit trust run by the Bank of New York) actually came before WEBS, and the DIAMONDS (a unit trust based on the Dow Jones Index Industrial Average and run by State Street Bank) and the Nasdaq 100 (a unit trust run by the Bank of New York) were introduced later. The Select Sector SPDRs used a mutual fund structure similar to the WEBS and were introduced in late 1998.

Barclays Global Investors, a major institutional index portfolio manager, launched iShares (mutual fund type ETFs based on a large number of benchmark indexes) in a bid to develop a retail branded family of financial products. The streetTRACKS Funds (another group of mutual fund type ETFs) represent State Street's first solo ETF effort in the United States. State Street is also behind the Hong Kong TraHKers Fund and other funds for investors outside the United States.[4]

ETFS AND OTHER TRADABLE BASKET PRODUCTS

While most readers think of the fund products described above as ETFs, various financial instruments, each referred to by some of its advocates as an exchange-traded fund, are designed to meet specific portfolio investment needs. In many cases, the needs met are practically identical; in other cases, they are quite different. In spite of some confusion about what the term ETF includes, most observers agree that a range of exchange-traded portfolio basket products compete for investors' dollars.

Our purpose in this section is to introduce the major categories of financial instruments which sometimes have been called "ETFs" or which compete with ETFs. We will appraise the features of each. Our objective is to provide a relatively straightforward comparison of features. The purpose of the comparison is not to suggest that one structure is always superior or that the emphasis should always be on competition between the products. In fact, folio customers have been

---

[4] For a slightly different perspective of the ETF landscape with more data on individual funds, see Albert J. Fredman, "An Investor's Guide to Analyzing Exchange-Traded Funds," *AAII Journal* (May 2001), pp. 8–13.

important users of the fund-type ETFs described in the previous section and of HOLDRs which are described below.

Closed-End Funds

Nuveen Investments began using the term "exchange-traded funds" for its closed-end municipal bond funds traded on the New York and American Stock Exchanges in the very early 1990s, several years before the first SPDRs began trading on the American Stock Exchange. The use of the name "exchange-traded funds" was selected to emphasize the fact that someone buying and selling these municipal bond fund shares enjoyed the investor protections afforded by investment company (fund) regulation and by the auction market on a major securities exchange.

"Open" Exchange-Traded Funds

The SEC requires that references to what we have been calling exchange-traded funds as open-end funds be made only in the context of a comparison with conventional open-end investment companies (mutual funds). We are about to make such a comparison so we will drop the quotes around open, and fully qualify the limits of openness in such funds. Shares in open ETFs are issued and redeemed directly by the fund at their net asset value (NAV) only in creation unit aggregations, typically 50,000 fund shares or multiples of 50,000 shares. The shareholder who wants to buy or sell fewer than 50,000 shares may only buy and sell smaller lots on the secondary market at their current market price. The secondary market participant is dependent on competition among the exchange specialist, other market makers and arbitrageurs to keep the market price of the shares very near the intra-day value of the fund portfolio. The effectiveness of market forces in promoting tight bid asked spreads and fair pricing has been impressive. ETF shares have consistently traded very, very close to the value of the underlying portfolio in a contemporaneously priced market.

For the typical retail or even institutional investor, purchasing and selling ETF shares is the essence of simplicity. The trading rules and practices are those of the stock market. ETF shares are purchased and sold in the secondary market, much like stocks or shares of closed-end funds, rather than being purchased *from* the fund and resold *to* the fund, like conventional mutual fund shares.

Because they are traded like stocks, shares of ETFs can be purchased or sold any time during the trading day, unlike shares of most conventional mutual funds which are sold only at the 4:00 p.m. net asset value (NAV) as determined by the fund and applied to all orders received since the prior day's share trading deadline. While the opportunities for intra-day trading may not be important to every investor, they certainly have appeal to many investors during a period when there is concern about being able to get out of a position before the market close when prices are volatile.

Primary market transactions in ETF shares, that is, trades when shares are bought and redeemed with the fund itself as a party to the trade, consist of in-kind creations and redemptions in large size. There have been occasions when creation and redemption of fund shares has resulted in asset flows of $1 billion dollars or more in or out of the SPDR or the Nasdaq 100 Trust in a single day. Exchange specialists, market makers, and arbitrageurs buy ETF shares from the fund by depositing a stock portfolio and a cash balancing component that essentially match the fund in content and are equal in value to 50,000 ETF shares on the day the fund issues the shares. The same large market participants redeem fund shares by tendering them to the fund in 50,000 share multiples and receiving a stock portfolio plus or minus balancing cash equivalent in value to the 50,000 ETF shares redeemed. The discipline of possible creation and redemption at each day's market closing NAV is a critical factor in the maintenance of fund shares at a price very, very close to the value of the fund's underlying portfolio, not just at the close of trading, but intra-day. A proxy for intra-day net asset value per share is disseminated for each ETF throughout the trading day to help investors check the reasonableness of bids and offers on the market.[5]

An extremely important feature of the creation and, more particularly, the redemption process is that redemption-in-kind does more than provide an arbitrage mechanism to assure a market price quite close to net asset value. Redemption in kind also reduces the fund's transaction costs slightly and enhances the tax efficiency of the fund. While a conventional mutual fund can require shareholders to take a redemption payment in-kind rather than in cash for large redemptions, most funds are reluctant to do this, and most shareholders have fund positions considerably smaller than the $250,000 minimum usually required for redemption in-kind. As a consequence, most redemptions of conventional mutual fund shares are for cash, meaning that an equity fund faced with significant shareholder redemptions is required to sell shares of portfolio stocks, frequently shares that have appreciated from their original cost. When gains taken to obtain cash for redemptions are added to gains realized on merger stocks that are removed from the index for a premium over the fund's purchase price, many conventional index funds distribute substantial capital gains to their shareholders, even though the continuing shareholders who pay taxes on these distributions have made

---

[5] This proxy value does not have the status of a formal NAV calculation.

no transactions, and the fund, looked at from a longer perspective, has been a net buyer of its index's component securities.

The in-kind redemption process for exchange-traded funds enhances tax efficiency in a simple way. The lowest cost shares of each stock in the portfolio are delivered against redemption requests. In contrast to a conventional fund which would tend to sell its highest cost stocks first, leaving it vulnerable to substantial capital gains realizations when a portfolio company is acquired at a premium and exits the index and the fund, the lowest cost lot of stock in each company in the portfolio is tendered to ETF shareholders redeeming in multiples of 50,000 fund shares. The shares of stock in each company remaining in the portfolio have a relatively higher cost basis, which means that acquired companies generate smaller or no gains when they leave the index and are sold for cash by the fund.

One further feature of the existing exchange-traded funds which causes a degree of misunderstanding and which seems to create an expectation that all ETFs will be extremely low cost funds requires an explanation. First, the existing ETFs are all index funds. Index funds generally have lower management fees than actively-managed funds, whatever their share structure. Second, ETFs enjoy somewhat lower operating costs than their conventional fund counterparts. The principal reasons for lower costs are (1) the opportunity to have a somewhat larger fund because of the popularity of the exchange-traded fund structure, (2) slightly lower transaction costs due to in-kind deposits from and payments to buyers and redeemers in the primary market and, most importantly, (3) the elimination of the transfer agency function—that is, the elimination of shareholder accounting—at the fund level.

As all U.S. ETFs are "book entry only" securities, an exchange-traded fund in the United States has one registered shareholder: the Depository Trust Company (DTC). If you want a share certificate for a SPDR or QQQ position, you are out of luck. Certificates are not available. The only certificate is held by the Depository Trust Company, and the number of shares represented by that certificate is "marked to market" for increases and decreases in shares as creations and redemptions occur.

Shareholder accounting for ETFs is maintained at the investor's brokerage firm, rather than at the fund. This creates no problems for the shareholder, although it does have some significance for the distribution of exchange-traded funds. One of the traditional functions of the mutual fund transfer agent is to keep track of the salesperson responsible for the placement of a particular fund position, so that any ongoing payments based on 12b-1 fees or other marketing charges can be made to the credit of the appropriate salesperson. There is no way for the issuer of an ETF to keep track of salespeople because these fund positions do not carry the record keeping information needed to use the DTC Fund/SERV process. They are, in a word, just like shares of a stock—and a stock with no certificates at that. The elimination of the individual shareholder transfer agency function reduces operating costs by a minimum of five basis points and probably by much more in many cases. ETF expenses tend to reflect the cost savings on this function.

The trading price of an exchange-traded fund share will be subject to a bid-asked spread in the secondary market (although these are very narrow on most products) and a brokerage commission. A simple breakeven analysis divides the round-trip trading costs by the daily difference in operating expenses. Anyone planning to retain a reasonably large fund position for more than a short period of time and/or anyone who values the intra-day purchase and sale features of the exchange-traded funds will find the combination of the lower expense ratio and greater flexibility make the ETF share more attractive than a conventional mutual fund share.

Powerful advantages notwithstanding, there are a few disadvantages in the exchange-traded fund format for some investors. An investor cannot be certain of his or her ability to buy or sell shares at a price no worse than net asset value without incurring some part or all of a trading spread and a commission. It is the trading spread in the secondary market which covers the costs of insulating the ongoing shareholder from the cost of in-and-out transactions by active traders. These transaction costs in open market ETF trades means that, even with lower fund expenses, certain small investors will not find ETFs as economical as traditional funds if they are in the habit of making periodic small investments. Since most conventional mutual funds take steps to refuse investments from in-and-out traders if they trade in and out too frequently, the transaction costs associated with ETFs are simply a more equitable allocation of these costs among various fund shareholders. A long-term investor, particularly a taxable long-term investor will benefit greatly from the exchange-traded fund structure because in the long run that investor should enjoy lower fund expenses and a higher after-tax return than he would find in an otherwise comparable conventional fund. This allocation of costs and benefits is ironic given the only significant criticism which has been leveled at exchange-traded funds, i.e., that they encourage active trading. In fact, the long-term taxable investor enjoys the greatest benefits from the ETF structure. Even so, the ETF structure has probably reduced the active trader's costs as well, given the obstacles and special redemption fees these traders often incur when they use conventional funds.

As noted, all current open exchange-traded funds are equity index funds. As time goes by, there will be a wider variety of funds available.

The introduction of fixed-income index funds, enhanced index funds and ultimately actively-managed funds seems inevitable. It is in the advance from simple indexation with full replication of the index in the portfolio that the investment management company structure shows its greatest advantages over the open UIT structure because the latter structure does not provide a mechanism for anything beyond full replication of an index. The open-end management investment company structure permits a portfolio to differ from the structure of an index fairly easily if the index structure is not consistent with the diversification requirements that allow the fund to qualify as a regulated investment company (RIC) for tax purposes. The UIT structure provides for replication of an index with limited variations based on rounding share positions and limited timing adjustments of index replicating transactions by advancing or deferring them for a few days.

Alternative portfolio or basket structures differ both from the UIT and the exchange-traded investment management company. These other structures have their own unique features. Foremost among these are HOLding company Depository Receipts, (HOLDRs), a structure pioneered by Merrill-Lynch, and Folios, which have been introduced by a number of firms that would otherwise be characterized primarily as deep discount brokers. Both HOLDRs and Folios are unmanaged baskets of securities which may have an initial structure based on an index, a theme, or just a diversification policy.

HOLding Company Depository Receipts (HOLDRs)

HOLDRs use a grantor trust structure which makes them similar to the open ETFs discussed above in that additional HOLDRs shares can be created and existing HOLDRs can be redeemed. The creation unit aggregation for the open ETF management company structures is typically 50,000 fund shares and the minimum trading unit on the secondary market is a single fund share. In contrast, the creation unit *and* the minimum trading unit in HOLDRs is generally 100 shares. Most brokerage firms will not deal in fractional shares or odd lots of HOLDRs.[6] An investor can buy and sell HOLDRs in the secondary market or an existing HOLDRs position can be redeemed (exchanged for its specific underlying

---

[6] DTC does not transfer fractional shares or fractions of the basic trading unit of a security, which is 100 shares in the case of the HOLDRs. However, some firms use trading and accounting systems that accommodate the New York Stock Exchange's Monthly Investment Plan (MIP). MIP was designed to let investors buy odd lots and fractional shares as a start in owning their share of America. Firms which can accommodate fractional share positions (including Foliofn) see the ability to handle fractional shares as a competitive advantage.

stocks). A new HOLDRs position can be created by simply depositing the stocks behind the 100-share HOLDRs unit with the Bank of New York.[7]

The creation/redemption fee for HOLDRs will generally be roughly similar in *relative* magnitude to the comparable fee on investment company ETFs and the pricing principles and arbitrage pricing constraints operate in a similar way. To the extent that one of the stocks in a HOLDRs basket performs poorly and the investor wants to use the loss on that stock to offset gains elsewhere, the HOLDRs can be taken apart and reassembled without affecting the tax status of any shares not sold. The ability to realize a loss on an individual position may give the HOLDRs structure a slight tax advantage over the investment company-based ETFs. On the other hand, unlike the redemption in-kind of the shares of an open ETF, the HOLDRs structure does not permit elimination of a low-cost position in the HOLDRs portfolio without realization of the gain by the investor.

The principal disadvantages of HOLDRs are that they lack the indefinite life of an investment company and there is no provision for adding positions to offset attrition through acquisitions of basket components by other companies. No HOLDRs component that disappears in a cash merger or bankruptcy can be replaced in the HOLDRs basket. If some stocks do well and others do poorly, there is no mechanism for rebalancing positions.

The HOLDRs share one very important characteristic with the index ETFs: It is frequently less costly to trade the basket in the form of HOLDRs than it is to trade the individual shares, particularly for a small- to mid-sized investor who might be trading odd lots in many of the basket components if HOLDRs or ETFs were unavailable.

Folios

In contrast to the other ETF variations and competitors described here, Folios are not standardized products nor are they investment companies or some kind of trust. They are baskets of stocks that can be modified one position at a time or traded with a single order through a brokerage firm. The firms which advocate and provide Folio baskets for trading do provide semi-standardized baskets—in some cases based on indexes, and in other cases based on a simple diversification rule. In practice, however, each investor's implementation of the Folio basket may be slightly different.

Because Folio baskets will not be standardized, Folios cannot be traded like fund shares or like HOLDRs. Each of the stocks in a Folio will

---

[7] The stock basket underlying a 100-share HOLDRs unit will initially consist of whole shares of the component stocks. In the event of a merger affecting one of the companies, any cash proceeds will be distributed. The surviving company's whole shares will usually be retained in the HOLDRs basket.

trade separately. While the brokerage firm can provide low-cost commissions and even the opportunity to execute trades against its other customer trades at selected times during the day, if the basket does not trade as a standardized basket, the investor will miss some of the transaction cost advantages which traders in standardized basket shares often enjoy.

A tax advantage of Folios over investment companies in certain circumstances is similar to a tax feature of HOLDRs. An investor can sell one position out of a Folio to take a loss and use that loss to offset gains obtained elsewhere—outside the Folio basket. In contrast, a fund taxed as a regulated investment company cannot pass losses through to shareholders. If the fund experiences large losses, an investor can take a loss on the fund shares by selling the share position; but losses on an individual portfolio component are not available to the investor who continues to hold the shares as a passthrough. In a reasonably bullish market environment, the ability of the UIT or management company ETF to modify its portfolio with creations and redemptions without taxable gain realizations will probably be more important to an individual investor than the ability to take specific losses in either HOLDRs or Folios. Other market environments may make the selected loss realization opportunity of the HOLDRs or Folios more valuable.

In contrast to the ETFs' fund structure, there is no "tax-realization-free" mechanism for reducing the impact of a very successful position in either HOLDRs or Folios. In the regulated investment company structures (exchange-traded unit trusts or funds), tax rules would limit the size of any single stock to 25% of the assets of the fund under most circumstances. Reductions in the commitment to a particular position in a regulated investment company with redemptions in-kind might be obtainable without realization of taxable gains. This would not be possible for very successful positions underlying HOLDRs or for components of a Folio. Basket mechanisms that do not offer a way to reduce a large, successful position without capital gains realization force the investor to choose between tax deferral and diversification.

A Side-by-Side Comparison of Tradable Basket Products[8]

Exhibit 27.1 provides an eclectic comparison of the mutual fund-style and UIT-style versions of open exchange-traded funds and conventional mutual funds to the other basket products we have discussed. Most of the items on this comparison table are relatively straightforward and readily understandable from the previous text, but several items do require some discussion.

---

[8] For a slightly different but useful perspective, see Albert J. Fredman, "Sizing Up Mutual Fund Relatives: Low-Cost Alternative Investing," *AAII Journal* (July 2001), pp. 9–14.

EXHIBIT 27.1 Basket Product Comparisons

Feature/Product Structure	Open ETFs	Open UITs	Conventional Mutual Funds	Closed ETFs	HOLDRs	Folios
Creation of Shares—primary market	In-kind deposit	In-kind deposit	Cash deposit with fund	IPO	IPO/in-kind deposit	NA
Purchase of Shares—secondary market	Open market purchase	Open market purchase	NA	Open market purchase	Open market purchase	Open market purchase
Sale of Shares—secondary market	Open market sale	Open market sale	NA	Open market sale	Open market sale	Open market sale
Redemption of Shares—primary market	In-kind redemption	In-kind redemption	Cash redemption	NA	In-kind redemption	NA
Underlying portfolio structure (available today)	Index	Index	Index or managed	Managed	Preset basket	Investor's choice
Tax structure	RIC	RIC	RIC	RIC	Structure is tax transparent	No structure
Tax-efficiency factors	Redemption in-kind	Redemption in-kind	Cash redemption	Cash redemption	Separable losses	Separable losses
Investor tax-efficiency rating	1	1	5	4	3	2
Effect of structure on shareholder's trading cost	Usually reduces	Usually reduces	Usually reduces	Usually reduces	Usually reduces	No effect except discount brokerage
Investor's Trading cost rating	1	1	2	1	1	3
Shareholder attention required	Minimal dividend reinvestment	Minimal dividend reinvestment	Minimal dividend reinvestment	Minimal dividend reinvestment	Dividend reinvestment principal reinvestment tax loss sales and replacements significant	Dividend reinvestment principal reinvestment tax loss sales and replacements significant

Ratings 1 = best, 5 = worst. See text for discussion

In assigning tax-efficiency ratings, we have placed significantly greater value on the redemption in-kind feature of the open ETFs and open UITs than on the separable loss feature available in Folios with no particular change and in HOLDRs through the exchange of the HOLDR for the basket of underlying securities followed by realization of the loss, re-establishment of the position that incurred the loss after the wash sale period is past and reconstitution of the HOLDR—a relatively complex and non-user-friendly process.

Closed-end funds are rated higher than conventional mutual funds on tax-efficiency because they are characterized by a closed portfolio and do not face the forced realization of gains which can come about through cash redemptions in an open-end mutual fund.

The investor's trading cost ratings are based on the advantages associated with trading a basket at the share level versus transacting separately in all the securities making up the basket. All of the standardized ETFs are ranked highly because trading in the composite share should be more efficient than trading in the underlying positions separately. It is certainly possible to differentiate among individual products in terms of the cost of trading the product or trading the underlying securities separately, but the difference is more related to the nature of the underlying market and the quality of the market in the basket product than it is on anything systematically related to the product structure. The conventional mutual funds are rated slightly below the exchange-traded products other than the unstructured Folios on the assumption that, on average, a redemption charge or other obstacles to short-term trading will increase an investor's costs of trading.[9] Folios are rated least favorably on trading cost simply because they do not provide any of the advantages associated with trading the other products as portfolios or baskets. Even when the transactions in a Folio are aggregated, each stock is traded separately. None of the Folio providers have reached a size that permits them to match and offset many customer orders to eliminate the bid-asked spread.

HOLDRs and Folios require somewhat greater investor (or manager) attention than the conventional fund or exchange-traded fund products for at least two reasons: First, to the extent that any of the companies in the HOLDRs or Folios are taken over in a cash acquisition, the shares will automatically be turned into cash and the shareholder will have to deal with reinvestment of the principal. Also, both these less structured products provide for their variety of tax-efficiency by permitting tax loss

---

[9] An investor can do an in-and-out trade in some conventional mutual funds with almost no transaction cost, but many funds will probably not accept a repeat order from that investor.

sales of individual securities. Folios, which are marketed principally as a way to take advantage of the automatic diversification a portfolio of stocks provides, require some kind of replacement or re-balancing activity to maintain a useful degree of diversification. With the other products, either a portfolio manager or the process for weighting or re-weighting the index and insuring regulated investment company diversification compliance in the fund will retain a minimal level of diversification without action by the investor or an advisor employed to manage the investor's position.

Investing in Real Estate and Alternative Investments

Real Estate Investment

Susan Hudson-Wilson, CFA
Chief Executive Officer
Property & Portfolio Research, LLC

This chapter covers the real estate asset class. It focuses on the investment and capital market aspects (the supply of and demand for the investment) and not on the space market aspect (the supply of and demand for space to lease) of real estate.[1]

COMPOSITION OF REAL ESTATE MARKET

Real estate comprises one-third of the value of global capital assets and represents approximately $10 trillion of value in the U.S. alone. Of this $10 trillion, approximately $3 to $4 trillion falls into the category of commercial and multifamily investment grade real estate, which excludes farmland, timber, raw land, hotels, and owner-occupied residential real estate. Hotels, farmland, timber, and raw land are sometimes included and sometimes excluded from institutional investors' definition of real estate, but for simplicity they are not discussed in this chapter. Owner-occupied residential real estate is a separately studied class of investment.

The commercial and rental residential real estate property types covered are:

---

[1] Jeffrey Fisher, Susan Hudson-Wilson, and Charles Wurtzebach, "Equilibrium in Space and Capital Markets," *The Journal of Portfolio Management* (Summer 1993), pp. 101–107.

- *Office* buildings, such as central business district assets, suburban buildings, office parks, and offices attached to mixed-use projects
- *Retail* centers, including malls, strip centers, big box retail, high street retail, neighborhood centers, and factory outlet projects
- *Industrial* projects, including both individual buildings and those located in industrial parks, and industrial buildings of all sizes and ceiling clear heights
- *Apartment* complexes located in the inner city, suburban garden style units, high-rise high end urban projects, tax exempt buildings, and condominiums converted to rental units

Real estate investments are characterized by the following structures:

- *Private commercial real estate equity,* held as individual assets or in commingled vehicles
- *Private commercial real estate debt,* held as either directly issued whole loans or commercial mortgages held in funds and/or commingled vehicles
- *Public real estate equity* structured as REITs or real estate operating companies (REOCs)
- *Public commercial real estate debt* structured as commercial mortgage-backed securities (CMBS)

These structures represent the quadrants of the modern real estate investment universe. Exhibit 28.1 shows the approximate value and percentage shares of each quadrant through time. Clearly the real estate investment universe has changed appreciably over the past 20 years. In the past, the private debt and equity markets dominated the real estate investment universe. While public equity had long played a small role in the real estate capitalization structure, the role has grown sharply since the early 1990s when many distressed private owners of real estate turned to the public markets to recapitalize and thereby save their companies from extreme capital shortfalls. Real estate debt markets also turned to the public markets for capital and so the commercial mortgage-backed securities industry developed.

Debt and equity and public and private markets are all covered in this chapter on real estate because while the traditional definition of real estate was limited to private equity, this definition has given way to a more modern and appropriate definition. Prior to the early 1990s, the public debt and equity markets were not of significant size and the private debt market was the province of a handful of the largest insurance companies and, therefore, was not routinely considered accessible to an institutional investor.

EXHIBIT 28.1   Capitalization Shares of Each Quadrant—1982 to 2001(E)

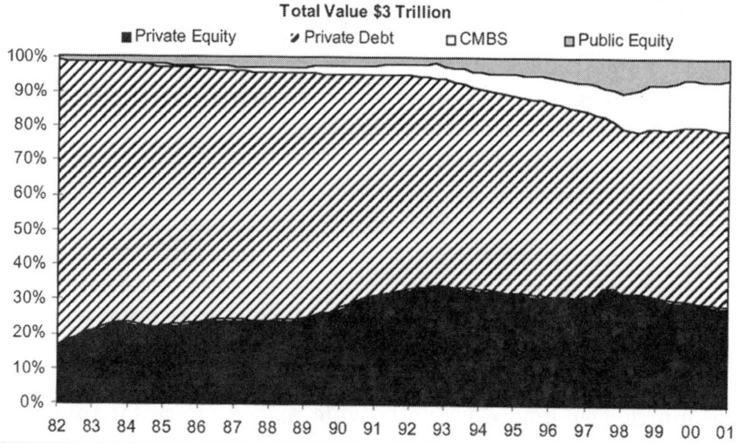

Total Value $3 Trillion

■ Private Equity   ⚊ Private Debt   ☐ CMBS   ▣ Public Equity

Source: Investment Property & Real Estate Capital Markets Report

TWO DISTINGUISHING CHARACTERISTICS OF REAL ESTATE INVESTMENTS

Two distinguishing characteristics of real estate are that it is a debt/equity hybrid and that real estate values rarely disappear.

Real Estate is a Debt/Equity Hybrid

A mix of debt-like and equity-like behaviors drives every real estate investment's performance. For example, consider the extreme case of a building leased in its entirety on a long-term triple net lease to a credit tenant. The contractually bound fixed lease payments to the building's owner are analogous to the payments to a bondholder and are not similar in character to the payments to an equity investor. The value of this asset varies in step with the same types of influences to which a mortgage holder or a bondholder is subject; interest rate movements, inflation, and the creditworthiness of the tenant. At the other extreme, the value of a totally vacant building is tied to conditions in the space and capital markets and not nearly as influenced by interest rates and, of course, is not influenced at all by tenant credit. There are no cash flows to equate to bond flows. As the building becomes leased it evolves from pure equity to a debt-equity hybrid, with some of the influences on value elicited from the debt markets and others from the equity markets. If the building is ultimately leased to long-term credit tenants then it becomes more debt-like than equity-like. On the other hand, if the triple net lease building loses its tenant, then it very quickly reverts to a pure equity investment. Equity-oriented value generators like the demand for and the supply of space, local market economic health, the building's location, and other building-specific attributes increase in their influence on value and on volatility, and, therefore, on the investment characteristics of the asset.

Commercial mortgages also exhibit this equity-like and debt-like convolution of behaviors. The creditworthiness of a building that is the collateral underlying a mortgage is dependent upon the lease structure as described previously. This creditworthiness can shift on a dime under some conditions. Most commercial mortgages are non-recourse to the borrower, but are recourse to the asset. Thus there are times when a foreclosed mortgage becomes an unintentional (or, as a deliberate strategy, an intentional) equity holding. A CMBS issue is generally comprised of a pool of mortgages, placed on underlying real estate collateral. The cash flows from the mortgages are then carved up to produce high-grade bond cash flows and low-grade or unrated equity-like cash flows from the most subordinated pieces. The tranches between the top and bottom tranches are characterized by varying degrees of equity-like and debt-like behaviors driven largely by the nature of the underlying collateral.

Real Estate Values Rarely Disappear

The second most important characteristic of real estate investments is that the asset is highly likely to have residual value no matter what kind of battering it may have suffered in the space and capital markets. All types of investments in real estate are ultimately grounded upon a physical asset. Real estate is not an "idea" for a business, nor is it a business that is dependent upon the employment of specific people—without whom the enterprise is valueless. Instead, a building is a physical structure that can probably be put to some use in some way over some period of time. This means that only in the rarest of circumstances does the value of an asset go to zero and stay there. This reality alone puts real estate and all of its variants in a distinct class.

Using the Debt-Equity Mix

Given the definition of real estate as a debt-equity hybrid, it only makes sense for the real estate investor to consider real estate an asset for which the debt and equity components can be purposefully weighted to suit the investor's needs. Investors increasingly use all of the quadrants to create a debt-equity mix that exposes them to the influences to which they most wish to be exposed and protects them from undesirable influences. As well, real estate investors can use the public and private trading market to execute arbitrage strategies and to manage liquidity and transactions costs.

THE NATURE OF THE INVESTORS

Who holds these real estate investments? The lion's share of the market has been, and continues to be, controlled by life insurance companies, banks, and private investors. Although the life company holdings as a percent of the total have declined significantly because some have gone public and wanted to purge their asset bases of the less well understood and valued holdings, and also because many experienced a tough cycle in the early 1990s. It is interesting that even in the face of that tough cycle, banks have held their relative position, as have pension funds and private investors. While pension funds look like real players at a 10% share of the institutional real estate market, in fact the portion of the average pension fund portfolio that is comprised of commercial and multifamily debt and equity is only about 4% of their total investment portfolio. Within the pension fund community, many funds have no holdings in real estate, whatsoever. Life companies and banks have always used real estate investing to extract a differential spread on the more debt-like aspects of the investment universe.

Foreign investors' share of the market is likely to expand, as cross-border investing is increasingly a part of all investors' approach to their investment strategy. As domestic investors look offshore and foreign investors look to the large markets of the U.S., the foreign investors' share will inevitably rise.

THE INVESTMENT CHARACTERISTICS OF EACH QUADRANT

Exhibit 28.2 presents each quadrant's mean return and standard deviation over time.[2]

---

[2] The calculation of the private equity and public debt returns is as follows. For private equity returns, Property & Portfolio Research (PPR) cap-weighted private equity index was used, incorporating returns for all the major metropolitan markets and property types weighted by the true market capitalization in each of those markets. Public debt returns are measured by the PPR CMBS model which applies typical CMBS structures to a variety of pools of mortgage cash flows and incorporates defaults and prepayments as well as changes in rating, spread, and overall interest rates. Other available CMBS indices, such as the new Lehman Brothers index, are either calculated at the tranche level or are too recent for this study.

EXHIBIT 28.2   Returns for Components of the Real Estate Investment Universe, 1982:1–2000:3

1982:1–2001:3	Private Equity	Private Debt	CMBS	Public Equity
Standard Deviation	5.3%	8.3%	7.2%	15.9%
Historical Mean	7.6%	11.4%	7.0%	13.7%

Sources: PPR; Giliberto-Levy Mortgage Index; NAREIT

Private Equity

Private equity is the least volatile of all of the real estate quadrants. At a mean historic return of 7.6% and a standard deviation of 5.3%, private equity real estate appears to be an effective asset. As explained in Chapter 2, in a mean-variance analysis to determine the allocation to real estate, it is necessary to have a good estimate of the expected return and volatility as measured by the standard deviation. Also demonstrated in that chapter are the problems associated with using historical data to obtain the necessary inputs. In the case of private equity, how good is the estimate of volatility?

One could make the case that volatility is understated. The reason is that the policy of most investors to mark their private assets to market only once each year creates a falsely tame picture of true mark-to-market performance. Certainly, if one were to assess the value of a stock equity only once each year its volatility would diminish significantly. On the other hand it is reasonable to ask whether the volatility of stock equity is perhaps *over*stated. Doesn't there seem to be a considerable amount of noise around the mean value that cannot be explained by income volatility or by shifts in expectations or perceptions of risk? Thus, while it is likely the case that infrequent valuations do produce a dampening, it is not clear that much greater frequency would generate the truth.

Also, for the most part, private equity real estate investors are "self-policing" and conduct and pay for the valuations themselves. This self-valuation is inherently conflicted and has indeed caused real concern. After the real estate market crash of the late 1980s, there was much discussion and debate around valuation methodology and control and several significant investors took steps to separate themselves from the valuation process of the real estate assets they managed. To address these legitimate concerns, two important steps were taken by an increasing number of institutional investors. First, the valuation process is placed in the control of an independent third-party valuation enterprise and second, the valuations are conducted with greater frequency and timeliness. Both of these changes, especially the one regarding frequency, have made differences, yet we have not observed a radical shift in the volatility of the returns. So, this leads the industry to additional explanations for the low volatility of private real estate equity.

The cash flows emanating from real estate investments are in fact highly stable. Thus the values, based in large part on cash flows, are also relatively stable. Long leases, buildings rented to either single users, or those with many different users on staggered leases generate demonstrably stable cash flows that are not subject to short-lived shifts in the economic environment.

The second explanation for low volatility is that real estate is, by its very nature, a debt-equity hybrid and so each building is essentially a mixed asset portfolio in which the cross-correlation between the two differently driven behaviors operates to reduce overall volatility. Further, we know from studying the performance of different urban area markets and property types within markets that there is a great range of different cycles occurring simultaneously—in part driven by the differences in the degree of debt-like and equity-like behaviors. Thus in real estate, when the buildings and the markets are pooled into indexes, there is room for significant risk mitigation within the index. The cross-correlations among real estate market sectors are quite low. The result is that the volatility for the overall private equity real estate market looks, and may very well be, truly low.

Public Equity

Public equity is a structure applied to a pool of real estate assets that allows them to trade in the public market. The two primary structures (traditional corporate structures are permissible as well) are the Real Estate Investment Trust (REIT) and the Real Estate Operating Company (REOC). The REOC is simply a regular corporation that operates real estate as its primary business activity. The REIT is explained below.

Contrary to its name, a REIT is not a trust—it is a tax election. A REIT is a company that offers shares for trade in the public market and generally acts as a perpetual ownership vehicle of one building or a pool of individual buildings. REITs are subject to certain rules to maintain their special tax status. For example, a REIT is required to pay out at least 90% of their accrual accounting-based earnings generated from the operations of the properties. Until 2000, REITs were encouraged to behave somewhat passively by rules constraining the volume of sales a REIT could execute in a year. These rules have been relaxed somewhat. In exchange for adherence to these rules, the income of the REIT is taxed at the investor level and not at the operating company level.

Most REITs employ leverage at the entity level and, therefore, experience greater volatility than is the case for unlevered private portfolios.

The mean return for the all equity National Association of Real Estate Equity Trusts (NAREIT) was 13.7% and the standard deviation was 15.9%. Of course, the REIT also experiences public market price volatility and, therefore, leverage alone does not explain the difference between the volatility of a REIT and that of a pool of private equity. Total returns for REITs over the period 1982 to 2001 have ranged from a high of 50% to a low of less than –20% (excluding hotels, which are not always included in the core definition of real estate).

The volatility in returns comes from how the income is priced and not from the income itself. The behavior of the income derived from private equity and that from public real estate equity should be identical. Both income streams are derived from the cash flows obtained from leased buildings. And, in fact, the income streams are identical in character. One study showed that when public equity cash flows were priced using private market cap rates, the performance of the private market was replicated.[3] Analogously, when private market cash flows were priced using public market yields, the performance of the public market was again replicated. So, it's all in the pricing. But which is right? Are REITs real estate or are REITs a creature of the larger stock equity markets with an entirely distinct and overwhelming pricing algorithm? This is an important question to investors who are contemplating using REITS as their sole exposure to the real estate asset class.

The answer to the question can be pursued by examining the correlation between REITs and the S&P 500 through time. The evidence suggests that while REITs were *not* real estate in the early 1980s up until the real estate market crash of the late 1980s, they were decidedly *not* stock equity in the most recent time period. In between those two extreme periods was a protracted period where REIT issuance was surging and where the correlation between REITs and the general stock market was generally drifting down. So what is the correct view to take on the question of whether or not REITs are real estate? It depends on what is happening in the larger stock equity market and the private real estate market. For example, when both the public stock equity market and the private real estate markets are rising, the correlation is likely to be very high; the two cycles feed one another. When real estate market fundamentals turn down, the divergence will rise. And, as has been the case in the 2000s, when the stock equity market is in bear mode, but property market fundamentals are structurally sound, again, the markets will experience divergent behaviors. The difference between the general stock market and the real estate market will be captured by both the

---

[3] Michael Giliberto and Anne Mengden, "REITs and Real Estate: Two Markets Reexamined," *Real Estate Finance* (Spring 1996), pp. 56–60.

public real estate markets as well as by the private markets. In other words, when the investor needs to see that real estate is real estate, and stock equity is stock equity, the difference asserts itself.

Private Debt—Commercial and Multifamily Mortgages

Private commercial and multifamily mortgages comprise the largest portion of the real estate investment universe and are exactly what they appear to be; loans based on the value of a building for which the underlying building is collateral. As explained in Chapter 17, these loans are almost universally non-recourse to the borrower and so the influence of the performance of the underlying collateral is of crucial importance to the performance of the loan. These loans can be fixed or floating rate, on one building or on a portfolio of buildings, cross-collateralized or not, and amortizing or interest only. Each loan is essentially privately negotiated; there are no standards to guide underwriting, the magnitude of the proceeds, or any other aspect of the loan or the documentation of the loan.

The spreads of American Council of Life Insurers (ACLI) loans over Treasuries are generally quite strong with the period following the real estate crash of the late 1980s posting very high spreads, and at a time when the risk was perhaps the lowest (construction had essentially shut down and the economy was recovering). Real estate markets are not immune from the general, and increasingly the global, capital markets as was evidenced by the great leap in spreads following the Russian default. Towards the end of 2001, spreads again rose as the perception of a new recession became a reality.

Commercial Mortgage-Backed Securities

A newly emerged structure for holding commercial and multifamily mortgages is the commercial mortgage-backed security (CMBS), a product described in Chapter 17. CMBS has created a new type of lender— the conduit lender. The conduit lender is any entity able to originate, underwrite, and securitize loans. Each part of the origination and management process is identified and de-linked, increasingly executed by experts in each area. Originators, servicers, special servicers, master servicers, third-party inspectors, and environmental inspectors abound. Essentially, the whole loan has been decomposed into its dimensions of risk and each dimension is managed and invested in by an appropriate entity.

This represents a far more sophisticated re-engineering of a real estate investment than does the advent of REITs. REITs are no more than a publicly-traded portfolio of private equities while each tranche of each CMBS is not at all similar in behavior and risk to the underlying mortgage from which it is created. The commercial mortgage-backed security represents a revolution in real estate finance.

CMBS spreads have generally tracked spreads in the whole loan market (i.e., market for unsecuritized commercial mortgage loans) except that the spreads really widen out (i.e., increase) for the lower and unrated tranches. As of January 2002, for example, the B rated tranches traded at 900 basis points over U.S. Treasuries while AAA rated tranches traded at 150 basis points. Spreads widened with the Russian default and a the general heightened level of concern for credit risk in 1998. In fact, just prior to that crisis the spread of CMBS to U.S. Treasuries (even for the lowest rated and unrated tranches) became very tight due to competition from conduits seeking to acquire commercial and multifamily loans to create CMBS products.

If the underwriting standards for commercial and multifamily loans can be maintained, the CMBS market will prosper. This is because it makes a great deal of intuitive sense. Each commercial and multifamily loan is very large, limiting the number of lenders that can offer financing. The possibly excessive spread (at least relative to corporate debt at the same credit levels) could be competed away if there were more lenders able to raise capital from smaller and smaller investors, even from individuals, as the securitized pieces can be infinitely divided. Investors in whole loans have to accept the entire return and risk spectrum while investors in CMBS can select exactly where they wish to be in the risk/return hierarchy. From a portfolio management perspective, this structure transforms an unwieldy investment into a precise tool for getting exactly what is needed for a portfolio.

REAL ESTATE IN THE MIXED ASSET PORTFOLIO

There are five primary reasons to consider real estate for inclusion in an investment portfolio:

1. Reduce the overall risk of the portfolio by combining asset classes that respond differently to expected and unexpected events.
2. Achieve a high absolute return.
3. Hedge against unexpected inflation.
4. Constitute a part of a portfolio that is a reasonable reflection of the overall investment universe (an indexed, or market-neutral portfolio).
5. Deliver strong cash flows to the portfolio.

EXHIBIT 28.3   PPR Real Estate Investment Universe Index (PPR REI),
1982:1–2001:3

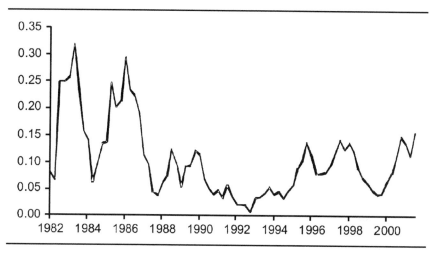

Source: PPR

Whether or not real estate can accomplish any of these goals, in the
short term as well as over the long haul, has not been an easy question
to answer. Two decades of research has yielded little bullet-proof evidence that real estate has a significant role to play in an institutional
portfolio. In the analysis below a cap-weighted index comprised of the
components of the real estate investment universe is used to capture the
performance of real estate (see Exhibit 28.3). The cap-weighted index
only represents one way to take advantage of the risk mitigation opportunities inherent across the quadrants of the real estate investment universe (all of the cross-correlations within real estate are below 0.6).
Other weighting schemes could be, and are, used by investors.

Real Estate as a Portfolio Diversifier/Risk Reducer

Using the real estate investment universe index (PPR REI), we can calculate the optimal allocation for real estate in a mixed asset class portfolio
of stocks, bonds, and cash. (The procedure for calculating the optimal
allocation is the mean-variance optimization methodology described in
Chapter 2.) The overall bond market is measured by the Lehman Cor-
porate/Government bond index, the stock market is measured by the
S&P 500, and cash is measured by the Treasury bill rate. The parameters for the optimization (using quarterly returns from 1987 through
2001:3) are shown in Exhibit 28.4 and the results of the optimization
are shown in Exhibit 28.5.

EXHIBIT 28.4   Real Estate Return and Risk Parameters for Optimization, 1987:1–2001:3

	Return	Risk	PPR REI	Stocks	Bonds	Cash
			Correlations 1982:1–2001:3			
PPR REI	7.5%	3.8%	1.000			
Stocks	15.4%	16.1%	0.395	1.000		
Bonds	7.7%	5.4%	0.763	0.311	1.000	
Cash	5.4%	1.6%	0.487	−0.031	0.481	1.000

Source: PPR

EXHIBIT 28.5   Multi-Asset Class Efficient Frontier, 1987–2000

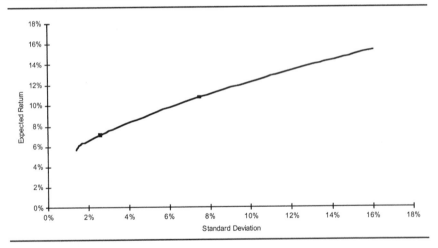

The correlations between real estate and stocks, real estate and bonds, and real estate and cash suggest that real estate can play a significant role in a mixed asset portfolio. Real estate's role extends from the lowest risk end of the efficient frontier to just past the midpoint of the mixed asset frontier. This makes sense as real estate is both a low-risk asset itself and a risk reducer in a stock and bond portfolio. Clearly, investors who wish to simply go for broke and seek the highest possible return, regardless of risk, will choose to allocate heavily toward stocks and will have no allocation to real estate as defined here. This evidence suggests that real estate is suitable for investors interested in capital preservation and who need to earn a useful rate of return. At one point along the lower half of the frontier, the model calls for an allocation of 16% to real estate. This weight drops to zero as one moves up the frontier.

Real Estate as an Absolute Return Enhancer

The second possible reason to include real estate in an investment portfolio is to bring high absolute and/or risk-adjusted returns to the portfolio. The data in Exhibit 28.4 show that, on average, real estate did not outperform stocks and bonds in absolute terms for the period 1987 through the third quarter of 2001. When assessed in terms of total return per unit of risk, real estate outperforms both stocks and bonds. However, employing the more commonly used Sharpe ratio and assuming a risk-free rate of 5.4% (the cash return for the period), real estate fails to outperform stocks but does outperform bonds on a risk-adjusted basis.

Thus, in the aggregate, it would not be justifiable to include real estate in a portfolio for the sole reason of bringing high absolute or risk-adjusted returns to the overall portfolio. There are, however, several other questions to ask about real estate's ability to deliver high absolute and risk-adjusted returns:

1. Did real estate outperform stocks or bonds in *some* quarters? Yes, there are periods in which the full quadrant definition of real estate is able to outperform stocks and bonds (i.e., 2000 . . . and again in 2001!).
2. Do some *components* of the real estate investment universe outperform stocks or bonds on average over the period? Yes, public equity real estate well outperforms bonds during the period, but none of the components of the real estate index outperform the overall stock average.
3. Do each of the components of real estate outperform stocks or bonds in individual quarters? Yes, each of the four components of the real estate investment universe experienced periods in which the real estate components' returns were above stock or bond returns. There are a good number of quarters when *each* component beat bonds, and even a few quarters in which all four components beat stocks.

The conclusion is that, in its aggregate investment universe form, real estate does not reliably produce high returns relative to the stock and bond investment classes. However, some real estate components provide absolute return benefits and real estate's lower volatility offers the investor some useful protection.

Real Estate as an Inflation Hedge

Conventional wisdom has held that real estate performs as an inflation hedge. This means that if inflation is greater than expected, real estate returns will compensate for the surprise and will help offset the negative response of the other assets in the portfolio. The rationale is important if it is accurate. Real estate returns have a complicated relationship with inflation. Inflation elicits different responses in the different property types through divergent impacts on the income and value components of return, and through variation in the effects of both past and the most recent inflation. Below, we first look at the response of private equity to inflation.

Past inflation is partially embedded in rents set previously because every seller of every product, including sellers of rental space, wishes to keep prices level or rising in real terms. Thus current net operating income (NOI), a measure explained in Chapter 17, is partly a function of past inflation; rising if past inflation has been greater, and falling (or rising less) if past inflation has been tame. The speed with which such inflation affects NOI, or the time lag necessary to capture inflation's impact on current NOI, depends on the structure of leases, which, in turn, varies with property type. Current office NOI reflects the inflation experience of one to ten years ago while apartment NOI reflects more recent inflation. The impact of past inflation is positive for all four major property types.

Current inflation impacts the levels of current rents and expenses. Current inflation raises NOI by increasing the rental rate on new leases, but lowers NOI by raising all expenses. In the office, warehouse, and apartment markets, current inflation causes NOIs to fall as the rise in current rents associated with recent leases does not fully offset the increase in expenses, which impact the entire asset. However, in the retail sector, current inflation raises NOI, as the impact on rents and percentage rents (which apply to all or much of the square footage in the building) more than offsets the impact on the few expenses that are not passed through. Retail, then, has two characteristics (percentage rents and the generous pass-through of expenses) that render it a very capable transmitter of inflation to asset performance.

Inflation impacts the capital value return in two ways. First, it impacts current NOI, as described above, which feeds through to value via the capitalization rate. This feed is especially strong for retail assets. In addition, inflation affects the cap rate directly by influencing NOI growth expectations and, therefore, investors' demand for real estate investments. The direct capital value impact of inflation is significantly positive for apartment and office properties, but not significantly different from zero for warehouse.

Thus, the empirical assessment shows that private equity real estate is a partial inflation hedge. That said, it is also clear that the degree of inflation-hedging capacity is not uniform across property types.

As with most debt, real estate debt is not a good inflation hedge because unexpected inflation and concomitant increases in nominal interest rates negatively impact the value of outstanding securities (mortgages and CMBS). Publicly traded forms of equity real estate will capture some of the benefits of the inflation hedge but are less successful transmitters of this value than private equity because of links to the stock market, which is generally damaged by inflation. So, if inflation hedging is a key reason why an investor chooses an allocation to real estate, that investor must tilt the portfolio toward private equity.

Real Estate as a Reflection of the Investment Universe

Real estate may have a role in a balanced investment portfolio simply because real estate is an important part of the investment universe. Any portfolio that does *not* include real estate is based on a bet that real estate will perform less well than is implied by the market-driven relative prices. Indeed, any allocation to real estate that does not reflect real estate's overall share in the investment universe implies a different bet from that of an indexed portfolio.

Unfortunately, determining the size of the total real estate investment universe to set the weight for real estate in an indexed portfolio has proven difficult. Using some broadly correct figures for the size of the market and data from the Flow of Funds report from the Federal Reserve Board for the size of the stock, bond, and cash sectors puts real estate at approximately 6% of the current investment universe. More recent shifts towards continued value growth in real estate and distress in the stock market, all compounded by recession, will cause further shifts in the relative weights.

Strong Cash Flows

An important dimension of the total return derived from a real estate investment is the proportion of that return that is derived from income. On average, real estate produces a long-term average cash yield of about 9% which compares with a cash dividend from stocks that averages about 3% and a yield from bonds that averages almost 8%. If an investor is concerned with the degree of certainty of return and has a need for cash returns, then real estate can serve a useful function.

Relevance to the Investor

It is clear that real estate has more than one role to play and that the investor needs to think about *how* to invest in real estate as well as *whether* to invest. But, in order to reach a conclusion about the role of real estate in a particular investment portfolio, it is important to think through the different types of investors and their needs.

A Risk-Tolerant Investor

Real estate is a risk reducer at low to moderate risk and return levels and so has no role in highly risk-tolerant portfolios. Thus, investors willing and able to seek the greatest return and unconcerned with capital preservation or volatility in returns would not be inclined to allocate any part of their portfolios to real estate as defined in this chapter. Such an investor is not concerned with real estate's size in the context of the overall investment universe and presumably is not concerned about inflation. While some parts of the real estate universe do periodically outperform stock equities, on average real estate is not a way to earn the greatest return. Such risk-tolerant investors might include individuals with "money to burn" or extremely over-funded corporate pension funds where the corporation wishes to go for broke as a way to add to earnings. A final category of investor might be an extremely underfunded pension fund that needs to stretch to achieve full funding (although this behavior would be inconsistent with the risk management mantra of ERISA). There are more fiduciarily responsible ways to achieve this particular objective. There are very few investors in this group because it is somewhat irresponsible to completely disregard risk.

A Risk-Sensitive Investor

The application of real estate as a partial solution to an investor's needs depends on the risk-sensitivity of the investor. If the investor is mostly concerned with capital preservation and has a typical actuarial return requirement, real estate will be an important part of the portfolio. The lower the return requirement and the greater the concern about risk, the greater will be the preferred allocation to real estate, up to the 16% level indicated by the allocations presented earlier in this chapter. As these investors' concern for capital preservation eases somewhat and their need for return rises, they will use less and less real estate until they have crossed the midpoint of the frontier when they will use none. The territory to the left of the midpoint of the frontier is the area relevant to low to moderate risk investors; pension funds with known liabilities and moderate actuarial rates of return, families wishing to ensure that wealth is preserved for future generations, and insurance companies and banks matching liabilities with well-understood cash flows and risk levels.

Risk-sensitive investors also generally prefer to line up with the larger investor community and are therefore interested in the size of the real estate market relative to other asset classes. An allocation that is seriously over- or underweight relative to the true investment universe represents a bet away from an important norm.

Risk-sensitive investors and those who have heavy demands for cash to satisfy liability streams will also have an interest in an asset like real estate with its relatively high yields. Returns derived from capital gains are riskier than those generated in tangible, realized cash. While overall returns might be lower than those for lower-yielding assets such as stocks, the certainty and size of the cash return is greater.

An Inflation-Sensitive Investor

If an investor must pay out a liability stream in real dollars, the inflation-hedging role of real estate is of interest. One of the best examples of such an investor is a defined-benefit pension fund. These entities are required to pay beneficiaries in real goods and services, not in nominal cash. Clearly, the cost of providing these health and retirement benefits is going to be greatly impacted by the incidence and the level of inflation. Another example would be a foundation or endowment interested in using a part of the cash flow from the investment portfolio to purchase art, provide students with scholarships, or create new physical plant (e.g., museums or educational facilities). All of these uses of the return from the portfolio are measured in real terms and would suffer from erosion in the purchasing power of the cash flows.

Real estate is truly one of the only vehicles able to partially preserve its value during a period of inflation. Inflation-indexed Treasury instruments, described in Chapter 16, are an assured way to hedge, but at the cost of lower returns. The time to put a hedge in place is before, not once, inflation occurs, so investors with real liabilities need an exposure to inflation hedges at all times.

LEVERAGE

While owners of residences routinely use leverage as a means to avail themselves of a home, it is less routinely used by institutional investors in real estate. This is because the use of leverage raises some philosophical and operational issues for institutional investors who are invested in multiple asset types. For purposes of this chapter, positive spread leverage at "reasonable" levels is discussed.

Leverage is the simple act of borrowing money based on the value and the security of the underlying collateral, in this case a building. Again the focus is on non-recourse (to the borrower) debt. Because of the non-recourse structure, for the borrower the use of leverage is analogous to short-selling the asset. The borrower takes the proceeds and can "put" the asset to the lender at any time with no further penalties by defaulting on the loan. As mentioned earlier, while it is rare for an asset's value to go to zero and stay there, it is not unheard of for a borrower to be unable to support the mortgage payment through a rough market cycle. Further, it is not unheard of for a lender to lend too much, based on an artificially inflated value. Thus the option value of the put is quite real.

An investor would choose to use leverage for one or more of the following reasons:

1. Increase the total return on an asset.
2. Hedge the downside risk of an asset's value.
3. Enable a fixed amount of capital to be spread over a larger number of individual investments.
4. Increase the yield and cash flow generated from a fixed pool of assets.
5. Reduce exposure to an asset or a pool of assets as a way of reducing exposure to the asset class.
6. Enhance the ability of real estate to act as a diversifier vis-à-vis the other assets in the mixed asset portfolio.

The final reason warrants further exposition. As discussed at the start of this chapter, real estate is a debt-equity hybrid. Thus, applying leverage to a building encumbered by one or more leases is a way of essentially "shorting out" the debt-like aspects of the asset's behavior. This then creates a heightened role for the equity-like aspects of the asset's behavior. This has the additional effect of enhancing the diversification effect of real estate in the context of a mixed asset portfolio; essentially "pure" real estate equity behavior is what remains.

Of course, leverage increases risk as measured by the volatility of the total return of the leveraged asset. This is inescapable. However, volatility has positive and negative dimensions to it. It often makes sense to apply leverage to assets that are, in other ways, less risky than average, thus the application of leverage does not imply that risk rises to unacceptable levels. The condition of the market when the debt is applied will greatly impact the ultimate health of the debt.

For institutional investors investing in multiple asset classes, there are benefits and issues with using leverage on the real estate portfolio. First, the diversification of the real estate portfolio itself can be enhanced with the use of leverage, assuming that appropriate allocations are made with the real estate portfolio. Second, the real estate asset produces enhanced diversification vis-à-vis stocks, bonds, and bills when it is leveraged.

However, the mixed-asset investor must also wrestle with the following question—does it ever make logical sense for the same investor to be a borrower and a lender (by making fixed income investments) at the same time? And, even worse, typically the rate at which the borrowing occurs will be greater than the like-credit rate at which the lending occurs. Don't these two approaches essentially neutralize one another while also incurring transaction costs? Of course, in the stock equity world this situation is routine, because most securities are issued by companies that use leverage. The stock investor, however, does not have a choice while the real estate investor (except the REIT investor) does.

So perhaps the fixed-income side of an institutional investor could lend to the real estate side? Right up until the moment where there were no problems, there would be no problems, then the trouble would begin. The two sides of the same investor organization would be conflicted and the situation would be untenable. This would be especially true in a typical situation where the portfolio manager for each asset class is expected to defend his own return and is not accountable for the overall fund level return.

Finally, leverage must be regarded as way for the borrower to raise capital, not to use capital. If a fund is not fully deployed in highly productive investment activities, it is hard to see why leverage would make sense.

Leverage then is a useful portfolio management tool as long as the philosophical issues are put aside and the real estate portfolio manager is judged on his or her independent performance.

INVESTMENT EXECUTION

In general, real estate is brought into the portfolio via:

1. Dedicated portfolios of individual assets executed by an in-house staff or by hiring outside managers, and/or via
2. Commingled funds that are either open or closed ended. These funds may be structured as insurance company separate accounts, private REITs, trusts, or public REITs.

Real estate investment carries with it significant execution costs both in terms of the staff required (either in-house or third party) to invest and manage and in terms of the actual costs of executing any transaction. The execution costs include expected costs such as brokerage fees, but also include more subtle ones such as search and underwriting costs. Much effort can be expended on transactions that are ultimately either deemed unworthy or are lost to a competitive bid.

Because of this reality, real estate investing, with the sole exception of investors who invest in public equity, is the province of the institutional player. There are a few commingled open and closed end vehicles available to smaller institutional investors, but there is close to nothing available for small institutions, endowments, foundations, and families, and certainly nothing (except REITS) of any magnitude available for individual investors. Given the nature of the investment process—one deal at a time, with large pools of capital required for each investment—real estate is virtually a closed shop.

This will change as the very nature of the institutional investor is changing. The U.S. is rapidly moving from defined-benefit pension plans to defined-contribution plans. The participants in the defined-contribution plans will absolutely want to be able to access a risk mitigator like real estate, and over time the investment industry will figure out how to meet their needs. REITS are a good start as they control the same types of assets that are controlled by the private vehicles. CMBS presents another opportunity for the democratization of real estate investing. As baby boomers age and begin to be more interested in cash flow and less in the volatility associated with growth, commercial real estate debt investing will take on new interest. But until the nut is cracked, the large institutions will dominate the field and reap the benefits of including real estate in their portfolios.

ADDITIONAL ISSUES

We conclude this chapter with some brief comments on additional issues associated with investing in real estate.

Valuation

As alluded to in the discussion of private equity, valuation continues to be an issue, especially for private equity, but then by extension for any collateral underlying any mortgage or tranche of CMBS. Even with public market pricing in the world of public equity, constant debate exists about the true net asset value of each REIT. While there is no magic bullet for this problem there are some sensible changes that could be made to the methods used in the valuation industry.

Currently, appraisal professionals exist who use the three methods to estimate an asset's value: the *cost approach*, the *comparables approach*, and the *income approach*. In the world of modern finance only the income approach has any real merit, as it is essentially a discounted cash flow method, exactly as used for other assets. The cost approach can only be interesting to a researcher who might want to know whether values are at or below cost for the purpose of estimating the likelihood of new supply appearing in the market. Clearly, when values exceed the cost of construction, it is likely that new supply will occur. Other than that, there is absolutely no reason why value should bear any short-run relationship to cost. The comparables approach is flawed as it is inherently backward looking and valuation is inherently forward looking. When markets move, this approach is virtually guaranteed to provide an incorrect perspective.

Thus, the industry truly needs to increase the rigor of the income approach. Discount rates should be linked to careful analysis of relative risk, and future rent growth and vacancy scenarios should be better linked to thorough market analysis. The analysis should be re-run as soon as any variable in the cash flow forecast changes. Thus, values would be constantly adjusted as new information was received and there would be less room for judgements and looking over one's shoulder. The deficiency of the valuation system presents a serious challenge for the industry.

Performance Measurement

There are several calculations employed to measure the performance of real estate investments, and several associations collect and disseminate performance statistics on certain dimensions of the real estate investment universe. The National Council of Real Estate Investment Fiduciaries (NCREIF) collects data on the income and capital value returns for a group of private equity assets held by tax-exempt investors. Commercial Mortgage Securitization Association (CMSA) and Lehman Brothers have begun the work of documenting the performance of CMBS. The National Association of Real Estate Investment Trusts (NAREIT) collects and disseminates performance data on the publicly traded REIT industry. A private firm, The John B. Levy company, produces a modeled statistic on the performance of private debt. Unfortunately, none of these sources is as comprehensive as one would like and so each "benchmark" must be used with a great deal of knowledge of the specific inclusions and limitations of the data.

In real estate, different investors use different calculations to measure performance—the internal rate of return, the time-weighted return, the average annual return, and the since-inception return are some of the measures used. (These measures are explained in Chapter 5.) In some cases, investors estimate a value in order to calculate the return and in other cases investors simply look at the cash-on-cash return of an investment. The bottom line is that there is no single standard by which real estate performance is measured.

Attribution analysis—covered in Chapter 13 for common stock—is in a very preliminary stage of development in the real estate investment community. This is partly because the data to support such analysis are weak and partly as a reflection of the generally less analytic predisposition of the investors (although this is changing).

Hold/Sell in the Traditional Private Equity Market

The inverse of the sell decision is the buy decision and any decision not to sell is a decision to rebuy. The criteria for the sell decision are multi-leveled. There are portfolio level considerations—does the market and property type exposure of the asset help or harm the investor's ability to achieve the investment goals of the overall portfolio? There are market level considerations—does the specific market in which the asset resides continue to provide the most effective way to bring the behavior of a desired sector to the portfolio? And there are asset level considerations—is the asset itself able to bring to the market, the sector, and the portfolio the behavior that is required of the asset?

While for other asset classes the hold/sell decision can be based substantially on the criteria presented above, in real estate there is one additional consideration—the cost of selling and redeploying the proceeds of the sale. Costs include staff time, commissions, taxes, and elapsed time. Particularly in the private portions of the real estate capital markets, costs are often significant and can reach levels where it is better to do nothing than it is to rebalance the portfolio.

CHAPTER 29

Hedge Funds

Mark J. P. Anson, CFA, Ph.D., CPA, Esq.
Chief Investment Officer
CalPERS

A hedge fund is a privately organized investment vehicle that manages a concentrated portfolio of public securities and derivative instruments on public securities, that can invest both long and short, and can apply leverage. In this chapter we will discuss the key features of hedge funds.

HEDGE FUNDS VERSUS MUTUAL FUNDS

Within this definition there are five key elements of hedge funds that distinguish them from their more traditional counterpart, the mutual fund, which was covered in Chapter 26.

First, hedge funds are private investment vehicles that pool the resources of sophisticated investors. Under one SEC rule, hedge funds cannot have more than 100 investors in the fund. Alternatively, a second rule allows hedge funds to accept an unlimited number of "qualified purchasers" in the fund. These are individuals or institutions that have a net worth in excess of $5,000,000.

Second, hedge funds tend to have portfolios that are much more concentrated than their mutual fund brethren. Most hedge funds do not have broad securities benchmarks. The reason is that most hedge fund managers claim that their style of investing is "skill-based" and cannot be measured by a market return. Consequently, hedge fund managers are not forced to maintain security holdings relative to a benchmark;

they do not need to worry about "benchmark" risk. This allows them to concentrate their portfolio only on those securities that they believe will add value to the portfolio.

Another reason for the concentrated portfolio is that hedge fund managers tend to have narrow investment strategies. These strategies tend to focus on only one sector of the economy or one segment of the market. They can tailor their portfolio to extract the most value from their smaller investment sector or segment.

Third, hedge funds tend to use derivative strategies much more predominately than mutual funds. Indeed, in some strategies the ability to sell or buy options is a key component of executing the arbitrage.

Fourth, hedge funds may go both long and short securities. The ability to short public securities and derivative instruments is one of the key distinctions between hedge funds and traditional money managers. Hedge fund managers incorporate their ability to short securities explicitly into their investment strategies. This is very different from traditional money managers that are tied to a long-only securities benchmark.

Finally, hedge funds use leverage, sometimes, large amounts. Mutual funds, for example, are limited in the amount of leverage they can employ; they may borrow up to 33% of their net asset base. Hedge funds do not have this restriction. Consequently, it is not unusual to see some hedge fund strategies that employ leverage up to 10 times their net asset base.

We can see that hedge funds are different than traditional long-only investment managers.

HEDGE FUND STRATEGIES

Hedge funds invest in the same equity and fixed-income securities as traditional long-only managers. Therefore, it is not the alternative "assets" in which hedge funds invest that differentiates them from long-only managers, but rather, it is the alternative investment strategies that they pursue.

In this section we describe several alternative strategies that hedge funds apply. In general, some hedge funds have considerable exposure to the financial markets. This would be the *long/short, global macro hedge fund or short selling players*. Other hedge funds take little market exposure, but use leverage to magnify the size of their bets. These are the *arbitrage hedge funds*. Last there are hedge fund strategies that take little credit or market risk. These are the *market neutral* and *market timing strategies*.

Equity Long/Short

Equity long/short managers build their portfolios by combining a core group of long stock positions with short sales of stock or stock index options/futures. Their net market exposure of long positions minus short positions tends to have a positive bias. That is, equity long/short managers tend to be long market exposure. The length of their exposure depends on current market conditions. For instance, during the great stock market surge of 1996–1999, these managers tended to be mostly long their equity exposure. However, as the stock market turned into a bear market in 2000, these managers decreased their market exposure as they sold more stock short or sold stock index options and futures.

For example, consider a hedge fund manager in 2000 who had a 100% long exposure to tobacco industry stocks and had a 20% short exposure to semiconductor stocks. The beta of the S&P Tobacco index is 0.5, and for the Semi-Conductor index it is 1.5. The weighted average beta of the portfolio is:

$$[1.0 \times 0.5] + [-0.20 \times 1.5] = 0.20$$

Beta is a well-known measure of market exposure (or systematic risk). A portfolio with a beta of 1.0 is considered to have the same stock market exposure or risk as a broad-based stock index such as the S&P 500.

According to the Capital Asset Pricing Model, the hedge fund manager has a conservative portfolio. The expected return of this portfolio according the model is:[1]

$$6\% + 0.20 \times (-9.5\% - 6\%) = 2.9\%$$

However, in 2000, the total return on the S&P Tobacco Index was 98% while for the Semi-conductor Index it was –31%. This "conservative" hedge fund portfolio would have earned the following return in 2000:

$$[1.0 \times 98\%] + [-0.20 \times -31\%] = 104.20\%$$

This is a much higher return than that predicted by the Capital Asset Pricing Model.

---

[1] The Capital Asset Pricing Model is expressed as:

E(Return on Portfolio) = Risk-free rate + Beta
$\qquad\qquad\qquad \times$ (Return on the Market – Risk-free rate)

In 2000, the return on the market, represented by the S&P 500 was –9.5%, while the risk-free rate was about 6%.

This example serves to highlight two points. First, the ability to go both long and short in the market is a powerful tool for earning excess returns. The ability to fully implement a strategy not only about stocks and sectors that are expected to increase in value but also stocks and sectors that are expected to decrease in value allows the hedge fund manager to maximize the value of his market insights.

Second, the long/short nature of the portfolio can be misleading with respect to the risk exposure. This manager is 80% net long. Additionally, the beta of the combined portfolio is only 0.20. From this an investor might conclude that the hedge fund manager is pursuing a low risk strategy. However, this is not true. What the hedge fund manager has done is to make two explicit bets: that tobacco stocks will appreciate in value and that semiconductor stocks will decline in value.

The Capital Asset Pricing Model assumes that investors hold a well-diversified portfolio. That is not the case with this hedge fund manager. Most hedge fund managers build concentrated rather than highly diversified portfolios. Consequently, traditional models (such as the Capital Asset Pricing Model) and associated risk measures (such as beta) may not apply to hedge fund managers.

Equity long/short hedge funds essentially come in two flavors: fundamental or quantitative. *Fundamental long/short hedge funds* conduct traditional economic analysis on a company's business prospects compared to its competitors and the current economic environment. These managers will visit with corporate management, talk with Wall Street analysts, contact customers and competitors, and essentially conduct bottom-up analysis. The difference between these hedge funds and long-only managers is that they will short the stocks that they consider to be poor performers and buy those stocks that are expected to outperform the market. In addition, they may leverage their long and short positions.

Fundamental long/short equity hedge funds tend to invest in one economic sector or market segment. For instance, they may specialize in buying and selling internet companies (sector focus) or buying and selling small market capitalization companies (segment focus).

In contrast, *quantitative equity long/short hedge fund managers* tend not to be sector or segment specialists. In fact, quite the reverse. Quantitative hedge fund managers like to cast as broad a net as possible in their analysis.

These managers use mathematical analysis to review past company performance in light of several quantitative factors. For instance, these managers may build regression models to determine the impact of market price to book value (price/book ratio) on companies across the universe of stocks as well as different market segments or economic sectors. Or, they may analyze changes in dividend yields on stock price performance.

Typically, these managers build multi-factor models, both linear and quadratic, and then test these models on historical stock price performance. Backtesting involves applying the quantitative model on prior stock price performance to see if there is any predictive power in determining whether the stock of a particular company will rise or fall. If the model proves successful using historical data, the hedge fund manager will then conduct an "out of sample" test of the model. This involves testing the model on a subset of historical data that was not included in the model building phase.

If a hedge fund manager identifies a successful quantitative strategy, it will apply its model mechanically. Buy and sell orders will be generated by the model and submitted to the order desk. In practice, the hedge fund manager will put limits on its model such as the maximum short exposure allowed or the maximum amount of capital that may be committed to any one stock position. In addition, quantitative hedge fund managers usually build in some qualitative oversight to ensure that the model is operating consistently.

Global Macro

As their name implies, global macro hedge funds take a macroeconomic approach on a global basis in their investment strategy. These are top-down managers who invest opportunistically across financial markets, currencies, national borders, and commodities. They take large positions depending upon the hedge fund manager's forecast of changes in interest rates, currency movements, monetary policies, and macroeconomic indicators.

Global macro managers have the broadest investment universe. They are not limited by market segment or industry sector, nor by geographic region, financial market, or currency. Additionally, global macro may invest in commodities. In fact, a fund of global macro hedge funds offers the greatest diversification of investment strategies.

Global macro funds tend to have large amounts of investor capital. This is necessary to execute their macroeconomic strategies. In addition, they may apply leverage to increase the size of their macro bets. As a result, global macro hedge funds tend to receive the greatest attention and publicity in the financial markets.

The best known of these hedge funds was the Quantum Hedge Fund managed by George Soros. It is well documented that this fund made significant gains in 1992 by betting that the British pound would devalue (which it did). This fund was also accused of contributing to the "Asian Contagion" in the fall of 1997 when the government of Thailand devalued its currency, the baht, triggering a domino effect in currency movements throughout southeast Asia.

In recent times, however, global macro funds have fallen on hard times.[2] One reason is that many global macro funds were hurt by the Russian bond default in August 1998 and the bursting of the technology bubble in March 2000. These two events caused large losses for the global macro funds.

A second reason, as indicated above, is that global macro hedge funds had the broadest investment mandate of any hedge fund strategy. The ability to invest widely across currencies, financial markets, geographic borders, and commodities is a two-edged sword. On the one hand, it allows global macro funds the widest universe in which to implement their strategies. On the other hand, it lacks focus. As more institutional investors have moved into the hedge fund marketplace, they have demanded greater investment focus as opposed to free investment reign.

Short Selling

Short selling hedge funds have the opposite exposure of traditional long-only managers. In that sense, their return distribution should be the mirror image of long-only managers: They make money when the stock market is declining and lose money when the stock market is gaining.

These hedge fund managers may be distinguished from equity long/short managers in that they generally maintain a net short exposure to the stock market. However, short selling hedge funds tend to use some form of market timing. That is, they trim their short positions when the stock market is increasing and go fully short when the stock market is declining. When the stock market is gaining, short sellers maintain that portion of their investment capital not committed to short selling in short-term interest rate bearing accounts.

The past 10 years has seen predominantly a strong bull market in the United States. There have been some speed bumps: the short recession of 1990–1991 and the soft landing of 1994. But for the most part, the U.S. equity market has enjoyed strong returns in the 1990s. As a result, short sellers have had to seek other markets such as Japan, or result to more market timing to earn positive results.

Convertible Bond Arbitrage

Hedge fund managers tend to use the term "arbitrage" somewhat loosely. Arbitrage is defined simply as riskless profits. It is the purchase of a security for cash at one price and the immediate resale for cash of the same security at a higher price. Alternatively, it may be defined as

---

[2] See *New York Times* (May 6, 2000).

the simultaneous purchase of security A for cash at one price and the selling of identical security B for cash at a higher price. In both cases, the arbitrageur has no risk. There is no market risk because the holding of the securities is instantaneous. There is no basis risk because the securities are identical, and there is no credit risk because the transaction is conducted in cash.

Instead of riskless profits, in the hedge fund world, arbitrage is generally used to mean low risk investments. Instead of the purchase and sale of identical instruments, there is the purchase and sale of similar instruments. Additionally, the securities may not be sold for cash, so there may be credit risk during the collection period. Last, the purchase and sale may not be instantaneous. The arbitrageur may need to hold onto its positions for a period of time, exposing him to market risk.

Convertible arbitrage funds build long positions of convertible bonds and then hedge the equity component of the bond by selling the underlying stock or options on that stock. Equity risk can be hedged by selling the appropriate ratio of stock underlying the convertible option.[3]

Fixed-Income Arbitrage

Fixed-income arbitrage involves purchasing one fixed-income security and simultaneously selling a similar fixed-income security. The sale of the second security is done to hedge the underlying market risk contained in the first security. Typically, the two securities are related either mathematically or economically such that they move similarly with respect to market developments. Generally, the difference in pricing between the two securities is small, and this is what the fixed-income arbitrageur hopes to gain. By buying and selling two fixed-income securities that are tied together, the hedge fund manager hopes to capture a pricing discrepancy that will cause the prices of the two securities to converge overtime.

Fixed-income arbitrage does not need to use exotic securities. It can be nothing more than buying and selling U.S. Treasury bonds. In the bond market, the most liquid securities are the on-the-run Treasury bonds. These are the most currently issued bonds issued by the U.S. Treasury Department. However, there are other U.S. Treasury bonds outstanding that have very similar characteristics to the on-the-run Treasury bonds. The difference is that *off-the-run* bonds were issued at an earlier date, and are now less liquid than the on-the-run bonds. As a result, price discrepancies occur. The difference in price may be no more than one-half or one quarter of a point ($25) but can increase in times

---

[3] For an illustration of how this is done, see Mark J.P. Anson, *The Handbook of Alternative Investments* (New York: John Wiley & Sons, 2002).

of uncertainty when investor money shifts to the most liquid U.S. Treasury bond.

Nonetheless, when held to maturity, the prices of these two bonds should converge to their par value. Any difference will be eliminated by the time they mature, and any price discrepancy may be captured by the hedge fund manager. Fixed-income arbitrage is not limited to the U.S. Treasury market. It can be used with corporate bonds, municipal bonds, sovereign debt, or mortgage backed securities.

A subset of fixed-income arbitrage uses mortgage-backed securities (MBS). MBS represent an ownership interest in an underlying pool of individual mortgage loans. Therefore, an MBS is a fixed-income security with underlying prepayment options. MBS hedge funds seek to capture pricing inefficiencies in the U.S. MBS market.

MBS arbitrage can be between fixed-income markets such as buying MBS and selling U.S. Treasuries. This investment strategy is designed to capture credit spread inefficiencies between U.S. Treasuries and MBS. MBS trade at a credit spread over U.S. Treasuries to reflect the uncertainty of cash flows associated with MBS compared to the certainty of cash flows associated with U.S. Treasury bonds.

What should be noted about fixed-income arbitrage strategies is that they do not depend on the direction of the general financial markets. Arbitrageurs seek out pricing inefficiencies between two securities instead of making bets on the market. Consequently, we do not expect fixed-income arbitrage strategies to have a high correlation with either stock market returns or bond market returns.

Merger Arbitrage

Merger arbitrage is perhaps the best known arbitrage among investors and hedge fund managers. Merger arbitrage generally entails buying the stock of the firm that is to be acquired and selling the stock of the firm that is the acquirer. Merger arbitrage managers seek to capture the price spread between the current market prices of the merger partners and the value of those companies upon the successful completion of the merger.

The stock of the target company will usually trade at a discount to the announced merger price. The discount reflects the risk inherent in the deal; other market participants are unwilling to take on the full exposure of the transaction-based risk. Merger arbitrage is then subject to event risk. There is the risk that the two companies will fail to come to terms and call off the deal. There is also the risk that another company will enter into the bidding contest, ruining the initial dynamics of the arbitrage. Last, there is regulatory risk. Various U.S. and foreign regulatory agencies may not allow the merger to take place for antitrust reasons. Merger arbitrageurs specialize in assessing event risk and building a diversified portfolio to spread out this risk.

Merger arbitrageurs conduct significant research on the companies involved in the merger. They will review current and prior financial statements, EDGAR filings, proxy statements, management structures, cost savings from redundant operations, strategic reasons for the merger, regulatory issues, press releases, and competitive position of the combined company within the industries it competes. Merger arbitrageurs will calculate the rate of return that is implicit in the current spread and compare it to the event risk associated with the deal. If the spread is sufficient to compensate for the expected event risk, they will execute the arbitrage.

Once again, the term "arbitrage" is used loosely. As discussed above, there is plenty of event risk associated with a merger announcement. The profits earned from merger arbitrage are not riskless. As an example, consider the announced deal between Tellabs and Ciena in 1998.

Ciena owned technology that allowed fiber optic telephone lines to carry more information. The technology allowed telephone carriers to get more bandwidth out of existing fiber optic lines. Tellabs made digital connecting systems. These systems allowed carriers to connect incoming and outgoing telephonic lines as well as allow many signals to travel over one phone circuit.

Tellabs and Ciena announced their intent to merge on June 3, 1998 in a one for one stock swap. One share of Tellabs would be issued for each share of Ciena. The purpose of the merger was to position the two companies to compete with larger entities such as Lucent Technologies. Additionally, each company expected to leverage their business off of the other's customer base. Tellabs price at the time was about $66 while that of Ciena's was at $57.

Shortly after the announcement, the share price of Tellabs declined to about $64 while that of Ciena's increased to about $60. Still, there was $4 of merger premium to extract from the market if the deal were completed. A merger arbitrage hedge fund manager would employ the following strategy:

Short 1000 shares of Tellabs at $64
Purchase 1000 shares of Ciena at $60

Unfortunately, the deal did not go according to plan. During the summer, Ciena lost two large customers, and it issued a warning that its third quarter profits would decline. Ciena's stock price plummeted to $15 by September. In mid-September the deal fell apart. The shares of Ciena were trading at such a discount to Tellabs' share price that it did not make economic sense to complete the merger, when Ciena's shares could be purchased cheaply on the open market. In addition, Tellabs share price declined to about $42 on earnings concerns.

By the time the merger deal fell through, the hedge fund manager would have to close out his positions:

> Buy 1000 shares of Tellabs stock at $42
> Sell 1000 shares of Ciena at $15

The total return for the hedge fund manager would be:

Gain on Tellabs shares:	$1000 \times (\$64 - \$42)$	=	$22,000
Loss of Ciena shares:	$1000 \times (\$15 - \$60)$	=	−$45,000
Short rebate on Tellabs:	$4.5\% \times 1000 \times \$64 \times (110/360)$	=	$880
Total:		=	−$22,120

For a total return on invested capital of:

$$-\$22,120 \div \$60,000 = -36.87\%$$

Further, suppose the hedge fund manager had used leverage to initiate this strategy, borrowing one half of the invested capital from his prime broker for the initial purchase of the Ciena shares. The total return would then be:

Gain on Tellabs shares:	$1000 \times (\$64 - \$42)$	=	$22,000
Loss of Ciena shares:	$1000 \times (\$15 - \$60)$	=	−$45,000
Short rebate on Tellabs:	$4.5\% \times 1000 \times \$64 \times (110/360)$	=	$880
Financing cost:	$6\% \times 500 \times \$60 \times (110/360)$	=	−$550
Total:		=	−$22,670

The return on invested capital is now:

$$-\$22,670 \div \$30,000 = -75.57\%$$

On an annualized basis, this is a return of −247%. This example of a failed merger demonstrates the event risk associated with merger arbitrage. When deals fall through, it gets ugly. Furthermore, the event risk is exacerbated by the amount of leverage applied in the strategy. It is estimated that Long Term Capital Management of Greenwich, Connecticut had a 4 million share position in the Tellabs-Ciena merger deal, much of it supported by leverage.

Some merger arbitrage managers only invest in announced deals. However, other hedge fund managers will invest on the basis of rumor or speculation. The deal risk is much greater with this type of strategy, but so too is the merger spread (the premium that can be captured).

To control for risk, most merger arbitrage hedge fund managers have some risk of loss limit at which they will exit positions. Some hedge fund managers concentrate only in one or two industries, applying their specialized knowledge regarding an economic sector to their advantage. Other merger arbitrage managers maintain a diversified portfolio across several industries to spread out the event risk.

Like fixed-income arbitrage, merger arbitrage is deal driven rather than market driven. Merger arbitrage derives its return from the relative value of the stock prices between two companies as opposed to the status of the current market conditions. Consequently, merger arbitrage returns should not be highly correlated with the general stock market.

Relative Value Arbitrage

Relative value arbitrage might be better named the smorgasbord of arbitrage. This is because relative value hedge fund managers are catholic in their investment strategies; they invest across the universe of arbitrage strategies. The best known of these managers was Long Term Capital Management (LTCM). Once the story of LTCM unfolded, it was clear that their trading strategies involved merger arbitrage, fixed income arbitrage, volatility arbitrage, stub trading, and convertible arbitrage.

In general, the strategy of relative value managers is to invest in spread trades: The simultaneous purchase of one security and the sale of another when the economic relationship between the two securities (the "spread") has become mispriced. The mispricing may be based on historical averages or mathematical equations. In either case, the relative value arbitrage manager purchases the security that is "cheap" and sells the security that is "rich." It is called relative value arbitrage because the cheapness or richness of a security is determined relative to a second security. Consequently, relative value managers do not take directional bets on the financial markets. Instead, they take focussed bets on the pricing relationship between two securities regardless of the current market conditions.

Relative value managers attempt to remove the influence of the financial markets from their investment strategies. This is made easy by the fact that they simultaneously buy and sell similar securities. Therefore, the market risk embedded in each security should cancel out. Any residual risk can be neutralized through the use of options or futures. What is left is pure security selection: the purchase of those securities that are cheap and the sale of those securities that are rich. Relative value managers earn a profit when the spread between the two securities returns to normal. They then unwind their positions and collect their profit.

We have already discussed merger arbitrage, convertible arbitrage, and fixed income arbitrage. Two other popular forms of relative value arbitrage are stub trading and volatility arbitrage.

Stub trading is an equity-based strategy. Frequently, companies acquire a majority stake in another company, but their stock price does not fully reflect their interest in the acquired company. As an example, consider Company A whose stock is trading at $50. Company A owns a majority stake in Company B, whose remaining outstanding stock, or stub, is trading at $40. The value of Company A should be the combination of its own operations, estimated at $45 a share, plus its majority stake in Company B's operations, estimated at $8 a share. Therefore, Company A's share price is undervalued relative to the value that Company B should contribute to Company A's share price. The share price of Company A should be about $53, but instead, it is trading at $50. The investment strategy would be to purchase Company A's stock and sell the appropriate ratio of Company B's stock.

Let's assume that Company A's ownership in Company B contributes to 20% of Company A's overall revenues. Therefore, the operations of Company B should contribute one fifth to Company A's share price. Therefore, a proper hedging ratio would be four shares of Company A's stock to one share of Company B's stock.

The arbitrage strategy is:

Buy four shares of Company A stock at $4 \times \$50 = \$200$
Sell one share of Company B stock at $1 \times \$40 = \$40$

The relative value manager is now long Company A stock and hedged against the fluctuation of Company B's stock. Let's assume that over three months the share price of Company B increases to $42 a share, the value of Company A's operations remains constant at $45, but now the shares of Company A correctly reflect the contribution of Company B's operations. The value of the position will be:

Value of Company A's operations:	$4 \times \$45$	$= \$180$
Value of Company B's operations:	$4 \times \$42 \times 20\%$	$= \$33.6$
Loss on short of Company B stock:	$1 \times (\$40 - \$42)$	$= -\$2$
Short rebate on Company B stock:	$1 \times \$40 \times 4.5\% \times 3/12$	$= \$0.45$
Total:		$= \overline{\$212.05}$

The initial invested capital was $200 for a gain of $12.05, or 6.02% over three months. Suppose the stock of Company B had declined to $30, but Company B's operations were properly valued in Company A's share price. The position value would be:

Value of Company A's operations:	$4 \times \$45$		= $180
Value of Company B's operations:	$4 \times \$30 \times 20\%$		= $24
Gain on short of Company B's stock:	$1 \times (\$40 - \$30)$		= $10
Short rebate on Company B's stock:	$1 \times \$40 \times 4.5\% \times 3/12$	=	$0.045
Total:			= $214.45

The initial invested capital was $200 for a gain of $14.45, or 7.22% over three months. For stub trading to work there must be some market catalyst such that the contribution of Company B is properly reflected in Company A's share price.

Volatility arbitrage involves options and warrant trading. Option prices contain an *implied* number for volatility. That is, it is possible to observe the market price of an option and back out the value of volatility implied in the current price using various option pricing models. The arbitrageur can then compare options on the same underlying stock to determine if the volatility implied by their prices are the same.

The implied volatility derived from option pricing models should represent the expected volatility of the underlying stock that will be realized over the life of the option. Therefore, two options on the same underlying stock should have the same implied volatility. If they do not, an arbitrage opportunity may be available. Additionally, if the implied volatility is significantly different from the historical volatility of the underlying stock, then relative value arbitrageurs expect the implied volatility will revert back to its historical average. This allows hedge fund managers to determine which options are priced "cheap" versus "rich." Once again, relative value managers sell those options that are rich based on the implied volatility *relative* to the historical volatility and buy those options with cheap volatility relative to historical volatility.

Event Driven

Event driven hedge funds attempt to capture mispricing associated with capital market transactions. These transactions include mergers and acquisitions, spin-offs, tracking stocks, reorganizations, bankruptcies, share buy-backs, special dividends, and any other significant market event.

By their nature, these special events are non-recurring. Consequently, the market may take time to digest the information associated with these transactions, providing an opportunity for event driven managers to act quickly and capture a premium in the market. Additionally, some of these events may be subject to certain conditions such as shareholder or regulatory approval. Therefore, there is event risk associated with this strategy. The profitability of this type of strategy is dependent upon the successful completion of the transaction within the expected time frame.

We should not expect event driven strategies to be influenced by the general stock market, since these are company specific events, not market driven events.

Market Neutral

Our last two categories are different from the previous hedge fund strategies in that they employ little or no leverage and maintain little or no market exposure. In fact, the very nature of their programs is to limit or eliminate market exposure altogether. We start with market neutral hedge funds.

Market neutral hedge funds also go long and short the market. The difference is that they maintain integrated portfolios which are designed to neutralize market risk. This means being neutral to the general stock market as well as having neutral risk exposures across industries. Security selection is all that matters.

Market neutral hedge fund managers generally apply the rule of one alpha.[4] This means that they build an integrated portfolio designed to produce only one source of alpha. This is distinct from equity long/short manages that build two separate portfolios: one long and one short, with two sources of alpha. The idea of integrated portfolio construction is to neutralize market and industry risk and concentrate purely on stock selection. In other words, there is no "beta" risk in the portfolio either with respect to the broad stock market or with respect to any industry. Only stock selection, or alpha, should remain.

Market neutral hedge fund managers generally hold equal positions of long and short stock positions. Therefore, the manager is dollar neutral; there is no net exposure to the market either on the long side or on the short side.

Market neutral investors generally apply no leverage because there is no market exposure to leverage. However, some leverage is always inherent when stocks are borrowed and shorted. Nonetheless, the nature of this strategy is that it has minimal credit risk.

Generally, market neutral managers follow a three-step procedure in their strategy. The first step is to build an initial screen of "investable" stocks. These are stocks traded on the manager's local exchange, with sufficient liquidity so as to be able to enter and exit positions quickly, and with sufficient float so that the stock may be borrowed from the hedge fund manager's prime broker for short positions. Additionally, the hedge fund manager may limit his universe to a capitalization segment of the equity universe such as the mid-cap range.

---

[4] See Bruce Jacobs and Kenneth Levy, "The Law of One Alpha," *The Journal of Portfolio Management* (Summer 1995).

Second, the hedge fund manager typically builds factor models. These are linear and quadratic regression equations designed to identify those economic factors that consistently have an impact on share prices. This process is very similar to that discussed with respect to quantitative equity long/short hedge fund manages. Indeed, the two strategies are very similar in their portfolio construction methods. The difference is that equity long/short managers tend to have a net long exposure to the market while market neutral managers have no exposure.

Factor models are used for stock selection. These models are often known as "alpha engines." Their purpose is to find those financial variables that influence stock prices. These are bottom-up models that concentrate solely on corporate financial information as opposed to macroeconomic data. This is the source of the manager's skill—his or her stock selection ability.

The last step is portfolio construction. The hedge fund manager will use a computer program to construct his portfolio in such a way that it is neutral to the market as well as across industries. The hedge fund manager may use a commercial "optimizer"—computer software designed to measure exposure to the market and produce a trade list for execution based on a manager's desired exposure to the market—or he may use his own computer algorithms to measure and neutralize risk.

Most market neutral managers use optimizers to neutralize market and industry exposure. However, more sophisticated optimizers attempt to keep the portfolio neutral to several risk factors. These include, size, book to value, price/earnings ratios, and market price to book value ratios. The idea is to have no intended or unintended risk exposures that might compromise the portfolio's neutrality.

Market neutral programs tend to be labeled "black boxes." This is a term for sophisticated computer algorithms that lack transparency. The lack of transparency associated with these investment strategies comes in two forms. First, hedge fund managers, by nature, are secretive. They are reluctant to reveal their proprietary trading programs. Second, even if a hedge fund manager were to reveal his proprietary computer algorithms, these algorithms are often so sophisticated and complicated that they are difficult to comprehend.

Market Timers

Market timers, as their name suggest, attempt to time the most propitious moments to be in the market, and invest in cash otherwise. More specifically, they attempt to time the market so that they are fully invested during bull markets, and strictly in cash during bear markets.

Unlike equity long/short strategies or market neutral strategies, market times use a top-down approach as opposed to a bottom-up approach.

Market timing hedge fund managers are not stock pickers. They analyze fiscal and monetary policy as well as key macroeconomic indicators to determine whether the economy is gathering or running out of steam.

Macroeconomic variables they may analyze are labor productivity, business investment, purchasing managers' surveys, commodity prices, consumer confidence, housing starts, retail sales, industrial production, balance of payments, current account deficits/surpluses, and durable good orders.

They use this macroeconomic data to forecast the expected gross domestic product (GDP) for the next quarter. Forecasting models typically are based on multi-factor linear regressions, taking into account whether a variable is a leading or lagging indicator and whether the variable experiences any seasonal effects.

Once market timers have their forecast for the next quarter(s) they position their investment portfolio in the market according to their forecast. Construction of their portfolio is quite simple. They do not need to purchase individual stocks. Instead, they buy or sell stock index futures and options to increase or decrease their exposure to the market as necessary. At all times, contributed capital from investors is kept in short-term, risk-free, interest bearing accounts. Treasury bills are often purchased which not only yield a current risk-free interest rate, but also can be used as margin for the purchase of stock index futures.

When a market timer's forecast is bullish, he may purchase stock index futures with an economic exposure equivalent to the contributed capital. He may apply leverage by purchasing futures contracts that provide an economic exposure to the stock market greater than that of the underlying capital. However, market timers tend to use limited amounts of leverage.

When the hedge fund manager is bearish, he will trim his market exposure by selling futures contracts. If he is completely bearish, he will sell all of his stock index futures and call options and just sit on his cash portfolio. Some market timers may be more aggressive and short stock index futures and buy stock index put options to take advantage of bear markets. In general though, market timers have either long exposure to the market or no exposure. Consequently, this is a conservative hedge fund strategy in the same mode as market neutral programs.

SHOULD HEDGE FUNDS BE PART OF AN INVESTMENT PROGRAM?

A considerable amount of research has been dedicated to examining the return potential of several hedge fund styles. Additionally, a number of studies have considered hedge funds within a portfolio context, i.e., hedge funds blended with other asset classes.

The body of research on hedge funds demonstrates two key qualifications for hedge funds. First, that over the time period of 1989–2000, the returns to hedge funds were positive. The highest returns were achieved by global macro hedge funds, and the lowest returns were achieved by short selling hedge funds. Not all categories of hedge funds beat the S&P 500. However, in many cases, the volatility associated with hedge fund returns was lower than that of the S&P 500, resulting in higher Sharpe ratios.

Second, the empirical research demonstrates that hedge funds provide good diversification benefits. In other words, hedge funds do, in fact, hedge other financial assets. Correlation coefficients with the S&P 500 range from −0.7 for short selling hedge funds to 0.83 for opportunistic hedge funds investing in the U.S. markets. The less than perfect positive correlation with financial assets indicates that hedge funds can expand the efficient frontier for asset managers.

In summary, the recent research on hedge funds indicates consistent, positive performance with low correlation with traditional asset classes. The conclusion is that hedge funds can expand the investment opportunity set for investors, offering both return enhancement as well as diversification benefits.

IS HEDGE FUND PERFORMANCE PERSISTENT?

This is the age-old question with respect to all asset managers, not just hedge funds: Can the manager repeat her good performance? This issue, though, is particularly acute for the hedge fund marketplace for two reasons. First, hedge fund managers often claim that the source of their returns is "skill-based" rather than dependent upon general financial market conditions. Second, hedge fund managers tend to have shorter track records than traditional money managers.

Unfortunately, the evidence regarding hedge fund performance persistence is mixed. The few empirical studies that have addressed this issue have provided inconclusive evidence whether hedge fund managers can produce enduring results. Part of the reason for the mixed results is the short track records of most hedge fund managers. A 3-year or 5-year track record is too short a period of time to be able to estimate an accurate expected return or risk associated with that manager.

In addition, the skill-based claim of hedge fund managers makes it more difficult to assess their performance relative to a benchmark. Without a benchmark index for comparison, it is difficult to determine whether a hedge fund manager has outperformed or underperformed her performance "bogey." As a result, the persistence of hedge fund manager performance will remain an open issue until manager databases with longer performance track records can be developed.

A HEDGE FUND INVESTMENT STRATEGY

The above discussion demonstrates that hedge funds can expand the investment opportunity set for investors. The question now becomes: What is to be accomplished by the hedge fund investment program? The strategy may be simply a search for an additional source of return. Conversely, it may be for risk management purposes. Whatever its purpose, an investment plan for hedge funds may consider one of three strategies. Hedge funds may be selected on an opportunistic basis, as a hedge fund of funds, or as an absolute return strategy.[5]

Opportunistic Hedge Fund Investing

The term "hedge fund" can be misleading. Hedge funds do not necessarily have to hedge an investment portfolio. Rather, they can be used to expand the investment opportunity set. This is the opportunistic nature of hedge funds—they can provide an investor with new investment opportunities that she cannot otherwise obtain through traditional long only investments.

There are several ways hedge funds can be opportunistic. First, many hedge fund managers can add value to an existing investment portfolio through specialization in a sector or in a market strategy. These managers do not contribute portable alpha. Instead, they contribute above market returns through the application of superior skill or knowledge to a narrow market or strategy.

Consider a portfolio manager whose particular expertise is the biotechnology industry. She has followed this industry for years and has developed a superior information set to identify winners and losers. On the long only side the manager purchases those stocks that she believes will increase in value, and avoids those biotech stocks she believes will decline in value. However, this strategy does not utilize her superior information set to its fullest advantage. The ability to go both long and short biotech stocks in a hedge fund is the only way to maximize the

---

[5] A fourth possible strategy is a joint venture where an investor provides seed capital and investment capital for a new hedge fund manager. The investor receives professional hedge fund management plus a "piece of the action."

value of the manager's information set. Therefore, a biotech hedge fund provides a new opportunity: the ability to extract value on both the long side and the short side of the biotech market.

The goal of this strategy is to identify the best managers in a specific economic sector or specific market segment that complements the existing investment portfolio. These managers are used to enhance the risk and return profile of an existing portfolio, rather than hedge it.

Opportunistic hedge funds tend to have a benchmark. Take the example of the biotech long/short hedge fund. An appropriate benchmark would be the AMEX Biotech Index that contains 17 biotechnology companies. Alternatively, if the investor believed that the biotech sector will outperform the general stock market, she could use a broad based stock index such as the S&P 500 for the benchmark. The point is that opportunistic hedge funds are not absolute return vehicles (discussed below). Their performance can be measured relative to a benchmark.

As another example, most institutional investors have a broad equity portfolio. This portfolio may include an index fund, external value and growth managers, and possibly, private equity investments. However, along the spectrum of this equity portfolio, there may be gaps in its investment line-up. For instance, many hedge funds combine late stage private investments with public securities. These hybrid funds are a natural extension of an institution's investment portfolio because they bridge the gap between private equity and index funds. Therefore a new opportunity is identified: the ability to blend private equity and public securities within one investment strategy. We will discuss this strategy further in our section on private equity.

Alternative "assets" are really alternative investment strategies, and these alternative strategies are used to expand the investment opportunity set rather than hedge it. In summary, hedge funds may be selected not necessarily to reduce the risk of an existing investment portfolio, but instead, to complement its risk and return profile. Opportunistic investing is designed to select hedge fund managers that can enhance certain portions of a broader portfolio.

Another way to consider opportunistic hedge fund investments is that they are finished products because their investment strategy or market segment complements an institutional investor's existing asset allocation. In other words, these hybrid funds can plug the gaps of an existing portfolio. No further work is necessary on the part of the institution because the investment opportunity set has been expanded by the addition of the hybrid product. These "gaps" may be in domestic equity, fixed-income, or international investments. Additionally, because opportunistic hedge funds are finished products, it makes it easier to establish performance benchmarks.

EXHIBIT 29.1 Implementing an Opportunistic Hedge Fund Strategy

Diversified Hedge Fund Portfolio	Equity-Based Hedge Fund Portfolio
Equity Long/Short	Equity Long/Short
Short Selling	Short Selling
Market Neutral	Market Neutral
Merger Arbitrage	Merger Arbitrage
Event Driven	Event Driven
Convertible Arbitrage	Convertible Arbitrage
Global Macro	
Fixed Income Arbitrage	
Relative Value Arbitrage	
Market Timers	

Constructing an opportunistic portfolio of hedge funds will depend upon the constraints under which such a program operates. For example, if an investor's hedge fund program is not limited in scope or style, then diversification across a broad range of hedge fund styles would be appropriate. If, however, the hedge fund program is limited in scope to, for instance, expanding the equity investment opportunity set, the choices will be less diversified across strategies. Exhibit 29.1 demonstrates these two choices.

Hedge Fund of Funds

A *hedge fund of funds* is an investment in a group of hedge funds, from five to more than 20. The purpose of a hedge fund of funds is to reduce the idiosyncratic risk of any one hedge fund manager. In other words, there is safety in numbers. This is simply modern portfolio theory (MPT) applied to the hedge fund marketplace. Diversification is one of the founding principles of MPT, and it is as applicable to hedge funds as it is to stocks and bonds.

Absolute Return

Hedge funds are often described as "absolute return" products. This term comes from the skill-based nature of the industry. Hedge fund managers generally claim that their investment returns are derived from their skill at security selection rather than that of broad asset classes. This is due to the fact that most hedge fund managers build concentrated portfolios of relatively few investment positions and do not attempt to track a stock or bond index. The work of Fung and Hsieh shows that hedge funds generate a return distribution that is very different from mutual funds.[6]

Further, given the generally unregulated waters in which hedge fund managers operate, they have greater flexibility in their trading style and execution than traditional long-only managers. This flexibility provides a greater probability that a hedge fund manager will reach his return targets. As a result, hedge funds have often been described as absolute return vehicles that target a specific annual return regardless of what performance might be found among market indices. In other words, hedge fund managers target an absolute return rather than determine their performance relative to an index.

All traditional long-only managers are benchmarked to some passive index. The nature of benchmarking is such that it forces the manager to focus on his benchmark and his tracking error associated with that benchmark. This focus on benchmarking leads traditional active managers to commit a large portion their portfolios to tracking their benchmark. The necessity to consider the impact of every trade on the portfolio's tracking error relative to its assigned benchmark reduces the flexibility of the investment manager.

In addition, long-only active managers are constrained in their ability to short securities. They may only "go short" a security up to its weight in the benchmark index. If the security is only a small part of the index, the manager's efforts to short the stock will be further constrained. The inability to short a security beyond its benchmark weight deprives an active manager of a significant amount of the mispricing in the marketplace. Furthermore, not only are long-only managers unable to take advantage of overpriced securities, but they also cannot fully take advantage of underpriced securities because they cannot generate the necessary short positions to balance the overweights with respect to underpriced securities.

The flexibility of hedge fund managers allows them to go both long and short without benchmark constraints. This allows them to set a target rate of return or an "absolute return."

Specific parameters must be set for an absolute return program. These parameters will direct how the hedge fund program is constructed and operated and should include risk and return targets as well as the type of hedge fund strategies that may be selected. Absolute return parameters should operate at two levels: that of the individual hedge fund manager and for the overall hedge fund program. The investor sets

---

[6] See William Fung and David Hsieh, "Empirical Characteristics of Dynamic Trading Strategies: The Case of Hedge Funds," *The Review of Financial Studies* (Summer 1997).

target return ranges for each hedge fund manager but sets a specific target return level for the absolute return program. The parameters for the individual managers may be different than that for the program. For example, acceptable levels of volatility for individual hedge fund managers may be greater than that for the program.

The program parameters for the hedge fund managers may be based on such factors as volatility, expected return, types of instruments traded, leverage, and historical drawdown. Other qualitative factors may be included such as length of track record, periodic liquidity, minimum investment, and assets under management. Liquidity is particularly important because an investor needs to know with certainty her timeframe for cashing out of an absolute return program if hedge fund returns turn sour.

Exhibit 29.2 demonstrates an absolute return program strategy. Notice that the return for the portfolio has a specific target rate of 15%, while for the individual hedge funds, the return range is 10% to 25%. Also, the absolute return portfolio has a target level for risk and drawdowns, while for the individual hedge funds, a range is acceptable.

However, certain parameters are synchronized. Liquidity, for instance, must be the same for both the absolute return portfolio and that of the individual hedge fund managers. The reason is that a range of liquidity is not acceptable if the investor wishes to liquidate her portfolio. She must be able to cash out of each hedge fund within the same timeframe as that established for the portfolio.

SELECTING A HEDGE FUND MANAGER

The hedge fund industry is still relatively new. Most of the academic research on hedge funds was conducted during the 1990s. As a result, for most hedge fund managers, a two- to three-year track record is considered long term. In fact, Park, Brown, and Goetzmann find that the attrition rate in the hedge fund industry is about 15% per year and that the half-life for hedge funds is about 2.5 years. Liang documents an attrition rate of 8.54% per year for hedge funds. Weisman indicates that relying on a hedge fund manager's past performance history can lead to disappointing investment results.[7] Consequently, performance history, while useful, cannot be relied upon solely in selecting a hedge fund manager.

---

[7] See Park, Brown, and Goetzmann, "The Performance Benchmarks and Survivorship Bias of Hedge Funds and Commodity Trading Advisors"; Bing Liang "Hedge Fund Performance: 1990–1999," *Financial Analysts Journal* (January/February 2001), pp. 11–18; and Andrew Weisman, "The Dangers of Historical Hedge Fund Data," working paper (2000).

EXHIBIT 29.2   An Absolute Return Strategy

Absolute Return Portfolio	Individual Hedge Fund Managers
Target Return: 15%	Expected Return: 10% to 25%
Target Risk: 7%	Target Risk: 5% to 15%
Largest Acceptable Drawdown: 10%	Largest Drawdown: 10% to 20%
Liquidity: Semi-annual	Liquidity: Semi-annual
Hedge Fund Style: Equity-based	Hedge Fund Style: Equity L/S, Market Neutral, Merger Arbitrage, Short Selling, Event Driven, Convertible Arbitrage
Length of Track Record: 3 years	Minimum Track Record: 3 years

Beyond performance numbers, there are three fundamental questions that every hedge fund manager should answer during the initial screening process. The answers to these three questions are critical to understanding the nature of the hedge fund manager's investment program. The three questions are:

1. What is the investment objective of the hedge fund?
2. What is the investment process of the hedge fund manager?
3. What makes the hedge fund manager so smart?

A hedge fund manager should have a clear and concise statement of its investment objective. Second, the hedge fund manager should identify its investment process. For instance, is it quantitatively or qualitatively based? Last, the hedge fund manager must demonstrate that he or she is smarter than other money managers.

The questions presented are threshold issues. These questions are screening tools designed to reduce an initial universe of hedge fund managers down to a select pool of potential investments. They are not, however, a substitute for a thorough due diligence review.

Investment Objective

The question of a hedge fund manager's investment objective can be broken down into three questions:

1. In which markets does the hedge fund manager invest?
2. What is the hedge fund manager's general investment strategy?
3. What is the hedge fund manager's benchmark, if any?

Although these questions may seem straightforward, they are often surprisingly difficult to answer. Consider the following language from a hedge fund disclosure document:

> The principal objective of the Fund is capital appreciation, primarily through the purchase and sale of securities, commodities and other financial instruments including without limitation, stocks, bonds, notes, debentures, and bills issued by corporations, municipalities, sovereign nations or other entities; options, rights, warrants, convertible securities, exchangeable securities, synthetic and/or structured convertible or exchangeable products, participation interests, investment contracts, mortgages, mortgage and asset-backed securities, real estate and interests therein; currencies, other futures, commodity options, forward contracts, money market instruments, bank notes, bank guarantees, letters of credit, other forms of bank obligations; other swaps and other derivative instruments; limited partnership interests and other limited partnership securities or instruments; and contracts relating to the foregoing; in each case whether now existing or created in the future.

Let's analyze the above statement in light of our three investment objective questions.

Question 1: In which markets does the hedge fund manager invest? Answer: In every market known to exist.

By listing every possible financial, commodity or investment contract currently in existence (or to exist in the future), the hedge fund manager has covered all options, but has left the investor uniformed. Unfortunately, the unlimited nature of the hedge fund manager's potential investment universe does not help to narrow the scope of the manager's investment objective.

Question 2: What is the hedge fund manager's general strategy? Answer: Capital appreciation.

This answer too, is uninformative. Rarely does any investor invest in a hedge fund for capital *depreciation*. Generally, hedge funds are not used as tax shelters. Furthermore, many institutional investors are tax-exempt so that taxes are not a consideration. Capital appreciation is assumed for most investments, including hedge funds. The above language is far too general to be informative.

Question 3: What is the manager's benchmark, if any? Answer: There is no effective benchmark. The manager's investment universe is so widespread as to make any benchmark useless.

Unfortunately, the above disclosure language, while very detailed, discloses very little. It does cover all of the manager's legal bases, but it does not inform the investor.

Where does this manager fall within the hedge fund spectrum? The very broad nature of this hedge fund's investment objective places it in the global macro category. Its investment universe is far too broad to be an arbitrage fund. By the same token, its strategy is too expansive to be considered an equity long/short program. Its only appropriate category is global macro.

By contrast, consider the following language from a second hedge fund disclosure document.

> The Fund's investment objective is to make investments in public securities that generate a long-term return in excess of that generated by the overall U.S. public equity market while reducing the market risk of the portfolio through selective short positions.

This one sentence state answers all three investment objective questions. First, the manager identifies that it invests in the U.S. public equity market. Second, the manager discloses that it uses a long/short investment strategy. Lastly, the manager states that its objective is to outperform the overall U.S. equity market. Therefore, a suitable benchmark might be the S&P500, the Russell 1000, or a sector index.

This hedge fund is clearly identified as an equity long/short strategy. Its primary purpose is to take on market risk, not credit risk.

In summary, long-winded disclosure statements are not necessary. A well-thought out investment strategy can be summarized in one sentence.

Investment Process

Most investors prefer a well-defined investment process that describes how an investment manager makes its investments. The articulation and documentation of the process can be just as important as the investment results generated by the process. Consider the following language from another hedge fund disclosure document:

> The manager makes extensive use of computer technology in both the formulation and execution of many investment decisions. Buy and sell decisions will, in many cases, be made and executed algorithmically according to quantitative trading strategies embodied in analytical computer software running the manager's computer facilities or on other computers used to support the Fund's trading activities.

This is a "black box." A black box is the algorithmic extension of the hedge fund manager's brain power. Computer algorithms are developed to quantify the manager's skill or investment insight.

For black box managers, the black box itself is the investment process. It is not that the black boxes are bad investments. In fact, the hedge fund research indicates that proprietary quantitative trading strategies can be quite successful.[8] Rather, the issue is whether good performance results justify the lack of a clear investment process.

Black box programs tend to be used in arbitrage or relative value hedge fund programs. Hedge fund managers use quantitative computer algorithms to seek out pricing discrepancies between similar securities or investment contracts. They then sell the investment that appears to be "expensive" and buy the investment that appears to be "cheap." The very nature of arbitrage programs is to minimize market risk. Leverage is then applied to extract the most value from their small net exposure to market risk.

A black box is just one example of process versus investment results. The hedge fund industry considers itself to be "skill-based." However, it is very difficult to translate manager skill into a process. This is particularly true when the performance of the hedge fund is dependent upon the skill of a specific individual.

Let's consider another, well publicized skill-based investment process. In the spring of 2000, the hedge funds headed by George Soros stumbled leading to the departure of Stanley Druckenmiller, the chief investment strategist for Soros Fund Management. The *Wall Street Journal* documented the concentrated skill-based investment style of this hedge fund group:

> For years, [Soros Fund Management] fostered an entrepreneurial culture, with a cadre of employees battling wits to persuade Mr. Druckenmiller to invest.

> "[Mr. Druckenmiller] didn't scream, but he could be very tough. It could be three days or three weeks of battling it out until he's convinced, or you're defeated."[9]

---

[8] See CrossBorder Capital. "Choosing Investment Styles to Reduce Risk," *Hedge Fund Research*, (October 1999); Goldman, Sachs & Co. and Financial Risk Management Ltd., "The Hedge Fund "Industry" and Absolute Return Funds," *The Journal of Alternative Investments* (Spring 1999); and "Hedge Funds Revisited," *Pension and Endowment Forum* (January 2000).

[9] *Wall Street Journal*, "Shake-Up Continues at Soros's Hedge-Fund Empire," May 1, 2000, page C1.

The above statement does not describe an investment process. It is a description of an individual. The hedge fund manager's investment analysis and decision-making is concentrated in one person. This is a pure example of "skill-based" investing. There is no discernible process. Instead, all information is filtered through the brain of one individual. In essence, the institutional investor must trust the judgment of one person.

Mr. Druckenmiller compiled an exceptional track record as the manager of the Soros Quantum Fund. However, the concentration of decision-making authority is not an economic risk, it is a process risk.

Investors should accept economic risk but not process risk. Soros Fund Management is a well-known global macro hedge fund manager. The fundamental risks of an investment in a global macro fund are credit risk and market risk.

Investors are generally unwilling to bear risks that are not fundamental to their tactical and strategic asset allocations. Process risk is not a fundamental risk. It is an idiosyncratic risk of the hedge fund manager's structure and operations.

Generally, process risk is not a risk that investors wish to bear. Nor is it a risk for which they expect to be compensated. Furthermore, how would an investor go about pricing the process risk of a hedge fund manager? It can't be quantified, and it can't be calibrated. Therefore, there is no way to tell whether an institutional investor is being properly compensated for this risk.[10]

Process risk also raises the ancillary issue of lack of transparency. Skill-based investing usually is opaque. Are the decisions of the key individual quantitatively based? Qualitatively based? There is no way to really tell. This is similar to the problems discussed earlier with respect to black boxes.

To summarize, process risk cannot be quantified and it is not a risk that investors are willing to bear. Process risk also raises issues of transparency. Investors want clarity and definition, not opaqueness and amorphousness.

What Makes the Hedge Fund Manager so Smart?

Before investing money with a hedge fund manager, an investor must determine one of the following. The hedge fund manager must be able to demonstrate that he or she is smarter than the next manager. One way to be smarter than another hedge fund manager is to have superior

---

[10] See James Park and Jeremy Staum, "Fund of Funds Diversification: How Much is Enough?" *The Journal of Alternative Investments* (Winter 1998). They demonstrate that idiosyncratic process risks can largely be eliminated through a diversified fund of funds program. They indicate that a portfolio of 15 to 20 hedge funds can eliminate much of the idiosyncratic risk associated with hedge fund investments.

skill in filtering information. That is, the hedge fund manager must be able to look at the same information set as another manager but be able to glean more investment insight from that data set.

Alternatively, if the hedge fund manager is not smarter than the next manager, he must demonstrate that he has a better information set; his competitive advantage is not filtering information, but gathering it. To be successful, a hedge fund manager must demonstrate one or both of these competitive advantages.

Generally speaking, quantitative, computer-driven managers satisfy the first criteria. That is, hedge fund managers that run computer models access the same information set as everyone else, but have better (smarter) algorithms to extract more value per information unit than the next manager. These managers tend to be relative value managers.

Relative value managers extract value by simultaneously comparing the prices of two securities and buying and selling accordingly. This information is available to all investors in the marketplace. However, it is the relative value managers that are able to process the information quickly enough to capture mispricings in the market. These arbitrage strategies expose an investor to credit risk.

Alternatively, hedge fund managers that confine themselves to a particular market segment or sector generally satisfy the second criteria. They have a larger information set that allows them to gain a competitive edge in their chosen market. Their advantage is a proprietary information set accumulated over time rather than a proprietary data filtering system.

Consider the following statement from a hedge fund disclosure document:

> The Adviser hopes to achieve consistently high returns by focusing on small and mid-cap companies in the biotechnology market.

The competitive advantage of this type of manager is his or her knowledge not only about a particular economic sector (biotechnology), but also, about a particular market segment of that sector (small and mid-cap). This type of manger tends to take more market risk exposure than credit risk exposure and generally applies equity long/short programs.

Identifying the competitive advantage of the hedge fund manager is the key to determining whether the hedge fund manager can sustain performance results. We indicated earlier that the issue of performance persistence is undecided.

Therefore, an investor cannot rely on historical hedge fund performance data as a means of selecting good managers from bad managers.

Furthermore, every hedge fund disclosure document contains some variation of the following language:

Past performance is no indication of future results.

Essentially, this statement directs the investor to ignore the hedge fund manager's performance history.

To asses the likelihood of performance persistence, the investor must then determine whether the hedge fund manager is an information gatherer or an information filterer. Consider the following language from a hedge fund disclosure document.

The General Partner will utilize its industry expertise, contacts, and databases developed over the past 11 years to identify _____ company investment ideas outside traditional sources and will analyze these investment opportunities using, among other techniques, many aspects of its proven methodology in determining value.

This hedge fund manager has a superior information set that has been developed over 11 years. It is an information gatherer. This manager applies an equity long/short program within a specific market sector.

Finally, consider the following disclosure language from a merger arbitrage hedge fund manager:

[The] research group [is] staffed by experienced M&A lawyers with detailed knowledge of deal lifecycle, with extensive experience with corporate law of multiple US states, US and foreign securities laws regarding proxy contests, and antitrust laws (both of the US and EU), and who have made relevant filings before regulators and have closed a wide variety of M&A transactions.

This hedge fund manager is an information filterer. Its expertise is sifting through the outstanding legal and regulatory issues associated with a merger and determining the likelihood that the deal will be completed.

To summarize, a good lesson is that successful hedge fund managers know the exact nature of their competitive advantage, and how to exploit it.

CHAPTER 30

Private Equity

Mark J. P. Anson, CFA, Ph.D., CPA, Esq.
Chief Investment Officer
CalPERS

The private equity sector purchases the private stock or equity-linked securities of non-public companies that are expected to go public or provides the capital for public companies (or their divisions) that may wish to go private. The key component in either case is the private nature of the securities purchased. Private equity, by definition, is not publicly traded. Therefore, investments in private equity are illiquid. Investors in this marketplace must be prepared to invest for the long haul; investment horizons may be as extended as long as 5 to 10 years.

"Private equity" is a generic term that encompasses four distinct strategies in the market for private investing. First, there is venture capital, the financing of start-up companies. Second, there are leveraged buyouts (LBOs) where public companies repurchase all of their outstanding shares and turn themselves into private companies. Third, there is mezzanine financing, a hybrid of private debt and equity financing. Last, there is distressed debt investing. These are private equity investments in established (as opposed to start-up) but troubled companies.

VENTURE CAPITAL

Venture capital is the supply of equity financing to start-up companies that do not have a sufficient track record to attract investment capital from traditional sources (e.g., the public markets or lending institutions). Entrepreneurs that develop business plans require investment capital to implement those plans. However, these start-up ventures often lack tangible assets that can be used as collateral for a loan. In addition, start-up companies are unlikely to produce positive earnings for several years. Negative cash flows are another reason why banks and other lending institutions as well as the public stock market are unwilling to provide capital to support the business plan.

It is in this uncertain space where nascent companies are born that venture capitalists operate. Venture capitalists finance these high-risk, illiquid, and unproven ideas by purchasing senior equity stakes while the firms are still privately held. The ultimate goal is to make a buck. Venture capitalists are willing to underwrite new ventures with untested products and bear the risk of no liquidity only if they can expect a reasonable return for their efforts. Often, venture capitalists set expected target rates of return of 33% or more to support the risks they bear. Successful start-up companies funded by venture capital money include Cisco Systems, Cray Research, Microsoft, and Genentech.

The Role of a Venture Capitalist

Venture capitalists have two roles within the industry. Raising money from investors is just the first part. The second is to invest that capital with start-up companies.

Venture capitalists are not passive investors. Once they invest in a company, they take an active role either in an advisory capacity or as a director on the board of the company. They monitor the progress of the company, implement incentive plans for the entrepreneurs and management, and establish financial goals for the company.

Besides providing management insight, venture capitalists usually have the right to hire and fire key mangers, including the original entrepreneur. They also provide access to consultants, accountants, lawyers, investment bankers, and most importantly, other businesses that might purchase the start-up company's product.

In seeking viable start-up companies to finance, venture capitalists focus on certain aspects of the entrepreneur's business opportunity. These are a business plan, intellectual property rights, prior history of the company, prior history of the management team, regulatory matters, and an exit plan.

Business Plans

The most important document upon which a venture capitalist will base her decision to invest in a start-up company is the business plan. The business plan must be comprehensive, coherent, and internally consistent. It must clearly state the business strategy, identify the niche that the new company will fill, and describe the resources needed to fill that niche.

The business plan also reflects the start-up management team's ability to develop and present an intelligent and strategic plan of action. Therefore, the business plan not only describes the business opportunity but also gives the venture capitalist an insight to the viability of the management team.

Last, the business plan must be realistic. One part of every business plan is the assumptions about revenue growth, cash burn rate, additional rounds of capital injection, and expected date of profitability and/or IPO status. The financial goals stated in the business plan must be achievable. Additionally, financial milestones identified in the business plan can become important conditions for the vesting of management equity, the release of deferred investment commitments, and the control of the board of directors.

Intellectual Property Rights

Most start-ups in the technology and other growth sectors base their business opportunity on the claim to proprietary technology. It is very important that a start-up's claim and rights to that intellectual property be absolute. Any intellectual property owned by the company must be clearly and unequivocally assigned to the company by third parties (usually the entrepreneur and management team). A structure where the entrepreneur still owns the intellectual property but licenses it to the start-up company is disfavored by venture capitalists because license agreements can expire or be terminated leaving the venture capitalist with a shell of a start-up company.

Generally, before a venture capitalist invests with a start-up company, it will conduct patent and trademark searches, seek the opinion of a patent counsel, and possibly ask third parties to confidentially evaluate the technology owned by the start-up company.

Additionally, the venture capitalist may ask key employees to sign non-competition agreements, where they agree not to start another company or join another company operating in the same sector as the start-up for a reasonable period of time. Key employees may also be asked to sign non-disclosure agreements because protecting a start-up company's proprietary technology is an essential element to success.

Prior Operating History

Venture capitalists are not always the first investors in a start-up company. In fact, they may be the third source of financing for a company. Many start-up companies begin by seeking capital from friends, family members, and business associates. Next they may seek a so called "angel investor," a wealthy private individual or an institution that invests capital with the company but does not take an active role in managing or directing the strategy of the company. Then come the venture capitalists.

As a result, a start-up company may already have a prior history before presenting its business plan to a venture capitalist. At this stage, venture capitalists ensure that the start-up company does not have any unusual history such as a prior bankruptcy or failure.

The venture capitalist will also closely review the equity stakes that have been previously provided to family, friends, business associates, and angel investors. These equity stakes should be clearly identified in the business plan and any unusual provisions must be discussed. Equity interests can include common stock, preferred stock, convertible securities, rights, warrants, and stock options. There must still be sufficient equity and upside potential for the venture capitalist to invest. Finally, all prior security issues must be properly documented and must comply with applicable securities laws.

The venture capitalist will also check the company's articles of incorporation to determine whether it is in good legal standing in the state of incorporation. Further, the venture capitalist will examine the company's bylaws, and the minutes of any shareholder and board of directors meetings. The minutes of the meetings can indicate whether the company has a clear sense of direction or whether it is mired in indecision.

The Start-up Management Team

The venture capitalist will closely review the resumes of every member of the management team. Academic backgrounds, professional work history and references will all be checked. Most important to the venture capitalist will be the professional background of the management team. In particular, a management team that has successfully brought a previous start-up company to the IPO stage will be viewed most favorably.

In general, a great management team with a good business plan will be viewed more favorably than a good management team with a great business plan. The best business plan in the world can still fail from inability to execute. Therefore, a management team that has demonstrated a previous ability to follow and execute a business plan will be given a greater chance of success than an unproven management team with a great business opportunity.

However, this is where a venture capitalist can add value. Recognizing a great business opportunity but a weak management team, the venture capitalist can bring his or her expertise to the start-up company as well as bring in other, more seasoned management professionals. While this often creates some friction with the original entrepreneur, the ultimate goal is to make money. Egos often succumb when there is money to be made.

Last, the management team will need a seasoned chief financial officer (CFO). This will be the person primarily responsible for bringing the start-up company public. The CFO will work with the investment bankers to establish the price of the company's stock at the initial public offering. Since the IPO is often the exit strategy for the venture capitalist as well as some of the founders and key employees, it is critical that the CFO have IPO experience.

Legal and Regulatory Issues

We have already touched on some of the legal issues regarding non-competition agreements, non-disclosure agreements, and proper filings for the issuance of equity and debt securities. In addition, the venture capitalist must also determine if patent protection is needed for the start-up's proprietary intellectual property, and if so, initiate the legal proceedings.

Also, in certain industries, federal regulatory approval is necessary before a product can be sold in the United States. Nowhere is this more important than in the biotechnology and healthcare sectors. The business plan for the company must also address the time lag between product development and regulatory approval. Additionally, the venture capitalist must consider the time lag before operating profits will be achieved after regulatory approval of a new healthcare product.

Finally, there should be no litigation associated with the start-up company or its management team. Litigation takes time, money, and emotional wear and tear. It is can be a distraction for the company and its key employees. Outstanding or imminent litigation will raise the hurdle rate even higher before a venture capitalist will invest.

Exit Plan

Eventually, the venture capitalist must liquidate her investment in the start-up company to realize a gain for herself and her investors. When a venture capitalist reviews a business plan she will keep in mind the timing and probability of an exit strategy.

An exit strategy is another way the venture capitalist can add value beyond providing start-up financing. Venture capitalists often have many contacts with established operating companies. An established company may be willing to acquire the start-up company for its technology as part of a strategic expansion of its product line. Alternatively, venture capitalists maintain close ties with investment bankers. These bankers will be necessary if the start-up company decides to seek an IPO. In addition, a venture capitalist may ask other venture capitalists to invest in the start-up company. This helps to spread the risk as well as provide additional sources of contacts with operating companies and investment bankers.

Venture capitalists almost always invest in the convertible preferred stock of the start-up company. There may be several rounds (or series) of financing of preferred stock before a start-up company goes public. Convertible preferred shares are the accepted manner of investment because these shares carry a priority over common stock in terms of dividends, voting rights, and liquidation preferences. Furthermore, venture capitalists have the option to convert their shares to common stock to enjoy the benefits of an IPO.

Other investment structures used by venture capitalists include convertible notes or debentures that provide for the conversion of the principal amount of the note or bond into either common or preferred shares at the option of the venture capitalist. Convertible notes and debentures may also be converted upon the occurrence of an event such as a merger, acquisition, or IPO. Venture capitalists may also be granted warrants to purchase the common equity of the start-up company as well as stock rights in the event of an IPO.

Other exit strategies used by venture capitalists are redemption rights and put options. Usually, these strategies are used as part of a company reorganization. Redemption rights and put options are generally not favored because they do not provide as large a rate of return as an acquisition or IPO. These strategies are often used as a last resort when there are no other viable alternatives. Redemption rights and put options are usually negotiated at the time the venture capitalist makes an investment in the start-up company (often called the Registration Rights Agreement).

Usually, venture capitalists require no less than the minimum return provided for in the liquidation preference of a preferred stock investment. Alternatively, the redemption rights or put option might be established by a common stock equivalent value that is usually determined by an investment banking appraisal. Last redemption rights or put option values may be based on a multiple of sales or earnings. Some redemption rights take the highest of all three valuation methods: the liquidation preference, the appraisal value, or the earnings/sales multiple.

In sum, there are many issues a venture capitalist must sort through before funding a start-up company. These issues range from identifying the business opportunity to sorting through legal and regulatory issues. Along the way, the venture capital must assess the quality of the management team, prior capital infusions, status of proprietary technology, operating history (if any) of the company, and timing and likelihood of an exit strategy.

Venture Capital Investment Vehicles

As the interest for venture capital investments has increased, venture capitalists have responded with new vehicles for venture financing.

These include limited partnerships, limited liability companies, and venture capital fund of funds.[1]

Limited Partnerships

The predominant form of venture capital investing in the United States is the limited partnership. Venture capital funds operate either as "3(c)(1)" or "3(c)(7)" funds to avoid registration as an investment company under the Investment Company Act of 1940.

All partners in the fund will commit to a specific investment amount at the formation of the limited partnership. However, the limited partners do not contribute money to the fund until it is called down or "taken down" by the general partner. Usually, the general partner will give one to two months notice of when it intends to make additional capital calls on the limited partners. Capital calls are made when the general partner has found a start-up company in which to invest. The general partner can make capital calls up to the amount of the limited partners' initial commitments.

An important element of limited partnership venture funds is that the general partner/venture capitalist has also committed investment capital to the fund. This assures the limited partners of an alignment of interests with the venture capitalist. Typically, limited partnership agreements specify a percentage or dollar amount of capital that the general partner must commit to the partnership.

Limited Liability Companies

A recent phenomenon in the venture capital industry is the limited liability company (LLC). Similar to a limited partnership, all items of net income or loss as well as capital gains are passed through to the shareholders in the LLC. Also, like a limited partnership, an LLC must adhere to the safe harbors of the Investment Company Act of 1940.

The managing director of an LLC acts like the general partner of a limited partnership. She has management responsibility for the LLC including the decision to invest in start-up companies the committed capital of the LLC's shareholders. The managing director of the LLC might itself be another LLC or a corporation. The same is true for limited partnerships; the general partner need not be an individual, it can be a legal entity like a corporation.

In sum, LLCs and limited partnerships accomplish the same goal—the pooling of investor capital into a central fund from which to make venture capital investments. The choice is dependent upon the type of

---

[1] There are also corporate venture funds. However, they do not provide a vehicle for outside investors.

investor sought. If the venture capitalist wishes to raise funds from a large number of passive and relatively uninformed investors, the limited partnership vehicle is the preferred venue. However, if the venture capitalist intends to raise capital from a small group of knowledgeable investors, the LLC is preferred.

Venture Capital Fund of Funds

A venture capital fund of funds is a venture pool of capital that, instead of investing directly in start-up companies, invests in other venture capital funds. The venture capital fund of funds is a relatively new phenomenon in the venture capital industry. The general partner of a fund of funds does not select start-up companies in which to invest. Instead, she selects the best venture capitalists with the expectation that they will find appropriate start-up companies to fund.

A venture capital fund of funds offers several advantages to investors. First, the investor receives broad exposure to a diverse range of venture capitalists, and in turn, a wide range of start-up investing. Second, the investor receives the expertise of the fund of funds manager in selecting the best venture capitalists with whom to invest money. Last, a fund of funds may have better access to popular, well-funded venture capitalists whose funds may be closed to individual investors. In return for these benefits, investors pay a management fee (and, in some cases, an incentive fee) to the fund of funds manager. The management fee can range from 0.5% to 2% of the net assets managed.

Fund of fund investing also offers benefits to the venture capitalists. First, the venture capitalist receives one large investment (from the venture fund of funds) instead of several small investments. This makes fund raising and investor administration more efficient. Second, the venture capitalist interfaces with an experienced fund of funds manager instead of several (potentially inexperienced) investors.

Specialization within the Venture Capital Industry

Like any industry that grows and matures, expansion and maturity lead to specialization. The trend towards specialization in the venture capital industry exists on several levels, by industry, geography, stage of financing, and "special situations."

Specialization by Industry

Specialization by entrepreneurs is another reason why venture capitalists have tailored their investment domain. Just as entrepreneurs have become more focused in their start-up companies, venture capitalists have followed suit. The biotechnology industry is a good example. Specialized start-up biotech firms have led to specialized venture capital firms.

Specialization by Geography

With the boom in technology companies in Silicon Valley, Los Angeles, and Seattle, it is not surprising to find that many California based venture capital firms concentrate their investments on the west coast of the United States. Not only are there plenty of investment opportunities in this region, it is also easier for the venture capital firms to monitor their investments locally. The same is true for other technology centers in New York, Boston, and Texas.

Stage of Financing

Venture capitalists also distinguish themselves by the point at which they will invest in a start-up company. Some venture capitalists provide first stage, or "seed capital" while others wait to invest in companies that are further along in their development. For a first time entrepreneur, seed financing can be difficult to find. Without a prior track record, most venture capitalists are skeptical of new product ideas.

Seed financing is usually in the range of $500,000 to $3 million. First stage venture capitalists tend to be smaller firms because large venture capital firms cannot afford to spend the endless hours with an entrepreneur for a small investment, usually no greater than $1 to $2 million.

A new development to fill this niche is the venture capital "feeder fund." These have been established where large venture capitalists provide capital to seed venture capitalists in return for the opportunity to make a later stage investment in the start-up company if it is successful.

Most venture capital firms invest either in mid or late stage rounds of equity. Later stage financing provides for a quicker return of capital as well as a lower risk investment. Returns are expected to be lower than that for seed financing. In many cases the start-up company has a viable product by the time a second or third round of venture financing is sought. Also, with the increase flow of money into venture funds, venture capitalists have found that they have larger pools of capital to deploy. Later stage financing provides the most efficacious means to deploy large chunks of investor capital.

Special Situation Venture Capital

In any industry, there are always failures. Not every start-up company makes it to the IPO stage. However, this opens another specialized niche in the venture capital industry: the turnaround venture deal. Turnaround deals are as risky as seed financing because the start-up company may be facing pressure from creditors. The turnaround venture capitalist exists because mainstream venture capitalists may not be sufficiently well-versed in restructuring a turnaround situation.

LEVERAGED BUYOUTS

Leveraged buyouts are a way to take a company with publicly traded stock private, or a way to put a company in the hands of the current management (sometimes referred to as *management buyouts* or *MBOs*). LBOs use the assets or cash flows of the company to secure debt financing either in bonds issued by the corporation or bank loans, to purchase the outstanding equity of the company. In either case, control of the company is concentrated in the hands of the LBO firm and management, and there is no public stock outstanding.

LBOs represent a mechanism to take advantage of a window of opportunity to increase the value of a corporation. Leverage buyouts can be a way to unlock hidden value or exploit existing but underfunded opportunities.

A Theoretical Example of a Leveraged Buyout

In a perfect world, everyone makes money, and no one is unhappy. We will discuss some spectacular LBO failures below. In the meantime, we describe how a theoretical LBO should work.

Imagine a company that is capitalized with a market value of equity of $500 million and a face value of debt of $100 million. The company generates an EBITDA (earnings before interest and taxes plus depreciation and amortization) of $80 million. EBITDA represents the free cash flow from operations that is available for the owners and debtors of the company. This is a 13.3% return on capital for the company's shareholders and debtholders.

An LBO firm offers $700 million to purchase the equity of the company and to pay off the outstanding debt. The debt is paid off at face value of $100 million and $600 million is offered to the equity holders (a 20% premium over the market value) to entice them to tender their shares to the LBO offer.

The $700 million LBO is financed with $600 million in debt (with a 10% coupon rate) and $100 million in equity. The company must pay yearly debt service of $60 million to meet its interest payment obligations. After the LBO, the management of the company improves its operations, streamlines its expenses, and implements better asset utilization. The result is that the cash flow of the company improves from $80 million a year to $120 million a year.[2] By foregoing dividends and using the free cash flow to pay down the existing debt, the management of the company can own the company free and clear in about seven years.

This means that, after seven years, the LBO firm can claim the annual cash flow of $120 million completely for itself. Using a growth rate of 2% per year and a discount rate of 12%, this cash flow is worth:

$$\$120 \text{ million}/(0.12 - 0.02) = \$1.2 \text{ billion}$$

Therefore, the total return on the investment for the LBO transaction is:

$$[\$1.2 \text{ billion}/\$100 \text{ million}]^{1/7} - 1 = 42.6\%$$

The amount of 42.6% represents the annual compounded return for this investment.

As this example demonstrates, the returns to LBO transactions can be quite large, but the holding period may also be commensurately long. At the end of seven years, the management of the company can reap the $1.2 billion value through one of four methods:

1. The management can sell the company to a competitor or another company that wishes to expand into the industry.
2. Through an initial public offering. Consider the example of Gibson Greetings. This company was purchased from RCA for $81 million with all but $1 million financed by bank loans and real estate lease-backs. When Gibson Greetings went public, the 50% equity interest owned by the LBO firm was worth about $140 million, equal to a compound annual rate of return of over 200%.
3. Another LBO. The management of the company doubled its value from $600 million to $1.2 billion. They can now refinance the company in another LBO deal where debt is reintroduced into the company to compensate management for their equity stake. In fact, the existing management may even remain as the operators of the company with an existing stake in the second LBO transaction, providing them with the opportunity for a second go round of leveraged equity appreciation.
4. Straight refinancing. This is similar to number 3 above, where a company reintroduces debt into its balance sheet to pay out a large cash dividend to its equity owners.

---

[2] Studies of LBOs indicate that coporate cash flows increase 96% from the year before the buyout to three years after the buyout. See Michael Jensen, "The Modern Industrial Revolution, Exit, and the Failure of Internal Control Systems," *The New Corporate Finance*, 2nd Edition, Donald H. Chew, Jr. (ed.) (New York: Irwin/ McGraw Hill, 1999).

How LBOs Create Value

The theoretical example given above is a good starting point for describing an LBO transaction, but there is no standard format for a buyout, each company is different, and every LBO deal has different motivations. However, there are five general categories of LBOs that illuminate how these transactions can create value.[3]

LBOs that Improve Operating Efficiency

A company may be bought out because it is shackled with a non-competitive operating structure. For large public companies with widespread equity ownership, the separation of ownership and management can create agency problems with ineffective control mechanisms. Management may have little incentive to create value because it has a small stake in the company, and monitoring of management's actions by a diverse shareholder base is likely to be just as minimal.

Under these circumstances, management is likely to be compensated based on revenue growth. This may result in excess expansion and operating inefficiencies resulting from too much growth. Safeway Corporation is an example where value creation came not from entrepreneurial input, but rather from greater operating efficiencies.

Unlocking an Entrepreneurial Mindset

Another way an LBO can create value is by helping to free management to concentrate on innovations. Another frequent LBO strategy is the unwanted division. Often an operating division of a conglomerate is chained to its parent company and does not have sufficient freedom to implement its business plan. An LBO can free the operating division as a new company, able to control its own destiny. Duracell Corporation which was taken private in 1988 is an excellent example of an entrepreneurial LBO.

The Overstuffed Corporation

One of the mainstream targets of many LBO firms are conglomerates. Conglomerate corporations consist of many different operating divisions or subsidiaries, often in completely different industries. Wall Street analysts are often reluctant to follow or "cover" conglomerates because they do not fit neatly into any one industrial category. As a result, these companies can be misunderstood by the investing public, and therefore,

---

[3] For case illustrations, see Chapter 15 in Mark J.P. Anson, *Handbook of Alternative Assets* (New York: John Wiley & Sons, Inc., 2002).

undervalued. Beatrice Foods (a food processing conglomerate) LBO in 1986 purchased for $6.2 billion is an example.

Buy and Build Strategies

Another LBO value creation strategy involves combining several operating companies or divisions through additional buyouts. The LBO firm begins with one buyout and then acquires more companies and divisions that are strategically aligned with the initial LBO portfolio company. The strategy is that there will be synergies from combining several different companies into one. In some respects, this strategy is the reverse of that for conglomerates. Rather than strip a conglomerate down to its most profitable divisions, this strategy pursues a "buy and build" approach. This type of strategy is also known as a "leveraged build-up."

LBO Turnaround Strategies

With a slowdown in the United States as well as global economies throughout 2000, turnaround LBOs have become increasingly popular. Unlike traditional buyout firms that look for successful, mature companies with low debt to equity ratios and stable management, turnaround LBO funds look for underperforming companies with excessive leverage and poor management. The targets for turnaround LBO specialists come from two primary sources: (1) ailing companies on the brink of Chapter 11 bankruptcy and (2) underperforming companies in another LBO fund's portfolio.

LBO Fund Structures

In this section we discuss how LBO funds are structured as well as discuss their fees. While LBO funds are very similar to venture capital funds in design, they are much more creative in fee generation.

Fund Design

Almost all LBO funds are designed as limited partnerships. This is very similar to the way hedge funds and venture capital funds are established. In fact many LBO funds have the name "partners" in their title.

Every LBO fund is run by a general partner. The general partner is typically the LBO firm, and all investment discretion as well as day-to-day operations vest with the general partner. Limited partners, as their name implies, have a very limited role in the management of the LBO fund. For the most part, limited partners are passive investors who rely on the general partner to source, analyze, perform due diligence, and invest the committed capital of the fund.

Some LBO funds have advisory boards comprised of the general partner and a select group of limited partners. The duties of the advisory board are to advise the general partner on conflicts of issue that may arise as a result of acquiring a portfolio company or collecting fees, provide input as to when it might be judicious to seek independent valuations of the LBO fund's portfolio companies, and to discuss whether dividend payments for portfolio companies should be in cash or securities.

Fees

If there was ever an investment structure that could have its cake and eat it too, it would be an LBO firm. LBO firms have any number of ways to make their money.

First, consider how LBO firms gather capital. KKR for instance, received in 2000 a $1 billion capital contribution from the State of Oregon pension fund for its newest LBO fund, the Millennium Fund. LBO firms charge a management fee for the capital committed to their investment funds. The management fee generally ranges from 1% to 3% depending on the strength of the LBO firm. On KKR's newest fund, for instance, the management fee offered to some investors is 1% per year. Given that KKR expects to raise between $5 billion and $6 billion, this would indicate an annual management fee in the range of $50 to $60 million a year.

In addition, LBO firms share in the profits of the investment pool. These incentive fees usually range from 20% to 30%. Incentive fees are profit sharing fees. For instance, an incentive fee of 20% means that the LBO firm keeps one dollar out of every five earned on LBO transactions.

LBO firms also may charge fees to the corporation that it is taken private of up to 1% of the total selling price for arranging and negotiating the transaction. As an example, KKR earned $75 million for arranging the buyout of RJR Nabisco, and $60 million for arranging the buyout of Safeway Stores.

Not only do LBO firms earn fees for arranging deals, they can earn break-up fees if a deal craters. Consider the Donaldson, Lufkin & Jenrette LBO of IBP Inc. This $3.8 billion buyout deal, first announced in October, 2000 was subsequently topped by a $4.1 billion takeover bid from Smithfield Foods Inc. in November, 2000. This bid was in turn topped by a $4.3 billion takeover bid from Tyson Foods Inc. in December 2000. Despite losing out on the buyout of IBP, as part of the LBO deal terms, DLJ was due a $66.5 million breakup fee from IBP because it was sold to another bidder.

In addition to earning fees for arranging the buyout of a company or for losing a buyout bid, LBO firms may also charge a divestiture fee for arranging the sale of a division of a private company after the buyout has been completed. Further, a LBO firm may charge director's fees to a buyout company if managing partners of the LBO firm sit on the company's board of directors after the buyout has occurred. In fact there are any number of ways for a LBO firm to make money on a buyout transaction.

RISKS OF LBOs

LBOs have less risk than venture capital deals for several reasons. First, the target corporation is already a seasoned company with public equity outstanding. Indeed, many LBO targets are mature companies with undervalued assets.

Second, the management of the company has an established track record. Therefore, assessment of the key employees is easier than a new team in a venture capital deal.

Third, the LBO target usually has established products or services and a history of earning profits. However, management of the company may not have the freedom to fully pursue their initiatives. An LBO transaction can provide this freedom.

Last, the exit strategy of a new IPO in several years time is much more feasible than a venture capital deal because the company already had publicly traded stock outstanding. A prior history as a public company, demonstrable operating profits, and a proven management team make an IPO for a buyout firm much more feasible than an IPO for a start-up venture.

The obvious risk of LBO transactions is the extreme leverage used. This will leave the company with a high debt to equity ratio and a very large debt service. The high leverage can provide large gains for the equity owners, but it also leaves the margin for error very small. If the company cannot generate enough cash flow to service the coupon and interest payments demanded of its bondholders, it may end up in bankruptcy, with little left over for its equity investors. "Leveraged Fallouts" are an inevitable fact of life in the LBO marketplace.

DEBT AS PRIVATE EQUITY

In this section we discuss two forms of private equity that appear as debt on an issuer's balance sheet. Mezzanine debt is closely linked to the leveraged buyout market, while distressed debt investors pursue companies whose fortunes have taken a turn for the worse. Like venture capital and LBOs, these strategies pursue long-only investing in the securities of target companies, and these strategies can result in a significant equity stake in a target company. In addition, like venture capital and LBOs, these two forms of private equity investing provide alternative investment strategies within the equity asset class.

Since mezzanine debt and distressed debt investors purchase the bonds of a target company, it may seem inappropriate to classify these strategies within the equity asset class. However, we will demonstrate in this chapter that these two strategies derive a considerable amount of return as equity components within a company's balance sheet.

For now, it is important to recognize that mezzanine debt and distressed debt investing can be distinguished from traditional long-only investing. The reason is that these two forms of private equity attempt to capture investment returns from economic sources that are mostly independent of the economy's long-term macroeconomic growth. For instance, the debt of a bankrupt company is more likely to rise and fall with the fortunes of the company and negotiations with other creditors than with the direction of the general stock market. While the direction of the stock market and the health of the overall economy may have some influence on a distressed company, it is more likely that the fortunes of the company will be determined by the hands of its creditors.

Mezzanine Debt

Mezzanine debt is often hard to classify because the distinction between debt and equity can blur at this level of financing. Oftentimes, mezzanine debt represents a hybrid, a combination of debt of equity. Mezzanine financing gets its name because it is inserted into a company's capital structure between the "floor" of equity and the "ceiling" of senior, secured debt. It is the in between nature of this type of debt from which mezzanine derives its name.

Mezzanine financing is not used to provide cash for the day-to-day operations of a company. Instead, it is used during transitional periods in a company's life. Frequently, a company is in a situation where its senior creditors (banks) are unwilling to provide any additional capital and the company does not wish to issue additional stock. Mezzanine financing can fill this void.

Mezzanine Financing to Bridge a Gap in Time

Mezzanine financing has three general purposes. First, it can be financing used to bridge a gap in time. This might be a round of financing to get a private company to the IPO stage. In this case, mezzanine financing can either be subordinated debt convertible into equity, or preferred shares, convertible into common equity upon the completion of a successful IPO.

Examples of this time-gap financing include Extricity, Inc. a platform provider for business-to-business relationship management. In May 2000, Extricity raised $50 million in mezzanine financing from a broad group of corporate and financial investors. Within a matter of days after its mezzanine round, Extricity also filed a registration statement for an IPO, but subsequently withdrew its registration statement as the market for IPOs cooled off. However, the mezzanine round of financing was sufficient to get Extricity through the next 10 months until March 2001, when the company was purchased for $168 million by Peregrine Systems Inc., a business-software maker.

Mezzanine Financing to Bridge a Gap in the Capital Structure

A second and more common use of mezzanine financing is to bridge a gap in the capital structure of a company. In this case, mezzanine financing is used not because of time constraints but rather because of financing constraints between senior debt and equity. Mezzanine financing provides the layer of capital beyond what secured lenders are willing to provide while minimizing the dilution of a company's outstanding equity.

Mezzanine debt is used to fill the gap between senior debt represented by bank loans, mortgages and senior bonds, and equity. Consequently, mezzanine debt is junior, or subordinated, to the debt of the bank loans, and is typically the last component of debt to be retired.

Under this definition, mezzanine financing is used to fund acquisitions, corporate re-capitalizations, or production growth. More generally, mezzanine financing is used whenever the equity component of a transaction is too low to attract senior lenders such as banks and insurance companies. Senior lenders may require a lower debt-to-equity ratio than the borrower is willing to provide. Most borrowers dislike reducing their equity share price through offerings that dilute equity ownership.

Mezzanine Financing to Bridge a Gap in an LBO

The third popular use of mezzanine debt is a tranche of financing in many LBO deals. For instance, LBO target companies may not have the ability to access the bond markets right away, particularly if the target company was an operating division of a larger entity. It may not have a separate financial history to satisfy SEC requirements for a public sale of its bonds. Consequently, a mezzanine tranche may be necessary to complete the financing of the buyout deal. Alternatively, a buyout candidate may not have enough physical assets to provide the necessary collateral in a buyout transaction. Last, bank lenders may be hesitant to lend if there is not sufficient equity committed to the transaction. Mezzanine debt is often the solution to solve these LBO financing problems.

Mezzanine Funds

Mezzanine funds must pay attention to the same securities laws as hedge funds, venture capital funds, and buyout funds. This means that mezzanine funds must ensure that they fall within either the 3(c)(1) or the 3(c)(7) exemptions of the Investment Company Act of 1940. These "safe harbor" provisions ensure that mezzanine funds do not have to adhere to the filing, disclosure, record keeping, and reporting requirements as do mutual funds.

There are two key distinctions between venture capital funds and mezzanine funds. The first is the return expectations. Mezzanine funds seek total rates of return in the 15% to low twenties range. Compare this to LBO funds that seek returns in the mid-to-high twenties and venture capital funds that seek returns in excess of 30%.

For example, senior bank debt in a private equity transaction is usually priced at 200 to 250 basis points over Libor, while mezzanine financing usually bears a coupon rate of 400 to 500 basis points over Libor. In addition, mezzanine financing will contain some form of equity appreciation such as warrants or the ability to convert into common stock that raises the total return towards 20%.

Mezzanine financing is the most expensive form of debt because it is the last to be repaid. It ranks at the bottom of the creditor totem pole, just above equity. As a result, it is expected to earn a rate of return only slightly less than common equity.

Second, mezzanine funds are staffed with different expertise than a venture capital fund. Most venture capital funds have staff with heavy technology related experience including former senior executives of software, semiconductor, and Internet companies. In contrast, mezzanine funds tend to have financial professionals, experienced in negotiating "equity kickers" to be added on to the mezzanine debt offering.

Mezzanine funds have not attracted the flow of investor capital compared to venture capital funds or leveraged buyout funds. Part of the reason is that with a robust economy throughout most of the 1990s, mezzanine debt was not a necessary component of many transactions. Second, mezzanine financing tends to be small, generally in the $20 million to $300 million range. Last, mezzanine debt, while it yields greater returns than junk bonds, cannot compete with the returns earned by venture capitalists and leveraged buyout funds.

Mezzanine funds look for businesses that have a high potential for growth and earnings, but do not have a sufficient cash flow to receive full funding from banks or other senior creditors. Banks may be unwilling to lend because of a short operating history or a high debt to equity ratio. Mezzanine funds look for companies that, over the next 4 to 7 years, can repay the mezzanine debt through a debt refinancing, an initial public offering, or an acquisition.

Mezzanine funds are risk lenders. This means that in a liquidation of the company, mezzanine investors expect little or no recovery of their principal. Consequently, mezzanine investors must assess investment opportunities outside of conventional banking parameters. Existing collateral and short-term cash flow are less of a consideration. Instead, mezzanine investors carefully review the management team and its business plan to assess the likelihood that future growth will be achieved by the issuing company. In sum, similar to stockholders, mezzanine debt investors assume the risk of the company's success or failure.

Investors in mezzanine funds are generally pension funds, endowments, and foundations. These investors do not have the internal infrastructure or expertise to invest directly in the mezzanine market. Therefore, they enter this alternative investment strategy as limited partners through a mezzanine fund.

Similar to hedge funds, venture capital funds and LBO funds, mezzanine funds are managed by a general partner who has full investment discretion. Many mezzanine funds are managed by merchant banks who have experience with gap financing or by mezzanine professionals who previously worked in the mezzanine departments of insurance companies and banks.

Advantages of Mezzanine Debt to the Investor

Mezzanine debt is a hybrid. It has debt-like components but usually provides for some form of equity appreciation. This appeals to investors who are more conservative but like to have some spice in their portfolios.

High Equity-Like Returns The high returns to mezzanine debt compared to senior debt appeals to traditional fixed-income investors such as insurance companies. Mezzanine debt typically has a coupon rate that is 200 basis points over that of senior secured debt. Additionally, given an insurance company's long-term investment horizon, it may be less concerned with short-term earnings fluctuations.

Further, mezzanine debt often has an equity kicker, typically in the form of warrants. These warrants may have a strike price as low as $0.01 per share. The amount of warrants included is inversely proportional to the coupon rate. The higher the coupon rate, the fewer the warrants that need to be issued.

Nonetheless, the investor receives both a high coupon payment plus participation in the upside of the company should it achieve its growth potential. The equity component can be significant, representing up to 5% to 20% of the outstanding equity of the company. For this reason, mezzanine debt is often viewed as an investment in the company as opposed to a lien on assets.

Priority of Payment   Although mezzanine debt is generally not secured by collateral, it still ranks higher than equity and other unsecured creditors. Therefore, mezzanine debt is senior to trade creditors.

Schedule of Repayment   Like senior secured debt, mezzanine debt usually has a repayment schedule. This schedule may not start for several years as senior debt is paid off, but it provides the certainty of when a return of capital is expected.

Board Representation   A subordinated lender generally expects to be considered an equity partner. In some cases, mezzanine lenders may request board observation rights. However, in other cases, the mezzanine lender may take a seat on the board of directors with full voting rights.

Restrictions on the Borrower   Although mezzanine debt is typically unsecured, it still may come with restrictions on the borrower. The mezzanine lender may have the right to approve or disapprove of additional debt, acquisitions made by the borrower, changes in the management team, and the payment of dividends.

Distressed Debt

Distressed debt investing is the practice of purchasing the debt of troubled companies. These companies may have already defaulted on their debt or may be on the brink of default. Additionally, distressed debt may be that of a company seeking bankruptcy protection.

The key to distressed debt investing is to recognize that the term "distressed" has two meanings. First, it means that the issuer of the debt is troubled—its liabilities may exceed its assets—or it may be unable to meet its debt service and interest payments as they become due. Therefore, distressed debt investing almost always means that some workout, turnaround, or bankruptcy solution must be implemented for the bonds to appreciate in value.

Second, "distressed" refers to the price of the bonds. Distressed debt often trades for pennies on the dollar. This affords a savvy investor the opportunity to make a killing if she can identify a company with a viable business plan but a short-term cash flow problem.

Vulture Investors and Hedge Fund Managers

Distressed debt investors are often referred to as "vulture investors," or just "vultures" because they pick the bones of underperforming companies. They buy the debt of troubled companies including subordinated debt, junk bonds, bank loans, and obligations to suppliers. Their investment plan is to buy the distressed debt at a fraction of its face value and then seek improvement of the company.

Sometimes this debt is used as a way to gain an equity investment stake in the company as the vultures agree to forgive the debt they own in return for stock in the company. Other times, the vultures may help the troubled company to get on its feet, thus earning a significant return as the value of their distressed debt recovers in value. Still other times distressed debt buyers help impatient creditors to cut their losses and wipe a bad debt off their books. The vulture in return waits patiently for the company to correct itself and for the value of the distressed debt to recover.

There is no standard model for distressed debt investing, each distressed situation requires a unique approach and solution. As a result, distressed debt investing is mostly company selection. There is a low covariance with the general stock market.

The returns for distressed debt investing can be very rewarding. Distressed debt obligations generally trade at levels that yield a total return of 20% or higher. For example, by the beginning of 2001 an estimated 15% to 20% of all leveraged bank debt loans traded at 80 cents on the dollar or less.[4]

Distressed Debt and Bankruptcy

Distressed debt investing and the bankruptcy process are inextricably intertwined. Many distressed debt investors purchase the debt while the borrowing company is currently in the throws of bankruptcy. Other investors purchase the debt before a company enters into bankruptcy proceedings with the expectation of gaining control of the company.

Using Distressed Debt to Recycle Private Equity

LBO firms are a great source for distressed debt. "Leveraged fallouts" occur frequently, leaving large amounts of distressed debt in their wake. However, this provides an opportunity for distressed debt buyers to jump in, purchase cheaply non-performing bank loans and subordinated debt, eliminate the prior private equity investors, and assert their own private equity ownership.

---

[4] See Riva D. Atlas, "Company in Trouble? They're Waiting," *New York Times* (January 21, 2001).

Distressed Buyouts

Even as leveraged buyout firms create distress situations, they also actively invest in this arena. After all, bankruptcy court and creditor workouts provide opportunities to purchase undervalued assets. Often, creditors are sufficiently worried about receiving any recovery that they bail out of their positions when possible, opening up the door for buyout firms to scoop up assets on the cheap.

Converting Distressed Debt to Private Equity in a Pre-Packaged Bankruptcy

In February 2001, Loews Cineplex Entertainment Corp., the largest publicly traded U.S. movie theater chain, and one of the largest movie theater chains in the world, filed for Chapter 11 Bankruptcy. At the same time, it signed a letter of intent with Oaktree Capital Management, LLC and the Onex Corporation to sell Loews Cineplex and its subsidiaries to the investor group. This was a "pre-packaged" bankruptcy where the debtor agrees in advance to a plan of reorganization before formerly filing for Chapter 11 Bankruptcy.

The letter agreement proposed that Onex and Oaktree convert their distressed debt holdings of about $250 million of senior secured bank debt and $180 million of unsecured company bonds into 88% of the equity of the reorganized company. Unsecured creditors, including subordinated debtholders, would receive the other 12% of equity.[5] All existing equity interests would be wiped out by the reorganization. Last, the remaining holders of bank debt would receive new term loans as part of the bankruptcy process equal in recovery to about 98% of the face amount of current debt.

In this prepackaged example, Onex and Oaktree became the majority equity owners of Loews by purchasing its bank and subordinated debt. Furthermore, their bank debt was converted to a private equity stake because all public shares of Loews were wiped out through the bankruptcy proceedings. Loews' two largest shareholders, Sony Corporation (40% equity ownership) and Vivendi Universal SA (26%) lost their complete equity stake in Loews. In effect, the bankruptcy proceeding transformed Loews from a public company to a private one.

Distressed Debt as an Undervalued Security

Distressed debt is not always an entrée into private equity; it can simply be an investment in an undervalued security. In this instance, distressed debt investors are less concerned with an equity stake in the troubled

---

[5] Oaktree Capital also owned about 60% of Loews' senior subordinated notes.

company. Instead, they expect to benefit if the company can implement a successful turnaround strategy.

Distressed Debt Arbitrage

If there is any way to skin an arbitrage, hedge fund managers will think of it. While this is not a private equity form of investing, it is a form of equity arbitrage best suited for hedge fund managers.

The arbitrage is constructed as follows. A hedge fund manager purchases distressed debt which she believes is undervalued. At the same time, she shorts the company's underlying stock. The idea is that if the bonds are going to decline in value, the company's stock price will decline even more dramatically because equity holders have only a residual claim behind debtholders.

Conversely, if the company's prospects improve, both the distressed debt and equity will appreciate significantly. The difference then will be between the coupon payment on the debt versus dividends paid on the stock. Since a company coming out of a workout or turnaround situation almost always conserves its cash and does not pay cash stock dividends, the hedge fund manager should earn large interest payments on the debt compared to the equity.

Risks of Distressed Debt Investing

There are two main risks associated with distressed debt investing. First, business risk still applies. Just because distressed debt investors can purchase the debt of a company on the cheap does not mean it cannot go lower. This is the greatest risk to distressed debt investing; a troubled company may be worthless and unable to pay off its creditors. While creditors often convert their debt into equity, the company may not be viable as a going concern. If the company cannot develop a successful plan of reorganization, it will only continue its spiral downwards.

It may seem strange, but creditworthiness doesn't apply. The reason is that the debt is already distressed because the company may already be in default and its debt thoroughly discounted. Consequently, failure to pay interest and debt service has already occurred.

Instead, vulture investors consider the business risks of the company. They are concerned not with the short-term payment of interest and debt service, but rather, the ability of the company to execute a viable business plan. From this perspective, it can be said that distressed debt investors are truly equity investors. They view the purchase of distressed debt as an investment in the company as opposed to a lending facility.

The second main risk is the lack of liquidity. The distressed debt arena is a fragmented market, dominated by a few players. Trading out of a distressed debt position may mean selling at a significant discount to the book value of the debt.

In addition, purchasers of distressed debt must have long-term investment horizons. Workout and turnaround situations do not happen overnight. It may be several years before a troubled company can correct its course and appreciate in value.

SIX

Asset Allocation

CHAPTER 31

Active Asset Allocation

Robert D. Arnott
Managing Partner
First Quadrant LP

In this chapter, we explore asset allocation. However, "asset alloca-tion" means different things to different people in different contexts. Asset allocation can loosely be divided into three categories: long-term policy asset allocation, short-term or intermediate-term tactical asset allocation, and dynamic asset allocation strategies for asset allocation designed to reshape the return distribution. There are many variants on each of the three themes, each of which deserves a brief overview. Before we can begin to review asset allocation issues, it is important to define our use of these terms.

Long-term asset allocation, or *policy asset allocation,* is the evalua-tion of the needs of an investor and the assessment of the appropriate asset mix required to meet those needs. Long-term asset allocation is not an active strategy. Rather, it is the identification of the normal asset mix policy which will represent the best compromise between a need for sta-bility and a need for performance. This is sometimes called *strategic asset allocation.* The intent of long-term or policy asset allocation is to shape the normal risk profile of a portfolio to meet the long-term needs of a plan. This involves careful balancing of the need for return against the investor's aversion to risk.

Active asset allocation encompasses a number of strategies. *Tactical asset allocation* refers to an active management process in which the investor seeks to opportunistically respond to the changing risk and return patterns in the capital markets. The objective of tactical asset allo-cation is to make money by shifting the asset mix (i.e., the relative

841

amounts of the major asset classes) in response to changing opportunities. This is also sometimes called either *strategic asset allocation* or *dynamic asset allocation*. The objective in tactical asset allocation is performance. The intent is to shift the asset mix to respond to the changing risk and return opportunities which are available in the markets. Tactical asset allocation is typically an inherently "buy low, sell high" process.

Dynamic asset allocation strategies are also active asset allocation strategies. The best known dynamic asset allocation strategy is portfolio insurance. The intent of this strategy is not necessarily to make money by responding to opportunities in the marketplace. Rather, the objective of portfolio insurance is to protect against adverse consequences. Effectively, the strategy synthetically replicates the performance of put options. As explained in Chapter 14, the buyer of a put option has upside potential but sets a limit on the downside. Rather than buying a put option on a portfolio, a synthetic put does this via the trading of the portfolio. Consequently, portfolio insurance is really designed for the primary purpose of protecting against unacceptable adverse consequences or, in other words, to reshape the distribution of likely returns.

The reason for this discussion of semantics should be clear—the same words are often used for two or more concepts. As shown in Exhibit 31.1, even among these three discrete classes of asset allocation, the distinctions blur.

EXHIBIT 31.1 Asset Allocation Objective

Policy Asset Allocation
Establish long-term normal asset mix consistent with long-term portfolio objectives

Tactical Asset Allocation
Add value; opportunistically respond to changing patterns of reward
Behavior Pattern: buy low, sell high

Strategic Asset Allocation
Ambiguous. Can refer to either Policy Asset Allocation, Tactical Asset Allocation or a hybrid, intermediate-term Tactical Asset Allocation

Portfolio Insurance
Protect against unacceptable performance
Behavior Pattern: sell low, buy high

Dynamic Asset Allocation
Ambiguous: can refer to either Tactical Asset Allocation or Portfolio Insurance

ASSET ALLOCATION AND OPTIMIZATION

In the early 1950s, Harry Markowitz pioneered the use of mean-variance optimization (also known as quadratic programming or quadratic optimization) as a tool for balancing the quest for return against the need for risk management in a portfolio. When applied to the optimization puzzle, an optimizer will produce the "optimal" asset mix, by its very nature. If we can estimate the return and the variance (a measure of volatility) on any asset or market, and the covariance between assets or markets (a measure of how similarly they behave), an optimizer will identify an "efficient frontier" of portfolios. Each portfolio on the "efficient frontier" offers the best expected return for any level of expected portfolio risk or, conversely, the lowest risk at any level of expected return.

An optimizer is exquisitely sensitive to the inputs. Modest differences in estimates for variance or covariance, or small differences in expected returns, can actually make a very substantial difference in the indicated asset mix. There is nothing wrong with this: The correct answer does, in fact, change considerably with small changes in our forecasts.

One consequence is that an optimizer may suggest a portfolio which, for various reasons, we would be unwilling to hold. The low correlations between, say, real estate or emerging markets and the more conventional markets, can lead to a very large allocation to the unconventional choice. This is not an incorrect answer. But, even if a 50% allocation to emerging markets offers the best trade-off between risk and return, few investors will find such a choice palatable. The risk in using an optimizer is that an investor may adjust these expectations for the future until the optimizer recommends the asset mix that they want!

Another issue for optimization is time horizon. Optimization can as easily be used for long-term policy asset allocation as for short-term tactical asset allocation. The appropriate use of an optimizer for policy asset mix will be based on long-term expected return and risk. Over the life of a pension portfolio or the life of an investor, what return is expected from stocks, bonds, and other assets? For tactical asset allocation, the goal is the same but the time horizon is very different, seeking returns over the next year or so, rather than over the coming decades.

Near-term expectations for risk and return may be very different from long-term expectations, due to market or economic conditions or due to the sentiment in the marketplace. If this is the case, optimization for tactical purposes will lead to an asset mix which differs from the long-term policy asset mix. If return expectations for one market are higher near-term than long-term, that would lead to a tactical bet favoring that market. If near-term risk is less than the expected long-term risk, or if near-term correlations with other markets are likely to be lower, this same result will apply.

Many tactical asset allocation models behave in much the same way, boosting exposure to the markets that are expected to produce higher returns or lower risk than their "normal" return or risk. In this fashion, a tactical asset allocation model which does not use an optimizer may make choices similar to those that an optimization-based process would make.

Mean-variance optimization is a more theoretically robust way to make asset allocation choices, but the simpler tactical framework may be more intuitive to the investor or the client. So long as it would make similar decisions to the optimization-based approach, it can produce results similar to the more robust mean-variance optimization process, and so may be preferred on the basis of simplicity. But, the basic roots of both the policy asset allocation and tactical asset allocation decision hearken back to Harry Markowitz's seminal work in mean-variance optimization. All else equal, one should be willing to invest more in a market which has higher return, lower risk, or lower correlations with other markets.

POLICY ASSET ALLOCATION

The policy asset mix decision can loosely be characterized as a *long-term asset allocation decision* in which the investor seeks to assess an appropriate long-term "normal" asset mix which represents an ideal blend of controlled risk and enhanced return. The strategies that offer the greatest prospects for strong long-term rewards tend to be inherently risky strategies. The strategies that offer the greatest safety tend to offer only modest return opportunities. The balancing of these conflicting goals is what is referred to as a "policy" asset allocation.

Even within this definition of policy asset allocation, there are many considerations that the investor must address. Policy asset allocation is the balancing of risk and reward in assessing a long-term "normal" asset mix. But what risks and what rewards are to be contemplated in this evaluation? For the investor with a short-investment horizon and a need to preserve capital, the relevant definition of risk is very different from a long-horizon investor such as a pension or endowment fund. Ironically, the lowest risk strategy for a short-horizon investor may be a very high-risk strategy for a long-horizon investor.

For many investors, there is more than one definition of risk that has a bearing on the policy asset allocation decision. The risks faced by various institutional investors were discussed in earlier chapters of this book. For example, the pension sponsor needs to be concerned with volatility of assets, volatility of liabilities, volatility of the surplus (or difference between assets and liabilities), as well as a handful of other factors. But risk is not just volatility. Rules for U.S. corporate defined benefit pension funds are such that if the present value of liabilities exceed the pension assets, the corporation is required to report the deficit on its balance sheet as a liability. We touch on the role of liabilities in this decision in Chapter 1.

In assessing the policy asset allocation, there are a host of different tools at the investor's disposal. Should the investor use optimization techniques? The most basic optimization technique is the model described in Chapter 2 which employs mathematical programming to maximize expected return while minimizing risk as measured in terms of the standard deviation. Should optimization techniques with a shortfall constraint be the basis for the policy asset mix decision? How does the suitable policy mix shift with different investor circumstances? All of these are questions which can and must be addressed in assessing the policy asset allocation decision.

Rebalancing and Cash Reserves

Two important elements of managing the policy mix are the rebalancing decision and the treatment of cash reserves. One way to view these two elements of the investment process is that both represent opportunities to lose money as a consequence of carelessness or "slippage." Let's examine each separately.

Periodic rebalancing of institutional portfolios is no mere option—that is, it is unavoidable. As asset values change, rebalancing will occur to bring the asset mix to the policy mix. For example, a portfolio set at a 50/50 stock/bond mix can after a few years deviate significantly from a 50/50 mix. No investment manager can allow a portfolio to drift indefinitely with the market. Failure to confront this problem in a disciplined fashion that will result in an asset mix that is subject to the whims of market movements. A carefully planned rebalancing process is required. Moreover, the literature on rebalancing suggests that disciplined rebalancing can boost risk-adjusted returns as much as a fairly large shift in the policy mix itself. For instance, the policy choice between 60% or 50% in stocks means *less* than the decision on how and when to rebalance.

Rational investors set an explicit asset allocation policy incorporating allowable ranges for each major asset class. Suppose, for example, that a pension sponsor decides that the fund's optimal normal mix is 60% stocks, 30% bonds, and 10% alternative investments. Typically, the pension sponsor might determine that rebalancing is necessary when any class strays more than five percentage points from its benchmark. Such a response is inadequate. A disciplined framework for rebalancing is demonstrably superior to the laxness implied by this kind of range.

What of the other aspect of policy mix "slippage," namely cash reserves? Most institutional portfolios do not intend to hold cash as part of their policy asset mix. Most funds are neither so conservative nor so short-term in their focus as to require the security of cash reserves, except as a tactical defense at times when the market is vulnerable. Cash balances can be invested through futures, or more directly invested back into the markets. During bear markets, this strategy will exact a cost, while during bull markets it can be immensely profitable.

Rebalancing Alternatives

Owners rebalance for various reasons and in different ways. Here are some of them:

- *Calendar Rebalancing.* The calendar has advanced a month, quarter, or year (or a board of trustees meeting is coming up). The asset mix is returned to "normal."
- *Rebalancing to Allowed Range.* This assures that the asset mix does not depart from the extremes of the allowed range. For example, consider a 60% normal equity mix, with five percentage points of tolerance. This signals a sale of 1% when stocks reach 66% of assets.
- *Threshold Rebalancing.* This approach assigns much more weight to the wisdom of the original policy. Here, a move beyond the tolerance range dictates a return all the way to the normal mix. Our hypothetical institution with a 66% stock weight and a 60% policy would reduce its equity commitment by 6% of assets in the same situation.
- *Drifting Mix.* One might (through inattention or ignorance) choose to "go with the flow," drifting with the markets. An investor who adopts this alternative evidences little respect for the normal policy mix.
- *Tactical Rebalancing.* This is a little-used approach that may be among the more interesting available. With tactical rebalancing, an investor combines simple rebalancing with a disciplined framework for tactical asset allocation. As the mix drifts away from the intended normal policy mix, a tactical asset allocation discipline is used to determine whether to rebalance back to the normal mix. If a market is rallying above its intended policy mix, and if it is attractive, why sell it? With tactical rebalance, the tactical asset allocation discipline cannot be used to take on additional active bets, only to take bets off the table when market movements introduce unintended active bets.

ATTRIBUTES OF TACTICAL ASSET ALLOCATION

Once the policy asset allocation has been established, and once the use of dynamic strategies, if any, has been decided upon, the investor can turn attention to the issue of "tactical" asset allocation. Here, once again, things are not as simple as they would appear on the surface. Tactical asset allocation is not a single, clearly defined strategy. There are many variations and nuances involved in building a tactical allocation process. Also, semantics can intervene to create needless complexity in understanding the tactical asset allocation issues.

Tactical asset allocation broadly refers to active strategies which seek to enhance performance by opportunistically shifting the asset mix of a portfolio to the changing patterns of reward available in the capital markets. Notably, tactical asset allocation tends to refer to disciplined processes for evaluating respective rates of return on various asset classes and establishing an asset allocation response intended to capture higher rewards. In the area of tactical asset allocation, there are different investment horizons and different mechanisms for evaluating the asset allocation decision. These also merit a brief review.

The structure of tactical asset allocation disciplines covers a wide spectrum. Some are simple objective comparisons of available rates of return. Others seek to enhance the timeliness of these value-driven decisions by incorporating macroeconomic measures, sentiment measures, volatility, and even technical measures. We believe that these more elaborate approaches are superior to purely value-driven models because as undervalued stock can get more undervalued, so too an undervalued asset class can grow more undervalued. The investor who buys an asset as soon as it becomes undervalued does less well than the investor who buys that same asset class shortly before it finally turns up.

Tactical asset allocation can refer to an intermediate-term process or a short-term process. There are tactical processes which seek to measure the relative attractiveness of the major asset classes and which seek to participate in long-term significant movements in the stock or bond markets, spanning a handful of years. Other approaches are more short-term in nature, designed to capture interim movements in the markets.

The shared attributes of these tactical asset allocation processes are several:

- In one sense tactical asset allocation is comparable to sector rotation, except that instead of rotating among the economic sectors of the equity market we are rotating among the sectors of the capital markets, or asset classes.
- They tend to be driven primarily by objective measures of prospective values within an asset class. We know the yield on cash, we know the yield to maturity on long bonds. And the earning yield on the stock market represents a reasonable and objective proxy for long-term rewards available in stocks. These objective measures of reward lead

inevitably to a value-oriented process. Some organizations use fewer asset classes, while others use more. Nonetheless, the strategy involves a disciplined, quantitative structure for measuring available returns.
■ Most important, tactical asset allocation is a strategy that provides the discipline to take a contrarian position. Tactical asset allocation processes tend to buy after a market decline and sell after a market rise. In each of the tactical asset allocation strategies currently employed by various practitioners, the tendency will be to buy the out-of-favor asset class.

By objectively measuring which asset classes are offering the greatest prospective rewards, tactical asset allocation disciplines measure which asset classes are the most out of favor; they steer investment into the unloved asset classes. These assets are priced to reflect the fact that they are neglected and the corresponding fact that investors demand a premium reward for an out-of-favor investment. Therein lies the potential for tactical asset allocation disciplines. At bear market lows, the returns available in the equity markets can be most impressive relative to bond returns or money market (i.e., cash) returns. There is a reason for this—equities are severely out of favor at bear market lows. It takes a great deal of courage to buy stocks in that environment. A tactical asset allocation discipline can give an investor the confidence to take that contrarian stance.

How Does Rebalancing Relate to Tactical Asset Allocation?

Tactical asset allocation and rebalancing are related strategies, tending to buy on weakness and sell into strength. They are not, by any means, identical. Using tactical asset allocation is no substitute for a disciplined rebalancing structure.

An investor either views the markets as efficient, making active asset allocation inappropriate, or perceives them as offering periodic profit opportunities. In either case, an investor must be alert to any drift in asset mix which affects the *non-tactical* portion of the asset base.

Consider an institution which allots 50% of its portfolios to stocks, 30% to bonds, and 20% to tactical asset allocation. In effect, it has established a 60/40 normal mix with leeway to deviate up to ten percentage points in either direction. With this structure, a falling stock market might prompt the tactical asset allocation strategy to put 5% more into stocks, while the non-tactical asset allocation assets drift 5% out of stocks. Volatile markets, causing drift in the non-tactical asset allocation assets, can actually *cancel* tactical asset allocation shifts, which tend to counter recent market moves. To recapture the value of the tactical asset allocation component, we still need to rebalance the non-tactical assets.

Systematic Management of Active Asset Allocation

How do most organizations handle asset allocation? The long-term asset allocation is typically established based on a careful analysis. The trade-offs between uncertainty and performance are carefully weighed in light of the long-term needs of the investor. Short-term adjustments are typically handled through cash flows with little or no formal analysis. Indeed, short-term adjustments are often handled in a way which is far from contrarian. The most important attribute of tactical asset allocation is that it can provide a disciplined framework. The use of futures represents an interesting opportunity, facilitating these short-term adjustments with very low transaction costs.

In looking at tactical asset allocation, perhaps the first question to be addressed is whether or not it is possible to add value by shifting the asset mix. One way to look at this question is to consider the flows between the markets. If Microsoft becomes severely undervalued relative to Oracle, money can and eventually will flow readily from Oracle into Microsoft, to exploit the opportunity. This pattern of capital flows helps to keep securities from straying very far from fair value. Intriguingly, we observe far less fluid capital flows between asset classes. If yields soar, stock market portfolio managers typically do not rush to buy bonds. That is "not their job." If cash yields rise sharply, bond and stock managers typically do not rush to sell their holdings in order to capture those cash yields. In short, while there are some flows between asset classes, they tend to happen gradually and in relatively modest size. If capital flows do not occur, then markets can stray far from fair value. This is the fundamental reason that asset allocation may represent an opportunity to enhance performance.

A disciplined structure for asset allocation is generally predicated on three key assumptions. First, the capital markets indicate what rates of return are available in the various asset classes. We *know* the yield on cash. We *know* the yield to maturity on long bonds, and we *know* the price/earnings ratio on the stock market, which can give us some indication of the long-term rewards available in stocks. The second key assumption is that there is a normal relationship among these implied returns. The third and most critical assumption is that the capital markets correct disequilibrium conditions when they occur. As equity returns stray from their normal relationship relative to bond returns, the forces of the capital markets will pull them back into line towards normalcy.

Suppose the yields on long-term Treasury bonds are 1% higher than the yield on Treasury bills. This is a difference that can be sustained for a very long time. If the gap opens wide, for example with long bond yields rising 5% above Treasury bill yields, then typically either the bond yield will come down or the cash yield will rise, in time. The same thing holds true in the comparison between stocks and bonds. For instance, suppose $100 will buy you either $10 of annual income on a long-term government bond (a bond yield of 10%) or $4 worth of earnings on a well-diversified stock portfolio (a stock market "earnings yield" of 4%, or a P/E ratio of 25). This was the case just before the 1987 stock market crash. Then, it's a fair bet that either bond market yield will come down or stock market earnings yield will rise (in other words, P/E ratios must fall). This comparison of a simple measure of prospective future returns is referred to as a "risk premium." It is one of the central elements of almost all tactical asset allocation programs.

All tactical asset allocation processes function essentially in this fashion. There are many differences, which make some tactical asset allocation processes more effective than others, and which allow different processes to disagree. For example, there are differences which lead to biases towards one asset class or another over an extended period of time. Also, there are subtle differences which lead some asset allocation processes to time market tops and bottoms rather poorly. The best asset allocation strategies will often combine several key decisions:

- A measurement of disequilibrium conditions—where do the opportunities lie?
- An evaluation of economic implications—can the markets sustain a return to equilibrium?
- A measure of market opportunities in a global context—will foreign capital be drawn to our markets?
- Considerations of patterns of sentiment—is the opportunity now or later?

Such strategies begin with a systematic evaluation of these kinds of market opportunities. The measurement of how far the markets have strayed from equilibrium relationships must lie at the foundation of any successful asset allocation approach. However, it is important to recognize that opportunities lie not only in markets *which have* strayed from equilibrium, but also in economic conditions *which can* sustain a *return to* equilibrium. It is this tendency to return to equilibrium that is the profit mechanism of any asset allocation strategy. It can also be useful to assess the sentiment at work in the marketplace. Will the markets move *now* or *later?*

Nonetheless, most tactical asset allocation products share this fundamental risk premium basis. In so doing, most tactical asset allocation processes share a highly disciplined structure and an inherently contrarian nature. Finally, most tactical asset allocation processes share in the fact that they have enhanced performance over time.

Tactical Asset Allocation: Why Bother?

The next question confronting an investor is whether it even makes sense to contemplate active shifts in asset mix. But consider the alternative: Should we make no active shifts in mix in response to changing market opportunities? Is it preferable to permit the shifting of asset mix to be driven by the wandering movements of the market or by a systematic structure designed to exploit opportunities?

Even modest improvements in performance can make a huge difference over time. Suppose the market produces 10% returns. This is sufficient to turn $100 into $270 in ten years. Suppose we can improve that result by just 1% per year. This translates into an additional $25 for every $100 that we started with, after just 10 years. That's an important improvement in returns. The historical evidence suggests that a simple rebalancing strategy, like the ones described earlier in this chapter, can boost returns by up to 0.5% per year. It is not unreasonable that an active asset allocation process, which boosts exposure when markets are out of favor and trims them when they are popular and expensive, can do far better than this.

ASSET ALLOCATION IMPLEMENTATION

With respect to implementation, first and foremost, it should be noted that implementation *must* be as disciplined as the investment decision process itself. Without a disciplined implementation process, one should not even consider managing asset allocation decisions.

With a disciplined implementation process, asset allocation can be affected either with or without the use of futures. Implementation of asset allocation is significantly improved if futures are used. The transactions incurred by tactical asset allocation, both with and without futures, can be considerable. Any avenue for cutting transaction costs is important. Nonetheless, implementation without futures is not without merit. If stock or bond holdings are actively managed, not indexed, implementation without futures forces the continual upgrading of the holdings within each asset class.

Let's go through an example. As Exhibit 31.2a shows, the typical portfolio is made up of holdings which might be categorized by an investor as buy candidates or hold candidates. The hold candidates are issues which are not attractive enough to be buy candidates, but not unattractive enough to justify the transaction costs which would be incurred in selling the stock. Thus, the typical portfolio consists of holdings which are deemed to be quite attractive and holdings which are deemed to be only mildly attractive. Active asset allocation forces the improvement of the portfolios within the asset classes. Why is this so? If the asset allocation decision prompts a shift *into* stocks, the investor most assuredly will not add stocks that are deemed only marginally attractive. The investor will buy stocks which are deemed to be quite attractive, namely the buy candidates. If an asset allocation decision prompts a sale of stocks, the stocks sold will most assuredly not be the buy candidates, as shown in Exhibit 31.2b. They will come from the marginally attractive sector of the portfolio, or the hold candidates. In so doing, the remaining stocks in either case will generally be the buy candidates. The same pattern applies to the bond holdings.

EXHIBIT 31.2   Asset Allocation, Portfolio Upgrade Phenomenon
a. Portfolio Upgrades from New Assets

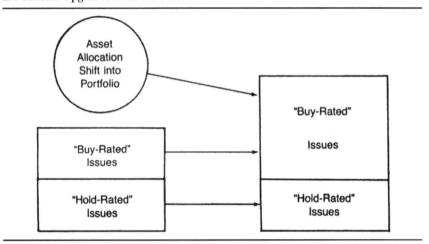

b. Portfolio Upgrades from Asset Withdrawals

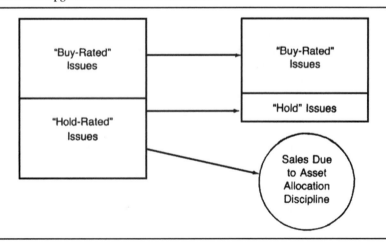

As a result, the holdings will be subject to a continual process of upgrading and will contain more issues from the most attractive portions of the market than equities held in an account that is not subject to asset allocation. The same holds true for the bond holdings or for the holdings of any other asset class subject to asset allocation.

Clearly, this does not assure that the stocks in an asset allocation portfolio will outpace the stocks in a portfolio that does not engage in asset allocation. It only implies that the *merits or demerits* of the stock and bond selection disciplines will be magnified by the asset allocation process. The stocks and bonds held in an asset allocation portfolio will be dominated by issues which are judged by the investor to be more attractive.

The Possible Role of Futures

Transaction costs represent the principal disadvantage of active asset allocation without the use of futures. Transaction costs have been estimated to be at any of a number of levels. Let's suppose the trading costs (commissions and price impact of our trading) for moving from stocks into bonds, or from bonds into stocks, are 1% each way. Both a tactical asset allocation and a portfolio insurance strategy will likely trigger trading amounting to perhaps 100% of a portfolio per annum. This will cost 1% of portfolio value in trading costs. This means that an active asset allocation discipline must add at least 1% per annum or it is not worth employing. Most tactical asset allocation disciplines do indeed offer rewards several times that. Therefore, tactical asset allocation does not *require* the use of futures. It can be implemented effectively and very profitably without resorting to the use of futures.

The advantages of implementation of an asset allocation strategy using futures are:

- Transaction costs minimized
- Excellent liquidity; rapid execution
- One day settlement; simultaneous trades
- Does not disrupt management of underlying assets
- Stabilizes portfolio income stream
- Potential for favorable mispricing

As these advantages suggest, the merits of futures in asset allocation trading are considerable. The commissions on a futures trade are trivial. $20 round-trip commission for purchase and subsequent sale of $100,000 worth of stock market exposure is fairly typical. This amounts to 2 basis points for a round-trip transaction. The market impact can also be trivial, since buying or selling $100 million worth of exposure in the stock market or bond market will represent 1%–2% of an average days' volume of the futures exchanges. Thus, transaction costs are slashed to very low levels. Instead of an asset allocation discipline having to add 150 basis points, it need only add 10 to 20 basis points to cover the transaction costs.

Second, these markets are very deep and liquid. Stock index futures now trade some $5–$10 billion each day. Bond futures are the most liquid single market in the world, routinely trading over $25 billion daily. As such, an investor can execute a $100 million asset allocation shift in minutes with relative ease. Today the stock index futures trade as much as two to four times the volume of the stocks on the NYSE.

Third, futures permit simultaneous trades. If investors want to sell $100 million worth of bond exposure and buy $100 million worth of stock market exposure without using futures, they can eliminate the bond exposure in minutes, since the Treasury markets are highly liquid. However, on the equity side, they will have to carefully craft a buy program consistent with their investment management disciplines, and have their trading desk and brokers work the order carefully—all of which can take days.

This is mitigated to some extent if the trades are managed through index funds, where a program trade can be effected quickly. But even with index funds the manager can still run into a thorny problem with the differences in settlement times. The stocks settle in three days while Treasury bonds settle in a day. This would mean that there would be $100 million completely uninvested for four days in order to synchronize settlement dates. Investors can make a $100 million shift in their asset mix in minutes using futures, without any concern for settlement or other operational difficulties.

Fourth, a shift in mix implemented by futures is not disruptive to the management of the underlying assets. If investors want to sell $100 million stocks and buy $100 million in bonds, they have to carefully design a sell program that will not alter the characteristics of the equity portfolio in unintended ways. This step alone can take days. They then have to execute the trade, carefully working the order in conformity of available liquidity. Then they have to do the same thing on the bond side. The whole process could take many days. With futures, the underlying stock and bond portfolios are not disrupted. Indeed, the futures strategy can be overlaid on top of another manager without the other manager even being aware of the trades. For taxable investors, the taxes triggered by selling stocks or bonds can be a substantial, additional trading cost which futures can avoid.

This separation of the futures positions from the asset managers has another advantage. If the active asset managers are outperforming the index, the use of futures permits the investor to fully capture the value added by management *within* the asset classes. The futures only reflect the index return, while the assets are earning the index return plus something extra. Thus, any excess returns stay with the portfolio, regardless of shifts in mix effected through futures. However, the reverse is also true: Any *underperformance* within the asset classes, relative to the index, also stays with the portfolio.

Fifth, for organizations where income is a consideration, the use of futures does not disrupt the income stream. If the portfolio is shifted from stocks into bonds, the income rises, which is nice. If a few months later it is shifted back to stocks, the income drops, which might be an unpleasant dose of reality. With the use of futures, the underlying asset mix need not change, and the income stream generated by those assets need not change, either. However, the value of the futures will fluctuate as the markets move, resulting in gains and losses on the futures position. These changes might be considered more as capital gains then as income; when accounted for in this way, the income can remain stable even though the asset mix is shifting.

Sixth, the futures may be favorably mispriced. If a futures trading strategy uses the futures mispricing as part of the decision rule, a strategy can be designed which benefits from any ongoing pattern of futures mispricing. Futures sometimes do stray from the fair value relative to the underlying assets, which, as explained in Chapter 14, is called *basis risk*. In the experience of the author, there are many times where the futures are favorably mispriced when tactical asset allocation shifts are made. In short, the mispricing has been advantageous for most conventional tactical asset allocation processes.

As noted earlier, tactical asset allocation disciplines are inherently contrarian. It is often a buy low, sell high discipline. When equities sag, equity exposure is boosted sharply. This usually happens at a time when, due to the drop in the stock market, there is a good deal of pessimism and the futures are underpriced relative to fair value. Equity exposure is often cut after significant market rallies. This is typically a period of euphoria in which the futures are overpriced relative to fair value. In short, asset allocation disciplines, because they are contrarian, reap considerable benefits from futures mispricing.

The Mechanics of Implementation Through Futures

To illustrate the asset allocation decision, consider the following two examples. In the first example, we accomplish asset allocation by using the underlying assets. In this case, we start with the portfolio of $50 million of equity and $50 million of bonds. If we want to shift the asset allocation mix from 50% equity and 50% bonds to 60% equity and 40% bonds, we would sell $10 million worth of bonds and buy $10 million worth of equity exposure. The resulting portfolio would be shifted to $60 million worth of equity and $40 million worth of bonds.

EXHIBIT 31.3   Asset Allocation Shifts Using Futures

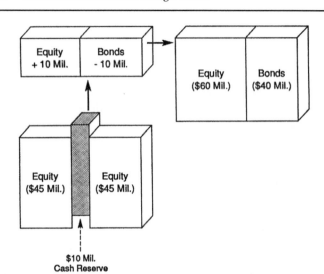

Now, consider the asset allocation shift using futures. First, the use of futures requires a liquidity reserve in order to fund the margin requirements for the futures positions. (Margin requirements for futures were discussed in Chapter 14.) In the second example in Exhibit 31.3 we begin with a portfolio totaling $100 million composed of $45 million worth of equity and $45 million worth of bonds, and $10 million in cash equivalents. The cash reserve is used as collateral for the futures positions. In order to accomplish the asset allocation shift it is required that we buy $15 million worth of equity exposure and sell $5 million worth of bond exposure. With these futures transactions equity exposure in the portfolio would total $60 million. This is achieved by having $45 million of equity exposure in the underlying stocks and $15 million of equity exposure through the futures market. The bond exposure in the portfolio would be reduced to $40 million from the initial $45 million by the short position in $5 million worth of bond futures. As a result of the futures transactions, the total portfolio exposure has been changed to 60% equities and 40% bonds, while leaving the underlying assets in place.

The Pitfalls of Futures

Though having important advantages, the use of futures for asset allocation does have some disadvantages. In the first place, even though the use of futures often allows for favorable mispricing, there is the potential for unfavorable mispricing. These periods of unfavorable mispricing will increase the cost of the asset allocation move using futures relative to making the shift using the underlying assets. However, the mispricing would have to be quite severe before it would actually be more advantageous to trade the underlying securities. With current arbitrage activity it is unlikely that such levels would occur very often, if at all.

A second disadvantage of using futures for asset allocation comes about because of the administrative work which is required on a daily basis to mark to market the futures positions. Any gains or losses in the futures contracts are required to be settled daily, requiring transfers-of funds between the investor and the broker. This daily back office work requires constant attention and can be both costly and time consuming.

A third disadvantage of using futures is that a cash liquidity reserve is necessary to accommodate the margin requirements and daily settlement of the futures positions. Funding this liquidity reserve often forces the investor to liquidate some assets currently invested in stocks and bonds. Though the underlying reserve is invested in cash equivalents, a full investment exposure can be achieved by buying equity index or bond futures to overlay the cash position. This replaces the active asset returns which might be had from investing in actual stocks and bonds with index-like performance tied to the futures contracts. To the extent that active asset management can add value relative to the index, this differential return is sacrificed because of the necessity to fund the liquidity reserve and achieve full exposure indirectly using a futures overlay.

MANAGING THE ASSET MIX

All too often, an investor asks the wrong questions when considering how to handle the asset allocation in a portfolio. Too often the question is framed in terms of "yes or no." Should we rebalance the portfolio? Should we be careless about idle cash reserves? Should we engage in tactical asset allocation in order to try to add a bit of value from active asset allocation? Should we use a dynamic asset allocation strategy to protect ourselves against a bear market? Should we use futures in our asset mix management?

Too often, the core question is not asked: What asset mix, and what response to a changing world, will best enable us to achieve our long-term return objectives? If we begin with this question, our own best answers to the more specific questions become easier to discern.